Jeffrey A. Parker

GLOBAL PUBLIC GOODS

INTERNATIONAL
COOPERATION
IN THE 21ST CENTURY

"It is not beyond the powers of political volition to tip the scales towards more secure peace, greater economic well-being, social justice and environmental sustainability. But no country can achieve these global public goods on its own, and neither can the global marketplace. Thus our efforts must now focus on the missing term of the equation: global public goods".

Kofi Annan
Secretary-General of the United Nations
New York
1 March 1999

GLOBAL PUBLIC GOODS

INTERNATIONAL COOPERATION IN THE 21ST CENTURY

EDITED BY

INGE KAUL

ISABELLE GRUNBERG

MARC A. STERN

PUBLISHED FOR

THE UNITED NATIONS DEVELOPMENT PROGRAMME
(UNDP)

NEW YORK   OXFORD
OXFORD UNIVERSITY PRESS
1999

Oxford University Press

Oxford   New York

Athens   Auckland   Bangkok   Bombay
Calcutta   Cape Town   Dar es Salaam   Delhi
Florence   Hong Kong   Istanbul   Karachi
Kuala Lumpur   Madras   Madrid   Melbourne
Mexico City   Nairobi   Paris   Singapore
Taipei   Tokyo   Toronto

and associated companies in
Berlin   Ibadan

Published by Oxford University Press, Inc.
198 Madison Avenue, New York, New York, 10016

Oxford is a registered trademark of Oxford University Press

Library of Congress Cataloging-in-Publication Data

Kaul, Inge
Global public goods: international cooperation in the 21st century/ edited by Inge
    Kaul, Isabelle Grunberg, Marc A. Stern.
    p. cm.
    Includes bibliographical references and index.
    ISBN 0-19-513051-0 (cloth). — ISBN 0-19-513052-9 (paper)
1. Public goods. 2. International cooperation. I. Kaul, Inge. II. Grunberg, Isabelle
    III. Stern, Marc A.
HB846.5.G55 1999
363—DC21   99-10940
                                                                    CIP
                                                                    Rev.

Cover and design: Gerald Quinn, Quinn Information Design, Cabin John, Maryland

Editing and production management: Communications Development Incorporated, Washington, DC

"With the publication of this volume, UNDP has again proved to be a leading intellectual agency, as well as an important operational body".

Kazuo Takahashi
Director
International Development Research Institute
Tokyo

"This volume introduces a framework for facilitating and reinforcing international development through an equal partnership model of cooperation. I find it enlightening, and hopefully reflective of the changing values of this era".

Ismail Razali
Chairman
Central Bank of Malaysia

"This book embarks into new dimensions of thinking".

Klaus Schwab
President
World Economic Forum, Davos

"We need better international cooperation to ensure that human beings have full access to necessary public goods. This volume is an invaluable tool to bring this goal closer".

Paul Kennedy
Yale University

"How can self-interest be harnessed for the public good? This volume will prove useful to anyone interested in answering that question".

Jose Goldemberg
Former Minister of the Environment, Brazil

"At a time when many are saying that globalization has gone too far, UNDP has produced a wide and deep study of global public goods. The volume deals with peace and trade, but also with global warming, transnational pollution, disease and financial crises—all public bads—and their suppression, which constitutes a good. The subject is complex but of paramount importance to a world experiencing, or approaching, multidimensional crises".

Charles Kindleberger
Massachusetts Institute of Technology

"This volume is bound to be an important reference for future work and public debate".

Ralph C. Bryant
The Brookings Institution

"This is an important piece of work on one of the most interesting and urgent problems of our time. An increasing number of issues, including those of the developing world, are an international responsibility. This volume does a distinctively important service by drawing this fact to our attention. I admire the effort that has gone into it. I particularly endorse the result".

John Kenneth Galbraith
Harvard University

"The concept of public good offers a useful analytical framework for the continuing debate over the usefulness of aid because, among other things, of its focus on the mutuality of benefits. In particular, regional public goods must be a critical part of the strategy for Africa's growth and development and for improving Africa's competitiveness".

Kwesi Botchwey
Former Minister of Finance, Ghana

CONTENTS

CONTENTS

PROLOGUE

I am very pleased to write the prologue to this important volume. I consider this an important book for three reasons.

First, I believe that the book breaks new ground by extrapolating the concept of "public goods" from the national level to the global level. The book makes a convincing argument that the two tests of a public good, non-rivalry and nonexcludability, can be applied at the global level to such things as environment, health, culture and peace. In particular, I am persuaded that financial stability, the Internet and knowledge can be considered as global public goods.

Second, I agree with the book's thesis that we live in an increasingly integrated and interlinked world. In this new world, the sovereignty of the state is changing owing to two opposing developments. On the one hand, states are forced to cooperate in order to solve their problems. This applies to the environment, health, peace, knowledge and, as we have witnessed recently, financial stability. On the other hand, the trend is towards subsidiarity or the principle of devolving the power of decision-making to the lowest possible level.

Third, I think the book makes a persuasive argument for the need to rethink the nature of international assistance. It is no longer enough to target international assistance at recipient countries or at specific sectors. The reason is that some global public goods cut across several sectors. How do we finance global public goods? Are existing institutions adequate? If not, how should they be reformed? Do we need new institutions? How do we incorporate into our institutions the ethos of tripartism: government, business and civil society?

This book seeks to answer these and many other important policy questions. It provides us with a new intellectual framework with which to think about international assistance. It also offers a powerful new argument for increased international cooperation in order to provide the global public goods that are needed to give globalization a human face.

Professor Tommy Koh
Ambassador-at-Large
Ministry of Foreign Affairs
Singapore

Executive Director
Asia-Europe Foundation

FOREWORD

National public goods have been part of the economic theory of government for centuries. As any student of public policy knows, the idea that society needs government to overcome the failures of the market in achieving efficiency and equity in the allocation and distribution of resources is hardly new. It is, moreover, a conservative idea. It assumes that private goods and services will always constitute the bulk of people's purchases. Markets must be allowed to function. Yet some outside party must supply those "collective consumption goods" that society also needs, but which the private sector has inadequate incentives to provide.

One might side with Adam Smith in focusing the state, as the provider of public goods, on a few areas: maintaining the money supply, enforcing property rights, promoting competitive markets, providing national defence and administering justice. Or one might assert that people-centred societies call for a wide range of publicly supplied goods, from social security, health services and student aid to public transportation, national parks and food stamps. But whatever position one takes in the debate, it is widely understood that national public goods and services are fundamental to people's well-being and that governments and markets must work together to provide them.

This book takes the concept of public goods across the national frontier. In doing so, it transforms the dimensions of the debate and elevates the concept to a new and urgent plane of importance. The authors start with the observation that, in many areas of public policy, what were once considered to be purely national issues now spill across borders and are global in reach and impact. They suggest that a globalizing world requires a theory of global public goods to achieve crucial goals such as financial stability, human security or the reduction of environmental pollution. Indeed, they point out that many of today's international crises have their roots in a serious undersupply of global public goods.

Consider, for example, the case of global human security. Early in this emerging discussion, the 1994 *Human Development Report* analysed threats to world peace in terms of a series of transborder challenges: unchecked population growth, disparities in economic opportunities, environmental degradation, excessive international migration, narcotics production and trafficking and international terrorism. The report argued that the world needs a new framework for international cooperation to deal with global threats of this kind. That argument remains sharply relevant today, as we reflect on how best to address a range of international public policy issues—from human rights and health to labour and the environment. A theory of global public goods would be an essential part of such a new framework, providing a new motivation for a different type of development assistance.

After all, society has always been willing to spend money on national public goods. We should be equally willing to pay for global goods that serve our common interest, be they shared systems of environmental controls, the destruction of nuclear weapons, the control of transmittable diseases such as malaria and HIV/AIDS, the prevention of ethnic conflicts or the reduction of refugee flows. And we should be prepared to finance such goods through innovative mechanisms based on the principles of reciprocity and collective responsibility, principles that go beyond the concept of official development assistance (ODA).

Of course, we still need ODA, reformed and redirected. Its chief purpose should be to help eradicate extreme poverty through sustainable human development. In fact, with the wealthiest 20% of humanity now as much as 135 times richer than the poorest 20%, and with poverty spreading in all societies, but especially in developing countries, there is an urgent need to increase the level of ODA.

But poverty cannot be stopped if we do not have peace or financial stability or environmental security. Sustainable human development cannot be achieved if we do not prevent conflicts, manage markets wisely or reverse the depletion of soils, energy, fresh water and clean air. Equity within and between generations is not feasible without an international system for identifying and apportioning environmental costs, for dealing with the destabilizing effects of weak financial architecture or for helping people everywhere to benefit from the accumulated stock of global knowledge. The responsibility for and the origins and effects of such challenges transcend national borders. Beyond ODA, we therefore need a new form of international cooperation that embraces trade, debt, investment, financial flows and technology, and that includes payments and incentives to countries to ensure an adequate supply of global public goods. Some ideas on how such a system might be built and financed can be found in this volume.

I expect this book to lend fresh momentum to the debate on the future of international cooperation in the new millennium. It is a book that deserves to be read closely and discussed vigorously by all who have a stake in that future. In a globalizing, increasingly interdependent world, this implies a wide readership indeed. We all stand to benefit enormously from a world that places people at its centre and delivers equity, sustainability and peace for generations to come.

James Gustave Speth
Administrator
United Nations Development Programme

ACKNOWLEDGEMENTS

This volume would not have been possible without the many valuable contributions, comments and suggestions we received from a large number of individuals and organizations. Special thanks go to James Gustave Speth, Administrator of the United Nations Development Programme (UNDP), who challenged us to take a fresh look at the current system of international cooperation. Throughout, we have benefited from his visionary leadership and his interest in and commitment to this project.

We would also like to express our gratitude to Eimi Watanabe, Assistant Administrator and Director of UNDP's Bureau for Development Policy, for her unwavering support and substantive comments. We appreciate in particular her interest in making the analysis relevant to the world's most vulnerable people.

The contours of the volume emerged from an expert meeting held in New York in November 1997. Contributors then presented chapter drafts at a meeting in June 1998. We are grateful to the participants in those meetings and others who shared their ideas and observations with us. We would like to thank in particular Kwesi Botchwey, Ralph C. Bryant, Richard Cooper, Barry Eichengreen, Poul Engberg-Pedersen, Marco Ferroni, Albert Fishlow, Catherine Gwin, Jessica Mathews, Rohinton Medhora, Jean-Claude Milleron, Sanjay Reddy, Oscar de Rojas, Alfredo Sfeir-Younis, John Sewell, Paul Streeten, and Klaus Winkel.

We would also like to thank the representatives of UN member states in New York who made themselves available for consultations on earlier drafts. The Overseas Development Council has been an intellectual partner throughout, and in particular initiated the research discussed by Rajshri Jayaraman and Ravi Kanbur in this volume.

We would especially like to acknowledge the support we received from Todd Sandler, who was extremely generous with his time and expertise and who worked tirelessly for a better manuscript. Any flaws that remain in the text are entirely the responsibility of the editors.

Special thanks are also due to our UNDP colleagues who raised probing questions and provided thoughtful comments: Adel Abdellatif, Rafeeuddin

Ahmed, Thelma Awori, Jean Barut, Nardos Bekele-Thomas, Neil Buhne, Suely Carvalho, Berhe Costantinos, Siba Das, Abdoulaye Dieye, Moez Doraid, Gana Fofang, Fawaz Fokeladeh, Sakiko Fukuda-Parr, Michael Heyn, Nay Htun, Zahir Jamal, Bruce Jenks, Richard Jolly, Terence Jones, Henning Karcher, Anton Kruiderink, Normand Lauzon, Roberto Lenton, Carlos Lopes, Elena Martinez, Peter Matlon, Paul Matthews, Jan Mattsson, Charles McNeill, Brenda McSweeney, Saraswathi Menon, Achola Pala Okeyo, Minh Pham, Frank Pinto, Ravi Rajan, Jordan Ryan, Jakob Simonsen, Jerzy Szeremeta, Sarah Timpson, Mourad Wahba, Augustine Zacharias and Fernando Zumbado. The views expressed here, however, do not necessarily reflect those of UNDP.

We are deeply indebted to Priya Gajraj, whose help in undertaking background research, editing, trouble-shooting and organizing proved invaluable at every stage of the volume's production.

The volume also benefited from the help of Ken MacLeod at Oxford University Press, the design work of Gerald Quinn, and the editing and prepress production work of Bruce Ross-Larson and his team at Communications Development Incorporated. We are most appreciative of the excellent collaboration we received from all of them.

Finally, we are grateful to Flora Aller, Rocio Kattis and Zipora Vainberg-Rogg, who provided valuable administrative support to our work.

Your comments on this publication would also be highly appreciated. Please send your observations and other inquiries about the book to UNDP Bureau for Development Policy/Office of Development Studies (ODS), UH-401, 336 East 45th Street, New York, NY 10017, USA.
Fax: (212) 906–3676
Email: ods@undp.org

CONTRIBUTORS

SCOTT BARRETT
London Business School

NANCY BIRDSALL
Carnegie Endowment for
International Peace

RICHARD A. CASH
Harvard Institute for International
Development

LINCOLN C. CHEN
Rockefeller Foundation

LISA D. COOK
Harvard University

TIM G. EVANS
Rockefeller Foundation

PRIYA GAJRAJ
United Nations Development
Programme

ISABELLE GRUNBERG
United Nations Development
Programme

DAVID A. HAMBURG
Carnegie Commission on
Preventing Deadly Conflict

GEOFFREY HEAL
Columbia University

JANE E. HOLL
Carnegie Commission on
Preventing Deadly Conflict

RAJSHRI JAYARAMAN
Cornell University

RAVI KANBUR
Cornell University

ETHAN B. KAPSTEIN
University of Minnesota

INGE KAUL
United Nations Development
Programme

ROBERT Z. LAWRENCE
Harvard University

LISA L. MARTIN
Harvard University

RUBEN P. MENDEZ
Yale Center for International and
Area Studies

J. MOHAN RAO
University of Massachusetts,
Amherst

JEFFREY SACHS
Harvard Institute for International
Development

TODD SANDLER
Iowa State University

AMARTYA SEN
Cambridge University

ISMAIL SERAGELDIN
World Bank

DEBORA L. SPAR
Harvard Business School

MARC A. STERN
United Nations Development
Programme

JOSEPH E. STIGLITZ
World Bank

J. HABIB SY
Partners for African Development

CHARLES WYPLOSZ
Graduate Institute of International
Studies, Geneva

MARK W. ZACHER
University of British Columbia

INTRODUCTION

INGE KAUL, ISABELLE GRUNBERG AND MARC A. STERN

We live in a volatile world. New opportunities hold ever-greater promise for well-being and prosperity. But caught in a web of tension and contradiction, this world is going through crisis upon crisis.

Economic miracles were hard-won in such places as East Asia; today financial turmoil and social distress dominate. The end of the Cold War raised hopes for a lasting peace and a peace dividend; instead, civil strife, conflict and even genocide have again scarred the landscape. No sooner did people world-wide begin to enjoy the prospects of a longer and healthier life, when new dis-eases—and some old ones—took their toll once again and challenged medical progress. And while technological advances had seemingly freed us from many natural constraints, including time and space, ecosystems are becom-ing overloaded with waste and pollution. Meanwhile, the continuing rise in global inequity, measured by the difference between the world's poorest and the world's richest, places continued strain on the global social fabric. If today's trends are allowed to persist, and crises to fester, the promise of a bet-ter world will recede even further.

Crises are costly. They cause human suffering, strain the environment and are extremely inefficient—a waste of investments and a drain on future resources for development. These facts are well known, and they have engen-dered a growing literature on how to ensure more sustainable growth and human development.

INTRODUCING GLOBAL PUBLIC GOODS

To understand better the roots of global crises, whether loud (financial crashes) or silent (poverty), we propose to look at today's policy challenges through the lens of global public goods.

First, what is a public good? We know that the marketplace is the most efficient way of producing private goods. But the market relies on a set of goods that it cannot itself provide: property rights, predictability, safety, nomenclature and so on. These goods often need to be provided by nonmarket or modified market mechanisms. In addition, as discussed in our chapter on "Defining Global Public Goods", people need both public and private goods, whether or not they engage in market transactions—peace is a case in point. Public goods are recognized as having benefits that cannot easily be confined to a single "buyer" (or set of "buyers"). Yet once they are provided, many can enjoy them for free. Street names are an example. A clean environment is another. Without a mechanism for collective action, these goods can be underproduced.

Or take education, which benefits the person being educated. To calculate the benefits, we take the income a person earns over a lifetime with education, and subtract that which she would get without an education. But that figure does not tell the whole story. What about the numerous employers the person will have over a lifetime, and the savings realized because these employers do not have to train her in-house? What about the benefits that literacy brings to all the companies that rely on the written word to advertise? The benefits to those who issue public warnings, put out signs or seek to implement laws? If one were to put a figure on all these benefits, they would dwarf the amount that accrues strictly to the educated person. This difference between the public and the private benefits is called an externality. And because of its substantial externalities, education is a public good.

Financial stability, like many topics covered in this volume, has public good qualities. A bank or financial institution can generate much profit through risky lending. All it stands to lose is its capital if it fails. But in a complex and interdependent financial system, the costs of a single institution defaulting are in fact much higher—often a multiple—because one default can lead to more failures and defaults. The difference between the private cost to the bank and the public cost, again, measures the externalities in risky behaviour—in this example, the negative externalities.

While public goods are understood to have large externalities (and diffuse benefits), a stricter definition relies on a judgement of how the good is consumed: if no one can be barred from consuming the good, then it is nonexcludable. If it can be consumed by many without becoming depleted, then it is nonrival in consumption. Pure public goods, which are rare, have both these attributes, while impure public goods possess them to a lesser degree, or possess a combination of them.

Looking again at education can help us understand why public goods are difficult to produce in proper quantities. Suppose there are many illiterate people and many eager employers. A person's first employer would be the one to shoulder the burden of educating her. But why should that first employer pay all the costs, while future employers will reap the benefits for free? This prospect is what might discourage any employer from paying the cost to educate her workforce. The solution is for all employers to pool resources to jointly finance education or at least to bridge the gap between the benefits education brings to the individual—for which she could pay herself—and the extra benefits they jointly get. But since nonemployers benefit as well, the whole community is usually brought into this effort.

This, in a simplified form, is the dilemma of providing public goods. And with globalization, the externalities—the "extra" costs and benefits—are increasingly borne by people in other countries. Indeed, issues that have traditionally been merely national are now global because they are beyond the grasp of any single nation. And crises endure perhaps because we lack the proper policy mechanisms to address such global public goods. In addition, the pervasiveness of today's crises suggests that they might all suffer from a common cause, such as a common flaw in policy-making, rather than from issue-specific problems. If so, issue-specific policy responses, typical to date, would be insufficient—allowing global crises to persist and even multiply.

In applying the concept of global public goods, we look for goods whose benefits reach across borders, generations and population groups. All public goods, whether local, national or global, tend to suffer from underprovision. The reason is precisely that they are public. For individual actors, it is often the best and most rational strategy to let others provide the good—and then to enjoy it, free of charge. At the international level, this collective action problem is compounded by the gap between externalities that are becoming more and more international in reach, and the fact that the main policy-making unit remains the nation state.

WHAT THIS BOOK IS ABOUT

Our proposition is that today's turmoil reveals a serious underprovision of global public goods. To explore that proposition, we investigate two main questions. The first is whether—and to what extent—the concept of global public goods is useful in describing and analysing global challenges. If it is, the second question is whether we can find feasible policy options and strategies that would apply across the board to ensure a more reliable supply of global public goods—from market efficiency to equity, health, environmental sustainability and peace. Without these global public goods, human security and development will be elusive.

How this book is structured

These questions are investigated in relation to selected areas of global policy concern, in case studies that form the core of the volume. Brief summaries of the case studies are provided at the beginning of each cluster of chapters in the second part of the book. Framing the case studies are two additional sections, one on concepts, and the other on policy implications.

The first part of the volume sets the stage. The chapter by Kaul, Grunberg and Stern explores the literature on public goods and provides a definition of global public goods. Todd Sandler elaborates on intergenerational public goods, looking in particular at the strategic aspects of their provision and discussing institutional arrangements for their allocation. Lisa Martin then presents an overview of current theories of international cooperation, drawing our attention to the roles of international organizations and nonstate actors in helping states realise the benefits of cooperation. In this respect, perhaps the most useful function of international organizations is reducing uncertainty—providing information about the issue at hand and about the preferences and behaviours of those who have a stake in the issue—states, nongovernmental organizations and so on.

After the Case Studies, the third part of the volume deals with cross-cutting policy implications. The chapter by Rajshri Jayaraman and Ravi Kanbur asks the question: when should donor countries fund the provision of global public goods through aid? They find that aid best contributes to public goods provision when these goods depend on the "weakest link". For example, success in eradicating a disease such as malaria or smallpox depends on the effort of the last countries to harbour these diseases. Public goods expenditures in poor countries are also especially recommended when those countries have a pivotal role to play in a certain issue-area, as with the preservation of tropical species, for example. Lisa Cook and Jeffrey Sachs discuss the need for greater focus on regional public goods, both to provide for the specialized needs of individual regions and to coordinate regional contributions to global public goods. Noting the minimal funding currently targeted to the regional level, Cook and Sachs recommend a number of steps for improving the ability of international aid organizations to help nations work together towards regional public goods. Considering the success of the Marshall Plan in post–Second World War development cooperation in Europe, the authors suggest that regional development cooperation in the future could follow a similar model.

A synthesis of all chapters, distilling from them the findings and policy messages that help answer the book's two main questions, is presented in the concluding chapter. There, the reader will also find ample references to individual chapters. This has been done in order to link the more general conclusions to concrete findings, and also to show how some of the broader points apply to particular issue-areas.

WHAT THIS BOOK IS BUILDING ON

We are not starting from scratch. The systematic formulation of the theory of public goods began with Paul Samuelson's (1954) "The Pure Theory of Public Expenditure". Mancur Olson's (1971) *The Logic of Collective Action* analysed provision problems at length. The application of the concept of public goods to global challenges started in the late 1960s, especially with Garrett Hardin's (1968) "The Tragedy of the Commons", followed by Bruce Russett and John Sullivan's (1971) "Collective Goods and International Organization". More than a decade later, Charles Kindleberger's (1986) *The World in Depression 1929–1939* analysed the economic crisis of the 1930s as a failure to provide key global public goods, such as an open trading system and an international lender of last resort. More recent contributions to the debate include Ruben Mendez's (1992) *International Public Finance* and Todd Sandler's (1997) *Global Challenges: An Approach to Environmental, Political, and Economic Problems*. So, public good analysis has been applied to global problems. But there has been surprisingly little examination of what global public goods really are—and few attempts to map out a typology of such goods.

Closely linked to the issue of providing global public goods is the political science question: why do states cooperate and abide by, or defect from, international agreements? A rich literature of different strands has developed on this question, especially since the 1980s (see, for example, Keohane 1984; Krasner 1986; Gilpin 1987; Mayer, Rittberger and Zurn 1993; and Brookings Institution 1994–98). Much of this literature is focused on intergovernmental cooperation. In our analysis, we extend the debate to take into account the fact that we live in a multiactor world.

We also draw on the development literature, which asks how economic activity can be translated into wider human choices and improved well-being for people (see, among others, Sen 1987; Dasgupta 1995; and UNDP various years). So far, this literature has been concerned primarily with developing countries. Yet the division of the world into "developed" and "developing" countries is no longer valid in its traditional form. It is becoming evident that high income is no guarantee of either equitable or sustainable development. The challenge of ensuring human security exists in the South as well as in the North, albeit often in different forms. And global public goods are likely to be critical to meeting this challenge in all countries.

In addition, we have consulted the aid literature (such as Riddell 1996; Stokke 1996; Berg 1997; World Bank 1998; and UNDP 1999) which, surprisingly, does not always build on theories of international regimes. Those theories have, in large measure, focused on international treaty making and the role of international organizations. Aid—the operational side of international cooperation, as opposed to the norm- and standard-setting side—has been primarily country-centred and guided by national development priorities. It has had few, if any, systematic linkages with international agreements. But in response to today's global challenges, the aid agenda needs to be expanded. Besides moral and ethical reasons linked to their "purely" national development concerns, poor countries need transfers to contribute to the provision of global public goods—in the mutual interest of all. The beneficiaries may be, for example, countries that forgo development opportunities in order to conserve pristine forests that harbour biodiversity or absorb carbon monoxide, or countries that require help in devising good institutions and practices for the safety of the world financial system.

This discussion benefits, too, from a wealth of issue-specific analyses. Without all of these different literatures (each referenced in the chapters), it would not have been possible to undertake the multidisciplinary and multilevel analysis we are attempting here. We are seeking to combine these literatures because the different issues they address have begun to intersect. Today's global challenges cannot be adequately understood by relying on any one strand of literature.

The multidisciplinary, multilevel and multi-issue approach has also allowed us to offer a comparative perspective on the study of global challenges. While environmental concerns are often addressed in a public goods framework, such other issues as financial stability, equity or culture have rarely been treated from this viewpoint. Elements of the environment paradigm no doubt inform much of the analysis here.

The main policy messages

We have entered a new era of public policy, defined by a growing number of concerns that straddle national borders. That is the overarching policy message emanating from this work, and it poses a dual challenge. One is the need to transform international cooperation from its traditional place as "external affairs" into policy-making applicable to most, if not all, domestic issue areas. The second challenge is to develop the concepts and instruments needed to overcome problems of collective action. In particular this will require actions to "internalize externalities"—to deal with potentially contagious phenomena at the source, before they spill across borders.

All the subjects examined in the case studies constitute, in one sense or another, global public goods. They also illustrate the new nature of many global public goods—what we call, in table 1 of the concluding chapter, *global policy outcomes*. Unlike other global issues that concern relations between countries—or at-the-border issues, such as transportation or tariffs—many of today's international policy problems require behind-the-border policy convergence and, increasingly also, joint facilities. This may include organizations that provide services on behalf of all countries, such as surveillance of global trends or rescue arrangements for countries in crisis.

Several factors are behind this new type of global public goods. Among them is the increasing openness of countries—which facilitates the travelling of global "bads". Another is the growing number of global systemic risks—which require more respect for thresholds of sustainability. A third is the strength of nonstate transnational actors, such as the private sector and civil society, which has stepped up the pressure on governments to adhere to common policy norms, from basic human rights to technical standards.

Under these conditions such global actions as reducing pollution, eradicating disease or supervising banks effectively are important to national policy objectives. Without policy achievements by the national governments that "matter" in particular issue areas, global public goods—such as environmental sustainability, health or financial stability—are not likely to emerge. And that, in turn, jeopardizes national policy goals in many countries, creating a global public bad.

Most of these changes have been in the making for decades. But only recently have the accumulating effects of these changes attracted serious attention from policy analysts, political leaders and the general public. They are debated from the viewpoint of managing globalization. It is not too surprising, then, to find that policy-making has not yet been fully adjusted. That makes it more interesting to identify precisely where, and why, the present system fails in addressing the new issues effectively.

The case studies in this volume point to three key weaknesses in the current arrangements for providing global public goods.

- *The jurisdictional gap*, that is, the discrepancy between a globalized world and national, separate units of policy-making. Indeed, with policy-making still predominantly national in both focus and scope, a gap arises due to the simple fact that many of today's challenges are global. The anxiety of national policy-makers over their loss of sovereignty to global markets and civil society can be traced in part to the absence of a clear strategy for linking national policy objectives to international diplomacy. Many governments are only just awakening to this mismatch between their traditional approaches to policy-making and the demands of the new international policy environment.

- *The participation gap*. The past decades have witnessed the emergence of important new global actors. But international cooperation is still primarily an intergovernmental process in which other actors participate on the fringes, undermining the effectiveness of traditional efforts to address global policy issues. This participation gap also extends to marginal and voiceless groups, despite the spread of democracy. By expanding the role of civil society and the private sector in international negotiations, governments can enhance their leverage over policy outcomes while promoting pluralism and diversity in the process. Keeping in mind issues of legitimacy and representativeness, the decision-making structures in many major multilateral organizations are due for re-evaluation, given the steady privatization and deconcentration of political and economic power in recent decades.

- *The incentive gap*. International cooperation today is broader in scope, having moved from between-country and at-the-border issues—that is, international traffic rules—to behind-the-border issues. This makes the implementation, or the operational side, of international agreements ever more important. But the operational follow-up to these agreements relies too exclusively on the aid mechanism, ignoring many other practical policy options that could make cooperation a preferred strategy for both developing and industrial countries.

Global public goods thus suffer from many types of collective action problems. A major obstacle is uncertainty about the problem and the feasibility of possible policy options. But even when uncertainty is resolved, other constraints remain. Public policy-making and its mechanisms and tools still reflect more of yesterday's realities than today's. To turn global public bads into global public goods, policy adjustments are urgently needed. Indeed, debates on reform are under way in many areas—from health to finance to peace.

Many of the proposals here echo these debates. But they also add an important dimension. They show that reform needs to go beyond controlling bads. Patchwork corrections to the present system will not be sufficient. In order to move beyond constant crisis prevention and management and be able to set our sights again on positive, constructive development, we need to review the fundemental principles of policy making. Two basic changes are called for. First, international cooperation must form an integral part of national public policy making. Clearly, the dividing line between internal and external affairs has become blurred, requiring a new approach. Second, international cooperation must be a fair proposition for all if it is to be successful. With consensus on these two points, the rest might even be quite easy to achieve.

The volume's main policy recommendations on the steps that could be taken to close the three identified policy gaps demonstrate this point.

CLOSING THE JURISDICTIONAL GAP

A broad recommendation emerges from the chapters suggesting that governments must assume full responsibility for the cross-border effects their citizens generate. In other words, countries should apply to these spillovers a policy principle that is well established nationally: the principle of "internalizing externalities". Many public goods as well as bads are the result of externalities—or the benefits and costs that actors do not consider in their decision-making. This is also an important reason for public goods to be undersupplied and public bads to be oversupplied.

The purpose of extending the applicability of this principle to international spillovers is to strengthen the capacity of nation states to cope with global interdependence. The implication is to let international cooperation start "at home", with national policies meant, at a minimum, to reduce or avoid altogether negative cross-border spillovers—and preferably to go beyond that to generate positive externalities in the interest of all.

A first step in this direction could involve establishing national externality profiles to help bring each nation's spillovers, both positive and negative, into focus. These profiles should facilitate bargaining among nations by increasing the transparency of the impacts that states have on each other and the global commons. Such profiles would also make countries more likely to take responsibility for the externalities generated within their borders.

A policy of internalizing externalities may also require that national government ministries develop a clear mandate for international cooperation. This would be especially important for ministries with extensive external linkages, such as labour, health, environment, trade or finance. As a corollary, it could be useful for ministries to have a two-track budget—one for domestic expenditures and one to finance international cooperation, while ensuring effective coordination of these external activities.

Several authors emphasize that regional cooperation is an important input into the provision of global public goods—as an intermediary between national and global concerns. This applies to the process of setting priorities—deciding which global public goods to produce and how much to provide—and to implementation—translating global concerns into concrete, lower-level follow-up actions. For example, because priorities and needs differ regionally, often even subregionally, there is no one standard approach to, say, agricultural or medical research. Furthermore, while harmonizing policies and standards may be critical to enhanced market efficiency, uniformity is often an inappropriate solution. Thus a careful effort must be made in providing global public goods to adhere to the principle of subsidiarity—moving decision-making on priorities and implementation as close to the local level as possible. In many cases this means strengthening regional bodies and entrusting them with responsibility for intermediation between the national and global levels.

To the extent that national or regional level internalization of externalities is not a feasible or efficient option, or where there are no markets, international organizations can facilitate "externality exchanges" between countries or between governments and other global actors. Many international organizations, including those of the UN system, were originally concerned with strengthening sectors—such as health, education, culture, food production, labour markets and industry. But they took too little account of the linkages to arrive at concrete outcomes—such as food security, peace, balanced growth or shared knowledge.

These outcomes often result from a combination of several efforts: not only capacity development in each sector, but also cross-sectoral and international linkages. That is why bargaining across countries and across issues to get results will become an important form of international cooperation in the new political landscape. Some reorganization of present institutions may also be warranted. For example, the United Nations Educational, Scientific and Cultural Organization (UNESCO) could be linked with the World Intellectual Property

Organization (WIPO) to become a major "knowledge bank", combining two complementary concerns—the creation of knowledge and its dissemination.

In sum, the policy-making process required for dealing effectively with global public goods is a circular one, a loop. Its roots are at the national level, where for reasons of efficiency and effectiveness the primary responsibility for the internalization of externalities must lie. Global-level action is a second-best option, because international cooperation has cost implications—in particular, the transactions costs for negotiations among a large group of actors. But to avoid collective action problems and to ensure fair burden sharing, such costs are in some instances unavoidable—and probably modest compared with the costs of inaction. International cooperation is no longer just a matter of external affairs. It is first and foremost a process of national policy formulation.

CLOSING THE PARTICIPATION GAP

The foregoing section has discussed the sharing of responsibility for the provision of global public goods across different levels—the national, the regional and the global. This section looks at the horizontal distribution of the opportunities among all major actors—government, people, civil society and business—to contribute to the production and consumption of public goods, and to setting priorities among various kinds of public goods. In order for the provision process to work, these three stages must be fully participatory. All actors must have a voice, have an appropriate opportunity to make the contribution expected of them and have access to the goods that result. If these requirements are not met, the publicness of public goods will stay a potentiality, not a reality. And instead of acting as an "equalizer", global public goods could worsen inequities. As the relevant chapters in this volume argue, the Internet is a global public good whose publicness has to be deliberately sought.

The fact that some public goods have access problems may sound paradoxical, because public goods are, at least partially, nonexcludable. Yet barriers to access are different from excludability. In theory, anyone can access the Internet and, therefore, the Internet appears to be a nonexcludable good. But in practice, the poor often cannot because they lack the money to pay for a subscription to a server, to obtain computer training or, even more basic, to buy a computer, or, if the option is available to them, they may lack the time to access a public computer facility, let us say, in a library or post office.

Likewise, one cannot take full advantage of good roads, even toll-free roads, unless one has a motor vehicle. To benefit from the public good of a good justice system, one often needs resources to pay a lawyer. And many children cannot benefit from a free education system because they cannot travel to school or because they have to work to support the family.

Access to public goods matters in part for equity considerations. When access is very costly, public goods end up benefiting only that part of the population that can afford to make the connection. When financed by taxes, the provision of public goods can then become regressive, in the fiscal sense of redistributing resources from the poor to the rich. But efficiency also comes into play. By enlarging access to the goods, one can bring widespread benefits at a lower cost since, once connection is paid for, it usually costs very little for an additional consumer to benefit from the public good.

At a global level, it is equally important to ensure that global public goods are accessible to all, especially if the production effort has been a shared endeavour. For example, many opportunities to take advantage of (free) knowledge are lost due to illiteracy. But concern about access is also important in order to ensure that public policy is not reinforcing existing undesirable trends, such as growing inequity. Since equity is a critical lubricant of international cooperation, the provision of global public goods across the board could suffer if equity issues are not addressed—as illustrated by the example of global climate change, where progress has been stalled not only by issues of scientific uncertainty, but also by concerns about the fairness and equity of some of the policy options.

To ensure that all concerned actors have a voice in determining global public good priorities, there are at least four dimensions that are needed for the reform of current institutions.

- One, there is a need for better North-South representation in the governance of many international organizations. We share the view that some analysts have advanced (Sachs 1998) that an important step would be to expand the G–8 group of major industrial countries into a G–16 by adding eight major developing countries.

- Two, civil society and the private sector have formed transnational alliances far beyond the reach of national governments. Similarly, their actions sometimes determine policy outcomes far more than government actions. Since effective solutions to pressing global problems are unlikely to emerge from forums that exclude these important actors, a new tripartism is recommended, involving government, business and civil society.

- Three, there are powerful incentives to solve today's problems at the expense of future generations, particularly since these future societies have no voice in current deliberations. To ensure that this will not be the case, special efforts must be made to take the longer term into account and to properly value the future. We suggest a new United Nations Global Trusteeship Council to act as a custodian of sustainable, or "steady-course" development.[1]

- Four, it is important in the newer, more issue-oriented international organizations to ensure enhanced interdisciplinarity, or put differently, a proper representation of all related concerns and interests. For example, if representatives of social concerns were present when financial rescue packages are negotiated, the social costs of financial crises could be considerably reduced.

The world is already moving in these directions, in particular towards the fuller involvement of civil society and business in intergovernmental processes—a new form of tripartism. One issue still unresolved is how to square the indirect representation of civil society and business by governments with their direct representation in international forums. The concern is that these groups might ultimately be overrepresented. But judging from the reflections on this point in the chapters here, notably those on equity, it appears that people have many concerns that are not linked to their nationality or citizenship—such as those of environmentalists, lawyers, doctors or feminists. Many individuals act internationally not only as a national of a particular country but also as a "global citizen". Nevertheless, we agree that a more systematic approach to the representation of civil society and business in intergovernmental forums is urgently needed—especially because this new tripartism appears so important to ensuring the publicness of global public goods.

As several authors argue, countries sometimes shy away from an international commitment because they are not sure that they have the resources—and capacities—to meet the new commitments. This frequently is a major reason for the underprovision of global public goods, from health surveillance to pollution reduction. In such cases it would often be more efficient for the international community to support poor countries in meeting their commitments than to shoulder the costs of the resulting overproduction of global public bads. True participation requires that all actors with a stake in cooperation be able to engage in the debate over global priorities, in that they have the capacity to be represented and that they can meet their international commitments. The need to support states unable to muster the resources to participate fully in international negotiations is thus an important part of ensuring the validity of a global public goods agenda. Just as important, when global public goods depend on contributions by most, or all, nations, it will be necessary to support capacity building in some states to enable them to meet their international commitments.

In sum, enhancing participation in the decision-making, the production and the consumption of global public goods is critical to ensuring equity in international policy-making. Without it, this process would lack legitimacy.

CLOSING THE INCENTIVE GAP

To be durable and to yield expected results, cooperation must be incentive-compatible. That is, it must offer clear net benefits to all participating parties, and all actors must perceive the benefits as fair. This is a message that comes out loud and clear from all the chapters. The authors' suggestions on how to achieve such incentive-compatibility are far-ranging, but they remain focused on practical steps of use to policy-makers. Among the most promising ideas, the following stand out.

Two low-cost approaches to improving the provision of global public goods are taking advantage of adoption spillovers and opportunities to combine national (or private) with global (or public) gains.[2] Both seek to piggyback public benefits on self-interested actions by states, firms and individuals. A viable example is, among others, the Montreal Protocol (United Nations 1987), which provides for the phase-out of ozone-depleting substances. Its adoption was made possible by a confluence of private and public interests.

Compensatory payments will form an important element of any incentive strategy for global public goods. Such payments may be required where the policy preferences and priorities of countries diverge. The Global Environment Facility as well as the Multilateral Development Fund established under the Montreal Protocol illustrate this approach.

Where the benefits of a global public good can be at least partially limited, a "club" approach can be attempted to ensure that those who benefit most from the good pay the largest share of the costs. Many organizations—the World Trade Organization, the Organisation for Economic Co-operation and Development, the North Atlantic Treaty Alliance—require their members to meet certain criteria before granting admission. One innovative idea to emerge from this study is the possibility of applying this same approach to the liberalization of international financial markets—creating clubs of countries with similar levels of institutional sophistication and capital account liberalization. A country's commitment to policies in support of financial stability would bring club membership and, with it, benefits such as collective support in case the country is affected by financial contagion.

There are also many important opportunities to use market forces and the price mechanism to improve the provision, or preservation, of common goods. Many public goods (clean air, fresh water, ocean fisheries) are underpriced while others (technological knowledge in certain areas) are overpriced. Getting the prices right, and where necessary establishing the basic frameworks for markets to emerge, are critical steps that the international community must take in some policy areas to secure desired policy outcomes. In fact, this policy practice has already begun—fishing rights and pollution entitlements are, in some instances, already tradable.

These recommendations show that in addition to aid, there are many more financing rationales and methods that could pay for the costs of providing global public goods. Yet official development assistance (ODA) is often used to finance global public goods, such as protecting the ozone layer or meeting the costs of financial crises, making it ever scarcer for the poorest countries, which have to rely on aid to meet even their most basic national development concerns. For example, many governments contribute to the Global Environment Facility out of their aid budget, and aid funds are used for initiatives to prevent and manage global financial crises. We estimate that one aid dollar in four supports global public goods rather than just the purely national concerns of poor countries. Our suggestion is to label the present ODA stream as ODA(C), for country allocations to assist poor states in their national endeavours—and to establish a new account code, ODA(G), for global priorities.

Against this account code, one could then list all expenditures related to global public goods, many of which now escape recording. Examples include payments for services procured through market-based arrangements, compensations, as well as the additional aid that might be motivated by making global public goods accessible to all.

As explained above, ensuring that developing countries have the capacity to engage in the global policy debate and take action on their priorities is a crucial element of international cooperation in an era of global public goods. For this reason it may not suffice to consider equity and access only on an issue-by-issue basis. It is also important that poor countries have the means to play an active role in negotiating externality exchanges, policy convergence and other forms of international cooperation in support of global objectives. We suggest the creation of a "Global Participation Fund", self-administered by developing countries, to support the fair involvement of all in global arrangements. Such a fund would expand on the work of the United Nations Conference on Trade and Development in support of developing countries. Similar proposals emerge from the case studies for self-administered arrangements at the regional level, such as aid funds and regional versions of the International Monetary Fund.

Many of these new financing methods cannot work without adjusting national public finance procedures to recognize the international dimension of many sectoral ministries. The two-track budgeting recommended above, whereby a portion of the budgets of national ministries would be earmarked for international cooperation, is crucial to opening new possibilities for tackling cross-border spillovers, and for promoting cooperation in the production of positive global externalities.

GLOBAL PUBLIC GOODS: WHO BENEFITS?

What do states and people gain from this new toolkit of international cooperation? At the most general level, improving international cooperation will strengthen the capacity of national governments to achieve their national policy objectives. As global integration proceeds, domestic policy objectives—such as public health, economic growth or environmental protection—are increasingly subject to international forces. To attain their national goals, governments must increasingly turn to international cooperation to achieve some control over transboundary forces that affect their people. Little surprise, then, to find that international consultations in areas as diverse as trade, finance, waste disposal, food safety and population have attracted more interest in national policies and actions. There is thus a broad justification for a more systematic and integrated approach to international cooperation. To accomplish this, national and international policy-making must form a continuum, where issue experts become diplomats, and diplomats add technical expertise to their skills.

For developing nations the prospect of a systematic approach to global public goods brings hope of a more equitable allocation of global resources to address priorities that matter to them. By establishing objective criteria for defining a global public good, the Northern and Southern development agendas that frequently seem to be in conflict become more comparable—and therefore negotiable. While preventing global warming and expanding access to the world knowledge stock are both global public goods, different groups of countries, for various compelling reasons, accord them different priority. But since they both constitute global public goods, the possibility of a quid pro quo suggests itself much more strongly than if one argues that each is essentially a "private" good—a "Northern" and a "Southern" good, without a common public denominator.

But this is only the first and most obvious benefit. Many global public goods, such as a free trade regime or well-functioning financial markets, require a strong network of global participants, and this provides a rationale for efforts at national capacity building. These activities, by definition, are in support of global public goods, even if they have large positive benefits for the country. So, to the degree that better regulation or administrative capabilities in developing countries bring about desirable outcomes globally, the international community has an incentive to support these activities. Funding for these activities, then, should come from non-aid accounts, as suggested by the ODA(G) account. By distinguishing between global public good financing and aid, developing countries can refocus development assistance on national development priorities. In addition, they would have a voice in decisions on how to allocate non-aid resources—through the participatory dialogue on ranking global public goods.

For industrial countries the prospect of a more orderly approach to managing global policy concerns should lighten the financial burden they currently bear when international crises erupt—whether in capital markets, health, environment or peace. The present method of dealing with these issues treats them as independent problems, precluding important opportunities for reciprocal deal-making that could improve cooperation. A more formal process for identifying and ranking global public goods would allow states to explore potential trade-offs of mutual support that could bring gains to all sides. Furthermore, burden sharing could be brought into a more universal environment, allowing some states to claim credit for the global public goods that they are already providing—and to ask similar contributions of others. Without a structure to promote issue linkage and mutual reciprocity, distrust and animosity can prevent states from joining together even when all would benefit from cooperation.

As we survey the costly economic, military, humanitarian and social crises of the past decade, it is clear that the international system is typically caught reacting to devastating circumstances—in whatever issue area—well after the main damage has been done. Preventing crises before they occur, and being better prepared for those that are unanticipated, is a far more efficient and effective way to manage our affairs. Thus there is a very practical argument for re-evaluating national and international policy-making.

The political momentum for such a re-evaluation could come from the energy that greater equity and fairness in international relations could unleash. This explains the strong emphasis here on more participatory decision-making, on forging a new tripartism among governments, civil society and business, on creating a United Nations Global Trusteeship Council for public goods and on expanding the G–8 to a G–16. Ignoring the need for such reforms could easily result in a continuing series of global crises, raising the likelihood of public backlash against globalization.

These concerns, and the notion of shared global priorities, have been with us for a long time. They inspired the efforts of political leaders and others following the two devastating world wars of the 20th century. The lessons from the horrors of those conflicts tempted leaders to pursue new mechanisms for international cooperation in the hope that conflicts between nations could be settled peacefully, and that the economic and social seeds of conflict could be attacked before they took root. But these leaders were not just idealists. Their concerns were the most practical of all—to prevent war, to eliminate want.

It is time to reclaim this ambition. Looking out on a world whose institutions are increasingly out of synch with the economic, social and human realities of our era, we see a compelling need to revisit our comfortable patterns of diplomacy and to bring them up to date. There is still time to address this dramatic disconnect between institutions and reality. Doing so requires leadership, vision and faith that our future is not merely the work of destiny but ours to shape.

NOTES

The views presented here are entirely those of the authors and not necessarily those of the institution with which they are affiliated.

1. To be clear, this proposal suggests the creation of a new trusteeship council, not a revitalization of the Trusteeship Council that was established under the Charter of the United Nations to supervise the administration of the former Trust Territories. That Trusteeship Council suspended operation in October, 1994, with the independence of Palau.

2. Adoption spillovers appear each time existing users of a standard, for example, benefit from the adoption of that standard by a new member. They also come into play when the adoption of a new standard (for example, cars that run only on lead-free gasoline) forces others to follow suit.

REFERENCES

Berg, Elliot. 1997. *Rethinking Technical Cooperation: Reforms for Capacity Building in Africa.* New York: United Nations Development Programme.

Brookings Institution. 1994–98. Project on Integrating National Economies Series. Washington, DC.

Dasgupta, Partha S. 1995. *An Inquiry into Well-Being and Destitution.* Oxford: Clarendon Press.

Gilpin, Robert G. 1987. *The Political Economy of International Relations.* Princeton, NJ: Princeton University Press.

Hardin, Garrett. 1968. "The Tragedy of the Commons." *Science* 162 (December): 1243–48.

Keohane, Robert O. 1984. *After Hegemony: Cooperation and Discord in the World Political Economy.* Princeton, NJ: Princeton University Press.

Kindleberger, Charles P. 1986. *The World in Depression 1929–1939.* Berkeley: University of California Press.

Krasner, Stephen D. 1986. *International Regimes.* Ithaca, NY and London: Cornell University Press.

Mayer, Peter, Volker Rittberger and Michael Zurn. 1993. "Regime Theory: State of the Art and Perspectives." In Volker Rittberger and Peter Mayer, eds., *Regime Theory and International Relations.* New York: Oxford University Press.

Mendez, Ruben P. 1992. *International Public Finance: A New Perspective on Global Relations.* New York: Oxford University Press.

Olson, Mancur. 1971. *The Logic of Collective Action.* Cambridge, MA: Harvard University Press.

Riddell, Roger. 1996. *Aid in the 21st Century.* ODS Discussion Paper 6. New York: United Nations Development Programme, Office of Development Studies.

Russett, Bruce M., and John D. Sullivan. 1971. "Collective Goods and International Organization." *International Organization* 25(4): 845–65.

Sachs, Jeffrey. 1998. "Making it Work." *The Economist.* 12 September.

Samuelson, Paul A. 1954. "The Pure Theory of Public Expenditure." *Review of Economics and Statistics* 36 (November): 387–89.

Sandler, Todd. 1997. *Global Challenges: An Approach to Environmental, Political, and Economic Problems*. Cambridge: Cambridge University Press.

Sen, Amartya K. 1987. *On Ethics and Economics*. Oxford and New York: Basil Blackwell.

Stokke, Olav, ed. 1996. *Foreign Aid Toward the Year 2000: Experiences and Challenges*. London: Frank Cass.

United Nations. 1987. *Montreal Protocol on Substances that Deplete the Ozone Layer*. UN Treaty Series 26369. Montreal, Canada.

UNDP (United Nations Development Programme). Various years. *Human Development Report*. New York: Oxford University Press.

———. 1999. *The Future of Aid: Regional Perspectives*. ODS Discussion Paper 17. New York: UNDP, Office of Development Studies.

World Bank. 1998. *Assessing Aid: What Works, What Doesn't, and Why*. A Policy Research Report. New York: Oxford University Press.

CONCEPTS

DEFINING GLOBAL PUBLIC GOODS

INGE KAUL, ISABELLE GRUNBERG AND MARC A. STERN

Weekends are great days for shopping—in cities like Manila, Nairobi, Cairo, Buenos Aires and London but also in many smaller towns and rural areas. People hustle through crowded bazaars and air-conditioned supermarkets with their baskets and carts filled with goods: bread, rice, vegetables, shoes and perhaps toys and sweets. Rarely, if ever, has someone been seen shopping for traffic lights. Yet few of our weekend shoppers could do without them. They would be stuck in gridlock traffic or unable to cross busy streets and highways. Without traffic lights, some might even have serious accidents on their way to the market. The reason nobody carries traffic lights in their shopping cart is that everybody expects to find them outside, as a public good. Inside the market, shoppers' attention is focused on private goods.

For their well-being people need both private and public goods. This chapter focuses on public goods, on the world outside the market places. First we introduce the concept of public goods and describe some of its main elements. Then we refine this generic definition and identify the distinguishing characteristics of *global* public goods, the main subject of this chapter and this volume. While there is a rapidly growing literature on the globalization of economic activity and its implications for public policy, not much attention has been paid to the notion of global public goods. Yet we know that domestically efficient economic activity and people's well-being require appropriate public goods. The question is, how does the expansion of economic activity across national borders affect the demand for public goods? In particular, does it entail a need for global public goods? To answer this question, it is important to understand the main properties and distinguishing features of international public goods, including regional and global public goods.

Global public goods must meet two criteria. The first is that their benefits have strong qualities of publicness—that is, they are marked by nonrivalry in consumption and nonexcludability. These features place them in the general category of public goods. The second criterion is that their benefits are quasi universal in terms of countries (covering more than one group of countries), people (accruing to several, preferably all, population groups), and generations (extending to both current and future generations, or at least meeting the needs of current generations without foreclosing development options for future generations).[1] This property makes humanity as a whole the *publicum,* or beneficiary of global public goods.

PUBLIC GOODS: THE GENERIC DEFINITION

To understand what a public good is, it is useful to examine its counterpart, a private good, and to discuss what it means to have a market for private goods. In a market transaction a buyer gains access to a good (or service) in exchange for money or, sometimes, in exchange for another good. Buyers and sellers meet through the price mechanism, and if everything works in a textbook-perfect way, the economy can reach a state of maximum efficiency in which resources are put to their most productive uses. A key condition for a market transaction, however, is that the ownership or use of a good can be transferred or denied conditional on the offsetting exchange—the payment of its price. Thus private goods tend to be excludable and rival in consumption. A piece of cake, once consumed, cannot be enjoyed by others. With public goods, matters are different.

The main properties of public goods:
nonrivalry in consumption and nonexcludability

The concept of public goods has its roots in 18th century scholarship. David Hume discussed the difficulties inherent in providing for "the common good" in his *Treatise of Human Nature,* first published in 1739. Some 30 years later Adam Smith analysed similar questions in his *Inquiry into the Nature and Causes of the Wealth of Nations.* We will not attempt to summarize the literature on the topic that has emerged since then. As Shmanske (1991, p.4) notes, it is "a literature so vast and varied that the mention of public goods brings to mind a dozen different issues, each of which brings along its own idiosyncratic model and relies on its own set of special assumptions". Rather than offer an exhaustive summary, we will map out, in nontechnical language, the most important characteristics of public goods and clarify some of the key issues involved—notably those that help us understand the nature of *global* public goods.[2]

PURE PUBLIC GOODS. The ideal public good has two main qualities: its benefits are nonrivalrous in consumption and nonexcludable. To elaborate, consider again the example of the traffic light. If one person crosses a street safely thanks to a well-functioning traffic light (and thanks to obedience on the part of the drivers facing the red signal), this does not distract from the light's utility for other persons. Hence the light's benefits are nonrivalrous in consumption. At the same time, it would be extremely difficult in political and social terms and quite costly in economic terms to reserve usage of the light for one person or group and to make all other people walk long distances to find a safe cross-way elsewhere. Thus the traffic light's benefits are nonexcludable, or excludable only at prohibitive costs. In fact, one could argue that as more people obey the light's signals, its benefits to each individual grow. This is because frequent use indicates broad public acceptance of the light's role in regulating traffic flows. Without such acceptance, its utility would be low and could even turn into disutility.

Strictly speaking, there is a market for traffic lights: they can be bought and sold, though perhaps not put in a shopping cart. But the traffic light *regime*—the lights, their shared meaning and the behavioural expectations they entail—is a public good.

Peace is another example of a pure public good. When it exists, all citizens of a country can enjoy it; and its enjoyment by, say, rural populations does not distract from its benefits for urban populations. A similar case can be made for law and order or good macroeconomic management (see Jervis 1988; Cowen 1992; and Mendez 1997).

IMPURE PUBLIC GOODS. Few goods are purely public or purely private. Most possess mixed benefits. Goods that only partly meet either or both of the defining criteria are called impure public goods. Because impure goods are more common than the pure type, we use the term "public good" to encompass both pure and impure public goods. As the discussion here and in other chapters of this volume shows, many of the implications of publicness remain salient even when a good is only partly nonrival or partly nonexcludable. Thus our general use of the term "public good" is a useful simplification.

In line with this definition, we suggest looking at "pure private" and "pure public" as the extremes of a public-private continuum. Even an activity such as consuming a nutritious meal, which at first glance seems to be highly private, upon closer examination has public benefits. A good meal adds to people's good health, and good health enhances their ability to acquire skills and to work productively. This, in turn, benefits not only them but also their families and society as a whole. The immediate benefits, however, are mostly private.

Impure public goods fall into two categories. Goods that are nonrivalrous in consumption but excludable are club goods (table 1; see also Cornes and Sandler 1996). Goods that are mostly nonexcludable but rivalrous in consumption are common pool resources (see G. Hardin 1968; Wijkman 1982; Stone 1993; Cooper 1994; Carraro and Siniscalco 1997; Dasgupta, Mäler and Vercelli 1997; and Sandler 1997). Public goods with an existence value are purchased not because they can be consumed but because people derive value from the knowledge that the good exists. Biodiversity would fall into this class of goods, as would the preservation of monuments and art. Merit goods are goods subsidized by the polity because their existence or their consumption (as in the case of art) is highly valued by the community (see Mead 1993 and Loomis 1996).

Externalities

Externalities arise when an individual or a firm takes an action but does not bear all the costs (negative externality) or all the benefits (positive externality; Stiglitz 1997) of the action. For example, educating women has positive effects on child survival and on slowing population growth. Releasing pollutants into a river, by contrast, can harm nature and human beings. Put differently, externalities are by-products of certain activities—spillovers into the public sphere. Cornes and Sandler (1996, p. 6) argue that public goods, notably pure public goods, "can be thought of as special cases of externalities".

TABLE 1

Private and public goods

	Rivalrous	Nonrivalrous

Excludable	Private good	Network
		Club good (mostly
		  nonrivalrous inside
		  the club)

Nonexcludable	Good subject to congestion
	  or depletion, yet
	  accessible to all
	Some global commons
	  (geostationary orbit)
		Pure public good
		Existence value
		Some global commons
		  (high seas, ozone layer)

Note: Public goods are in the shaded areas.

The foregoing discussion raises the question of what is positive and what is negative. For economists, positive and negative externalities are distinguished by their positive or negative utilities to third parties. Thus here we will reserve the term "public good" for goods and activities with positive utility, including positive externalities. If a public disutility is involved, we will use the term "public bad".

While utility and disutility are commonly accepted notions, they ignore the issue of prioritization. At the local, national and global levels most judgements of what is desirable can only be the result of a political process, given the tremendous disparities in living conditions and value systems that exist within countries, let alone the world. Thus the measuring rod has to be found within existing policy consensus. For example, if society values knowledge, a library could be said to be a good with a high positive utility. Other communities, however, may prefer to spend resources on roads. Likewise, prioritization exists de facto in global policy-making. It has to be made transparent and participatory.

Supply problems of public goods

Because they are nonrivalrous in consumption and nonexcludable, public goods typically face supply problems, and so are often referred to as a case of market failure (see Bator 1958; Davis and Hulett 1977; and Malinvaud, Milleron and Sen 1998). They elicit patterns of behaviour that, from the individual agent's viewpoint, are quite rational. Yet from a collective viewpoint— such as that of a local community, a nation or humanity as a whole—the result is suboptimal and can be disastrous. The two main problems affecting the provision of public goods are known in the literature as "free riding" and the "prisoner's dilemma".

THE FREE-RIDER PROBLEM. As noted, Hume first described the free-rider phenomenon in the mid-18th century. In his view, gaining the cooperation of a thousand citizens to jointly work for the common good would fail in the face of an individual's incentive to "free himself of the trouble and expense, and . . . lay the whole burden on others" (Hume 1961, p. 478). Garrett Hardin reprised the problem in his famous essay "The Tragedy of the Commons". In his formulation, shepherds sharing common pasture are "locked into a system that compels (each one) to increase his herd without limit" (G. Hardin 1968, p. 1244), thus leading to overgrazing and land degradation. Olson (1971, p. 113) argues that even altruism or common purpose would not overcome the powerful incentive to avoid contributing personal resources to common endeavours. People may fear that indicating an interest, say, in better roads, will trap them into also having to foot the bill. Whatever the reason, the temptation to free ride, easy ride or simply not express one's preferences sends the wrong signal to suppliers. As a result supply and demand cannot reach an equilibrium, public goods are undersupplied and resource allocations are suboptimal.

Markets are good at providing private goods. For the provision of public goods, however, we need additional mechanisms such as cooperation. Yet as we will see in the following, cooperation is easier said than done.

THE PRISONER'S DILEMMA. In game theory the prisoner's dilemma describes a situation in which lack of information impedes collaboration between two prisoners (see R. Hardin 1971; Brams 1973; Riker and Ordeshook 1973; Kimber 1981; Conybeare 1984; and Oye 1986). The prisoners are held in separate cells and so are unable to agree on a common story in support of their defence. Thus each prisoner must independently reason through his or her best strategy for dealing with the police: deny the crime, or confess. The prosecutors, meanwhile, spell out the penalties as follows: if both prisoners deny the crime, they will each get a year in prison on a lesser charge that can be proven without a confession. If one confesses while the other denies, the one who collaborates will be rewarded with freedom, while the other will get five years in prison for the crime and for lying. If both confess, each will serve a reduced sentence of three years.

Prisoner A quickly realizes that no matter what prisoner B chooses (deny or confess), he is always better off confessing to the crime. If prisoner B denies the crime, prisoner A can get off with no punishment by confessing. If prisoner B confesses, prisoner A faces three years in jail if he also confesses the crime, and five years if he denies it. Thus prisoner A will confess. Prisoner B, facing identical choices, will also confess. The result: both prisoners will confess to the crime and will each serve three years in jail (table 2).

The prisoner's "dilemma" arises from the fact that both would be better off cooperating—by denying the crime—than defecting—by confessing. If they could maintain their silence, they could each serve one year rather than three. Lacking the ability to communicate, and thereby an opportunity to collaborate for mutual gain, they both lose out, serving a total of six years behind bars rather than just two. The four extra years of punishment represent the cumulative loss to the two prisoners resulting from their inability to create a cooperative outcome for themselves.

The prisoner's dilemma is of great interest to students of international relations and other areas of conflict and cooperation, because it represents in

TABLE 2

The prisoner's dilemma

		Prisoner A	
		Denies	Confesses
Prisoner B	Denies	A and B each get 1 year	A gets 0 years B gets 5 years
	Confesses	A gets 5 years B get 0 years	A and B each serve 3 years

simple terms many real-life situations in which two or more parties face similar incentives to "defect" from cooperation unless mechanisms are established to facilitate communication and build trust. One real-life example is labour standards. In the absence of industry-wide negotiating forums, individual firms wishing to improve labour conditions would have to act in isolation. They would most likely be reluctant to improve work conditions, arguing that it would increase costs and jeopardize their competitiveness. The effect could be that no firm would improve work conditions. Indeed, under competitive pressures a perverse incentive emerges to lower labour standards even if many—or most—firms would prefer to raise their standards. Thus we see in a practical case how a lack of communication and ability to agree on a common strategy can lead to a suboptimal strategy—even though each firm acted rationally from its own point of view.

In a national context the solution to market failures and collective action problems is often to bring the state in to improve conditions for cooperation by, among other things, establishing new or clearer property rights, setting norms and standards or providing fiscal incentives. In some cases the coercive power of government produces socially optimal outcomes. In many other instances the state plays an essential catalytic role. Nevertheless, the supply of public goods also suffers from state failures, such as rent seeking on the part of policy-makers and bureaucrats, public expenditure biases in favour of influential population segments or political stalemate between competing interest groups (Olson 1971; see also Strange 1996 and World Bank 1997). Thus public goods often face a double jeopardy: market failure compounded by government failure. In such cases cooperation is often spurred by civil society advocacy on behalf of a public concern (such as pollution control) or by the threat of an impending or actual disaster (such as a "tragedy of the commons").

TAKING PUBLIC GOODS TO THE GLOBAL LEVEL

The assumption tacitly underpinning the discussion above, as with so many other discussions on the subject, is that public goods are national in character. Until recently this assumption could be sustained in many, if not most, cases. But today international, and particularly global, public goods are becoming more central to national and individual well-being. Within the class of public bads, examples include banking crises (which often have world-wide ripple effects), Internet-based crime and fraud, and increased risks of ill-health due to increased trade and travel but also due to the world-wide spread of such hazardous practices as drug abuse and smoking. Among public goods, a striking example is the rapidly growing number of international regimes providing common frameworks for international transport and communication, trade, harmonized taxation, monetary policy, governance and much more. In most if not all of these areas, policy questions that have traditionally been settled at the domestic level are now subject to international scrutiny and coordination.

This is not the place to examine why public goods and bads are going global; we leave that to other chapters in this volume. The important issue here is rather to rethink from a global perspective the characteristics of a public good—that is, its qualities of nonrivalry and nonexcludability. The main issue to clarify is what criteria we should use to identify a global public good. Of particular importance is the question of who should be the beneficiaries—the *publicum*—of a public good in order for it to qualify as global. This issue is important because we live in a highly divided and inequitable world where some actors are more influential than others in setting public policy agendas and where some goods, even supposedly public goods, are more easily accessible to some people than to others. Answering the beneficiary question and assessing the good's scope of publicness will, furthermore, help in analysing—and correcting—supply problems. For example, it can provide clues to who might be free riding on whom and need incentives to cooperate. A concept of global public goods is crucial to effective public policy under conditions of increasing economic openness and interdependence among countries. As noted, the term "global public good" has not received much attention, despite the rapidly proliferating literature on globalization and its effects on national policy-making (see Kindleberger 1986; Streeten 1995; and Sandler 1998).

Identifying the global public

Despite the vanishing of the East-West divide in the late 1980s and increased economic openness and market integration, the world continues to be marked by sharp disparities and clear dividing lines. Thus it is no simple matter to determine the reach that a public good should have to qualify as global. Three divisions seem to be of special significance in our context—namely, the division of the world's population into countries, socio-economic groups and generations.

COUNTRIES. Nation states form important core elements of the international community. Since the Peace of Westphalia in 1648, nation states have enjoyed formal policy sovereignty and played a key role in shaping human activity—economic, social, cultural and political—within their borders. For a variety of reasons and purposes, states (countries) form groups such as regional forums (for example, in Asia, Latin America, Sub-Saharan Africa or Europe), trade blocs (such as the North American Free Trade Agreement or South American Common Market, or Mercosur), defence alliances (such as NATO, the North Atlantic Treaty Organization), and clubs (such as the Oganisation for Economic Co-operation and Development, G–7, or G–77).

Thus a first requirement for a global public good is that it covers more than one group of countries. If a public good were only to apply to one geographic region—say, South America—it would be a regional public good, and possibly a club good (that is, a good with excludable benefits).

SOCIO-ECONOMIC GROUPS. As trend analyses of human development over the past 50 years have shown, socio-economic disparities are growing both between and within countries (UNDP 1998). The rich are getting richer and the poor are getting poorer, not only in terms of income but also in many other respects, including access to knowledge, information and technology. Being rich or poor is not just a matter of being a citizen of a poor or a rich country. Rather, wealth and deprivation exist side by side in poorer and in richer countries. Hence, even though a public good has world-wide benefits in the sense of reaching all (or at least, a large number of nations belonging to different country groups), its benefits may be accessible only to better-off population segments, further marginalizing the poor.

The Internet, for example, entails such a risk because it has a high access price (the costs of a computer, a telephone line, and sometimes the subscriber fee for the Internet service provider). Similarly, global public bads, such as malaria or tuberculosis, if left unaddressed often hurt the poor more than the rich. This is because the poor may be unable to afford medical treatment and protection or because the poor's only asset is often their health and physical strength. But the world is not only divided along income lines. Ethnicity, gender, religion, political affiliations and other factors also separate people. Hence for a public good to be global, its benefits must reach not only a broad spectrum of countries but also a broad spectrum of the global population.

GENERATIONS. The preceding two points suggest that ideally, humanity as a whole should be the beneficiary of global public goods. But an individual's life is limited. Thus it is important to specify which generation we have in mind when we say "humanity". The environmental movement has reminded us of the importance of a longer-term perspective. As argued in the Brundtland Commission's report, *Our Common Future* (World Commission on Environment and Development 1987, p. 43), sustainable development is "development that meets the needs of the present without compromising the ability of future generations to meet their own needs". This definition of sustainability applies not only to environmental debt (that is, irreversible damage to natural resources) but also to financial and other forms of debt. Any type of collective borrowing from the future raises questions of intergenerational equity.

Some authors, including Sandler in this volume, draw a distinction between intragenerational and intergenerational global public goods. As Sandler notes, we are often faced with trade-offs between these two types of goods. One of his examples is nuclear energy: it can increase the availability of energy for present generations, but in the long run it creates nuclear waste. Thus we believe that intergenerational spillovers should be included in the general definition of a global public good. Hence the third qualifying mark of a global public good is that it meets the needs of present generations without jeopardizing those of future generations.

The definition of a global public good suggested here is demanding. It describes the ideal type of a global public good. But as noted, a pure public good is rare—and so is a pure *global* public good. Bearing this in mind, a practical way of summarizing the foregoing discussion is to offer a maximal definition of a pure global public good and a minimal definition of an impure global public good. A pure global public good is marked by universality—that is, it benefits all countries, people and generations. An impure global public good would tend towards universality in that it would benefit more than one group of countries, and would not discriminate against any population segment or set of generations.

In the same way we use the term "public good" to denote pure and impure public goods, we will use the term "global public good" to denote both purely global and impurely global public goods. The justification is again practical: both types of global public goods pose similar policy challenges. Chief among them is the issue repeatedly raised in the literature on international relations and cooperation: in the international sphere, where there is no government, how are public goods produced? (See Kindleberger 1986.)

Distinguishing global and nonglobal public goods

Our notion of global is not merely geographic—that is, global as opposed to local, national or regional. Rather, it is multidimensional, including, besides the geographic dimension, a sociological and temporal dimension. We have chosen this multidimensional definition to do greater justice to the complexities of the real world. The result, however, is a more complex definition. Thus it is useful to reflect not only on what a global public good is but also on what type of goods would not qualify.

Clearly, if a public good were to benefit only one country or region, it would not be global, but national or regional. Similarly, the security services that NATO provided during the Cold War for Western bloc countries were a public good for the alliance or, in more general terms, a club good. And if a multilateral investment guarantee scheme were to yield benefits exclusively for private international investors, it would be a world-wide club good, possibly even a private good—but not a global one according to our definition.

On the other hand, a poverty alleviation programme for Sub-Saharan Africa could be a global public good if, by meeting the needs of local populations, it were also to contribute to conflict prevention and international peace, reduce environmental degradation of potentially international consequences and improve global health conditions. By contrast, donations to disaster victims are a voluntary redistribution of private goods, from one owner to another, motivated primarily by empathy rather than by global concerns. Private transfers and public goods provision do not necessarily differ in a moral or ethical sense. They merely have different technical characteristics: (non)rivalry and (non)excludability.

All of this shows that it is important to guard against a hasty categorization of public goods as global or nonglobal. A decision on this issue requires careful assessment and impact analysis as well as a participatory policy dialogue among all concerned actors and beneficiaries.

A typology of global public goods

We have already distinguished between pure and impure global public goods. In what follows we will sort global public goods according to another criterion, namely, their place in the production chain. We suggest here a distinction between final and intermediate global public goods.

- Final global public goods are outcomes rather than "goods" in the standard sense. They may be tangible (such as the environment, or the common heritage of mankind) or intangible (such as peace or financial stability).
- Intermediate global public goods, such as international regimes, contribute towards the provision of final global public goods. Note that global public goods such as economic growth arise from a mixture of public and private inputs.

Again, this distinction has significant policy relevance. To illustrate, there is nothing intrinsically good about agreeing to reduce chlorofluorocarbons (CFCs). To achieve this objective—as an intermediate product—matters primarily in terms of the final good, an intact ozone shield. In general, the publicness of the final good matters most and may give rise to international collective inaction. Typically, global public goods are the results of many activities, private and public. The purpose of identifying intermediate global public goods is to highlight the area, or areas, where international public intervention may be needed to provide a particular global public good. To stay with the example of the ozone layer, the needed intermediate global public good could be an agreement such as the Montreal Protocol.

Perhaps the most important intermediate public goods are international regimes. Such regimes provide a basis for many other intermediate products with global public benefits—including, for example, international surveillance systems, international infrastructure or international aid programmes. International regimes take different forms that may be closely intertwined but that should nevertheless be distinguished:

- International agreements are statements of commitment typically setting forth policy priorities, principles, norms or standards as well as decision-making procedures and obligations.
- Organizations are bodies or mechanisms, usually resulting from international agreements, intended to, among other things, facilitate consultations and negotiations among member parties, monitor treaty compliance or provide other types of information, or undertake operational activities (for more details on international regimes, see Keohane 1984; Krasner 1986; and Ruggie 1993).

Among international organizations, a distinction exists between those that support consultation and negotiation, those intended to provide vital information to states through monitoring and surveillance, and those dedicated to operational activities. A growing number of international agreements require operational follow-up at the country level.

International regimes cover an ever-growing range of activities, from transportation and communication to health, the environment, demographics, judicial systems, human rights and macroeconomic policy. While many global regimes are intergovernmental in nature, international civil society organizations and the private sector play an increasing role in international norm and standard setting as well as in international operational activities. Just think of international human rights organizations such as Amnesty International or Human Rights Watch, or humanitarian organizations such as the Red Cross or Médecins sans Frontières. Another example is the International Standards Organization (ISO), which is a public-private partnership.

The benefits of global regime building are enhanced predictability in international relations and transborder activities, which reduce the risk of conflict and misunderstanding. As a result transactions costs are reduced, encouraging cooperation and improving efficiency. In some cases international regimes help promote—or restore—universalism, such as the universal recognition of basic human rights, including women's rights.

Yet as Olson (1973, p. 873) notes, "the desire for peace . . . for orderly financial arrangements for multilateral trade, for the advance of basic knowledge, and for an ecologically viable planet are now virtually universal, yet these collective goods are only episodically or scantily supplied". In the next section we offer some explanations for this inaction and undersupply of global public goods.

The supply problems of global public goods

Public goods are essentially defined by the existence of a provision problem; by their nature, they cannot easily be provided by the "invisible hand" of the market. Examining the issue of international trade from the public good viewpoint, Conybeare (1984, p. 7) notes that "in the public good game the degree of suboptimality is normally considered to be a function of the extent to which the qualities of publicness are present and of the number of beneficiaries". As noted, global public goods can vary in their qualities of nonrivalry and nonexcludability. In this respect they are no different from any other public good. In terms of beneficiaries, however, most global public goods do vary from other public goods: their beneficiary groups are likely to be extremely large, often reaching into the billions. As a consequence, the beneficiaries of global public goods are more diverse, including developing and industrial countries, poor and rich, and people of different cultures living in different ecosystems and coming from different historical backgrounds. Thus one has to expect that interests and concerns will vary and cooperation will not be easy to achieve due in part to differences in policy priorities and other preferences—perhaps often simply due to lack of information and mutual understanding and trust.

Certainly, billions of people do not negotiate directly with each other. In many instances their governments do it on their behalf, reducing the number of negotiating partners to about 185—still an unwieldy group for creating cooperative arrangements. But as Cooper and others (1989) and Putnam (1988) point out, intergovernmental negotiations are often two-tier processes. While negotiating with each other internationally, governments also have to consult with their diverse constituencies back home on emerging compromises or other proposals on the negotiating table. This requirement automatically increases the number of parties involved in any negotiation by a multiple. In addition, as various chapters in this volume demonstrate, inter-governmental negotiations increasingly come under close scrutiny from international civil society, so nongovernmental organizations (NGOs) are another factor to reckon with. So are the international organizations of business, such as the International Chambers of Commerce, as well as individual multinationals and other corporations. Given the large number of actors and beneficiaries and the tremendous uncertainty that results from their presence (in addition to the technical uncertainties that often surround issues under negotiation), one can expect collective action problems, such as free riding or prisoner's dilemmas, to abound.

Moreover, as explained by Martin in this volume, states internationally behave like private actors, motivated by national self-interest. This tendency raises the issue of who exists at the global level to cut the Gordian knot of col-lective inaction. At the national level that role is often assumed by the state, although state failures in this respect also occur domestically. Globally, how-ever, the risk of "state" failure is systemic due to the absence of a global sov-ereign. This makes it all the more important to examine the role of nonstate actors in providing global public goods.

Despite these difficulties, which could potentially impede the supply of global public goods, there is an impressive—and growing—volume of inter-national regimes as well as many other examples of successful international cooperation.

CONCLUSION

In today's rapidly globalizing world, people's well-being depends on striking a careful balance not only between private and public goods but also between domestic, regional and global public goods. Thus it is important to have a clear definition and understanding of global public goods.

We have defined global public goods as outcomes (or intermediate products) that tend towards universality in the sense that they benefit all countries, population groups and generations. At a minimum, a global public good would meet the following criteria: its benefits extend to more than one group of countries and do not discriminate against any population group or any set of generations, present or future.

Our discussion has shown that in a highly divided world, global public goods raise the familiar issue of how to ensure their provision, given that internationally there is no equivalent to a national institution of government. But global public goods also raise two other issues: Who defines the political agenda, and hence the priorities for resource allocations? And who determines whether global public goods are in fact accessible to all population groups? Both issues—prioritization and access—are important areas for further research and policy debate.

NOTES

The views presented here are solely those of the authors and not necessarily those of the institution with which they are affiliated.

1. This definition of the generational distribution of the benefits of global public goods draws on the definition of sustainable development provided by the World Commission on Environment and Development (Brundtland Commission) (1987).

2. An early description of public goods was made by economists Knut Wicksell and Erik Lindhal in the interwar period. Italian economists (such as Francesco Ferrara) in the 1850s and 1860s were forerunners. Many of these early classics were translated and introduced in Musgrave and Peacock (1959). For English-speaking readers, classic texts on public goods include Musgrave (1959), Samuelson (1954) and Buchanan (1968).

REFERENCES

Bator, Francis M. 1958. "Anatomy of Market Failure." *Quarterly Journal of Economics* 72: 351–79.

Brams, Steven. 1973. *Game Theory and Politics*. New York: MacMillan.

Buchanan, James. 1968. *The Demand and Supply of Public Goods*. Chicago: Rand MacNally.

Carraro, Carlo, and Domenico Siniscalco, eds. 1997. *New Directions in the Economic Theory of the Environment*. New York: Cambridge University Press.

Conybeare, John A. C. 1984. "Public Goods, Prisoners' Dilemmas and the International Political Economy." *International Studies Quarterly* 28: 5–22.

Cooper, Richard N. 1994. *Environment and Resource Policies for the World Economy*. Washington, DC: Brookings Institution.

Cooper, Richard N., and others. 1989. *Can Nations Agree? Issues in International Economic Cooperation*. Washington, DC: Brookings Institution.

Cornes, Richard, and Todd Sandler. 1996. *The Theory of Externalities, Public Goods, and Club Goods*. 2nd ed. Cambridge: Cambridge University Press.

Cowen, Tyler. 1992. "Law As a Public Good." *Economics and Philosophy* 8: 249–67.

Dasgupta, Partha, Karl-Göran Mäler and Alessandro Vercelli, eds. 1997. *The Economics of Transnational Commons*. New York: Oxford University Press.

Davis, J. Ronnie, and Joe R. Hulett. 1977. *An Analysis of Market Failure: Externalities, Public Goods, and Mixed Goods*. Gainesville: University Press of Florida.

Hardin, Garrett. 1968. "The Tragedy of the Commons." *Science* 162: 1243–48.

Hardin, Russell. 1971. "Collective Action As an Agreeable n-Prisoner's Dilemma." *Behavioral Science* 16: 472–81.

Hume, David. 1961 [1739]. *A Treatise of Human Nature*. Garden City, NJ: Dolphin Books.

Jervis, Robert. 1988. "Realism, Game Theory and Cooperation." *World Politics* 15(3).

Keohane, Robert. 1984. *After Hegemony: Cooperation and Discord in the World Political Economy*. Princeton, NJ: Princeton University Press.

Kimber, Richard. 1981. "Collective Action and the Fallacy of the Liberal Fallacy." *World Politics* 33: 178–96.

Kindleberger, Charles P. 1986. "International Public Goods without International Government." *American Economic Review* 76(1): 1–13.

Krasner, Stephen D. 1986. *International Regimes*. Ithaca, NY and London: Cornell University Press.

Loomis, John B. 1996. "How Large Is the Extent of the Market for Public Goods: Evidence From a Nationwide Contingent Valuation Survey." *Applied Economics* 28: 779–82.

Malinvaud, Edmond, Jean-Claude Milleron and Amartya K. Sen, eds. 1998. *Development Strategy and the Market Economy.* New York: Oxford University Press.

Mead, Walter J. 1993. "Review and Analysis of Recent State-of-the-Art Contingent Valuation Studies." In Jerry A. Hausman, ed., *Contingent Valuation: A Critical Assessment.* Amsterdam: North Holland Press.

Mendez, Ruben P. 1997. "War and Peace from a Perspective of International Public Economics." In Jürgen Brauer and William Gissy, eds., *Economics of Peace and Conflict.* Aldershot, UK: Avebury.

Musgrave, Richard A. 1959. *The Theory of Public Finance.* New York: McGraw Hill.

Musgrave, Richard A., and Alan T. Peacock, eds. 1959. *Classics in the Theory of Public Finance.* London: Macmillan.

Olson, Mancur. 1971. *The Logic of Collective Action.* Cambridge, MA: Harvard University Press.

———. 1973. "Increasing the Incentives for International Cooperation." *International Organization* 27(2): 866–74.

Oye, Kenneth, ed. 1986. *Cooperation under Anarchy.* Princeton, NJ: Princeton University Press.

Putnam, Robert. 1988. "Diplomacy and Domestic Politics: The Logic of Two-Level Games." *International Organization* 42(3): 427–60.

Riker, William H., and Peter C. Ordeshook. 1973. *An Introduction to Positive Political Theory.* Englewood Cliffs, NJ: Prentice Hall.

Ruggie, John Gerard, ed. 1993. *Multilateralism Matters: The Theory and Praxis of an Institutional Form.* New York: Columbia University Press.

Samuelson, Paul A. 1954. "The Pure Theory of Public Expenditure." *Review of Economics and Statistics* 11: 387–89.

Sandler, Todd. 1997. *Global Challenges.* Cambridge: Cambridge University Press.

———. 1998. "Global and Regional Public Goods: A Prognosis for Collective Action." *Fiscal Studies* 19(1): 221–47.

Shmanske, Stephen. 1991. *Public Goods, Mixed Goods, and Monopolistic Competition.* College Station: Texas A & M University Press.

Smith, Adam. 1993 [1776]. *Inquiry into the Nature and Causes of the Wealth of Nations.* New York: Oxford University Press.

Stiglitz, Joseph E. 1997. *Economics.* 2nd ed. New York: W.W. Norton.

Stone, Christopher D. 1993. *The Gnat Is Older than Man: Global Environment and the Human Agenda.* Princeton, NJ: Princeton University Press.

Strange, Susan. 1996. *The Retreat of the State.* Cambridge: Cambridge University Press.

Streeten, Paul. 1995. *Thinking about Development.* Cambridge and New York: Cambridge University Press.

UNDP (United Nations Development Programme). 1998. *Human Development Report 1998.* New York: Oxford University Press.

Wijkman, Per Magnus. 1982. "Managing the Global Commons." *International Organization* 36(3): 511–35.

World Bank. 1997. *World Development Report 1997: The State in a Changing World.* New York: Oxford University Press.

World Commission on Environment and Development (Brundtland Commission). 1987. *Our Common Future.* New York: Oxford University Press.

INTERGENERATIONAL PUBLIC GOODS

Strategies, Efficiency and Institutions

Todd Sandler

We live in a "brave new world" where allocative decisions on public goods today can have consequences that cross political and generational boundaries. Although the international aspects of public goods have received much attention in recent years, particularly with respect to environmental activities,[1] intergenerational public goods have received relatively scant attention.[2] An intergenerational pure public good (bad) provides benefits (costs) that are nonrival and nonexcludable within and among generations. For example, a genetically engineered medicine that cures cancers can benefit people worldwide during the discovering generation's lifetime and for generations to come. Similarly, lost biodiversity can have adverse global consequences for today's generation and all subsequent generations. Other intergenerational public goods include eradicating disease, curbing global warming, limiting ozone shield depletion, preserving culture, restraining ethnic conflict and developing cultural norms. For ethnic conflicts, atrocities committed by one generation can create hatreds that fuel conflicts for generations to come, as evident in Bosnia, Kosovo, northern Ireland, parts of the Middle East and some areas of Africa. Cultural norms and laws that promote cooperative behaviour within or among generations can have immense intergenerational benefits.

Although it is tempting to apply standard remedies for transnational public goods problems to transgenerational public goods, it is not necessarily effective. For example, fostering greater transnational cooperation can exacerbate intergenerational inefficiency if this cooperation leads to an even larger provision of an activity that benefits the current generation at the expense of future generations (John and Pecchenino 1997; Sandler 1978). Thus the expansion of nuclear energy through international cooperation improves the welfare of contemporaries but creates an even greater nuclear waste containment problem for future generations. Similarly, foreign aid intended to develop a country's natural resources so as to alleviate poverty—such as World Bank financing of dams in South America—can result in enormous losses to biodiversity, limiting opportunities for future generations. This last example concerns sustainable development, associated with the preservation of natural capital so as to maintain the opportunities of future generations.[3]

Other aspects that distinguish remedies for transnational public goods from those for transgenerational public goods involve bargaining, strategic interactions and institutional design. For intergenerational public goods the natural sequencing of generations has profound implications for the design of institutional structures and the kinds of strategizing that can occur among concerned parties. An earlier generation might, for example, exploit a first-mover's advantage, placing more of the burden for an intergenerational public good on the next generation. The sequencing of generations can affect the bargainers' threat points, associated with a failure to reach an agreement. When institutions are designed to correct for market failures tied to transgenerational public goods, the calculation of net linkage gains depends on the outcome in the absence of an agreement. This status quo point also represents the participants' well-being that must be improved if an institutional arrangement is to make everyone better off. A rich array of strategic interactions exists for intergenerational public goods because collective action problems can arise within nations, among nations, among generations or among both nations and generations.

This chapter has five main purposes. First, it presents a taxonomy of public goods with benefits spanning generational or national boundaries. Second, it describes the implications for economic efficiency of a variety of public goods that affect nations or generations. Third, it explores the strategic aspects of intergenerational public goods. Fourth, it offers design principles for institutional arrangements, intended to address concerns about the allocation of transgenerational public goods. Fifth, the analysis is applied to specific cases of intergenerational public goods throughout.

A number of policy insights derive from this analysis. At the national level, decision-makers are unlikely to achieve optimal levels of these public goods. If intergenerational awareness of public goods spillovers is only encouraged within a country, then that country's well-being may actually deteriorate as others free ride on its enhanced far-sightedness. Thus cooperation and increased awareness of spillovers must have both an international and an intergenerational dimension for all nations to gain. If institutions are properly designed to provide these intergenerational public goods, then the extent of policy-makers' awareness on both dimensions must be anticipated. Simple club arrangements can efficiently allocate resources for intergenerational public goods with excludable benefits. Markets can operate reasonably well for intergenerational public goods that display a large share of nation-specific or generation-specific benefits. When intervention is needed, supranational structures must be designed to account for associated transactions costs and benefits. Loose or unstructured linkages, which conserve on transactions costs, should be tried first.

A PUBLIC GOODS TAXONOMY

The creation of a taxonomy for public goods that provide benefits across nations or generations poses choices about which attributes of those goods to highlight. Two distinctions are essential for intergenerational public goods—namely, between intragenerational and intergenerational spillovers of benefits and between regional and global spillovers of benefits. The spatial dimension of the public good determines the relevant decision-makers— for example, the executive branch for national public goods, a regional social planner (that is, a hegemon) or individual nations for regional public goods and a world body or regional collectives for global problems. If no further attributes are considered, the resulting 2 x 2 classification scheme is identical to that of Sandler (1997, pp. 67–68). Curbing global warming fits the intergenerational category because greenhouse gases (such as carbon dioxide) have long residency in the atmosphere; it also fits the global category because atmospheric heating affects temperatures world-wide. In contrast, managing a terrorist incident is apt to yield only localized public benefits to the current generation.

This earlier taxonomy can now be extended. Although nonrivalry and nonexcludability can themselves be associated with a whole continuum of categories, a useful approach is to focus on, say, four types of public goods that affect the need for and form of institutional structures to correct for market failures. To expand the 2 x 2 taxonomy to 16 categories, I list pure public goods, impure public goods, club goods, and public goods possessing joint products. For its range of recipients, pure public goods provide benefits that are both completely nonrival and nonexcludable, whereas impure public goods yield benefits that are partially rival and/or partially nonexcludable. If, say, congestion detracts from the good's benefits available to others, then these benefits are partially rival. An important subclass of impure public goods consists of club goods, which possess partially rival benefits that can be excluded. At a national level, clubs provide an opportunity for members to allocate resources privately to a public good without government intervention. Similarly, nations can form a club to share an excludable public good without the need for a supranational government structure. Thus the International Telecommunications Satellite Organization (Intelsat), a private consortium with nations and firms as members, operates as a club to share a communications satellite network that carries most international phone calls and television networks. A fourth class includes public good activities that yield two or more outputs that vary in their degree of publicness. For example, "tied" foreign aid can, by financing a developing country's infrastructure or fostering its people's well-being, yield public benefits to the recipient and to the world at large. Because the aid is tied to the interests of the donor country, the donor is expected to obtain one or more country-specific benefits from providing its donation. If, for example, a donor is granted military bases on the recipient's soil, then both a security and foreign interest benefit are conferred on the donor.

The 16-cell taxonomy is provided in table 1, complete with four examples of each type. Intragenerational and intergenerational public goods are distinguished by regional and global spillovers, as well as by the four classes of public goods. Insofar as the suppression of a forest fire provides regional purely public benefits to just a current generation, it is placed in the top left-hand cell along with groundwater pollution that can be cleansed within a generation's lifespan. Flood control and animal disease control are also instances of regional pure public goods.

In the pure public column, the cleanup of ocean pollution provides global spillover benefits to the current generation. Weather forecasts of El Niño represent a global public good because this phenomenon affects large portions of the earth. These forecasts are intragenerational because such weather phenomenon are short-lived. Other, more localized weather forecasts would be regional. Atmospheric monitoring stations and the World Court represent additional intragenerational public goods. Insofar as the World Court is open to all nations to hear disputes for settlement, it provides nonexcludable benefits world-wide. The court's ability to resolve a dispute between one set of nations does not limit its ability to address additional disputes between others, so its benefits are also nonrival.

TABLE 1

Taxonomy of public goods based on good's characteristics

		Pure public
Intragenerational	Regional	• Forest fire suppression • Groundwater pollution cleanup • Animal disease control • Flood control
	Global	• Ocean pollution cleanup • Weather forecasts • Monitoring stations • World Court
Intergenerational	Regional	• Wetland preservation • Lake cleansing • Toxic waste cleanup • Lead emissions reduction
	Global	• Ozone shield protection • Global warming prevention • Disease eradication • Knowledge creation

Some public goods may fall into more than one category depending on how they are defined. Intergenerational, regional pure public goods include wetland preservation, lake cleansing, toxic waste cleanup and curbing of lead emissions, whereas intergenerational, global pure public goods involve stemming the thinning of the ozone layer, curbing global warming, eradicating disease and creating knowledge. All these examples provide nonrival benefits that are nonexcludable. The removal of a pollutant provides benefits to everyone residing in the region of spillovers. Within this spillover area, everyone receives the benefits from the cleanup. If the impact of the pollution removal is sufficiently long-lived, it can benefit future generations.

Impure public	Club	Joint products
• Waterways	• Common markets	• Peacekeeping
• Rivers	• Crisis management	• Military forces
• Highways	forces	• Medical aid
• Local parks	• Electric grid	• Technical assistance
	• Information networks	
• Electromagnetic	• Canals	• Foreign aid
spectrum allocation	• Air corridors	• Disaster relief
• Satellite transmissions	• Internet	• Drug interdiction
• Postal service	• Shipping lanes	
• Disease control		
• Acid rain reduction	• National parks	• Peacekeeping
• Fisheries protection	• Irrigation systems	• Flood control
• Hunting grounds	• Lakes	• North Atlantic Treaty
protection	• Cities	Organization
• VOC emissions reduction		• Cultural norms
• Overuse of antibiotics	• Transnational parks	• Tropical forest
• Ocean fisheries	• Geostationary orbits	preservation
• Antarctica protection	• Polar orbits	• Space colonies
• Revolution making	• Barrier reefs	• United Nations
		• Poverty alleviation

In the impure public good column, examples range from waterways that allow for the local transport of goods and services to the overuse of antibiotics that affects the well-being of current and future generations. For all the impure public goods listed, crowding or congestion reduces the quality of services available to users as overall utilization increases. As more vessels ply a waterway, transit time increases. Noise and interference characterize congestion for the electromagnetic spectrum because increased utilization requires that smaller bandwidths separate users. For antibiotics, an intertemporal form of congestion occurs when greater utilization of antibiotics today raises the likelihood that surviving bacteria will develop an immunity, decreasing the future effectiveness of the antibiotics. Acid rain is impurely public because its dispersion is based on a spatial rivalry—that is, the further a country is from the source of the sulphur or nitrogen oxide emissions, the less of these emissions are deposited on that country's soil (Murdoch, Sandler, and Sargent 1997; Sandnes 1993). A similar phenomenon applies to the emission of volatile organic compounds (VOCs). By causing long-run degradation to the environment, acid rain and VOCs have intergenerational effects. Because exploitation of fisheries and hunting grounds can result in smaller species populations or even extinction, use of these goods also implies intergenerational consequences.

Table 1 lists 16 club goods. For these club goods an exclusion mechanism can charge a toll to users so as to internalize the crowding costs associated with a unit of utilization. If the toll is to achieve efficiency, then the toll must equal the marginal crowding costs that another visit or unit of utilization imposes on the membership. Users' total toll payments equal their visits times the toll per visit; visitors with a strong preference for the club good will visit more frequently and pay higher total payments. Regional club goods include goods—common markets, crisis-management forces, electric grids, national parks, highways—whose users are region specific. In contrast, global club goods—the Panama Canal, straits, air corridors, the Internet, polar orbits—are shared by countries world-wide. The distinction between intragenerational and intergenerational club goods has to do with the nature of congestion and whether there is an intergenerational consequence to utilization. For intergenerational club goods, congestion takes both the standard form, in which utilization today detracts from the consumption experience of current users, and an intertemporal form, in which utilization today affects the quality of the club good for current and future users. The latter form of rivalry is known as depreciation due to utilization (Sandler 1982).

Consider a national park. Once visits surpass a park's carrying capacity—that is, its limit for withstanding use and being able to regenerate to its natural state by the next period—its environment begins to deteriorate. As another example, an irrigation system may build up silt through use, resulting in reduced efficiency or depreciation due to utilization. Yet another global intergenerational club involves the sharing of geostationary orbits some 22,300 miles above the equator, at which altitude a satellite orbits the earth in sync with the earth's rotation, so that the satellite remains stationary over a point on the earth's surface. When placed in this orbital band, only three satellites are required to provide point-to-multipoint service throughout the earth (except at the poles). Congestion takes the form of atemporal signal interference and the possibility of collisions, which may involve discarded and functioning satellites that drift up to 100 miles. Leaving discarded satellites in orbit, a standard practice, poses an intertemporal crowding externality. Intergenerational club goods can be managed efficiently by a collective of members, called an *intergenerational club* (see below).

The last column in table 1 indicates public goods in which an activity gives rise to two or more jointly produced outputs as benefits. Thus a country's military forces may provide purely nation-oriented goals of civil defence and terrorism crisis management while also deterring aggression at home and against a country's allies. Deterrence is purely public to all allies. Similarly, disaster relief yields a world-wide public benefit by helping a country in need; this relief may also contribute to the providing nation's standing in the world community. If an intergenerational benefit is derived, the good is placed in the two bottom cells of the column. Peacekeeping may give intragenerational or intergenerational benefits; hence its placement in two cells. When peacekeeping inhibits the acquisition of hatred that can be passed from one generation to the next, an intergenerational public good is achieved. Similarly, foreign aid or poverty alleviation may, by improving the health of a country's people, benefit current and future generations. Preserving tropical forests provides intergenerational public benefits on a global scale because of carbon sequestration and biodiversity. Flood control can give more localized joint products that are partly intergenerational in character if a dam is long-lived. By providing scientific discoveries, space colonies may produce global intergenerational benefits. Cultural norms that foster the cooperative provision of public goods may also yield benefits to current and future generations.

INTERGENERATIONAL PURE PUBLIC GOODS: SPILLOVER AWARENESS

To provide a flavour of the allocative efficiency problems posed by an intergenerational public good, a simplified model is sketched in which there are two regions, $r = 1, 2$, with three generations, $j = 1, 2, 3$, in each region. Each generation lives for one period so that, in the initial analysis, there are no overlapping generations within either region. The set of people in the jth generation of the rth region is denoted by Ω_{jr}. As an intergenerational public good, good q is produced by each region in period 1 and then lasts for three periods. In the first and subsequent periods a private good, y, is produced and fully consumed during the period of production; thus the private good has no intergenerational aspects. Initially, the public good is only allowed to be produced in period 1.

The modelling details are presented in appendix 1. In essence there are three ingredients in the model: a utility function for each individual, a constraint requiring consumption of private goods in each period to equal production of private goods, and a multiperiod, multiregional production possibility constraint. The utility functions represent individuals' tastes for the private good and the intergenerational public good, while the production possibility constraint indicates how much of each good can be produced with available resources at different points in time.

An efficiency criterion is required if the allocative aspects of an intergenerational public good are to be investigated. The concept of intergenerational Pareto efficiency (IPE) is employed and corresponds to a position from which it is not possible to improve the well-being of any person at any point in time without harming some other person in the current or some other generation (Page 1977; Sandler and Smith 1976). The intergenerational Pareto efficiency criterion applies the Pareto principle over time and space because it accounts for all relevant periods. In particular, intergenerational Pareto optimality requires the maximization of the ith individual's utility subject to the constancy of all other individuals' utility in the relevant regions and generations.[4] In addition, the production transformation function and the private good production-consumption constraints must be satisfied. To attain intergenerational Pareto efficiency, the provider of the intergenerational public good must account for the marginal benefits that the long-lived public good confers on people in the current *and* future generations in *both* regions (see appendix 1). Thus spillovers of public good benefits to other regions and future generations must be taken into account. Moreover, the required sum of these marginal benefits over regions and generations must be equated to the marginal costs associated with producing the public good in period 1. A similar condition holds for any region that provides the public good. This full awareness of spillovers is labelled *awareness rule 1* (AR1) and serves as an ideal benchmark. Such a far-sighted decision is anticipated only if some centralized social planner—such as a collective serving the two regions' interests—made the allocation decision while taking into account benefit spillovers over space and time. If more regions or generations were affected by the public good, then the marginal benefit must be summed over all relevant regions and generations.

Alternative awareness rules

When the allocative decision about the intergenerational public good is made at the regional or national level, the decision-maker is unlikely to account for the benefit spillovers conferred on other regions and future generations. At least three reduced levels of awareness are possible. First, an interregional social planner or institution can account for interregional spillover benefits but not for intergenerational benefits. In this case awareness rule 2 (AR2) would equate the marginal benefits of only the current generation in the two regions to the marginal costs (see appendix 2).[5] Insofar as AR1 includes more marginal benefit terms than AR2, AR2 implies a lower level of provision because a smaller aggregate marginal benefit is equated to marginal production cost. AR2 corresponds to a myopic supranational institution that is aware of the interregional consequences of the public good decision but is ignorant of the intergenerational consequences.

The next two awareness rules are the most relevant and indicate the provision decision for the intergenerational public good being made by a decision-maker in each region. In this scenario the regional planners or national governments are only interested in the Pareto principle as it applies to their people, so there is no concern for residents outside the region.[6] A third level of awareness has the regional social planners ignoring interregional spillovers while accounting for intergenerational spillovers, so that the marginal benefits are summed only over the region's own current and future generations before being equated to the marginal costs for the public good. For simplicity we assume that regional marginal costs for the public good equal the multiregional marginal costs in AR1, so that a provision comparison can be easily made between AR1 and AR3. Given the smaller number of marginal benefit terms in AR3 relative to AR1, the intergenerational public good is underprovided relative to the ideal. This follows because interregional spillover benefits are ignored.

The fourth level of spillover awareness, AR4, proves to be the most likely result, in which both interregional and intergenerational spillovers are ignored by the regional social planners. When AR4 applies, the provision level for the intergenerational public good is the smallest of the four rules in which only the current generation's gains in the providing region matters.

Diagrammatic representation

To apply a standard graphical apparatus to intergenerational public goods (Cornes and Sandler 1985; Sandler 1992), I assume that the regional planner's welfare is solely dependent on current residents' utility levels.[7] In figure 1 two (production) constrained iso-welfare contours for region 1's social planner are displayed as curves II and $I'I'$ for the case where AR4 applies so that each region looks out for just its own first generation. Production of q takes place in both regions, so that $q = q^1 + q^2$ and residents of either region derive a marginal benefit from either region's provision of the public good. For a given level of q^2, say q_0^2, AR4 is satisfied along curve II at point A, where the slope is zero.[8] Iso-welfare curve $I'I'$ represents a higher level of well-being for region 1 insofar as it receives a greater level of q^2 spillins for each level of its own provision of q^1. If the spillins are q_1^2, then AR4 is satisfied along $I'I'$ in figure 1 at point B, where the iso-welfare contour again attains a zero slope. The curve connecting the zero-sloped points on the various iso-welfare contours for different spillin levels from region 2 is the Nash reaction path, N_{AR4}^1, for region 1. This reaction

FIGURE 1

Nash reaction path for region 1

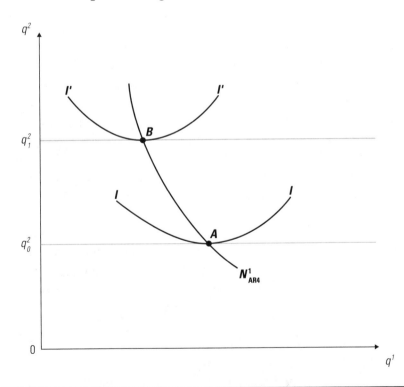

FIGURE 2

Nash equilibrium for two regions

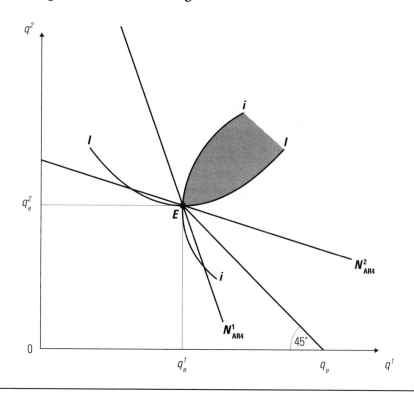

path is typically downward sloping, indicating that as region 2 provides more of the intergenerational public good, region 1 provides less as it free rides on region 2's provision.

Region 2's iso-welfare contours have their bottom points oriented to the q^2 axis. One such curve, ii, is depicted in figure 2. Similarly, region 2's Nash reaction path is derived by connecting these infinite-sloped points—see N^2_{AR4} in figure 2. Region 2's Nash reaction path is also negatively sloped, indicating that region 2 reduces its provision of the intergenerational public good as region 1 increases its provision.[9] If both regions abide by AR4, then a Nash equilibrium results at point E in figure 2 with region r providing q^r_e for $r = 1, 2$. If we draw a 45 degree line from point E to the q^1 axis, then the intercept of this line, q_e, is the total multiregional provision level. To the north-east of point E the shaded region between the respective regions' iso-welfare contours indicates allocations where both regions' welfare can be augmented. The strategic interaction associated with AR4 leads to a Pareto suboptimal outcome at E from which both regions' welfare could be improved if they both accounted for the spillins conferred spatially and temporally.

Suppose that region 1 assumes a more far-sighted view towards its future generation and accounts for intergenerational public good spillovers by satisfying AR3. Further suppose that region 2 continues to satisfy AR4. By abiding by AR3, region 1 includes more marginal benefits in its calculation when deciding its level q^1 for each level of spillins of q^2. As a result region 1's provision of the intergenerational public good will be greater for each level of q^2. This increased intergenerational awareness results in a rightward shift of region 1's Nash reaction path from N^1_{AR4} to N^1_{AR3} in figure 3. After this shift the new equilibrium is at E' where the overall level of the public good has

FIGURE 3

Increased intergenerational spillover awareness

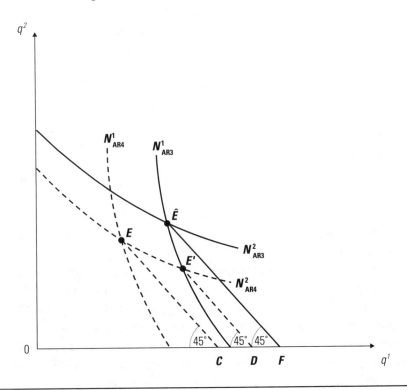

increased from $0C$ to $0D$, so that unilateral far-sightedness augments the overall level of the intergenerational public good. Region 2 is clearly better off because it contributes less to the public good but consumes more of it owing to increased spillins. Region 2's iso-welfare curve (not depicted in figure 3) through point E' is a greater welfare level than the iso-welfare curve through point E. A welfare comparison for region 1 is more troublesome because the iso-welfare contours associated with N^1_{AR3} and point E' are different than those associated with N^1_{AR4} and point E, insofar as the underlying social welfare function for the planner in region 1 has changed. The smaller is region 2's free riding on region 1's increased provision, the more likely that region 1 may also benefit from its increased concern for its future generations. Region 1's enhanced intergenerational spillover awareness could lose its net welfare if region 2's reaction path were sufficiently steep, so that region 1 loses sizable spillins from the other region's strategic response.

A better scenario occurs if region 2 also becomes more aware and also abides by AR3. If this were to occur, then region 2's Nash path would shift to N^2_{AR3} in figure 3 and the equilibrium $\hat{E}$ would result, where the overall level of provision is $0F$, which exceeds $0D$. The distribution of provision burdens at $\hat{E}$ relative to E depends on the relative rightward shifts of the Nash paths. The most likely scenario is that both regions will contribute more and be better off than at E. Because satisfying AR3 does nothing to internalize interregional spillovers, as required by AR1, the equilibrium at $\hat{E}$ does not result in intergenerational Pareto efficiency. Accounting for these interregional spillovers may require some form of supranational linkage between the regions.

FURTHER STRATEGIC INTERACTIONS

The analysis is now extended to investigate strategic behaviour both within a region and between regions for the provision of an intergenerational public good. Again just two regions are assumed, now labelled East and West. We further assume that in the East the young are expected to serve and carry on the wishes of their parents. In contrast, the parenting (earlier) generation often displays a responsibility for the next generation in the West region, and in so doing demonstrates a good deal of future-generation awareness. Thus the East and West labels distinguish between a region with backward-oriented responsibility and a region with forward-looking altruism. Within both regions there are two generations in which the first lives for two periods, $j = 1, 2$, and the second lives only for period 2. Thus generation 1 overlaps in time with generation 2.

The model

A sketch of the underlying model is given from the viewpoint of the East or backward-oriented region. Each generation is now represented by a single individual to simplify the presentation; the reader is invited to view this representative individual as a social planner for his or her generation. Once again a private good (y) and an intergenerational public good (q) are assumed, in which y_E^{ij} denotes the ith Eastern generation's consumption of the atemporal private good in period j and q_E^{ij} denotes the ith Eastern generation's provision of the intergenerational public good in period j. The first Eastern generation's multiperiod utility,

1. $V_E^1 = V_E^1 \left[u_E^{11} (\bullet), u_E^{12} (\bullet) \right]$

depends on the generation's single period utility functions during its lifetime. Eastern generation 2's multiperiod utility contains only $u_E^{22}(\bullet)$. In period 1 Eastern generation 1's consumption of the intergenerational public good is $q_E^{11} + q_W^{11}$ or the provision amount in the first period in both the East and West, where q_W^{11} is determined from abroad. In period 2 generation 1's consumption of the public good is $q_E^{11} + q_E^{12} + q_E^{22} + q_W^{11} + q_W^{12} + q_W^{22}$ or the provision amount in the first and second periods in both the East and West. The first and second generations are constrained by a multiperiod transformation indicating the ability of each generation to trade off production of the two goods.[10]

Each generation chooses its y's and q's to maximize its multiperiod utility function subject to its transformation function.[11] At the Nash solution the first generation has no incentive to provide the intergenerational public good in period 2, so q_r^{12} is zero in both the East and West. This follows because the marginal benefits derived from the intergenerational public good provision in period 1 is always greater than those from provision in period 2 because period 1 provision benefits the provider for two periods rather than one period. When making a multiperiod allocative decision, generation 1 foresees this consideration and provides the public good immediately, thus supplying just the private good in the second period.

Strategic considerations

If regional spillovers are taken as given, then strategic behaviour in the East involves the decision to provide q_E^{11} by generation 1 and q_E^{22} by generation 2, given q_W^{11} and q_W^{22}. This can be represented by the standard reaction paths based on the transformation-constrained iso-welfare curves for generations 1 and 2 in the East. In figure 4 q_E^{11} is placed on the horizontal axis and q_E^{22} on the vertical axis. Nash path N^1 connects the zero-sloped points on generation 1's iso-welfare contours for different levels of q_E^{22} as anticipated to come from generation 2 in the second period of generation 1's lifetime. Also in figure 4, N^2 denotes generation 2's reaction path to spillins of q_E^{11}. These Nash reaction paths assume that the level of interregional spillins from the West are fixed; an increase in these Western spillins would shift both Nash reaction paths leftward as spillins from abroad substitute for the region's own provision. A decrease in these interregional spillins would have the opposite effect.

If each generation in the backward-looking region or East acts according to its Nash reaction path, then the equilibrium is at E in figure 4, where $0G$ represents the aggregate two-period provision of the public asset. The sequencing of the generations allows for an alternative strategic response known as *leader-follower* behaviour (Sandler 1992; Cornes and Sandler 1996),

FIGURE 4

Eastern intergenerational strategizing

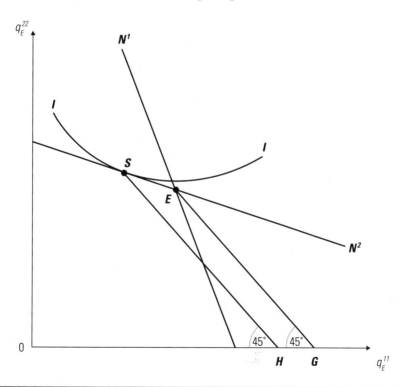

in which the first generation acts as the leader and the second as the follower. The leader knows that the follower, who goes second, will take the leader's provision amount as given; hence the follower continues to abide by its Nash reaction path. The leader, however, treats the follower's public good provision, q_E^{22}, as dependent on the leader's choice of q_E^{11} relative to the follower's Nash reaction path. Consequently, the leader attempts to achieve its greatest iso-welfare curve along generation 2's Nash reaction path. In figure 4 the leader-follower equilibrium in the East is S, where iso-welfare curve II is tangent to N^2. At S the aggregate multiperiod level of q_E has fallen from $0G$ to $0H$ as the first generation exploits its first-mover advantage and forces the second generation to assume a larger burden for the intergenerational public good. Generation 1's iso-welfare curve through S is higher than the one (not shown) through point E; the opposite is true for generation 2's welfare.

Regions that have very different views of the responsibilities that one generation has for the next may have profound effects on the manner in which resources are allocated to intergenerational public goods. This insight may partly help explain why industrial countries have more strongly supported environmental treaties, such as the Kyoto Protocol on global warming, while some developing countries have been hesitant.[12] Given its generational orientation, the East is apt to engage in a leader-follower strategy. In contrast, the West is anticipated to use a Nash strategy based on altruism to its future generation, much like the AR3 case encountered in the previous section. Figure 5 represents the strategic interactions and their consequences on the East and West; the provision of the intergenerational public good in the West is on the horizontal axis and the provision in the East is on the vertical axis. The dotted Nash West and East curves serve as benchmark cases and indicate the intergenerational response in each multigenerational region for alternative levels of spillins from the other region. In essence these paths depict the equilibrium aggregate quantity (for example, $0G$) of $q_E^{11} + q_E^{22}$ from figure 4 for alternative levels of q_W ($= q_W^{11} + q_W^{22}$), and hence shifts of N^1 and N^2. Each increase in q_W would cause curves N^1 and N^2 in figure 4 to shift to the left and down, so that equilibrium E would move to the south-west, implying a reduced provision of q_E ($= q_E^{11} + q_E^{22}$). As a result the Nash reaction curves relating q_E and q_W in figure 5 are negatively sloped for both the West and East as drawn.

In figure 5 the leader-follower reaction curve for the East is also negatively sloped, because an increase in q_W also displaces the equilibrium S to the south-west in figure 4, thus reducing q_E. Because the aggregate amount of q_E associated with leader-follower behaviour is always less than that of the Nash equilibrium in the East, the East's leader-follower curve must be below its Nash curve in figure 5. If the West adheres to its Nash path while the East abides by its leader-follower path, then the equilibrium would be at point R, where the aggregate level of the intergenerational public good is less than level 0J of the Nash equilibrium. The East would shift more of the burden for the public good onto the West owing to these regions' different dispositions to future generations. This burden-shifting tendency between the East and West is worsened if the West displays altruism towards future generations, analogous to a switch from AR4 to AR3, so that the Nash curve in figure 5 shifts to the altruistic Nash West curve. If this occurs, the equilibrium at F for the two solid paths would result in a greater overall level of q because 0K exceeds 0J. At F the West picks up much of the burden for the

FIGURE 5

East-West intergenerational strategizing

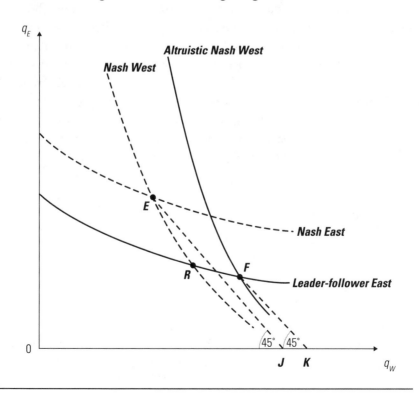

intergenerational public good. If the shifts were larger, a corner solution on the horizontal axis could follow with the East riding free. Whether or not the overall level of q increases at F relative to E hinges on the relative shifts of the two paths. The greater is the shift in the Nash West path relative to the leader-follower East path, the more likely it is that the aggregate level of q will increase.

These differences in intergenerational responsibilities imply that countries in a forward-looking region are more apt to supply such things as disease cures, environmental protection and research breakthroughs. Based on these results, sustainable development is predicted to be more difficult to maintain in backward-oriented countries than in forward-looking countries. Even more disturbing is the realization that efforts by some countries to achieve sustainable development, an intergenerational public good, may encourage other countries to reduce theirs.

JOINT PRODUCTS

Many different joint product scenarios are possible. Again consider the basic model of two regions (East and West) and three nonoverlapping generations, each of which lives for one period. Wherever possible the same notation is maintained. An intergenerational public activity (q) is assumed to yield a generation-specific and region-specific benefit (x) and an intergenerational pure public benefit (z). That is, good x benefits only the generation of the region supplying activity q during the generation's lifetime, while the benefits of good z spill over to the other region and generations. Further suppose that activity q is only supplied in the first of three periods. The joint product relations are

2. $x^{1r} = \alpha^r q^r$, $r = E, W,$

and

3. $z^r = \beta^r q^r$, $r = E, W,$

where α^r and β^r are positive constants representing how many units of the respective joint products are derived from each unit of activity q^r. The total amount of the intergenerational public good experienced by an individual in any generation is

4. $Z = z^E + z^W = \beta^E q^E + \beta^W q^W.$

During period 1 the utility function of individual i in region r is

5. $u^{ilr} = u^{ilr}\left(y^{ilr}, \; \alpha^r q^r, \; \beta^E q^E + \beta^W q^W\right), \qquad r = E, \; W, \qquad i \in \Omega_{lr},$

where I have substituted for x^{lr} and Z based on equations 2, 3 and 4. Individuals in generations 2 and 3 have only the private good y and the intergenerational public good Z in their utility functions because they do not supply activity q. The rest of the model is analogous to that described in the second section. As before, the multiperiod production trade-off is between the private good and the public activity.

In the providing generation and region the decision-maker for the intergenerational public good is anticipated to concentrate on the benefits derived by the current generation in just his or her own region. This behaviour implies that the weighted sum of the marginal benefits for the two jointly produced outputs is equated to the marginal costs of activity q.[13] The weights on the marginal benefits reflect the productivity of q in providing the region-specific and the region-wide outputs of x and Z, respectively, as given in equations 2 and 3. If the intergenerational activity is, say, more productive in yielding x than Z, then these region-specific benefits are emphasized to a greater extent when determining how much q to produce. The providing generation fails to account for the benefits that its provision of q supplies to the other region and future generations, leading to suboptimal provision. However, the greater is the generation-specific benefits derived from q, the more motivated is the generation to provide the public activity and the less the need for intervention.

Next, suppose that activity q gives rise to region-specific benefit x that also lasts for three generations. When acting alone, the first generation is still anticipated to focus on its gains from activity q, and, in so doing, ignores intergenerational benefits conferred through both x and Z. This means that unlike previous analyses of joint products, the appearance of provider-specific benefits may worsen suboptimality if temporal spillovers arise with respect to these latter benefits and are also ignored. In calibrating the extent of suboptimality, one must calculate the providing generation's sum of benefits from the public activity as a share of the total benefits received by both regions and all generations.[14] As this share increases towards one so that the providing generation receives most of the gains, the current generation has greater incentives to supply the public activity. Altruism towards future generations can also increase the providing generation's perceived marginal benefits, thus motivating it to account for future generations' spillovers.

The presence of joint products means that increased interregional cooperation through supranational structures may worsen the misallocation of resources. Consider a scenario in which each region receives region-specific private benefits and a jointly produced interregional public bad from an activity. Further, suppose that the private benefit affects only the current generation, while the public bad influences current and future generations. For example, the production of nuclear energy benefits the current generation but gives rise to wastes that place current and future generations world-wide at risk. Similarly, the burning of fossil fuels warms the current generation but adds to the accumulation of greenhouse gases, which may harm current and future generations world-wide. If a supranational link forms that furthers the interests of the current generation in the cooperating regions, then the cooperation-induced increased provision of the public activity adjusts for the current generation's interregional externalities, while increasing the negative externalities to future generations. With joint products, external effects concern regions, jointly produced outputs and generations. When negative externalities are present, agreements and linkages that attend to just one or two of these external-effects dimensions may worsen resource allocation relative to no agreement whatsoever. Some standard remedies may no longer apply when joint products possess alternative temporal characteristics.

INTERGENERATIONAL CLUBS

When forming a supranational structure to correct for market failures involving two or more regions, regional policy-makers must consider the transactions costs that accompany any mode of allocation. If these transactions costs are less than the transactions benefits attributable to an allocative mechanism that augments efficiency, then the institution may be warranted (Sandler 1997). Institutional arrangements that economize on transactions costs stand a better chance of being viable. One such institutional arrangement is a club, which can be formed when the public good's benefits are excludable at costs less than the allocative benefits achieved by matching tastes and user fees. Depending on the shared good, club participants can be firms, nations or individuals. For intergenerational club goods the required toll must account for crowding and depreciation losses that a visit imposes at the margin on current and future members. Depreciation due to utilization arises when a current visit affects the quality of the club good now and into the future. Users who visit more frequently pay more in total tolls but pay the same toll per visit.

Thus clubs are able to account for differences in tastes by monitoring visits and charging for each visit based on the associated costs imposed on the membership. If, for example, a visit causes a great deal of depreciation for current and future users, then the toll must be sufficiently high to reflect these losses. Visitors who visit early in an intergenerational club good's lifetime may have to pay relatively large fees for any resulting deterioration of the club good, insofar as any depreciation will affect a large number of subsequent generations and members. As the intertemporal component of the toll rises, individuals will be dissuaded from visiting, thus preserving the good. Toll proceeds are earmarked to maintain and to provide the club good, passed among the generations of members. If the tolls are properly designed, then tolls can finance the club good without the need for outside intervention. Clubs can be owned and operated by members (such as sovereign nations) for their own well-being.

One generation of members can reimburse an earlier generation's investment through equity shares, sold as the club good is transferred between generations. The value of these equity shares depends on the residual value of the club good. If a generation were myopic and ran down the club good's value through depreciation and collected tolls that did not reflect this depreciation, then the myopic generation would receive less in payments to support its retirement when the club asset is traded to the next generation (Sandler 1982). In such a club arrangement the current generation's actions are tied to the future consequences, thus motivating it to far-sighted behaviour. If the club investment were instead raised by debt, then the club's ability to repay its loan would depend on it collecting sufficient tolls to offset any depreciation through maintenance. The ability to refinance the loan between generations depends directly on the residual worth of the shared good—the collateral on which the debt is drawn. When a generation behaves myopically, less money can be raised during refinancing, and hence that generation is made to shoulder the burden of its short-sightedness. In fact, any form of leveraged financing of the club good would provide incentives for the current generation to collect the proper tolls. Intergenerational clubs represent a "private" means for a collective to internalize intergenerational externalities in the form of crowding and depreciation due to utilization.

As an example of an intergenerational club good, consider the Great Barrier Reef off the coast of Queensland, Australia. Visitors to the reef can be charged a user fee that reflects a visit's crowding effects and its long-run impact on the health of the reef. If these tolls are properly managed to internalize the externality to current and future generations, the visitation rate will be duly restricted to address the intergenerational concerns. The same arrangement can be applied to protect transnational parks (such as game reserves) and historical monuments (such as the Taj Mahal or the Egyptian pyramids). The management of tropical forests for ecotourism can also benefit from the application of club theory. Even population decisions and traffic control in cities can be decided with the help of the theory of intergenerational clubs. Perhaps the ultimate example of an intergenerational club is "spaceship earth", where membership is the world's changing population.

In passing an intergenerational club asset from an old generation to a new generation, the selling of the asset to the next generation helps determine pension assets. These pension revenues will be higher if a generation properly looked after a club good, thus providing motivation for far-sighted behaviour.

OTHER INSTITUTIONAL CONSIDERATIONS

When exclusion is not feasible, as in the case of some purely public intergenerational goods, a club arrangement is not an institutional alternative. For chlorofluorocarbon (CFC) reduction the resulting protection of the ozone layer yields benefits that cannot be withheld from nonpayers, now or into the future. Supranational structures (such as international organizations or treaties) intended to correct for the market failure associated with intergenerational public goods must adjust for a number of considerations. First, they must include an intergenerational perspective if the interregional linkage is to address both the spatial and temporal externalities. This intergenerational perspective may be fostered by including overlapping generations of young, middle-aged and old among the decision-makers (John and Pecchenino 1997). As the lifetimes of generations are lengthened by better medicine and nutrition, more generations will overlap at any one time and this can support greater intergenerational awareness.

Second, there is a need for long-lived institutional structures that can take and maintain an intergenerational perspective. Churches, for example, have been particularly adept at passing down religious doctrines from one generation to the next. A common concern (for example, the fear of hell) united generations and drew them together in a similar pursuit. As culture these church doctrines represent intergenerational public goods. To be effective these institutions must be sufficiently flexible to allow for evolution as generational tastes change over time.

Third, effective institutions for providing intergenerational public goods must supply the current generation with a sufficiently large share of the benefits so that they are properly motivated to act. Finally, there is less need for a formal institutional arrangement when the current generation's share of the public good's benefits is sufficiently large. If the institutional structure providing the public good can remain "loose" or unstructured, then this will economize on transactions costs. A structure is loose if there is no need for an enforcement mechanism, decisions are unanimous, meetings are infrequent and participants' autonomy is preserved (Sandler 1997). By economizing on transactions costs, these structures can then be viable because transactions benefits do not have to be very large to justify the institution.

In the case of ozone depletion, the benefits to the current generation and its immediate descendants were sufficiently large to balance the associated costs, so the current generation initiated drastic cuts in CFC use. The Montreal Protocol and its subsequent amendments to curb CFCs required little in the way of enforcement insofar as nations viewed the associated net benefits from participating as positive. Meetings on the protocol were infrequent and ad hoc. For acid rain the spatial weights relating emissions to depositions meant that the lion's share of a country's emissions befouled its own territory. This realization provided the right incentives to frame a treaty to curb sulphur emissions. If, analogously, a sufficient temporal share of the benefits from providing an intergenerational public good is specific to the current generation, then this bodes well for an action being taken. Any action that can increase the current generation's perceived share of the gain from providing an intergenerational public good will motivate its provision.

While the current generation's share of the benefits appears large from curbing CFC emissions, for which the immediate health threat from enhanced ultraviolet radiation exposure is experienced today, this is not necessarily the case for global warming, for which the adverse effects might not be noticeable for decades. This suggests that the global warming problem does not have the appropriate incentives from an intergenerational viewpoint to ensure proper action. Efforts to resolve uncertainty regarding the benefits associated with an intergenerational public good may increase the current generation's perceived share of benefits by more adequately identifying the immediate gains from an action and, as a consequence, motivate action.

Finally, consider the promotion of sustainable development where efforts are made to maintain the opportunities provided to the next generation (Solow 1986; Toman, Pezzey and Krautkraemer 1995). If the current generation is to form far-sighted transnational agreements, then it must perceive a high share of the resulting benefits. When today's generation has a better understanding of the losses associated with its decisions, its awareness of the ensuing benefits and costs can be fostered. This awareness can be furthered by instituting a change in national income accounting so as to include depreciation to the natural capital stock. Efforts to educate the public about the environmental consequences of today's actions can promote altruism to future generations and, consequently, should bolster sustainable development.

Conclusion

The strategic interaction between generations differs from that within generations. If an intergenerational public good yields benefits that spill over borders and generations, then policies designed to correct for just spatial transnational externalities may worsen the misallocation of resources. This is especially the case if the public activity provides positive near-term benefits and negative long-run costs. Moreover, the natural sequencing of generations gives the present generation a potential first-mover advantage. In a suggestive interregional example, a backward-looking region is depicted as abiding by a leader-follower model in which the current generation relies on the next generation, while a forward-looking region is represented as adhering to Nash behaviour with the current generation applying altruism towards future generations. The final outcome is that the forward-looking region assumes a larger burden than the backward-looking region for providing intergenerational public goods—an outcome that bodes poorly for environmental treaties involving world-wide pollutants.

Actions to increase the perceived share of the intergenerational public good benefits going to the current generation will motivate it to provide the good. Transnational linkages that achieve far-sighted solutions are facilitated if efforts to promote intergenerational awareness are successful for all participants of the linkage. Policies that increase the awareness of only some participants will result in lopsided outcomes where the burden of the intergenerational public good is shouldered by the far-sighted nations. If institutional linkages for providing intergenerational public goods can be kept loose or unintegrated, then transactions costs are economized, and this promotes the institution of the linkage. This looseness can be achieved if the current generation within each participant perceives significant generation-specific benefits.

Much research remains to be done on intergenerational public goods. For example, more work is needed on the issue of discounting (Doeleman and Sandler 1998). A more complete analysis is also required for representing strategic behaviour among generations. Yet another extension would examine the role of income redistribution policy between and within generations as a means for promoting public good provision.

APPENDIX 1

BASIC MODEL

This appendix describes the basic model used in the second section of the chapter. An individual's utility function is depicted as

1a. $\quad u^{ijr} = u^{ijr}\left(y^{ijr}, q\right), \qquad i \in \Omega_{jr}, j = 1, 2, 3 \text{ and } r = 1, 2.$

Each of these utility functions is assumed to be strictly increasing, quasi-concave, and twice differentiable. The total quantity of the private good produced during period j, denoted by Y_j, must equal the amount consumed during the jth period, so that

2a. $\quad Y_j = \sum_{r=1}^{2} \sum_{i \in \Omega_{jr}} y^{ijr}$

for $j = 1, 2, 3$. In equation 2a the y^{ijr} terms represent the ith individual's consumption of the private good during period j in region r. These individual consumption amounts are summed over the individuals alive during period j in a given region and then over the regions for each period. The multiregional, multiperiod production of the private good is

3a. $\quad Y = \sum_{j=1}^{3} Y_j$

or the sum of the production amounts in the three periods. A multiperiod transformation constraint for the two-region economy indicates how a given amount of resources can be transferred between the two production activities:

4a. $F(Y,\ q)\ =\ 0,$

where the multiperiod supply of resources is suppressed. This function is strictly increasing and strictly convex in its arguments to assure that first-order conditions are sufficient for a maximum.

For intergenerational Pareto efficiency the associated Lagrangean expression, L, is:

$$L = u^{111}(y^{111},\ q) + \sum_{r=1}^{2} \sum_{j=1}^{3} \sum_{i \in \Omega_{jr}} \lambda^{ijr}\left[u^{ijr}(y^{ijr},\ q) - k^{ijr}\right] - \sigma F\left(\sum_{j=1}^{3} Y_j,\ q\right),$$

where the sum over i in the second term on the right-hand side excludes the first individual. The λ's and σ are undetermined Lagrangean multipliers, while the k expressions are constant levels of utility. Maximization of the Lagrangean with respect to the y^{ijr} expressions and q yields the first-order condition in (AR1), after simplification to eliminate the Lagrangean multipliers:

AR1. $\displaystyle\sum_{r=1}^{2} \sum_{j=1}^{3} \sum_{i \in \Omega_{jr}} MRS_{qy}^{ijr} = MRT_{qy}.$

In equation AR1 the *MRS* expressions represent the marginal rate of substitution of the intergenerational public good for the private good. The marginal rate of substitution is the ratio of marginal utilities of the two goods and indicates the *marginal benefit* or value, in terms of the private good, that an individual derives from the intergenerational public good. From left to right, the superscripts on the *MRS* correspond to the individual, the period and the region. On the right-hand side of equation AR1 the marginal rate of transformation (*MRT*) of the public good for the private good denotes the ratio of marginal costs of the two goods.

APPENDIX 2

AWARENESS RULES AR2, AR3, AND AR4

The three additional awareness rules are as follows:

AR2. $\displaystyle\sum_{r=1}^{2} \sum_{i \in \Omega_{1r}} MRS_{qy}^{ilr} = MRT_{qy}$,

AR3. $\displaystyle\sum_{j=1}^{3} \sum_{i \in \Omega_{jr}} MRS_{qy}^{ijr} = MRT_{qy}^{r}$, $\qquad r = 1, 2$

AR4. $\displaystyle\sum_{i \in \Omega_{1r}} MRS_{qy}^{ilr} = MRT_{qy}^{r}$, $\qquad r = 1, 2$

where Ω_{1r} is the current generation in region r for AR2 and AR4. The superscript on MRT denotes the region.

NOTES

1. On transnational public goods, see, for example, Barrett (1993), Bryant (1995), Cornes and Sandler (1996, chapters 17–18), Helm (1991), Murdoch and Sandler (1997), Runge (1993), Sandler (1992, 1996, 1997, 1998) and Sandler and Sargent (1995).

2. The following papers consider intergenerational public goods: Amsberg (1995), Bromley (1989), Doeleman and Sandler (1998), John and Pecchenino (1994, 1997), John and others (1995) and Myles (1997).

3. Recent articles on sustainability include Buiter (1997), Doeleman and Sandler (1998), Howarth (1997) and Toman, Pezzey and Krautkraemer (1995). Solow (1986) distinguishes three types of capital: humanmade, human and natural. For weak sustainability the overall capital stock must be maintained, so any reduction in natural capital must be compensated by an increase in the other kinds of capital. In contrast, natural capital stocks cannot decline when satisfying strong sustainability.

4. This criterion applies a zero discount rate so as to treat benefits to each generation equally. For very long-lived projects this implied that the discount factor of unity is in the spirit of Heal's (1997) call for proportional discounting that places more value on future benefits.

5. The underlying Lagrangean is the same form as that in appendix 1 except that only the utility levels of the first generation are held constant.

6. The transformation function is now region specific and denoted by $F^{r}(Y^{r}, q^{r}) = 0$, where Y^{r} represents the multiperiod production amount for the private good and is summed over the three periods. Thus Y^{r} is the multiperiod sum of Y_{j}^{r}, which equals the sum of y^{ijr} over just the jth generation, while q^{r} is the intergenerational public good in period 1 in region r.

7. The underlying social welfare function is assumed to be utilitarian, which consists of a simple sum of the relevant individuals' utility functions.

8. In figure 1 the slope of an iso-welfare curve for region 1 is

$$\left(MRT_{qy}^{1} \middle/ \sum_{i \in \Omega_{11}} MRS_{qy}^{i\,11} \right) - 1.$$

If this equation is set equal to zero, then AR4 results.

9. In figure 2 the Nash path for region 2 is drawn flatter than the 45 degree line, while the Nash path for region 1 is drawn steeper than the 45 degree line. If both goods are normal with a positive income elasticity less than one, then these slopes result and the Nash equilibrium is unique and stable (Cornes and Sandler 1996).

10. The first generation's multiperiod transformation is denoted by

$$F_E^1\left(y_E^{11} + y_E^{12},\ q_E^{11} + q_E^{12} \right) = 0,$$

while the second generation's transformation function is given by

$$F_E^2(y_E^{22},\ q_E^{22}) = 0$$

11. The Lagrangean for Eastern generation 1 is

$$V_E^1\left[u_E^{11}\left(y_E^{11},\ q_E^{11} + q_W^{11} \right),\ u_E^{12}\left(y_E^{12},\ q_E^{11} + q_E^{12} + q_E^{22} + q_W^{11} + q_W^{12} + q_W^{22} \right) \right] - \sigma F_E^1(\bullet),$$

and the Lagrangean for generation 2 is

$$V_E^2\left[u_E^{22}\left(y_E^{22},\ q_E^{11} + q_E^{12} + q_E^{22} + q_W^{11} + q_W^{12} + q_W^{22} \right) \right] - \psi F_W^2(\bullet).$$

12. Income disparity between the East and West also explains some of the differences in environment-supporting behaviour, but the strategic differences introduced here represent influences that go beyond income disparity to explain alternative environmental policies.

13. This condition is

$$\sum_{i \in \Omega_{1r}} \left(\alpha^r MRS_{xy}^{ilr} + \beta^r MRS_{zy}^{ilr} \right) = MRT_{qy}^r,\ r = E, W.$$

14. The intergenerational optimality condition for full awareness is

$$\sum_{j=1}^{3} \sum_{i \in \Omega_{jr}} \alpha^r MRS_{xy}^{ijr} + \sum_{r = E, W} \sum_{j=1}^{3} \sum_{i \in \Omega_{jr}} \beta^r MRS_{zy}^{ijr} = MRT_{qy}^r.$$

References

Amsberg, Joachim von. 1995. "Excessive Environmental Risks: An Intergenerational Market Failure." *European Economic Review* 39(8): 1447–64.

Barrett, Scott. 1993. *Convention on Climate Change: Economic Aspects of Negotiations.* Paris: Organisation for Economic Co-operation and Development.

Bromley, Daniel W. 1989. "Entitlements, Missing Markets, and Environmental Uncertainty." *Journal of Environmental Economics and Management* 17(2): 181–94.

Bryant, Ralph C. 1995. *International Coordination of National Stabilization Policies.* Washington, DC: Brookings Institution.

Buiter, William H. 1997. "Generational Accounts, Aggregate Savings and Intergenerational Distribution." *Economica* 64(4): 605–26.

Cornes, Richard, and Todd Sandler. 1985. "The Simple Analytics of Pure Public Good Provision." *Economica* 52(2): 103–16.

———. 1996. *The Theory of Externalities, Public Goods, and Club Goods.* 2nd edition. Cambridge: Cambridge University Press.

Doeleman, Jacobus A., and Todd Sandler. 1998. "The Intergenerational Case of Missing Markets and Missing Voters." *Land Economics* 74(1): 1–15.

Heal, Geoffrey. 1997. *Valuing Our Future: Cost-Benefit Analysis and Sustainability.* ODS Discussion Paper 13. New York: United Nations Development Programme, Office of Development Studies.

Helm, Dieter, ed. 1991. *Economic Policy towards the Environment.* Oxford: Blackwell.

Howarth, Richard B. 1997. "Sustainability As Opportunity." *Land Economics* 73(4): 569–79.

John, A. Andrew, and Rowena A. Pecchenino. 1994. "An Overlapping Generation's Model of Growth and the Environment." *Economic Journal* 104(6): 1393–1410.

———. 1997. "International and Intergenerational Environmental Externalities." *Scandinavian Journal of Economics* 99(3): 371–87.

John, A. Andrew, Rowena A. Pecchenino, David E. Schimmelpfennig and Stacey L. Schreft. 1995. "Short-Lived Agents and the Long-Lived Environment." *Journal of Public Economics* 58(1): 127–41.

Murdoch, James C., and Todd Sandler. 1997. "The Voluntary Provision of a Pure Public Good: The Case of Reduced CFC Emissions and the Montreal Protocol." *Journal of Public Economics* 63(2): 331–49.

Murdoch, James C., Todd Sandler and Keith Sargent. 1997. "A Tale of Two Collectives: Sulphur versus Nitrogen Oxides Emission Reduction in Europe." *Economica* 64(2): 281–301.

Myles, Gareth D. 1997. "Depreciation and Intergenerational Altruism in the Private Provision of Public Goods." *European Journal of Political Economy* 13(4): 725–38.

Page, Talbot. 1977. "Discounting and Intergenerational Equity." *Futures* 9(5): 377–82.

Runge, C. Ford. 1993. "International Public Goods, Export Subsidies, and Harmonization of Environmental Regulations." In Mathew D. Shane and Harald von Witzke, eds., *The Environment, Government Policies, and International Trade: A Proceedings.* Washington, DC: US Department of Agriculture, Economic Research Service.

Sandler, Todd. 1978. "Interregional and Intergenerational Spillover Awareness." *Scottish Journal of Political Economy* 25(3): 273–84.

———. 1982. "A Theory of Intergenerational Clubs." *Economic Inquiry* 20(2): 191–208.

———. 1992. *Collective Action: Theory and Applications.* Ann Arbor: University of Michigan Press.

———. 1996. "A Game-Theoretic Analysis of Carbon Emissions." In Roger Congleton, ed., *The Political Economy of Environmental Protection: Analysis and Evidence.* Ann Arbor: University of Michigan Press.

———. 1997. *Global Challenges: An Approach to Environmental, Political, and Economic Problems.* Cambridge: Cambridge University Press.

———. 1998. "Global and Regional Public Goods: A Prognosis for Collective Action." *Fiscal Studies* 19(1): 221–47.

Sandler, Todd, and Keith Sargent. 1995. "Management of Transnational Commons: Coordination, Publicness and Treaty Formation." *Land Economics* 71(2): 145–62.

Sandler, Todd, and V. Kerry Smith. 1976. "Intertemporal and Intergenerational Pareto Efficiency." *Journal of Environmental Economics and Management* 2(3): 151–59.

Sandnes, Hilda. 1993. *Calculated Budgets for Airborne Acidifying Components in Europe, 1985, 1987, 1988, 1989, 1990, 1991, and 1992.* EMEP/MSC-W Report 1/93. Oslo, Norway: Norske Meteorologiske Institutt.

Solow, Robert M. 1986. "On the Intergenerational Allocation of Natural Resources." *Scandinavian Journal of Economics* 88(1): 141–49.

Toman, Michael A., John Pezzey and Jeffrey Krautkraemer. 1995. "Neoclassical Economic Growth Theory and 'Sustainability.'" In Daniel W. Bromley, ed., *The Handbook of Environmental Economics.* Oxford: Blackwell.

The Political Economy of
International Cooperation

Lisa L. Martin

Over the past 15 years the field of international relations has produced a great deal of work on international cooperation and international institutions. This work has immediate relevance for conceptualizing a new era and a new approach to international development cooperation. Once we understand development cooperation as a problem of providing global public goods, our attention is immediately drawn to the problems of strategic interaction and opportunistic behaviour that confront states as they attempt to cooperate in the pursuit of mutually beneficial goals.

Drawing on public goods models and related concerns, the literature on international cooperation identifies strategic problems that states must overcome if they are to cooperate effectively—and how international organizations can facilitate state efforts to cooperate, primarily through the provision of information. This chapter summarizes the central claims of political science about the conditions for international cooperation and the roles of international organizations and nonstate actors in helping states achieve the benefits of cooperation. It concludes that the most useful functions of international organizations involve the provision of information about state preferences and behaviour—particularly about standards and causal knowledge.

Theories of International Cooperation

Since the early 1980s the field of international relations has largely been dominated by debates about the concept of international cooperation (Oye 1986). Stimulating this theoretical innovation were developments in the new institutional economics and game theory, which used ideas of self-enforcing agreements, opportunistic behaviour and lack of legal obligation that nicely characterize the international arena (Keohane 1984). The modern literature on international cooperation departed from earlier liberal, or "idealist", conceptions of cooperation in important ways. It attempted to show that, even making fairly pessimistic assumptions about state interests and intentions, we could identify conditions under which states would find it beneficial and possible to cooperate with one another. The literature has specified conditions that should facilitate cooperation and the various types of information needed. Examination of the need for information has drawn theorists' attention to the role of international organizations, considered in more detail below.

Theories of international cooperation made a big leap forward by accepting the assumption that states are self-interested and have conflicts of interest with one another. Theorists accepted the challenge of showing how cooperation might nevertheless emerge—and even show some stability. The key set of articles in this area is the volume edited by Kenneth Oye (1986), *Cooperation under Anarchy*. The emphasis on anarchy was an especially important part of the research agenda because it ruled out the possibility that cooperation would be enforced by outside agents. As Oye explains, "nations dwell in perpetual anarchy, for no central authority imposes limits on the pursuit of sovereign interests" (1986, p. 1). The statement that international relations is an anarchical realm simply means that agreements among states will last only if they are self-enforcing. International organizations may play a major role, as elaborated below, but it is a mistake to conceive of this role as direct enforcement of agreements. International organizations, if they have any enforcement powers, have only minimal capability to force states to do anything they do not want to do. Instead, organizations assist cooperation by creating the conditions that make agreements self-enforcing.

Before going into the specifics, it is important to stress one of the main premises of these studies. From their perspective, international institutions are not seen as a form of world government, as a failed attempt at world government or as a precursor to world government. Nor are international institutions conceptualized as sitting above states, handing down mandates to them and enforcing agreements. "World government", in fact, has little if anything to do with what political scientists see as the functions that international institutions can perform. Instead these institutions are seen as actors that acquire authority and powers only as the result of acts of delegation by their member states.

For the most part, delegated powers consist of various kinds of information provision, such as monitoring, setting standards and distributing scientific expertise. Enforcement of international agreements nearly always continues to be decentralized in the hands of member states rather than the organization itself. Some international organizations, such as the World Trade Organization and European Court of Justice, are increasingly involving themselves in dispute resolution. But even with these functions organizations are properly seen as assisting states in resolving their cooperation dilemmas, rather than acting as an authoritative enforcer of rules and norms. By providing guidance on how to interpret international agreements and the specifics of state behaviour, dispute resolution is properly seen as one more type of information provision.

The basic model of state interests adopted by the new literature on cooperation is that of the prisoner's dilemma. The prisoner's dilemma captures the logic of mixed motives, in which states can gain from reaching cooperative agreements but also confront incentives to renege on these commitments. In games with a definite, foreseeable termination, the prisoner's dilemma logic leads inexorably to defection, with actors unable to achieve potential gains from cooperation. But when a prisoner's dilemma game is repeated indefinitely, actors can adopt strategies of reciprocity that allow them to reach cooperative, and mutually beneficial, equilibria. Reciprocity consists of such strategies as tit-for-tat, where cooperation is met with cooperation, and defection with defection. Theories of international cooperation define cooperation as mutual adjustment of state policies to achieve outcomes that all prefer to the status quo (Keohane 1984). Cooperation is clearly differentiated from harmony, in which states pursue policies that other states prefer without any explicit mutual adjustment. Because prisoner's dilemma situations present states with incentives to renege on cooperative arrangements, they make the distinction between harmony and cooperation particularly clear and compelling.

Drawing on the logic of the prisoner's dilemma, theorists have identified generic conditions for international cooperation. The basic issue here is what allows strategies of reciprocity to operate effectively. Fundamental to their success is reliable information about various aspects of the situation, including others' actions and intentions, their beliefs, the relevant standards of behaviour and the relationship between actions and outcomes (that is, causal knowledge). Strategies of reciprocity require that states can monitor one another's behaviour and retaliate when others fail to live up to their commitments. Poor monitoring capacities, resulting in "noise" in observations of state actions, can quickly undermine the practice of reciprocity and so the possibility of stable cooperation. Axelrod (1984), in an experimental setting, shows how small mistakes in monitoring actors' behaviour in a prisoner's dilemma can quickly lead to feuds and cycles of retaliation, making the achievement of cooperation highly problematic. Poor information of any type can undermine the use of reciprocity to sustain cooperation, making information provision one of the keys to successful international cooperation. For this reason the rest of this chapter focuses on how international organizations and other actors can provide various types of information, thus facilitating international cooperation.

As discussed below, the prisoner's dilemma is not the only appropriate model for international cooperation. But it is extremely important in drawing attention to the mixed motives that states face—and to certain generic obstacles to international cooperation. It is also a fruitful model in that it concentrates research on the question of reciprocity, a common strategy for maintaining cooperation in international relations. Cooperative behaviour requires the establishment of conditions in which strategies of reciprocity can work effectively, particularly conditions of good information.

THE ROLE OF INTERNATIONAL ORGANIZATIONS

According to contractual theory (see, for example, Krasner 1983; Keohane 1984; and Goldstein 1996), states often face problems like the prisoner's dilemma, in which individually rational behaviour gives rise to outcomes that leave all unhappy. In economics such a situation is called market failure because a properly functioning market should prevent suboptimal outcomes. In international relations this situation has been called a game of collaboration, drawing attention to the fact that states must collaborate to reach their own, individually specified goals (Martin 1992; Snidal 1985; Stein 1983).

The motivation behind institutional creation and maintenance is to allow states to reach the Pareto frontier, the set of outcomes at which no more joint gains are available. At the Pareto frontier any gain to one state by definition results in losses for others. Reaching the Pareto frontier in a prisoner's dilemma requires good information about the situation and the other players. One way to think about what information does is to conceive of it as removing or making transparent the walls that separate the prisoners from one another. Freed from these walls, they can learn about each other's intentions and actions, agree on standards of behaviour and learn about the relationship between their actions and outcomes.

Keohane (1984) spells out how international institutions can help states overcome collective action dilemmas. He argues that market failure should not occur if transactions costs are negligible and property rights are clearly defined. As he explains, "the Coase theorem could be interpreted...as predicting that problems of collective action could easily be overcome in international politics through bargaining and mutual adjustment" (Keohane 1984, p. 86). Under these conditions states should be able to make and maintain mutually beneficial agreements. But in international politics transactions costs are high and property rights are often poorly defined. Thus states often may fail to overcome collective-action problems because of fear that others will renege on deals, because they are unable to adequately monitor others' behaviour or learn about others' preferences or because they act opportunistically since punishment mechanisms are inadequate.

Institutions enter the picture at this point—to allow states to overcome such problems and reach mutually beneficial agreements. The primary function of institutions in this framework is to allow strategies of reciprocity to operate efficiently (Keohane 1986). Institutions perform this function by providing information about others' preferences, intentions, behaviour, standards of behaviour and causal knowledge. Thus in contractual theory the primary effect of institutions is an efficiency effect, in that they allow states to reach agreements that are closer to the Pareto frontier. Institutions, in this rationalist model, do not modify underlying state interests. Instead, by changing the informational environment, they change state strategies in such a way that self-interested states find it easier to cooperate reliably with one another.

A similar conclusion has been reached in the literature on common-pool resources. One finding of this literature is that cooperation is facilitated when users of a common-pool resource can monitor each other's compliance with joint rules at a reasonable cost. In other words, information about compliance becomes central to the resolution of common-pool resource dilemmas—as is the case in such real-world examples as conserving global whale populations, controlling the trade of endangered species and protecting regional marine environments.

Some authors have responded to contractual theory by pointing out that collaboration problems are not the only impediments to cooperation facing states. States also face distributional, coordination and bargaining problems (Krasner 1991; Fearon 1998). All these problems revolve around disputes over where states will find themselves on the Pareto frontier—not the less contentious question of how to reach the Pareto frontier. In any institutionalized pattern of cooperation there are a number of ways to cooperate, and many may not be readily distinguishable from one another in terms of efficiency (that is, they are all on the Pareto frontier). States that agree to coordinate their exchange rates will disagree on precisely what the appropriate parities are; states that cooperate with one another in a military alliance will disagree on precisely how much each should contribute to mutual defence.

Initial studies of international regimes argued that such coordination problems were easier to solve than collaboration problems—and that regimes had little to contribute to their resolution (Stein 1983). But this argument has come under serious attack. Bargaining problems can be just as devastating to prospects for international cooperation as can collaboration problems. In addition, bargaining problems are resolved under different conditions. Fearon (1998) has shown, for example, that while a long shadow of the future may enhance the prospects of finding mutually beneficial agreements, it also intensifies bargaining problems because any deals struck will have consequences that reach far into the future. Only coordination problems with no distributional consequences—a rare category—will lend themselves to quick resolution. In other cases states will delay, make threats, hide or distort information, and generally engage in all the time-honoured techniques of statecraft that make international politics a fascinating yet grim business.

How do bargaining problems get resolved? Krasner (1991) follows the traditional realist line, arguing that a straightforward exercise of state power determines which of the possible outcomes gets chosen. The most powerful state simply chooses the outcome it prefers; other states have little choice but to go along. Power is not the only possible solution to the bargaining problem. Garrett and Weingast (1993) point to the role of focal points in resolving coordination problems. The concept of a focal point dates back to Schelling (1960) and initially referred to solutions that had an "obvious", natural ring to them: meeting at Grand Central Station if two people become separated in New York City, or dividing the benefits of cooperation 50-50.

Garrett and Weingast extend the notion to include "constructed" focal points, those intentionally chosen and promoted by international actors. They concentrate especially on the European Court of Justice, arguing that its choice of the norm of mutual recognition as a method to complete the internal European Union (EU) market is an important example of a constructed focal point. They claim that the court's ability to establish focal points explains why it has been so influential in European integration, even though it lacks (at least until recently) enforcement power.

So, using the constructed focal point analogy, analysts have found that international institutions can operate to resolve coordination problems. This analysis of bargaining and coordination is important because it reinforces the central argument of this chapter that information is essential to international cooperation. Bargaining is about choosing one among a number of sustainable solutions to a problem, and states will generally disagree about which of these solutions they prefer. As analysis of bargaining problems evolves to consider notions such as focal points, we discover that bargaining problems are largely information problems. By constructing a focal point, which generally involves setting a standard, organizations can provide the information needed to allow states to overcome bargaining problems, as the European Court of Justice did when specifying mutual recognition as the path to completion of the internal EU market. This provision of focal point or standard-setting information can potentially be undertaken by powerful states (or even firms) rather than by international organizations. But because other states will always be suspicious of the motives of the powerful states, relying on organizations to set standards and identify focal points is often more effective, as members of the European Union have discovered.

In sum, rationalist approaches to international institutions assume that states turn to institutions in an attempt to solve cooperation problems. These cooperation problems are defined by patterns of state interests. In this perspective institutions change patterns of state behaviour not by changing fundamental state goals but by changing strategies and beliefs—by influencing the informational environment. They provide information about others' preferences, behaviour and intentions. They also provide information about means-ends relationships—how particular policies will lead to different outcomes. Such causal knowledge is essential, for example, to understanding how the choice of a particular exchange rate regime will affect key macroeconomic variables. Equilibria in rationalist models are defined by a combination of beliefs and strategies (Morrow 1994), and institutions operate directly on both.

The cases discussed in other chapters in this book illustrate many of the general arguments made here. The chapters on distributive justice, for example, make more concrete the discussion of bargaining and the importance of information in resolving bargaining problems, as distributive justice and bargaining both refer to the distribution of the benefits of cooperation. Sen (in this volume) and Rao (in this volume) analyse equity as a global public good, and Kapstein (in this volume) discusses how concepts of distributive justice were integrated with the international system developed after the Second World War. As the foregoing discussion of bargaining suggested, concerns about equity can impede the creation of international institutions and be addressed by well-designed institutions.

We can also see a growing consensus that failure to assure a relatively equitable distribution of benefits from cooperation can prevent, or at least greatly delay, the creation of cooperative mechanisms. While legal scholars, sociologists and philosophers tend to trace this fact to deeply embedded norms of fairness, political scientists focus more on bargaining incentives and the desire of actors to increase their share of any benefits produced. If lack of equity prevents the creation of cooperative mechanisms that could benefit all, equity comes to take on some characteristics of a public good. These arguments about distributive justice suggest that we should turn our attention to how international organizations can operate to enhance the equitable distribution of the benefits of cooperation.

In many cases considered in this book, such as environmental issues, compensation of losers from agreements may be key both to increasing effectiveness and to enhancing equity. But providing compensation to those who lose in the short term from international agreements raises a host of strategic problems, most having to do with gaining access to high-quality information. The losers have incentives to exaggerate their losses, thus increasing their claim on compensation. Meanwhile, those who must provide the compensation face incentives to minimize the calculations of losses, and to find excuses not to come through with promised resources.

International organizations can step in to alleviate these strategic dilemmas in several ways. They can provide expert analyses of the claims of losers for compensation—say, by evaluating the extent of economic losses from participation in international agreements. Organizations can also set standards for contributions to provision pools and publicize information about states that fall short of their obligations in this respect. The discussion of equity and distributive justice thus clarifies some of the kinds of information that are necessary if states are to resolve bargaining and coordination problems—and highlights the role that international organizations can play in providing such information.

The chapters in this book on environmental agreements, by Barrett and by Heal, also provide concrete examples of the strategic problems that states face in attempting to cooperate with one another and how lack of information can impede cooperation. Technology and the creation of markets for rights to pollute will greatly alleviate the difficulties in increasing provision of environmental goods, as these chapters show. But reliance on technology and markets alone is unlikely to put international organizations out of the business of helping to protect the environment. Even if technology facilitates the conclusion of global accords, temptations to fall out of compliance with these accords will persist. Poor countries in particular will be concerned about the costs of turning to new technology and may be tempted to ignore the terms of environmental agreements, especially if they believe that their compliance will go unnoticed and unrewarded (or that cheating will go unpunished). This is the classic problem of incomplete information considered by theories of international cooperation, and leads in a straightforward way to the proposition that international organizations can be valuable in monitoring compliance with international agreements and publicizing this information. Such monitoring is likely to be perceived as less intrusive than monitoring by other states.

Similarly, relying on tradable rights to pollute can work as an effective solution only if information about compliance with permit limits is widely available. One problem that has plagued the implementation of tradable permit systems is precisely the difficulty of monitoring whether participants in the schemes are exceeding their limits. Theories of cooperation strongly suggest that this is precisely the kind of situation in which assigning monitoring functions to international organizations (or, in some cases, to nonstate actors) can improve the welfare of all by limiting the extent of cheating. Environmental cooperation illustrates the demand for monitoring and reliable information about whether states are complying with international agreements—and the potential role of international organizations in providing this information.

NONSTATE ACTORS: NGOS AND EPISTEMIC COMMUNITIES

The problem of development cooperation increasingly requires that states interact productively with nonstate actors. These actors can facilitate development cooperation or, in the worst case, significantly interfere with the pursuit of global public goods. Nongovernmental organizations (NGOs) and epistemic (or expert) communities provide various kinds of information that are relevant to the pursuit of collective goals. NGOs also have important effects on agenda setting and the evolution of public attention to global goals (Sen in this volume). A focus on the information provision functions of international organizations leads us to the question of whether some types of information could be provided as effectively by other types of actors, such as NGOs and epistemic communities.

Nonstate actors should be viewed as complements to international organizations rather than as substitutes for them. While nonstate actors can and do provide vital information to facilitate cooperation, the tasks of filtering, sorting, publicizing and authenticating this information properly fall to international organizations. The issue, from this perspective, is to find ways for these actors to work together, complementing one another's strengths rather than looking to put one another out of business.

First, consider the rapidly expanding role that NGOs play in global politics. NGOs have moved well beyond the nationally based groups of the early 20th century. Increasingly, they are transnational in organization, membership and objectives (Keck and Sikkink 1998). Working as advocacy networks, they shape agendas, publicize events throughout the world, raise public awareness and issue reports on compliance with international standards of behaviour. Because NGOs are typically built on a foundation of strongly held principles and have networks at the grass roots and throughout many countries, they acquire legitimacy and persuasiveness in their approach to global problems. As Sen (in this volume) notes, some nongovernmental groups transcend individual or even national interests to promote universal—global—interests. In the short term the greatest contribution of these groups to the provision of global public goods may be in their activities of publicizing failures to comply with international norms, such as human rights or environmental norms. In the longer term they can make an even more significant contribution by changing public attitudes towards such issues, as they did on slavery and women's rights.

A concept closely related to that of NGOs is epistemic communities (Haas 1992). Like NGOs, epistemic communities are advocacy networks. But they add an element of scientific or expert knowledge, specializing in knowledge-based advocacy. They thus provide what I have called causal knowledge. The activities of epistemic communities in environmental issues are especially notable. As scientific knowledge about environmental topics evolves and epistemic communities reach a consensus on how human activity changes the environment, this knowledge is filtered through to domestic politics, national governments and international negotiations. Like NGOs, epistemic communities provide information and, over the longer run, change public attitudes. Their distinctive contribution, and one that is growing, may be their ability to have a direct impact on international negotiations on issues of global concern. Experts present at negotiations on the environment or on economic issues can greatly influence the negotiations and the framework for international agreements. One institutional question is whether such representation is most effective in constructing efficient, well-designed international agreements if experts play only an informal, advisory role, or if they are given a more formal place at the negotiating table.

To make these arguments about NGOs and epistemic communities more concrete, I turn to public health. Zacher (in this volume) concentrates on one aspect of global public health, the provision of information about the incidence of infectious disease. Two strategic problems seem central here: the provision of reliable information about disease and the willingness of governments to publicize outbreaks of infectious disease in their territories when such revelations might have negative economic consequences. Zacher emphasizes that multiple sources of information, such as the Internet, are becoming available.

At first glance this may suggest that the provision of information does not face a supply problem and that international organizations have little value to add in information provision, contrary to the major lesson of theories of international cooperation. But the availability of multiple sources of information does not automatically solve the information provision problem. It is entirely possible that some nongovernmental sources are biased or prone to error. Multiplication of information providers could, in practice, result in proliferation of noise and inaccurate information, rather than the high-quality information that states need to adequately address public health threats.

This analysis suggests that it may make more sense to conceive of the role of international organizations as one of filtering available information rather than directly providing it. When reports of infectious disease surface, it could be extremely valuable to the international community to have an expert, unbiased, reliable actor who could assess these reports and provide some indication of their likely accuracy. International organizations are likely to be better placed than states to perform this filtering.

If international organizations took on this filtering, they would contribute to resolution of the second strategic problem—getting governments to reveal information about disease in their territories. Governments may be dissuaded from issuing preliminary reports of disease by the fear that these would be publicized by the Internet and media outlets, without allowing for experts to come in and first establish the accuracy of the reports. Being able to turn, perhaps discreetly, to an unbiased expert body could greatly enhance the willingness of legitimately worried governments to report disease outbreaks in a timely and open manner.

As the information about the disease example suggests, private actors and international organizations have offsetting strengths and can usefully work together to enhance international cooperation. NGOs have the advantage of being close to the ground, spread around the world and tied together in networks. They are highly important, therefore, in providing rapid, initial information about such problems as the outbreak of infectious disease. Epistemic communities, in contrast, work on a smaller scale, providing scientific information that enhances the ability of actors to develop strategies that will achieve their desired outcomes.

International organizations generally cannot compete with NGOs in having grass-roots access—or with epistemic communities in having direct access to the latest scientific knowledge. But they do have the advantages of high visibility and a level of authority that comes from the powers delegated to them by their member states. Thus they can vitally complement the activities of private actors even where NGOs and epistemic communities are highly engaged. As in public health, they can filter information from NGOs; as in the environment, they can structure the input of epistemic communities to international negotiations. In addition, where cooperation requires direct monitoring of government activities—for example, to ascertain compliance with formal international agreements—there seems little substitute for the authoritative activities of international organizations. They have a legitimacy not achieved by private actors, and thus are the best placed to engage in potentially invasive monitoring of governments' behaviour.

CONCLUSION

Studies of international cooperation and public goods combine theoretical and empirical analysis of the conditions for self-interested actors to cooperate with one another in a stable, sustainable manner. One does not need to assume that actors are altruistic or idealistic to explain why they might cooperate with one another. All one needs to do is demonstrate that all can benefit from cooperative endeavours. But analysts then need to confront obstacles to cooperation. Resolution of these problems requires high-quality information about states' preferences, actions and intentions, about relevant standards of behaviour, and about causal or scientific knowledge. In all these areas, international organizations are designed to provide, either on their own or in collaboration with NGOs and epistemic communities, the relevant information.

As the practice of international development aid moves away from the traditional donor-recipient model to more multilateral, cooperative models, these generic obstacles to cooperation will increasingly come to bear. As we move into an era where development is conceptualized as a problem of providing global public goods rather than as a direct transfer of resources, the structure of future development cooperation institutions will change. One of the key lessons is that international organizations can substantially facilitate the pursuit of global cooperative goals, often through the provision of high-quality, reliable information about the characteristics and actions of states.

NOTE

The author is grateful to Mark Zacher for useful comments.

REFERENCES

Axelrod, Robert. 1984. *The Evolution of Cooperation.* New York: Basic Books.

Fearon, James D. 1998. "Bargaining, Enforcement, and International Cooperation." *International Organization* 52(2): 269-305.

Garrett, Geoffrey, and Barry Weingast. 1993. "Ideas, Interests, and Institutions: Constructing the EC's Internal Market." In Judith Goldstein and Robert Keohane, eds., *Ideas and Foreign Policy.* Ithaca, NY: Cornell University Press.

Goldstein, Judith. 1996. "International Law and Domestic Institutions: Reconciling North American 'Unfair' Trade Laws." *International Organization* 50(4): 541–64.

Haas, Peter, ed. 1992. "Epistemic Communities and International Policy Coordination." *International Organization* 46 (1).

Keck, Margaret E., and Kathryn Sikkink. 1998. *Activists beyond Borders: Advocacy Networks in International Politics.* Ithaca, NY: Cornell University Press.

Keohane, Robert O. 1984. *After Hegemony: Cooperation and Discord in the World Political Economy.* Princeton, NJ: Princeton University Press.

———. 1986. "Reciprocity in International Relations." *International Organization* 20(1): 1–27.

Krasner, Steven D., ed. 1983. *International Regimes.* Ithaca, NY: Cornell University Press.

———. 1991. "Global Communications and National Power: Life on the Pareto Frontier." *World Politics* 43(3): 336–56.

Martin, Lisa L. 1992. "Interests, Power, and Multilateralism." *International Organization* 46(4): 765–92.

Morrow, James D. 1994. "Modeling the Forms of International Cooperation." *International Organization* 48(3): 387–423.

Oye, Kenneth A., ed. 1986. *Cooperation under Anarchy.* Princeton, NJ: Princeton University Press.

Schelling, Thomas C. 1960. *The Strategy of Conflict.* Cambridge, MA: Harvard University Press.

Snidal, Duncan. 1985. "Coordination versus Prisoners' Dilemma: Implications for International Cooperation and Regimes." *American Political Science Review* 79(4): 923–42.

Stein, Arthur A. 1983. "Coordination and Collaboration: Regimes in an Anarchic World." In Steven D. Krasner, ed., *International Regimes.* Ithaca, NY: Cornell University Press.

CASE STUDIES

EQUITY AND JUSTICE

MARKET EFFICIENCY

ENVIRONMENT AND CULTURAL HERITAGE

HEALTH

KNOWLEDGE AND INFORMATION

PEACE AND SECURITY

EQUITY AND
JUSTICE

EQUITY IN A GLOBAL PUBLIC GOODS FRAMEWORK
J. Mohan Rao

DISTRIBUTIVE JUSTICE AS AN INTERNATIONAL PUBLIC GOOD:
A HISTORICAL PERSPECTIVE
Ethan B. Kapstein

GLOBAL JUSTICE: BEYOND INTERNATIONAL EQUITY
Amartya Sen

At first sight the global public goods framework does not easily lend itself to discussions of distributive issues such as equity. After all, global public goods seem to involve primarily shared benefits, rather than the question of "who gets what"? The three chapters in this section demonstrate, however, that equity is at the core of both the concept of public good and its implementation.

As indicated in the chapter "Defining Global Public Goods", some global public goods are final objectives and outcomes (such as peace) and some are intermediate (such as international regimes). Equity is both. These three chapters shed light on issues of definition and provision for this key public good and illuminate its global dimensions.

The chapter by J. Mohan Rao provides the backbone of the theoretical argument. Equity, Rao argues, underpins and sustains social order and cooperation, which are indispensable for the joint provision of public goods—including at the global level. In addition, equity is needed not just to organize the supply of public goods but also to define the demand for public goods and answer the question: whose public good should be on the agenda? Finally, equity itself is a public good: although many people desire an equitable society, this objective is rarely achieved when individuals act in isolation. People need to jointly commit to a common view of equity and follow up with joint action.

While Rao tends to rely on formal institutions—whether states, local governments or international organizations—for the provision of public goods, Amartya Sen highlights the fact that nonstate actors, operating across borders, are often at the forefront of global norms and standards of equity and justice. People's judgement on what is just and fair depends only marginally on their citizenship, and more on their personal and professional identities. So in essence, justice has an inescapable global quality. As Sen points out, it is important to distinguish between equity within countries and in a global, transnational setting.

A concern for distributive justice is to some extent embedded in the current institutions of the world economy, according to Ethan B. Kapstein. Kapstein reminds us that a just economic order has long been valued as a global public good, especially after the Second World War, when the Bretton Woods system was designed. For leaders reflecting on the causes of the war, the links between economic distress and global conflict were all too evident. Kapstein shows that the postwar architecture relied on two pillars: creating wealth and distributing it. Wealth was to be created primarily through free international trade, while redistributing it was the responsibility of domestic institutions. Yet this approach became less and less effective over time. The only way forward now, Kapstein argues, is to address these concerns at the international level.

EQUITY IN A
GLOBAL PUBLIC GOODS
FRAMEWORK

J. MOHAN RAO

As the new millennium approaches, a true global economy is taking shape and a global culture emerging. Driven by real-time communications and revolutions in information technology, by the rapid convergence in national policies and by the increased interchange of ideas, images and lifestyles across national and cultural boundaries, this era of globalization presents new opportunities and unusual threats. Yet global democracy is nowhere in sight. Rules and principles to prevent, even to manage, economic crises are either nonexistent or ad hoc and incomplete. Enforceable rules and standards for the protection of the global environment and labour and human rights have yet to be widely accepted, much less implemented. While the size of a middle class plugged into new global networks (and with the wherewithal to be part of global consumerism) has grown and spread, huge segments of the world's population remain marginalized. But whether included or excluded, few are free from a growing sense of vulnerability to global forces.

At the same time, global integration has diminished the management capacities of the nation state and poses risks of national disintegration. The effectiveness of a state's macroeconomic policy and fiscal capacity in dealing with shocks and instabilities are increasingly constrained by privatization, market liberalization and the growing mobility of capital. In industrial countries disintegration manifests itself as falling wages or growing unemployment of the semi-skilled, increased wage dispersion and a rising share of profit (relative to wages) in national income. In developing countries neither market nor state is able to include and integrate large parts of the population that have long been on the fringe, due to rising wage differentials between the semi-skilled and the unskilled and the slow growth of formal jobs relative to informal employment. Many nations are not prepared to face the social and political effects of large shocks, even though the nation state remains the last resort for the (political) resolution of adjustment choices.

Thus economic and cultural globalization seem to have ushered in an awkward and potentially unstable period of transition for the world. Even if one supposes that free trade and unrestricted capital mobility can eventually result in global factor price equalization and international equality, the transition may take decades—if not centuries. Meanwhile, many areas of pressing global concern can be successfully addressed only through international collective action. But can effective and efficient solutions be found if questions of distribution, equity and justice are side-stepped?

At stake are questions of how to distribute the costs incurred, and the benefits to be derived, from cooperative action to create global public goods or minimize global public bads. Questions of equity are also implicated in the origins of the global problems themselves. International negotiations are influenced by unequal economic and bargaining strengths and the diverse stages of development at which nations find themselves. These negotiations would be comparatively easy if economically unequal nations were converging in living standards and if the global pie was briskly growing bigger. But except in restricted samples, such as Organisation for Economic Co-operation and Development (OECD) countries, international economic divergence—rich countries growing faster than poor ones—has been the rule, while the rate of world income growth was slower in 1980–95 than in the "golden age" (1950–79).[1]

These difficulties are compounded by the fact that the world is having to pay more attention to the welfare of future generations, who face growing environmental threats. For example, disagreements between rich and poor countries today over the sharing of the global quota of pollution sinks may affect decisions on the global quota itself, which will have consequences for nations tomorrow. Disagreements may also spill over into unrelated areas of international negotiation. Although past costs and inequities are rationally not supposed to matter for present and future decisions, equity considerations render such "bygones" at least indirectly relevant in international negotiations. They have also played a part in the long history of negotiations at the General Agreement on Tariffs and Trade (GATT). Often, however, ignorance and special interests camouflage distributional considerations or keep them off the open agenda in international discussions. Failure to confront those considerations in an informed, transparent and democratic fashion not only defeats procedural and substantive justice but also may produce inefficient, even ineffective, solutions. In the end such failures can undermine the legitimacy and sustainability of the new globalism.

Hence the basic argument of this chapter—that equity and distributional criteria must be at the core of a global public goods framework for international cooperation. In the course of elaborating the argument, account will also be taken of standard economic considerations in the treatment of public goods in a national context, as well as prevalent rationales for (or against) incorporating equity, justice and social cohesion as criteria in the pursuit of international cooperation. In this respect, key differences and similarities between the international and national contexts will be emphasized.

Does equity play a major role in the provision of global public goods? Arguably, some combination of international cooperation and coercion to produce such goods seems possible, even on the basis of self-interest alone. This would not seem absolutely to require social cohesion across national boundaries—including accepted notions of equity and other cultural norms. Yet this view does not recognize the pervasive presence and potential influence of equity considerations in global cooperation. This influence may be considered at three levels. First, equity and justice promote cooperative behaviour, itself needed for the provision of public goods. Although social cohesion may not be an absolute precondition in the supply of public goods, its value lies in making cooperation easier and giving global rules greater legitimacy and sustainability. This is the pervasive instrumental aspect of equity in a global public goods context.

Second, when the system is perceived to be fair and equitable, nations will participate in it willingly. Otherwise their contributions individually and collectively will tend to be insufficient to make the system work well, or at all. With public goods, both supply and demand are fundamentally influenced by equity in the finance and distribution of those goods and access to them. At a minimum, notions of horizontal equity (the equal treatment of equals) and vertical equity (a progressive distribution of burdens) in financing are often invoked. In addition, when resources are limited and not all public goods can be supplied, equity issues may arise in the choice of goods to be supplied because not everyone desires or needs the same goods equally. Thus equity concerns permeate the definition of public goods, bargaining for the provision of public goods and the question of access, even in a global context.

Third, global equity is itself a public good that, without cooperation or coercion (that is, in a decentralized setting), may be undersupplied. The undersupply may be because, for example, there is no private market through which nations or individuals may meet their need to give.

The first section of this chapter sets the stage by outlining the continuing role of inequality among nations in shaping the world. The second section considers the potential instrumental value of social cohesion in public goods supply (equity for public goods). After that the chapter considers how distributional factors affect the demand and supply of public goods. Then it pursues the proposition (originally from Thurow 1971) that the distribution of income is itself a public good. The final section offers conclusions.

The rest of the chapter illustrates the value of equity for the production of public goods, in the distribution of public goods, and as a public good itself.

A WORLD IN NEED OF EQUITY

Strong claims for international convergence notwithstanding, international inequality is a powerful force. Arguably, it is the bulwark of international order (though, as the next section shows, there are important qualifications to this proposition). Two aspects of this order stand out. First, even when global action is coordinated (or orchestrated), vastly unequal national, military, economic and organizational capacities continue to be a powerful influence. Second, inherited inequalities of wealth and asymmetries in the division of labour continue to structure the world's markets, and hence market outcomes.

Today's world is one of great cultural diversity and of huge disparities in the economic status of nations. In this fragmented and unequal world not all nations or groups within nations are symmetrically and equally integrated with global markets. If everyone had free and competitive access to markets and was playing on a level field, then markets could be expected to produce equalizing forces. But playing fields are far from level, and access is hardly free and competitive. These locally determined circumstances generate powerful economic forces that make for, and sustain, unequalizing rather than equalizing developments both within and among nations.

To be sure, there have been significant changes—the rapid convergence of living standards and incomes among industrial countries by the late 1960s, the general decline in US economic hegemony, and policy changes, such as the abandonment of fixed exchange rates, the relaxation of capital controls and the rise of export competitiveness to virtual parity with domestic welfare as the object of macroeconomic policy. Similarly, convergence in economic regimes has been accelerated by the end of the Cold War and the collapse of the Soviet Union. These events also partly revived US hegemony and had a major impact on rule-making.[2] For example, the demand is growing for level playing fields in areas as diverse as trade in services and foreign investment—and even in labour standards and child labour legislation.[3]

How big a change is this? That can be judged only in relation to the demand for a "new international economic order", which seemed to be the rallying cry of all but the OECD nations until just 10 years ago. Witness the Uruguay Round of GATT negotiations, which abandoned the principle of special treatment for developing countries. This was an extraordinary shift from the principle of differentiated rules to that of one rule for all. Optimists might claim this to be the only equitable principle, equality before the law applied to nations. Pessimists might see it as abandoning the elementary principles of horizontal and vertical equity. The difference reflects opposite views of how real-world markets function.

New divisions in social classes and economic interests are also appearing, both within nations and across them, in direct response to globalization—cleavages between those making it in the globalized economy and those caught in its backwash.[4] While many developing countries seem to be slipping in the economic hierarchy, individual gainers and losers abound. For both rich and poor countries globalization appears to be reducing the space available for the pursuit of autonomous policies. Even accountability to voters seems to be diminishing, as politicians of every hue must increasingly placate global markets and ensure competitiveness.

There is also unequal capacity to participate in a meaningful way in international negotiations. Governments remain the key actors in negotiations, although nongovernmental bodies and multinational companies have emerged as powerful pressure groups. Yet many poor countries lack the technical and financial wherewithal to identify their interests, much less pursue them with vigour. In this sense new international rules of the game are being written without the involvement of many of the players and teams.[5] The following issues exemplify the kind of distributional implications involved in the current global agenda:

- *Environmental policy.* While developing countries point their fingers at the profligate per capita use of natural resources by industrial countries, industrial countries readily condemn the continuing rapid population growth in developing countries.[6]
- *International trade.* Even while institutions for free trade have been strengthened, no effort has been made to ensure that poor countries do not suffer the worst effects from price declines and price instability for their exports. These ills arise, at least in part, from the uncoordinated growth of exports from poor countries and from the protectionism of rich countries.[7]
- *Finance.* Debt forgiveness is not high on the agenda of many countries—including those (such as Germany) whose postwar prosperity

was at least partly built on debt forgiveness. Financial system externalities can be grossly inequitable both internationally and domestically, as the recent Asian crisis shows. Failure to control market volatility has a much harsher impact on developing than industrial countries primarily because shocks expose the inadequacy of safety nets and any weakness in political systems.

- *Global transactions and national economies.* Some global public goods (enforcement of free trade, for example) may be viewed as eroding national public goods or creating negative externalities. Thus free trade may increase wage inequalities within a country and erode social consensus on a broad front or, even more specifically, it may alter national norms on what are otherwise considered inalienable rights— labour standards, for instance. Yet global rule-making and implementing institutions are generally fundamental to world order and examples of global public goods that must be centrally supplied.

EQUITY FOR PUBLIC GOODS

The inability of markets to supply public goods is a classic case of market failure. Provision of public goods, whether national or global, is the result of cooperation or coercion, not market competition. Cooperation of all agents is not a necessary precondition because, in principle, a subset of agents may acquire a private monopoly in the provision of the public good, or monopoly rights may be exercised by a dominant state. Moreover, whether of the few or the many, a cooperative agreement has to be enforced, and this may require coercion. Even when it is the result of cooperation, efforts to supply public goods may produce conflict (actual or latent) over the sharing of costs or over the scale of the public good. Hence the following question: is order, rather than equity, the true precondition for joint provision of public goods? "Yes" is the answer given by three schools of Western thought: Hobbesianism, liberalism and hegemonic stability theory.

The Hobbesian view

According to Thomas Hobbes, the war of all against all will arise with or without pre-existing inequalities among agents. But inequalities may greatly exacerbate conflict in the supply of public goods. It should come as no surprise, then, that a dominant tradition among political thinkers focuses intensely, if not exclusively, on international inequality as the fundamental determinant of world order. For order (whether produced by a formal world government or otherwise) is a necessary condition for the production of other public goods. If order is the mother of all national public goods, it cannot be otherwise at the international level.

The global economy reflects prevailing social, political and economic rules or arrangements. These are the result not of chance but of "human decisions taken in the context of man-made institutions and sets of self-set rules and customs" (Strange 1988). According to the dominant tradition of political thought, international order is the result of a strict international hierarchy of coercion. Nation states are not selfish seekers of power ex hypothesis. Rather, the Hobbesian motive of "eminence" is imposed on them by their very existence and the resulting competition. Without hierarchy, there can be only anarchy.

The liberal tradition

Liberal thought, particularly liberal economics since Adam Smith, has resisted the mercantilist implication that, in a hierarchical world, national economic policy must be designed in a zero-sum framework. The liberal stance in international relations—particularly since the neoclassical revolution of the 1870s—is built from the ground up, starting with the individual rather than the nation state, and is quite consistent with its intranational stance. Distributional considerations hold no essential place in the scientific quest of conventional economics, a position that fits well with the egoistic actor model that is its foundation. Because order is not the object of inquiry, neither eminence nor any other source of initial inequality plays an essential role. Instead the nation state is taken to be somehow constructed as a social contract to promote value-creating competition (the rule of the market) and to suppress destructive competition (the law of the jungle). It is easy to see that once the rule of the market is in place, the classic liberal problem of reining in the state asserts itself and thence the liberal solution of laissez faire.[8] Although the possibility of cooperation among self-interested agents remains a difficult theoretical barrier, it is not insuperable.

The liberal viewpoint is reinforced when moving from a national to an international context. In the liberal view global order and efficiency can be secured by a market system so long as nation states do not interfere in cross-border transactions among agents except to enforce property and contractual rights. Here it appears that state minimalism is carried one step further than in the national context. Contractual freedom ensures that the world economy is not any less automatically harmonized by the market than the national economy. In addition, however, a globalized market based on laissez faire within and among nations automatically disciplines would-be predatory states (the traditional concern of liberalism) and limits the capture and control of public policy (the primary concern of the recently evolved doctrine of neoclassical political economy). In other words, while accepting that policies are endogenous, neoliberalism sees the global market as the solution for the ills of the national political economy (see Srinivasan 1985). Market globalism is the ideal antidote to state dirigisme.

Hegemonic stability theory

A more symmetric treatment of national and global order comes from Kindleberger (1970) and others. It begins with the observation that periods of high prosperity for the world economy have also been times of high international order—that is, periods when international public goods (free trade, peace and security) and a way to balance international payments were secured. This affirms the liberal economics tenet of gains from trade. But in this view international order typically rests on the free-rider problem being overcome by a hegemonic power. This says nothing, however, about the possibility that the predatory problem may be reproduced at the global level (that is, by imperialism). No doubt, the premier economic power would be the main beneficiary of its hegemony. Thus there is no resolution of the question whether the hegemon acts as a true monopolist or as a benevolent dictator, prepared to use its coffers to subsidize the needy or bribe the recalcitrant (a form of noblesse oblige).

By the yardstick of internal consistency, none of the three positions carries more weight than the other two. Moreover, none posits any primordial ties of connection, solidarity, equity or social cohesion among individuals or national groupings. And while the liberal theory may be sanguine about the possibility of cooperation among self-seekers or agnostic as to the origin of national or global order, the Hobbesian and hegemonic theories rely on hierarchy and coercion to produce order from anarchy. The liberal paradigm affirms the values of democracy and equality, which the Hobbesian and hegemonic paradigms reject as unrealistic.

But the liberal position also ignores the role that inequality (or equality) may play in the construction of a political order. Equity and justice are neither necessary prerequisites nor necessary consequences of the order produced. In short, it would seem quite possible to construct a theory of public goods without any room for equity. In such a world equity is neither a public good nor necessary for the provision of "proper" public goods.

Does it follow that equity and justice play no role in the world order? Certainly, equity and justice figure prominently in international discussions and negotiations on the identification, supply and distribution of public goods. But this may be an illusion. Perhaps considerations of equity derive from self-interest. Talk of justice often disguises the underlying realities of more or less organized bargaining power. In other words, self-interest is the real object, the language of justice the bargaining currency. If equity considerations prevail, it is because they may be instrumental in ensuring feasible and reasonably efficient arrangements for the supply of public goods.

The mainstream model of self-interested and rational players, however, is bound to run into difficulties. Strictly speaking, self-interest implies that equity has neither instrumental value nor value in itself. Moreover, in a closed model of self-interest, such as the one provided by neoclassical political economy, all public policy will be captured by self-seeking groups. In such a view of individual agents, groups and states, normative exhortations have no place and policy seems to enter a determinist cul de sac. Even innovations must be confined to changes in technologies, resources or knowledge.

Self-interest also yields intertwined paradoxes in the construction of social values and democracy—that is, the process by which social choices are made. Ordinarily, democracy is understood to be the realization of the public interest through participation. But the Arrow paradox shows that the public interest is not meaningfully or consistently defined by the democratic aggregation of individual preferences. On the other hand, democracy (voting) is itself a paradox akin to the prisoner's dilemma: it is a public good that can only be realized if individual citizens do not yield to the rational temptation of riding free by not voting. Yet people still vote, some even on the basis of the public interest. And these paradoxes have not stopped theorists from taking normative positions on both procedural and substantive justice. The apparent contradiction between positive and normative positions is reconciled by distinguishing between mere self-interest and enlightened self-interest.

Enlightened self-interest
Strict self-interest often results in a failure to provide the public good. For example, everyone could help a stranger in need. But each person has an incentive to ride free (that is, to leave it to others), and if everyone thinks that way, no one is helped. Each avoids the small cost of helping but pays the heavy price of not getting help when in need. An older but still common view is that such problems of cooperation can be addressed even by self-interested indi-

viduals (or nations) provided only that they are enlightened about where their self-interest lies.

Yet Keynes (1963 [1926], p. 312) pointed out long ago that it is a mistake to suppose that "enlightened self-interest always operates in the public interest. Nor is it true that self-interest generally is enlightened; more often individuals acting separately to promote their own ends are too ignorant or too weak to attain even these".[9] In effect, whenever the dilemma of cooperation is resolved, individuals may be seen as exercising enlightened self-interest. But this after-the-fact description tells us nothing about the before-the-fact distinction between mere self-interest and enlightened self-interest.

One meaning of enlightened self-interest emerges from the analysis of repeated games of the prisoner's dilemma type. When a game of prisoner's dilemma is repeated, players are able to forgo immediate gains in exchange for the promise of future benefits in the course of subsequent games. Provided that they care about future benefits (that they have a sufficiently low discount rate), a cooperative solution can emerge. Enlightenment is a not-too-defective telescope with which the future is viewed. But one must be wary of generalizing this solution to all public goods situations. In particular, one must worry whether this solution can make sense in providing social order—because all agents must implicitly agree beforehand to suspend the law of the jungle long enough for the orderly prisoner's dilemma game to be repeated and the cooperative solution found. Clearly, this assumes the solution rather than providing it.

Social embeddedness and legitimacy

The idea that all economies are embedded socially has been around for a long time. A classic in this respect is Karl Polanyi's *Great Transformation*. "Disembedding" the economy from its social and political moorings can never be complete and never more than temporary. Hence a society, including its provision of public goods, is not founded on self-interest alone. Reciprocity, mutual concern, fair play and justice must count among the fundamental motivations of human action and cooperation.[10] In terms coined first by Hirschman (1970), exit and voice, the standard mechanisms of resource allocation in markets and states, are insufficient. Loyalty—social commitments and norms that create and sustain social cohesion—provides the missing link. As in the realist and individualist arguments, public goods are proximately provided through cooperation and coercion; but cohesion is the basis for both.

Justice and equality are inseparable. Thus the search for global standards implicitly appeals to the notion of equality, not merely a formal one but a substantive one. For it is hard to see how even the most basic human right—the right to life—can be separated from the capacity and opportunity to obtain the means to life. No wonder the Universal Declaration of Human Rights claims pointedly that "Everyone has the right to work. . . . Everyone has the right to a standard of living adequate for the health and well-being of himself and of his family, including food, clothing, housing and medical care, necessary social services, and the right to security in the event of unemployment. . . . Everyone has the right to education" (United Nations Department of Public Information 1998, Articles 23 and 25). As Speth (1997) points out, the 1993 Vienna Declaration is a powerful statement affirming that the right to development implies that states in the international community have a duty to promote this right.

More generally, the political construction of rules, laws, institutions and public goods proceeds within a moral context. This means that even social bargaining is conditioned by moral premises. While it can be argued that the production of public goods and the distribution of their costs depend on the bargaining power of the agents involved, it would be a mistake to see it purely in those terms. Bargaining is conducted in a social or moral context that defines a criterion of legitimacy, a concept that has no meaning in a world of self-interest. While individuals and groups may exercise their powers of disruption (or threaten to do so) to achieve their ends, what ends they consider appropriate and what means legitimate are influenced and conditioned by their social embeddedness.

To a sceptic it may seem obvious that the global economy cannot be morally embedded because the world lacks a common culture or the cohesion born of national or tribal solidarity. Such an assumption is explicit in King's (1998) view of European monetary union relative to German unification:

> Do you really think it would have been politically possible [for West Germany] to have made fiscal transfers of billions of dollars to a foreign country? Suffering pain for compatriots [East Germans], albeit new ones, is one thing. Suffering to share a currency with foreigners is less inspiring. (p. 6)

True, cultural differences are usually more pronounced between countries than within countries. But nations and tribes are no more an eternal construct than is the comity of nations. King's statement freezes history not merely in his view of the German nation, but by denying a similar possibility to the idea of a truly united Europe. Conversely, nations often lack cohesion when elites control the state. Nor is international solidarity just a figment of someone's imagination. Loyalty, solidarity and social cohesion know no frontiers other than those erected by history.[11]

EQUITY IN THE SUPPLY OF—AND DEMAND FOR—PUBLIC GOODS

Whether the social bargain creating public goods is driven by self-interest or communal ties, achieving it requires that public goods or externalities be identified and costs and benefits determined, opinion and influence mobilized, public financing secured and production of the goods arranged and effectively monitored. Distributive and equity considerations may enter the process at any of these points. Insofar as public goods are centrally produced, financing requires an equitable sharing of burdens. Inequalities of resources, organization and capacities can affect the supply of public goods (including order). Distribution is an important demand-side determinant of public goods provisioning, although its influence is mediated by social bargaining that is likely to be governed by existing inequalities. And inequalities influence the information, ideas, media and language through which claims are made or rejected.

Financing public goods

Consider first the burden sharing. Not only is this unavoidable, but it is bound to create inefficiencies. In the rarefied world of welfare economics, inefficiencies are avoided through lump-sum transfers. In reality, however, real taxes and transfers are endogenously determined through real politics. In addition to the influence of blatant self-interest, horizontal and vertical equity are, in practice, invoked as the standards for sharing burdens and determining ability to pay. In this regard there is no evident asymmetry between the global and national contexts. Past practice has already entrenched ability to pay criteria in many areas—for example, contributions to the UN system or the Bretton Woods institutions or for ad hoc emergencies. Similar criteria seem likely to play a major role in future burden sharing in relation to, for example, environmental protection.

Supply of public goods

Second, inequality has a potent influence on the supply of public goods. Public goods (or bads), including social order (or disorder), are often joint products of the state, civic institutions and citizens. Acts of both omission and commission are involved. Thus an ethnic or occupational group may disrupt order to press its claims, thereby imposing costs on the rest of society. In other words, even though social order can properly be viewed as a public good, its production cannot be wholly centralized. Instead, it results from an explicit or implicit social bargain, because private groups can actively externalize costs of disorder onto others. That also applies, though in differing degrees, to other public goods or quasi-public goods. For example, medical standards are jointly produced by state regulations, professional codes and individual practices.

Social groups may be more or less organized and more or less capable of wielding individual and collective influence to shift the distribution of wealth and income—including the provision of public goods—in their favour. In doing so, they must confront other groups with the same objective. Naturally, these groups are differentiated from each other by inequality, which creates a potential for social conflict. Hence inequality can impose direct conflict-related costs and costs of stalemates or other suboptimal solutions. In short, the size of the pie is not independent of the way the pie is sliced. Norms of equity may evolve in part to limit the costs of conflict.

Granted, public goods are heavily involved in preserving existing inequalities. The effective demand for various public goods (including rules of property or market regulation) will reflect those inequalities. Yet as we have seen, overall equity, including in the provision of public goods, can be a stabilizing and efficiency-enhancing element in the social bargain.

Applications to global policy-making

Needless to say, only groups with some power will elicit redistribution as payment for social peace. In the global (as in the national) context it might be argued that the poor are powerless. For example, indebted poor countries have virtually no exit options open to them. More generally, the absence of a global state organ with even a modicum of democratic representation may be seen as a particular handicap to the global participation and influence of poor countries. Political negotiation in the present setup is fragmented across various international agencies and forums with highly uneven representation. Because the top security and financial agencies are grossly unrepresentative, weaker members of the world community are at a disadvantage in pressing their claims even in other forums. Finally, the usual give and take of a broadly integrated political process within nations is fragmented at the global level.

This makes it more difficult for nations to be informed about possible trade-offs on different issues, making coherent and flexible bargaining difficult at the international level. Thus the mechanism of voice is rather weak in the global context.

But it may appear that the exit option is considerably stronger since aggrieved groups can simply choose to stay out of particular proposals and thus weaken international cooperation. In a national context such recalcitrance would be speedily met with coercive state sanctions. How far this difference extends depends on the coherence and effectiveness with which international organizations can regulate national action.

Demand for public goods

The third main channel of influence of inequality is through the demand for public goods. International inequality implies that nations are at different stages of development, which affects both their needs for global public goods and their capacity to help supply them. Willingness to pay for public goods seems likely to be sharply differentiated (in economic parlance, the Engel elasticities of the demand for public goods may well be different from unity). There may be differences between industrial and developing countries with respect to the need for global public goods such as protection of intellectual property rights, protection of the global environment, regulation of multinational corporations or capital mobility, worker safety and other labour standards, and so on.

Apart from the varying income elasticities, the other primary reason for differences in demand for global public goods has to do with the cost and availability of "private" (that is, national) alternatives. For example, developing countries are far more vulnerable to financial shocks because they lack the internal shock absorbers of rich countries. The "technology" of self-provisioning is not available uniformly across nations. Yet another reason for demand-side variations has to do with the complementarity between global and national actions. Effective access to public goods may be a function of domestic resource expenditures and actions. Thus a country cannot avail itself of international codes against corruption or criminal activity if it lacks the means to implement them at home. On the contrary, it may become a crime haven.

Globalization increases the demand for international rules. Yet it also makes it more difficult to agree on rules. Growing competition for global markets is producing heightened international conflict over standards in such areas as labour relations and the workplace, the relations between transnational corporations and nations, and environmental impacts. Tensions have emerged between globalized capital and national interests. Concern is mounting about fraud in global securities markets, security of banks, unruliness of exchange markets, and lack of standards in telecommunications, safety, health and environment. Some of these are clearly beyond the control of individual nation states. In some cases attempts at control can only damage whatever benefits states may derive from the operation of the relevant enterprises or resource flows. Regarding transnational enterprises, even assignment of profits to subsidiaries or other parts of their international networks is resolved internally and so must reflect the powers and interests of managers—an arbitrary element that has significant implications for taxation and other policies (Vernon 1993). Competition for foreign capital in the form of lower tax rates and other fiscal concessions must follow, with particularly adverse effects in developing countries.

To summarize, there are many similarities, rather than differences, in the distribution of public goods at the global and national levels. But the absence of reasonably representative formal organs of state power at the global level is the most important difference. The state is not just the preeminent instrument of coercion in society, it also has the potential to be a powerful instrument of equity, justice and efficiency. When it is broadly representative, the state can reconcile conflicting demands, especially by allowing redistributive bargains. At present, a combination of representative and hegemonic institutions helps capture some of the benefits of true cooperation. But the full range of benefits is not realized.

EQUITY AND JUSTICE AS PUBLIC GOODS

This chapter argues that norms, which produce social cohesion and define moral motives, can be instrumental in achieving and sustaining cooperation without which public goods would be undersupplied. It also argues that norms of fairness and justice provide focal points around which social conflict can be mitigated and efficiency-enhancing social bargains made. These enabling and lubricating functions of equity stabilize and legitimize the political order. But social justice may have a third important connection with the provision of public goods—social equity and justice are themselves public goods.

As noted, moral motives and historical contingencies have an important role to play in the construction of order and public goods; at the very least, the self-interest basis of public goods provision is substantively problematic. But this argument also has an important normative counterpart. Just as equity and justice may be among a society's important building blocks, a society may find itself in the paradoxical position of not providing as much equity as its citizens desire. In other words, while equity may help provide for other public goods, equity itself may be neglected as a public good. According to Thurow (1971), who was the first to make this point, when people derive utility from giving gifts, from the incomes of other persons and from income distribution itself, achieving economic efficiency may entail substantial income redistributions. That is, achieving equity is itself an aspect of achieving efficiency.

When people care about income distribution, it emerges as a pure public good. This is because everyone in society faces the same income distribution, which implies that their "consumption" of this good is both nonexclusionary and nonrival. As with other public goods, there is the likelihood of under-provisioning in the absence of adequate institutions for ensuring cooperation. As Mary Wollstonecraft (1792, cited in UNDP 1994) noted, "it is justice, not charity, that is wanting in the world". The paradox of injustice amid charity arises essentially as an assurance game or as a prisoner's dilemma. Suppose each of us cares for the poor or unfortunate but have no sensible instruments with which we can express our sympathy. For example, the ability to identify the needy or unfortunate might be beyond the reach of individuals. Such information and administration problems might be easily and efficiently solved through collective means. Converting sympathy and fellow-feeling into genuine opportunity and real freedom for all—from economic want, political oppression and cultural denial—is a matter of collective action and social arrangements. While an arm's-length market economy thrives on isolated individualism, equity may suffer due to the paradox of isolation.

All these arguments give a circular picture of the place of equity in social organization. On the one hand, equity can be a powerful instrument of social cooperation. On the other, equity may be neglected for want of social cooperation. This has two crucial implications. First, observable data cannot be relied on to accurately gauge the true strength of the demand for equity and justice at any given time and place. A low level of social cohesion may account for weak cooperation and, hence, low provisioning of public goods. But then, low social cohesion itself can be accounted for by low public provisioning for equity.[12] Second, over time there may be positive feedback involving equity and social cohesion on the one side, and cooperation and public goods provision on the other. It is in this light that Parfit's (1978) urging to take equity seriously and cultivate it can be understood:

> *Few political solutions [to public goods provision] can be introduced by a single person...But a [political] solution is a public good, benefiting each whether or not he does his share in bringing it about. In most large groups, it will not be better for each if he does his share...The problem is greater when there is no government...The problem is greatest when its solution is opposed by some ruling group...The moral solutions are, then, often best;* and they are often the only attainable solutions. *We therefore need the moral motives. How could these be introduced? Fortunately, that is not our problem. They exist. That is how we solve many Prisoner's Dilemmas. Our need is to make these motives stronger, and more widely spread.*
>
> (pp. 38–39, emphasis added)

Self-interest will not suffice. Equity is to be taken seriously. Equity must be cultivated to better reap the favourable dynamic effects on cooperation. But also recognized must be the self-referential element in the whole argument—not merely describing the social phenomenon but actively intervening in it.

CONCLUSION

The transition to a globally integrated market has exposed two kinds of deficiency in institutional arrangements for managing markets. On the one hand, globalizing markets have eroded the autonomy and blunted the policy instruments that nation states wield. On the other hand, international institutions and rules to meet the emerging challenges have remained inadequate. On both counts, there is increased vulnerability to unpredictable market forces. Moreover, at both the national and international levels, there is a perception that new rules of the game are being fashioned on uneven playing fields, and that the ideals of equity and justice seem fairly remote from the concerns of national and international technocrats and policy-makers. Thus concerns about economic vulnerability are likely to be joined by questions about political legitimacy and effective democracy.

In a sense these are still early days for global integration. Much of the world's population and economy remain marginalized. Indeed, whether global integration can succeed in including the marginalized within and across nations is still an open question. On the other hand, it is reasonable to suppose that the dynamic parts of developing and transition economies will see rapid economic and export growth. Such an export push, particularly when coming from countries such as Brazil, China and India, will likely produce sharp dislocations in OECD countries in terms of wage and overall inequalities.

These propositions are scarcely disputable. Thus the implication is self-evident: not only does the world need a big push towards greater cooperation for establishing adequate rules and institutions for the emerging global economy, but the creation of these global public goods must pay special attention to the criteria of equity, legitimacy and democracy. World-wide stability, security, democracy and peace cannot be founded on a system of rules that leaves too much of value for real people and communities to the whims of the market. In particular, equity, legitimacy and democracy are not only important means to effect cooperation, but valuable ends. The time seems too far away when nations will be fully integrated, factor prices equalized and the national unit essentially forgotten, so that attention can be paid to world-wide individual inequality. But the time is also gone when inequality could be treated as an exclusively national affair.

NOTES

1. See Rao (1998b) for an analysis of income divergence in 1960–79 and 1980–95.

2. For a general analysis of the role of politics in structuring global markets, see Cox (1994) and Underhill (1994).

3. But multinational companies have successfully resisted attempts to incorporate labour standards in the North American Free Trade Agreement (NAFTA) or social clauses in GATT (Collingsworth, Goold and Harvey 1994). NAFTA and GATT focused on protecting property rights of the business community, and in thousands of pages of rules did not mention the basic rights of workers.

4. The novelty of such divisions should not be exaggerated. After all, similar differences arose under colonialism. Nevertheless, the differences have arisen so rapidly and pervasively (in both industrial and developing countries) as to constitute a new and powerful force of national disintegration.

5. This unevenness is the basis of Susan Strange's (1988) concept of "structural power"—that is, the power to shape the rules of the game itself.

6. See Agarwal and Narain (1991) for a critique of the marginal-use criterion based on equity considerations.

7. For an analysis of the recent terms of trade history of developing countries, see Avramovic (1992). For the implications of liberalization, see Bleaney (1993).

8. Put differently, liberal thought and prescription are concerned primarily with the prevention of the monopoly or predatory solution to the public goods problem, not with how alternative solutions emerge.

9. It is not clear what Keynes had in mind by way of a solution, other than perhaps belief in the progress of knowledge to overcome ignorance and of a corresponding technocracy to overcome weakness.

10. Even if human motives are diverse, it does not follow that they are necessarily invariant across time and place. For a discussion of possible approaches, see Rao (1998a).

11. Even from a descriptive point of view of the world, nations influence each other in economic-behavioural terms. As Gerschenkron (1962) argued, altered expectations produced by international interdependence are a driving force of the modern history of capitalism.

12. This is not the only problem that arises when we seek to assess the relative importance of equity in different times and places. Self-interest is often cloaked by the language of rights and social justice, and we cannot easily tell the true influence of power from that of norms.

REFERENCES

Agarwal, Anil, and S. Narain. 1991. *Global Warming in an Unequal World.* New Delhi: Center for Science and Environment.

Avramovic, Dragoslav. 1992. *Developing Countries in the International Economic System: Their Problems and Prospects in the Markets for Finance, Commodities, Manufactures and Services.* Human Development Report Occasional Paper 3. New York: United Nations Development Programme.

Bleaney, Michael. 1993. "Liberalization and the Terms of Trade of Developing Countries: A Cause for Concern?" *World Economy* 16: 452–66.

Collingsworth, Terry, J. William Goold and Pharis J. Harvey. 1994. "Time for a Global New Deal." *Foreign Affairs* 73: 8–14.

Cox, Robert W. 1994. "Global Restructuring: Making Sense of the Changing International Political Economy." In Richard Stubbs and Geoffrey R.D. Underhill, eds., *Political Economy and the Changing Global Order.* New York: St. Martin's Press.

Gerschenkron, Alexander. 1962. *Economic Backwardness in Historical Perspective.* Cambridge, MA: Harvard University Press.

Hirschman, Albert. 1970. *Exit, Voice and Loyalty.* Cambridge, MA: Harvard University Press.

Keynes, John Maynard. 1963[1926]. "The End of Laissez Faire." In *Essays in Persuasion.* New York: W.W. Norton.

Kindleberger, Charles. 1970. *Money and Power: The Economics of International Politics and the Politics of International Economics.* New York: Basic Books.

King, Edmund. 1998. Letter to the Editor. *The Economist,* 16 May: 6.

Parfit, Derek. 1978. "Prudence, Morality, and the Prisoner's Dilemma." *Proceedings of the British Academy 65.* Oxford: Oxford University Press.

Polanyi, Karl. 1944. *The Great Transformation.* New York: Farrar and Rinehart.

Rao, J. Mohan. 1998a. "Culture and Economic Development." In *World Culture Report: Creativity and Markets.* Paris: United Nations Educational, Scientific, and Cultural Organization.

————. 1998b. "Development in the Time of Globalization." United Nations Development Programme, New York.

Srinivasan, T.N. 1985. "Neoclassical Political Economy, the State and Economic Development." *Asian Development Review* 3: 38–58.

Speth, James Gustave. 1997. "Freedom from Poverty: A Fundamental Human Right." Open seminar to the Swedish Development Forum, Stockholm.

Strange, Susan. 1988. *States and Markets: An Introduction to International Political Economy.* New York: Basil Blackwell.

Thurow, Lester. 1971. "The Income Distribution As a Public Good." *Quarterly Journal of Economics* 85: 327–36.

Underhill, Geoffrey R.D. 1994. "Introduction: Conceptualizing the Changing Global Order." In Richard Stubbs and Geoffrey R. D. Underhill, eds., *Political Economy and the Changing Global Order.* New York: St. Martin's Press.

United Nations Department of Public Information. 1998. *Universal Declaration of Human Rights.* New York: United Nations Department of Public Information.

UNDP (United Nations Development Programme). 1994. *Human Development Report 1994.* New York: Oxford University Press.

Vernon, Raymond. 1993. "Sovereignty at Bay: Twenty Years Later." In Lorraine Eden and Evan H. Potter, eds., *Multinationals in the Global Political Economy.* New York: St. Martin's Press.

Wollstonecraft, Mary. 1792. *A Vindication of the Rights of Woman.* London: J. Johnson.

DISTRIBUTIVE JUSTICE AS AN INTERNATIONAL PUBLIC GOOD

A Historical Perspective

ETHAN B. KAPSTEIN

As the Allies began to liberate Western Europe from the Nazis in the summer of 1944, a group of international financial bureaucrats from the victorious powers met in Bretton Woods, New Hampshire, to shape the postwar economic order. While their grand design of peace and stability would never be fully realized in a battle-scarred world that would soon enter a Cold War, they nonetheless gave the global economy its basic shape and vision. Simply put, that economy would combine the utilitarian, wealth-producing benefits of free trade with the social benefits of the welfare state. The postwar leaders who devised this system hoped to reconcile national demands for social justice with global peace and prosperity. In that sense social justice was highly valued as an international public good.

Distributive policies had the character of an international public good, and as such, ways had to be found to ensure that these policies would not be underprovided. This was a central task facing the international organizations of the United Nations family (including the World Bank and the International Monetary Fund). These organizations would advance the dual approach to distributive justice by ensuring that the international division of labour developed alongside the national welfare state.

This model served workers in industrial countries reasonably well for the first few decades after the war, although it is questionable how well it has done by workers in developing countries. Today the foundations of that structure are beginning to show their age.

The commitment to social justice that was embedded in the initial institutions has weakened, raising several questions. How well did the postwar leaders do in giving the global economy a social dimension? How stable is the structure they built? And what are the possible modifications or alternatives to ensure distributive justice in the global economy?

LEARNING FROM HISTORY: SOCIAL JUSTICE AS AN INTERNATIONAL PUBLIC GOOD

At a meeting off the coast of Newfoundland in August 1941, months before Japan's attack on Pearl Harbor, US President Franklin Roosevelt and British Prime Minister Winston Churchill laid the cornerstones of their wartime collaboration and postwar cooperation. They pledged that at the war's end they would seek to secure "for all countries and peoples improved labour standards, economic advancement, and social security". They also vowed to provide "freedom from fear or want" (*Atlantic Charter* 1941).

Their Atlantic Charter was inspired by the failure of the Treaty of Versailles and the League of Nations to achieve a lasting peace, and by the collapse of the world economy during the Great Depression, with its disastrous political effects (Wilson 1991). Indeed, lessons of the past hung heavily over postwar planners. They wanted to rebuild a global economy but recognized that international economic issues could not be treated in isolation from domestic social change. Social disruption, they believed, was the Achilles' heel of the globalization of the 19th century. Faced with domestic turmoil in the face of rapid industrialization and modernization, states chafed under the gold standard, lacking the economic policy wherewithal to respond with social safety nets. Radical politics fed the longings of the disenfranchised for a voice in policy-making. The upshot—as taught in such influential works as Peter Drucker's *The End of Economic Man* (1939) and Karl Polanyi's *The Great Transformation* (1944)—was inevitably fascism and war.

At the same time, far from promoting prosperity and peace, the international economy had become a battleground by the late 19th century. Britain's policy of "free trade", built on its industrial and financial power and the Empire, showed little evidence that gains from trade were widely distributed. Germany had rejected free trade by the 1870s, and the United States had never adopted it. The First World War had failed to reconcile the economic tensions among the great powers, though the great boom of the 1920s eased them. The Great Depression, however, launched a new spiral of conflict. By the 1930s the world economy had broken down, and rival blocs formed around the great powers. Again, the inevitable result was war.

Thus postwar planners had to find a way to ease tensions both within and between states. The 19th century models of balance of power politics and laissez-faire economics had failed, and the wartime years saw the protagonists working feverishly on new designs for the future. They became open to a host of ideas about how the world ought to be.

Thus the search for social justice and policies that became associated with it was more than a realist's response to the failures of early 20th century governments to maintain peace and prosperity. It was also an ideological rejection of much of 19th century economic and political thought. Postwar leaders rejected the Darwinian strand of laissez-faire economics (exemplified by Herbert Spencer) that seemed to justify misery as inevitable, even healthy, in market economies; that view was inconsistent with domestic stability and world peace. Spencer's view that "justice requires that individuals shall severally take the consequences of their conduct. . . . The superior shall have the good of his superiority; and the inferior the evil of his inferiority" (cited in Hawkins 1997, p. 86) seemed a certain recipe for political disruption. Rather than focus solely on the individual as being responsible for his or her fate, societies as a whole would bear some responsibility for the economic well-being of citizens.

This alternative vision of political economy was famously represented by John Maynard Keynes, but it had deep historical roots on both sides of the Atlantic. Indeed, as industrial capitalism took its toll on working people in the 19th century, various religious, political and labour groups articulated alternative political-economic models that rejected laissez-faire and the status quo of widespread poverty and suffering. Socialists, chartists and utopians were among those who wrote, spoke and agitated on behalf of working people, and they called, among other things, for factory laws, suffrage, minimum wages, unemployment insurance, pensions and collectives. In short, they sought to de-commodify labour and remove its fate from the alleged laws of nature and the market. While only the socialist movement would have a widespread political impact in advanced industrial countries, other groups promoted ideas that would eventually reach a broad audience and, when the moment was ripe (during the Great Depression, for example, and at the end of the Second World War), help shape the policy debate.

In the United States the 19th century saw the rise of the social gospel movement and its new political economy. The movement's members regarded the philosophy of laissez-faire economics as selfish, inhumane, unchristian, unethical, immoral and barbaric. It was, in the words of one preacher, "the science of extortion, the gentle art of grinding the faces of the poor". Asked another: "Is it not evident that our economic system is diametrically opposed to Christian teaching?" (cited in Fine 1964, p. 175).

Historian Sidney Fine says that "the main problem treated by the exponents of the social gospel was the relations between capital and labor". The movement's leaders accused classical economics of treating labour as "but a commodity to be bought in the cheapest market and sold in the dearest". They argued that working people were entitled to more than that, and that "the employer must remember in dealing with his employees that he is not dealing with merchandise from which he is to make a profit but with the children of God, whose welfare must be his concern" (cited in Fine 1964, p. 175).

Thus Social Christians pleaded for an end to the wage system and called on employers to pay a just wage—one that would enable workers to maintain a decent standard of living. They felt that ethics rather than profit must be at the centre of economic life. As the influential preacher Washington Gladden said, "economics without ethics is a mutilated science—the play of Hamlet without Hamlet" (cited in Fine 1964, p. 177).

The ideas of the social gospel movement and the new political economy gradually began to permeate the US polity. As the squalid conditions of working people and their families became a regular topic of newspaper reporting and photography, and as labour unions grew stronger, public policy slowly responded to workers' demands. Within these groups and their ideas were the roots of US progressivism and the New Deal.

As Roosevelt explained in his penultimate message to Congress, in January 1944, "we have come to a clear realization of the fact that true individual freedom cannot exist without economic security and independence. . . . We have accepted, so to speak, a second Bill of Rights under which a new basis of security and prosperity can be established for all—regardless of station, race or creed". He then listed various economic rights, including the right to a job and to "earn enough to provide adequate food and clothing and recreation" (cited in Israel 1966, p. 2881).

Among economists, Keynes was central to this social movement, which focused on the role of the state in bringing about opportunity and security for all citizens. "The outstanding faults of the economic society in which we live", he wrote in *The General Theory*, "are its failure to provide for full employment and its arbitrary and inequitable distribution of wealth and incomes" (Keynes 1964, p. 372ff). Keynes directed his work to redressing these faults, and his theories formed the hard core of the postwar welfare state.

The idea of a social minimum for all had wide ideological acceptance at the war's end. Even Friedrich Hayek asserted that there were two forms of economic security—a minimum level of sustenance for all, and security of a given standard of living—and the first was, to him, beyond debate. "There is no reason why", he wrote, "in a society which has reached the general level of wealth which ours has attained the first kind of security should not be guaranteed to all". He went on to claim that "there can be no doubt that some minimum of food, shelter, and clothing, sufficient to preserve health and the capacity to work, can be assured to everybody" (Hayek 1944, p. 133). Nowhere did he argue that the market acting on its own would provide this social minimum.

In tracing the renewed spread of religious and moral ideas onto the international political arena after the Second World War, David Lumsdaine (Lumsdaine 1993) observes that they filled an intellectual vacuum. The tragedies of the early 20th century only seemed to confirm the grim prophecies preached by members of the social gospel and associated movements. The failure of laissez-faire economics to recognize the dignity of man, the weakness of the state to care for the needy and the seeming inability of governments to work cooperatively towards common objectives all pointed to the need for a new international order, built with multilateral organizations at its core. These organizations would suppress ancient rivalries, meet emergency economic requirements and promote a just social order in the interest of peace and prosperity.

The United Nations was the centrepiece of these organizations. In the spirit of the Treaty of Versailles, the United Nations Charter related economic welfare to political stability. Thus article 55 states that "with a view to the creation of conditions of stability and well-being which are necessary for peaceful and friendly relations among nations . . . the United Nations shall promote: a. Higher standards of living, full employment, and conditions of economic and social progress and development" (United Nations 1945). And Article 23 of the Universal Declaration of Human Rights proclaims that "everyone has the right to work, to free choice of employment, to just and favorable conditions of work and to protection against unemployment". Slavery and servitude were also banned: "Everyone has the right to life, liberty, and the security of person" (United Nations 1948).

International labour was enthusiastic about the emerging postwar structure. The World Federation of Trade Unions (WFTU), founded in 1945, believed that it would play a crucial role in international organizations and help lead the nations of the world to a peaceful plane. In the words of the great British trade unionist Walter Citrine, "The UN could not be a success without the support of the people . . . if the WFTU pulled out, the UN would collapse" (cited in Silverman 1990, p. 15). Union leaders now envisioned a corporatist world in which "all elements of society" would be represented in economic and political debates (cited in Silverman 1990, p. 17).

As this brief review suggests, postwar leaders resolved to build a global economy that would be far more institutionalized and constitutionalized than it was in the 19th century, and they would do so in the interests of political stability, economic growth and social justice—all inextricably linked in the minds of postwar leaders. As originally conceived, international political stability would be provided by the United Nations, backed by the enforcement powers of the Security Council. But as the postwar structure evolved, hopes for the United Nations dissipated and the United States and Soviet Union assumed nearly hegemonic power within their spheres of influence.

Economic growth would be promoted by free multilateralism and the international division of labour, facilitated by organizations such as the General Agreement on Tariffs and Trade, the World Bank and the International Monetary Fund. Social justice, in turn, would be the province of the welfare state, through full employment and social policies that promised working people jobs at a living wage and universal education for their children, coupled with a social safety net to buffer the hard times. Indeed, the new international economic system, unlike the 19th century system, was to be fashioned so as to leave the state considerable autonomy in the social realm.

The overarching notion was that free trade promoted peace through interdependence, while it promoted prosperity through efficiencies that came with the division of labour. Thus free trade was optimal from the cosmopolitan perspective.

Yet free trade also had distributive consequences, both within and between states. Within states trade produced both winners and losers, and welfare policies would enable losers to adjust to structural change, while income redistribution schemes, when needed, would be introduced in the interests of social cohesion. Trade also produced winners and losers between states. Thus foreign aid, investment, technology flows and preferential tariffs would be granted to developing countries to help them become full partners in the global economy. In this way the demands of both efficiency and equity would be served.

THE TWO PILLARS OF THE POSTWAR GRAND DESIGN

The two pillars of the grand design for the postwar era were built at the national level, in the form of the welfare state, and at the international level, in the form of free trade.

At the national level: the welfare state

In the postwar order the welfare state loomed large as the provider of social justice. At the end of the war no other political-economic objective became more crucial to advanced industrial countries—with the partial and crucial exception of the United States—than full employment. As Harvard University's most influential Keynesian, Alvin Hansen wrote in a survey of postwar planning that it was clear that "throughout the world, leaders in government and in industry are more and more committed to a program of sustained full employment" (Hansen 1945, p. 19). During the war and its immediate aftermath the governments of most Allied countries pledged to adopt full employment policies, something they had never done. These policies were viewed as necessary for domestic political purposes but they also had the character of an international public good, since most postwar leaders believed that unemployment was the main cause of political instability.

The pace-setter was Britain, operating under the sway of Keynesian ideas and bruised by the experience of a history that had hammered home one point: European peace depended, above all, on the economic security of its working people. In 1944 Churchill's Tory government issued its White Paper on Employment, which began with the now-famous words: "The Government accept as one of their primary aims and responsibilities the maintenance of a high and stable level of employment after the war" (Her Majesty's Government 1944, p. 1). With those words the welfare state took its place as the cornerstone of postwar economic planning.

What was meant by full employment? One of its most influential advocates, William Beveridge (author of the 1942 British White Paper on Social Insurance and the influential 1944 tract *Full Employment in a Free Society*), defined it in the following terms: "Full employment . . . means having always more vacant jobs than unemployed men, not slightly fewer jobs. It means that the jobs are at fair wages, of such a kind, and so located that the unemployed men can reasonably be expected to take them; it means, by consequence, that the normal lag between losing one job and finding another will be very short" (Beveridge 1944, p. 18).

And how would full employment be achieved? Here Beveridge and others who shared his sympathies accepted the Keynesian analysis that governments—the state—must engage in active demand-side management through manipulation of monetary and fiscal policy. As Beveridge wrote of the state's new responsibilities, "no one else has the requisite powers . . . to ensure adequate total outlay and by consequence to protect its citizens against mass unemployment". It was the state's task no less than its function "to defend citizens against attack from abroad and against robbery and violence at home" (Beveridge 1944, p. 29). In other words, full employment was now a fundamental task of every government.

Britain was not alone in making this commitment to its workers and veterans. At the end of the war Australia, Canada, France, New Zealand and many other countries adopted similar policies, and Australia would prove to be a particularly vociferous spokesperson for that policy goal in international forums. But one country ultimately rejected the concept of full employment as the beacon of its postwar economic policy—the United States.

In fact, the position of the United States was complicated and ambiguous. During the war the Roosevelt administration had given several nods in the direction of full employment in both domestic and international policies. But there was stiff opposition from Congressional conservatives, who saw it as a first step on the dreaded road to economic planning that must inevitably result in socialism. These same conservatives had already fought the New Deal, saving the United States from the worst excesses of the Roosevelt administration. In the usual American way a compromise on employment would be reached, which nonetheless, in tune with the times, placed a growing burden on the government for economic management.

The failure of full employment legislation was somewhat surprising in that New Deal officials, like their British counterparts, had made it their central economic goal for the postwar period. As historian Alan Brinkley writes, "full employment was necessary . . . not just to spare individuals the pain of joblessness, but also—and more important—to provide the nation with the largest possible body of consumers" (Brinkley 1995, p. 229). To be sure, the quest for full employment would involve government planning to ensure "the expansion of civilian consumption" (Brinkley 1995, p. 231). And it was exactly that aspect—the government as planner—that awakened the sensibilities of conservative critics.

America's failure to declare full employment as its explicit policy objective caused its wartime allies deep concern as plans for the postwar world were debated and drafted. Countries feared that when the war was over, the United States would fall into recession, even depression, dragging the world economy down with it. As the world's biggest economy, any decisions—or nondecisions—by the United States during a slow-down would necessarily reverberate world-wide. In essence, the United States might end up providing public bads to other countries instead of public goods, as it had done during the Great Depression with the passage of the notorious Smoot-Hawley tariff. If Washington was unwilling to promise that it would adopt aggregate demand policies aimed at maintaining full employment, where did that leave smaller countries that would suffer as a result?

The battle over full employment reached its peak following President Roosevelt's 1944 State of the Union address, in which he claimed that political rights alone were "inadequate to assure us equality in the pursuit of happiness". "Economic security and independence", he said, "were fundamental to human freedom" (cited in Israel 1966, p. 2881). With these words Roosevelt indicated that he remained a committed New Dealer as he faced the postwar world.

Emboldened by the speech, a coalition of liberal groups, with intellectual support from academics such as Alvin Hansen, pressed for adoption of a Full Employment Bill. Such a bill was finally introduced in early 1945 by Senator James Murray of Montana; it stated that "all Americans able to work and seeking work have the right to a useful and remunerative job. . . . It is essential that continuing full employment be maintained in the United States". Under the bill the president would be required to prepare a national production and employment budget that would estimate "the number of jobs needed during the ensuing fiscal year or years to assure continuing full employment" (cited in Brinkley 1995, p. 261).

With the death of President Roosevelt the Full Employment Bill found its main champion in President Harry Truman. He called it a "middle way" between statism and an unregulated marketplace. But the bill's opponents saw it as the first step on the slippery slope to socialism. The bill's claim of a right to work could easily become the basis for a "vast state bureaucracy that would compel everyone to work and determine what jobs they could have" (Brinkley 1995, p. 262). The bill had no chance of passage in an increasingly conservative Congress. Ultimately, the United States would pass instead the 1946 Employment Act, which called on the government "to use all practicable means . . . to foster and promote . . . conditions under which there will be afforded useful employment for those able, willing and seeking to work, and to promote maximum employment, production, and purchasing power" (cited in Brinkley 1995, p. 262). Despite the more cautious language, however, the United States had joined its wartime allies in recognizing that the state must play a more active role in assuring the economic well-being of its citizens.

At the international level: free trade

The welfare state provided only one piece of the postwar economic puzzle. The other would be provided by free multilateralism. Free trade would serve as the engine of global peace and prosperity. It would promote peace through interdependence, as had been argued since the times of Adam Smith and Immanuel Kant. It would promote prosperity through the division of labour, which liberated factors of production and enabled them to focus on their most effective use. (The concept of "embedded liberalism" is described, for example, in Ruggie 1983.)

But modern trade theory has also been the subject of significant debate since its introduction by David Ricardo. From the perspective of political economy, free trade inevitably causes harm to well-organized special interests—producers and workers who seek protection against import competition. From the point of view of national security, free trade implies dependence on foreign producers for strategic military requirements. And at the international level, free trade raises the question of relative gains or the distribution of gains from trade. As Richard Gardner wrote in *Sterling-Dollar Diplomacy*, "although free trade can be shown to maximize real income for the world as a whole, it may not do so for each of its constituent parts. Multilateralism can be shown to benefit everybody only if some mechanism exists for distributing the gains both within and between nations" (Gardner 1996, p. 14).

The wisdom of adopting free trade as a first principle for the world economy's constitution was a major issue that divided the United States from its allies in the postwar years. For Britain and other industrial countries it was not obvious that openness to trade and investment flows was consistent with domestic economic objectives. Americans held an evangelical belief that this was the case, but the British and others were less certain; this is somewhat ironic given Britain's long experience with free trade, which the United States did not share. To the British trade openness had much to recommend it in terms of global efficiency, but advancing national socio-economic goals was not necessarily among its attributes. In any event, the British believed that without achieving the most important domestic policy objective (full employment), international economic cooperation simply could not be sustained.

Developing countries were also suspicious of free trade ideology. In the early postwar years the literature on the economic development of less developed countries was dominated by critics of free trade. Most prominently, Raul Prebisch and Gunnar Myrdal, both of the United Nations, "rejected the classical theory of international trade as inapplicable to less developed countries and argued that, far from acting as an engine of economic growth, international trade had been responsible for hindering development". Instead Prebisch and his colleague Hans Singer claimed that developing countries would inevitably face declining terms of trade for primary products, while Myrdal argued that international trade produced unequal returns to factors of production. "The chief policy inference" from these analyses "was an urgent need for rapid industrialisation based on import substitution" (Arndt 1987, p. 73). It was further argued that industrial countries should aid and abet rapid industrialization through preferential tariffs, foreign aid and technology transfers. In essence, Singer and Myrdal were calling for a policy of international redistribution.

Neoclassical trade economists disputed these assertions. Thus Gerald Meier argued that the statistical foundations for the Prebisch-Singer-Myrdal line of attack were extremely weak, while the analytical reasoning was unconvincing. "It is difficult," he argued, "to entertain seriously the argument that the slow pace of development has been due to a worsening in the terms of trade". In seeking the root cause of slow development, Meier pointed to domestic rather than international factors. Indeed, when domestic impediments to the efficient use of factors were removed, he was certain that trade would prove an "engine of growth" (Meier 1963, p. 175ff).

Both sides to this debate found common ground in calling for development assistance. The World Bank had been created at Bretton Woods "to assist in the ... development of territories of members by facilitating the investment of capital for productive purposes". While the Bank's objective was "to promote private foreign investment" (IBRD, p. 1, Article 1) through the use of country risk guarantees, it recognized the need to use its own capital to finance infrastructure projects and, over time, to reduce poverty. Bilateral foreign aid programs also developed throughout the postwar era. US foreign economic assistance was promoted by Harry Truman's "Point Four" programme of 1949, in which he called on the country to "embark on a bold new program for making the benefits of our scientific advances and industrial progress available for the improvement and growth of underdeveloped areas" (cited in Espy 1950, p. 3). From an economic perspective (these programs also had a Cold War security rationale) the objective was to make it possible for developing countries to profit from the international division of labour.

Despite misgivings about free trade and the perceived necessity of aid to hasten economic development, many policy-makers acted on the assumption that the adoption of liberal economic policies by all states would lead to convergence in economic performance. In this view natural resource endowments did not determine the evolution of living standards over the long term. Economic success was ultimately a function of the interaction between human capital and free markets, coupled with good governance and sound policies (for example, openness, macroeconomic stability and fiscal discipline). Because capital-short countries enjoyed higher returns to scarce capital, capital would flow there. Because countries with abundant unskilled labour would focus on the production and export of goods making intensive use of that factor, returns to unskilled labour would increase. Over the long term convergence in productivity (itself a function of increased market integration) would lead to convergence in income.

GLOBAL DISTRIBUTIVE JUSTICE: WHERE ARE WE NOW?

Did the grand design have the intended effects? Has the postwar global economy widened or narrowed the gap between winners and losers, both within and between countries? The answer to that question will surely depend on whether or not one has been its beneficiary. Yet that alone points to the enduring gap between winners and losers in global economic relations.

By the late 1950s there was little evidence that any convergence was happening. Instead, developing countries were failing to catch up. In 1961 the United Nations Commission for Europe produced a report, *Europe and the Trade Needs of the Less Developed Countries*, which projected "third world" exports and imports over the next 20 years. It predicted that official aid flows and exports of primary products would meet only two-thirds of developing country import needs, leaving a gap of at least $15 billion. The report concluded that this amount would have to be filled by exports of manufactures, and it proposed a generalized system of preferences for developing country exporters. This scheme would be adopted by the European Economic Community in 1971 and by the United States five years later. In essence, the Generalized System of Preferences amounted to an income transfer from industrial to developing countries; thus it was redistributive. Yet, to the extent that this transfer was used to finance additional imports from industrial countries, the Generalized System of Preferences brought gains to these countries and their export sectors.

The postwar record does not justify early optimism about trade as an engine of growth. In the 1990s the International Monetary Fund (IMF) reported that "most developing countries have failed to raise their per capita incomes toward those of the industrial countries". Asia was the only region "to have registered significant progress" (although with the financial collapse in 1997–98, even those gains are now in doubt). But the IMF did not hold the structure of the international system responsible. Instead it concluded that the extent to which countries' per capita incomes converged in the long term was "determined by their own policies and resources" (IMF 1997, p. 77ff).

Overall, the evidence suggests that convergence in incomes did occur in the immediate postwar years—particularly within and among industrial countries. More recently, however, incomes have again begun to deviate, especially between industrial and developing countries. Today, in the words of World Bank economist Lant Pritchett, there is "divergence, big time" (Pritchett 1995).

In the past 30 years the poorest 20% of the world's people saw their share of global income fall from 2.3% to 1.4%. Meanwhile, the share of the richest quintile grew from 70% to 85%. As a result the ratio of the share of the richest to that of the poorest grew from 30:1 to 61:1 (UNDP 1996).

The reasons for this change are still a matter of debate. It may be that there was some incompatibility between the two pillars of the postwar strategy: a globalized economy was bound to create an increasingly challenging environment for conducting distributive policies at the national level. Indeed, increasing globalization, particularly capital mobility, raised questions worldwide about whether state autonomy over economic policy was eroding. The IMF asserted that "globalization may be expected increasingly to constrain governments' choice of tax structures and tax rates, especially in smaller countries" (IMF 1997, p. 70). Moreover, by increasing policy interdependence, globalization poses formidable collective action problems.

In Richard Cooper's classic account, "increasing interdependence complicates the successful pursuit of national economic objectives in three ways. First, it increases the number and magnitude of the disturbances to which each country's balance of payments is subjected, and this in turn diverts policy attention and instruments of policy to the restoration of external balance.

Second, it slows down the process by which national authorities, each acting on its own, are able to reach domestic objectives. Third, the response to greater integration can involve the community of nations in counteracting motions which leave all countries worse off than they need be" (Cooper 1968, p. 148).

As Cooper suggests, the assumption underlying interdependence theory is that the consequences of domestic economic policy and performance cannot be easily contained within national borders. Certainly, a theory similar to this one was held by the postwar planners as they rebuilt the world economy. Ironically, that is why they built international institutions—to contain domestic crises and allow a measure of policy-making autonomy at the national level.

Yet there are growing questions, even among mainstream economists, about whether the political-economic framework, as it has evolved, is successful in reconciling national autonomy in social policy with increasing integration. In a widely cited book, Dani Rodrik argues that capital mobility has reached a point where it is undermining the ability of the state "to generate the public resources needed to finance social insurance schemes" (Rodrik 1997, p. 73). Cooper, of course, pointed towards this danger some 30 years earlier. The architects of Bretton Woods never imagined such a high level of capital integration and Keynes, for one, hoped that financial markets would remain national.

The dilemmas of interdependence were already present, if muted, at the birth of the postwar order—together with the concern for policy-making autonomy. One great fear of postwar planners was that, as in the 1930s, a depression in one country (particularly the United States) would quickly spread abroad, engulfing the world. This risk meant that each country had to make good on its commitment to pursue something like full employment policies—that is, to provide public goods. Thus, in the event of a recession, countries would have to stimulate aggregate demand in Keynesian fashion. That requirement created the classic problem for international enforcement: by what right could states pressure another government for failing to provide the public good of stimulating its domestic economy? Where countries relied on IMF or World Bank assistance, loan conditionality could be used to press for reforms, and bilateral assistance programs might play a similar role. Even in these cases, however, it was unclear exactly how much influence outsiders would have on domestic economic decision-making.

That general issue remains today. To what extent can (or should) one group of countries seek to influence the economic policies of another? After all, it would seem that there is no universal formula for good economic policy. As John Stuart Mill taught, the distribution of wealth and resources "is a matter of human institution only. The things once there, mankind, individually or collectively, can do with them as they like. They can place them at the disposal of whomsoever they please, on whatever terms. The distribution of wealth, therefore, depends on the laws and customs of society" (Mill 1970, p. 350).

POLICIES FOR A JUST WORLD: THE WAY AHEAD

What policies can reconcile efficiency and fairness in the global economy? In a world of increasing trade flows and capital mobility, national policies aimed at achieving distributive justice will, at least to some degree, be constrained by external economic forces. This naturally leads us to a consideration of the role that international institutions can play in shaping economic outcomes that are consistent with our social concerns. Organizations like the World Bank and the IMF, for example, loom large in the economies of several of their member countries, and their effect on the international economic system goes way beyond their capital base. Through the policy advice they articulate and the signals they send about national economic performance, their influence ripples broadly throughout the world's capital markets, and in turn throughout labour markets as well.

It is ironic that these same organizations often make the claim that responsibility for social welfare rests squarely with the nation state and its capacity for good governance. Thus the IMF states that a country's long-term per capita income levels are determined by its own policies and resources. Yet at the same time the IMF tells us that "globalization may be expected to increasingly constrain governments' choices of tax structures and tax rates" (IMF 1997, pp. 70). If governments lack the power to shape tax policy, it is hard to see what sort of powers they have over economic performance. These contradictions do not inspire much confidence in the IMF's ability to provide sound advice.

To claim that states alone are responsible for their fate in a global economy is disingenuous on several counts. First, it begs the question that if good national policy were enough to ensure good economic outcomes, why were international organizations ever needed, and why are they still needed today? Second, to the extent that globalization undermines national policy-making capacity—as the IMF and the World Bank admit it does to some degree—

alternative methods must be found for making good governance a reality. Third, because the benefits of globalization are not evenly distributed among nations, international mechanisms are needed to ensure that all players gain sufficiently to keep them in the game. Finally, because globalization requires international policy coordination and information sharing with respect to the activities of both state and nonstate actors, efforts at international governance are needed by definition.

These points are not made in defence of an argument that what we need is world government. International institutions, including the most advanced among them (such as the European Union), are fundamentally creatures of their member states. But member states can use these organizations in any number of ways. In some cases state elites exploit international organizations as a way of escaping domestic politics, claiming that the government's hands are tied on this or that issue. The IMF serves this purpose for developing country leaders who seek to make economic policy reforms in the face of domestic opposition. For this reason critics of international institutions frequently point to a democratic deficit between them and the citizens of their member countries.

In this section I provide policy recommendations that give voice to those who have the least influence in shaping the global economy. My basic argument is that international organizations should play a more positive and active role in ensuring that fairness no less than efficiency considerations shape economic policies (for a similar argument in the European context, see Scharpf 1996). Such policies are in the long-run interests of all those who seek to advance globalization and believe in its contributions to world peace and prosperity. By helping the world's disadvantaged realize their talents and live in dignity, we promote productivity, stability and justice. In essence, then, social justice is an international public good.

A new Bretton Woods

The institutional foundations of the world economy are beginning to show their age. The world economy has learned to live with flexible exchange rates, but whether that has improved or impaired its health is a matter of debate. While correlation is not causation, the shift from fixed to flexible rates that occurred in the 1970s also saw the beginning of much slower industrial country investment and growth and higher unemployment and inequality—conditions that remain with us to the present day (Davidson 1998, p. 819). Tremendous capital mobility (threatened and real), to an extent never anticipated by the postwar architects, is emerging. Increasing trade flows are raising the spectre of zero-sum international labour competition. With these developments unskilled workers are becoming fearful of their futures, as well they might in the midst of unemployment, poverty, inequality and insecurity.

If the great powers wish to restore confidence in the global economy, they would do well to convene another Bretton Woods conference. The purpose of the meeting would be to address such questions as, How is globalization doing in terms of the least advantaged, and what can be done to improve their lot? And is the current financial system consistent with growth and stability, or must a new order be contemplated? This latter issue would seem especially pertinent as Western Europe introduces its new common currency.

Migration policy is among the most significant issues that any new Bretton Woods would have to address. Even the World Bank admits that, while myriad international agreements have been struck aimed at promoting capital mobility and free trade, "international migration of people in search of work is the laggard in this story" (World Bank 1997, p. 134). People are no more free to migrate than they were a generation ago, and much less so in many cases than their grandparents. The role of labour mobility and migration in the global economy is an issue of the first order, and it must be addressed in the interests of assuring working people the greatest possible opportunity set. There is little reason for an individual to invest in education, training and self-improvement if no jobs are available.

A second issue that a new Bretton Woods should seek agreement on is how to give workers a voice in international institutions. Postwar planners initially contemplated the creation of an international trade organization that would concern itself with commercial and employment policies. With the failure to establish such an entity, trade and labour concerns went on separate paths, but workers have unfortunately stumbled onto a dead end. Mechanisms for ensuring labour representation at the IMF, the World Bank and other such institutions would be one way to promote a more equitable global order, and a possible model might be found at the Organisation for Economic Co-operation and Development (OECD), which has done perhaps the most of any multilateral organization to solicit labour input.

A third issue for this meeting's agenda should be consideration of an international social minimum. This does not mean that we can expect agreement on a global minimum wage or anything of the sort. Instead it means that each country should define what constitutes a decent standard of living for all citizens, including access to education and health care, working wages and entitlement to social safety nets. An international organization, perhaps the World Bank or UNDP, should be charged with producing an annual social policy report, just as the IMF produces studies of macroeconomic performance in its member countries. Gaps in providing the social minimum should be highlighted as targets for national economic reform efforts and international assistance.

Finally, a new Bretton Woods would have to reconsider capital liberalization, and how mobile capital can best be harnessed in the interests of efficiency and fairness. Proposals like a "Tobin tax" on financial transactions must be considered (see below) and a world tax organization contemplated. Because of their centrality to the current debate, these ideas are discussed in greater detail below.

In thinking about the possibility of a future Bretton Woods, we must be realistic and recognize that the last one occurred only after a generation of world conflict and depression that enveloped the major powers. Today war and economic deprivation have largely been removed from the global economy's core countries; instead they fester in the developing world periphery, where they tragically draw less attention. What this means is that a sense of crisis is lacking in world capitals, making it unlikely that bold initiatives will be forthcoming anytime soon. In the interests of political reality, then, I offer in the following paragraphs some recommendations that fall between a full-scale Bretton Woods conference on the one hand and the sort of marginal fixes now popular on the other.

Link trade liberalization with labour standards and worker compensation programmes

Trade and labour policy have mainly travelled on separate tracks since the end of the Second World War. The General Agreement on Tariffs and Trade, and its successor World Trade Organization, focused on reducing trade barriers, while the International Labour Organization was responsible for advancing core labour standards. That dualistic approach has run its course, and it is time to join the issues.

The great fear that policy-makers and economists usually express on this matter is that tying trade agreements to core labour standards (freedom of association and collective bargaining, nondiscrimination in hiring and prohibition of child and forced labour) will lead world trade down the slippery slope of trade protection. The failure of countries to achieve international labour standards, it is claimed, could be used as an excuse to halt trade with them, or it could raise their labour costs to the point where they are no longer competitive.

But these arguments are absurd for several reasons. First, core international labour standards, promulgated by the International Labour Organization, already exist. Second, international trade is not a right but a privilege, and countries that seek to barter and truck with the community of nations should accept common standards. Third, the possibility of free trade and membership in the World Trade Organization should be held out as a carrot to states that violate core labour standards; if it is not, what incentives can be offered? (for an excellent overview of the labour standards debate, see OECD 1996.)

The international system has often responded with sanctions to countries exhibiting various kinds of "bad behaviour". India and Pakistan were slapped with US trade sanctions after their nuclear tests in 1998. Iraq has been the target of a United Nations embargo since 1990, and Iran has had only limited access to world markets since its Islamic revolution. Other countries that remain ostracized include Cuba, the Democratic People's Republic of Korea (also known as North Korea), and Libya. In short, sanctions are widely used, but for some reason have not been applied to states that violate core labour standards.

The world trading system could put great pressure on countries that fail to adopt these standards. Countries like China would find their economic opportunities severely limited. But here is a case where the trading system seems to be basically operated by and for large multinational corporations, which consistently reject tying trade agreements to labour rights.

It is worth noting that the vigorous adoption of core labour standards by the international community would indicate the acceptance of new, associated responsibilities. A country that is willing to abolish child labour, for example, may need foreign assistance to expand its school system. That is the sort of collective response that a world community bent on a just form of globalization should be willing and able to make.

As countries pursue free trade agreements, they must also be sensitive to how trade will affect working people, and put in place programs that assist displaced workers. Indeed, compensation should be another core labour standard. Traditionally, such compensation programmes have been solely a national responsibility. But with a growing number of developing countries and transition economies entering the trading system, international assistance on this issue could be of tremendous value and could help maintain political support for continued globalization. Again, if the benefits of trade are so great, why not be generous to those who find themselves on the losing end of this policy change?

Establish greater supervision over the activities of multinational enterprises and banks

Trade and finance cross borders with relative ease, workers less so and governments not at all. That tension is at the heart of all efforts aimed at greater international supervision of multinational activities. While international policy coordination over multinational business has traditionally been an information-sharing exercise, it is increasingly becoming a supervisory activity that seeks to prevent international competition from sparking a destructive race to the bottom in which countries end up relieving themselves of all tax and regulatory authority. With the recent financial crisis in East Asia, calls for tighter controls over cross-border capital flows have grown in intensity and volume.

Already there is significant activity in this area. Banks and investment firms face the common capital adequacy standards set by the Basle Committee of Bank Supervisors and the International Organization of Securities Commissions, and the European Union is responsible for regional regulation over such areas as competition and antitrust policy (Kapstein 1994). The OECD and the United Nations Conference on Trade and Development (UNCTAD) have also established codes of conduct for multinational enterprises regarding consumer protection and the like. Three issues of rising international salience, however, concern worker rights, capital controls and international taxation.

Worker rights and labour standards have already been discussed. Here I will simply add that, in the absence of international agreements linking trade and labour standards, an alternative or complementary path would be to establish minimum codes of conduct on how multinationals treat their workers. These codes would include the core labour standards as well as provisions for a living wage and compensation in the event of worker displacement. Efforts have already been made along these lines by minority shareholders of some major corporations—almost always over the objections of boards of directors—but they have generally failed to win the needed votes at shareholder meetings. Governments, nongovernmental organizations (NGOs) and international organizations like UNCTAD could thus play a useful role in shaping these standards, publicizing them and monitoring enterprise performance. Indeed, in the absence of positive government action in this direction at the national level, code setting could provide an interesting case of how NGOs and international organizations might form transnational alliances for the benefit of labour interests.

With respect to portfolio investment or "hot money" flows, it appears that governments and international organizations are again giving serious thought to capital controls of some type, either through tax policy or quantitative restrictions on inflows. With respect to tax policy, perhaps the most prominent idea is that of economist James Tobin for a tax on all cross-border financial transactions, in the hope of decreasing such flows and making them more manageable. Other approaches include taxes graduated according to the length of time investors keep their money in a given country. Such graduated policies, which have been adopted with great success in Chile, seek to penalize short-term portfolio investors and reward long-term direct investment.

The national orientation of these measures, however, may mean that they will lose their effectiveness over time. States will be tempted to use different policies on capital controls, including taxation, to the advantage of their domestic economies and financial institutions. Because large banks and investment firms tend to have a significant voice in domestic policy-making, given their prominent role in economic activity and money creation, officials are sensitive to their competitive concerns and will develop regulatory policies that are in their interests (Kapstein 1994). In addition, monetary and financial policies tend to be obscure to many voters, and labour often has failed to understand how such policies will affect workers. Thus decisions on capital and labour markets become dissociated, often to labour's disadvantage.

These comments suggest that there are several problems associated with capital mobility that must be dealt with at the international level. One of the most prominent problems in light of the East Asia crisis concerns the destabilizing effects of capital mobility on national economies. Thus there is increasing discussion of international financial cooperation aimed at, for example, supervising or even limiting cross-border loans made by banks and other financial institutions (see Wyplosz in this volume). Because labour has been so hard-hit by these destabilizing effects, its representatives should have a seat at the policy table when decisions in this area are made. Unfortunately, the centre of action in this debate has been the IMF, which has hardly shown itself to be sensitive to workers' concerns or open to their participation in its deliberations.

A second and potentially more significant issue in terms of reshaping the international political economy concerns international taxation of mobile capital. As we know from the public finance literature, the effective tax rate on mobile capital is zero. As we know from the data, tax rates on mobile capital are falling. While tax competition has been used by states in the interests of attracting direct investment, it has had many negative effects as well, including declining revenues for government coffers. The fact that tax competition can easily lead to a race to the bottom among states—in which mobile capital gets away with paying virtually nothing to any government—suggests a possible role for international coordination in this area.

Probably the leading advocate of a world tax organization has been IMF official Vito Tanzi. He argues that such an organization could have the following functions:

- Identifying the main trends in tax policy among its member countries.
- Compiling cross-country tax statistics.
- Preparing an annual world tax development report.
- Providing technical assistance in tax policy and tax administration.
- Developing basic principles and norms for tax policy.
- Creating an international forum for discussion and debate on tax matters.
- Arbitrating frictions among countries with respect to their tax policies.
- Surveying tax developments and making policy recommendations (Tanzi 1996).

Again, any such organization must give voice to labour concerns in its decision-making.

Overall, the comments here point to the growing gap between multinational enterprises and national economic institutions, including labour markets. Closing that gap will be a major item on the international agenda as we look towards the future. In shaping policies that aim to achieve that objective, the concerns of workers must be taken firmly into account. The current structure of international institutions does not give sufficient voice to labour, and reforms in this direction are needed if new policy ideas are to succeed.

Ensure that conditional lending by the World Bank and the IMF is sensitive to equity considerations

If we know one thing about the aftermath of an economic crisis, it is that the rich usually get richer and the poor get poorer. In the interests of macroeconomic stability, states end up cutting programs that benefit workers and the disadvantaged. Further, interventions by international organizations such as the IMF and the World Bank seem to do nothing to alter that outcome. To the contrary, the IMF only suggests targets for budget spending, and generally avoids making recommendations on which items should be cut.

The economic and moral arguments made in this volume indicate that the World Bank and the IMF should give greater thought to the distributional consequences of their policy-based lending. They should place more emphasis on the needs of the disadvantaged and ensure that education and compensation programs receive adequate funding. In this regard the World Bank's announcement that it would seek to create 75 million jobs in East Asia through its post-crisis project loans is welcome news (Solomon 1998, p. A17). The Bank has also said that it will give significant attention to poverty alleviation in its lending programs to this troubled region.

Similarly, the IMF could take a more aggressive line in advocating for the poor and disadvantaged in its macroeconomic stabilization programs. In so doing it should consult with labour, NGOs and other interest groups to assure that it is hearing a representative set of political voices. The IMF's assumption that a balanced budget is politically neutral is fundamentally flawed, and it must pay greater attention to those who win and those who lose from its recommendations.

Invest in health care and public health

Normally when one thinks of international cooperation in health care, it is in terms of humanitarian assistance. That is all to the good, but in fact good health care is a major contributor to economic performance as well. In the words of World Health Organization director Gro Brundtland, new research "is making it increasingly clear that ill health leads to poverty in individuals, populations, and nations" (cited in Altman 1998, p. B10). By recognizing its contributions to worker productivity and well-being, we can see that health care should be given significant attention by those who promote globalization.

That does not seem to be the case, however. Around the world, millions of people die each year from infectious diseases. More than 1 billion people do not have access to clean water, and nearly 2 billion lack proper sanitation facilities. At least 840 million people go hungry every day. As a result nearly one-third of the population in the developing world is not expected to reach age 40 (UNDP 1997, p. 5). It is hard to develop an economy when large numbers of workers are dying in what should be the prime of life.

These facts seem far removed from industrial countries, which have made great strides in controlling disease and famine, protecting the environment and providing basic human needs. But even here the gap between the haves and the have-nots is dramatic. In the United States nearly 50 million people are without health insurance. Some urban slums are once again seeing the reemergence of diseases like tuberculosis, stumping health care experts who thought these enemies had been defeated. Indeed many US slums have health care statistics that are more like those of developing countries than industrial countries.

In most post-communist transition economies the health care situation verges on the catastrophic. Soviet-style planning left a legacy of environmental devastation that has poisoned two generations and will take at least that long to clean up. Alcoholism, drug use and poor nutrition further contribute to premature deaths. And poorly paid doctors face a terrible shortage of medical equipment and drugs in outdated hospitals and clinics.

These public health issues should be treated as economic problems for several reasons. First, an unsanitary and polluted environment is a barrier to one's life chances. People living in these conditions are more likely to become ill and thus less capable of realizing their talents. The result is a waste of human resources. The more work or education days that are lost to illness, the more society suffers. Work and education are important investments, and if people are incapacitated, that investment goes to waste.

Second, people and companies are more likely to invest in countries where health risks are manageable. Where the threat of illness, epidemic or famine looms large, investors will understandably wish to go elsewhere. Not surprisingly, a strong correlation exists between health and wealth.

Creating a healthy environment, then, would seem to make good economic sense. Thus it ought to receive greater consideration in debates over economic reform, alongside macroeconomic stabilization measures, trade policy and the like. Again, making this case could be the job for new transnational coalitions that join labour unions with health care experts and environmentalists. Health care has traditionally been the exclusive province of medical experts and their various national and international institutions. But the encouraging words of World Health Organization director Gro Brundtland cited above (and it should be noted that Brundtland was both a medical director and former prime minister of Norway) suggests that the time may be ripe for new initiatives in this area.

Make foreign aid more effective

Foreign aid is needed to compensate for the polarizing effects of globalization and to combat the trend towards increased inequality in the world economy. Yet foreign aid accounts for a small fraction of both industrial country and recipient country budgets. According to the OECD, in 1996 official foreign aid totalled $59.9 billion, down almost 6% from 1995. Moreover, this aid accounted for no more than 0.25% of the combined gross domestic product of OECD members—"the lowest ratio recorded over the nearly thirty years since the United Nations established a goal of 0.70 percent" (World Bank 1997, p. 140). While private investment flows to developing countries have increased in recent years, these are not a direct substitute for foreign aid.

How effective is aid to developing countries? What do governments do with the money? In principle they can do two things: invest in projects ranging from education to health care to infrastructure, or transfer it to citizens through tax policy or cash payments—but to whom?

In a recent study Peter Boone (1996) found that, rather than transfer money to the poor, some governments gave it to their wealthy supporters. Aid often went to consumption by elites rather than to social investment. Of course, aid (especially bilateral aid) is sometimes given precisely to exercise leverage over a country's elites, rather than to help the neediest. So Boone's results are hardly surprising.

Conversely, the World Bank (1998) found that aid did the most good where governments were committed to effective policies. This finding suggests that donors should do more to ensure that their funds are being used to help the neediest in target countries. Rather than abandon aid altogether, ways should be sought to improve its impact on the poor. This means working closely with recipient countries in ensuring that funds go to education, health care and the development of a social safety net. In short, aid should be used to support the broad objective of transforming the least advantaged into the most productive. In that way aid would also be in the long-run interests of increased economic integration.

Conclusion

Distributive justice was central to the design of the postwar order. If a half-century of war, depression and revolution had taught statesmen and postwar planners anything, it was that economic distress inevitably leads to conflict. As Franklin Roosevelt said in his 1944 message to Congress, "people who are hungry and out of a job are the stuff of which dictatorships are made" (cited in Israel 1966, p. 2881). Moreover, instability and war bred in one country had shattered international peace. The Bolshevik revolution in 1917 and interwar Germany demonstrated that economic deprivation anywhere could lead to political conflict everywhere. Thus it can be argued that social justice is a global public good—and once provided by one country, it benefits everyone everywhere through its contribution to world peace and stability.

But that conclusion implies a danger that the public good might be underprovided, either because states lack the fiscal wherewithal to make good on social policy promises or because national ideologies fuel domestic turmoil, with the potential for international spillover.

In the minds of postwar planners, social justice was to be provided with a two-fold strategy. At the international level, liberalization of trade and finance was to spread economic opportunity around the globe. The polarizing effects of free markets, however, were to be corrected at the national level, largely through the welfare state.

As globalization accelerated in the 1970s, it became more difficult for states to pursue full employment and redistributive policies in a world of free trade and free capital movements. It is interesting to note, however, that free capital movements were not part of the original postwar vision. Indeed, the original purpose of the IMF was to manage fixed parities and coordinate the interventions necessary to sustain the Bretton Woods regime. If distributive justice (a prerequisite for peace) is to be actively pursued, this dilemma will need to be squarely addressed and a new international policy agenda formulated. Perhaps the agenda sketched above can inform current discussions on a new architecture for the world economy.

References

Altman, Lawrence K. 1998. "Next WHO Chief Will Brave Politics in Name of Science." *New York Times*. 3 February.

Arndt, Heinz Wolfgang. 1987. *Economic Development: The History of an Idea.* Chicago, IL: University of Chicago Press.

Atlantic Charter. 1941. http://www.msstate.edu/archives/history/USA/WWII/charter.txt

Beveridge, William Henry. 1944. *Full Employment in a Free Society: A Report.* London: George Allen.

Boone, Peter. 1996. "Politics and the Effectiveness of Foreign Aid." *European Economic Review* 40: 290–329.

Brinkley, Alan. 1995. *The End of Reform.* New York: Vintage.

Cooper, Richard. 1968. *The Economics of Interdependence.* New York: McGraw-Hill.

Davidson, Paul. 1998. "Post Keynesian Employment Analysis and the Macroeconomics of OECD Unemployment." *The Economic Journal* 108(May): 817–31.

Drucker, Peter D. 1939. *The End of Economic Man.* New York: The John Day Co.

Espy, Willard. 1950. *Bold New Program.* New York: Harper & Brothers.

Fine, Sidney. 1964. *Laissez-Faire and the General-Welfare State.* Ann Arbor, MI: University of Michigan Press.

Gardner, Richard N. 1996. *Sterling-Dollar Diplomacy.* Oxford: Clarendon Press.

Hansen, Alvin. 1945. *America's Role in the World Economy.* New York: Norton.

Hawkins, Mike. 1997. *Social Darwinism in European and American Thought.* New York: Cambridge University Press.

Hayek, Friedrich A. 1944. *The Road to Serfdom.* Chicago, IL: University of Chicago Press.

Her Majesty's Government. 1944. *White Paper on Employment.* London: Her Majesty's Stationery Office.

IBRD (International Bank for Reconstruction and Development). *Articles of Agreement.* As amended through February 16, 1989. Washington, DC.

IMF (International Monetary Fund). 1997. *World Economic Outlook* (May). Washington, DC.

Israel, Fred, ed. 1966. *The State of the Union: Messages of the Presidents, 1790–1966.* New York: Chelsea House.

Kapstein, Ethan B. 1994. *Governing the Global Economy: International Finance and the State.* Cambridge, MA: Harvard University Press.

Keynes, John Maynard. 1964. *The General Theory of Employment, Interest and Money.* New York: Harvest.

Lumsdaine, David H. 1993. *Moral Vision in International Politics: The Foreign Aid Regime 1949–1989.* Princeton, NJ: Princeton University Press.

Meier, Gerald. 1963. *International Trade and Development.* New York: Harper & Row.

Mill, John Stuart. 1970. *Principles of Political Economy.* New York: Penguin.

OECD (Organisation for Economic Co-operation and Development). 1996. *Trade, Employment and Labor.* Paris.

Polanyi, Karl. 1944. *The Great Transformation.* New York: Farrar and Rinehart.

Pritchett, Lant. 1995. "Divergence, Big Time." *Journal of Economic Perspectives* 11:3–17.

Rodrik, Dani. 1997. *Has Globalization Gone Too Far?* Washington, DC: Institute for International Economics.

Ruggie, John Gerard. 1983. "International Regimes, Transactions and Change: Embedded Liberalism in the Postwar Economic Order." In Stephen D. Krasner, ed., *International Regimes.* Ithaca, NY and London: Cornell University Press.

Scharpf, Fritz. 1996. "Economic Integration, Democracy and the Welfare State." Cologne, Germany: Max-Planck-Institut für Gesellschaftsforschung.

Silverman, Victor I. 1990. "Stillbirth of a World Order: Union Internationalism from War to Cold War in the United States and Britain, 1939–1949." Ph.D. dissertation. University of California, Berkeley.

Solomon, Jay. 1998. "World Bank Says It Was Wrong on Indonesia." *Wall Street Journal.* 5 February.

Tanzi, Vito. 1996. "Is There a Need for a World Tax Organization?" Paper presented at the International Institute of Public Finance, 26–29 August, Tel Aviv, Israel.

United Nations. 1945. *Charter of the United Nations and Statute of the International Court of Justice.* New York.

———. 1948. *Universal Declaration of Human Rights.* New York. (Available at http:// www.un.org/Overview/rights.html)

UNDP (United Nations Development Programme). 1996. *Human Development Report 1996.* New York: Oxford University Press.

———. 1997. *Human Development Report 1997.* New York: Oxford University Press.

United Nations Commission for Europe. 1961. *Europe and the Trade Needs of the Less Developed Countries.* Geneva.

Wilson, Theodore. 1991. *The First Summit.* Lawrence, KS: University Press of Kansas.

World Bank. 1997. *World Development Report 1997: The State in a Changing World.* New York: Oxford University Press.

———. 1998. *Assessing Aid: What Works, What Doesn't, and Why.* A Policy Research Report. New York: Oxford University Press.

GLOBAL JUSTICE
Beyond International Equity

AMARTYA SEN

Global equity is sometimes identified with international equity. The two, however, are very different notions—both in terms of their constitutive contents and with respect to their policy implications. In this chapter I examine the nature of the distinction, which I believe is quite central to political philosophy as well as policy scrutiny. Its implications for the understanding of global public goods are also quite extensive. The contrast between global and international equity relates to quite deep differences in:

- The domain of *social justice:* whether relations of justice apply primarily *within* nations, with relations across borders being seen as relations *between* nations.

- The concept of a *person:* whether our identities and responsibilities are parasitic on nationality and citizenship, which must lexicographically dominate over solidarity based on other classifications such as group identities and viewpoints of class (including relations between workers or between businesspeople with particular ethics), gender (including feminist concerns beyond local borders), professional obligations (including the commitments of doctors, educators and social workers without frontiers) and political and social beliefs (with loyalties that compete with other identities).

Something quite important is involved in these distinctions, which have far-reaching implications on the nature of practical reason at the global level and the choice of actions of potential agents. Ideas of justice—and corresponding actions—that cut across borders must not be confused with international relations in general, or with demands of international equity in particular.

RAWLSIAN JUSTICE AS FAIRNESS

As in many other discussions of social justice, it is quite helpful to begin with the Rawlsian notion of "justice as fairness" (Rawls 1971, 1993). The framework of political and social analysis initiated by John Rawls's classic contributions has had a profound impact on contemporary understanding of the nature of justice. Even though, as I argue below, a serious departure from the ramifications of Rawlsian analysis will ultimately be needed, the basic idea of "justice as fairness" is an appropriate starting point.

In the Rawlsian framework, fairness for a group of people involves arriving at rules and guiding principles of social organization that pay similar attention to everyone's interests, concerns and liberties. In working out how this may be understood, the Rawlsian device of the "original position" has proved useful. In the hypothetical original position, which is an imagined state of primordial equality, individuals are seen as arriving at rules and guiding principles through a cooperative exercise in which they do not yet know exactly who they are going to be (so that they are not influenced, in selecting social rules, by their own vested interests related to their actual situations, such as their respective incomes and wealth).

Rawlsian analysis proceeds from the original position to the identification of particular principles of justice. These principles include the priority of liberty (the "first principle") giving precedence to maximal liberty for each person subject to similar liberty for all. The "second principle" deals with other matters, including equity and efficiency in the distribution of opportunities, and includes the Difference Principle, which involves the allocational criterion of "lexicographic maximin" in the "space" of holdings of primary goods (or general-purpose resources) of the different individuals, giving priority to the worst-off people in each conglomeration.

Questions can be raised about the plausibility of the specific principles of justice that Rawls derives from his general principles of fairness, and it can, in particular, be asked whether the device of the original position must point inescapably to these principles of justice (my own scepticism on this point is presented in Sen 1970 and 1990). The adequacy of Rawls's focus on primary goods, which makes his Difference Principle resource-oriented rather than freedom-oriented, can be particularly questioned.[1] With those specific debates I am not primarily concerned in this chapter (though, when the more basic groundwork regarding the idea of the original position is completed, the bearing of these differences on the application of the groundwork will have to be taken up in the analysis to follow).

THREE CONCEPTS OF GLOBAL JUSTICE

My concentration in this chapter is on the more elementary issue of the composition of the "original position" and its implications for the understanding of fairness as well as its manifest practical consequences. In particular, who are the individuals who are seen, hypothetically, as having gathered together in the original position to hammer out deals on rules and guiding principles? Are they all the people in the world—irrespective of their nationality and citizenship—who are seen as arriving at rules that are going to govern the affairs of the whole world? Or are they instead the citizens of each nation, each country separately, gathered together in their own original positions?

These two different conceptions can be identified, respectively, as "universalist" in a most comprehensive sense and "particularist" in its nation-based orientation.

- *Grand universalism.* The domain of the exercise of fairness is all people everywhere taken together, and the device of the original position is applied to a hypothetical exercise in the selection of rules and principles of justice for all, seen without distinction of nationality and other classifications.

- *National particularism.* The domain of the exercise of fairness involves each nation taken separately, to which the device of the original position is correspondingly applied, and the relations between nations are governed by a supplementary exercise involving international equity.

Even though the original position is no more than a figment of our constructive imagination, the contrast between these rival conceptions can have very far-reaching implications on the way we see global justice. The formulation of the demands of global justice as well as the identification of the agencies charged with meeting those demands are both influenced by the choice of the appropriate conception and the characterization of the domain of fairness. Even the understanding of the nature of the twin concepts driving this volume—"global public goods" and "global housekeeping"—cannot but be influenced in the choice of domain and the concept of justice. Questions such as *whose* house is to be kept in shape and *which* joint and indivisible results are to be seen as the relevant public goods invoke the underlying issues regarding the domain of reciprocal concern and the identification of appropriate agencies.

I shall presently argue that neither of these two conceptions—grand universalism and national particularism—can give us an adequate understanding of the demands of global justice, and that there is a need for a third conception with an adequate recognition of the plurality of relations involved across the globe. But let me first elaborate a little on the claims of each of these two classic conceptions.

Grand universalism has an ethical stature that is hard to match in terms of comprehensive coverage and nonsectarian openness. It rivals the universalism of classical utilitarianism and that of a generalized interpretation of the Kantian conception of reasoned ethics (see Kant 1785; Bentham 1789; Mill 1861; Sidgwick 1874; Edgeworth 1881; and Pigou 1920). It can speak in the name of the whole of humanity in a way that the separatism of national particularist conceptions would not easily allow.

And yet grand universalism is hard to adopt in working out the institutional implications of Rawlsian justice as fairness. The exercise of fairness through a device like the original position is used, in Rawlsian analysis, to yield the choice of the basic political and social structure for each society, which operates as a political unit and in which the principles of justice find their application. There are great difficulties in trying to apply this mode of reasoning to the whole of humanity without an adequately comprehensive institutional base that can implement the rules hypothetically arrived at in the original position for the entire world. It would not be, I hope, taken to be disrespectful of our host institution—the United Nations—to suggest that it is in no way able to play this role. Indeed, even the very conception of the United Nations—as its name indicates—is thoroughly dependent on drawing on the basic political and social organizations prevalent in the respective national states.

All this may forcefully suggest that we seek the tractability and coherence of the nationalist particularist conception of Rawlsian justice. That is, in fact, the direction in which Rawls himself has proceeded, considering separately the application of justice as fairness in each political society, but then supplementing this exercise through linkages between societies and nations through the use of intersocietal norms. These interactions take the form of what Rawls calls "the law of peoples" (see Rawls 1996). The "peoples"—as collectivities—in distinct political formations consider their concern for each other (and the imperatives that follow from such linkages). The principle of justice as fairness can be used to illuminate the relation between these political communities (and not just between individuals, as in the original Rawlsian conception).

It must be noted, however, that in this particularist conception the global demands of justice primarily operate through *intersocietal* relations rather than through *person-to-person* relations, which some may see as central to an adequate understanding of the demands of global justice. The nation-based characterization identifies, in fact, the domain of *international* justice, broadly defined. The imperatives that follow, despite the limits of the formulation, have far-reaching moral content, which has been analyzed with characteristic lucidity by Rawls. However, the restrictions (identified in the introduction of this paper) of an "international"—as opposed to a more directly "global"— approach apply forcefully to this approach, which limits the reach of the Rawlsian "law of peoples".

How should we take note of the role of direct relations across borders between different people whose identities include, inter alia, solidarities based on classifications other than partitioning according to nations and political units such as class, gender or political and social beliefs? How do we account for professional identities (such as being a doctor or an educator) and the imperatives they generate, without frontiers? These concerns, responsibilities and obligations may not only not be parasitic on national identities and international relations, they may also occasionally run in contrary directions to international relations. Even the identity of being a "human being"—perhaps our most basic identity—may have the effect, when fully seized, of broadening our viewpoint, and the imperatives that we may associate with our shared humanity may not be mediated by our membership in collectivities such as "nations" or "peoples". As I write this chapter sitting in Calcutta, with the Indian subcontinent still shaking with the aftershocks of nuclear explosions, the perspective of direct *interpersonal* sympathies and solidarities across borders has a cogency that can substantially transcend the national particularism of the estranged polities.

We do need, I believe, a different conception of global justice—one that is neither as unreal as the grand universalism of *one* comprehensive "original position" across the world, nor as separatist and unifocal as national particularism (supplemented by international relations). The starting point of this approach—I shall call it "plural affiliation"—can be the recognition of the fact that we all have multiple identities, and that each of these identities can yield concerns and demands that can significantly supplement, or seriously compete with, other concerns and demands arising from other identities.

With *plural affiliation* the exercise of fairness can be applied to different groups (including—but not uniquely—nations), and the respective demands related to our multiple identities can all be taken seriously (irrespective of the way any conflicting claims are ultimately resolved). The exercise of "fairness", which can be illustrated with the device of the original position, need not look for a unique application. The original position is a rich way of characterizing the discipline of reciprocity and within-group universalization, and it can be used to provide insights and inspirations for different group identities and affiliations. Nor is it entirely necessary, in order to benefit from Rawls's foundational characterization of fairness, to work out an elaborate system—as in Rawls's own theory—of detailed specification of a stage-by-stage emergence of basic structures, legislation and administration. The device of the original position can be employed in less grand, less unique and less fully structured forms without giving complete priority to one canonical formulation involving national particularism.

For example, a doctor could well ask what kind of commitments she may have in a community of doctors and patients, but the parties involved need not necessarily belong to the same nation. (It is well to remember that the Hippocratic oath was not mediated—explicitly or by implication—by any national contract.) Similarly, a feminist activist could well consider what her commitments should be to address the special deprivation of women in general—not necessarily only in her own country. The obligations that are recognized cannot, of course, each be dominant over all competing concerns, because there may well be conflicting demands arising from different identities and affiliations. The exercise of assessing the relative strength of divergent demands arising from competing affiliations is not trivial, but to deny our multiple identities and affiliations just to avoid having to face this problem is neither intellectually satisfactory nor adequate for practical policy. The alternative of subjugating all affiliations to one overarching identity—that of membership in a national polity—misses the force and far-reaching relevance of the diverse relations that operate between persons. The political conception of a person as a citizen of a nation—important as it is—cannot override all other conceptions and the behavioural consequences of other forms of group association.

INSTITUTIONS AND MULTIPLICITY OF AGENCIES

There are a great many agencies that can influence global arrangements and consequences. Some of them are clearly "national" in form. These include domestic policies of particular states as well as international relations (contracts, agreements, exchanges) between states, operating through national governments. However, other cross-border relations and actions often involve units of economic operation quite different from national states—such as firms and businesses, social groups and political organizations, nongovernmental organizations and so on—that may operate locally as well as beyond the frontiers. Transnational firms constitute a special case of this. There are also international organizations, which may have been set up directly by individual states acting together (such as the League of Nations or United Nations) or indirectly by an already constituted international organization (such as the International Labour Organization, United Nations Children's Fund, United Nations University, or World Institute for Development Economics Research). Once formed, these institutions acquire a certain measure of independence from the day-to-day control of individual national governments.

Still other institutions involve nongovernmental, nonprofit entities that operate across borders, organizing relief, providing immunization, arranging education and training, supporting local associations, fostering public discussion and engaging in a host of other activities. Actions can also come from individuals in direct relation to each other in the form of communication, argumentation and advocacy that can influence local social, political and economic actions (even when the contacts are not as high profile as, say, Bertrand Russell's writing to Nikita Kruschev on the nuclear confrontations of the Cold War). For an adequate understanding of global justice (and a fortiori for seeing the role of "global public goods", not to mention "global housekeeping"), it is extremely important to take adequate note of the multiplicity of agencies and of the rationale of their respective operations.

In operating across boundaries, cross-national institutions (and more generally, cross-national contacts) inevitably have to face issues of purpose, relevance and propriety, and these issues cannot really be dissociated from concerns of justice. In dealing with this requirement, one approach would be to repudiate the direct linkages across borders and to embed every cross-boundary relation within the limited structure of "international relations", including the "law of peoples". This can be achieved, but only at the cost, I would argue, of great impoverishment of content and reach, and certainly of massive circumlocution.

A more appropriate alternative is to pose the issue of justice—and that of fairness—in several distinct though interrelated domains involving various groups that cut across national boundaries. These groups need not be as universally grand as the collectivity of "all" the people in the world, nor as specific and constrained as national states. There are many policy issues that cannot be reasonably addressed in either of these two extremist formats.

How should a transnational conglomerate treat the local labour force, other businesses, regional customers or—for that matter—national governments or local administration? If there are issues of fairness involved, how should these issues be formulated—over what domain? If the spread of business ethics (generating rules of conduct, fostering mutual trust or keeping corruption in check) is a "global public good", then we have to ask how the cogency and merits of particular business ethics are to be evaluated. Similarly, if the solidarity of feminist groups helps to generate social change across borders (perhaps by providing support for local groups, by generating critiques of policies of governments or businesses or simply by helping to place the addressing of neglected inequalities on the agenda for public discussion), then the claim of such organizations—and indeed of such modes of thinking—may well be integrated with the class of global public goods. But we need to address the question as to how the affiliations and interactions, and their consequences, are to be normatively assessed, invoking such ideas as justice and fairness. All this calls for extensive use of the perspectives of plural affiliations and the application of the discipline of justice and fairness within these respective groups.

A CONCLUDING REMARK

In this chapter I have argued for the need to distinguish between global and international equity. The distinction has, I believe, far-reaching implications for public policy as well as for conceptual clarity. I have tried to examine some of these implications.

Individuals live and operate in a world of institutions, many of which operate across borders. Our opportunities and prospects depend crucially on what institutions exist and how they function.

Not only do institutions contribute to our freedoms, their roles can be sensibly evaluated in the light of their contributions to our freedoms. To see development as freedom provides a perspective in which institutional assessment can systematically occur (see Sen forthcoming).

Even though different commentators have chosen to focus on particular institutions (such as the market, the democratic system, the media or the public distribution system), we have to consider them all to be able to see what they can do, individually or jointly. Many of these institutions—not just the market mechanism—cut vigorously across national boundaries and do not operate through national polities. They make contributions that have strong elements of indivisibility and nonexclusiveness that are characteristic of public goods, and their claim to be seen as "global public goods" is quite strong. The literature has to take note of this important issue.

NOTE

1. The contrast in the informational perspective in the conceptual framework can have many practical implications, which I discuss in Sen (1985b). On their relevance for economic policy and related issues, see also Sen (1984, 1985a), Hawthorn (1987), Drèze and Sen (1989), Griffin and Knight (1989), UNDP (1990), Anand and Ravallion (1993) and Desai (1995).

REFERENCES

Anand, Sudhir, and Martin Ravallion. 1993. "Human Development in Poor Countries: On the Role of Private Incomes and Public Services." *Journal of Economic Perspectives* 7(1): 133–50.

Bentham, Jeremy. 1789. *An Introduction to the Principles of Morals and Legislation.* London: Payne. Republished Oxford: Clarendon Press (1907).

Desai, Meghnad. 1995. *Poverty, Famine and Economic Development.* Aldershot: Elgar.

Drèze, Jean, and Amartya K. Sen. 1989. *Hunger and Public Action.* Oxford: Clarendon Press.

Edgeworth, Francis Y. 1881. *Mathematical Psychics.* London: Kegan Paul.

Griffin, Keith, and John Knight, eds. 1989. "Human Development in the 1980s and Beyond." *Journal of Development Planning* 19 (special issue).

Hawthorn, Geoffrey, ed. 1987. *The Standard of Living.* Cambridge: Cambridge University Press.

Kant, Immanuel. 1785. *Fundamental Principles of Metaphysics of Ethics.* English translation by T.K. Abbott. Republished London: Longman (1907).

Mill, John Stuart. 1861. *Utilitarianism.* London: Longman.

Pigou, A.C. 1920. *The Economics of Welfare.* London: Macmillan.

Rawls, John. 1971. *A Theory of Justice.* Cambridge, MA: Harvard University Press.

———. 1993. *Political Liberalism.* New York: Columbia University Press.

———. 1996. *A Theory of Justice.* Oxford: Oxford University Press.

Sen, Amartya K. 1970. *Collective Choice and Social Welfare.* San Francisco, CA: Holden-Day. Republished Amsterdam: North Holland (1979).

———. 1984. *Resources, Values and Development.* Oxford: Blackwell and Cambridge, MA: Harvard University Press.

———. 1985a. *Commodities and Capabilities.* Amsterdam: North-Holland.

———. 1985b. "Well-being, Agency and Freedom: The Dewey Lectures 1984." *Journal of Philosophy* 82.

———. 1990. "Justice: Means versus Freedoms." *Philosophy and Public Affairs* 19.

———. Forthcoming. *Development As Freedom.* Based on lectures given at the World Bank as a presidential fellow under the title "Public Policy and Social Justice," fall 1996, Washington, DC.

Sidgwick, Henry. 1874. *The Method of Ethics.* London: Macmillan.

UNDP (United Nations Development Programme). 1990. *Human Development Report 1990.* New York: Oxford University Press.

MARKET
EFFICIENCY

In an efficient economy, as modelled by the theory of general equilibrium, prices reflect the balance between supply and demand, and resources (land, labour, capital and so on) go to their most productive uses. Thus the overall "pie" is bigger even with the same amount of inputs—and this could be said to be a public good outcome. Governments aim for greater market efficiency by setting basic parameters for markets (rules, property rights, licensing) and try to balance efficiency with other objectives. Increasingly, programmes to boost market efficiency have become international. These two chapters discuss these issues with particular reference to international trade and finance.

Nancy Birdsall and Robert Z. Lawrence analyse the new agenda for trade liberalization: the harmonization of policies "behind the border". Indeed, free trade can be distorted not only by barriers at the border (such as tariffs or quotas) but also by differences in the way domestic markets are regulated. For example, two countries with different safety regulations do not offer a level playing field to investors and exporters. The need to harmonize these domestic rules and policies presents challenges and opportunities to developing countries, say Birdsall and Lawrence. Against advantages such as fighting races to the bottom, one needs to weigh the risk of loss of sovereignty and legitimacy when regulatory systems are imported whole cloth. The authors conclude by recommending an increasing role for developing countries in international rule-making to harmonize standards and practices, as well as increased technical and financial assistance to facilitate this process.

Analysing international finance, Charles Wyplosz takes a slightly different starting point: he points out the market inefficiencies that prevail even in highly liberalized global markets and proposes solutions for these market failures. The global financial and economic crisis that started in South-East Asia in 1997 and spread to Russia, Eastern Europe and Latin America in 1998 and 1999 provides the background to his study on international financial stability as a global public good. Wyplosz disentangles the web of market failures at work, draws out a rationale for international policy action both to prevent and cure crises, outlines the system currently in place and offers a plan for improvement that turns much of the current practice on its head. For example, he advocates policy competition rather than the policy monopoly enjoyed by the International Monetary Fund, slowing rather than accelerating international financial liberalization and ex ante rather than ex post conditionality.

While both chapters consider efficient markets essential to prosperity, they point out the difficulties in ensuring market efficiency on a global scale. Birdsall and Lawrence analyse the challenges from a political economy standpoint. Wyplosz concentrates on the difficulties that arise from an economic standpoint and advocates interventions to restore market efficiency in this context.

DEEP INTEGRATION
AND TRADE AGREEMENTS
Good for Developing Countries?

NANCY BIRDSALL AND ROBERT Z. LAWRENCE

The transactions of international trade are voluntary and generate benefits for the participants. When nation states agree formally with other nation states to rules governing trade, the benefits to them and their citizens are likely to exceed the costs, though within nations some citizens will gain more than others and some may be absolutely worse off (at least in the absence of side payments by the gainers to the losers). Over the past 20 years trade agreements among nations have gone beyond tariff and other border barrier reductions to agreement on domestic rules of the game—intellectual property rights, product standards, internal competition policy, government procurement and, to a lesser degree, labour and environmental standards. These more complex agreements bring deeper integration among participating nations—integration not only in the production of goods and services but also in standards and other domestic policies. As a result they imply many more trade-offs and raise new issues concerning the sharing of the gains from trade—which nations benefit and within nations, which groups.

These "deep integration" agreements also have implications at the global level. The integration of the global economy in trade and finance creates pressure for common rules of the game across the world. On the one hand, such global coordination can have benefits for all. On the other hand, pressure to agree too quickly may lead to inappropriate rules that do not adequately reflect individual societies' preferences and needs. A rush to adopt such rules could create a backlash, especially if agreement in participating countries does not reflect an open and democratic process that provides political legitimacy or is not supported by an internal capacity to administer new rules even-handedly. In that case attempts to achieve common rules and standards may end up undermining global coordination.

In this chapter we explore the costs and benefits for developing countries of the "deep integration" that characterizes international trade relations today—what we will also refer to as "modern trade", often associated with membership in a "modern trade club"—for example, multilaterally in the World Trade Organization (WTO) or regionally in the North American Free Trade Agreement (NAFTA), Asia-Pacific Economic Cooperation (APEC) or the South American Common Market (Mercosur). We put particular emphasis on developing countries because the income gap between them and highly industrialized nations suggests that the pressures for harmonization that modern trade and modern trade clubs bring raise particularly interesting questions for them and thus ultimately for global welfare. In the first section we discuss how the trend towards deep integration has ended the special treatment of developing countries in postwar trade agreements. Then we discuss how the modern multilateral character of trade agreements, by increasing the overall efficiency of world trading markets, can generate benefits at the global level, some of which are particularly relevant for developing countries. In the third section we consider additional benefits that are specific to developing countries as a result of their participation. After that we explore the potential costs facing developing countries with the trend towards common rules. Following a brief aside on regional trade agreements for developing countries, we conclude with reflections on the political challenges to the international community and to governments posed by the ongoing negotiation of global trading rules.

Of course, at the global level modern trade clubs are only one of the many clubs that nations join—dealing not only with trade but also with human rights, the environment, finance, security and other issues among nations. These various clubs of nations together constitute the infrastructure of today's global cooperation. Trade clubs are among the most visible and powerful parts of this infrastructure, so their contributions or their costs for developing countries and thus for global cooperation broadly conceived are particularly important.

In this chapter we do not explicitly focus on the benefits of openness for economic growth in developing countries, nor on the gains from tariff and other border barrier reductions.[1] Instead we work from the premise that trade linkages have fostered growth, based on a large body of evidence.[2] We focus on the implications of the trade agreements themselves and in particular on the implications of the deeper nonborder measures that modern trade agreements of the past 10 years increasingly include.

CHANGING INTERNATIONAL TRADE POLICY AND
DEVELOPING COUNTRIES

Over the past 50 years international trade policy has evolved, with changing effects on developing countries. Closed markets and shallow integration have been followed by open markets and deepening integration, especially among industrial countries, and, with deepening integration reaching some developing countries, the end of preferential treatment.[3]

Closed markets and shallow integration

In the immediate postwar period two ideas about developing countries governed their involvement in international trade. One was that they should try to develop with only limited engagement in the overall global economy. In part this view was a response to the disastrous international environment that had prevailed in the 1930s. In part it reflected a scepticism about the potential of market forces and a faith in the capacity of governments to plan development and allocate resources. In addition, there was a view that political factors such as neocolonialism had created a system that was biased against developing countries, and in particular against producers of primary products. As a result most developing countries adopted import substitution policies and maintained high tariff barriers and restrictive quotas.

The second idea was that when developing countries do enter into world trade, they should be given special treatment. For example, the General Agreement on Tariffs and Trade (GATT), which reduced tariffs on a most-favoured-nation basis, was amended to provide for special and differential treatment of developing countries. In principle, developing countries had considerable freedom to pursue whatever policies they chose. Developing countries were granted leniency in the use of infant industry protection and trade restrictions for balance of payments purposes, and given special market access under the Generalized System of Preferences (GSP). They were able to receive most-favoured-nation treatment from other GATT members without undertaking much liberalization at home. (To be sure, these principles were not always fulfilled, as exemplified by industrial countries' failures to liberalize agricultural trade and the discriminatory treatment of developing country exports of textiles in the Multi-Fibre Arrangement.)

The context for the limited engagement and special treatment of developing countries was what can be called "shallow integration". When barriers at nations' borders were high, as they were in the immediate postwar period, governments and citizens could sharply differentiate international policies from domestic policies. International policies dealt with the border barriers, but nations were sovereign over domestic policies without regard for the impact on other nations. In its original form GATT, signed in the 1940s, emphasized this approach. Tariffs were to be reduced on a most-favoured-nation basis and discrimination against foreign goods was to be avoided by according them national treatment. But the rules of the trading system by and large left nations free to pursue domestic policies in other areas such as competition, environment, taxation, intellectual property and regulatory standards.[4] To the degree that there were international agreements in other policy areas—indeed, there were international multilateral agreements on business practices, labour standards, intellectual property and the environment—these occurred outside GATT, and in the absence of enforcement or sanctions, compliance was, for practical purposes, voluntary. This was the case, for example, when nations signed conventions on international labour standards in the International Labour Organization (ILO) or codes of conduct for multinational corporations at the United Nations.

Open markets and deep integration

In the 1980s the notion that developing countries should develop behind high barriers began to change. Developing nations responded both to success and to failure by moving towards liberalization and outward orientation. In East Asia success led to external pressures on Taiwan (province of China) and the Republic of Korea to liberalize. Elsewhere shifts towards an outward orientation were induced by debt problems, the East Asian example, the need to attract new forms of capital and the encouragement of the International Monetary Fund (IMF) and the World Bank. The collapse of communism brought a large new group of nations into the international marketplace. China, the world's largest and most rapidly growing developing country, is only the most visible of these nations. Although complete removal of border barriers has not been achieved, the leaders of most nations agree in principle that free trade is desirable, and many are prepared to commit their countries to achieving it in the foreseeable future. In late 1994, for example, 34 nations in the Western Hemisphere and 18 members of the APEC forum committed themselves to eventually achieving full regional free trade and investment.

Deep integration among developed countries

Meanwhile, among developed countries pressures were building for deeper international integration—that is, for the harmonization and reconciliation

of domestic policies. A host of new issues emerged on the international negotiating agenda, including services trade, intellectual property, rules for foreign
investors, product standards, competition policies and labour and environmental standards.

A combination of political and commercial forces has driven this trend
towards deep integration. As the barriers to trade have been dismantled, the
impact of different domestic policies has become apparent, especially as it
affects international competition. Increasingly, the major political actors in
society (business, labour and civil society groups concerned with the environment) have called for a level playing field. For coalitions representing business, the problem is product dumping, for labour it is "social dumping", and
for environmentalists it is "eco-dumping". Trade agreements offer these
groups a vehicle to lobby for changes at home, either by directly changing the
trading rules or by using trade as a weapon to enforce agreements achieved
elsewhere.

Even more powerful commercial forces are driving the trend towards
deep integration. Foreign trade and foreign investment have become increasingly complementary. Competing successfully in foreign markets increasingly
requires access to marketing, sales and customer service expertise in those
markets. Acquiring innovative small foreign firms in major markets has
become vital for competitive success. Furthermore, as international competition intensifies, small cost advantages have large consequences. Particular
national locations are not necessarily well suited for the complete manufacture of complex products. With improvements in communications and transportation, firms are increasingly able to produce products by sourcing from
multiple locations. Raw materials might best be sourced in one country,
labour-intensive processes performed in a second and technologically sophisticated processes performed in a third.

These commercial forces have increased investors' attention to barriers
that indirectly inhibit trade, to the degree of ease with which foreign firms can
enter new markets through both acquisition and new establishment and to
the effects of domestic regulations and taxes on the conditions under which
such firms can operate. The United States, for example, increasingly argues
that barriers to foreign investment in Japan constitute nontariff barriers to
trade. More generally, firms that plan to source in one country and sell in others want security about the rules and mechanisms governing trade. Firms also
prefer secure intellectual property rights and compatible technical standards
and regulations.

Deep integration and the end of preferential treatment

A logical outcome of the shift among developed countries towards deep integration and the increasing outward orientation of developing countries has been pressure—political and commercial—for deep integration between developed and developing countries. Adding to the pressure have been the privatization programmes of many developing countries and those countries' larger efforts to attract foreign investment capital. These pressures have undermined the logic of preferential treatment for developing countries. Special treatment was straightforward when trade agreements related to barriers at the border; developed countries could simply adopt lower tariffs than developing countries. In contrast, agreements that embody adherence to common rules by their nature imply reciprocal obligations.

A shift towards reciprocal treatment is evident in both regional and multilateral arrangements. The only preference developing countries now typically receive is in the form of a longer transition period to full reciprocity. Under the Uruguay Round of multilateral trade negotiations, developing countries were given longer periods in which to adopt new disciplines such as intellectual property, but they were generally not exempted to anywhere near the same degree as they had been earlier. Likewise, recent agreements signed by the European Union with Eastern European, Middle Eastern and North African nations envisage much more complete reciprocity. Under NAFTA, once the transition period has elapsed the obligations assumed by Mexico and its more developed NAFTA partners (Canada and the United States) are reciprocal. In the APEC agreements developing countries are given an additional 10 years to adopt complete free trade and investment by 2002, but their obligations are ultimately similar to those of their developed country counterparts.

DEEP INTEGRATION: IMPROVED MARKETS FOR ALL

A more open and competitive international market can be thought of as a global public good in itself. As noted, a more open international market has been for most developing as well as industrial countries associated with increased economic growth and reduced poverty, as trade opening has made local producers more competitive in global markets, increased access to new technology and stimulated foreign investment.[5] In turn, increased growth and reduced poverty in developing countries have implied a more secure and stable global postwar system.[6] But what are the additional global benefits of the growing emphasis on common rules and deeper integration in recent trade agreements?

Avoiding races to the bottom

As competition for international direct investment flows becomes more important, the increasingly clear international rules on measures to attract foreign investment and to a lesser but growing extent on environmental and labour standards that characterize modern trade agreements can in principle help all countries avoid a race to the bottom in international competition.[7] Whether in fact clear rules do help is not straightforward, but, as discussed below, depends on the specifics. But certainly in the case of investment competition and for those who would otherwise free ride on the benefits of, for example, global environment agreements like the Montreal Protocol,[8] the emerging emphasis on clear and common rules creates the potential to offset incentives for regulatory competition. Voluntary codes of conduct and socially conscious programmes, the reach of which is expanded by trade and trade-related investment, can also help avoid a race to the bottom.

Establishing rules of the game can be particularly important to developing countries, which otherwise can be subject to constant pressure from potential investors for lower standards in order to attract new investment. For example, in the absence of agreed rules, there is already concern in countries like Honduras that investors are prepared to move relatively mobile clothing manufacturing operations to neighbouring countries unless new tax, regulatory or other privileges are bestowed by the national government or by local governments. This situation is perfectly analogous to the regulatory competition problem faced within US states in the absence of agreed federal standards.

Controlling opportunism

International rules and oversight of trade agreements benefit all countries to the extent that they limit the ability of large firms to exploit monopoly power. This is particularly important for developing countries because these countries are not as likely to be positioned to take advantage of market imperfections. Firms in developed economies often have monopoly or market power in international trade, so that the international market in the product they produce or consume deviates markedly from the competitive model. Developed countries may then be in a position to adopt policies that enhance the market power of their own firms—so-called strategic trade policies—or improve the terms on which they trade by using a so-called optimal tariff. To illustrate, countries with market power can lower the world price of the goods they import by limiting demand through a tariff. (These gains from lower import prices can more than offset the distortions to domestic consumption and production associated with the tariff; see Krugman and Obstfeld 1994, pp. 253–55.)

Restraining protectionism

Agreed rules can also preempt protectionists in their efforts to use the domestic political process to resist trade opening. This can be particularly beneficial to developing countries. For example, from a health or environmental point of view a lack of agreed rules on product standards buttresses domestic protectionist groups in industrial countries in their fight against the opening of markets such as agriculture and textiles on grounds that imports may not meet local standards.

Attaining scale economies

Harmonization of standards or mutual recognition of different product standards can realize economies of scale across countries. Thus international agreements may allow countries, including poor countries, to better exploit their comparative advantage by realizing economies of scale. This improves the global market for everyone by reducing the average costs of production world-wide.[9]

More contestable international markets

All exporting countries have an interest in seeing that international markets are more readily contestable—that is, that anticompetitive practices of existing producers or the natural monopolies that can emerge in some sectors do not make it impossible for new producers to enter, permanently shielding current producers from the healthy threat of competition. To the degree that international agreements on competition policy, standards, regulation and other measures that create barriers to entry succeed in making global markets more open, developing countries will gain.

DEEP INTEGRATION: SOME ADDITIONAL BENEFITS FOR DEVELOPING COUNTRIES

Developing countries that participate directly in modern trade agreements can capture some additional benefits.

Low-cost importing of best-practice institutions

The common rules of deep integration often mean that developing countries that participate can benefit from adopting institutions and the associated infrastructure of rules and rule-making without having to pay the costs of developing them. Participation in international agreements provides a forum through which developing countries can "import" new institutions and regulatory systems that may not match domestic conditions precisely, but that are ready-made, pre-tested and provide international compatibility. For nations in Eastern Europe, for example, adopting policies that conform to the norms of the European Union (EU) is particularly attractive because they can be seen as the first steps towards full membership in the union.

Such "importing" of institutions and regulatory systems can be seen in the widespread adoption of financial reform across developing countries. Because modern trade relations create the commercial pressures for investment links described above, deep integration will naturally involve integration of financial sector arrangements as countries seeking to attract foreign investment seek also to assure foreign investors (and creditors) of the soundness of their financial systems. Many developing countries, especially in Latin America, are adopting the banking supervision and prudential regulatory requirements recommended by the international financial community (the Basle Committee). These usually involve importation not only of regulatory standards but of specific accounting and auditing standards as well. Some countries, including Argentina and Mexico, have opened up their banking systems to foreign ownership,[10] so many banks are owned partially or completely by foreign banks. An advantage of this opening is that these countries have instantly imported the institutional capacity and human resources associated with meeting the standards of Organisation for Economic Co-operation and Development (OECD) banking systems. This is no different from countries "importing" standards of the US Food and Drug Administration (FDA) when they announce that they will permit use only of drugs approved by the FDA; or airline customers throughout the world preferring airlines that the US Federal Aviation Administration has approved.

Enhancing domestic reforms

When developing countries enter into modern trade agreements, they often make certain commitments to particular domestic policies—for example, to antitrust or other competition policy. Agreeing to such policies can be in the interests of developing countries (beyond the trade benefits directly obtained) because the commitment can reinforce the internal reform process. Indeed, participation in an international agreement can make feasible internal reforms that are beneficial for the country as a whole that might otherwise be successfully resisted by interest groups. For example, trade negotiations may help mobilize more diffuse but ultimately more representative groups, such as consumers (as well as potential exporters), who will benefit from increased trade and whose interests more accurately represent overall welfare, thereby offsetting the influence of organized producers and workers who compete with imports. In many cases domestic forces interested in liberalization will find their case strengthened if they can present their policies as fitting part of an international liberalization agreement.

Furthermore, participation in international agreements may increase the credibility of the reform process itself. This is particularly important for developing countries because the more credible and sustainable a trade liberalization reform is, the more confident investors will be and the more rapid and deep will be the shift in production from inefficient to efficient sectors. Before firms will undertake the necessary investments to serve foreign markets, they need to be confident that access to these markets will be forthcoming. When countries, particularly those with a long history of protection, proclaim their newfound allegiance to open trade and investment, local as well as foreign investors often react quite sceptically. By undertaking commitments that could lead to international sanctions if broken, countries lock in reforms and make them less susceptible to political changes. Thus when Mexico became party to NAFTA, it provided additional insurance to US investors that it would maintain an open trade regime and avoid the risks of a beggar-thy-neighbour trade war with the United States.

Catalyzing more open and democratic decision-making

The need to establish and sustain reforms associated with international commitments or more generally with the opening of trade regimes has encouraged the creation of new mechanisms for developing political and social consensus for the reforms themselves. A recent example of consensus building for reform is from Chile at the time of its transition from a military regime to democracy. A tripartite agreement signed in 1990 by the government, labour and business articulated a model of equitable and democratic development that built on the open-market economic policies adopted under the military regime. The agreement reflected an ideological shift, identifying the private firm as the principal agent in development and an open competitive market as a principal factor for growth and distribution. This and successive consultations resulted in additional agreements in the following years on a broad range of subjects, including the opening of new markets and the pursuit of environmental protection, and also led to the swift adoption of labour reform.

Similarly, as governments recognize the danger that public distrust poses to the acceptance of trade agreements, they are increasingly inviting business, labour and other civil society groups to participate in the negotiation process. Prior to launching trade negotiations for the Free Trade Area of the Americas, for example, the United States pushed for creation of a Committee on Civil Society to speak for the interests of various groups. The idea of the committee was not particularly welcomed by other countries, and its involvement and value remain to be seen, but its very creation marks a change from prior trade negotiations that did not deal with the kinds of domestic issues that modern agreements cover. In any event, the point is that the deep integration process, by encouraging domestic policy reform and bringing those reform issues to the international arena, can inspire more open and democratic processes in countries where policy-making has traditionally been from the top down.

A less obvious benefit of deep integration with other countries can accrue to developing countries with immature democratic regimes. In 1996, for example, the democratically elected government of Paraguay was threatened by a military coup, and it was not clear that then-President Juan Carlos Wasmosy was willing or able to take the necessary steps to resist a takeover. Paraguay is a member of the Mercosur trade agreement, along with Argentina, Brazil and Uruguay. Strengthened by their role as fellow members of a trade arrangement important to Paraguay, the governments of the three other Mercosur countries put immediate and strong pressure on relevant groups in Paraguay, implicitly threatening expulsion from the trade group. This benign pressure may well have played an important role in preventing the unravelling of Paraguay's young democratic regime. Similarly, though not yet obviously with a happy outcome, other Asian members of the Association of Southeast Asian Nations (ASEAN) trade group have expressed concern to the government of Malaysia about the detention in the fall of 1998 of former Finance Minister Anwar Ibrahim.

Exploiting multilateralism

The potential for large, rich economies to use strategic trade policies to enhance the market power of their firms was mentioned above. It is one example of how developing countries, lacking much international power, have a particular interest in seeing that the rules of the game are set in a multilateral setting in which they can actively participate, rather than fought out in the context of bilateral arrangements in which individual developing countries are likely to be at a negotiating disadvantage with a larger, more powerful trading partner.

Rule-making rather than rule-taking

More generally and over the long run, active participation in the negotiation and ongoing monitoring of deep integration agreements can change the nature of the dialogue between developing and developed countries—making developing countries actors rather than spectators on the world scene and thus putting them in a much better position to assert their interests. Indeed, the acts of dialogue and coalition building are themselves important protocols to establish for international affairs. (Similarly, developing countries may have a more effective voice in the context of international agreements on cross-border and global environmental problems that are another source of market failure than they can have in one-to-one bilateral negotiations with neighbouring rich countries. See Heal in this volume.)

DEEP INTEGRATION: RISKS FOR DEVELOPING COUNTRIES

There are benefits to developing countries of participation in modern trade agreements, but there are also risks. The large differences in levels of income and development between developing and industrial countries and the dominance of larger, richer industrial countries in global markets create risks and thus potential costs for developing countries. The key challenge is therefore how to manage those risks and minimize any costs while capturing the benefits of greater integration into world markets. What are the risks?

A weak hand in multilateral settings

A multilateral setting has potential advantages, but only if developing countries have sufficient financial and human resources to be active and effective negotiators of their interests. Involvement in complex trade negotiations often extends over many years and requires a critical minimum of resources. Lack of adequate resources means that many countries, especially those that are small as well as poor, are at a distinct disadvantage in the negotiating process. It comes as no surprise that Latin American countries are seeking training and technical assistance from the Inter-American Development Bank to strengthen their capacity to negotiate—and, in contrast to the past, are willing to borrow to finance these programmes.

Protectionist politics in developed country markets

As noted, agreement on common rules has the advantage for developing countries that it may limit the types of actions and the nature of complaints that protectionist groups in rich countries bring to impede imports from developing countries. On the other hand, the enforcement mechanisms and sanctions built into trade agreements may also provide an additional incentive for protectionist groups to try to use the system to restrict competition. Thus developing countries justifiably fear that trade agreements that cover product standards will be used as a vehicle by politically powerful protectionist interests in developed countries to deny access to developing country producers. These fears are based in part on a history of past use of US antidumping legislation against low-cost foreign producers. The potential for protectionist interests to invoke antidumping rules has created considerable market uncertainty and entailed high legal costs for potential and actual producers outside the United States, even when in the end they have prevailed in US courts. The costs of this uncertainty, in terms of lost investment in new activities and direct legal costs, are likely to be relatively higher for developing country producers if only because they tend to be smaller and more likely to be entering markets newer to them.

This history causes developing countries to fear that agreeing to common competition rules and international investment standards will lead to abuse of these common rules by private, powerful parties in richer countries. Developing countries are also concerned that adopting common standards in these areas will preclude what they see as legitimate government efforts in their countries to help their firms enter new markets through special programmes or subsidies.

Inappropriate standards: labour and environment

It is inevitable that there will be pressure on developing countries seeking to join international arrangements to adopt rules and institutions that may not be appropriate given their level of development or needs. Developing countries are particularly sensitive to pressure to incorporate environmental and labour standards into trade agreements because of the history of effective exploitation of common commercial standards by powerful groups in developed countries. As with competition standards, standards in these new areas can be used by protectionist interests in rich countries to close markets to poor countries. Indeed, developing countries face the same negotiating disadvantage on these standards as on the commercial details of trade agreements; rule-making mechanisms in the WTO are still being developed, raising ongoing questions of legitimacy.[11]

Moreover, if history and political barriers could be overcome and agreement on common standards could be reached, poor countries with limited institutional capacity would be more vulnerable to adjudication based on their inadequate enforcement of these standards. Developing countries have less capacity and face higher costs with respect to any regulatory regime—indeed, this is why in areas like drug approvals and bank supervision, they benefit (as noted) from importing standards whole cloth. The potential direct and indirect costs of internal management of agreed common standards are illustrated by recent decisions in the NAFTA context, which make a participating country potentially liable if its domestic regulations can be shown to cause foreign firms to lose business and revenue. The government of Canada, for example, felt it prudent to compensate a US corporation for losses associated with Canada's environmental ban on a fuel additive.

The more fundamental issue is whether it is in the economic and social interests of developing countries to enter agreements that would generally require enforcing higher local standards in labour and environment.[12] In areas like labour and environment a consensus has to be reached in each society on what standard is appropriate if standards are to be sustained. Because developed countries are richer (by definition) they tend already to have reached agreement within their societies on standards that are more costly for private agents to honour than are analogous standards of poorer countries. The prominent fear on the domestic front for developing countries is that committing to measures on the environment or labour could retard their development. It is common for developing countries to point out the existence of a double standard: when they were poor, the developed countries of today did not adhere to the norms they are now trying to require of others.

Consider first the environment issue, using as an example pollution intensity—that is, pollution per unit of output. There are at least three reasons to expect higher pollution levels and higher pollution intensity in developing countries (see Birdsall and Wheeler 1993). First, environmental amenities are normal goods; higher income in developed countries produces greater demand for clean air and water. Similarly, at lower levels of income and higher discount rates, income gains and jobs may be more valued relative to health and other costs of pollution. Second, the relative costs of monitoring and enforcing pollution standards are higher in developing countries, given the scarcity of trained personnel, difficulty of acquiring sophisticated equipment and high marginal costs of undertaking new government activity when the policy focus is on achieving and maintaining price stability and managing market reforms. Third, growth in developing countries is associated with a shift out of agriculture into industry with rapid urbanization and heavy investment in urban infrastructure; this transition is more likely to imply increasing levels of pollution for each unit of output. In developed countries, by contrast, growth is associated with a shift out of industry into services, and thus with decreasing levels of pollution for each unit of output.

Each of these structural differences is consistent with what might be called the "social cost" comparative advantage of developing countries in pollution-intensive production. If there is such a comparative advantage, it is likely to be reinforced by free trade—implying greater pollution intensity.[13] In this context it is politically difficult for a government to agree to a more demanding local standard because such an agreement would apparently offset the economic advantage of the increase in trade that is sought in the first place. Put another way, because higher environmental standards are a consequence of the higher demand for such standards that comes with higher incomes, they are difficult to import—all the more so if they are seen as a necessary accommodation to a foreign trading partner. Moreover, imposing a higher standard that is not consistent with a country's level of development and the preferences of its citizens will likely reduce rather than enhance the level of trade, and undermine the very growth process that is the key to eventually raising standards in poor countries.

There is, of course, a possibility that the true social costs of pollution are not appropriately reflected in current environmental standards in some developing countries, where fiscal and regulatory arrangements do not particularly reflect society's views. Obvious examples include the former Soviet Union and other communist states, where heavy industrial pollution was an outcome of the politics of a planned economy; and public enterprises in Latin America and Asia, which prior to privatization were in practical terms exempt from local environmental standards. In these cases it is possible that adherence to agreed minimum standards in the context of trade agreements would actually bring local practices more closely into alignment with society's preferences.

But such an argument goes against the deeply rooted notion of national sovereignty and needs to be made with great care. Regulatory standards may bring benefits, but they also necessarily impose costs, and are not likely to be enforced or politically sustained if they are the result of pressure from those who do not pay the costs—that is, outsiders—to use trade arrangements to impose their will on insiders. Rather, to be sustained such realignments of local practices and societal preferences need to percolate up through democratic processes.

In developing countries where the growth process is working and investment rates are healthy, the pressure of global competition is probably driving many firms to use the most efficient and usually simultaneously the cleanest production methods anyway. In these settings some formal harmonization of environmental standards is possible because it is consistent with market forces. Formalization of harmonization could benefit developing countries in these circumstances by accelerating the process of adjustment to cleaner standards. But the benefits of harmonization are much more difficult to realize in developing countries that are poorer or that are not growing and thus not benefiting from new investments that embody efficient and cleaner technology. Put another way, the benefits of harmonization can probably only be realized in developing countries that are approaching the income levels of developed countries, and that also already benefit internally from a reasonably open and deliberative political process for the setting of rules.

What about labour standards? Currently these are among the most controversial aspects of the trade policy debate. Most of those who advocate introducing labour standards into trade agreements are careful to emphasize that they are not talking about detailed requirements, such as a specific minimum wage or specific regulatory requirements, which might price the products of some countries out of international markets. Instead they have in mind something close to the core standards that have been developed by the International Labour Organization (ILO).[14] These include freedom of association, the right to form organizations, the right to collective bargaining, the suppression of forced labour, nondiscrimination, equal pay for men and women and rules restricting child labour (for example, that the minimum age for work should not be lower than the age of completion of compulsory learning).[15]

It is certainly possible that by accepting such obligations in an international setting, developing countries may be able to increase the credibility of their commitment to achieve such standards. It is also possible that such standards could enhance the perception in developed economies that international competition is more fair. But the crucial issue, for labour as for environmental standards, is not only whether harmonization of standards across countries makes sense (in the case of a limited set of core labour standards, which almost all countries already recognize, it may make sense). The crucial issue is whether the use of trade sanctions, formalized in the context of trade agreements, to accelerate the development and enforcement of labour standards in developing countries would be effective, beneficial and sustainable. It is one thing to argue the need for international agreements on labour (or the environment) and quite another to argue that trade clubs should be the vehicle to enforce them in developing countries.

Developing countries resist the linking of trade and standards for at least two reasons. First, it is developing countries that would inevitably be the target of enforcement sanctions, since almost by definition they are "behind" in the enforcement if not the rhetoric of such standards. The costs to them of handling trade disputes, whether legitimate or not, would no doubt escalate, since were the potential for sanctions available, domestic political groups within developed countries, particularly labour, would be constant and powerful advocates of using WTO trade dispute mechanisms, in a manner analogous to business groups' use of antidumping rules. Yet in most developing countries the threat of or actual invocation of trade sanctions would not be effective, and could even be counterproductive, in helping to enforce child labour standards or in generating the internal political support for enforcing collective bargaining rights.

Second, developing countries fear the slippery slope that enforcement of standards through trade sanctions could imply. Though many developing countries have formally endorsed such core labour standards as collective bargaining rights and minimal workplace safety, they are legitimately concerned that opening the door for sanctions in trade agreements on core standards would generate additional pressure for inappropriate requirements—for example, on wage levels. Their fears are stoked by a combination of domestic political pressures in rich countries, the emphasis on trade sanctions (relative to less coercive approaches) of groups concerned with labour issues and the reality that such pressures would arise in the international arena, where developing countries, once they give up their veto power, are at a distinct negotiating disadvantage.

India's position is illustrative. India has ratified most ILO conventions yet continues to object strenuously to the introduction of such standards at the WTO. In fact, in Singapore in 1996, WTO members agreed that the ILO rather than the WTO was the appropriate multilateral venue for agreement on enforcement of labour standards.

There are alternatives to enforcement of standards through trade sanctions that would be more effective in raising standards in developing countries while supporting trade expansion and its growth benefits and supporting the domestic political process that ultimately has to support sustainable higher standards. Alternatives would take better account of the perspective and constraints faced by developing countries. The international community could agree on a formal programme of assistance to developing countries, including financial incentives for domestically agreed core labour standards.[16] Instead of resorting to coercive trade sanctions, more emphasis could be placed on noncoercive measures that could be used to help countries that agree to comply with higher standards—such as reporting requirements, multilateral monitoring and consultation, and publication and other transparency measures (see Hart 1998). These alternative measures have the advantage of building on and strengthening progress that is consistent with market forces. They also can reinforce the benefits of voluntary codes of business conduct and other programmes that rely on consumer preferences in developed countries.

More generally, it seems obvious that on the issue of standards, the global community would benefit from more dialogue and compromise between high-income and low-income countries, and from the recognition in such dialogue that the often vast gap in levels of development across trading countries inevitably generates domestic economic and political pressures that are bound to create legitimate conflicts. Trade itself and trade-related investments are already accelerating a healthy process of improved standards for labour and environment in developing countries; the challenge is to find more effective and, for the developing countries, less risky vehicles for accelerating that process.

AN ASIDE ON REGIONAL TRADE CLUBS

There is ongoing debate about whether regional trade clubs undermine the larger goal of multilateral free trade. It is worth noting that for developing countries, the evidence increasingly suggests that there are trade as well as nontrade benefits associated with regionalism.

For developing countries the most obvious benefits of regional arrangements with deep integration are strictly commercial—for example, when they involve the elimination of differences in production and product standards, they lower production costs. It is true that deeper agreements, by making regional firms more efficient, might lead to a reduction of external trade. But this would not necessarily constitute trade diversion that reduced the efficiency of global markets or overall welfare, as long as the new regime makes the local producer sufficiently more efficient. For example, changes in domestic regulations could give internal firms cost advantages over outsiders that result in both fewer imports from outside the region and in lower internal costs. (The adoption of a common standard within the region could also make it less costly for producers outside the region to sell their products.) Investment is also made more credible and secure if a regional agreement brings improved governance mechanisms and secure access to large foreign markets that is unhindered either by customs officials or by domestic actions such as antidumping.

Regional trade clubs also offer noncommercial advantages for developing countries. From a political standpoint, it is easier for a government to liberalize with respect to neighbours than to do so multilaterally. And regional clubs can bring intraregional political benefits by creating a culture of coordination that can be drawn on during times of crisis, as the Paraguay and Mercosur example above illustrates. Regional clubs can also deal more effectively with regional nontrade challenges such as environmental protection and migration. Regionalism can also create regional goodwill as countries' interests become increasingly vested in their neighbours' well-being.

Regional trade groups illustrate a fundamental point about the issue of standards. There is no reason, a priori, to assume that the provision of regulatory regimes and other public goods should be the sole responsibility of the nation state or, alternatively, of a single global arrangement. Some goods and rules are better provided locally, while for others bilateral and multilateral international arrangements may be more appropriate. In the case of regional agreements, this point seems even more important for developing countries, because regional agreements are more likely to reflect appropriate standards and more likely to involve possible nontrade spillovers for developing countries.

Conclusion

As the scope of international trade agreements is enlarged, so too is the potential for realizing the benefits of international economic integration more fully. The international provision of rules that maintain open and contestable markets for goods and services and that enhance the international compatibility of standards and policies are worthwhile goals. At the same time, however, negotiating appropriate rules presents formidable political challenges for the international community in general and for developing countries in particular. As Robert Putnam (1988) emphasizes, there are two levels to international negotiations. One level involves the international negotiation among national governments; the other level involves the domestic negotiation within countries between the government and its citizens. Deeper international economic integration naturally raises concerns on both levels.

Internationally these negotiations are different from those dealing only with border barriers. Under the assumption that markets are competitive, economic theory suggests that the reduction of border barriers such as tariffs will benefit both the importing and the exporting nation. Accordingly, traditional trade agreements can be presumed to be win-win. But theory does not suggest that this will necessarily be the case for deeper agreements that deal with behind-the-border policies. Indeed, such agreements could well be win-lose. For example, an international agreement to enforce intellectual property rights could on balance harm a country that has little or no domestic innovation and has previously simply copied foreign innovations. Thus such an agreement entails greater risks for nations that are less powerful and points to the need for packaging agreements so that on balance all nations perceive that they have gained. In the Uruguay Round, for example, many developing countries were only willing to conclude an agreement on intellectual property in return for the elimination of the Multi-Fibre Arrangement, which restricted textiles exports from developing countries.

For developing countries reconciled or harmonized policies may or may not be more efficient than the domestic policies they replace or discipline. Therefore, in contrast to the free flow of goods and services, which by definition generates benefits for developing countries as trading parties, the deep integration of modern trade agreements is likely to require careful assessment of benefits relative to costs. Because deeper does not automatically mean more efficient (or more equitable, as the imposition of deep integration in the form of colonialism reminds us), each advance towards more common rules requires for each country an assessment of the benefits relative to the risks. In short, the devil lies in the details.

Negotiations to achieve deeper integration will inevitably tempt powerful countries to use access to their markets as a carrot to achieve agreements that are in their interests. But it would be unfortunate if an international trade order that reflected market power were to be established. In the short run such a system would be damaging to developing countries. In the long run it would hurt developed countries as well. Indeed, it behoves large developed economies to reflect that a system based on market power is not in their long-run interest because the largest markets in the global economy of the future are likely to be in countries such as China and India.

The second complicating factor is that these agreements also affect domestic political relationships. As international agreements increasingly constrain domestic policies, they bring a whole range of new actors into the debate over their desirability. Indeed, we have already observed that one possible benefit of these agreements is to alter the internal debate among domestic interest groups. But this could also create a cost. While in developing countries commitments to international agreements may strengthen desirable domestic reform efforts, they may also antagonize powerful antitrade domestic lobby groups. Meanwhile, in such high-income countries as the United States, opposition to trade agreements has increased among groups on both the left (who want to use trade agreements to achieve multiple other goals) and the right (who complain about the erosion of sovereignty).

There are two implications for policy at the global level. First, as developing countries become more fully integrated into the international marketplace, international trade institutions, most notably the WTO, will experience additional challenges with respect to the legitimacy of modern agreements and international implementation capacity. As international rule-making mechanisms evolve, the major trade powers will need to accept the logic of an increasing role for developing countries in rule-making in these institutions.

Second, if modern regional and multilateral trade agreements are to generate maximum global benefits, developing countries must be able to participate actively and effectively in their negotiation and have the resources and institutional capacity needed for their implementation. This has always been true, of course, but it is more crucial and more salient today given the growing complexity of modern agreements and their domestic policy implications. This means that developing countries need technical and financial assistance to take their place at the table. It is in the enlightened self-interest of richer and more powerful economies to finance such assistance—if only to ensure their own participation in the international benefits.

Notes

The authors are grateful to Lesley O'Connell for excellent research assistance.

1. These benefits are substantial. Martin and Winters (1996) refer to studies, including one by the WTO, indicating global steady-state gains from merchandise

trade liberalization under the Uruguay Round of between $40 billion and $258 billion in 1992 prices, depending on various assumptions. Gains to developing countries are much larger than to developed countries as a share of GDP—in one study 1.6% compared with 0.7%.

2. See, for example, Sachs and Warner (1995). Earlier work by Krueger (1974) suggested why trade openness in developing countries would be likely to foster growth, by encouraging competitiveness and discouraging rent seeking.

3. This section borrows heavily from Lawrence (1998).

4. The charter for the World Trade Organization originally covered a broader range of issues, including restrictive business practices and labour standards, but it was never adopted.

5. There is a large literature supporting the view that trade and integration have enhanced growth in developing countries (see, for example, Sachs and Warner 1995). Whether open capital markets have been salutary is more controversial.

6. It is true that the liberalization and integration of capital markets in the 1990s have made many developing countries increasingly vulnerable to financial contagion. Contagion has affected especially those developing countries that rely heavily on short-term public or private borrowing to finance local investment or consumption, including some with relatively sound macroeconomic policies. The effects of open capital markets are treated in Wyplosz (in this volume). Here we are concerned with the effects of trade and of long-term investment (relative to short-term debt flows).

7. The theoretical conditions for a race to the bottom to occur are complicated and are dependent on assumptions about available tax and subsidy instruments and the nature of market imperfections. In fact, under some circumstances environmental and other regulations could be set too high and there could be a race to the top—the "not in my backyard" phenomenon. For a discussion see Wilson (1996).

8. Signatories to the Montreal Protocol have agreed to prohibit trade in goods containing chlorofluorocarbons (CFCs) in products produced by nonsignatory countries.

9. Where these benefits are great they may involve a trade-off. On the one hand, local specific regulations may match preferences more closely; on the other, international norms may yield benefits from scale economies.

10. Of course, the initial impetus to do so was to attract resources to recapitalize weak banking systems, particularly after the late 1994 "tequila" crisis that started in Mexico and affected Argentina.

11. The WTO bodies that draft common health and environmental standards (for example Codex Alimentarius) have been accused of being undemocratic and unresponsive, at least to the interests of consumer groups and nongovernmental organizations.

12. We do not discuss international environmental problems here. For international problems such as the risk of global warming, the case for international agreement is much clearer than for problems confined within national borders, though even in international agreements, different countries would probably face different timetables and financial burdens to meet agreed goals.

13. Ironically, the evidence suggests for Latin America that the effect of free trade has been to lower pollution intensity, all other things being equal, by inducing shifts of productive capacity away from protected industries that tend to be highly pollution-intensive (Birdsall and Wheeler 1993).

14. These are detailed on the ILO Web site; see http://www.ilo.org.

15. The US government in particular has advocated introducing these standards into the WTO, but the stunning fact is that although in practice it adheres to these conventions, the United States has only ratified one of these fundamental human rights: the abolition of forced labour.

16. Anderson (1996) suggests linking a schedule of gradually increasing standards in developing countries to the incentive of improvements in access to OECD markets.

REFERENCES

Anderson, Kym. 1996. "The Intrusion of Environmental and Labor Standards into Trade Policy." In Will Martin and L. Alan Winters, eds., *The Uruguay Round and the Developing Countries.* New York: Cambridge University Press.

Birdsall, Nancy, and David Wheeler. 1993. "Trade Policy and Industrial Pollution in Latin America: Where Are the Pollution Havens?" *Journal of Environment and Development* 2(1): 137–49.

Hart, Michael. 1998. "A Question of Fairness: The Global Trade Regime, Labor Standards, and the Contestability of Markets." In Geza Feketekuty and Bruce Stokes, eds., *Trade Strategies for a New Era: Ensuring U.S. Leadership in a Global Economy.* New York: Council on Foreign Relations and the Monterey Institute of International Studies.

Krueger, Anne O. 1974. "The Political Economy of the Rent-Seeking Society." *American Economic Review* 64(3): 291–303.

Krugman, Paul R., and Maurice Obstfeld. 1994. *International Economics: Theory and Policy.* 3rd ed. New York: Harper Collins.

Lawrence, Robert Z. 1998. "Regionalism, Multilateralism and Deeper Integration: Changing Paradigms for Developing Countries." Paper prepared for the Organization of American States conference on Multilateral and Regional Trade Arrangements: An Analysis of Current Trade Policy Issues, 26–27 May, Washington, DC.

Martin, Will, and L. Alan Winters. 1996. "The Uruguay Round: A Milestone for the Developing Countries." In Will Martin and L. Alan Winters, eds., *The Uruguay Round and the Developing Countries.* New York: Cambridge University Press.

Putnam, Robert D. 1988. "Diplomacy and Domestic Politics: The Logic of Two-Level Games." *International Organization* 42(3): 427–60.

Sachs, Jeffrey D., and Andrew Warner. 1995. "Economic Reform and the Process of Global Integration." *Brookings Papers on Economic Activity 1.* Washington, DC: Brookings Institution.

Wilson, John Douglas. 1996. "Capital Mobility and Environmental Standards: Is There a Theoretical Basis for a Race to the Bottom?" In Jagdish Bhagwati and Robert E. Hudec, eds., *Fair Trade and Harmonization: Prerequisites for Free Trade?* Cambridge, MA: MIT Press.

INTERNATIONAL FINANCIAL INSTABILITY

CHARLES WYPLOSZ

It is a sad truth in the postwar world that most initiatives to reinforce international financial cooperation have been taken under the pressure of some kind of financial crisis.

—BIS 1996, p.169.

This chapter looks at instability as a challenge to the international financial system and investigates the "public bad" nature of the phenomenon. The conclusion: financial instability is an international public bad, but not a classical one. Instability is not purely a technical by-product of the production of financial services. Rather, it is the outcome of market failures, for reasons not yet fully understood. Having laid out this diagnosis, the chapter looks at how existing institutions and policies deal with international financial instability, both to limit its acuity and to deal with its implications. The main emphasis is on drawing lessons from recent experiences (Europe, Mexico, East Asia) and recent theoretical advances, especially those that have improved our understanding of crises. The chapter presents five main proposals.

- Proceed with caution in promoting capital liberalization. Not only should the "consensus" of the past 10 years—that the sooner the capital account is liberalized, the better—be toned down, but the logic should also be reversed. Countries should apply for liberalization, and a list of preconditions is presented.

- Avoid the restrictive macroeconomic policies, huge loans and deep structural policies of recent packages. Contractionary policies are not always well adapted to financial instability. Big loans are not always needed either. And structural policies that target long-standing practices and institutions should be avoided as part of ex post conditionality, because they are excessively intrusive and cannot be implemented fast enough in a crisis.

- Complement today's ex post conditionality with ex ante conditionality. Structural policies that target long-standing practices and institutions are better dealt with when they are prepared and implemented over time, if only because they require capacity building. Countries should be given a long period to complete a number of tasks vital for financial stability. Those that do so successfully can be offered enhanced access to multilateral funding.

- Suspend debt repayment in the event of a major crisis accompanied by a collapse of the exchange rate. Both sovereign and private debtors trapped in such a situation must be offered orderly workouts.
- End the monopoly of the International Monetary Fund (IMF) by creating regional IMFs. The chapter presents the case for competition in the business of international policy advice.

FINANCIAL INSTABILITY AND ITS COST

Financial crises are not a new feature of the world of finance, as is well documented by Kindleberger (1939). Financial markets are inherently volatile because asset prices are driven by expectations about the future. There is no "weight of history" to tie down asset prices, which promptly react to any information that might affect future returns. It does not matter whether the information will be proven correct or whether the analysis of its impact on asset prices is exact. This is already tomorrow's information and tomorrow's volatility. Yet volatility is not synonymous with instability.

A key function of financial markets is to price risk. Asset prices reflect both expected returns and the uncertainty surrounding these returns. It is normal for prices to vary constantly. Instability arises when asset prices—which include exchange rates—display excessive volatility, which occurs when the markets' reaction is not justified by currently available information.[1] Panics, herd behaviour and belated realization of the significance of past events are examples of what creates financial instability.[2] Market overreaction is not necessarily a symptom of irrational behaviour. Instead, it is the unavoidable consequence of an inherently risky activity. Herd behaviour, for instance, reflects the natural tendency to hide in the pack when the going gets rough. Nor is it the case that large movements of capital are necessarily a sign of instability. They may represent stabilizing market responses to changing opportunities, much as the instantaneous drying up of capital movement into a country may be the excessive symptom of market anxiety over the situation in that country.

Financial instability can be very costly, and financial institutions are first in line. When one fails, the others are immediately under threat because of extensive mutual links—and because the public at large feels threatened. Bank runs offer a vivid example of "rational panic": when many depositors rush to cash in their savings, it is rational for all depositors to do the same because no bank can ever pay back all deposits upon request. Bank crises typically compel the authorities to come to the rescue because no country can tolerate a collapse of its banking system. The costs borne by the budget during recent bank rescue operations, by any standard, are huge (table 1).

But the costs of financial instability are not just budgetary. Asset price changes affect people's wealth and their standards of living and consumption. They also affect asset issuers' ability to carry out business, including investment and employment, sometimes even leading to disastrous waves of bankruptcies. This in turn affects aggregate spending and can precipitate major recessions, often quickly followed by political crises.

TABLE 1

Estimates of costs of banking crises

(percentage of GDP)

Country	Years	Cost
Argentina	1980–82	55
Benin	1988–90	17
Bulgaria	1990s	14
Chile	1981–87	41
Côte d'Ivoire	1988–91	25
Finland	1991–94	<10
Hungary	1987–present	10–15
Israel	1977–83	30
Japan	1990s	10
Mauritania	1984–93	15
Mexico	1994–present	12–15
Poland	1991–present	<10
Senegal	1988–91	17
Spain	1977–85	10–15
Sweden	1990–93	<10
Tanzania	1987–95	10
United States	1980s	2.5–3.0
Venezuela	1994–present	18

Source: BIS 1997; Crockett 1997.

FIGURE 1

Effects of currency crashes in developing countries

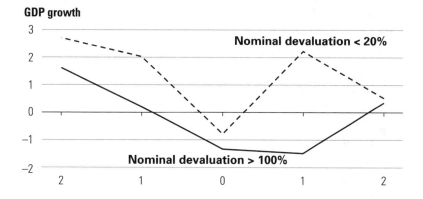

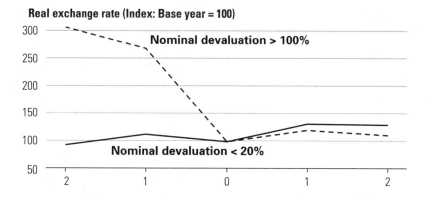

Note: The figure plots the effects of currency crashes identified by Frankel and Rose (1996) using an index composed of changes in exchange rates and drops in foreign exchange reserves. The two groups represented in the figure correspond roughly to the top and bottom quintiles (in terms of real devaluation) of about 100 crises identified by Frankel and Rose and for which there are GDP and exchange rate data in IMF (1998). Year 0 is the year of the currency crash.
Source: IMF 1998; Frankel and Rose 1996.

The East Asian crisis provides a vivid example. A more systematic, if less dramatic, description of the effects of currency crises in developing countries is shown in figure 1. The figure shows the evolution of GDP growth and of the real exchange rate against the US dollar from two years before to two years after the crash. When the real exchange rate depreciates by more than 100%— a clear sign of financial instability—GDP growth falls by about 3 percentage points for two years, and subsequent recovery is weak. When the real depreciation is less than 20%—most likely corresponding to a "normal" correction of macroeconomic imbalance—the recession is less deep and shorter lived. Crises are thus different from adjustments.

IS FINANCIAL STABILITY AN INTERNATIONAL PUBLIC GOOD?

Financial stability can be seen as an international public good because financial instability is a potential public bad that spreads across countries. But collective action problems have led so far to an underprovision of the international public good, with severe redistributive effects. To see why, financial stability is better approached from its mirror image—instability, as defined in the previous section. When asset prices exhibit excessive volatility, millions of decisions (consumption by individuals, investment by firms) are affected. When capital flows suddenly swell in one direction or another, not only does the private sector face the need for immediate reaction, but national authorities suddenly face unpleasant choices with potentially adverse political backlash. Such effects are clearly nonrival and nonexcludable: financial instability is undoubtedly a public bad.

Instability as a public bad: negative externalities

Traditionally, public bads occur through negative externalities. A good example is water pollution. It is unavoidable that certain chemical production processes contaminate water. When this water is discharged into a river, all downstream residents suffer from a negative externality. Does this call for policy action and, if so, which one? A further distinction is necessary.

Some externalities are pecuniary, transmitted by the price mechanism. For instance, city congestion results from the agglomeration of people in a narrow patch of land. Each resident is, in some sense, a nuisance for the others. This externality (ignoring air and noise pollution, as well as positive externalities that come with agglomeration) does not call for policy action because a market mechanism is at work. Housing rents, transportation costs and the prices of goods and services are higher than in emptier areas: city dwellers buy the economic right to contribute to congestion. In this sense the congestion mechanism is self-regulating.

Other externalities are nonpecuniary because they cannot be taken care of by markets. Take water pollution, for which there is no market. Yet public action may create a market and make this externality pecuniary. To that effect, legislators only have to define property rights. If it is decided that each citizen has the right to clean water, chemical plants will have to choose between depolluting water or paying compensation to citizens downstream. Pollution rights may be auctioned to establish the "right" level of fines. Alternatively, legislators may set as a principle the right to pollute. Downstream residents can still decide to pay the firm to depollute its water before disposal. In both cases, once the property right is set, a market for rights can be established. Importantly, the choice of a particular right has distributive effects: if it is the right to clean water, firms face costs; if it is the right to pollute, residents bear costs. Presumably, in a democracy, the decision is best left to politics.

Not all externalities can be made pecuniary, though. Air pollution travels far away and in haphazard ways, depending on shifting winds and random rainfalls. It becomes impossible to define precisely the firms that cause pollution and the victims. Establishing the principle of clean air remains a possibility, but relying on the market will not work. For example, firms will not be able to compensate all affected citizens if they wish to. Nonmarket action will be needed, such as emission norms and fines.

Financial instability, as argued, is a natural by-product of the business of dealing with risk. "Normal" volatility is priced and thus requires no public intervention. For example, rising financial instability leads to increasing risk premiums, higher interest rates and possibly exchange rate movements. In fact, financial markets design instruments that permit dealing with the resulting uncertainty, and a wide array of products suit varied needs and tastes for risk.

But the "excessive" volatility that leads to crises is not priced. It is a negative externality, and it is nonpecuniary because, as with air pollution, its sources and victims are too diffuse to be identified. Bank runs, for example, are triggered by depositors alarmed by uncontrollable rumours, and then affect all depositors. No price mechanism is available. The usual solution is to require that bank deposits be insured if banks do not see it in their own interest (under the pressure of competition) to do so spontaneously. The insurance market may set a price to reduce the potential costs suffered by depositors in the event of bank runs, hopefully reducing their incidence. Yet not all risks can be insured. Insurance itself is a risky business and suffers from some of the same defects as financial services.

Instability as a public bad: market failures
Another side to financial instability further complicates the situation. Contrary to a widely held view, financial markets do not function well, for

they are prone to failures. This matters because, along with nonpecuniary externalities, market failures are the most powerful argument in favour of policy intervention. Financial market failures occur because of the widespread presence of information asymmetries.[3]

The generic source of information asymmetry is quite simple: a lender usually knows less about a borrower's financial situation than the borrower does. Because the availability and cost of any loan depend on financial health, a borrower has the incentive to misrepresent the true situation. This is an unavoidable feature of financial markets since any financial instrument is, ultimately, a loan. The results are moral hazard, adverse selection and multiple equilibria.

- *Moral hazard* occurs in financial markets when, for example, a borrower accumulates excessive debt, gambling that the lender will eventually agree to easier terms. The lender may not be innocent, betting on government support if many loans sour because bankruptcy could trigger a bank run or endanger other financial institutions. Moral hazard is the outcome of a market failure: when people do not face the full cost of risky behaviour, they take socially excessive risk.
- *Adverse selection* occurs in financial markets when, for example, following an increase in interest rates, the credit market dries up because lenders refuse to lend, fearing that only desperate borrowers are willing to take up expensive loans. "Good" borrowers refrain from borrowing because the cost is becoming excessive. This adverse selection may prevent the market from functioning because it has become too risky. A particular aspect of the phenomenon is credit rationing: lenders simply refuse to grant loans to potential borrowers perceived as too risky, while the normal price mechanism would be a high risk premium.
- *Multiple equilibria* seem, in practice, quite specific to financial markets.[4] Asset prices are driven by expectations. The future, in turn, may be affected by current conditions. For example, a financial crisis today may worsen growth and affect stock prices or the exchange rate in the future. When dark expectations justify a crisis today, the crisis confirms the validity of these predictions. This is a "bad" equilibrium that may well coexist with a "good" equilibrium where markets remain optimistic, boosting asset prices and future growth. The existence of multiple equilibria, deeply linked to uncertainty, opens the possibility that financial markets themselves are the source of a crisis: another instance of rational herd behaviour with irrational economic effects.

Thus there are good reasons for financial markets to generate instability. And insurance faces a similar problem of asymmetric information, leading to both moral hazard and adverse selection and keeping insurance from helping to solve a number of financial market deficiencies, as explained in the discussion of self-fulfilling exchange rate crises.

Instability as a global public bad

Instability is a national public bad. Indeed, governments have long dealt with it at the national level. The subsidiarity principle suggests that this is where the provision of the public good of financial stability should start: each country should deal with the markets under its jurisdiction. But this is not enough—for three good reasons.

INTERNATIONAL SPILLOVERS. A case of externality. Markets typically know no borders, especially financial markets. Shares of the same firm can usually be traded world-wide. Exchange rate markets are, by definition, international. Banks and other financial institutions operate in many countries. As a result excessive price changes are not contained within national borders, and sharp shifts in capital flows to and from a country can be triggered by events far away. The world financial market is not just an amazingly powerful institution—it is also a vehicle for powerful externalities.

Many of these externalities are pecuniary: country and exchange risk premiums are usually based on an extensive credit rating industry, which monitors, at a cost, economic and political conditions around the world. But even the business of credit rating faces the problem of asymmetric information. The failure of rating agencies, which did not issue adequate warning signals ahead of the Asian crisis (except for Thailand), has been widely noted. One consequence was a market failure of massive proportions: financial markets did not adequately price, ahead of time, the risks of the crisis to come.

Not only do markets fail to price pecuniary externalities, but some externalities are non-pecuniary. For example, as the crisis occurred in Thailand, markets reacted violently (adverse selection) and indiscriminately, spreading the crisis throughout South-East Asia and beyond to Brazil, Poland, Russia and several other countries. This externality cannot be priced adequately. There is an emerging market premium, but it fails to take into account the phenomenon of contagion.

MARKET FAILURES. The asymmetric information problem is more acute internationally than nationally. First, the discrepancy of information between lenders and borrowers is made more difficult by distance, cultural differences and the ability to decipher local (economic, political and other) idiosyncrasies. Large multinational financial institutions respond by developing subsidiaries, but even still some of the failures have been spectacular (Barings,

Daiwa, Drexel). Globalization opens new weaknesses, as operators attempt to exploit legal international loopholes.

Second, as noted, when instability becomes acute in a particular country, lenders' reaction is to abruptly limit or even to cut lending to "similar" countries. In typical herd behaviour, as uncertainty rises, financial institutions tend to protect themselves by sticking to the pack. At best only blue-chip companies retain access to foreign borrowing, leading to serious cases of adverse selection. Worse still, when the herd runs for the door as all lenders try to get out of the danger zone, stock and exchange rate markets collapse.

Third, moral hazard becomes geopolitical. Banks and other financial institutions tend to rely on the assumption that excessive international lending cannot be sanctioned by systemic default. When an indebted country's financial instability becomes acute, foreign lenders, rather than opt for costly and uncertain litigation, lobby for international official bailouts. Ex ante they refuse to include in their loan contracts clauses that could cover the gray area between faithful debt service and outright default. Ex post they even embark on speculative behaviour. The costs of instability are shifted from lenders and borrowing countries to governments of lending countries. In addition, a de facto alliance of borrowers and lenders often aims to extract support from international organizations and such well-off countries as those of the G–7 or G–10. Quite often, officials have less information than the lenders and the borrowers.

RACES TO THE BOTTOM. When national authorities intervene to deal with market failures, they inevitably impose costly prudential measures that affect the profitability of financial institutions. The result is a competition among regulatory systems: more regulated financial systems may be safest but they also operate at a competitive disadvantage. Safety could be sufficiently valued by customers to warrant the extra cost. But if that were the case, banks would have spontaneously exploited this market niche, and that has not really happened so far. The result is that regulators tend to shy away from appropriate policy action, which leaves stability-enhancing measures underprovided.

Market failures may have redistributive effects. Here again the Asian crisis provides a striking illustration. The costs to South-East Asia of the financial crisis have been massive: a deep recession, sharply rising unemployment, widespread bankruptcies and political turmoil. Viewed from the West, where lending institutions typically have escaped unscathed, there is little incentive to advocate or even monitor the adoption by borrowing countries of economically and politically costly measures that could prevent a crisis.

In addition, with nonpecuniary externalities, purely national regulators will not take into account the effects on other countries of the measures that they adopt. Strictly motivated by national interest, they may underestimate the damage to other countries. This pattern reinforces the presumption that there is too little provision of stability-enhancing measures internationally.

The special case of self-fulfilling exchange rate crises

Among nonpecuniary externalities, the multiple equilibria in financial markets need to be emphasized, if only because their practical importance is still not yet widely recognized. Multiple equilibria were the root cause of self-fulfilling exchange rate crises in Europe in 1992–93 (Eichengreen and Wyplosz 1993), in Mexico in 1995 (Sachs, Tornell and Velasco 1996) and in Asia in 1997 (Krugman 1998; Wyplosz 1998b). Self-fulfilling attacks on a fixed exchange rate occur when markets come to expect that a crisis will force the authorities to adopt new policies. The markets calculate that, once an attack has forced a devaluation or the abandonment of the fixed exchange rate regime, the best course for the authorities is a policy that would have been incompatible with the previous situation, typically a relaxation of the monetary stance.

Self-fulfilling crises are a case of multiple equilibria because, without the "bad equilibrium" attack, the best policy would have been a continuation of the pre-crisis policy stance—the "good" equilibrium that was sustainable. This has led Eichengreen, Rose and Wyplosz (1996) to distinguish two sorts of crises. First-generation crises are caused by the wrong fundamentals, such as an excessively expansionary monetary policy or unsustainable budget deficits. With these crises it is a matter of when, not if. Second-generation crises are self-fulfilling: they may or may not happen. Both good and bad equilibria are possible, and it is quite arbitrary which one actually occurs. In a nutshell, second-generation crises occur because they are expected to occur.

To be sure, self-fulfilling attacks cannot arise unless some underlying weakness prevents the authorities from preserving the "good" equilibrium. Such weaknesses—fragile banking systems, high unemployment, political instability, large debts—are necessary but not sufficient for a crisis. It is likely that most countries suffer from some weakness that could lead to a self-fulfilling attack, but only a small minority ever falls victim. Self-fulfilling attacks are inherently unpredictable (see Wyplosz 1998c). Four important implications follow.

First, the unpredictability (at least given current knowledge) of self-fulfilling attacks means that markets cannot adequately price a risk that is far too diffuse.[5] Thus it is not surprising that rating agencies failed to predict the recent crises. Even if they had spotted weaknesses, they had no way of telling if and when a particular economy might shift from one equilibrium to another.

Second, self-fulfilling attacks create an additional channel for contagion. A crisis in one country may lead traders, the public or investors to reinterpret their views of financial stability in other countries. Black Tuesday in 1987, the tequila crisis in 1995 and Asia in 1997 offer examples.[6] Similarly, bank failures can spread across borders not because of bank cross-holdings but because of a reinterpretation of the available information.

Third, policy-makers and international financial institutions have been trained to see a crisis as the sanctioning of bad macroeconomic policies. Self-fulfilling attacks can occur even when the traditional fundamentals—the budget, inflation, the current account, monetary policy—are "right". At work is a weakness that had not generally been previously associated with speculative attacks. Still, policy-makers and international financial institutions tend to react with classic contractionary measures, compounding a market failure with a "policy failure" (see Sachs and Radelet 1998 and Wyplosz 1998a).

Fourth, financial instability—defined as excessive volatility in prices or flows—has important national and international redistributive implications. In any financial market, be it global or national, an amount of risk must be borne by someone. This risk results from the shocks that continuously buffet national and world economies (called extrinsic uncertainty) and from the occasionally destabilizing reaction of markets (intrinsic uncertainty).

Financial intermediaries offer financial services to reduce their customers' exposure to risks, performing implicitly an insurance role. In so doing, they absorb risk (at a cost). They then typically pool risk among themselves, buying and selling their commitments to end users until the risk borne by each intermediary is small enough. Implicitly, financial intermediaries provide each other with insurance. While they therefore absorb some of the global risk, they are very careful to limit their exposure. When a crisis occurs, suddenly swelling the amount of global risk, they are rarely willing to step in. It is the end users (national authorities, firms, individuals) that stand to face a large dose of noninsurable risk, which soon translates into losses.

Clearly, wealthier and more financially savvy end users are rarely caught off-guard and seldom suffer large losses. Less sophisticated asset-holders end up absorbing the greater part of risks and losses. Wage earners and taxpayers are not insured or are only partially insured (for example, through unemployment benefits where they exist) against crises. Thus crises redistribute wealth from the poorer to the wealthier, nationally and internationally, from low to high human capital. This statement can be illustrated by contrasting Sweden and South-East Asia. Like Asia in 1997, following a collapse in housing prices—itself the consequence of imprudent lending—most Swedish banks had become insolvent in the early 1990s. Sweden subsequently went into recession, but its fate comes nowhere close to the current Asian crisis.

So, while some crises fulfil the useful role of imposing financial discipline on private and public agents, this process is inefficient and unfair. True, self-fulfilling crises would not occur without pre-existing weaknesses, but the ratio of punishment to misbehaviour is excessive. Policy interventions are therefore needed to separate normal from excessive financial market reactions.

THE MECHANISMS OF INTERNATIONAL FINANCIAL STABILITY

This section presents and comments on existing mechanisms designed to promote financial stability nationally and internationally.

National provision of financial stability
ADEQUATE MACROECONOMIC AND STRUCTURAL POLICIES. Policy itself can be a source of instability.[7] Price stability and steady and predictable macroeconomic policies—including fiscal discipline, a sustainable current account and an adequate exchange rate policy—are preconditions for financial stability. Structural requirements include a proper policy process, distortion-reducing taxation, efficient labour markets and healthy financial and banking systems.

Not controversial, this is more a wish list than a description of what most countries can achieve over the next 10 years. But even though most countries will not live up to such exacting standards, few of them will face the kind of crises that have been witnessed in South-East Asia. No matter how inherently desirable it is, this list is neither necessary nor sufficient for financial stability.

ADEQUATE LEGAL FRAMEWORK. Property rights must be clearly established and rigorously enforced. This includes bankruptcy and private property legislation, including stakeholder commitments in case of failure by financial institutions. The aim is to ensure that stakeholders have the incentive to monitor financial institutions adequately because they know that they will face consequences if they fail to do so. Lender-of-last-resort interventions must be unpredictable to avoid moral hazard. There is little doubt that this list is indeed a necessary condition for financial stability.

ACCOUNTING. Economists' description of markets is often seen as unrealistic because it assumes that an incredibly high level of information is shared by all economic agents. This criticism is valid, but there is more than one way to deal with it. Rather than opt for "realism" and settle for second (or *n*th) best policies that tinker with the market logic and ultimately harm growth, a major objective should be to ensure that markets resemble as much as possible their theoretical structure. Accounting standards, truthful and timely reporting, auditing, transparency in risk-taking and revealing consolidated accounts all work towards achieving this aim—and all require adequate legislation and thorough implementation. There is little doubt that sound accounting practices provide wide benefits to society as a whole.

EFFICIENT AND DEEP FINANCIAL MARKETS. Financial markets are more stable when they function well—providing a wide variety of instruments, safe payment systems, open competition and private ownership of financial firms (to avoid conflicts of interest). And the more efficient are financial markets, the more complex they tend to be. Complexity can reflect a high degree of performance and sophistication, but it can also generate a lack of transparency, both internal and external. There is a tendency towards infatuation with sophistication, partly because regulators sometimes feel that they are less technically alert than financial engineers. Sophisticated internal and external controls must accompany product sophistication.

REGULATION AND SUPERVISION. The widespread existence of regulation and supervision represents a healthy admission that financial markets cannot be allowed to function completely freely. This admission is a source of tension with the equally widespread view that financial liberalization is a step forward on the road to development. In principle, liberalization should not proceed faster than regulation. More realistically, because regulation and supervision are unlikely to be entirely effective, it must be recognized that each liberalization step raises instability.

MONITORING CAPITAL FLOWS. Free capital movements are seen as a condition of efficiency. Yet financial crises rarely occur in countries that limit capital movements. There is a clear trade-off between the efficiency costs of restricting capital movements and the cost of promoting financial stability. In addition, capital flows can be restrained selectively by using such new-generation "Tobin taxes" as the required deposits operating successfully in Chile. Such tools discourage speculative short-term flows without harming efficient long-term capital flows.[8]

International institutions: a tour d'horizon

Formally, the IMF is in charge of international financial stability. By providing support and advice to countries that face external payment difficulties, the IMF clearly aims at maintaining orderly exchange markets and, when a crisis erupts, at preventing internal turmoil and international contagion. Viewed this way, the IMF fulfils many of the requirements just stated.

The World Bank is in charge of financial sector reform, among other tasks. It provides financing and advice to countries that want to establish the kind of institutions just listed, and regional development banks operate alongside it.

Both the IMF and the World Bank (along with regional banks) intervene country by country. Thus they do not deal directly with externalities but instead seek to prevent contagion by circumscribing bush fires. They also spread best practice through accumulated experience. Yet neither the IMF nor the World Bank have been involved in setting up rules to prevent or limit free riding. The vacuum has been filled by various organizations explicitly set up to promote international financial cooperation.

The G–7 was born out of early attempts to stabilize exchange rates following the end of the Bretton Woods system. It has evolved towards broadly based mutual surveillance among some of the largest economies. Many of the same functions are formally performed by the Organisation for Economic Co-operation and Development (OECD) for a broader grouping of advanced economies. Financial stability is often an important concern of both the G–7 and the OECD, but not operationally so. Other groupings, such as the G–10 and the G–24, operate with similarly vague tasks.

The Bank for International Settlements (BIS) is a central bankers' forum for discussions that often aim at financial stability. Along with the IMF and the OECD, the BIS collects data and makes them available to markets. The BIS houses, but does not manage, the Basle Committee on Banking Supervision, an institution explicitly set up to foster common regulatory practices. The Basle Committee is perhaps the most advanced form of international efforts to achieve financial stability through the adoption of measures designed to strengthen banks by reducing risky behaviour and encouraging stakeholder monitoring.

A similar approach has led to the establishment of two other international institutions. Stock market regulation is dealt with by the International Organization of Securities Commission (IOSCO), while the International Accounting Standards Committee (IASC) is concerned with accounting practices. In contrast with the Basle Committee, IOSCO and IASC recommendations are not automatically adopted by member countries.

The proliferation of institutions of different status and membership reflects the nature of the process adopted so far. There has been no grand design similar to the Bretton Woods system. Problems are dealt with ad hoc by groups of concerned countries or professional associations (IOSCO, IASC). Existing institutions (IMF, World Bank, BIS, OECD) spread their domain of intervention, sometimes overlapping with each other, sometimes leaving cracks in between. Most of these efforts are spearheaded by the advanced economies case by case, largely on a voluntary basis. Following the Mexican crisis, the recent G–10 effort led to the Draghi report (BIS 1997), nonbinding and for the time being more a list of good intentions than an instrument for dealing with international financial instability.

The Asian crisis, following the Mexican crisis, has revealed many cracks. Investor enthusiasm with emerging markets has created a situation where risks are very large for emerging market countries and increasingly less negligible for advanced economies. This development justifies a rethinking and presumably lies behind the debate on the "new architecture" for international financial markets.

We have probably passed the stage in history where global plans like Bretton Woods can be agreed on. Grand schemes require either a hegemon or an international consensus. There is no hegemon anymore and, as noted, financial instability leads to large-scale income redistribution, and any reform is bound to alter the way the costs of crisis are shouldered in and across countries. Given the amounts involved, there is little hope of achieving consensus. Thus the "new architecture" is likely to become a messy stone-by-stone construction, much as necessity has led to the creation of the G–7, G–10, G–24, IOSCO, IASC and Basle Committee.

Central but unresolved issues

The financial and exchange rate crises of the 1990s share several new features. Trade openness has spread. Industrial policies have declined. Direct controls over domestic financial markets have been phased out. And capital accounts have been liberalized. Among the reasons behind this broad evolution are the demise of the Soviet bloc, the disenchantment with state interventions and the examples from successful reformers on all continents. The outcome has been broader growth performance around the world, led by the stunning results in South-East Asia.[9]

This is what makes the 1997 crisis emblematic. Except for Thailand, these countries did not exhibit the kind of macroeconomic mismanagement traditionally associated with foreign exchange crises (see Krugman 1998; Sachs and Radelet 1998; and Wyplosz 1998b). Despite some structural but widespread weaknesses around the world (unhedged foreign currency indebtedness and weak bank regulation), the crisis was not foreseen by international organizations, rating agencies and foreign investors. Generalized gross negligence is one interpretation. The self-fulfilling crisis is another. The fact that "surprising" crises are more frequent after a wave of financial liberalization supports the interpretation that these attacks are self-fulfilling. They reflect the greater ability of markets to force policy-makers' hands, even when there is no gross mismanagement.

A particularly disquieting aspect is "wisdom after the fact", a regular feature of this new generation of crises. Once a crisis has occurred, there is near unanimity on its cause. Each new crisis reveals a hitherto neglected weakness, and the list of weaknesses grows with each crisis. Weaknesses that looked familiar and benign beforehand are recognized as fatal afterwards. With the passage of time, we will know more: whether there really exist self-fulfilling crises, and what features can be qualified ex ante as serious weaknesses. (This research has already started; see Eichengreen, Rose and Wyplosz 1995, 1996; Frankel and Rose 1996; and Milesi-Ferretti and Razin 1998.) At this stage, however, we have to accept that most countries are likely to exhibit some casual-looking weakness, leaving them open to sudden acute financial instability for reasons not currently understood. The implications of this appraisal cannot be overemphasized. They call for a careful rethinking about how to prevent crises and how to deal with crises once they have erupted.

Instability prevention

SURVEILLANCE: TOWARDS BETTER MACROECONOMIC POLICIES. Bad policies are a standard source of financial instability, so why don't countries spontaneously do what is best for them? Quite often the blame is laid on national politics. When political reforms are too difficult, one solution is to bring in an outside "referee" to propose and impose a Pareto-superior solution.[10]

Why would international institutions work better than national ones? One reason is that most of the reforms that raise total welfare simultaneously redistribute incomes, both nationally and internationally. Potential winners are naturally circumspect while potential losers organize resistance, often creating domestic political logjams. Outside institutions are sometimes seen as a referee with the authority to impose welfare-enhancing solutions, the financial resources for Pareto transfers to compensate the losers or both.

The IMF does both. It draws its authority from its technical knowledge, and it offers financial support, both direct (its own resources) and indirect (official bilateral aid or private funds tied to adherence to IMF programmes). IMF interventions can be seen as a Pareto transfer from the international community to a country that is in difficulty and threatening international financial stability. That is not enough, however, because stability-enhancing measures have redistributive effects within the country. But Pareto transfers within a country are not part of IMF procedures, which raises the question of why IMF programmes work. Furthermore, few countries apply to programmes before the crisis has set in. This precludes the IMF from preventing instability.

INFORMATION. The current official view (IMF, G–7, G–10, G–24) emphasizes the merits of better information (quantity, quality and timeliness). Better information can help, but for two reasons it would be seriously misleading to limit efforts to improving information. First, information is never enough. For instance, information and supervision procedures are highly developed in OECD countries, yet financial crises and bank runs have occurred recently in Norway, Sweden and the United Kingdom. Policy and management errors cannot be eliminated, and cover-ups are instinctive when difficulties arise.

Second, in a world of multiple equilibria, the best that can be done is to draw up lists of potential weaknesses. We know too little to pretend that we have the analytical ability to interpret the available information. This implies that current efforts at building up early warning signals are doomed to fail. As shown in Wyplosz (1998c), early warning signals tend to be either silent when crises occur or ringing when there is none, the familiar problem with type I and type II errors.[11] A third type of error corresponds to the possibility that the warnings may provoke a crisis.

These issues explain well the current ambivalence about whether the IMF should reveal its information. In efforts to increase the flow of information, the IMF has come under pressure to divulge more (all?) of its information. Its reaction has been lukewarm, for it is concerned about "talking too much", thus betraying confidence and triggering a crisis while losing access to confidential information. In addition, it remains to be shown that the IMF has a comparative advantage in information relative to private investors. Former IMF staff members do not believe that it does (CEPR 1998, p. 29).

REGULATION AND SUPERVISION. Efforts at establishing international norms for regulation and supervision are recent, mostly dating to the crisis of 1987. The public good nature of financial stability calls for public action. The risk that competitive pressure results in ever lower levels of regulation calls for international coordination to set a level playing field along with proper safety nets.

In banking, developed countries have adopted the Basle Committee's recommendations, but developing countries trail behind. Except in a few Latin American countries, good intentions have not been translated into action. An important issue is whether developing countries should adopt the same rules as developed ones. Since financial institutions from developing countries start at a competitive disadvantage, should they not start with milder rules? Quite to the contrary, the severity of the rules should be inversely related to the development of the financial system. The less developed is the financial system, the riskier it is and the worse the consequences of a crisis. In addition, weaker institutions will be better able to compete internationally if they are known to be subject to stricter rules.

WHEN INSTABILITY PREVAILS: CRISIS MANAGEMENT

Crisis prevention is already well established, with good hopes of significant progress in developing countries. Crisis management is more rudimentary at the international level. It is also more controversial, both in its analysis and its implementation.

Crisis diagnosis and prognosis

Once instability boils over, its causes and likely effects need to be quickly and correctly grasped. In the wake of the Asian crisis, the heated public debate between the IMF and its critics has shown how difficult the exercise can be. The reason lies with the many poorly understood issues listed earlier. Fundamentals-based crises are reasonably well understood, leaving limited room for disagreement. But for self-fulfilling crises, there is an urgent need to develop a strategy for their possible occurrence. The danger is to apply an old medicine to a new illness.

- First it is essential to determine the kind of crisis that is developing, even if that takes time and markets and governments panic.
- Second, some policies are always appropriate whenever instability rises— and can be implemented immediately while the diagnosis is being fully

worked out. For example, giving up (temporarily, maybe) a fixed exchange rate regime always seems to be the right response.

- Third, IMF programmes should have built-in flexibility so that they can be quickly adapted, without a loss of confidence or discipline, when the diagnosis firms up. During the Asian crisis much time was lost when it emerged that tight fiscal policy may not have been the proper recommendation. Part of the delay had more to do with saving face than with proper policy-making.

- Fourth, policy design should be less secretive, to allow different views to be aired before decisions are made. While public debates could fuel financial instability, policy mistakes are even more detrimental.

In this respect it is surprising that letters of agreement for IMF programmes are not released to the public. There are good democratic reasons to make commitments public. There are also good economic reasons: signals to markets can help stabilize the situation if the programme is well adapted. And if it is not, timely public and professional scrutiny is highly desirable.

Similar considerations apply to prognosis. Financial instability implies high uncertainty. Forecasts, always the Achilles' heel of macroeconomics, become nearly impossible to make with any reasonable degree of accuracy in the midst of acute financial instability. The accepted wisdom that policy programming must be built around forecasts creates formidable difficulties. As with diagnosis, prognosis should be the object of considerable caution. In particular, policies based on forecasts need to be contingent on further analysis and findings. The popular argument that programmes, to establish credibility and discipline, must be set in concrete is particularly naive. Upholding policies that are based on assumptions that clash with the evidence is like driving a car on ice without proper tires.

Contagion and national interests

Financial instability is often contagious. Confining the contagious patient to quarantine can be seen as good policy for society as a whole. But it is not always so.

Contagion may be based on fundamentals. One country's depreciation and recession provokes a contraction in the demand addressed to its trade partners or competitors, who then undergo a decline in asset prices and an exchange rate depreciation. Further ripples may affect more countries. That is the rationale for containment. But this does not imply the economic equivalent of quarantine—forcing a country in the midst of a financial crisis to adopt policies that prevent any transmission of the shock. Ideally, policy coordination implies some compromise between international and purely national interests. In addition, if the initially affected country is asked to adopt policies that prevent contagion but at some cost to itself, improving international welfare justifies compensatory Pareto transfers from the healthier countries.

Self-fulfilling crises are another channel for contagion. For example, when a self-fulfilling crisis arises in one country, markets may reinterpret information on another "similar" country as an indication that a crisis is highly likely there too. Asia in the wake of the Thai crash is again a case in point—a case in which contagion prevention becomes trickier. First, as noted, classic policies may not work when a crisis is self-fulfilling; they could actually make matters worse (Sachs and Radelet 1998). Second, the diffuse nature of what triggers self-fulfilling crises makes it difficult to foresee where the contagion may spread.

Moral hazard and debt relief

This section considers the moral hazard of the public sector. Another moral hazard, for the behaviour of private lenders, is taken up below. Typically, a country facing an exchange crisis needs to suspend the servicing of its external debt. Initially the exchange rate tends to undergo a deep undervaluation, which is eventually corrected. During the interim the domestic currency value of the foreign debt is inflated, justifying some suspension of payments. But debt relief can open the question of moral hazard. As noted, international support, by absorbing part of the costs of instability, may provide incentives for private lenders to underestimate risks—and for national authorities to refrain from adopting national measures that provide stability (prudent macroeconomic policies, regulation and supervision). IMF conditionality deals with the second risk by ensuring that national authorities face a serious cost. In particular, the IMF has systematically rejected debt suspension.

Given the considerable costs of financial crises—economic and otherwise—it is hard to believe that national authorities nurture, or just willingly ignore the dangers of, financial instability.[12] Punishing a country in crisis by denying debt suspension may thus be ill advised. Yet so far the concern with moral hazard has blocked international support for a standstill. Developing countries, which in the past frequently resorted to unilateral moratoria when faced with financial crises, have carefully refrained from doing so recently. One reason is that developing countries increasingly borrow from private sources, making debt management more commercial and less

FIGURE 2

Net capital flows into Asia and Latin America

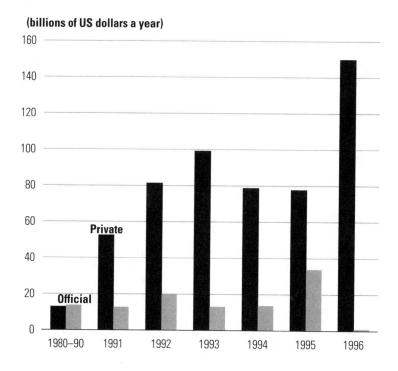

(billions of US dollars a year)

Source: BIS 1997.

political (figure 2). Another reason is that the 1980s led both borrowers and lenders to be more cautious. In addition, IMF-led programmes have involved significantly larger official loans along with the requirement that debt servicing not be discontinued. Yet there is movement. Quietly, the IMF has started to accept that its loans be used to serve debts, a practice that it used to ban. Standstills are still resisted on moral hazard grounds.

The risk of adverse selection

Information asymmetries also create the problem of adverse selection. The first effect is the drying up of international credit. When private lenders become concerned that previously healthy-looking borrowing countries will not be able to service debts, they abruptly interrupt credit flows. This market failure can have dramatic effects and justify that public lenders (international financial institutions and governments) step in urgently. This is reasonably well understood and practised. Yet another manifestation of the adverse selection phenomenon, little noted, is the other side of the coin of moral hazard prevention: tough IMF conditionality to minimize moral hazard scares away countries in the pre-crisis phase.

Countries facing mounting financial instability can choose between asking for an IMF programme and trying to ride out the storm on their own. Quite often, it seems, they would rather take the risk of going it alone than face the certainty of IMF conditions that they perceive as excessively tough. An example is Mexico's last-ditch effort at converting its peso debt into dollar debt. In so doing, not only does a country deepen its own wounds, it also endangers other countries susceptible to contagion.

This behaviour followed the Thai crisis: months passed before the last country to be hit, the Republic of Korea (later referred to as Korea), caved in under market pressure and called in the IMF, following the pattern previously set by Malaysia and Indonesia. What happens is that only the most desperate cases appear in the "market" for IMF programmes. Moderate cases eschew IMF conditionality, implicitly stigmatizing countries that do apply. The unfortunate result: when the IMF finally comes in, the situation has become more desperate and intractable—and harder to circumscribe than if it had been treated in good time. The delay may make all the difference between a soft and a hard lending, and between an isolated case and a wave of contagious attacks.

New directions in crisis management

INSTABILITY IS NOT ALWAYS ASSOCIATED WITH BAD MACROECONOMIC POLICIES. Instinctively, it seems, the IMF associates financial instability with policy mismanagement. But the likely existence of multiple equilibria calls for a reappraisal. So far, resistance has been fierce. Because self-fulfilling crises occur only in the presence of some weakness, acute financial instability can always be explained ex post by some form of policy mistake even if one is not detected ex ante. Each major round of crisis teaches us new sources of weakness in a never-ending process of wisdom after the fact. Opponents to an aggiornamento typically emphasize the latest wisdom.

Structural microeconomic weaknesses do not systematically call for strict macroeconomic policies. One striking feature of the Asian crisis has been the official denial that the lessons from the Great Depression and subsequent financial crises applied (especially the crisis of October 1987, as well as the

Scandinavian, UK and US banking crises of the 1980s and 1990s). Crises quickly produce a credit crunch that, if not treated adequately, is soon followed by a sharp contraction. In Asia as elsewhere, quickly rising unemployment, factory closures, relapse into poverty and lost incomes—not to mention political crises with profound longer-term implications—remind us of 1929. In contrast, at the outset of the more recent crises, country authorities promptly reacted by reliquifying financial markets and recapitalizing financial institutions with budgetary resources. Why not Asia?

In addition, excessive preoccupation with moral hazard leads to overlooking the trade-off with adverse selection. The systematic imposition of tight macroeconomic policies may discourage and delay applying for IMF programmes until it is too late. There must be an incentive for early application—and a cost for late application. The tools can be the traditional mix of conditionality and loan size.

SMALL LOANS ARE MORE EFFICIENT. A striking feature of the Mexican and Asian crises has been the massive increase in the size of packages organized by the IMF and financed by the World Bank and large bilateral donors. The IMF has provided little explanation for this new phenomenon (which also leads to an unhealthy blurring of the distinction between the IMF and the World Bank). Ostensibly, these amounts correspond to external debt repayment that comes due over some unspecified horizon. There also seems to be a belief that large amounts are needed to quiet markets as they start panicking. This is illusory. The IMF's pockets are far too shallow to raise the ante in a world of free capital movements.

When speculative attacks occur, no finite amount of money can stop liberalized financial markets. There is a better strategy. The IMF's stamp of approval—based on the technical competence of its staff, not on the amount of funds committed—remains highly valuable. For decades the IMF's strategy has been leverage: small IMF loans would trigger larger amounts of private lending once the private sector has been reassured by the Fund's conditionality and surveillance. This strategy remains even more valid today.

LIMIT INTRUSIVE INTERVENTIONS. The IMF has developed expertise in dealing with macroeconomic mismanagement, a controversial practice because it effectively suspends some elements of sovereignty while inevitably redistributing income. But for its defence, the IMF can rely on two main arguments. First, market failures and international spillovers justify international interventions. Second, there is a fairly broad consensus of what constitutes "good" macroeconomic policies.

For many microeconomic policies, the second argument vanishes. In addition, the trade-off between intrusion and externalities is less favourable in this case. Many microeconomic externalities are pecuniary (a weak financial system leads to higher risk premiums), and most microeconomic interventions affect deeper aspects of sovereignty, particularly as they touch on property rights and income distribution. In the midst of a crisis such interventions are inevitably seen as blackmail. And they take time to be implemented: once the crisis is over, they tend to be conveniently forgotten. Instead they ought to be part of a long-term strategy, as discussed in the next section.

ADAPTING POLICIES TO CAPITAL MOBILITY: TOWARDS A COHERENT APPROACH

This section brings together the foregoing analysis and makes concrete proposals, some of which are under study by the IMF as it reacts to the Asian crisis, and so could materialize shortly. Others will be controversial, but the evolution of official thinking has been so rapid since the end of 1997 that these proposals may soon look less outlandish.

Capital liberalization: reversing the logic

Financial market liberalization brings rewards in efficiency and resilience to shocks, but it also generates instability. Facing decades-old resistance—from governments, interest groups and often public opinions—the promoters of capital liberalization seem to have gambled that regulation and supervision would follow more or less automatically. It mostly has not. This approach is proving to be costly, leading to massive output losses, human distress and political turmoil, seriously weakening the valid case for liberalization.

SEQUENCING. International financial market liberalization should be the last step of a series that starts with the adoption of proper accounting standards and prudential measures consistent with the stage of development of markets—as well as the establishment of supervisory authorities. Accounting standards do not seem to be controversial and can be readily imported. Regulation is more complicated. For example, the Basle Committee's rules have been designed for developed country banks. Neither the risk weights nor the internal models are necessarily appropriate for developing countries. Similarly, supervision in developed countries is carried out by bodies that need to accumulate considerable experience and human capital before they are fully operational.

AUTHORIZATION TO LIBERALIZE. Current practice is to encourage countries to open up as soon as possible, often overlooking prudential measures. A better approach would be to reverse the logic and to set preconditions for the admission of liberalizing countries into international financial markets. Given the presence of powerful international externalities, individual countries should not be free to design prudential regulation if they intend to open up their financial markets.

If this logic is accepted, is it possible to cut off emerging financial institutions from global markets until they have adopted adequate prudential procedures? This is routinely done individually in the private sector as each financial institution carefully chooses with whom it conducts business. This selection process can be strengthened in five ways.

- First, Basle-type international standards can stipulate that financial deals with counterparts based in countries that are not implementing appropriate practices be assigned a special high-risk rating.
- Second, financial institutions from nonaccredited countries should not have direct access to payment systems. They would have to operate through institutions from accredited countries, which would have to reflect the associated risk.
- Third, foreign ownership of local financial institutions has proven to be an efficient way of spreading good practice. Emerging market authorities often want to nurture a fledgling domestic industry. Infant industry arguments usually conceal untold private interests at the expense of financial stability. Removing such protection should be a precondition.
- Fourth, rating agencies, which have done particularly poorly recently, should be supervised by an international agency, public or private. Although these services are privately provided and bought, past failures have been shown to have systemic effects that justify public concern. Some events may be truly unpredictable, but rating agencies may also be caught in conflicts of interests as well as collusive or herd behaviour.
- Fifth, international and national authorities should refrain from offering "too big to fail" guarantees to financial institutions, guarantees that can undermine the vigilance of private financial institutions.

EXCHANGE RATE REGIME. Exchange rate anchors tend to be kept in place long after their usefulness has been exhausted. The IMF, much as it was enforcing fixed exchange rates under the Bretton Woods system, could now do more to encourage exchange rate flexibility for countries that liberalize their capital accounts. Flexibility does not necessarily mean free floating. Bands of fluctuation allow significant flexibility if they are wide enough; if they are adjusted (discretely or through a crawl) to ensure that the equilibrium exchange rate is included in the band and if the monetary authorities refrain from enforcing implicit mini-bands inside the larger bands.

Some countries may decide to retain a fixed exchange rate regime. They should, as a precondition for capital liberalization, be requested to make the regime sturdy. One possibility is to explicitly establish the exchange rate anchor as the primary objective of monetary policy. In practice, this means either establishing a currency board or joining a monetary union. Another possibility is to establish market-friendly restrictions to capital movements of the type adopted in Chile, already mentioned.[13]

IMF interventions in the longer run: ex ante conditionality

The current period is, hopefully, one of transition.[14] As developing countries open to trade and capital movements, teething problems emerge. Living with some financial instability requires building institutions and accumulating human capital. Eventually, emerging economies will establish the kind of institutions now being refined in developed countries. In the meantime, the IMF invariably finds itself playing firefighter and subject to controversies because of the numerous trade-offs. The IMF's position would be more secure if, rather than deal with the consequences of instability, it were to promote faster adjustment. Its critics rightly argue that firefighting is a never-ending game—when pyromaniacs are allowed to roam freely. One possible approach is to complement traditional ex post conditionality with new ex ante conditionality.

The logic is simple. When financial markets are global, all countries have a stake in the financial conditions in any single country. A country that faces a crisis cannot be left alone: externalities, contagion and other market failures compel other countries to provide support. Moral hazard is unavoidable. In reaction, support is often too limited in speed and scope, harnessed by conditions better designed to protect the rescuers than the rescued and inevitably controversial. There is a "grand bargain": bailouts in exchange for surveillance and rule compliance. Bailouts without surveillance lead to moral hazard, but rule compliance reduces the likelihood of crises. Ex ante conditionality consists of creating "clubs" where this bargain could be replicated, with a credible threat of suspension of the guarantee in case of insufficient compliance.[15]

Ex ante conditionality is defined as follows. The IMF could set a number of rules that would have to be satisfied before a country is eligible for support. These rules would include the measures listed earlier: appropriate macroeconomic policies, information standards, established norms of regulation and supervision and possibly commitments for corruption, state intervention and openness. In most countries such standards cannot be achieved in a short time. The solution is for the IMF to make it known that, beyond a set date (possibly 10 years or more), it will support only countries that have been certified as satisfying all the preconditions.

How would such conditionality work? Many countries will undertake to match these conditions, and this alone should seriously diminish the likelihood of severe instability. In many ways these countries will have developed the kind of stability-enhancing measures in place in most developed countries. Severe instability will be rare, most likely the outcome of genuine bad luck or self-fulfilling attacks. Supporting such countries will not raise any of the moral hazard questions now plaguing rescue operations.

Other countries will be unable or unwilling to accept ex ante conditionality. If such a country faces acute financial instability, it will not be supported by an IMF loan. Undoubtedly its situation will then be disastrous, not just for the country but for others as well. That is why some important aspects need to be ironed out to make the proposal workable.

To start with, from the public good viewpoint, the question is whether other countries will suffer. Lenders and other parties to financial operations with that country will have known the situation beforehand and freely chosen risky behaviour. In most cases the externality will be pecuniary and thus not a justification for public intervention. But some cases will be more difficult. Trade partners and competitors will be underpriced once the exchange rate has crashed. In principle special protective measures could be temporarily imposed, but they would be too easy to evade. Similarly, trading partners will feel a decline in demand. In principle, ex post, some form of support is globally welfare-enhancing. The challenge is to design Pareto transfers that do not undermine the principle of ex ante conditionality. They could take the form of limited and severe ex post conditionality.

Who will be held accountable for rule compliance in each country? The private sector or the authorities? It will be the national authorities' responsibility to undertake the necessary reforms and build up adequate institutions. Countries could be eligible for technical and financial support—say, through World Bank loans. The national authorities will also have to exercise supervision over their private sectors. No one expects that supervision will be completely effective, but norms of regulation and supervisions can be developed and agreed on internationally.

Delinquent countries, while not eligible for loans, might still seek technical advice. There is no reason for the IMF, or any other agency, to turn down such requests. The IMF could even prepare and monitor full-fledged pro-grammes. And even without loans, such programmes will be attractive to a country in crisis if they help re-establish access to foreign private loans or if they result in lower interest premiums.

Objections can of course be raised. Clearly, the weak point is politics. Some countries are too big to fail and may gamble that they do not have to accept the conditions. What will happen if they are hit by a crisis? Once such a country is bailed out, what will be left of ex ante conditionality? But the same argument has not prevented the nearly universal adoption of bankruptcy laws, and truly exceptional bailouts of firms that are too big to fail seriously dent the integrity of bankruptcy proceedings.

A mellow version would be for the IMF, or another institution, to act as a watchdog of countries' compliance with proper financial stability-enhanc-ing standards, without the threat of denial of assistance in a crisis.

Institutions for orderly workouts

The recent crisis has brought to the forefront the moral hazard of private lenders to developing countries, in contrast to the moral hazard of the public sector discussed earlier. Claessens, Dooley and Warner (1995), among others, show that lenders typically escape unhurt from financial instability. They charge substantial premiums for loans to risky countries, sovereign and pri-vate. When a crisis erupts, they are the main beneficiaries of official assistance. This setup creates incentives for excessive and risky lending that in turn raises financial instability. Yet in a crisis the lenders still insist on full debt service, which often worsens the situation and further deepens instability. The two moral hazard problems (bailouts that weaken national discipline and bail-outs that encourage reckless lending) can be lessened by setting up proper institutions.

Eichengreen and Portes (1995) offer proposals for sovereign debtors, and some were adopted in the Rey Report commissioned by the G–10 (Group of Ten 1996). The aim is to allow for speedy agreed-on rescheduling of debt ser-vice. When there is a large number of creditors, each with both a veto right and the incentive to run for the door, it is hard to start negotiations—and even harder to reach agreement. The proposals contain two key elements. First, a clause incorporated into loan contracts would specify how a representative of the bondholders would be empowered to negotiate with a borrowing coun-try that faces a financial crisis. Second, the veto right would be replaced by qualified majority voting and sharing clauses. The proposals are sensible and were approved by the G–10 in June 1996. But implementation is bogged down by opposition from lenders, for obvious reasons.

The Rey Report's recommendations are not enough, however. The Asian crisis has revealed the importance of private borrowing in the mechanism that leads up to and deepens crises. Much as the Rey Report was prompted by the Mexican crisis of 1994–95, the Asian crisis of 1997 calls for similar arrangements for private borrowers. The need for standstills and reschedules for private borrowers is even more controversial than for sovereign borrowers.

Loans to private borrowers are normal commercial credit operations that fall under standard bankruptcy procedures in a default. Opponents to standstills have strong arguments. Why should a special clause be introduced just because the borrower is in a developing country? In addition, the Asian crisis has shown the danger of unhedged foreign currency borrowing. Hedging is standard practice in developed countries. Special covenants allowing firms to expect an easy way out of default would only worsen the moral hazard problem. There are, however, two crucially important counter-arguments.

First, markets may be missing: in most developing countries firms often cannot borrow internationally in their own currency and hedging instruments do not exist—or are prohibitively expensive. Second is the possibility of self-fulfilling crises. When the exchange rate depreciates to levels way below any sensible estimate of equilibrium, loans that were ex ante reasonable become unbearable (figure 3). Eventually the real exchange rate must return to equilibrium, either through a nominal appreciation, through inflation, or both. This will make it possible to resume debt service, but in the meantime burden-smoothing calls for a standstill on all debts, private and public.

This is achieved in three main steps. First, an institution must be put in charge of declaring a standstill. Second, international legislation has to apply to all arrangements, private as well as public, and to all debtors from the country declared in standstill. Third, a procedure must be established to organize subsequent negotiations on rescheduling. Each step raises formidable questions. Which institution should be in charge of declaring a standstill? The IMF has an obvious information advantage, but it faces conflicts of interest. It can be a lender itself, its board is dominated by lender countries and there exist obvious links between its own programmes, debt servicing and negotiations with debtors. A new, independent court might be needed for the task. The recent proposal to set up a world financial organization could be put to good use here.

This proposal clearly faces a serious moral hazard hurdle. It could make it too easy to reschedule private debts, and it could create constituencies

FIGURE 3

Real exchange rates in Asia

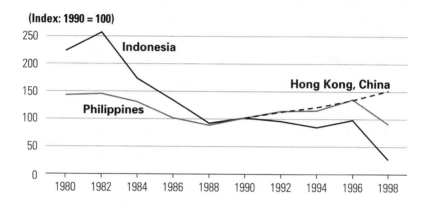

(Index: 1990 = 100)

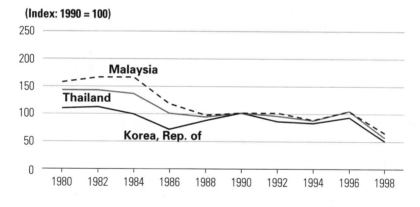

(Index: 1990 = 100)

Source: IMF 1998; The Economist, 20 June 1998.

within developing countries opposed to national efforts at establishing financial stability. In addition, lenders will react by raising the risk premium applied to all emerging market private borrowers, with possible negative effects on productive investment and growth. The first problem would be mitigated by ex ante conditionality, as proposed in the previous section. For the second issue, the prospect of the orderly resolution of a crisis might push down interest rates. In the end blanket private debt suspension is not unheard of: it occurred de facto in 1997–98, explicitly for the Republic of Korea and Russia, implicitly for Indonesia. The realistic question is not if but how.

Regional monetary funds

When capital has been liberalized, contagion can be rapid and widespread. During the Asian crisis the IMF had to react quickly to a rapidly deteriorating situation, facing all the trade-offs and difficulties described earlier. The mix of urgency and new challenges is a recipe for controversy and mistakes. Without passing judgement on that episode, one lesson is that the IMF is likely to commit errors in such a situation. Under the reasonable assumption that international financial stability will repeatedly come under stress in the years to come, it is highly likely that errors, small and big, will occur repeatedly. Good policy planning implies that this possibility be explicitly recognized and mitigating measures taken. The solution is diversification and debate.

An open debate before decisions are made can only help reduce the risk of major policy mistakes. The IMF is well known for the vigour of its internal debate, but also for its hierarchical structure. In the end, when all has been said and done, decisions are made by a very small number of people. This is as it should be for effectiveness, but it is conducive to errors. Furthermore, in a crisis there is a sharp limit on how much can be discussed publicly, so outside views, from observers who are not part of the hierarchy, are unlikely to be heard in good time.

Diversification in policy responses is made impossible by the de facto monopoly on policy advice that the IMF enjoys. The justification for monopoly is, presumably, that the IMF is the custodian of the world monetary order. Having more than one custodian would raise difficult issues of coordination and monitoring: rule enforcement cannot be subject to competition. But things have changed since Bretton Woods. The IMF is no longer enforcing a specific rule. Instead it is aiming to achieve the rather hazy goal of international financial stability. And it is not alone in this undertaking: other public and private, formal and informal institutions (G–7, G–10, IOSCO, IASC, the Basle Committee, rating agencies) share this responsibility. What makes the IMF unique is that it combines surveillance and conditional assistance. It alone can wag a stick and a carrot.

Surveillance does not require monopoly. Proximity to national authorities is an advantage in information and a disadvantage in freedom of speech and action. In fact, the IMF does not have a monopoly on surveillance. Its monopoly is limited to conditional assistance, and even there it has been pulling resources from other institutions and from governments. Its real monopoly lies in setting the terms of conditionality. This is where controversy lies and where mistakes can occur—and this is what has to be rethought.

How could there be competition in the realm of policy advice? Private advisers exist, but they do not provide multibillion-dollar loans.[16] Private financial institutions have already started to encroach on IMF territory. For example, George Soros has made large bridge loans to the Russian government. Because financial stability is a public good, competition should not come from the private sector, but there should be more IMFs. Much as the World Bank works alongside regional development banks, the IMF could operate alongside regional funds, as was suggested early on in the Asian crisis. This would be a step in the direction of subsidiarity.

The benefits would be competition in the design of stabilization programmes. Different approaches could be mooted, proposed, tried and analyzed. For example, the IMF's tight fiscal policy approach to the Asian crisis could have been implemented in some countries, while others could have opted for a different strategy of publicly funded stimulation of their imploded economies. It could be that, in the end, the experiment would have vindicated the IMF—but maybe not. Social experimentation is not to be encouraged because it can lead to dramatic social losses. But the IMF's unorthodox handling of the Asian crisis was clearly an experiment.[17]

This proposal is clearly far out on the scale of acceptability. No doubt, it is open to three serious objections. First, competition between regional IMFs could result in a decline of conditionality. Some regional funds might be tempted to increase their market share by offering lenient conditions, leading to disasters. That is a possibility. Yet only foolish funds would knowingly engage in such a competition. Easy-going funds would specialize in attracting governments eager to obtain international approval for mistaken policies. The result would be bad outcomes and costly salvage programmes. Ill-inspired funds would soon run out of resources. Their shareholders would replenish the coffers only if they expect to be in need of lenient treatment too. There would emerge clubs of bad countries and clubs of virtuous countries for all to see.[18] There is little doubt that, eventually, good policies would reward good funds and lead to the disappearance or reform of the bad funds. Of course, the transition could be disruptive and costly. This is not a valid argument for long-term institution building; what counts is the present value of the proposed architecture.

The second objection concerns the risk of politicization. Regional funds could pursue noneconomic goals and evolve into adversarial blocks. There is no evidence that the regional development banks have followed such a path. If successful, the existence of regional funds will dilute the power currently enjoyed by the large shareholders of the IMF. It is fair to recognize, however, that the current distribution of power in the IMF board is highly politicized, reflecting the political equilibrium of 1944. Some updating is long overdue—and should be seen as the natural and unavoidable consequence of the emergence of well-run economies around the world.

The third objection is that astute governments might use competition to withhold crucial information, providing some bits and pieces to the IMF and others to the regional funds, yet concealing the bigger picture. Given current efforts to disseminate accurate and complete information, this would be a step back. The solution would be an agreement to systematically share all available information among all the funds. But information asymmetries may be less at the regional level than at the international level, so regional funds could have a better understanding of their constituents' situations than the IMF does. This is the appeal of subsidiarity.

CONCLUSION

Financial instability is on the rise, the unavoidable consequence of the ongoing liberalization of capital movements. Financial instability hurts individual countries, but it also spreads across countries and continents. There is a need for the provision of financial stability as a world-wide public good.

Because financial instability originates in market failures, the first goal should be to correct these failures. This chapter argues that better information collection and dissemination, stability-oriented macroeconomic policies and improved regulation and supervision are steps in the right direction—but fall well short of eliminating instability, at least for many years to come. We have to accept financial instability as a fact and learn how to deal with crises when they occur.

The result is an exercise in policy actions that are second or third best. Making worse the inevitable trade-offs and judgement calls, financial markets generate multiple equilibria, opening the way not just for fundamentals-based crises but also for self-fulfilling crises. In a world of self-fulfilling crises, instability is no longer necessarily a result of bad policies or bad economic structures. This should lead us to rethink our policy prescriptions.

Part of the Asian debacle can be related to our ignorance of the mechanisms of financial instability. We do not have yet a clear view of what triggers self-fulfilling crises. We do not agree on how to prevent contagion without letting a country in crisis sink into recession. We do not understand well the trade-off between externalities and growth-enhancing policies. The dynamics of crises remain almost virgin territory, especially the tendency for exchange rates to depreciate beyond bounds. As a result policy responses tend to be designed with familiar analytical frameworks in mind, even though there is mounting evidence that these frameworks do not fit reality.

Part of the debacle is also related to conservative thinking. Yes, new ideas fresh from the academic press ought to be taken with a grain of salt. But the international policy-making establishment has been slow to recognize the new challenges of globalization. Too often, it seems, prudence is invoked to justify the continuing dominance of existing practices. The challenge is not just for economists to come up with better and more robust prescriptions. It is to rethink the world financial system.

This chapter has advanced precise proposals to rethink the world financial system. Some will appear doable—slowing down capital account liberalization, adopting market-friendly restrictions to capital flows, encouraging more exchange rate flexibility, designing a mechanism for orderly debt suspension and restructuring. Other proposals will seem unrealistic—setting preconditions for capital account liberalization, shifting to ex ante conditionality, establishing regional IMFs.

Before passing judgement, keep in mind that most of the doable proposals were considered highly unreasonable just a few years (or months) ago. The Asian crisis has given more respectability to views such as the need to retain capital controls until preconditions are met or the desirability of sovereign debt workouts. Under the unremitting pressure of events, conventional wisdom has been shaken up lately, and that is ultimately what always happens. It is hoped that the ideas here will be studied seriously before more crises create more disasters.

Notes

The author is grateful to Hans Genberg and Alex Swoboda for useful discussions and Xavier Debrun and Arjan Kadareja for excellent research assistance.

1. Crockett (1997) proposes a similar definition but also adds instability in financial institutions. Collapses of financial institutions either reflect sudden excessive asset price collapses and so are covered by the definition proposed here, or internal mismanagement in particular institutions (Continental Illinois, Barings, BCCI and so on) that is not systemic and should not be considered market instability.

2. While it is not clear when price responses are "excessive" (see Schiller 1981), the weight of evidence is that markets tend to overreact to news and occasionally even react to irrelevant news.

3. Information asymmetry has long been recognized as a major source of failure in financial markets. The seminal contribution of Stiglitz and Weiss (1981) has recently been applied to developing country crises by Calvo (1995), Mishkin (1996) and many others.

4. There is now a vast literature on multiple equilibria in financial markets, and in particular on foreign exchange markets following the seminal contribution of Obstfeld (1984). For overviews, see Krugman (1998) and Wyplosz (1998b).

5. The peso-problem effect means that the markets may still price the risk even if they put a very low probability on its occurrence. The argument presented here suggests that the markets may systematically underestimate the probability of self-fulfilling crises, for good reason. In that case the price is wrong.

6. Eichengreen, Rose and Wyplosz (1996) find that the occurrence of a crisis in one OECD country increases by 8 percentage points the probability of a crisis elsewhere in the OECD zone.

7. This section largely follows the classification presented in BIS (1997).

8. On the Tobin tax, see Haq, Kaul and Grunberg (1996). On the Chilean experience, see Cowan and de Gregorio (1997).

9. This statement needs to be qualified because simple statistics suggest otherwise. World average annual growth of GNP per capita (evaluated in 1987 US dollars) was 1.0% in the 1970s, 0.2% in the 1980s and 0.3% during 1990–93, so the early 1990s do not exhibit better performance. Nor has global growth become more uniform, as the standard deviation across countries increased from 1.3 during the 1970s and 1980s to 1.7 during 1990–93. Numerous other factors (such as wars) should be taken into account (World Bank 1997). Eatwell (1997) goes further, arguing that financial liberalization has actually hurt growth. This view is critically reviewed in Grunberg (1998).

10. For example, Giavazzi and Pagano (1988) argue that a fixed exchange rate regime is a way of constraining policy choices to deliver a better outcome. Similarly, Debrun (1997) argues that the Stability Pact, adopted as part of the European Monetary Union, is designed to bring outside pressure to bear on the design of stable fiscal policies.

11. In standard probability theory a type I error occurs when signals fail to detect an impending crisis. A type II error occurs when a warning is issued but no crisis actually takes place. The occurrence of type I errors is reduced by issuing more warnings, but this increases the number of type II errors, and conversely.

12. This statement ignores politics and corruption. There may exist (numerous) cases where politically motivated bilateral aid is large enough to prevent

crises and the need to apply for IMF support. It is also possible that the ruling class privatizes foreign support so that the balance of social costs and benefits becomes irrelevant.

13. For an analysis of market-friendly restrictions to speculative capital, see Eichengreen, Tobin and Wyplosz (1995). For a discussion of alternatives, see Wyplosz (1998c). For a description of the Chilean case, see Cowan and de Gregorio (1997).

14. The idea developed in this section originated in a discussion with Alan Meltzer who should not, however, be held responsible for the present formulation.

15. This principle is similar to the one that underpins George Soros's proposal to set up an international credit insurance corporation. Soros's idea is in fact closer to the "authorization to liberalize" proposal presented before.

16. The much-publicized feud between Jeffrey Sachs and the IMF reflects this situation. Sachs is acting as a private adviser who occasionally reaches different conclusions. To compete with the IMF he can only try to trigger financial support from other sources and, if that fails, to raise his voice.

17. Orthodoxy in the face of a demand collapse calls for Keynesian policies.

18. One merit of this process of self-selection is that it would deal with the problem of lack of legitimacy of the IMF. The IMF is often seen as a US-led agency bent on imposing technocratic views. By cooperating with regional funds, the IMF would establish itself as a willingly chosen partner. Currently the IMF is often used by governments as a scapegoat to impose policies that they privately support but cannot propose or defend for political reasons.

REFERENCES

BIS (Bank for International Settlements). 1996. *Annual Report.* Basle, Switzerland.

————. 1997. *Financial Stability in Emerging Market Economies.* Draghi Report of the Working Party on Financial Stability in Emerging Market Economies. Basle, Switzerland.

Calvo, Guillermo. 1995. "Varieties of Capital Market Crises." University of Maryland, Center for International Economics, College Park.

CEPR (Centre for Economic Policy Research). 1998. *Financial Crises and Asia.* CEPR Conference Report 6. London.

Claessens, Stijn, Michael Dooley and Andrew Warner. 1995. "Portfolio Capital Flows: Hot or Cool?" *World Bank Economic Review* 9(1): 153–74.

Cowan, Kevin, and José de Gregorio. 1997. "Exchange Rate Policies and Capital Account Management: Chile in the 1990s." Serie economica 22. University of Chile, Santiago.

Crockett, Andrew. 1997. "Why Is Financial Stability a Goal of Public Policy?" In Federal Reserve Bank of Kansas City, *Maintaining Financial Stability in a Global Economy*. Kansas City.

Debrun, Xavier. 1997. "A Simple Model of Fiscal Restraints under Monetary Union." Graduate Institute of International Studies, Geneva.

Eatwell, John. 1997. *International Financial Liberalization: The Impact on World Development*. ODS Discussion Paper 12. New York: United Nations Development Programme, Office of Development Studies.

The Economist. 1998. "Emerging Market Indicators." 20 June.

Eichengreen, Barry, and Richard Portes. 1995. "Crisis? What Crisis? Orderly Workouts for Sovereign Debtors." Centre for Economic Policy Research, London.

Eichengreen, Barry, and Charles Wyplosz. 1993. "The Unstable EMS." *Brookings Papers on Economic Activity 1*. Washington, D.C.: Brookings Institution.

Eichengreen, Barry, Andrew Rose and Charles Wyplosz. 1995. "Exchange Market Mayhem: The Antecedents and Aftermath of Speculative Attacks." *Economic Policy* 21: 249–312.

———. 1996. "Contagious Currency Crises: First Tests." *Scandinavian Journal of Economics* 98(4): 463–84.

Eichengreen, Barry, James Tobin and Charles Wyplosz. 1995. "Two Cases for Sand in the Wheels of International Finance." *Economic Journal* 105(428): 162–72.

Frankel, Jeffrey, and Andrew Rose. 1996. "Currency Crashes in Emerging Markets: An Empirical Treatment." *Journal of International Economics* 41(3–4): 351–66.

Giavazzi, Francesco, and Marco Pagano. 1988. "The Advantage of Tying One's Hands: EMS Discipline and Central Bank Credibility." *European Economic Review* 32(5): 1055–74.

Group of Ten. 1996. *The Resolution of Sovereign Liquidity Crises: A Report to the Ministers and Governors* (Rey Report). Basle, Switzerland.

Grunberg, Isabelle, ed. 1998. *Perspectives on International Financial Liberalization*. ODS Discussion Paper 15. New York: United Nations Development Programme, Office of Development Studies.

Haq, Mahbub ul, Inge Kaul and Isabelle Grunberg, eds. 1996. *The Tobin Tax*. New York: Oxford University Press.

IMF (International Monetary Fund). 1998. *International Financial Statistics*. CD-ROM. Washington, DC.

Kindleberger, Charles. 1939. "Speculation and Forward Exchange." *Journal of Political Economy* 47: 176–85.

Krugman, Paul. 1998. "Currency Crises." Massachusetts Institute of Technology, Department of Economics, Cambridge, MA.

Milesi-Ferretti, Gianmaria, and Assaf Razin. 1998. "Determinants and Consequences of Current Account Reversals and Currency Crises." International Monetary Fund, Washington, DC.

Mishkin, Frederic. 1996. "Understanding Financial Crises: A Developing Country Perspective." NBER Working Paper 5600. National Bureau for Economic Research, Cambridge, MA.

Obstfeld, Maurice. 1984. "Multiple Stable Equilibria in an Optimizing Perfect-Foresight Model." *Econometrica* 52(1): 223–28.

Sachs, Jeffrey, and Stephen Radelet. 1998. "The East Asian Financial Crisis: Diagnosis, Remedies, Prospects." Harvard University, Harvard Institute for International Development, Cambridge, MA.

Sachs, Jeffrey, Aaron Tornell and Andrès Velasco. 1996. "The Collapse of the Mexican Peso: What Have We Learned." *Economic Policy* 22: 13–64.

Schiller, Robert J. 1981. "Do Stock Prices Move Too Much to Be Justified by Subsequent Changes in Dividends?" *American Economic Review* 71(3): 421–36.

Stiglitz, Joseph, and Andrew Weiss. 1981. "Credit Rationing in Markets with Imperfect Information." *American Economic Review* 71(3): 393–410.

World Bank. 1997. *Global Development Finance.* CD-ROM. Washington, DC.

Wyplosz, Charles. 1998a. "Globalized Financial Markets and Financial Crises." Graduate Institute of International Studies, Geneva.

―――. 1998b. "International Capital Market Failures: Sources, Costs and Solutions." Graduate Institute of International Studies, Geneva.

―――. 1998c. "Speculative Attacks and Capital Mobility." Graduate Institute of International Studies, Geneva.

ENVIRONMENT AND CULTURAL HERITAGE

MONTREAL VERSUS KYOTO:
INTERNATIONAL COOPERATION AND THE GLOBAL ENVIRONMENT
Scott Barrett

NEW STRATEGIES FOR THE PROVISION OF GLOBAL PUBLIC GOODS:
LEARNING FROM INTERNATIONAL ENVIRONMENTAL CHALLENGES
Geoffrey Heal

CULTURAL HERITAGE AS PUBLIC GOOD:
ECONOMIC ANALYSIS APPLIED TO HISTORIC CITIES
Ismail Serageldin

Over the past 10 years international environmental cooperation has risen to the top of the international policy agenda. From the many environmental issues now on this agenda, we focus here on two, ozone depletion and climate change, to illustrate some of the critical policy challenges posed by global public goods. The first two chapters in this section address two key dimensions of cooperation—how to build effective international treaties to coordinate national policies that affect the global environment, and when and how to use markets for the provision of global public goods in the environmental arena. The third chapter examines a problem common to many environmental issues—establishing a sound valuation methodology for nontraded goods— and applies it to the preservation of culture and cultural goods.

Scott Barrett's chapter poses a seemingly simple question: if the Montreal Protocol has been so successful in reducing the production and use of ozone-depleting substances, why can't an effective treaty to control greenhouse gas emissions be put into place? His examination of these issues reveals two findings. First, the underlying economics of addressing climate change and ozone depletion are different. A study that guided policymakers at an early stage of ozone negotiations found that the costs of reducing ozone-depleting substances were small relative to the benefits. In contrast, the best studies available today suggest that the costs of reducing greenhouse gas emissions by a substantial amount match or exceed the benefits. Second, Barrett argues that in the absence of a central global authority, international treaties must be self-enforcing or must include credible incentives for compliance and disincentives to discourage noncompliance. Thus the Montreal Protocol, while effective, cannot simply be redrafted to address the climate change problem. Rather, reducing greenhouse gases poses new challenges for burden-sharing and effective implementation.

Geoffrey Heal's chapter describes the changing world of public goods. As he explains, privatization and technological advances have combined to change the very nature of public goods provision in many respects. In the environmental field, in addition, there exists a growing volume of privately produced global public bads, such as pollution. In response, Heal suggests using markets to foster the private provision of public goods. If properly structured, markets can solve the problems posed by this type of good. The chapter describes how a global market in pollution permits could reduce pollution levels while assuring an efficient and equitable distribution of the costs of emission reductions. In a second example of the power of markets to overcome cooperation dilemmas, Heal describes how early actions by large firms or countries can accelerate environmental reforms by smaller actors through a process of adoption spillovers.

Ismail Serageldin shows that crude cost-benefit analysis is often a poor guide to solving issues of the environment but also those of culture. Both can have economic as well as intrinsic value that is commonly recognized, if not valued. For methodologically similar problems such as these, cost-benefit analysis must be complemented by new analytical instruments. Beyond the criterion of use value, used for private goods, Serageldin highlights the relevance of nonextractive value, including existence value. For example, the value of a cultural site goes beyond the amount that the site is able to generate in terms of tourist dollars. Unique sites have value for the world at large, not just for residents and visitors. Serageldin suggests private-public partnerships to ensure the revitalization of priceless sites such as old cities, offering the examples of the historical districts of Hafsia, Tunis, and Fez, Morocco.

MONTREAL VERSUS KYOTO

International Cooperation and the Global Environment

Scott Barrett

Stratospheric ozone depletion and climate change have much in common. Both environmental problems are global in that all countries emit ozone-depleting substances and greenhouse gases, all are affected by such emissions and effective management of these problems requires cooperation involving many if not all countries. Reductions in the use of ozone-depleting chemicals and in the emission of greenhouse gases are global public goods. Ozone depletion and climate change are global public bads.

Although these problems are superficially similar, the provision of these public goods has been different. International agreements on stratospheric ozone depletion are effectively ridding the world of the most harmful ozone-depleting substances. By contrast, international agreements on global climate change, if implemented to the letter, will only dampen growth in greenhouse gas emissions. To be sure, international cooperation for both problems is still developing. Cooperation in ozone layer protection, codified in the Montreal Protocol and its associated agreements, could unravel, perhaps helped by a thriving black market in banned substances. Cooperation in climate protection could increase as the Kyoto Protocol is implemented and perhaps amended and revised. So far, however, cooperation has been more successful in the case of ozone depletion. Why?

The reason is not that climate change is a more recent discovery and subject to far greater uncertainties. That the world's climate would change as concentrations of greenhouse gases increased was observed a century ago, whereas the theory linking chemicals such as chlorofluorocarbons (CFCs) to ozone depletion was not published until 1974. And while the uncertainties about climate change are substantial, they are no more so than were the uncertainties about ozone layer depletion when the Montreal Protocol was negotiated in 1987. As Richard Benedick (1997), the chief US negotiator at the Montreal Protocol talks, put it:

> We seem to have forgotten that [the case for the Montreal Protocol] was completely theoretical. Measurements did not in fact record any thinning of the ozone layer, except over Antarctica, a seasonal occurrence which scientists at the time considered a special case, and for which there were numerous theories. There was, moreover, no evidence that CFCs were responsible. Finally, there was no sign of increased ultraviolet radiation actually reaching the Earth.

The reason for the different outcomes seems instead to spring from a lack of political will. But why should political will support more cooperation for ozone protection than for climate change mitigation?

This chapter shows that the relative success of international cooperation depends on the economics of the problem and the design of the treaty intending to remedy it. The economics of the problem—meaning the benefits and costs of providing a global public good—are largely given. The terms of the treaty intended to sustain cooperation, by contrast, are chosen. So the world's diplomatic corps can make a difference.

But a treaty is subject to some constraints; the most important is that it must be self-enforcing. This means that countries are free to choose whether to be a signatory to an agreement seeking to provide a global public good. Negotiating a treaty that sustains near-universal participation and requires that each signatory provide a substantial amount of environmental protection is the principal challenge to diplomacy.

The treaty mechanisms that diplomats can choose, when subject to the constraint of self-enforcement, depend in turn on the economics of the problem. It is easy enough for diplomats to design a self-enforcing treaty that promises to reward countries for participating (carrots) and threatens to punish them for not participating (sticks), just as it is easy to write a treaty that requires that every signatory undertake substantial abatement. Making these promises and threats credible is another matter. To be credible, the countries called on to punish nonparticipation, for example, must be better off in carrying out the threat than ignoring it. But in punishing others, a country almost always harms itself, the extent of which again depends on the economics of the problem. Too often the threats needed to deter nonparticipation (free riding) will not be credible. In other words, it is simplistic to say that the Montreal Protocol should serve as a template for a climate change agreement. If the economics of climate change are different, then the international system may not be able to replicate the success of Montreal in a climate change agreement.

In contrast to some other chapters in this volume, the analysis here is centred on the state. To be sure, other institutions—international organizations, firms, nonprofit organizations, research communities—also help determine outcomes. And in some cases these other institutions can even outperform governments in supplying public goods. But government is special. Unlike all other institutions, the state has the power to coerce; it can tax its citizens and use this money to pay for the provision of public goods. Moreover, I am concerned here with the performance of two treaties—and treaties are contracts between states. Other institutions will affect treaty outcomes, but for the problems investigated here, none is as important as the state.[1]

Still, the state is not a monolith, as I implicitly assume in parts of this chapter. The problem might be cast in a public choice framework—one that recognizes that a state's negotiators are influenced by a number of constituencies. But even this level of analysis would not suffice, for the theory should also explain how these constituencies are organized, how a state's political institutions take account of the interests of these constituencies and so on. Ultimately, the appropriate unit for the analysis of global public goods problems should be the individual, the citizen. The theory should explain the existence of all relevant institutions—including the state—as serving the interests of individuals, however imperfectly (if we require a unifying theory, it would probably be the theory of transactions costs; see Dixit 1996). Lacking such a theory, I rely on a state-centred approach in the analysis that follows, despite recent scholarship that hints at possible connections between domestic political institutions and the supply of global public goods.[2]

BACKGROUND TO THE NEGOTIATIONS

Stratospheric ozone depletion and the Montreal Protocol

In the mid-1970s atmospheric scientists predicted that CFC emissions could eventually deplete the ozone layer by as much as 7%, a level sufficient to increase skin cancers and cataracts and reduce agricultural and fishery productivity. Though inconclusive, these predictions motivated several countries, including the United States, to restrict unilaterally the production and use of CFCs. As a result global CFC consumption stabilized through the early 1980s. But with growth in the use of CFCs for other purposes (for example, use in the manufacture of computer chips more than doubled between 1975 and 1982) and in other countries, overall consumption and production began to increase.

In 1977 the United Nations Environment Programme (UNEP) convened an International Conference on the Ozone Layer, which recommended that negotiations begin on a treaty for ozone protection. The result of these efforts, the Vienna Convention for the Protection of the Ozone Layer, was completed in 1985. While the convention created a framework agreement to guide future cooperative efforts, it imposed no requirement on signatories to reduce CFC emissions.

Just two months after the agreement was reached, however, the British Antarctic Survey reported that between 1977 and 1985 the ozone layer over the Antarctic had been depleted by 40%. Coupled with renewed growth in global consumption of CFCs, the discovery of the ozone hole spurred the US Environmental Protection Agency and UNEP to join forces in a new atmospheric ozone study. This study, which confirmed the British findings, formed the basis for a new agreement and culminated in the signing of the Montreal Protocol in late 1987.

The protocol required that the production and consumption of some CFCs be halved (from 1986 levels) by 1999 and that production and consumption of some halons (used in fire protection) be held at 1986 levels. The protocol entered into force on January 1, 1989, with 30 signatories (including the then European Community) that together accounted for 83% of global consumption of the listed substances (Parson 1993).

But the Montreal Protocol was soon shown to be inadequate. Thus at the second meeting of the signatories, held in London in June 1990, the protocol was amended. The number of controlled substances was increased from 8 to 20, and the original 50% reduction was increased to a full phase-out. Furthermore, the London amendments sought to increase participation in the convention among developing countries. In line with this objective, industrial country parties offered to pay developing country parties for the incremental costs of complying with the agreement.

Further tightening of the convention was undertaken in Copenhagen in November 1992. Phase-out dates were brought forward (for CFCs, for example, to 1996 from 1999), and the number of substances covered was increased to 94. An additional amendment, negotiated again in Montreal, focused on noncompliance, introducing a licensing system and other steps to reduce black market trade in ozone-depleting substances. All the while, participation in the Montreal Protocol has risen. By late 1998, 165 countries were parties to the Montreal Protocol, and virtually all nonparties lack an effective municipal government.

Global climate change and the Kyoto Protocol

In 1896 Svante Arrhenius, a Swedish chemist, calculated that a doubling in the atmospheric concentration of carbon dioxide (CO_2), brought about by the burning of fossil fuels, would increase global mean temperature by about 5 degrees Celsius. In retrospect this was a remarkable prediction. But not until the 1980s did a near consensus begin to emerge about the direction of climate change and the need to reduce growth in atmospheric concentrations of greenhouse gases.

The Intergovernmental Panel on Climate Change (IPCC) was largely responsible for this progress. The panel was formed in 1988 to report on what was known about climate change, its potential impact and what could be done to forestall or adapt to it. The panel's first working group calculated in 1990 that emissions of the long-lived gases, including carbon dioxide, would have to be reduced by more than 60% just to stabilize their concentration at the current level (IPCC 1990).

After the panel's report was published, most OECD countries announced their intention to reduce their CO_2 emissions, though different countries chose different targets (see IEA 1992). But in contrast to the case of ozone depletion, most countries have not lived up to their unilateral commitments to reduce greenhouse gas emissions. Only a few countries backed their commitments with an implementation plan, and none guaranteed that its targets would be met.

In May 1992 the international community concluded more than a year's negotiations to produce a Framework Convention on Climate Change. The final text of the framework convention, which was signed by more than 150 countries at the Rio "Earth Summit," did not specify targets for greenhouse gas emissions reduction. Instead, article 2 of the agreement recognizes "that the return by the end of the present decade to earlier levels of anthropogenic emissions of carbon dioxide and other greenhouse gases" would be desirable, and that parties to the agreement should devise policies "with the aim of returning individually or jointly to their 1990 levels of these anthropogenic emissions".

In the spring of 1995 the first meeting of the Conference of Parties to the Framework Convention on Climate Change was held in Berlin. It was agreed that industrial countries should set limits on emissions and reduction target objectives within specified time frames. This move was intended to initiate negotiation of a protocol similar to the Montreal Protocol by the end of 1997.

Despite strong opposition in the US Senate to the formula agreed on in Berlin (calling for reduced emissions in industrial countries without similar obligations for developing countries), the Clinton administration endorsed this framework at the next Conference of Parties to the Framework Convention on Climate Change, held in 1997 in Kyoto, Japan. But the Kyoto Protocol will only become binding on the United States if it is ratified by the Senate, and without this ratification the Kyoto Protocol might not come into force. To come into force, the agreement must be ratified by 55 countries that together account for at least 55% of the 1990 CO_2 emissions of the so-called Annex I countries—that is, industrial countries, including the United States and European economies in transition. By October 1998, 59 countries had signed the protocol, including 21 Annex I countries (accounting for about 39% of Annex I emissions). Only one country has ratified the agreement (Fiji).

THE ECONOMICS OF GLOBAL ENVIRONMENTAL PROTECTION

Although these two sets of negotiations (one to protect the ozone layer, the other to reduce greenhouse gas emissions) have had very different results, much about these problems is similar. In both cases countries have recognized the need for international cooperation, scientists have been uncertain about the consequences of policy choices and different concerns have been voiced by rich and poor countries about who was responsible for taking action and paying for it.

But the differences are more striking. More unilateral abatement was undertaken to protect the ozone layer than the climate, and more international cooperation has been sustained for ozone layer protection than for climate change mitigation. Even before being amended, the Montreal Protocol required reductions in emissions of up to 50% by all parties, whereas the Kyoto Protocol asks for just a 5% reduction by a subset of countries.

The simple theory of international cooperation

Provision of a global public good (such as cutting CFC or CO_2 emissions) by any country benefits every country. But only the countries that provide the good pay for its provision. So each country may prefer that others provide the public good, with the result that little of the good will be provided in total.

Countries would do better if the public good were provided jointly. But because of incentives to free ride, this is easier said than done.

The essential problem is routinely described by the well-known prisoner's dilemma. However, this representation of international cooperation is usually not appropriate. The prisoner's dilemma is a 2 x 2 game, meaning that it is played by two players, each of which has a binary action set (each can, say, abate or pollute). The global public goods game is played by 200 or so countries, each of which has a continuous action set (each can abate anywhere from 0–100% of its gross emissions). The payoffs in the prisoner's dilemma make choosing to pollute a dominant strategy—meaning that each country would choose to pollute rather than abate, irrespective of the choices of all other countries. It is more likely, however, that the amount of abatement undertaken by any country will depend on the amounts undertaken by others. For some countries choosing to abate may be the preferred strategy, irrespective of what other countries do.

In the absence of an all-embracing agreement, countries are likely to provide too little abatement. But how much is too little? Full cooperation in providing a public good requires that each country provide an amount that equates the marginal cost of provision for each country to the aggregate marginal benefit—calculated as the sum of the marginal benefits to all countries. National self-interest, however, commends a different formula for provision: that each country provide an amount that equates the marginal cost of provision to its own marginal benefit.

One possible representation of the problem is shown in figure 1 for N symmetric countries (see also Barrett 1990, 1994). Here the marginal cost of abatement for a country increases with the quantity of abatement undertaken by that country. The marginal benefit of abatement, meanwhile, decreases with the total quantity of abatement undertaken by all countries. If countries fail to cooperate, they will each abate up to the level where $MB_i = MC_i$. If they cooperate fully, they will each abate up to the point where $N \cdot MB_i = MC_i$. The latter level is likely to exceed the former, with the magnitude of the difference depending on N and the slopes of the MB and MC schedules. All else being equal, the larger is N, the larger will be the gap between the noncooperative and fully cooperative outcomes.

If MC_i is flat and MB_i is steep, substantial abatement will be undertaken by all countries unilaterally. Cooperation will not improve matters much in this case. If MC_i is steep and MB_i is flat, very little abatement will be undertaken, even if countries cooperate fully. If MC_i and MB_i are both flat, there

FIGURE 1

The potential gains to cooperation

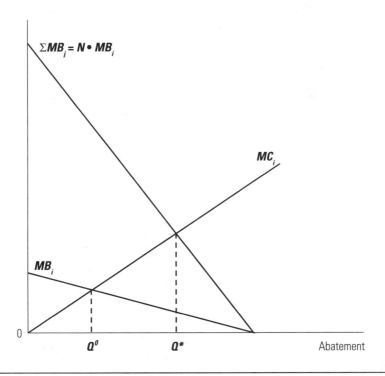

will be a substantial difference in the level of abatement undertaken in the noncooperative and full cooperative outcomes (that is, $Q^* - Q^0$ will be large) but this difference will not matter much in net benefit terms. Finally, if MC_i and MB_i are both steep, the difference in abatement between the two outcomes will be great, and so will be the difference in net benefit terms. It is for this type of problem that cooperation is needed most.

This is for symmetric countries. What happens when one considers important asymmetries? In general, asymmetry will shrink the difference between the noncooperative and fully cooperative outcomes (Olson 1965; Barrett 1998). Suppose, for example, that there are 100 countries, 3 of which are very large in the sense that they account for the bulk of global emissions and will benefit most from global abatement. Then it is almost as if there are only 3 countries; the other 97 do not matter much for this problem. The 3 large countries are likely to undertake substantial provision of the public good themselves because each will capture a large share of the total benefit of its own provision. The 97 others would do little if anything to provide the good, but their behaviour would not matter much relative to the total provision. It is in this sense that the need for global cooperation is less when countries are asymmetric.

This also assumes that the marginal abatement cost and benefit curves take on the shapes illustrated in figure 1 (that is, that the underlying total benefit and cost relations are quadratic). They may not take these shapes, and there is the added difficulty that these curves may be known only with uncertainty. Still, for many specifications the basic insights of the above analysis will hold.

The economics of ozone depletion

The economics of reducing ozone depletion have been outlined by the US Environmental Protection Agency (USEPA 1988a, 1988b). The USEPA presents three future scenarios for reducing ozone depletion—no controls are adopted by any country; only the United States adopts the requirements of the original Montreal Protocol; and, the most likely outcome, the original Montreal Protocol controls are adopted by 94% of industrial countries and 65% of developing countries, with all participating nations complying fully.

The USEPA concludes that the Montreal Protocol would reduce ozone depletion substantially—from 50% (if no controls were adopted) to only 1.2% if all signatories complied fully with the Montreal Protocol targets by 2100 (table 1).[3] The calculations also show that unilateral action by the United States alone would have a significant short-term effect on ozone depletion but virtually no impact by 2100, demonstrating yet again the need for international cooperation.

Benefits and costs for each of the three scenarios were calculated for the United States only. By far the largest benefit was the avoidance of cancer-related illnesses and deaths due to multilateral or unilateral policies. The study found that by 2165 implementation of the Montreal Protocol would avoid more than 245 million US cancer cases and more than 5 million early deaths. Costs for cancer illness were taken to be costs of treatment, and costs for cancer deaths were taken to be the value of a statistical life, estimated by the USEPA at $3 million. The present value of net benefits from avoided cancer deaths is counted in trillions of dollars. By contrast, the remaining benefits add up to only a few tens of billions.

TABLE 1

Implications of the Montreal Protocol and unilateral action on ozone depletion

Ozone depletion (%) by	No controls	Montreal Protocol	Unilateral implementation of Montreal Protocol by the United States
2000	1.0	0.8	0.9
2050	15.7	1.9	10.3
2100	50.0	1.2	49.0
Benefits and costs to the United States (billions of 1985 US dollars)			
Benefits	–	3,575	1,373
Costs	–	21	21
Net benefits	–	3,554	1,352

Source: USEPA 1988b.

The costs of abatement depend on the ease with which products that do not use ozone-depleting substances can be substituted for products that do use them, other substances can be substituted for ozone-depleting substances in the production of products that use them and the current stock of ozone-depleting substances can be reclaimed for future use. Estimation of these costs is complicated by the fact that innovation is required to develop substitutes for ozone-depleting substances and to engineer processes that can use these substitutes. Furthermore, the costs will depend on the policies used to implement the Montreal Protocol. If economic instruments were used instead of standards, for example, costs would likely be lower. However, these uncertainties are not crucial to our analysis.

As table 1 shows, the USEPA's estimated range of costs (in present value terms) is small relative to the benefits. The basic economics of stratospheric ozone policy thus imply that for the United States (and probably every other industrial country), the benefits of adopting the Montreal Protocol exceed the costs by a wide margin, irrespective of the behaviour of other countries.

That industrial countries had strong unilateral incentives to undertake substantial abatement is also suggested by the earlier unilateral abatement undertaken by the United States and some other countries. Still, the case for unilateral action is probably overstated by the USEPA's analysis, which ignores the possibility of leakage—that is, if one country (or group) cuts production of substances covered by the protocol, production may simply shift to other countries. If leakage is severe enough, unilateral abatement may only redistribute production and have no long-term effect on total emissions. One reason for having an international agreement would be to plug this potential leak. Another reason would be to create incentives for countries with less favourable unilateral incentives to also undertake abatement for the global good. These issues are taken up later in this chapter.

Amazingly, the economics of ozone policy became even more favourable after the USEPA produced its estimates—substitutes for CFCs proved easier and less costly to produce than expected. In February 1990 the US Council of Economic Advisors said that a complete phase-out was not only feasible but cheap. "Preliminary estimates," the council reported, "place the U.S. costs of a phase-out of CFCs and halons by 2000 at $2.7 billion over the next decade if the schedule of intermediate reductions currently incorporated in the Montreal Protocol is maintained" (p. 210). This estimate is almost a tenth of the USEPA's, which was calculated for meeting the much weaker targets specified in the original Montreal Protocol.

The economics of climate change

More controversial and more uncertain are the economics of climate change. Nordhaus's (1991) comprehensive analysis concluded that global emissions of CO_2 should be reduced only slightly (by about 2%). Cline (1992) questioned the assumptions underlying this work and concluded that an aggressive international abatement programme was justified. Later, Nordhaus (1994) refined his methodology, but again concluded that "a massive effort to slow climate change today would be premature given current understanding of the damages imposed by greenhouse warming". Although there are many studies on the economics of climate change, these two views succinctly represent the range of current economic opinion.

Drawing on the larger literature (as summarized in IPCC 1995), estimates of damage to the United States of a doubling in CO_2 concentrations (expressed as a percentage of GDP) are very similar, partly because most studies use similar data. In 1991 Nordhaus calculated damage to be around 0.25%

of GDP, though in 1994 he raised this to 1% to include "a precautionary guess as to the magnitude of 'surprises' from climate change". Although the data do not allow a direct comparison, the expected damages from climate change appear to be about the same order of magnitude as the expected damages from ozone depletion.[4]

Estimates of the costs of reducing CO_2 emissions in the United States are also broadly similar (table 2). All these estimated costs for modest reductions in CO_2 emissions are large relative to the damages. But if long-term warming is, say, 10 degrees Celsius, damages could climb as high as 20% of GDP (IPCC 1996).Because an abatement policy would be able to prevent only part of these damages, however, the total benefits from abatement would be less than 20% of GDP. So even under the most pessimistic damage scenario, the cost-benefit calculus for climate change looks very different from the estimates for ozone depletion. According to this analysis, the costs of undertaking substantial abatement would equal a large portion of the benefits thereby created.

Estimates for US damage associated with a doubling in CO_2 concentrations are at one point in time and in one location. To convert these figures into global marginal benefits requires a number of assumptions. Although there are some estimates of damages for the rest of the world, it is usually assumed that US damages can be prorated across the entire world (either in aggregate or by sector), and both Nordhaus and Cline proceed in this way. Information

TABLE 2

Selected estimates of climate change damage and CO_2 abatement costs for the United States

(% of GDP)

Study	Damage from a doubling of CO_2 concentrations	Cost model[a]	Abatement cost	
			Stabilization	20% reduction
Cline	1.1	Jorgenson-Wilcoxen	0.6	1.7
Fankhauser	1.3	Edmonds-Reilly	0.4	1.1
Tol	1.5	Manne-Richels	0.7	1.5
Nordhaus	1.0	Martin-Burniaux	0.2	0.9

a. Cost estimates are from a study by the Energy Model Forum of Stanford University, which ran 14 cost models using common assumptions and standardizing for the emission reduction scenarios shown above.
Source: IPCC 1996, tables 6.4 and 9.4; Nordhaus 1994.

is also needed about the nature of the damage function, and virtually nothing is known about this. Studies of damage costs have assumed that damages are anything from a linear to a quadratic to a cubic function of temperature change. Nordhaus (1994) claims that "there is evidence that the impact increases sharply as the temperature increases" (p. 56) and therefore assumes that damage is quadratic in temperature increases. Cline also considers the case where damage is quadratic. This assumption, by the way, is consistent with the damage function shown in figure 1.

Several estimates of the marginal benefit of abatement—that is, the damage avoided by a one ton reduction in CO_2 emissions—lie between the estimates calculated by Nordhaus and Cline (table 3). So we see again that these studies reflect the range of current opinion about the economics of climate change.

Where Nordhaus and Cline fundamentally disagree is in their assumed discount rates, and this accounts for much of the difference in their estimates of marginal benefit. If abatement is undertaken today, the costs are borne today, while the benefits will be realized slowly, over decades, even centuries. The more the future is discounted, the lower will be the current marginal benefit of abatement. Nordhaus (1991, 1994) discounts future benefits by 4–5%, while Cline uses a discount rate of about 2% (IPCC 1996). For purposes of comparison, the USEPA's analysis of the benefits of abating ozone-depleting substances used a 2% discount rate.

TABLE 3

Estimates of global marginal abatement benefit and global marginal abatement cost for CO_2

(US dollars per ton)

Study	Marginal benefit[a]	Cost model[b]	Marginal cost	
			Stabilization	20% reduction
Ayres and Walter	30–35	Jorgenson-Wilcoxen	20	50
Nordhaus	7	Edmonds-Reilly	70	160
Cline	8–154	Manne-Richels	110	240
Peck and Teisberg	12–14	Martin-Burniaux	80	170
Fankhauser	23	Rutherford	150	260
Maddison	8	Cohan-Scheraga	120	330

a. For most studies the marginal benefit increases over time. Estimates presented here are for 2001–10.
b. Cost estimates are from a study by the Energy Model Forum of Stanford University.
Source: IPCC 1996, tables 6.11 and 9.4.

It is sometimes claimed that the costs of abating a certain quantity of emissions is actually negative because of large inefficiencies in current energy policies. Indeed, IPCC (1995, p. 51) concludes that the potential improvements from reforms in energy policy is "large" and that the costs of mitigation could be "dramatically" affected by tax reforms. Whether this can be applied to global climate change policy is a matter of interpretation. If energy markets are inefficient because of inappropriate subsidies or institutional barriers to energy conservation, then these inefficiencies should be corrected even if climate change is not a worry. The same is true of an inefficient tax code that encourages energy consumption. It might be argued that such inefficiencies would be easier to remove for political reasons if they were tied to a climate change policy, but even with this interpretation the basic economics will not necessarily change significantly. Nordhaus (1994), considers a simulation in which emissions are reduced 30% by "no regrets" policies (that is, policies that make sense even if climate change does not occur) and finds that the optimal carbon tax does not change much. The main effect of the policy is a one-time gain in abatement. Nordhaus (1994) finds that tax reform could potentially justify a very high carbon tax ($59 in the decade starting in 1995), but the IPCC warns that inefficient use of tax revenues could increase costs.

These matters aside, there is a consensus that the marginal costs of abatement increase substantially, at least after adjustment for these effects, and this is reflected in the marginal cost figures (see table 3). Cline and Nordhaus agree that marginal costs rise at an increasing rate, and both of their analyses estimate cost curves using the outputs of other models. The difference between their assumptions about the costs of abatement is unimportant. Cline (1992, pp. 169–70) notes that "the central point about the Nordhaus analysis is that it counsels very limited action on the greenhouse problem not primarily because it identifies unusually high costs of abatement, but because it arrives at small estimates of the benefits of abatement". Similarly, Nordhaus (1994, p. 97) argues that the difference between his study and Cline's is that the latter "is not grounded in explicit intertemporal optimization, makes a number of assumptions that tilt toward stringent controls, and assumes a very low discount rate".[5]

Thus there are basically two views about climate change. Cline and Nordhaus agree that the marginal costs of abating CO_2 emissions increase fairly sharply (at least after any "no regrets" opportunities have been exploited). Where they disagree is in regard to the marginal benefits of abatement. Nordhaus contends that the marginal benefit of abatement is low for a doubling in CO_2 concentrations, implying, for a quadratic damage function, that the slope of the marginal benefit schedule is relatively small (in figure 1, Nordhaus essentially argues that Q^* is small). By contrast, Cline believes that the marginal benefit of abatement is relatively large for a doubling in CO_2 concentrations, suggesting that the slope of the marginal benefit curve is relatively steep (that Q^* is large).

These estimates may seem far removed from the climate change negotiations, but they are not. The Bush administration justified its opposition to European proposals by referring to similar estimates. The US Council of Economic Advisors (1990) cited a study predicting that meeting the Toronto target by 2100 (that is, reducing CO_2 20% from the 1988 level) would cost between $800 billion and $3.6 trillion.[6] The council noted that this was 35–150 times the cost of complying with the Montreal Protocol and argued that the benefits did not seem to justify the cost. The report concluded that "the highest priority in the near term should be to improve understanding in order to build a foundation for sound policy decisions. Until such a foundation is in place, there is no justification for imposing major costs on the economy in order to slow the growth of greenhouse gas emissions" (p. 223).

Summary

To sum up, the economics of ozone depletion suggest that at the very least rich countries had a strong unilateral incentive to substantially reduce their emissions. Available estimates also suggest that full cooperation would demand substantial global abatement. For climate change the incentives to reduce emissions unilaterally are much more muted. And while a case can be made that full cooperation requires substantial abatement, the opposite conclusion can also be supported by the data.

THE MONTREAL AND KYOTO PROTOCOLS

Comparing the Montreal and Kyoto Protocols is difficult because the Montreal Protocol has been around longer and has changed substantially since being first negotiated. By contrast, the Kyoto Protocol is new and has not had time to develop. In 10 years it may have achieved as much as the Montreal Protocol. Then again, in 10 years it may not even have entered into force. The Law of the Sea treaty did not enter into force until 12 years after it was negotiated, and some agreements—such as the 1988 Convention on the Regulation of Antarctic Mineral Resource Activities—are almost certain never to enter into force. Where appropriate, I try to correct for the relative youth of the Kyoto Protocol in the analysis that follows.

The Montreal and Kyoto Protocols have much in common (table 4). There are major differences, however, and these are perhaps even more important.

Completeness

The Montreal Protocol, even in its original form, imposes emission limits on every party. The Kyoto Protocol, in keeping with the Berlin Mandate, imposes limits only on the so-called Annex I signatories (industrial countries and Europe's transition economies); non-Annex I parties (that is, developing countries) are not subject to emission limits. This difference is important for two reasons.

The first is that leakage may at least partly shift emissions from countries bound by the Kyoto ceiling to those that are not, so that global emissions may fall less than if limits were imposed on all signatories. The other reason completeness matters is that if abatement is concentrated in a subset of countries, the total cost of reducing global emissions will be higher than if abatement were more widely distributed. If abatement is undertaken only in Annex I countries, the marginal cost of reducing emissions will be higher in those countries than in non-Annex I countries. Thus the total costs of reducing global emissions by the same amount could be reduced by shifting abatement towards the non-Annex I countries.

Joint implementation

In an attempt to address concern about developing countries not being subject to emission caps, the Kyoto Protocol allows an Annex I signatory to meet its emission limit by paying a developing country to carry out incremental abatement on its behalf—that is, by paying a developing country to undertake a project that reduces emissions of greenhouse gases, irrespective of the project's other merits. This "joint implementation" programme (called a "clean development mechanism" in the protocol) is welcome but it has some limitations.

First, Annex I and developing country partners in a joint implementation transaction must demonstrate to the other Kyoto signatories that their project will reduce emissions by the promised amount. This means (at least) having to estimate emissions from the non-Annex I country with and without the project—something that can never be done precisely. Second, attempting to calculate the emission savings from a project will be costly, and experience in

TABLE 4

Features of the Montreal and Kyoto Protocols

Feature	Montreal Protocol	Kyoto Protocol
Quantitative emission limits for:		
• Industrial countries	Yes	Yes
• Transition economies	Yes	Yes
• Developing countries	Yes	No
Emission offsets	Yes; subtracts from production the amount destroyed	Yes; subtracts from gross emissions removal by sinks
Comprehensive treatment of gross emissions	Yes; trade-offs allowed within categories of ozone-depleting substances	Yes; limitation applies to an aggregate of six pollutants
Nonuniform emission limits	Yes; developing countries have different limits, though limits are uniform within country categories	Yes; limits are country-specific, and transition economies are allowed to use an alternative base year
Emission limits permanent	Yes	No; limitation only for 2008–12; future limitations to be included as amendments
International trading in emission entitlements	Yes	Yes, though the system for emissions trading has not been established
Intertemporal trading in emission entitlements	No	Yes, insofar as the emission limits during 2008–12 must be met on average and countries can carry forward additional reductions to a subsequent control period

TABLE 4 *continued*

Feature	Montreal Protocol	Kyoto Protocol
Joint implementation	No; not needed because all signatories are subject to emission ceilings and trading is already allowed	Yes; countries subject to emission ceilings can engage in joint implementation with one another and can carry out joint implementation projects in countries not subject to emission ceilings
Reporting requirements	Yes	Yes
Verification procedure	Yes	Yes
Side payments	Yes; industrial country parties pay for the incremental costs of compliance by developing countries, and the Global Environment Facility offers assistance to transition economies	Not for mitigation, though some assistance is provided by the Global Environment Facility
Compliance incentives	Yes; carrots in the form of side payments and sticks in the form of trade sanctions	To be decided at a future Conference of Parties to the protocol
Free-rider deterrence mechanism	Yes; trade sanctions for nonparties on ozone-depleting substances and products containing them, plus the threat to ban trade in products made using ozone-depleting substances	No, with the possible exception of the minimum participation clause

(Table continues on next page.)

TABLE 4 *continued*

Feature	Montreal Protocol	Kyoto Protocol
Leakage prevention mechanism	Yes; in the form of a ban on imports from nonparties of ozone-depleting substances and related products and discouragement of the export to nonparties of technology useful to the production and use of ozone-depleting substances (These measures are not needed if the agreement sustains almost full participation)	No
Minimum participation	Enters into force after being ratified by 11 countries accounting for at least two-thirds of global consumption of ozone-depleting substances in 1986	Enters into force after being ratified by 55 countries, including Annex I countries, accounting for at least 55% of Annex I CO_2 emissions in 1990
Withdrawal	Allowed four years after ratification after giving one year's notice	Allowed three years after protocol enters into force for a party after giving one year's notice

the United States shows that, where transactions costs are high, the volume of such transactions will be limited.

Side payments
The Montreal Protocol established the principle of "common but differentiated responsibility", and in so doing separated the question of where abatement should be undertaken from who should pay for it. Although developing countries that signed the Montreal Protocol are subject to an emission ceiling, industrial country signatories agreed to compensate them for the incre-

mental costs of compliance. These side payments ensured that developing countries are not worse off for signing.

The Kyoto Protocol, on the other hand, imposes no ceiling on developing countries, and so need not offer to pay incremental costs. It does, however, provide full incremental costs to a developing country for any joint implementation agreement.

Permanent caps

Emission limits covered by the Montreal Protocol are permanent, whereas those covered by the Kyoto Protocol run only until 2008–12. (Establishing limits beyond that period will require amendments to the treaty). Whether limits are permanent or subject to review matters because many investments to reduce emissions involve projects with lifespans of 25 years or more. If future limits are expected to be very tight, then long-term emission-reducing investments make sense. But if controls are expected to be slack in the future, then long-term investments look less attractive. (With trading in emission entitlements, expected future constraints on all countries will determine the price of tradable entitlements.)

Of course, even "permanent" ceilings, such as those in the Montreal Protocol, can be moved down—or up. Indeed, the Montreal Protocol ceilings have been altered over time. What really matters is whether countries believe that the limits in the Montreal Protocol are permanent—a question of credibility.

The Kyoto Protocol partly sidesteps the problem with a provision for intertemporal trading. This allows a country to carry forward credits for "excessive" abatement undertaken in the current period (up to 2008–12). And so, the reasoning goes, the incentive not to reduce emissions now is muted. Even so, unless countries know now what future constraints will be, they will not know the value to them of making investments today.

The absence of permanent caps may also invite strategic behaviour. Suppose a country does invest in long-term emission reduction. The cost, once made, is sunk. Having already made the investment, then, the cost to this country of meeting tighter future limits will be reduced—and so its position at the bargaining table will be weakened. Strategic behaviour may then commend underinvestment in the short term.

Unseating free riders

Perhaps the most important difference between the two treaties is that the Montreal Protocol deters nonparticipation by restricting trade between signatories and nonsignatories, whereas the Kyoto Protocol does not contain a free-rider deterrent. The Montreal agreement bans trade between signatories and nonsignatories in substances covered by the treaty and in products containing them. According to Benedick (1991, p. 91), these sanctions were "to stimulate as many nations as possible to participate in the protocol". That is, the sanctions were intended to deter free riding.

Normally, trade sanctions damage the country that imposes them—one reason they are often ineffective. But the Montreal threat seems to work. Why? Because if the sanctions deter relocation of production or emissions, then the countries imposing the sanctions gain by imposing them. This, in turn, reinforces the credibility of sanctions. (For details on the importance of credibility, see Schelling 1960.)

Trade sanctions alone, however, are not enough to ensure full cooperation, because sanctions will only be credible if enough countries sign up. The minimum participation clause ensures that this threshold will be reached, that legally binding sanctions will only be imposed if enough countries are signatories (Barrett 1997). This works because, with sanctions, the payoff to being a signatory increases as the number of participating countries increases. If every country but one were a party to the agreement, then the nonparty would gain from free riding but lose from not being able to trade in some goods with the rest of the world. Provided the loss from trade is large enough, trade sanctions can deter free riding.

Though the Kyoto Protocol does not contain a free-rider deterrent mechanism like that in the Montreal Protocol, the minimum participation clause may act as one. As noted, the Kyoto Protocol will not come into force (and so will not be binding on any country) until it is ratified by 55 countries accounting for 55% of Annex I country emissions in 1990. How might this deter free riding? Suppose that accession by one more country would just tip the balance, and ensure that the minimum participation clause was triggered. Then, although this last signatory would incur a cost (of compliance), its accession would impel all parties to comply with the protocol's requirements. In a sense, accession by this key country is subsidized.

Once the minimum participation level is reached, however, the incentive to sign is reduced to zero, because each additional signatory will not influence the behaviour of any other party. Though every treaty has a clause on minimum participation, with few exceptions the actual number of signatories exceeds the specified minimum. This suggests that the clause is usually not intended to deter free riding but rather to coordinate behaviour. Suppose, for example, that it would be in a country's interests to ratify a treaty only if enough other countries did so. Then a minimum participation clause would help ensure that participation in the treaty was "tipped", so that enough other countries did in fact ratify the agreement. This effect could be important, but it is not the same as a free-rider deterrent.

Compliance enforcement

Lack of compliance incentives in the Kyoto Protocol might not seem like much of a problem. The Montreal Protocol also deferred a decision on compliance enforcement, although it did initially offer incentives for countries to participate in the treaty (and subsequently used these to enforce compliance). In other words, precisely the same instrument was used to enforce compliance as to deter free riding. Thus compliance enforcement is a potential problem with the Kyoto Protocol, because it has no mechanism to deter free riding.

Most countries almost always comply fully with treaties to which they are parties, and most agreements do not make provisions to punish noncompliance. Chayes and Chayes (1995) infer from these observations that sticks are not needed to ensure compliance. It is possible, however, that countries only choose to sign agreements that they want to comply with anyway (Downs, Rocke and Barsoon 1996). Put differently, if compliance really was not a problem, then countries might negotiate treaties differently from the ones that now make up the canon of international law.

In 1992 the parties to the Montreal Protocol agreed to an "indicative list of measures that might be taken by a meeting of the parties in respect of noncompliance with the Protocol". These were assistance, including "technology transfer and financial assistance"; "issuing cautions"; and "suspension . . . of specific rights and privileges under the Protocol . . . including those concerned with industrial rationalization, production, consumption, trade, transfer of technology, financial mechanism and institutional arrangements".

But would these measures ever be used? They were tested only recently. When it became apparent in 1996 that Belarus and Ukraine were unlikely to comply with the requirements of the protocol, a deal was reached with the Implementation Committee of the Montreal Protocol in which financial assistance for a phase-out programme would be provided if these states agreed to restrict exports of controlled substances (the purpose being to prevent transshipment, as neither Belarus nor Ukraine manufactures CFCs).

Russia's potential noncompliance, however, threw up a greater challenge. In 1995 Russia said that it would not be able to comply with its basic treaty obligations by 1996 and formally requested an extension. The Implementation Committee refused and instead offered Russia essentially the same deal it struck with Belarus and Ukraine. But Russia objected to the trade restrictions and conditions for receiving multilateral assistance, claiming that the decision did not consider the difficulties that transition posed for compliance.

After a tense stand-off, approval or rejection of the committee's decision was to be decided at the seventh meeting of the signatories, held in Vienna in December 1995. At the meeting the Russian environment minister warned that, if the recommendations were approved, "the process of replacing ODS [ozone-depleting substances] will significantly lose momentum . . . measures to strengthen export controls will not be taken, there will be a trend towards illegal production of ODS by producers and the use of these products by consumers"(Brack 1996, p. 104). Thus Russia argued that imposing sanctions would harm the other parties to the treaty, and not only itself.

But Russia's plea was unanimously rejected. Venezuela (a CFC producer) even argued that trade restrictions against Russia should be stiffened, leading the Russian delegation to denounce the proceedings and storm out of the meeting. In a February 1996 letter to the executive secretary of the Ozone Secretariat, however, the Russian environment minister struck a conciliatory tone, acknowledging "the current concern in the international community regarding possible deliveries of ODS from Russian sources during the period in which they are being phased out" and stating that Russia was taking steps "toward solving the problems of control within our borders". The Implementation Committee noted that "the Russian Federation had by its actions taken important steps to comply with [the above decision of the conference of the parties] and towards achieving full compliance with the control measures of the Protocol," and it said that it would "consider favourably additional steps to expedite financial assistance" as regards implementing the phase-out, thus approving plans by the Global Environment Facility to subsidize substitution of CFCs in Russia with a $35 million (on top of a previous $8.6 million) subsidy.[7]

At the ninth meeting of the parties, held in Montreal in September 1997, the Implementation Committee reported that Russia had submitted data requested by the committee, set up a system for controlling imports and exports of controlled substances, undertaken not to export controlled substances to nonsignatories other than members of the Commonwealth of Independent States, begun setting up recovery and recycling facilities, and reduced its production of ozone-depleting substances 60% since 1995. Russia was now on track to phase out its production completely by 2000.

This experience begs a couple of questions. What will happen if (or when) parties to the Kyoto Protocol announce that they will not be able to satisfy the requirements of the agreement? And how will parties to the Kyoto Protocol behave if there is doubt that their future obligations will be enforced?

Leakage

One problem with less-than-full participation is leakage—that, as some countries reduce their pollution, comparative advantage in the polluting activity may shift towards other countries, and emissions in these other countries may therefore increase.

Leakage is often associated with free riding but it is a different problem. Leakage can only arise where there is international trade. Free riding arises from the public good characteristics of environmental protection. So there can be free riding even if countries do not trade, and there can be leakage even if there is no free riding. But even though the problems are different, they are often simultaneously present—and when they are, leakage will magnify the free-riding problem.

Leakage can be eliminated by making sure that participation in an agreement is full, for then there will not be any "other" countries to which production can relocate. In principle, it can also be eliminated through the use of border tax adjustments (see Hoel 1996).

The Montreal Protocol has a number of mechanisms that limit leakage. First, in banning imports of ozone-depleting substances and goods incorporating them, the agreement reduces the incentive for production to relocate. Second, the agreement requires that parties undertake "to the fullest practicable extent to discourage the export to any State not party to this Protocol of technology for producing and for utilizing controlled substances". But perhaps most important in deterring free riding is that, by ensuring that participation is close to full, the agreement effectively eliminates leakage. The Kyoto Protocol does not provide such incentives. Of course, this does not mean that leakage will necessarily be a problem for the Kyoto Protocol. The available literature offers conflicting evidence on leakage for climate change (IPCC 1996). However, concerns about leakage are at the very least a political problem. Worries about possible leakage were one reason that the US Senate opposed the Berlin mandate.

Implications

The broad message is simple. Montreal has succeeded because it has attracted almost full participation, and it has done so using an ingenious combination of carrots and sticks—carrots in the form of payments to developing countries and transition economies for the incremental costs of complying with the agreement, and sticks in the form of a threat to impose trade sanctions against nonsignatories. The carrot ensures that no developing country or transition economy can lose by being a party to the agreement. The stick, coupled with the minimum participation clause, ensures that any country will lose by not signing. These mechanisms are credible by virtue of the economics of ozone policy. The carrot is attractive for industrial countries to offer because the benefit to them of ozone protection is much greater than the cost of a global phase-out of controlled substances. And the stick is credible because, should sanctions not be used, production might relocate to nonsignatory states.

Perhaps the Kyoto agreement can, with time, be amended to resemble the Montreal agreement. Putting the right words down on paper is not the problem, however. Rather, it is making the required mechanisms credible. A threat is credible only if everyone believes that, when push comes to shove, it will be carried out. Ultimately, the economics of public good provision determine not only the potential gains from cooperation but also the degree of cooperation that can be sustained by the anarchic international system. This is the basic lesson of the theory of international cooperation (Barrett 1994, forthcoming).

NOTES

1. It is well known that the decision by DuPont and other CFC manufacturers to stop producing these chemicals had an influence on the outcome. But even those decisions were not made independently of governments. First, DuPont's announcement came after the Montreal Protocol had been negotiated. Second, after DuPont made the announcement, the US government had little alternative but to demand anything short of a phase-out. However, DuPont would have known this. In other words, its announcement may have been motivated by the expectation that the US would require all manufacturers to phase out CFCs (a phase-out by all manufacturers would arguably be in DuPont's best interests). Moreover, DuPont may have seen the writing on the wall. The cost-benefit estimates presented later in this chapter were published only three months

after DuPont's announced phase-out, and DuPont's chairman later noted that the company's announcement was heavily influenced by new scientific findings showing that the Montreal Protocol restrictions were inadequate (see Barrett 1992).

2. Studies linking democracy to international environmental cooperation include Congleton (1992), Fredriksson and Gaston (1998), Murdoch and Sandler (1997) and Murdoch, Sandler and Sargent (1997). These linkages are complex, however, and these studies remain inconclusive. For example, whether one country will sign an agreement will typically depend on whether other countries also sign it.

3. In fact, the USEPA truncates depletion at 50%. The model used to evaluate ozone depletion indicates that depletion would exceed 50% if there were no controls.

4. The estimated future damages from climate change for the current US economy are about $60 billion a year. Over time the economy would expand, and as a result the current value of the damage would rise. In present value terms, however, the damage would not necessarily rise because future damage would be discounted. Suppose that the economy grows at rate ρ and that future damage is discounted at rate r. Assuming $r > \rho$ (for convergence), the present value of the future flow of damage would equal $\int_0^\infty 60e^{-(r-\rho)t}dt = 60/(r-\rho)$. In present value terms the value of the lives lost to ozone depletion if no controls are adopted is about $3.6 trillion. These two present value sums are equal if $r-\rho = 0.017$. Because this seems plausible, I conclude that the expected damages from climate change and ozone depletion in present value terms are roughly equal, at least for the United States.

5. The analyses by Cline and Nordhaus differ in another respect. Nordhaus solves for the policy that equates the global marginal benefit and cost of abatement. Cline's approach is different. He seeks to determine the conditions under which the benefits of a programme of substantial abatement exceed the costs. Cline's approach would be appropriate if the options before us were binary. But they are not, and his approach therefore requires certain care in interpretation. For example, in his discussion of his central estimate, in which the benefit-cost ratio is less than 1, Cline (1992) argues that "if it were certain that these were the stakes of global warming, the implication would be that abatement is too costly relative to the prospective damage and no action should be undertaken". This is a misreading of the message. What the central case advises is not that no action is justified but that only moderate abatement is justified. Similarly, when the benefit-cost ratio exceeds 1, it would be wrong to conclude that the programme of substantial abatement proposed by Cline should be undertaken. Net benefits may be higher under a somewhat more modest or even more extreme policy.

6. For comparison, the Kyoto Protocol requires that the United States reduce its emissions by 7% from the 1990 level by 2008–12.

7. The quotations in this paragraph are drawn from the March 1996 report of the Implementation Committee (UNEP 1996).

REFERENCES

Barrett, Scott. 1990. "The Problem of Global Environmental Protection." *Oxford Review of Economic Policy* 6: 68–79.

———. 1992. "Strategy and the Environment." *Columbia Journal of World Business* 27: 202–08.

———. 1994. "Self-Enforcing International Environmental Agreements." *Oxford Economic Papers* 46: 878–94.

———. 1997. "The Strategy of Trade Sanctions in International Environmental Agreements." *Resource and Energy Economics* 19: 345–61.

———. 1998. "Cooperation for Sale." London Business School.

———. Forthcoming. "A Theory of Full International Cooperation." *Journal of Theoretical Politics.*

Benedick, Richard E. 1991. *Ozone Diplomacy: New Directions in Safeguarding the Planet.* Cambridge, MA: Harvard University Press.

———. 1997. "The UN Approach to Climate Change: Where Has It Gone Wrong?" http://www.weathervane.rff.org/pointcpoint/pcp4/benedick.html.

Brack, Duncan. 1996. *International Trade and the Montreal Protocol.* London: Royal Institute of International Affairs.

Chayes, Abram, and Antonia H. Chayes. 1995. *The New Sovereignty.* Cambridge, MA: Harvard University Press.

Cline, William R. 1992. *The Economics of Global Warming.* Washington, DC: Institute for International Economics.

Congleton, Roger D. 1992. "Political Institutions and Pollution Control." *Review of Economics and Statistics* 74: 412–21.

Dixit, Avinash K. 1996. *The Making of Economic Policy: A Transaction-Cost Politics Perspective.* Cambridge, MA: MIT Press.

Downs, George W., David M. Rocke and Peter N. Barsoon. 1996. "Is the Good News about Compliance Good News about Cooperation?" *International Organization* 50: 379–406.

Fredriksson, Per G., and Noel Gaston. 1998. "Ratification of the 1992 Climate Change Convention: What Determines Legislative Delay?" World Bank, Environment Department, Washington, DC.

Hoel, Michael. 1996. "Should a Carbon Tax Be Differentiated Across Sectors?" *Journal of Public Economics* 59: 17–32.

IEA (International Energy Agency). 1992. *Climate Change Policy Initiatives*. Paris: Organisation for Economic Co-operation and Development.

IPCC (Intergovernmental Panel on Climate Change). 1990. *Climate Change—the IPCC Scientific Assessment*. Geneva: World Meteorological Organization and United Nations Environment Programme.

———. 1995. IPCC *Second Assessment: Climate Change 1995*. Geneva: World Meteorological Organization and United Nations Environment Programme.

———. 1996. *Climate Change 1995: Economic and Social Dimensions of Climate Change*. Cambridge: Cambridge University Press.

Murdoch, James C., and Todd Sandler. 1997. "Voluntary Cutbacks and Pretreaty Behavior: The Helsinki Protocol and Sulfur Emissions." *Public Finance Review* 25: 139–62.

Murdoch, James C., Todd Sandler and Keith Sargent. 1997. "A Tale of Two Collectives: Sulphur versus Nitrogen Oxides Emission Reduction in Europe." *Economica* 64: 281–301.

Nordhaus, William D. 1991. "To Slow or Not to Slow: The Economics of the Greenhouse Effect." *The Economic Journal* 101: 920–37.

———. 1994. *Managing the Global Commons*. Cambridge, MA: MIT Press.

Olson, Mancur. 1965. *The Logic of Collective Action*. Cambridge, MA: Harvard University Press.

Parson, Edward A. 1993. "Protecting the Ozone Layer." In Peter M. Haas, Robert O. Keohane and Marc A. Levy, eds., *Institutions for the Earth*. Cambridge, MA: MIT Press.

Schelling, Thomas C. 1960. *The Strategy of Conflict*. Cambridge, MA: Harvard University Press.

US Council of Economic Advisors. 1990. *Economic Report of the President*. Washington, DC: US Government Printing Office.

UNEP (United Nations Environment Programme). 1996. *Report of the Implementation Committee under the Non-Compliance Procedure for the Montreal Protocol on the Work of Its Thirteenth Meeting*. UNEP/OzL.Pro/ImpCom/13/3. Geneva.

USEPA (US Environmental Protection Agency). 1988a. "Protection of Stratospheric Ozone; Final Rule." *Federal Register* 53: 30566–30602.

———. 1988b. *Regulatory Impact Analysis: Protection of Stratospheric Ozone*. Washington, DC.

NEW STRATEGIES FOR THE PROVISION OF GLOBAL PUBLIC GOODS

Learning from International Environmental Challenges

GEOFFREY HEAL

The world of public goods has changed radically in the past quarter century, rendering some textbook discussions and examples quite dated. This is a good time to take a fresh look at both the nature of public goods and the policy options for managing their provision.

The first section of this chapter identifies key trends in the changing world of public goods. It shows that increasingly public goods are privately produced—by private enterprises, as a result of privatization, and by (often negative) externalities, as a result of myriad decentralized and independent decisions by actors world-wide. The second section examines mechanisms for the provision of this new type of privately produced public good, placing special emphasis on market-based mechanisms. Given the growing importance of natural-resource issues in discussions of global public goods, the examples come from the environmental field. Two main messages emerge from the discussion:

- Public goods, such as the reduction of greenhouse gas emissions, pose a new challenge: deciding who can—and should—produce the public good.
- Creating new markets can be an effective and efficient means of meeting this challenge.

THE CHANGING WORLD OF PUBLIC GOODS

Traditionally it has been assumed that public goods—such as law and order, defence, protection from extreme weather, essential social and economic infrastructure—should be provided by the public sector for the public as a whole. But today we know that private initiative and private actions also play an important role. Why? Because the nature of public goods has changed as a result of two major trends: privatization and externalities.

Privatization

Privatization of previously state-provided public goods and services has been captured in the popular rhetoric of "rolling back the frontiers of the state". In both industrial and developing societies the view of government has changed radically. Many sectors previously under state management and ownership— including water, power, telecommunications, transportation, broadcasting and health care—have been transferred to private management and owner- ship. Economists previously viewed many of these services as involving a com- bination of public goods and natural monopolies: transport systems were viewed as public goods, and power suppliers as natural monopolies.

The change in social and political perspectives on these industries has many roots. Among them are changes in technology that permit smaller pro- ducers and potentially more scope for competition. It is no longer the case that a power plant, to be efficient, has to operate on a massive scale. Gas-fired turbine generators can compete with massive conventional power stations in meeting peak demand—and operate efficiently at output levels correspond- ing to the needs of small communities or individual factories.

Also important is our new understanding of network industries. A net- work industry typically consists of a physical network—railways, telecom- munications channels, electric power cables—and a service that requires the use of this infrastructure. The past 10 years have seen a move towards unbundling, to seeing the provision of the physical network and that of the related services as different businesses. With unbundling, any power provider can use the grid to distribute its power and any phone company can access the network of any other. The underlying physical network has always had the characteristics of a public good, requiring large-scale provision to be effective. Together these two trends—technological changes permitting effi- cient small-scale power generation and the dissociation of distribution from production—permit substantial competition in the provision of power, changing the business radically. One effect: more competition in the provi- sion of services. Similar moves are under way with railways. Consider the UK rail system, with the track owned by RailTrack and train companies charged for its use.

Consider another example: broadcasting. It used to be impossible to exclude anyone in a broadcast's target area from receiving and using the broadcast. With no possibility of exclusion, and with no rivalry in consumption, broadcasting was a classic public good. But scrambling technologies have changed this. And if broadcasts are scrambled, only those who have paid for unscrambling technology can use them. There is still no rivalry in consumption, but there is perfect excludability. A public good has been privatized by technological change—not in the legal or financial sense but in the strict economic sense.

Political factors have also contributed to the drive towards privatization. Financing the provision of public goods or those provided by regulated natural monopolies has always posed a conceptual conflict between efficient pricing and breaking even. Efficient pricing has required marginal cost pricing and thus losses, although theoretical developments in the analysis of increasing returns make this an oversimplification (Heal 1998). The changing role of the state has led governments to look favourably on an institutional framework in which breaking even appears to be assured, and has moved the focus away from some of the traditional prescriptions for managing natural monopolies.

So there is real substance behind the privatization of traditional public goods and public sector activities. Changes in technology have made competition possible in some areas and made goods or services excludable in others. In parallel, public concern with state spending has focused political attention on the financing of publicly provided goods, always a difficult point. As a result the political balance has tipped in favour of privatization.

The growing importance of externalities

The past 20 years have seen a phenomenal increase in public concern about environmental public goods, to the extent that these are by now the "quintessential" public good. Here I focus on privately produced public goods—many of which are, unfortunately, not "good" but "bad". Take carbon dioxide, the principal gas responsible for global climate change. It is quite stable, remaining in the atmosphere for about 60 years after emission. It mixes easily, and within months the carbon dioxide emitted in New York or Beijing will be diffused around the globe. Thus the concentration of carbon dioxide in the atmosphere is rather uniform around the world, and its atmospheric concentration is a global public good.

How is all this carbon dioxide produced? It is the result of billions of decentralized and independent decisions by private households for heating and transportation and by corporations for these and other needs, all outside the government's sphere. The government can influence these decisions, but only indirectly, through regulations or incentives. The same is true for other atmospheric pollutants. Sulphur dioxide emissions are the result of home heating and power generation choices of people the world over. Ozone-depleting chlorofluorocarbons are produced for use in household refrigerators and air conditioners. The loss of biodiversity results from myriad independent decisions about changes in land use (changes that destroy previous habitats) and from decisions about pollution (including those that affect the climate). Farmers, ranchers, vacation home owners, suburban home owners—all have a direct impact on biodiversity through their lifestyles and land use.

The foregoing observations introduce a completely new element into the provision of public goods. For traditional public goods, three questions are to be answered:

- How much should be provided?
- How should this be financed?
- How can the state obtain the information to answer these questions?

The last point relates to the free-rider problem. Anyone who is asked how much he or she is willing to pay for a public good—and who expects that their payment will be affected by the response—has an obvious incentive to give a response that understates their true preference. For privately produced public goods, however, we have to ask a fourth question:

- Given a desirable target level of production, how do we attain it, and how is this target production to be divided among all the potential producers?

For example, in the case of reducing greenhouse gas emissions this question takes a very specific and difficult form: which countries should cut back emissions, and by how much? The same question will then be repeated within the country, and indeed probably within organizations and firms. This new question—how the production of the public good should be distributed among agents—interacts in surprising and interesting ways with the first trend of privatization and the increasing use of markets.

Before moving ahead, I will summarize some of what I have said about the characteristics of public goods in a diagram. Traditionally public goods have been seen as goods that are publicly produced and for which there is no rivalry in consumption and no excludability. Traditional private goods have been, and continue to be, the opposite. In figure 1 these three dimensions are shown as the three axes of a cube, with traditional public goods at one corner

FIGURE 1

Characteristics of private and public goods

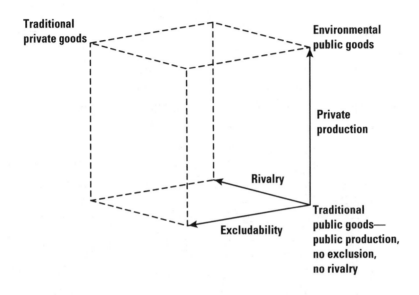

and private goods at the opposite corner. In the example of scrambling broad-casting and thus making it excludable (though not rival) in consumption, a change in technology moved the service from the origin along the horizontal excludability axis. Knowledge is also a privately produced public good, as it is nonrival in consumption and nonexcludable. Intellectual property rights are measures for making this good excludable, the equivalent of scrambling for broadcasts. Today we could find goods or services in almost any location on the cube, not just in the opposite corners.

PROVIDING MODERN PUBLIC GOODS

This section addresses the issue of how to manage the provision of modern public goods, notably privately provided public goods. Two mechanisms are reviewed: the creation of new markets for the right to pollute and the encouragement of adoption spillovers.

Example one: tradable pollution permits

As noted, privately produced public goods raise three standard questions on how much to provide, how to finance provision and how to ascertain the information needed to answer the first two questions. They also raise a fourth question, a new one in the world of public goods: who should produce how much of the total public good that ought to be provided?

I focus first on the fourth question, which in principle can be answered in several ways:

- One is the traditional command and control approach: take the total, divide it in some way among the possible producers and instruct each of them that this is what they will produce. In the most common case of privately produced public goods—environmental pollution—this approach typically takes the form of deciding that there will be an X% reduction in the output of the pollutant and instructing everyone to reduce pollution by X%.
- A maximum level of pollution can be set, uniform across all agents, consistent with a target total pollution level.
- The pollution can be reduced by taxation, trying to pick a tax rate that will bring about the desired pollution level.
- A market can be used to decide who produces how much by allocating pollution rights and allowing them to be traded.

Standard arguments indicate that either of the last two approaches—taxation or permit markets—is more cost-effective than command and control. Cost-effective here means that a given abatement level is achieved at a lower total cost. Of the two cost-effective approaches, markets are a better way of attaining a given target total pollution level, for the obvious reason that we can pick the total volume of pollution permits to equal the target pollution level.

The idea of trading rights to pollute goes back at least to Dales (1968) and the 1970s, although it could be argued that it has origins in Coase (1960) or even in Lindahl's work on public goods (Foley 1970). For a general review of the issues, see Chichilnisky and Heal (1994a, 1999).

What issues does the use of markets raise in answering the "who produces" question for privately produced public goods? It is important to understand exactly how the market will work in this case. A total production level has been chosen for pollution, the total permissible pollution level. The next step is to allocate tradable rights to pollute—also known as tradable emission quotas—up to a total of the chosen total production target. These are divided among potential polluters according to a procedure chosen by the authority controlling the pollution.

To make this concrete, consider sulphur dioxide emission permits in the United States. The US Environmental Protection Agency sets limits on the total emission of sulphur dioxide in a region, issues permits to emit sulphur dioxide adding up to this limit and allocates these permits between potential polluters. Once this is done, the potential polluters are free to pollute up to the limit set by the permits that they have received—or to pollute less and sell the permits for which they have no need, or to purchase additional permits from other potential polluters and then pollute up to a level given by their initial allocation of permits plus their purchases. The incentive to cut back on pollution is provided by the fact that an unused permit can be sold: the higher the market price, the stronger the incentive.

THE DISTRIBUTION OF QUOTAS. How would this mechanism work for a global public good such as carbon dioxide? In other words, what are its implications for the Kyoto Protocol on greenhouse gas emission? To introduce a regime of tradable emission quotas, we have to create property rights where none previously existed. These property rights must then be allocated to countries participating in the carbon dioxide abatement programme, in the form of quotas. Such quotas have market value—perhaps very great market value. Thus the creation and distribution of quotas could lead to a major international redistribution of wealth. This means that it is economically and politically important to fully understand the issues that underlie an evaluation of alternative ways of distributing emission quotas.

A clear precedent for this redistributive effect of international property rights can be seen in the Law of the Sea conference and the introduction of 200-mile territorial limits in the waters off a nation's coast. The limits established national property rights where none previously existed, and these rights could and frequently were distributed by governments to domestic firms. The property rights in offshore water thus effected a very substantial redistribution of wealth internationally.

There is no way to restrict countries' emissions of greenhouse gases without altering both their energy use and their overall production and consumption patterns. Thus the implementation of measures to decrease carbon emissions will have a significant impact on the ability of different groups and countries to produce goods and services for their own consumption and for trade. Because of this, the distributional impact of environmental policy—that is, the choice of who will bear the adjustment costs—is of major import. Under a tradable quota regime, payment for the provision of a public good—in this case payment for an atmosphere containing less greenhouse gases—takes the form of bearing the economic costs of adjusting to the quota regime and its prices. This makes the analysis of environmental policy particularly difficult because consensus on distributional considerations is typically quite difficult to achieve.

DISTRIBUTION AND EFFICIENCY. Market allocations are often recommended for their efficiency. This means that it is not possible to reallocate resources away from a market-clearing allocation without making someone worse off: there is no slack in the system. Market efficiency requires three key properties:

- Markets must be competitive.
- There must be no external effects—in Pigouvian terminology private and social costs must be equal, and in Coasian terminology there must be property rights in the environment.
- The goods produced and traded must be private.

The efficiency of market allocation is independent of the assignment of property rights. Ownership patterns are of great interest for welfare reasons, and different ownership patterns lead to different efficient allocations when traders achieve different levels of consumption and there are different distributions of income. But ownership patterns have no impact on market efficiency. The efficiency of the market independent of distribution is a crucial property underlying the organization of most modern societies.

Yet the efficiency properties that make the market so valuable for the allocation of private goods fail when the goods are public. With such goods it is not possible to separate efficiency from distribution. The public good nature of atmospheric carbon dioxide is a physical fact, derived from the tendency of carbon dioxide to mix thoroughly and stably. This simple fact is completely independent of any economic or legal institutions. It has profound implications for the efficiency of market allocations, for efficiency and distribution are no longer divorced as they are in economies with private goods. Instead they are closely associated. In economies with public goods, market solutions are efficient only with the appropriate distributions of initial property rights. Why?

When all goods are private, different traders typically end up with different amounts of goods at a market-clearing equilibrium because of their different tastes and endowments. The flexibility of the market in assigning different bundles of goods to different traders is crucial for efficient solutions. But traders with different preferences should reach consumption levels at which the economy-wide relative prices of any two goods are both equal to the marginal rate of substitution between those goods for every trader and equal to the rate of transformation between the two goods for every producer. This is an enormous task: it is a testament to the decentralized power of markets that this coincidence of values emerges at a market-clearing allocation.

When one good is public, however, there is a physical constraint: all traders, no matter how different, must consume the same quantity. This imposes an additional constraint, a restriction that does not exist in markets where all goods are private. Because of this restriction, some of the adjustments needed to reach an efficient equilibrium are no longer available in markets with public goods.

The number of instruments the market uses to reach an efficient solution—the goods' prices and the quantities consumed by all traders—is the same with private or public goods. But with a public good these instruments must now do more: at a market equilibrium the quantities of the public good demanded independently by each trader must be the same, no matter how different the traders are. As a result, in addition to equalizing price ratios to every trader's marginal rates of substitution and transformation, an additional condition must now be met for efficiency. The sum over all traders of the marginal rates of substitution between the public good and any private good must equal the marginal rate of transformation between them. It must also equal the relative price. This condition emerges from the simple observation that one additional unit of the public good produced benefits every trader simultaneously, which is implied by the fact that all consumers consume the same amount.

The physical requirement of equal consumption by all therefore introduces a fundamental difference between efficiency with public goods and efficiency with private goods. All this must be achieved by the market in a decentralized fashion. Traders must still be able to choose freely, maximizing their individual utilities, and therefore the previous condition of equating each trader's marginal rates of substitution and transformation to prices must still hold. Otherwise the market-clearing allocation would not be efficient. In other words, with public goods the market must perform one more task.[1]

An additional task calls for additional instruments. Because the market with n private goods has precisely as many instruments as tasks, with public goods new instruments must be enlisted. Some of the economy's characteristics can now be adjusted to meet the new goals. The traders' property rights to the public good, their rights to emit gases into the atmosphere, are a natural instrument for this purpose because they are in principle free and undefined until the environmental policy is considered. By treating the allocations of quotas as an instrument—that is, by varying the distribution of property rights on the atmosphere—it is generally possible to achieve a market-clearing solution where traders choose freely to consume exactly the same amount of the public good. Market efficiency can be achieved with public goods, but only with the appropriate distribution of property rights. Again, distribution and efficiency are no longer independent.

NORTH-SOUTH ASPECTS. The physical constraint of the public good is most acute when traders have rather different tastes and endowments, when they would naturally choose different consumption patterns and different levels of the public good. Tastes are often difficult to measure, but differences in endowments are measured more readily: national accounts often provide an adequate approximation. Income differences are very pronounced in the world economy, so it will be difficult internationally to achieve identical levels of demand for a public good, and correspondingly to attain market efficiency.

Think for simplicity of a world divided into a North and a South, the industrial and the developing. Endowments of private goods are much larger in the North than in the South; in a competitive market with private goods this naturally leads to very different patterns of consumption. Thus the North-South dimension of carbon dioxide abatement is likely to be an important aspect in the evaluation of environmental policy. While this point is widely understood in political negotiations between industrial and developing countries, it has not been clear until recent work that the political arguments have in fact an underpinning in arguments about economic efficiency.

Not only are distributional issues fundamental to achieving political good will and to building consensus, they are also fundamental in designing policies that aim at market efficiency. Market efficiency is crucial in reaching political consensus: negotiations often advance by removing inefficiencies and so producing solutions potentially favourable to all. Proposing an inefficient solution means neglecting potential avenues to consensus—a strategic mistake in negotiations where the achievement of consensus is key.

DISTRIBUTION AMONG COUNTRIES. From the previous arguments it follows that a judicious allocation of quotas among countries must not be viewed solely as a politically expedient measure to facilitate consensus. Nor should it necessarily be viewed as an attempt to reach fair outcomes at the expense of efficiency, or at least independent of efficiency. The appropriate allocation of quotas within a given world total of emissions may be an instrument for ensuring that competitive markets can reach efficient allocations. The fact that it plays this role comes from the physical constraints that a public good imposes on market functioning.

What remains to be determined, however, is the particular distribution of quotas needed to ensure that the market solution will be efficient. Distributional issues are delicate points in any negotiation, and the fact that market efficiency is involved makes the point apparently more complex. In reality, however, it can be seen to improve the dynamics of the negotiation process. The reason: the connection between distribution and efficiency means that an argument about distribution is not a zero-sum game, as it would be if the division of a fixed total between competing parties were all that were involved. Because some distributions of quotas are efficient and others are not, some lead to a greater total welfare than others and thus to an opportunity for all to gain relative to the other, inefficient distributions.[2]

Now, a conceptual overview of the problem. I work under the assumption that all countries have generally similar preferences for private goods and for environmental assets if they have comparable incomes.[3] This assumption is consistent with different trade-offs between private and environmental consumption in countries at different incomes. A second standard assumption is that the marginal utility of consumption decreases with income. This simply means that an additional unit of consumption increases utility less at higher levels of consumption than it does at lower levels. That is, adding one dollar's worth of consumption to a person with meagre resources increases the person's well-being more that adding one dollar's worth of consumption to a wealthy individual increases that person's well-being. I assume too that all countries have access to similar technologies and that their productive capacities differ only as a consequence of differences in capital stocks.

Under these assumptions it is possible to show that the allocation of quotas may have to favour developing countries proportionately more than industrial countries if we seek market efficiency (Chichilnisky and Heal 1994b). This holds true for any total target level of emissions.

Is there generally a connection between the distribution of income and the level of emissions? To answer this, consider one more fact about preferences between private and public goods: that environmental assets are normal goods. This means that the amount one is willing to spend on environmental amenities or assets increases with one's income. The more we earn the more we spend on every normal good, including environmental goods.

The final general condition invoked by the analysis here requires perhaps more thought: that environmental assets are necessary goods. This simply means that while the total amount spent on environmental assets increases with income, the proportion of income a person is willing to spend on environmental assets decreases as their income level rises. This assumption has been corroborated empirically in every known study in the United States, Europe and Africa (see Kristrom and Riera 1996), though such studies typically involve contingent valuation techniques, which can have weaknesses. The assumption can also be justified theoretically on the grounds that lower-income people are more vulnerable to their environment than are higher-income people. They cannot afford to choose or modify their environment, while higher-income people can. For example, a public park or access to potable water are environmental assets that have relatively more value to lower-income people than they do to those who can afford to build their own park or arrange their own water access. People in lower-income countries are known to be more vulnerable to global warming than are those in higher-income countries. My assumptions here are consistent with what has been established with remarkable regularity in most empirical studies: the income elasticity of demand for environmental assets is between 0 and 1 (most studies find it to be about 0.3; see Kristrom and Riera 1996).

If these points are correct, it is possible to establish that a redistribution of income towards lower-income individuals or countries will generally lead to an improvement in environmental preservation. Why? Because when preferences are similar and the income elasticity of demand is less than 1, a redistribution of income in favour of lower-income groups implies that relatively more income will be allocated to the environmental asset. If traders choose freely, they will choose more preservation. In the case here, higher abatement levels are to be expected when more resources are assigned to lower-income countries.

Example two: adoption spillovers
In recent years environmental commitments have expanded in most countries, industrial and developing, as a result of governments adopting new, legally binding environmental norms and standards. An example is the move towards unleaded gasoline in Germany and how the new gasoline policy in Germany affected—or produced spillover effects into—Italy.

Unleaded gasoline was introduced in Germany before it was introduced in Italy. Many Germans drive to Italy as tourists, and in some regions their business is an important source of income. After unleaded gasoline was introduced in Germany, Germans drove to Italy in cars requiring unleaded fuel, and their business was important enough that gas stations in the regions patronized by them began selling unleaded gas, even though there was no market for it among Italian drivers. This move required the establishment of facilities for the production and distribution of unleaded gasoline in Italy, which in turn required a considerable investment that historically has been one of the obstacles to the introduction of unleaded gasoline in any country. Because of this prior introduction to meet the requirements of German tourists, the incremental cost of requiring all vehicles to use unleaded gasoline in Italy was greatly reduced, making the eventual adoption of unleaded gasoline in Italy far easier than it would otherwise have been. This is a nice example of how the adoption of standards by one country has positive spillover effects to others and reduces their costs of adopting the same standards.

A second illustration of this point is more general. Emission abatement often requires the development and implementation of new technologies. In the case of unleaded gasoline the main requirement was the development of vehicle engines that could deliver undiminished performance without lead additives. The mandating of unleaded gasoline in the United States forced all of the world's main vehicle manufacturers to solve this problem, greatly reducing the costs and political obstacles to the later adoption of unleaded gas in other countries.

Both examples make an important general point: the more widely a standard is already adopted, the less costly are subsequent adoptions. For global environmental public goods whose provision requires new technical standards, getting one or two large countries to make the move first can greatly facilitate the widespread adoption of the appropriate new standards. The Montreal Protocol illustrates this: the development of chlorofluorocarbon-free refrigerants greatly reduced opposition to the protocol in industrial countries, and an agreement to transfer this new technology to developing countries then facilitated a world-wide agreement. In economic terms the point is that there are big fixed costs to the provision of global public goods, and many of these fixed costs can be for research and development. These research and development costs only have to be paid once because the requisite technologies only have to be developed once. If one country does this, others need not. So the first to adopt confers benefits on others (see Sandler 1998 for related points about the role of leader nations and the effect technology has on the stability of coalitions). The United States has usually been the first mover in these agreements.

How do these considerations apply to the Kyoto Protocol and the associated moves to reduce global emissions of greenhouse gases? Will a key technological breakthrough facilitate widespread progress, as in phasing out chlorofluorocarbons or lead additives? There are probably two strategic developments here: the development of clean vehicle engines and the commercialization of renewable energy sources. Japanese and German vehicle manufacturers are pressing hard for the development of fuel-cell technologies for cars, and British Petroleum and other energy companies are allocating rapidly rising research and development funds to renewable energy sources, mainly photovoltaic. The introduction of strict carbon dioxide emission standards by a few large economies could push these ventures to commercial viability—and start the process of widespread adoption.

There is another element to the role played by early adopters of a standard required for supporting the provision of a global public good. This additional effect interacts with reducing fixed costs. If some countries abate emissions of greenhouse gases, this confers benefits on nonabating countries and moves upwards the curve relating their benefits from abatement to the level of abatement and the costs they incur to abate. Nonabating countries now accrue positive benefits even when incurring no abatement costs, so that their cost-benefit relationship no longer goes through the origin (figure 2).

As a consequence of abatement by others, the net benefits from adoption in follower countries increase at all cost levels, and the maximum net benefit may increase from negative to positive. The net benefit curves have to be interpreted carefully. They show net benefits as a function of abatement at positive abatement levels, but at zero abatement the net benefit is always positive and given by the vertical intercept of the benefit curve. Why? Because even at zero abatement, a follower country benefits from the abatement activities of others. So the graph of net benefits relative to the abatement level for follower countries has a discontinuity at zero. Net benefits for these countries are positive at zero abatement because of benefits from the actions of others and the absence of abatement costs, but they jump down as soon as abatement begins because of the fixed costs incurred.

As other countries increase their abatement and move the benefit curves up, the fixed cost of abatement may also fall because of technological innovations, as explained above. This combination of circumstances can lead to a situation where the optimal abatement level for individual follower countries viewed on

FIGURE 2

Benefits increase when others abate

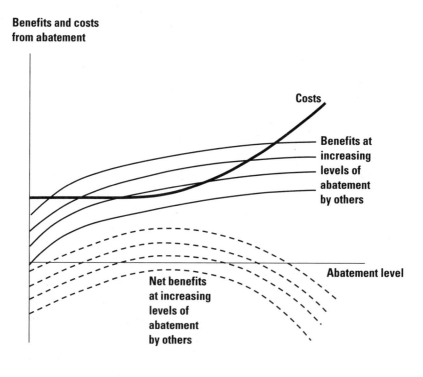

its own is positive (figure 3). There will be no tendency in such situations to totally opt out of an abatement agreement and free ride on others.

In sum, there are reasons to be guardedly optimistic about the possibility for durable agreements to support the provision of international public goods. Precedents are encouraging (though some are tragic), and features of the problem suggest that a self-interest in cooperation can emerge as costs fall following early investments by some countries.

COALITION FORMATION AND INTERNATIONAL POLITICS

Management of global public goods, including the creation of market-based mechanisms, implies global actions and global agreements. What is the nature of these agreements, and how can the international community relate to them?

To be effective, international agreements have to be attractive to all participants, because participation cannot be enforced, at least not in the way compliance with domestic laws can be enforced. The Montreal Protocol on Substances that Deplete the Ozone Layer has been effective because it is in the interests of all key players, and was carefully crafted to be so (Barrett in this volume). The remaining negotiations for the Kyoto Protocol have to achieve the same outcome, and make this protocol in the interests of developing and industrial countries. Crafting stable agreements of this type is challenging. But features of global public goods problems can, if properly exploited, help in attaining consensus on their provision.

Conventional wisdom runs counter to this, asserting that the free-rider problem is particularly destructive at the international level. The point here is that each country has an obvious incentive to let others cut back emissions

FIGURE 3

Costs fall when others develop the technology

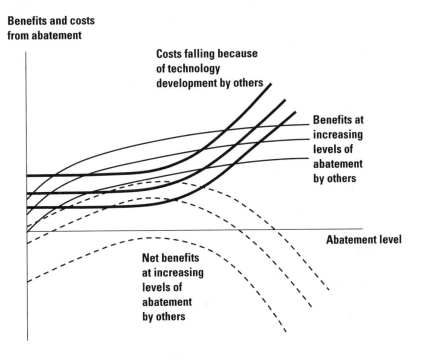

of global pollutants (and bear the costs of doing so) while it enjoys a share of the benefits. Precisely because a better global environment is itself a global public good, each country can benefit from improvements wrought by others at no cost to itself. Thus there is a sense in which a country's best course is to encourage others to go ahead and contribute to a better environment but not join them.

This rather cynical analysis misses the mark empirically: in 1990 there were about 150 international environmental treaties, and the number is still growing (Barrett 1994). Many are regional rather than global, but the issues are the same. Not all of them came into existence purely because of the altruism of their members: there has to be an element of self-interest, which the free-rider argument misses. Indeed, there seem to be two factors that help bring these treaties into existence and hold them together.

One has to do with the fact that the parties to these treaties are all members of a continuing international community in which they have interacted regularly for many years and expect to continue doing so. These interactions cover many areas, not just global or regional public goods: they cover security, trade, aid and many other issues. Analytically this means two things. One is that the countries involved in these agreements are picking moves in repeated games—that is, in strategic interactions that will continue indefinitely. The second is that the strategy spaces in these games are not restricted to moves concerning global public goods: the strategy spaces are much richer and contain many other dimensions. They include trade strategies, technology transfer strategies, security strategies and many more.

These two facts—repeated interaction and a complex strategy space—are important. A basic result in game theory tells us that there is much more scope for cooperative and mutually beneficial outcomes in strategic interactions that are repeated rather than once-off (Heal 1976). For example, if a prisoner's dilemma game is played once, the outcome for rational players is the inefficient one. But if it is repeated indefinitely, the efficient solution should emerge.[4] The complexity of the strategy space also helps. Another result in game theory tells us that efficient outcomes are more likely in games with high-dimensional strategy spaces.

What are the implications of this for managing the provision of international public goods? They are relatively simple: it helps to have a functioning international community that cooperates in many areas and that includes all countries likely to be involved in the provision and management of the public goods. Then we have the benefits of repeated interaction and of having many dimensions to negotiating strategies. If in addition a fair and equitable outcome can be realized, then, as stressed by Rao (in this volume), all countries will feel that they are a part of a beneficial repeated game and will have an interest in the long-run viability of the international community. This is clearly an argument against excluding countries from full participation in the international community as a way of exercising leverage over them.

CONCLUSION

The world of public goods continues to change. Many goods that were traditionally provided publicly have been privatized. Although publicly provided in the past, they are not necessarily strictly public goods, but often have an element of publicness through limited excludability or limited rivalry. For them, there has been a tendency to distinguish between the infrastructure, often a network, and the services provided on top of it. Privatization has tried to introduce competition in the provision of services that use the network—and to regulate the network provider.

In a distinct development that also involves the use of markets in the regulation of public goods, we have moved to a regime in which policy concerns focus on public goods that are privately produced. A growing tendency with such goods is to use the market to answer the "who will produce" question. This is associated with the growth of markets for emission permits and pollution rights.

Managing the provision of global privately produced public goods raises interesting questions that are currently on the agenda of the Framework Convention on Climate Change and the governments and agencies that want this convention to work. Many sceptics have focused on the free-rider issue and the prisoner's dilemma implicit in the efficient provision of public goods. This seems inappropriate, for it misses the context in which all of this occurs. There is an international community. The countries involved are a part of this community. And they are involved in many negotiations on a wide range of issues. In addition, there are adoption spillovers: the first adopter of policies to provide more of the global public good makes the task easier for those who come later.

These observations define a natural role for international diplomacy, with two parts. One is to fully involve countries whose cooperation is crucial in the international community on a continuing equitable basis and in many ways. The second, related to the adoption spillovers discussed earlier, is for the international community to encourage key actors to play a pump-priming role by making early moves towards new policies and standards, reducing the costs to those that will follow. Given the crucial role of early movers in establishing frameworks and technologies and in demonstrating feasibility, there may be a case for designing systems under which they will eventually recover some of the costs of being first, perhaps in the form of a type of intellectual property right.

NOTES

1. A Lindahl equilibrium provides extra instruments for this task—namely, extra prices—by considering personalized prices for public goods. Redistribution of endowments can substitute for the extra prices in a Lindahl equilibrium.

2. Although I cannot develop it here, this point is true even in a strictly second-best context where the total emission level being distributed between countries is not one associated with an efficient pattern of overall resource use. The connection between efficiency and distribution has long been known to be close in second-best policy choices.

3. By this I mean only that their income and price elasticities of demand are of the same order of magnitude. I am ruling out radically different valuations of private goods and the environment.

4. Martin (in this volume) makes the same point from a political science perspective.

REFERENCES

Barrett, Scott. 1994. "Self-Enforcing International Environmental Agreements." *Oxford Economic Papers* 46: 878–94.

Chichilnisky, Graciela, and Geoffrey M. Heal. 1994a. *Markets for Tradable Carbon Dioxide Emission Quotas: Principles and Practice.* A report to the Organisation for Economic Co-operation and Development. Washington, DC: OECD.

———. 1994b. "Who Should Abate Carbon Emissions? An International Viewpoint." *Economics Letters* 44: 443–49.

———, eds. 1999. *Environmental Markets.* New York: Columbia University Press.

Coase, Ronald H. 1960. "The Problem of Social Cost." *Journal of Law and Economics* 3: 1–44.

Dales, John H. 1968. *Pollution Property and Prices.* Toronto, Canada: University of Toronto Press.

Foley, Duncan K. 1970. "Lindahl's Solution and the Core of an Economy with Public Goods." *Econometrica* 38(1): 66–72.

Heal, Geoffrey M. 1976. "Do Bad Products Drive Out Good?" *Quarterly Journal of Economics* 90(3): 499–502.

———. 1998. *The Economics of Increasing Returns.* The International Library of Critical Writings in Economics. London: Edward Elgar.

Kristrom, Bengt, and Per Riera. 1996. "Is the Income Elasticity of Environmental Improvement Less than One?" *Environmental and Resource Economics* 7: 45–55.

Sandler, Todd. 1998. "Global and Regional Public Goods: A Prognosis for Collective Action." *Fiscal Studies* 19(1): 221–47.

CULTURAL HERITAGE AS PUBLIC GOOD

Economic Analysis Applied to Historic Cities

ISMAIL SERAGELDIN

As an essential part of humanity, culture is an end in itself. One of the least understood but most essential aspects of cultural identity is its contribution to a society's ability to promote self-esteem and empowerment for everyone, including the poor and the destitute. Thus cultural identity and cultural heritage appear very much as public goods that deserve public support.[1]

Culture is the complex of spiritual, material, intellectual and emotional features that characterize a society or social group. It includes not only arts and letters but also the beliefs, traditions, value systems, modes of life and fundamental rights of human beings. Conceptually, if we recognize the unique and the specific that so enrich us, we must also recognize the universal yearning for identity and meaning that binds us all in a common humanity. So, in addition to being valuable at the level of the community or the state, culture is also a global public good.

Granted, the substantive elements of a cultural heritage can evolve. In many parts of the world the defence of "tradition" and cultural specificity is used to legitimate the "authenticity" used to vitiate the new and to stifle creativity. Claims of cultural specificity justify the oppression of women and the perpetuation of intolerance and obscurantism. The pretence of that which deprives women of their basic human rights or mutilates them in the name of convention should not be given sanction. No society has progressed without making a major effort to empower its women through education and to end discrimination.

Thus a balance should be struck between the defence of particular traditions and other global public goods, such as universal standards and human rights. The approach to culture that I espouse here encourages diversity, creates a space of freedom in each society for the minority expression and the contrarian view and promotes inclusion and social cohesion. It is a rich and variegated concept.

Culture has been valued, nurtured and transmitted since the beginning of humanity. But only recently have attempts been made to understand it with the tools of economic analysis. The objective in this chapter is to review some methodological advances for the valuation of culture and cultural goods.

THE PROPER VALUATION OF CULTURE

The need for new tools is apparent if one briefly reviews what happens when cultural goods are treated like ordinary private goods. For example, one may be tempted to place a figure on the economic value of a particular monument by calculating the annual amount that tourists are spending to visit the site. But this approach could lead to three erroneous conclusions:

- That areas of the cultural heritage that do not generate a large enough tourist stream are not worth investing in. This conclusion denies the intrinsic worth of the cultural heritage, both for the people there and for the enrichment that it brings to the world at large by its very existence. After all, many of us will not visit any of the sites on the World Heritage List. But we would feel impoverished to know of the loss of such sites— and feel enriched by their continuing existence, even if we never visit them.

- That maximizing the number of tourists visiting the place and the amount that they spend would be desirable because it increases the benefit stream. In fact, in many cases such a development would destroy the charm of the place and denature the activities that are part of the cultural setting.[2]

- That if another and mutually exclusive investment—say, a casino on a beach—would increase the tourist dollars for the country, the old city should not be restored and the casino should be built.

None of these conclusions is justified or defensible. We must look for the intrinsic value of the cultural heritage above and beyond what it is likely to generate in terms of tourist dollars.

The special case of cultural heritage in historic cities

Much can be said about the nature of cultural expression and of cultural heritage. The discussion here is limited to the special case of historic cities in developing countries because it brings together so many aspects of the issue. Handling all these aspects effectively is akin to solving the elegant puzzle known as Rubik's Cube. In that puzzle aligning the mosaic of one face of the cube tends to undo the matched colours of the other faces. Similarly, promoting development and cultural heritage conservation in historic cities of the developing world—trying to accommodate sensitive architecture and urbanism, promote sound municipal finances, provide adequate incentives for the private sector, incorporate concern for the poor and the destitute and encourage community involvement and participation—while promoting socio-economic diversity and pluralism sometimes appears impossible. Like Rubik's Cube, however, the solution, though difficult, is possible. But it requires patience, dedication and imagination.

To understand better the faces of the Rubik's Cube in the case of historic cities, and the path to be followed for a solution, we must start by identifying the many actors, the levels of decision making and above all who pays and who benefits—a leitmotif that we must not lose sight of.[3] The actors are many: national and local governments, the international community and its agencies, the national and local tourists who visit historic cities, the international and national private firms that invest in the old historic core for commercial or real estate development, and the local residents, be they owners or renters. Special attention must be given to the poor, who risk being displaced by the unaffordability of the changes.[4] In addition, members of the local community, for whom this is not just home but also a fundamental part of their identity, can be agents of transformation. To do so, however, community members must be adequately mobilized and organized—especially women, who are primary agents in the networks of cooperation and reciprocity.[5] Strengthening these networks is critical to the maintenance of social solidarity.

HOW TO CONSERVE: ADAPTIVE REUSE AND FLEXIBILITY

What, how and why to conserve are questions that have long engaged many people.[6] Here I am concerned not just with the conservation and reuse of individual buildings—important as that is—but also with the more difficult challenge of conserving historical areas, an urban tissue, a sense of place[7] and an urban character (see Worksett 1969).[8] The need to preserve has to be matched by the need to provide flexibility of reuse. Excessively rigid adherence to restoration standards—where nothing is changed from the original—can lead to suboptimal use of properties.[9] This raises the need to review conservation practices[10] to ensure that purity of purpose does not constrain the ability to reuse buildings and thus strangle the economic and social revitalization of historic city cores.

Economics is the key

Whatever we do, we will not be able to mobilize the necessary amount of investment, or the right kind of investment, needed to fully accomplish the goals of revitalizing the economic base of an old city, restoring its glorious monuments, protecting its unique character and meeting the socio-cultural needs of its inhabitants[11] and the aspirations of its young. This inability raises a host of technical problems.[12] Solving them requires imagination and technical expertise, including imaginative reuse of old buildings (see Cantacuzino 1987 and Williams, Kellogg and Gilbert 1983, pp. 233–74), as well as money. And raising this money requires the application of rigorous economic and financial analysis that justifies the flows of public investments and creates adequate incentives for private action (see Lichfield 1988). Such analysis is not at present being applied systematically in the case of historic cities (see Burman, Pickard and Taylor 1995). The rest of this chapter is devoted to a discussion of the most recent thinking on the methodology of economic analysis for cultural heritage projects—and to some applications, namely Hafsia, Tunis (Tunisia), and Fez, Morocco.

THE ECONOMICS OF INVESTING IN CULTURAL HERITAGE

A full discussion of possible approaches to the problems of historic cities has been extensively debated elsewhere and is beyond the scope of this chapter. Most approaches generally involve some combination of the following:

- *Restrictions on activities in historic areas.* The most obvious restriction is not to destroy culturally significant structures. Restrictions may go further, however, by requiring particular standards of upkeep or specifying how that upkeep should be carried out—say, by requiring materials that match those originally used.[13] Public and private activities in such areas are also often restricted.
- *Conservation activities on particularly significant structures.*[14]
- *Measures to encourage conservation by other actors.* Because direct intervention to conserve all structures is impractical, conservation efforts depend on spontaneous efforts by others.

For conservation efforts in historic cities to succeed, a multiplicity of actors needs to undertake many disparate actions. Some of these actions can be deliberately chosen and directed by government decision-makers. But many others are outside their direct control and depend on independent decisions by private actors. Such efforts must include both an economic and a financial analysis. The economic (or social) analysis asks whether the proposed investments are worth undertaking: do their benefits to society exceed their costs? The financial (or private) analysis examines the costs and benefits that different groups will experience as a result of these investments and asks whether each group will gain or lose from them (see Squire and van der Tak 1975).

To some extent the techniques of standard urban economics can be used, and much solid work has been done within such a framework (see Couillaud 1997)—as with the excellent study of St. Petersburg by Butler, Nayyar-Stone and O'Leary (1996). But there is an added dimension that standard urban economics is poorly equipped to address: conservation investments in historic cities are also part of the total cultural heritage. I next discuss possible approaches to measuring the benefits of cultural heritage, drawing insight from environmental economics, which has been studying similar problems for some time.[15]

Building on the experience of environmental economics
Cultural heritage problems are qualitatively similar to problems encountered in conserving environmental assets. Analysis of the costs and benefits of protecting environmental assets has been at the heart of much of environmental economics.[16] Many of the services provided by environmental assets and by historic cultural heritage may not enter markets—or do so only indirectly and imperfectly. And many benefits are wholly intangible. Moreover, the benefits provided by cultural heritage sites are conceptually similar to those provided by, for example, national parks. Whether aesthetic benefits are derived from buildings or trees—and whether recreation benefits are derived from museum visits or fishing—makes little difference to the valuation problem. Recent advances in environmental economics are thus quite relevant to conducting a cost-benefit analysis of a project involving a cultural heritage site.

Categories of value
Cultural heritage sites differ from other sites because of their aesthetic, historical, cultural and social significance. Cultural heritage projects will have a wide range of effects. Some will be directly related to the cultural heritage dimension of the site. Others will not. Yet others will be a mix of both.[17] In similar circumstances, environmental economists generally take a comprehensive look at value using the concept of total economic value. Total eco-

nomic value is usually decomposed into categories of value. The breakdown and terminology vary slightly from analyst to analyst but generally contrast use value and nonuse value. Use value is further broken down into extractive (or consumptive) use value and nonextractive use value. Each is often further subdivided into additional categories. By disaggregating the value of a cultural heritage site into various components, the problem of measuring benefits generally becomes far more intelligible and tractable.

EXTRACTIVE USE VALUE. Extractive use value derives from goods that can be extracted from the site. For a forest, say, extractive use value would be derived from timber and other harvests. Buildings in historic living cities are being used as living, trading, and renting and selling spaces. Many of these categories of use are captured by markets and transactions in markets. But unlike a forest, the use of a historic city is not depleted unless the use is inappropriate or excessive, denaturing the beauty of the site or the character of the place. At some level a parallel exists to extractive use of a forest being kept at sustainable levels.

NONEXTRACTIVE USE VALUE. Nonextractive use value derives from the services the site provides. For example, wetlands often filter water, improving water quality for downstream users, and national parks provide opportunities for recreation. These services have value but do not require any goods to be harvested. The parallel for historic cities is clear: some people just pass through the city and enjoy the scenery without spending money there, and their use of the place is not captured by an economic or financial transaction.[18] Measuring nonextractive use value is considerably more difficult than measuring extractive use value.

A substantial part of environmental economics has been devoted to valuing such services,[19] and a variety of methods have been developed to do so (see Dixon and others 1994). This category of use value is extremely relevant to many aspects of cultural heritage areas—and is a key part of the discussion that follows. Among the nonextractive use values generally considered in environmental economics, those likely to have the most relevance to the valuation of cultural heritage are aesthetic and recreational value.

AESTHETIC VALUE. Aesthetic benefits are obtained when the fact of sensory experience is separate from material effect on the body or possessions. Aesthetic effects differ from nonuse value because they require a sensory experience, but aesthetic benefits are often closely linked to physical ones.

RECREATIONAL VALUE. Although the recreational benefits provided by a site are generally considered together as a single source of value, they are a result of different services that a site might provide. The extent of recreational benefits depends on the nature, quantity and quality of these services. A historic area could have rest areas, vistas and attractive meditation areas—in addition to shopping bazaars and monuments. The enjoyment derived by visitors from each of these depends on such factors as the cleanliness of the surroundings. Disaggregating the benefit into components eases the task of valuing it.

NONUSE VALUE. Nonuse value tries to capture the enrichment derived from the continued existence of major parts of the world heritage.[20] Even if one is not likely to visit these sites, one would feel impoverished if they were destroyed. In many cases this is referred to as existence value: the value that people derive from the knowledge that the site exists, even if they never plan to visit it. People place a value on the existence of blue whales even if they have never seen one and probably never will; if blue whales became extinct, many people would feel a definite sense of loss.

Other aspects of nonuse value include option value, the value obtained from maintaining the option of taking advantage of a site's use value at a later date (akin to an insurance policy), and quasi-option value, which derives from the possibility that even though a site appears unimportant now, information received later might lead us to re-evaluate it.[21] Nonuse values are the most difficult types of value to estimate, but they have obvious relevance for the assessment of cultural heritage sites.

Recognizing the beneficiaries

While the preservation of cultural heritage has diffuse externalities, many different actors are likely to benefit directly from an investment to protect the cultural heritage in historic cities. They include:

- Residents, making the distinction between renters and owner-residents, and absentee landlords, who qualify as a special category of investors (housing usually being regulated differently from businesses).
- Investors in businesses in the historic area, who may or may not be residents, including small traders and national and international private firms.
- Visitors to the historic city, some nationals, others international.
- Nonvisitors, distinguishing between national and international, which could be called "the world at large".

Further refinements are necessary for meaningful analysis: poor and rich, formal and informal and so on.

Measuring the benefits

Several methods are used in measuring benefits (see Stabler 1995; Pagiola 1996; and Serageldin and Pagiola 1998). Each has advantages and limitations.

MARKET PRICE METHODS. Although many benefits of cultural heritage sites do not enter markets, some do, most obviously when visitors pay a fee to enter a site.[22] The revenue from such fees provides a measure of the value people place on being able to visit the site. Some uses of cultural heritage sites have close substitutes that can be used to estimate the value of those uses. Thus the value of using a historic building as a school might be estimated by using the cost of the next best way to obtain the necessary space—for example, the cost of building and equipping a suitable structure. Cultural heritage sites might also induce a variety of economic activities, most obviously in the tourism industry (hotels, restaurants, shops). Standard techniques can be used to value these benefits. The difficulty generally arises in predicting the impact that changes in the cultural heritage site will have on the quantity of such services, not in estimating their value.

REPLACEMENT COST. The cost of replacing a good is often used as a proxy for its value (see Pearce 1993 and Winpenny 1991). This approach has two problems, however. First, it simply may not be possible to replace many cultural heritage sites, and where the site is only damaged, restoration cost might be used. Second, if the point is to decide whether a site is worth restoring, using the restoration cost as a measure of value is clearly of little use. Such an approach would argue that the more degraded the site, the costlier the restoration, and the greater the value. This is clearly faulty reasoning, though this measure may be appropriate for some critical aspects of the site where the value might reasonably be thought to be extremely high. In such cases the appropriate approach is cost-effectiveness rather than cost-benefit.

TRAVEL COST. The travel cost method uses information on visitors' total expenditure to visit a site to derive their demand curve for the site's services.[23] This method assumes that changes in total travel costs are equivalent to changes in admission fees. From this demand curve can be calculated the total benefit that visitors obtain. (Note that the value of the site is not given by the total travel cost; this information is used only to derive the demand curve.) The travel cost method was designed for and has been used extensively to value the benefits of recreation. But it depends on numerous assumptions, many of them problematic in international tourism, and is best used to measure the value visitors place on the site as a whole, rather than on specific aspects of the site.

HEDONIC METHODS. Many observed prices for goods are prices for bundles of attributes (see Rosen 1974). For example, property values depend on physical attributes of the dwelling (such as number and size of rooms and amenities such as plumbing and general condition); on the convenience of access to employment, shopping and education; and on a number of less tangible factors such as environmental quality. Because each house differs slightly from others, the influence of the various factors on its price can be broken down using statistical techniques known as hedonic methods if enough observations are available. This approach is of interest because many dimensions of cultural heritage are likely to be embodied in property values.[24] A historic structure, for example, may sell for more than an equivalent modern one. Hedonic techniques allow this effect to be measured holding other factors such as size and amenities constant. In essence the technique estimates the implicit prices for various attributes that together make up the sales price. Although these techniques have obvious applicability to the study of benefits of cultural heritage in urban settings, their use has often been limited by their considerable data requirements.[25]

CONTINGENT VALUATION. Contingent valuation is carried out by asking consumers directly about their willingness to pay to obtain an environmental good (see Bjornstad and Kahn 1996 and Jakobsson and Dragun 1996). A detailed description of the good accompanies details about how it will be provided. In principle contingent valuation can be used to value any environmental benefit. Moreover, because it is not limited to deducing preferences from available data, contingent valuation can be targeted quite accurately to ask about the specific changes in benefits that the proposed project would bring.

Contingent valuation has long been used to examine aesthetic benefits, and it is especially important in estimating existence value because it is the only way to measure it, since by definition existence value will not be reflected in behaviour. In developing countries contingent valuation has been used primarily to value publicly or privately provided goods such as water supply and sewerage in areas without existing services.

Contingent valuation methods have been the subject of severe criticism by some analysts (see Garrod and Willis 1990). But best practice guidelines have been developed for its use,[26] and it is now generally accepted that contingent valuation can provide useful and reliable information as long as these guidelines are followed. A pioneering example of the application of contingent valuation to cultural heritage conservation is presented below in the case study of Fez.

BENEFITS TRANSFER. Benefits transfer refers to the use of estimates obtained (by whatever method) in one context to estimate values in a different context. For example, an estimate of the benefit obtained by tourists viewing wildlife in one park might be used to estimate the benefit obtained from viewing wildlife in a different park. This approach must be used with considerable caution, however, because the commodity or service being valued must be extremely similar at both sites, as must the affected populations.

Because cultural heritage sites are unique, benefits transfer methods have little applicability. Yet there may be some relevance in considering benefits associated with international tourism. Since tourists at a historic site are likely to be drawn from the same pool of potential tourists as those at another site, it seems reasonable to assume they would place similar values on similar services. Thus, while this approach is probably of little use in valuing unique aspects of the site, it could be used for more generalized aspects. Of course, the original estimates being transferred must be reliable for any attempt at transfer to be meaningful.

Pitfalls in measuring benefits

The choice of technique depends on the problem being studied. Except in simple situations, a variety of techniques will likely be necessary to estimate the full range of benefits. Moreover, where substantial investments are contemplated, it might be desirable to cross-check estimates by deriving them from multiple sources. When bringing together the results of multiple techniques, two important points should be borne in mind: to avoid the twin dangers of underestimation (not measuring intangible benefits) and double-counting (using techniques that each capture part of the same benefit and adding them; see Serageldin and Pagiola 1998).

Another important pitfall comes from limiting the benefit stream to a fairly measurable, solid and understandable set: tourism revenues. As noted, a benefit stream that focuses exclusively on tourist revenue has many shortcomings. Yet another pitfall is the use of the likely impact of investment in (or expenditure on) restoring the heritage on gross domestic product (GDP). This approach equates the spending with the benefit of that spending. Thus letting a monument decay and then spending more on its restoration and conservation would appear to promote more benefits than avoiding the decay in the first place. These anomalies are common to GDP calculations and have been much debated in the economic literature.[27] Although some aspects of the issues can be addressed by such calculations—for example, spending on restoration projects has a higher multiplier effect than spending on other construction projects—they are likely to be misleading. This, despite their obvious attractiveness to decision-makers who have been conditioned to think of contributions to GDP growth as equivalent to increases in welfare and well–being.[28]

APPLICATIONS: HAFSIA AND FEZ

These methods, despite their promise, have not been widely applied. Two cases exemplify recent efforts in that direction: an analysis of public intervention in the Hafsia district of old Tunis and preparation of the project to revitalize Old Fez. The first is an ex post study of a completed experience; the second, an ex ante analysis that bears study, since it pioneers many aspects of the problems discussed here.

Hafsia, Tunis

This award-winning project exemplifies success in revitalizing the economic base and diversifying the social mix of the inhabitants of the old medina, the traditional city centre. The middle class has returned, making the old medina once more the locus of social and economic integration that it historically had been (see Davidson and Serageldin 1995). This project received widespread recognition in 1983, when it won the Aga Khan Award for Architecture (Cantacuzino 1985) because of its ability to contain the damage of earlier misguided efforts at large-scale development in the area. It did this by encircling the three apartment buildings and two schools, creating the covered souk that organically relinks the two parts of the old city texture and sensitively inserting some scaled housing that emulates the texture. The key questions raised then were whether a second phase would do more than just promote a physical implant of a few new houses. The response over the past 10 years has been spectacular. The second phase not only confounded the sceptics, it also won the unique distinction of a second Aga Khan Award for Architecture in 1995 (Davidson and Serageldin 1995).

In an amazing amalgam of public and private, the Municipality of Tunis, the Association pour la Sauvegarde de la Médina (ASM) and the Agence de Réhabilitation et Rénovation Urbaine (ARRU) have succeeded in reducing the high population densities in the old wekalas, dealing with the displaced through a sensitive resettlement scheme. Rehabilitation of the structures through credit schemes has worked extremely well in all but the rent-controlled, nonowner occupied structures. The success of the project in 1995 in nudging the government to finally remove the rent control law effectively lifted the remaining obstacle to commercially financed rehabilitation of these nonowner-occupied rental units (Harvard University Graduate School of Design 1994).

The second phase of the Hafsia project is financial, economic and institutional success. Cross-subsidies have made the project as a whole financially viable. Rates of return on public investment have been high. The multiplier effect of private to public funds has been on the order of three to one (Harvard University Graduate School of Design 1994). All this has been accompanied by a sensitive treatment of the urban texture and an integration of the old city with its surrounding metropolis. It is a project worthy of study and emulation (Serageldin 1986).

The results of the ex post financial analysis of revitalization efforts at Hafsia are summarized in table 1. As can be seen, the overall project was financially profitable thanks largely to the revenue from land sales and despite relatively high resettlement costs. The internal rate of return was found to be about 11% (Harvard University Graduate School of Design 1994).

TABLE 1

Project financial summary, Hafsia, Tunis
(millions of US dollars)

Upgrading component

Expenses		Revenues	
Infrastructure and community facilities	1.2	Repayment of home improvement loans	1.1
Home improvement loans	1.1	Profit sharing on land sales	1.2
Resettlement of displaced households	4.0	Repayment of resettlement loans	1.9
Subtotal	**6.3**		**4.2**

Rehabilitation component

Expenses		Revenues	
Land acquisition	1.4	Land sales to private developers	1.5
Construction	4.8	ARRU sales of housing and shops	7.8
Subtotal	**6.2**		**9.3**

Note: Data are from the perspective of the municipality and the parastatal implementing agency (ARRU).
Source: Harvard University Graduate School of Design 1994.

Fez, Morocco

Few cities have been as extensively studied as Fez. The most recent set of studies was completed in 1998 by many actors, including the Unit for Housing and Urbanization in Harvard University's Graduate School of Design, United Nations Educational, Scientific and Cultural Organization (UNESCO), Agence pour la Dédensification et la Réhabilitation de la Médina de Fès (ADER-FES) and the World Bank. Of particular note are the exemplary environmental impact assessment, the mapping of the socio-economic data and the analysis of urban market transactions, all of which yield fascinating insights into the dynamics of the urban situation in the old city. In addition, Carson and others (1997) is the first application of contingent valuation techniques to a cultural heritage conservation project.

The project for the rehabilitation of the old medina of Fez shows how a carefully designed operation can weave the different strands discussed in this chapter. The project is the most comprehensive effort to date to deal with the problems of a dense medina on the World Heritage List. Whether this project will be successfully implemented will depend on many things, not least the institutional arrangements chosen to implement it. But the project has already yielded an enormous amount of sophisticated analysis that should be a benchmark for future projects of this kind.

Briefly stated, the project will improve the infrastructure of the old medina, including better access for some parts of the area as well as an emergency road network; help owners and residents upgrade the dilapidated housing stock; and provide incentives for commercial activities and tourist visits. The project is conceived as a public-private partnership and designed in a participatory fashion, with ADER-FES playing an important role in grounding the operation in the community. External consultants from the Unit for Housing and Urbanization in Harvard University's Graduate School of Design have focused as much on innovative capacity building as on rigorous analysis.

The benefits of the project include improved infrastructure, especially the emergency road network; improved living conditions, including incentives for upgrading substantial parts of the residential housing stock; restored facets of a jewel of the world urban heritage; rejuvenated commercial activities in the old medina; and increased tourism revenues. The rate of return for the public investment appears to be quite robust (against downside scenarios of cost overruns on the order of 10–20%), remaining consistently above 10% after the eighth year.

In addition, a special study tried to capture the added value of the historic heritage. Three methods were used, in addition to the conventional estimation of added tourist revenues resulting from longer stays or increased spending per tourist.

- The first sample was of tourists who had visited Fez, and an estimate of how much they would be willing to invest to upgrade the old town yielded the figure of some $11 million.
- The second sample involved tourists in Morocco who had not visited Fez, and the estimate from that yielded some $33 million (because the number of tourists was larger, even if the per person willingness to pay was lower). This could be called an option value for the heritage of Fez because the interviewees could presumably visit there some day.
- The third sample involved a Delphi approach with Europeans who had never visited Morocco and who were not necessarily likely to visit in the near future. The estimates, when generalized to other European households, yield a nonuse value for the existence of the heritage in Fez of more than $300 million. The purpose of such numbers is not that they would be translated immediately into some added revenue for the maintenance and restoration of the Fez heritage, but that there is a large intrinsic value that goes beyond what is measured by or measurable by actual tourist revenues.

CONCLUSION

Much is being done to add rigor to the financial and economic analysis of cultural heritage conservation projects. What is important in this new work is that it gives context to the project intervention—its costs and benefits—in the reality of the multiplicity of interests and actors who make up the living city. In that sense the new work recognizes the externalities and tries to internalize them. Above all, this work tries to give due recognition to the intrinsic existence value of cultural heritage—not just as an object for tourists.

The estimation of such existence values is not a senseless academic exercise. It is an effort to grapple with and ultimately define the intrinsic worth of protecting the cultural heritage. It is similar to work that has been done in environmental economics to estimate the existence value of biodiversity. In that case analytical work over a number of years led to the recognition of the global benefits associated with the local costs of protecting the environmental asset—say, biodiversity in a rainforest. This was the foundation for creating the Global Environment Facility (GEF),[29] which has provided more than $3 billion in grants to poor countries to cover the incremental cost of protecting the global environment. (About $1 billion went for biodiversity projects.)

Surely the parallel with the cultural heritage of the world, especially that recognized as part of the World Heritage List, is striking. Conservation of the cultural built heritage needs to be seen in a fashion similar to the way we recognize conservation of the natural environment. Here too the costs of the conservation are local but the benefits are global. Perhaps we can hope to see a Global Cultural Facility that garners far more funds than are currently provided to the World Heritage Fund, which receives a mere fraction of what is needed to address the major challenges of conservation around the world.

NOTES

This chapter draws heavily on some of the author's prior publications, including Serageldin (1997a, b and forthcoming) and Serageldin and Pagiola (1998). The views expressed here are those of the author and should not be attributed to the World Bank or any of its constituent organizations.

1. A public good is a commodity for which use of a unit of the good by one agent does not preclude its use by other agents (Mas-Colell, Whinston and Green 1995).

Pure public goods are characterized by two features: nonexcludability and nonrivalry. If the benefits of the good are available to all once the good is produced, the good is said to be nonexcludable. Excluding others from consuming the good is either impossible or extremely costly. A good is nonrival if the consumption of the good by one agent does not diminish or prevent consumption by another agent. Hence nonrival benefits are consumed at zero marginal cost. Nonrivalry of consumption has also been referred to as the indivisibility of benefits. National defence, sunsets, pollution control devices and disease eradication programs are common examples of pure public goods. Conserving cultural heritage and promoting cultural identity, to the extent that it is not at the expense of minority cultures within the same society, fall into the category of public goods. On the other hand, some aspects of cultural heritage conservation can be privatized—for example, access to an individual site or moment can be restricted, and money charged. This becomes excludable but not rival, a form of impure public goods, and raises different theoretical questions.

Pure private goods are excludable and rival: the market price excludes consumers who are unwilling to pay the price, and consumption by the buyer prevents consumption by others. Between pure public and pure private goods are impure public goods with varying degrees of excludability and rivalry. Club goods are one particular subset of impure public goods for which membership exclusion exists but consumption is nonrival between members. For a thorough theoretical presentation on public goods and club goods, see Cornes and Sandler (1996).

2. This is also known as a problem of carrying capacity. Englin and Mendelsohn (1991) study this aspect in terms of congestion in visiting parks. They find that certain dirt roads on forest parks have attractive attributes that below certain saturation levels of utilization are considered an economic good, but beyond which they are seen as negative by users.

3. This essential principle is often overlooked in financial analysis, especially in the public finance setting. A long literature on the shifting and incidence of taxation forces us to be more discriminating in understanding the real ultimate beneficiaries and those who ultimately pay. The case is all the more important in the complex designs of projects and interventions dealing with historic cities, where general revenue may be used, where public and private intertwine and where cross-subsidies are almost invariably part of the arrangements.

4. Thoughtful practitioners of conservation have long called attention to the issue of the poor and minorities. See, for example, Williams, Kellogg and Gilbert (1983).

5. For a discussion of the importance of these networks of reciprocity for the poor, see Narayan (1997). For a discussion of how social capital helps the poor cope with difficulty in urban contexts, see Moser (1996). For a general discussion of the role of community action in dealing with urban problems, see Serageldin, Cohen and Leitmann (1995).

6. See Williams, Kellogg and Gilbert (1983) and Kain (1981). Kain's book discusses the origins of the conservation movement and its evolution with some references to experiences in Britain, Canada, France, Greece, Poland and the United States.

7. Dealing with such questions is always tricky, but several efforts have been made to bring rigor to what tends to be a very qualitative set of issues. See Morris (1983), which tries to use quantitative and qualitative methods to address the elusive quality of a sense of place.

8. Urban character tends to be defined by many factors in addition to prevalent architectural style. These factors include street alignment, variety of land use, variety of age of structures, mix of public, semipublic and private space, volumetric and height relations of structures and socio-economic activities of people. For a view that ties the external appearance of buildings to urban character, see Williams, Kellogg and Gilbert (1983).

9. A case from the United Kingdom is instructive. There were two buildings in Bath of identical appearance. One was completely remodelled on the inside, allowing a totally different layout while maintaining an unchanged façade. The second was maintained exactly as it was both inside and outside. The former rented at £18 per square foot, the going rate. The latter remained vacant for 2.5 years.

10. Despite excellent work, some conservationists can be too restrictive in their interpretations of the respect for the past. They would allow no improvements in buildings at all. In general, conservationists fall into different schools that do not necessarily have an agreed approach to restoration. See Serageldin and Zulficar (1989).

11. Today many special codes must be met, including historic codes, building codes and zoning regulations, including, for example, the need to make buildings more usable by people with disabilities (see Yatt 1998). This last has many pitfalls: see Evan Terry Associates (1998), which addresses the design requirements of the Americans with Disabilities Act.

12. Technical issues are difficult to address because ways of building and materials have changed. See New Landmarks Conservancy (1997), which includes success stories from the United States. For more recent historic buildings (built at the turn of the century and in the first half of the 20th century), see Ramsey and Sleeper (1998).

13. Many such restrictions are enforced in special management contracts for historic buildings owned by the public and given over to private use.

14. Conservation techniques can follow different philosophies, from minimal conservation efforts to efforts that recreate the grandeur of the original monument, sometimes making a point of showing the difference between the old and the new, other times just carefully identifying the new elements (tiles, bricks) in a nonvisible way, all the way to total reconstruction. This is in addition to questions of adaptive reuse of the building. For a discussion of this, see Serageldin and Zulficar (1989).

15. Although this idea has been discussed in the literature for some time (see Stabler 1995), the first quantitative application of these ideas to an actual historic preservation project for a city in the developing world is reported on here for Fez, Morocco.

16. For an excellent overview of environmental economics, see Schramm and Warford (1989); Markandaya and Richardson (1992); Munasinghe (1993); and Weiss (1994). Major new texts include Pearce and Turner (1990); Tietenberg (1992); Pearce and Warford (1993); and numerous volumes by Pearce, Barbier and others working in London. These include Pearce, Markandya and Barbier (1989, 1990); Barbier and others (1990); Barde and Pearce (1991); and Swanson and Barbier (1992).

17. To the extent that a site involves natural or human-made beauty, it may have enormous value independent of its historical or cultural value. Thus one can enjoy the charms of a medieval town centre without reference to the history of the individual monuments, although for many the city would evoke both memory and identity through its cultural heritage connotations.

18. In some ways the sense of place, the impact that it can have on behaviour and how it interacts with it are also intangible benefits that cannot be easily measured but are nevertheless real. See Serageldin (1996).

19. This work has a long tradition dating from the early efforts of Marion Clawson (see Clawson and Knetsch 1966) to the more recent work of David Pearce (see Pearce and Nash 1981 and Pearce and Warford 1993).

20. In fact, nonuse value can be an important part of the value of an environmental asset, and by extension, of cultural heritage. Lockwood, Loomis and DeLacy (1993) report on a contingent valuation method survey to estimate the willingness to pay for the conservation of national parks in Victoria, Australia. The survey highlighted the importance of existence values and bequest values, which accounted for 35% and 36% of the total valuation. In fact, nonuse value was three times use value.

21. There is a discussion of whether option value should be included with use values, since the intent of paying is to protect the possibility of future use, which arguably is different from existence values. On the other hand, because it does not involve current use, option value can legitimately be included with nonuse values.

22. The general view is that to the extent that there is a functional real estate market these benefits would be captured in the urban land and real estate price. Note that in many cases there is a proxy price for the property due to the presence of rent controls or other legal barriers to outright sale; key money and other informal transactions can be tracked for such values. An outstanding research effort of this type is given by Harvard University Graduate School of Design and others (1998).

23. Willis and others (1993) rightly argue that the travel cost method is best suited for measuring value only when the majority of the visitors to a site come from far away. Thus this method is largely inadequate for urban contexts

24. The quality of surroundings has been known to affect the price of residential property, so, by extension, the quality of a historic district can be a factor. Garrod and Willis (1991), for example, calculate the impact on residential prices of proximity to forest using a hedonic price method.

25. Efforts to include nonmarket factors have resulted in a number of efforts to develop scoring systems to value buildings of historic value or to prioritize government action. Canada's method of ranking based on a scoring system is reported on in Kalmann (1980). The United States has developed a similar ranking system, and the United Kingdom has used a "planning balance sheet analysis" form that was used to evaluate two alternative schemes in the Convent garden in the 1970s. All these are reviewed by Pickard (1995).

26. The NOAA panel set guidelines and burden of proof standards for producing legitimate contingent valuation results; see Arrow and others (1993). Critical assessments of how these criteria have fared can be found in Randall (1997) and Smith (1997).

27. Alberini and others (1997) transfer US mean willingness to pay to avoid air pollution–induced health effects to Taiwan (Province of China) and compare

results with contingent valuation findings obtained there. Bergland, Magnussen and Navrud (1995) evaluated and found unsatisfactory benefits transfer approaches as applied to two Norwegian river sites. Hanley and others (1998) discuss advantages and disadvantages of benefits transfer with contingent valuation and choice experiment valuation techniques. For general discussions of benefits transfer, see Boyle, Poe and Bergstrom (1992) and Desvousges, Naughton and Parsons (1992).

28. For a discussion of the technical pitfalls and issues of using GDP/GNP calculations, see Krishnan, Harris and Goodwin (1995, part V). Efforts to adapt national accounts to deal with environmental dimensions have been promising but limited; see Lutz (1993).

29. The limitations of the GNP/GDP concept were well captured by Robert F. Kennedy in 1968: "The Gross National Product does not allow for the health of our children, the quality of their education, or the joy of their play. It does not include the beauty of our poetry or the strength of our marriages; the intelligence of our public debate or the integrity of our public officials. It measures neither our wit nor our courage; neither our wisdom nor our learning; neither our compassion nor our devotion to our country; it measures everything, in short, except that which makes life worthwhile". Cited in Steer and Lutz (1994, p. 17).

30. The GEF provides grants to developing countries to cover the incremental cost of interventions that benefit the global environment where the local costs exceed the local benefits. Thus it provides direct payment for the global benefit part of the intervention. The GEF covers biodiversity, climate change, ozone and international waters.

REFERENCES

Alberini, Anna, Maureen Cropper, Tsu-Tan Fu, Alan Krupnick, Jin-Tan Liu, Daigee Shaw and Winston Harrington. 1997. "Valuing Health Effects of Air Pollution in Developing Countries: The Case of Taiwan." *Journal of Environmental Economics and Management* 34:107–26.

Arrow, Kenneth, Robert Solow, Paul Portney, Edward E. Leamer, Roy Radner and Howard Schuman. 1993. "Report of the National Oceanic and Atmospheric Administration Panel on Contingent Valuation." *Federal Register* 58(10): 4602–14.

Barbier, Edward B., Joanne C. Burgess, Timothy M. Swanson and David W. Pearce. 1990. *Elephants, Economics and Ivory*. London: Earthscan.

Barde, Jean-Philippe, and David W. Pearce, eds. 1991. *Valuing the Environment*. London: Earthscan.

Bergland, Olvar, Kristin Magnussen and Ståle Navrud. 1995. "Benefits Transfer: Testing for Accuracy and Reliability." Discussion Paper 95–03. Agricultural University of Norway, Department of Economics.

Bjornstad, David J,. and James R. Kahn, eds. 1996. *The Contingent Valuation of Environmental Resources: Methodological Issues and Research Needs.* New Horizons in Environmental Economics Series. Cheltenham, UK: Edward Elgar.

Boyle, Kevin, Gregory L. Poe and John C. Bergstrom. 1992. "Benefits Transfer Studies: Myths, Pragmatism and Idealism." *Water Resources Research* 28: 657–63.

Burman, Peter, Rob Pickard and Sue Taylor, eds. 1995. *The Economics of Architectural Conservation.* University of York, UK: Institute of Advanced Architectural Studies.

Butler, Stephen R., Ritu Nayyar-Stone and Sheila O'Leary. 1996. "The Law and Economics of Historic Preservation in St. Petersburg, Russia." Paper prepared for the US Agency for International Development. Urban Land Institute, Washington, DC.

Cantacuzino, Sherban. 1985. *Architecture in Continuity: Building in the Islamic World Today.* New York: Aperture.

———. 1987. *New Uses for Old Buildings.* London: Architectural Press.

Carson, Richard T., Robert C. Mitchell, Michael B. Conaway and Ståle Navrud. 1997. "Non-Moroccan Values for Rehabilitating the Fez Medina." Paper prepared for the World Bank on the Fez Cultural Heritage Rehabilitation Project. Harvard University Graduate School of Design, Cambridge, MA.

Clawson, Marion, and Jack L. Knetsch. 1966. *The Economics of Outdoor Recreation.* Baltimore, MD: Johns Hopkins University Press.

Cornes, Richard, and Todd Sandler. 1996. *The Theory of Externalities, Public Goods and Club Goods.* 2nd ed. New York: Cambridge University Press.

Couillaud, Michel. 1997. "Valorisation du Patrimoine de Fès: Rapport final." Fez: ADER-FES.

Davidson, Cynthia, and Ismail Serageldin, eds. 1995. *Architecture beyond Architecture.* London: Academy Editions.

Desvousges, William H., Michael C. Naughton and George R. Parsons. 1992. "Benefit Transfer: Conceptual Problems in Estimating Water Quality Benefits from Existing Studies." *Water Resources Research* 28: 675–83.

Dixon, John, Louise Fallon Scura, Richard A. Carpenter and Paul B. Sherman. 1994. *Economic Analysis of Environmental Impacts.* London: Earthscan.

Englin, Jeffrey, and Robert Mendelsohn. 1991. "A Hedonic Travel Cost Analysis for Valuation of Multiple Components of Site Quality: The Recreational Value of Forest Management." *Journal of Environmental Economics and Management* 21: 275–90.

Evan Terry Associates. 1998. *Avoiding the 100 Most Common ADA Design Errors.* New York: Wiley.

Garrod, Guy, and Ken Willis. 1990. "Contingent Valuation Techniques: A Review of Their Unbiasedness, Efficiency and Consistency." Countryside Change Unit Working Paper 10. University of Newcastle upon Tyne, UK.

————. 1991. "The Environmental Economic Impact of Woodland: A Two-Stage Hedonic Price Model of the Amenity Value of Forestry in Britain." *Applied Economics* 24:715–28.

Hanley, Nick, Douglas MacMillian, Robert E. Wright, Craig Bullock, Ian Simpson, Dave Parsisson and Bob Crabtree. 1998. "Contingent Valuation versus Choice Experiments: Estimating the Benefits of Environmentally Sensitive Areas in Scotland." *Journal of Agricultural Economics* 49(1): 1–15.

Harvard University Graduate School of Design. 1994. "Study of the Social and Economic Impact of the Hafsia Project." Project summary prepared by Harvard University Graduate School of Design, Unit for Housing and Urbanization; Association Sauvegarde de la Medina de Tunis; Agence de Réhabilitation et de Rénovation Urbaine; and République Tunisienne. Cambridge, MA.

Harvard University Graduate School of Design, Unit for Housing and Urbanization, World Bank, Government of Morocco, and ADER-Fez. 1998. "Rehabilitation of the Fez Medina: Project Summary Document." Cambridge, MA.

Jakobsson, Kristin M., and Andrew K. Dragun. 1996. *Contingent Valuation and Endangered Species: Methodological Issues and Applications.* New Horizons in Environmental Economics Series. Cheltenham, UK: Edward Elgar.

Kain, Roger, ed. 1981. *Planning for Conservation.* New York: St. Martin's Press.

Kalmann, Harold. 1980. *The Evaluation of Historic Buildings.* Ottawa, Canada: Ministry of the Environment.

Krishnan, Rajaram, Jonathan M. Harris and Neva R. Goodwin, eds. 1995. *A Survey of Ecological Economics.* Washington, DC: Island Press.

Lichfield, Nathaniel. 1988. *Economics in Urban Conservation.* Cambridge, UK: Cambridge University Press.

Lockwood, Michael, John B. Loomis and Terry DeLacy. 1993. "A Contingent Valuation Survey and Benefit-Cost Analysis of Forest Preservation in East Gippsland, Australia." *Journal of Environmental Management* 38: 233–43.

Lutz, Ernst, ed. 1993. *Towards Improved Accounting for the Environment.* Washington, DC: World Bank.

Markandaya, Anil, and Julie Richardson, eds. 1992. *Environmental Economics: A Reader.* New York: St. Martin's Press.

Mas-Colell, Andreu, Michael D. Whinston and Jerry R. Green. 1995. *Microeconomic Theory.* New York: Oxford University Press.

Morris, Colin. 1983. "Townscape Images: A Study in Meaning." In Roger Kain, ed., *Planning for Conservation*. New York: St. Martin's Press.

Moser, Caroline O.N. 1996. *Confronting Crisis: A Comparative Study of Household Responses to Poverty and Vulnerability in Four Poor Urban Communities.* ESD Studies and Monographs Series 8. Environmentally Sustainable Development Department. Washington, DC: World Bank.

Munasinghe, Mohan. 1993. *Environmental Economics and Sustainable Development.* Washington, DC: World Bank.

Narayan, Deepa. 1997. *Voices of the Poor: Poverty and Social Capital in Tanzania.* ESD Studies and Monographs Series 20. Environmentally Sustainable Development Department. Washington, DC: World Bank.

New Landmarks Conservancy. 1997. *Historic Building Facades: The Manual for Maintenance and Rehabilitation.* New York: Wiley.

Pagiola, Stefano. 1996. "Economic Analysis of Investments in Cultural Heritage: Insights from Environmental Economics." World Bank, Washington, DC.

Pearce, David W. 1993. *Economic Values and the Natural World.* London: Earthscan Publications.

Pearce, David W., Anil Markandya and Edward B. Barbier. 1989. *Blueprint for a Green Economy.* London: Earthscan.

———. 1990. *Sustainable Development: Economics and Environment in the Third World.* Aldershot, UK: Edward Elgar.

Pearce, David W., and C.A. Nash 1981. *The Social Appraisal of Projects.* London: Macmillan.

Pearce, David W., and Kerry Turner. 1990. *Economics of Natural Resources and the Environment.* Baltimore, MD: Johns Hopkins University Press.

Pearce, David W., and Jeremy J. Warford. 1993. *World without End: Economics, Environment, and Sustainable Development.* New York: Oxford University Press.

Pickard, Rob. 1995. "Setting the Scene: A Review of Current Thinking." In Peter Burman, Rob Pickard and Sue Taylor, eds., *The Economics of Architectural Conservation.* University of York, UK: Institute of Advanced Architectural Studies.

Ramsey, Charles, and Harold R. Sleeper. 1998. *Traditional Details for Building Restoration, Renovation and Rehabilitation.* New York: Wiley.

Randall, Alan. 1997. "The NOAA Panel Report: A New Beginning or the End of an Era?" *American Journal of Agricultural Economics* 79(5): 1489–94.

Rosen, Sherwin. 1974. "Hedonic Prices and Implicit Markets." *Journal of Political Economy* 82(1): 34–55.

Schramm, Gunter, and Jeremy J. Warford, eds. 1989. *Environmental Management and Economic Development.* Baltimore, MD: Johns Hopkins University Press.

Serageldin, Ismail. 1986. "Financing the Adaptive Reuse of Culturally Significant Areas." In Yudhishthir Raj Isar, ed., *The Challenge to Our Cultural Heritage: Why Preserve the Past?* Washington, DC: Smithsonian Institution Press and Paris: United Nations Educational, Scientific, and Cultural Organization.

———. 1996. "Architecture and Behaviour: The Built Environment of Muslims." In Suha Özkan, ed., *Faith and the Built Environment: Architecture and Behaviour in Islamic Cultures.* Lausanne, Switzerland: Architecture & Comportment.

———. 1997a. "Our Past Is Our Future: Investing in Our Cultural Heritage." Paper presented at the Organization of World Heritage Cities conference on Tourism and World Heritage Cities—Challenges and Opportunities, September 17–19, Evora, Portugal.

———. 1997b. "Solving the Rubik's Cube: Cultural Heritage in Cities of the Developing World." *Urban Age* 4(4): 5–7.

———. Forthcoming. "Revitalization of Historic Cities: The Need for a New Economic Analysis." In Doris AbuSeif-Behrens, ed., *Papers in Honor of Laila Ali Ibrahim.*

Serageldin, Ismail, and Stefano Pagiola. 1998. "Investments in Cultural Heritage: Preserving Historic Cities in Developing Countries." World Bank, Washington, DC.

Serageldin, Ismail, and Said Zulficar. 1989. "A Living Legacy." In Ismail Serageldin, ed., *Space for Freedom: The Search for Architectural Excellence in Muslim Societies.* London: Butterworth Architecture.

Serageldin, Ismail, Michael A. Cohen and Josef Leitmann, eds. 1995. *Enabling Sustainable Community Development.* ESD Proceedings Series 8. Environmentally Sustainable Development Department. Washington, DC: World Bank.

Smith, V. Kerry. 1997. "Pricing What Is Priceless: A Status Report on Non-Market Valuation of Environmental Resources." In Henk Folmer and Thomas Tietenberg, eds., *The International Yearbook of Environmental and Resource Economics.* Williston, VT: American International Distribution.

Squire, Lyn, and Herman van der Tak. 1975. *Economic Analysis of Projects.* Baltimore, MD: Johns Hopkins University Press.

Stabler, Michael. 1995. "Research in Progress on the Economic and Social Value of Conservation." In Peter Burman, Rob Pickard and Sue Taylor, eds., *The Economics of Architectural Conservation.* University of York, UK: Institute of Advanced Architectural Studies.

Steer, Andrew, and Ernst Lutz. 1994. "Measuring Environmentally Sustainable Development." In Ismail Serageldin and Andrew Steer, eds., *Making Development Sustainable: From Concepts to Action.* ESD Studies and Monographs Series 2. Environmentally Sustainable Development Department. Washington, DC: World Bank.

Swanson, Timothy M., and Edward B. Barbier, eds. 1992. *Economics for the Wilds: Wildlife, Wildlands, Diversity and Development.* London: Earthscan.

Tietenberg, Thomas H. 1992. *Environmental and Natural Resource Economics.* 3rd ed. New York: HarperCollins.

Weiss, John. 1994. *The Economics of Project Appraisal and the Environment.* Brookfield, VT: Edward Elgar.

Williams Jr., Norman, Edmund Kellogg and Frank B. Gilbert, eds. 1983. *Readings in Historic Preservation: Why? What? How?* New Brunswick, NJ: Center for Urban Policy Research.

Willis, Ken, Guy Garrod, Christopher T. Saunders and Martin Whitby. 1993. "Assessing Methodologies to Value the Benefits of Environmentally Sensitive Areas." Countryside Change Unit Working Paper 39. University of Newcastle upon Tyne, UK.

Winpenny, James T. 1991. *Values for the Environment.* London: Her Majesty's Stationery Office.

Worksett, Roy. 1969. *The Character of Towns: An Approach to Conservation.* London: Architectural Press.

Yatt, Barry D. 1998. *Cracking the Codes: An Architect's Guide to Building Regulations.* New York: Wiley.

HEALTH

The control of infectious diseases has been a staple of international diplomacy for more than a hundred years. Yet despite many advances, global health threats continue to loom large—and might even be on the rise. As global economic integration proceeds, health interdependence is deepening. The two chapters in this section reflect on both traditional and new types of global health risks.

In his chapter on global epidemiological surveillance, Mark W. Zacher points to two problems: the reluctance of governments to report disease outbreaks and the lack of capacity in many countries to adequately monitor public health and respond to outbreaks. Zacher suggests that increased involvement by nongovernmental organizations (NGOs) will help remedy at least part of the disclosure problem. "Bad" news travels faster today due to the spread of the Internet and the growth of international networks of health professionals. Still, Zacher emphasizes that the expanded role of NGOs and individuals in disclosure does not take away from the need for an international organization, such as the World Health Organization (WHO) to verify and legitimate outbreak reports and to coordinate international responses to outbreaks. In addition, international development assistance has an important role to play in improving the weak links in global prevention and surveillance systems. National capacities to prevent, report and control outbreaks can and should be improved in many developing countries in the interest of reducing the common global risk posed by infectious diseases.

The second chapter in this section explores the new context of global health interdependence in a world that increasingly resembles a global village. Lincoln C. Chen, Tim G. Evans and Richard A. Cash argue that today noncommunicable diseases have a global dimension. The reason is that bad consumption habits travel through global marketing and media, and new threats have emerged from such global bads as ozone depletion and climate change. The authors reason that in the future global health will increasingly be provided by private parties rather than state-run services—a development that will place greater stress on the poor. In response, the authors suggest a number of incremental steps to increase the effectiveness and fairness of national and international health policies. They envision the provision of global health as a multiactor process involving, besides governments, academics, private industry, NGOs and the media. Sometimes the interactions between different groups of actors will be harmonious, but at other times they may be conflictual. Regarding international organizations, the authors see their role primarily as a catalytic one—providing intermediate global public goods, such as relevant information, or negotiating norms and standards. Like Zacher, the authors emphasize the critical importance of development assistance aimed at enhancing national capacities and health performance in weaker countries. Similar recommendations could be made for international organizations facilitating the provision of other public goods.

GLOBAL EPIDEMIOLOGICAL SURVEILLANCE

International Cooperation to Monitor Infectious Diseases

MARK W. ZACHER

Infectious diseases have killed more people throughout history than war. During the Justinian era of the Roman Empire a third of the population died from what was probably the plague, and in the 14th century the Black Death killed almost a third of Europeans. In the 16th and 17th centuries between 60% and 90% of the native population of the Americas from Mexico southward died of smallpox, measles or influenza. In the 19th century millions died from seven cholera pandemics that spread from South Asia. Yellow fever was also a major killer during this time. Even as late as 1918–19 a swine flu ("the Spanish flu") killed roughly 22 million people throughout the world, with Europe being the hardest hit. Until the end of the 19th century more soldiers died from disease than combat (Hobson 1963; Howard-Jones 1975, 1981; McNeill 1976; Dols 1977).

The development of modern surveillance can be traced to 1897, when the states attending the International Sanitary Conference acknowledged the need for international health surveillance. In 1902 the new Pan-American Sanitary Bureau was directed to collect and disseminate information on patterns of disease outbreaks. In 1903 countries adopted the International Sanitary Convention, which called for the creation of an international organization to monitor the international ecology of diseases. This in turn led to the creation of the Organisation Internationale d'Hygiène Publique (OIHP) in Paris in 1907, which, as one of its central functions, gathered information on outbreaks for distribution to member states. Along with the Health Organization of the League of Nations (which conducted some surveillance), the OIHP was a precursor of the World Health Organization (WHO), established in 1948, in the field of international monitoring. While global interest in health surveillance was relatively weak between the 1940s and the 1980s, today there is a renewed interest in international cooperation.

There are many good reasons for this heightened interest, including new health risks and better communications. But it is also because in a world of increased mobility—of people and goods—health risks anywhere can pose a threat everywhere. Thus the knowledge generated through international health surveillance has an important public goods dimension. Because information about existing risks is often of great interest and benefit to all countries, it is increasingly difficult to withhold this information given the strength of civil society and the media.

Yet knowledge about disease outbreaks has a peculiar quality. While the international community may benefit, publicity about an outbreak can have national and private costs for an affected country in the form of trade embargoes or faltering tourism. As the following analysis shows, these possible adverse effects can serve as a powerful incentive not to comply with requests.

This chapter identifies policy measures that, based on experience, can help foster international cooperation in disease surveillance. The most important are:

- Countries must be encouraged to accurately report outbreaks, and this requires that other states not impose inappropriate and useless barriers to the entry of goods, travellers and carriers from the areas of outbreak. International organizations such as the WHO should play prominent roles in educating countries on particular outbreaks and appropriate responses.

- To avoid a moral hazard, emphasis should also be placed on the responsibilities of countries to strengthen their health systems, including surveillance. Preventing an outbreak is far easier than controlling and curing an epidemic later on.

- International development assistance is necessary so that developing countries can achieve speedy progress in building surveillance capabilities at the national level. It is encouraging that some aid donors are increasing their allocations to the health sector.

- International disease surveillance increasingly involves national governments, international organizations, nongovernmental organizations (NGOs) and professional groups and the private sector, and the multiplicity of actors strengthens global monitoring.

- Nevertheless, international organizations continue to play a crucial role. They validate information and, should the information reveal the need for action, they can coordinate responses and be a trusted partner of countries that need support.

This chapter describes the historical evolution of global epidemiological surveillance, analyses the factors that have influenced its strengths and weaknesses and evaluates some of the international surveillance programs and related regulations that have been accepted or considered in the 1990s. With regard to the explanatory analysis, there is an underlying focus on how the characteristics of epidemiological surveillance as an international public good have influenced international cooperation. A short section briefly discusses the chapter's general findings and arguments, especially regarding international health monitoring as a public good. The discussion then focuses on international surveillance efforts during several periods leading up to the 1990s, a time that has seen a dramatic increase in concern over emerging and re-emerging infectious diseases.

The chapter is largely confined to the surveillance of epidemic diseases that can suddenly infect and kill many people (for example, cholera) because international conferences have largely focused on these diseases. The paper does not focus on endemic diseases that are always prevalent and killing people (malaria, for instance), although they are discussed at certain points. Some diseases can be classified in both groupings, but for the most part diseases can be put in the endemic or epidemic categories (Lederberg, Shope and Oaks 1992; Garrett 1994; WHO 1996).

The discussion of past and present international epidemiological cooperation contributes to the growing realization that one of the most important roles of modern international organizations is to encourage states to share knowledge that, in turn, allows countries to make sounder decisions on strategies of cooperation. Robert Keohane's (1984) institutionalist theory of international cooperation focuses on the role of institutions in reducing uncertainty by enhancing the body of knowledge available to states (see also Martin in this volume). Dani Rodrik (1996) has also noted that perhaps the central role of international organizations is to improve the knowledge base on which officials can base their calculations of proposals for collaboration. While greater knowledge may not always lead to cooperation, collaboration is strengthened when it helps reduce uncertainty about the implications of alternative strategies.

INTERNATIONAL DISEASE SURVEILLANCE AS A GLOBAL PUBLIC GOOD

Knowledge about the world's health has many public goods aspects (Sandler 1992). It is, in large measure, nonrivalrous in consumption and nonexcludable.

Nonrivalry in consumption refers to the ability of all to benefit from a good once it is produced. In the case of epidemiological surveillance, all countries benefit in some way from knowledge of foreign outbreaks of infectious diseases because it allows countries to take measures to protect their people and prepare their medical institutions to cope with threatening diseases. And if improved knowledge leads to international activities to control diseases at their source, many countries benefit.

There are, however, some caveats. Not all diseases are likely to strike all countries, so some countries may have little concern about the spread of some diseases. And some countries believe that, even if a certain disease were discovered within their borders, they have the medical capabilities to care for citizens who contract it. At the same time, since there are always some diseases that concern all countries, a broad knowledge of global epidemiological trends benefits all.

Nevertheless, the data provided by international surveillance are of little benefit to countries that lack the medical, technological and financial resources to respond to new outbreaks. This is particularly true today for many developing countries. All countries can still benefit, however, from the activities of a few major states, NGOs and international organizations that have international health assistance programmes. Their work throughout the world supports the position that the benefits of epidemiological intelligence are nondivisible for all countries.

The second issue regarding surveillance as a public good concerns whether information on foreign disease outbreaks, or the remedial action taken, can be withheld from states, or whether the benefits are nonexcludable. To a degree, global epidemiological intelligence collected by individual countries, or even international organizations, may not or need not be internationally shared. In fact, the WHO's Rumor Outbreak Page is not distributed to all member states (see below). But through modern information technology and the global media, serious outbreaks are reported rapidly, and it would be difficult for a country, or even a few countries, to hide knowledge of one. Similarly, it would be difficult to deny medical information to afflicted countries once human lives are threatened. Any attempt to deny developing countries access to epidemiological intelligence because they could not afford it would be unacceptable.

HISTORICAL TRENDS

Adoption of the International Sanitary Convention and creation of the OIHP marked the beginning of international surveillance of infectious diseases in the 20th century. At the same time, a less formal reporting system was created under the Pan-American Sanitary Bureau.

At first states were only supposed to report outbreaks of a few diseases under the OIHP surveillance system, although states voluntarily provided information on other diseases as well. Initially, only reporting on cholera and plague was required, and subsequently, yellow fever, typhus and relapsing fever. These tended to be the diseases that Western European countries, which dominated the creation of the health regime, feared would spread from Asia, Africa, Latin America and Eastern Europe.

Although countries were not formally obliged to send information directly to the OIHP, and the OIHP was not obliged to disseminate information to member states, both the organization and the countries did disseminate information. The OIHP compiled and regularly distributed a bulletin containing disease information, and publication continued during the Second World War. The League of Nations Health Organization's similar *Weekly Epidemiological Record* also survived the war (Williams 1969; Goodman 1971, pp. 71–104; Howard-Jones 1975, 1978; Cooper 1989; Schepin and Yermakov 1991, pp. 183–228).

There is little indication, however, that the information that was collected and disseminated was greatly valued. Secondary literature on international health over the first four decades of this century contains no mention of any studies that evaluated the surveillance systems of the OIHP, the International Sanitary Convention, or the Health Organization of the League of Nations. The absence of such studies may reflect the fact that international mechanisms for surveillance were not particularly critical to the international health concerns of industrial countries.

The introduction of more modern public health programs and cleaner water (particularly on boats) reduced fears of the spread of cholera and plague across borders. In addition, industrial countries produced new medicines to treat these diseases. While yellow fever sometimes posed a serious problem in Latin America and Africa, the advent of a vaccine and better medical treatment reduced concern about it. Typhus and relapsing fever, diseases associated with squalid living conditions, armies and famine, largely disappeared after horrible outbreaks in Eastern Europe between 1918 and 1922, and were contained by the use of DDT during the Second World War.

Furthermore, at the time the OIHP data did not fill a crucial gap in information. Industrial countries already had first-hand access to information because the European powers knew a great deal about health conditions in their colonies and the United States was familiar with health conditions in Latin America. The Egyptian Quarantine Board, controlled by Britain, provided considerable intelligence about the movement of diseases between Asia and the Mediterranean, as well as health conditions at Muslim holy sites in Saudi Arabia.

The impact of the early surveillance was also limited because countries often did not report on disease outbreaks for fear of losing commerce. This pattern has held over the course of this century (Goodman 1971, pp. 71–104; Howard-Jones 1975, 1978; Brown 1979; Arnold 1988; Schepin and Yermakov 1991, pp. 183–228; Weindling 1995; Watts 1997, pp. 167–268).

From the late 1940s through the 1980s

After the Second World War the World Health Organization assumed the OIHP's task of convening conferences to revise the International Sanitary Convention (renamed the International Sanitary Regulations). Many (mostly minor) revisions were considered between 1949 and 1951, and none significantly concerned surveillance. Most important, members agreed that the International Sanitary Regulations now required approval by a two-thirds majority in the World Health Assembly (rather than by the traditional treaty-making conference) and were binding on all member countries unless they contracted out of all or specific obligations (Goodman 1971, pp. 151–86; Schepin and Yermakov 1991, pp. 246–48).

Even with the 1951 revision, there was little indication that members considered the new regulations any more important than the previous International Sanitary Convention. In the WHO committee that dealt with the regulations, there was more discussion of "excessive measures" than of disease surveillance or border controls for travellers (WHO documents for the Committee on International Quarantine, renamed in 1969 the Committee on International Surveillance of Communicable Diseases).

Even the process of decolonization, which reduced colonial powers' knowledge of health conditions in Asia and Africa, did not spark greater concern about surveillance. Despite exponential growth in international travel, and despite the fact that it was impossible to identify individuals with various diseases at borders, little effort was made to develop good surveillance that could help protect national populations (Delon 1975; Leive 1976, pp. 33–144; Belanger 1983, pp. 95–113; Fidler 1997, pp. 832–51).

This casual attitude of WHO member states towards the regulations was rooted in medical developments and attitudes that emerged in the period before the Second World War. In particular, the fear that countries could be swamped by outbreaks diminished with the availability of more advanced medical cures and preventive measures. The incidence of the international transmission of cholera, plague, yellow fever, typhus, relapsing fever and smallpox—particularly from developing to industrial countries—declined, and smallpox was completely eliminated in the 1970s. This was an era when people were increasingly confident that there was "a drug for every bug". In 1969 the US Surgeon General even remarked that it was time to "close the book" on infectious diseases and focus attention on noninfectious diseases such as cancer and heart disease (Fidler 1996b, p. 1).

At the same time, countries remained reluctant to report disease outbreaks that might cause other countries to impose restrictions on entry of their citizens and goods. In particular, governments balked at admitting an outbreak of cholera and plague because such announcements tended to attract harsh responses from other countries. In 1970 the WHO director-general took the unusual step of announcing an outbreak of cholera in Guinea after the government refused to do so. The director of the Pan-American Health Organization later took a similar step, calling the president of a country and asking him to announce an outbreak (Goodman 1971, pp. 247–80; Leive 1976, pp. 33–144; interviews).

Since 1951 states have been required by the International Sanitary Regulations (renamed the International Health Regulations in 1969) to notify the WHO within 24 hours of cases of designated diseases (including, as of 1981, those on airplanes and ships) and to obtain laboratory diagnoses. States are also required to inform the WHO and travellers of measures they intend to enact and to submit weekly reports on the development of outbreaks. In practice, however, many states have not reported outbreaks, and when the WHO has announced such occurrences, it is often some time after the fact. This rather weak system, hardly the fault of the WHO secretariat or its committees, reflected the lack of concern about the transmission of diseases among industrial countries and an unwillingness to suffer the consequences of reporting among many developing countries (Delon 1975; WHO 1983; Fidler 1997; interviews).

The transformation in the 1990s

The emergence of the human immunodeficiency virus (HIV) and acquired immune deficiency syndrome (AIDS) in the early 1980s and an increasing recognition of the problem of drug-resistant diseases (especially strains resistant to antibacterial drugs) provided the first real wake-up calls to countries on the importance of surveillance. For the first time in a long while, major industrial countries began to take a serious interest in controlling the international spread of infectious diseases.

The early and mid-1990s witnessed important outbreaks of new and old diseases in developing countries. Cholera struck Peru in 1991, Rift Valley fever hit Egypt in 1994 and plague struck India in 1994 and Chile in 1995. Ebola was found in Zaire and Gabon in 1996, Hantavirus in Chile in 1997, Rift Valley fever in Kenya in 1998 and Avian flu in Hong Kong, China in 1998. There were also highly publicized outbreaks of Lyme disease, Legionnaires disease, Hantavirus and water-borne and food-borne outbreaks of E. coli in the United States (WHO 1995a, 1996).

A surge in publications on infectious diseases also helped fuel concern. Among them in the early 1990s were the US Institute of Medicine's *Emerging Infections* (Lederberg, Shope and Oaks 1992), Laurie Garrett's *The Coming Plague* (1994), Richard Preston's *The Hot Zone* (1994), the US Centers for Disease Control's *Addressing Emerging Infectious Disease Threats* (CDC 1994) and the US National Science and Technology Council's *Infectious Diseases— A Global Health Threat* (CISET 1995). Most commentaries accurately stressed that it is impossible to prevent infected people from entering foreign countries and argued instead that early detection and control of diseases were needed at their source. David Fidler, after reviewing various analyses of the infectious disease threat, noted that they all identify surveillance as the most important strategy (1997, p. 822).

Lessons

Recent outbreaks of disease taught a number of lessons on surveillance— although they were largely the same lessons health experts learned long ago. The central lesson is that inadequate information on the risk of disease outbreaks can cause grave commercial harm. The 1991 cholera outbreak in Peru cost the country nearly $800 million in trade restrictions and lost tourism, largely because other countries did not understand the nature of the outbreak and the possible impacts quickly enough. The 1994 plague outbreak in India cost the country $1.5 billion in trade and travel restrictions. India refused to publicly acknowledge the outbreak for a long time despite Cable News Network (CNN) pictures of several hundred thousand people fleeing Surat. As it turned out, the number of deaths was small (fewer than 60) and there were no known cases of the plague's transmission outside India.

In many cases the international community overreacts. Incomplete media coverage, failure of governments to report an outbreak and ignorance of other countries can all conspire to make a country an international pariah. The image of panic broadcast by CNN during the Indian plague outbreak exacerbated the situation by fuelling groundless fears. When a minor outbreak of plague occurred in Peru in 1995, countries slapped restrictions on Peruvian travellers and goods throughout Latin America despite attempts by the Pan-American Health Organization to educate these countries on the realities of the outbreak. Some of the most advanced countries in Latin America imposed the most restrictive barriers. These events indicate that states will continue to show reluctance in reporting disease outbreaks as long as other states are not committed to avoiding "excessive measures" such as bans on planes and ships landing (WHO 1996; Fidler 1997, pp. 823–24).

The benefits of transparency

The dangers of mishandling an outbreak were demonstrated by the Indian experience in 1994. The failure to admit the plague outbreak or to invite international officials to provide public evaluations, combined with incomplete reporting by the media and the ignorance of other countries to the implications of the outbreak, wreaked serious economic harm on India. Other countries were also harmed by the restrictions they imposed on India. The Gulf states suffered a great deal from the barriers they imposed on the entry of Indian ships and planes, and Canada spent $750,000 monitoring travellers from India and establishing extra precautionary health measures at airports.

The value of inviting the WHO to appoint a public spokesperson was demonstrated during the Ebola outbreak in Zaire in 1995. The WHO spokesperson's media briefings on the development of the outbreak calmed the concerns of governments around the world.

However, when the WHO sought not only to be the official media spokesperson during an outbreak of Rift Valley fever in Kenya in 1998, but also to coordinate external medical responses, it became apparent that other international bodies, foreign governments and NGOs had their own medical agendas and did not want to follow the WHO's lead. The episode highlighted the need for protocols on how the WHO, international organizations, doctors from foreign laboratories, NGOs and local government officials should coordinate their surveillance and remedial activities.

Crises require "best-shot" strategies

Only a few countries have laboratories with the capability to diagnose a disease and prescribe a response, especially for diseases such as Ebola. Although there is a system of more than 200 WHO Collaborating Centers, which are laboratories that specialize in particular diseases, only a few are called on to respond to foreign outbreaks. The US Centers for Disease Control (CDC) is by far the most important, and within its organizational structure there are 22 WHO Collaborating Centers.

CDC personnel were central to international responses to most major outbreaks in recent decades. Other key national laboratories that respond to haemorrhagic fevers such as Ebola and Rift Valley fever are the Pasteur Institute in Paris, the Centre for Applied Microbiology and Research in Porton Down (Salisbury, UK) and the Institute of Virology in Johannesburg. In about half the cases where the CDC enters a country, it does so at the request of the WHO or the Pan-American Health Organization. In the other cases it enters at the request of the country. In certain circumstances, such as the 1994 plague outbreak in India, the integration of CDC personnel with a WHO operation was important to the political acceptability of the use of CDC epidemiologists. Four of the six doctors in the WHO mission to India were CDC personnel. (Etheridge 1992; WHO 1996; interviews).

Prevention rather than border controls

The international medical crises of the 1990s have shown that it is difficult and impractical—if not impossible—to monitor international travellers for signs of diseases at borders. And since most diseases have common incubation periods of several days to a few weeks, and leave no clearly discernible physical signs, there is no way to detect most infected persons. Instead many experts have concluded that resources could be better used to reduce the number of people with diseases in developing countries and to improve the medical capabilities of those countries to care for the ill. Financing better health infrastructure in developing countries remains a contentious issue, however (World Bank 1993; Fidler 1997, pp. 830, 863; interviews).

Some US international health policies clearly reflect doubts about the efficacy of border controls. The United States, for example, requires that all immigrants and refugees—about 500,000 people a year—be examined abroad by doctors. Yet there are no health requirements for the 45 million international travellers entering the country every year because there is no way to assess their health. The staff of the Quarantine Division of the CDC is only a fraction of what it was in the 1960s because it was realized that in the modern state, diseases cannot be stopped at borders.

Information provision benefits from multiplicity of effort

An important change in thinking about international epidemiological surveillance began in 1994 in response to the numerous outbreaks, recent field experiences and publications in the early 1990s. At this time state reporting on disease outbreaks under the International Health Regulations was poor. Many states were not vigilant or well prepared to track disease outbreaks, and they were fearful of foreign responses if they reported them. Major powers relied more on their own intelligence systems and increasingly on media reporting for information on diseases developing throughout the world. It was, however, recognized that information on some outbreaks in developing countries was slow in reaching national capitals and the outside world.

The first significant development in surveillance was in 1994, after a US international health specialist, Dr. Jack Woodall, proposed a monitoring system to link health professionals around the world. With funding from the National Academy of Science, the Rockefeller Foundation and other sources, ProMed-mail was founded in 1995 as a nongovernmental network of health professionals.

Health professionals send information to ProMed-mail in the United States, where medical specialists review the information and produce an edited version for about 15,000 subscribers in more than 150 countries. Almost 1 in 10 subscribers provides the network with information on diseases in their country. Subscribers can also exchange information on diseases through a message board on the Internet.

ProMed-mail does not pick up all important outbreaks, but it does identify many. One of the most important effects of ProMed-mail is that it sharply limits a state's ability to hide outbreaks. Because of ProMed-mail, states are more likely to volunteer information about outbreaks—ultimately benefiting the entire international community. But some health professionals are unwilling to send information to ProMed-mail for fear of being punished. For example, a Cuban doctor was jailed for providing information to the network (Manning 1997). ProMed-mail has also suffered when it has, on occasion, distributed inaccurate information on a disease outbreak, causing a country to suffer sanctions. This happened recently in two Latin American countries. Despite these problems, ProMed-mail has provided a new level of transparency on outbreaks and has encouraged states to be more honest about their medical crises. It has also helped WHO identify occurrences of diseases for its Rumor Outbreak Page (Manning 1997; interviews).

The network approach: an emerging trend

Responding to the new concern over outbreaks of infectious diseases, the WHO created a Division for Emerging Communicable Diseases in 1995 and began improving information dissemination. Until 1996 the WHO posted an Outbreak Page on the Internet, but the page only included the diseases listed in the International Health Regulations (cholera, plague and yellow fever), and only when the outbreaks were reported by states. In 1996 the WHO initiated the Rumor Outbreak Page on the Internet. Information for the page comes from WHO field representatives, other international organizations, NGOs, the media and ProMed-mail. Only about 75% of the outbreaks on the Rumor Outbreak Page are subsequently corroborated, so it is clear that the WHO must be careful in what it lists. The page is sent only to WHO regional offices, WHO Collaborating Centers, some governments and some medical organizations, and there is an understanding among the recipients that they will not publicize the information. Despite many limitations, the page is a revolution in thinking, since any earlier attempt by the WHO to disseminate information without states' permission would not have been permitted.

A unique supplement to both ProMed-mail and the Rumor Outbreak Page was launched by Canada in 1997 and made operational in 1998. Known as the Global Public Health Information Network, it is a system for scanning the Internet for information on disease outbreaks throughout the world. According to an agreement between the WHO and Canada, the collected data will initially be sent exclusively to the WHO. After several years of operation the information will probably be sent to other sources, although there are reservations about Canada's offending other states by circulating information about them. Some experts think that the network will not be able to sift through the vast amount of data on the Internet and identify the few important outbreaks, or that it will inundate the Canadian and WHO bureaucracies with so much information that they will be unable to digest it. While its effectiveness remains to be proven, the network is an innovative experiment to test the Internet's importance as a source of epidemiological intelligence. The use of the Internet by the network and by ProMed-mail has already considerably enhanced transparency in international health.

Other international surveillance activities also deserve comment. First, while media reports have been used to track disease outbreaks in the past, they are now perceived as much more valuable. The WHO has followed Agence France Presse and Reuters reporting for some time, but CNN and other television and print media have increased the importance of journalists in international health. CNN has a separate health segment in its broadcasts. Second, there is a complex network of health professionals throughout the world who are associated with universities, hospitals and governments. Some are actively involved in searching out emerging or re-emerging diseases throughout the world, and they regularly meet at professional conferences—for example, the American Society for Hygiene and Tropical Medicine and the Royal Society for Hygiene and Tropical Medicine. Medical specialists are linked through a plethora of professional and informal contacts, and they often communicate when problems arise. They constitute a system that could be called "the informal international college of health professionals", and it stands alongside the other surveillance systems in importance. In some cases the laboratories of professionals are formally linked into the WHO intergovernmental network through WHO Collaborating Centers. The WHO Division of Emerging Communicable Diseases is now trying to create an electronic network linking these Collaborating Centers.

The WHO has been successful in developing networks of specialists working on specific diseases. For example, in FluNet a network of flu specialists share information on the emergence of different strains of influenza. Specimens from about 80 national laboratories are sent to four WHO Collaborating Centers (in Australia, Japan, the United Kingdom and the United States) and an accord is reached each February on a flu vaccine for the coming year, at least for Northern states. This kind of nonobligatory international collaboration under the aegis of the WHO can be effective if there is a clear goal and if the best national laboratories are involved. A network concerned with drug-resistant diseases (called WHONET) has also been created, but it has not enjoyed the same success as FluNet. Few developing countries have the required expertise to contribute to the exchanges, and industrial countries generally have their own sources of information (interviews).

Third, there are national systems of international surveillance that are not formally organized, but which constitute parts of the intricate global surveillance network. The British, French, and Americans have the best surveillance capabilities in developing countries, but the US CDC is more active than the others—even though less than 5% of the 7,000 personnel focus explicitly on international issues. The CDC has five research field stations—in Thailand and Côte d'Ivoire for HIV, in Botswana for tuberculosis, in Kenya for malaria and in Guatemala for parasitic diseases. There are also 60 staff members who are on long-term assignments abroad with the US Agency for International Development or international organizations. The CDC also benefits from ties with six permanent laboratories maintained by the US Navy in Bangladesh, Egypt, Indonesia, Kenya, Peru and the Philippines. Also of great importance is the CDC's Field Epidemiological Training Program, which trains foreign health professionals at the center's headquarters in Atlanta (Georgia) and in short courses abroad. The ties established through the training program often lead to long-term exchanges that help the CDC learn about outbreaks and provide assistance. The CDC recently increased its international linkages as a result of cooperation with the European Union under the Transatlantic Agenda, with Japan under the US-Japan Common Agenda, with Russia under the Gore-Chernomrydin agreement and with South Africa under the Gore-Mbeke initiative. Some people in the international health field do not like the prominence of the CDC, but virtually all experts realize that it, and more broadly the US medical research establishment, provides a public good that benefits the international community. International disease surveillance by individual states is not the sole preserve of the CDC and WHO. Both the British and French (the latter especially in French-speaking West Africa through the Pasteur Institute's epidemiological training programme) are prominent in the international health field. A number of other countries also participate in national or regional surveillance (interviews).

NEXT STEPS: REVISING THE INTERNATIONAL HEALTH REGULATIONS

When the WHO agreed to revise the International Health Regulations in 1995 (on an initiative sponsored by the United Arab Emirates), it established a committee to produce a draft (WHO 1995b). By early 1998 this committee had produced a draft containing 57 new articles and 11 annexes. Several sections, including those on surveillance, have provoked considerable controversy.

In particular, a proposal that would require states to gather and analyse data for "the syndromic approach" has been sharply criticized. Instead of an obligation to report on outbreaks of specific diseases, this would require states to report on the epidemiological characteristics of different syndromes: acute haemorrhagic fever, acute respiratory, acute diarrhoea, acute jaundice, acute neurological and "other notifiable" (WHO 1998, article 2, annex III). This approach evolved from the realization that serious new threats have emerged and that the major international problems today are not plague, cholera and yellow fever. In addition, states are encouraged to report data on disease outbreaks in the absence of solid laboratory corroboration of what the diseases are.

Other new provisions include an obligation that states provide the WHO with information on the course of the outbreak, vectors connected to particular diseases (for example, mosquitoes) and preventive measures that the state has taken. The WHO, in turn, is obligated to distribute reported information to all member states, to assist reporting states in investigating outbreaks (which would generally involve calling on Collaborating Centers for assistance) and to comment on unreliable information. The WHO can obtain assistance in evaluating reports by seeking information from other international organizations, WHO Collaborating Centers, the governments of neighbouring states, and the public. This gives the WHO much greater latitude in gathering information on disease outbreaks than it has under the present International Health Regulations (WHO 1998, articles 4–9; WHO 1995a; Fidler 1996a, 1997).

Many changes could be made to the existing draft articles. The system for reporting on syndromes could be simplified, and some diseases could be identified in the reporting requirements. Arrangements to send outside experts to states with outbreaks could be spelled out in some detail. The powers of the WHO to draw on information from sources apart from the infected state could be curtailed because some countries are nervous about the WHO's ability to obtain information that would challenge their reports. The flexible provisions on the ability of states to control carriers and travellers at their borders and on the ability of the WHO to criticize excessive measures of states could be made clearer, although some kind of flexible compromise on the powers of state and WHO discretionary powers is likely to emerge. The final agreement on new International Health Regulations will probably make the WHO a more important actor in international epidemiological monitoring, but the accord is also likely to be general enough to allow an evolution of practices over time.

Conclusion

A sense of urgency has propelled the increase in international surveillance of disease following recognition that epidemic diseases and serious endemic diseases (such as malaria and HIV/AIDS) are much bigger threats than was previously thought. No longer is there "a drug for every bug". While haemorrhagic fevers such as Ebola get the headlines (and are cause for concern), what really worries experts are drug-resistant strains of old diseases and the potential for a lethal strain of influenza such as "the Spanish flu" of 1918–19.

Contemporary surveillance has also assumed greater importance due to the greater transparency of states in the information age and the number of organizations engaged in surveillance. While various surveillance efforts could be viewed as wasteful duplication, the multiplicity of activities is actually useful, because governments are becoming more willing to report on disease outbreaks to the WHO precisely because they realize that nongovernmental sources will eventually learn of, and publicize, outbreaks. The WHO is a beneficiary of what has developed at nongovernmental levels. Perhaps the greatest gap in the surveillance system is at the national level, where local surveillance and laboratory capabilities are weak. This is a crucial area for future international cooperation. The growing role of the World Bank in this area is a positive sign (World Bank 1993, 1997; Siddiqi 1995; Koivusala and Ollila 1997; Jayaraman and Kanbur in this volume).

NOTE

A great deal of the information for this chapter came from interviews with officials of the World Health Organization, the Pan-American Health Organization and the Canadian and US governments. The author benefited from the assistance and comments of Simon Carvalho and is grateful to Hilla Aharon, David Fidler and Lisa Martin for comments.

REFERENCES

Arnold, David, ed. 1988. *Imperial Medicine and Indigenous Societies.* Manchester: Manchester University Press.

Belanger, Michel. 1983. *Droit International de la Santé.* Paris: Economica.

Brown, E. Richard. 1979. *Rockefeller Medicine Men.* Los Angeles: University of California Press.

CDC (Centers for Disease Control). 1994. *Addressing Emerging Infectious Disease Threats: A Prevention Strategy for the United States.* Atlanta, GA.

CISET (National Science and Technology Council, Committee on International Science, Engineering, and Technology). 1995. *Infectious Diseases—A Global Health Threat.* Washington, DC: National Academy Press.

Cooper, Richard N. 1989. "International Cooperation in Public Health As a Prologue to Macroeconomic Cooperation." In Richard Cooper and others, eds., *Can Nations Agree?* Washington, DC: The Brookings Institution.

Delon, P.J. 1975. *The International Health Regulations: A Practical Guide.* Geneva: World Health Organization.

Dols, Michael W. 1977. *The Black Death in the Middle East.* Princeton, NJ: Princeton University Press.

Etheridge, Elizabeth W. 1992. *Sentinel for Health: A History of the Centers for Disease Control.* Berkeley: University of California Press.

Fidler, David P. 1996a. "Globalization, International Law, and Emerging Diseases." *Emerging Infectious Diseases* 2: 77–84.

———. 1996b. "Law and Emerging and Re-Emerging Infectious Diseases: The Legal Challenge for the American Bar." Paper presented at the American Bar Association's *Conference on Emerging and Re-Emerging Infectious Diseases,* April, Orlando, FL.

———. 1997. "Return of the Fourth Horseman: Emerging Infectious Diseases and International Law." *Minnesota Law Review* 81: 771–868.

Garrett, Laurie. 1994. *The Coming Plague: New Emerging Diseases in a World Out of Balance.* New York: Farrar, Strauss, and Giroux.

Goodman, Neville. 1971. *International Health Organizations and Their Work.* London: Churchill Livingstone.

Hobson, William. 1963. *World Health and History.* Bristol: John Wright.

Howard-Jones, Norman. 1975. *The Scientific Background of the International Sanitary Conferences,1851–1938.* Geneva: World Health Organization.

———. 1978. *International Public Health between the Two World Wars: The Organizational Problems.* Geneva: World Health Organization.

———. 1981."The World Health Organization in Historical Perspective." *Perspectives in Biology and Medicine* 24: 467–82.

Keohane, Robert M. 1984. *After Hegemony: Cooperation and Discord in the World Political Economy.* Princeton, NJ: Princeton University Press.

Koivusala, Meri, and Eeva Ollila. 1997. *Making a Healthy World: Agencies, Actors, and Policies in International Health.* London: Zed Books.

Lederberg, Joshua, Robert E. Shope and Stanley C. Oaks, Jr., eds. 1992. *Emerging Infections: Microbial Threats in the United States.* Washington, DC: National Academy Press.

Leive, David M. 1976. *International Regulatory Regimes: Case Studies in Health, Meteorology, and Food.* Lexington, MA: Lexington Books.

Manning, Anita. 1997. "Cuban Doctor Imprisoned for Warning of a Dengue Fever Outbreak." *USA Today* (July 16): 8D.

McNeill, William H. 1976. *Plagues and People*. Oxford: Oxford University Press.

Preston, Richard. 1994. *The Hot Zone*. New York: Random House.

Rodrik, Dani. 1996. "Why Is There Multilateral Lending?" In Michael Bruno and Boris Pleskovic, eds., *Annual World Bank Conference on Development Economics 1995*. Washington, DC: World Bank.

Sandler, Todd. 1992. *Collective Action: Theory and Applications*. Ann Arbor: University of Michigan Press.

Schepin, Oleg, and Waldermar Yermakov. 1991. *International Quarantine*. Madison, WI: International University Press.

Siddiqi, Javed. 1995. *World Health and World Politics: The World Health Organization and the UN System*. London: C. Hurst.

Watts, Sheldon. 1997. *Epidemics and History: Disease, Power, and Imperialism*. New Haven, CT: Yale University Press.

Weindling, Paul. 1995. *International Health Organizations and Movements, 1918–1939*. Cambridge: Cambridge University Press.

WHO (World Health Organization). 1983. *International Health Regulations (as revised in 1981)*. Geneva.

———.1995a. *The International Response to Epidemics and Applications of the International Health Regulations*. Geneva.

———. 1995b. "Revision and Updating of the International Health Regulations." WHA 48.7. Geneva.

———. 1996. *World Health Report 1996: Fighting Disease, Fostering Development*. Geneva.

———. 1998. *International Health Regulations: First Annotated Edition*. Geneva.

Williams, Green. 1969. *The Plague Killers*. New York: Charles Scribner's Sons.

World Bank. 1993. *World Development Report 1993: Investing in Health*. New York: Oxford University Press.

———. 1997. *Sector Strategy: Health, Nutrition, and Population*. Washington, DC.

HEALTH AS A
GLOBAL PUBLIC GOOD

Lincoln C. Chen, Tim G. Evans and Richard A. Cash

In a companion chapter in this volume, Mark W. Zacher argues that infectious disease surveillance is a global public good as defined by the criteria of "nondivisibility" and "nonexcludability". Nondivisibility refers to the ability of all to benefit from the public good once it is produced, and nonexcludability to the inability to exclude any individual or group from the benefits.

History makes a strong case that surveillance of infectious diseases is a global public good (McNeill 1976). The Athenian plague of 430 BC was the first recorded transnational epidemic, with the pathogen probably spread from Ethiopia through Egypt by troop movements during the Peloponnesian War, although the exact cause is debated (Zinsser 1963).[1] Since the European Black Death in 1347, successive waves of plague and cholera have been associated with international trade, the most recent being the Latin America cholera epidemic of the 1990s (Lederberg 1997).[2] In the 17th century European conquest of the New World introduced new viruses to previously unexposed indigenous populations. Measles and smallpox devastated Native Americans, exerting a death toll that greatly exceeded that from combat (Berlinguer 1992).[3] Indeed, the 1969 update of the International Health Regulations by the World Health Organization (WHO) marked more than a century of interstate cooperation in the control of key infectious diseases for mutual health protection (Cooper 1989).

Thus control of infectious diseases can be considered a global public good. But can the same be said for noncommunicable diseases? Are noncommunicable diseases primarily private rather than public goods? Or in this era of globalization, have health circumstances so changed that the customary balance between public and private in health is shifting?[4] In other words, can global health, rather than a group of transmissible diseases, be considered more a public than a private good? And if so, what are the implications for global health? How would such thinking affect international health cooperation and global health governance?

These are the questions we address in this chapter. We argue that although health may have both public and private properties, globalization may be shifting the balance of health to a global public good. By compressing time and distance, globalization is profoundly affecting the world economy, politics, culture and ideas—virtually all aspects of human life, including health. The global revolution in information and life sciences, we hypothesize, is likely to offer the potential for powerful new interventions. Under these conditions of rapid social change, a central challenge is to resolve inherent tensions between global health equity and social exclusion. We conclude by discussing how diverse institutional actors, both old and new, might develop more effective mechanisms of international cooperation for global health protection.

GLOBALIZATION AND HEALTH

A traditional typology of disease is tripartite—communicable disease, noncommunicable disease and injury. A first generation of diseases is linked to poverty—common infections, malnutrition and reproductive health hazards mostly affecting women and children. These mostly (but not entirely) communicable diseases are concentrated among the poor in developing countries. A second generation of primarily chronic and degenerative diseases—such as cardiovascular disease, cancer, stroke and diabetes—predominate among the middle-aged and elderly in all countries. Susceptibility to these noncommunicable diseases is linked to lifestyle and health-related behaviour. To these two groups of diseases should be added injury, which is also prevalent in both rich and poor countries.

The dividing line between public and private among these diseases is traditionally believed to be rather clear-cut. Because of externalities, the control of communicable diseases is a public good, but treatment for noncommunicable diseases and injury is mostly private. After all, the risk factors associated with noncommunicable diseases are related to individual choices in lifestyle and human behaviour—unhealthy diet, lack of exercise, consumption of tobacco or unsafe habits. Because private choices have personal consequences, there is an appropriate match between individual risk and the private burden of sickness.

As our knowledge of health advances, however, this rigid divide appears to oversimplify a more complex situation. Moreover, globalization is blurring the traditional line between public and private in health (table 1). Some have observed that we are witnessing the emergence of an unprecedented "third wave" of health threats—emerging infections, new environmental threats and behavioural pathologies. This blend of new as well as resurgent older diseases is planetary in scope and threatens all countries, rich and poor. As a result the traditional categorization of diseases demands serious reconsideration. Most of these threats have characteristics of a global public bad, and their ultimate

TABLE 1

Health and global change

Global transnational factor	Consequences and probable impact on health status
Macroeconomic	
Structural adjustment policies and downsizing	Marginalization, poverty, inadequate social safety nets[a]
Structural and chronic unemployment	Higher morbidity and mortality rates[b]
Trade	
Trade of tobacco, alcohol and psycho-active drugs	Increased marketing, availability and use[b]
Dumping of unsafe or ineffective pharmaceuticals	Ineffective or harmful therapy[b]
Trade of contaminated foodstuffs and feed	Spread of infectious diseases across borders[b]
Travel	
More than 1 million people crossing borders every day	Infectious disease transmission and export of harmful lifestyles (such as high-risk sexual behavior)[c]
Migration and demographic	
Increased refugee populations and rapid population growth	Ethnic and civil conflict and environmental degradation[c]
Food security	
Increased demand for food in rapidly growing economies (such as those in Asia)	Structural food shortages as less food aid is available and the poorest countries are unable to pay hard currency[b]
Increase in global food trade continuing to outstrip increases in food production, and food aid continuing to decline	Food shortages in marginalized areas; increased migration and civil unrest[a]

TABLE 1 *continued*

Global transnational factor	Consequences and probable impact on health status
Environmental degradation and unsustainable consumption patterns	
Resource depletion, especially access to fresh water	Global and local environmental health impact[b]
Water and air pollution	Epidemics and potential violence within and between countries
Ozone depletion and increases in ultraviolet radiation	Introduction of toxins into human food chain and respiratory disorders
Accumulation of greenhouse gases and global warming	Immunosuppression, skin cancers and cataracts
	Major shifts in infectious disease patterns and vector distribution, death from heat waves, increased trauma due to floods and storms and worsening food shortages and malnutrition in many regions
Technology	
Patent protection of new technologies under trade-related intellectual property rights agreements	Benefits of new technologies developed in the global market are unaffordable to the poor[c]
Communications and media	
Global marketing of harmful commodities such as tobacco	Active promotion of health-damaging practices[b]
Foreign policies	
Policies based on national self-interest, xenophobia and protectionism	Threat to multilateralism and global cooperation required to address shared transnational health concerns[c]

a. Possible short-term problem that could reverse in time.
b. Long-term negative impact.
c. Great uncertainty.
Source: Yach and Bettcher 1998a.

resolution will require global cooperation beyond the capability of any single actor or nation state.

Since the global spread of the human immunodeficiency virus (HIV) began in the early 1980s, 29 new bacteria or viruses have been identified, many capable of global spread (map 1). With more than 1 million travellers flying across national boundaries every day, many of these new pathogens have the capacity to reach anywhere in the world within 24 hours (Lederberg 1997). Moreover, many infectious agents are not new but well-known pathogens rekindled by changing conditions. Rapid urbanization, urban poverty and urban squalor, for example, created conditions conducive to recent epidemics of dengue fever in Jakarta, Indonesia and Mexico City and a plague outbreak in Surat, India (IOM 1997). Acceleration of international trade has precipitated new epidemics (cholera in Latin America), sparked local epidemics in previously protected populations (cyclospora in the United States, where one-third of fruits and vegetables are imported) and generated unprecedented health fears ("mad cow disease", or bovine spongiform encephalitis, in Europe). At the same time, one of our most powerful defences against bacterial infection, antibiotics, may be rendered impotent by the emergence of antibiotic resistance—for example multidrug-resistant tuberculosis or chloroquin-resistant malaria (CISET 1995).[5]

In a manner paralleling emerging infections, the control of new environmental threats can also be considered a global public good (McMichael and Haines 1997). The health effects of ozone depletion, global warming and the disposal of toxic wastes are planetary. No one can fully escape their health consequences, and all would benefit from global control. The air pollution in Southeast Asia in 1997, caused by the burning of Indonesian forests and exacerbated by El Niño, vividly demonstrates the transnational implications of atmospheric change.

With globalization, even some noncommunicable diseases traditionally considered to be private goods are developing stronger public characteristics. Two examples: tobacco and illicit drugs. Scientific evidence has firmly established that tobacco consumption, after decades of latency, can increase the risk of lung and bladder cancer and heart and lung disease. The world's 1.1 billion smokers, 800 million of whom are in developing countries, account for about 3 million tobacco-related deaths a year (Nakajima 1997, p. 327). In part due to an annual expenditure of $6 billion in global marketing campaigns, smoking is increasing by 2.5% a year in developing countries—while declining by 0.5% a year in industrial countries. Strangely, trade in tobacco is considered legitimate international commerce, but the international movement of addictive psychoactive substances is considered illegal.[6] The WHO estimates that there are about 15 million users of psychoactive drugs, one-third by injection, leading to 200,000 deaths a year (Nakajima 1997, p. 329).

Consumption of tobacco is usually considered voluntary. Yet we now recognize that individual choice is not entirely free from structural workplace constraints, peer pressures or the biology of addiction. Indeed, many behavioural health risks and consequences are not strictly private. While addiction to tobacco may be voluntary, studies have confirmed the powerful behavioural influence of commercial advertising, often targeted at teenagers and women. Moreover, neither the health effects of tobacco use nor the costs of treatment are entirely private, because passive smoke is hazardous to nonsmokers, and most tobacco-related costs are passed on to the public through medical insurance or social security.

Thus global tobacco control has strong public goods characteristics.[7] A more obvious public goods case is the control of illicit addictive substances. Global networks for the production and distribution of illicit drugs are clear examples of public bads. With globalization, transnational trafficking in illegal drugs has become far more difficult to control due to the mobility of sites for production and processing, expanding avenues for transnational shipment and hard-to-detect money laundering. A strong argument can be made that controlling smoking and illegal drug use is a global public good.

In sum, due in part to globalization, health is becoming more of a global public good through two forces. First, enhanced international linkages in trade, migration and information flows have accelerated the cross-border transmission of disease and the international transfer of behavioural and environmental health risks. Second, intensified pressures on common-pool global resources of air and water have generated shared environmental threats. Globalization is not simply accelerating long-term trends but is ushering in contextual changes that are qualitatively and quantitatively different in disease risk, health vulnerability and policy response. "Although responsibility for health remains primarily national, the determinants of health and means to fulfill that responsibility are increasingly global" (Jamison, Frenk and Knaul 1998, p. 515).

EQUITY, MARKETS AND OPPORTUNITY

If global health is treated as a public good, three broad themes are underscored—equity, markets and opportunity.

Map 1

New infectious diseases in humans and animals since 1976

Countries where cases first appeared or were first identified

1982
E. coli
0157:H7
United States

1989
Hepatitis C
United States

1981
AIDS
United States

1976
Cryptosporidiosis
United States

1976
**Legionnaire's
disease**
United States

1991
**Venezuelan
haemorrhagic fever**
Venezuela

1994
**Brazilian
haemorrhagic fever**
Brazil

a. Animal cases only.
Source: WHO 1996.

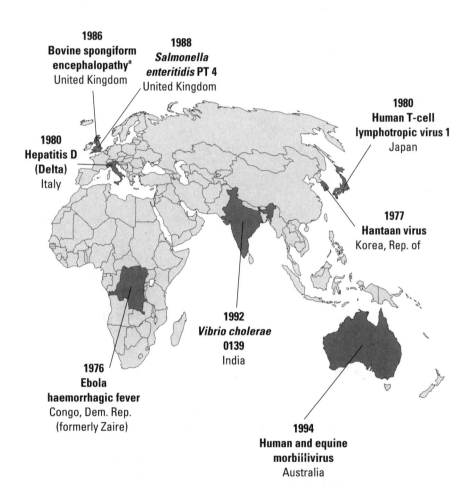

1986
Bovine spongiform
encephalopathy[a]
United Kingdom

1988
Salmonella
***enteritidis* PT 4**
United Kingdom

1980
Human T-cell
lymphotropic virus 1
Japan

1980
Hepatitis D
(Delta)
Italy

1977
Hantaan virus
Korea, Rep. of

1992
Vibrio cholerae
0139
India

1976
Ebola
haemorrhagic fever
Congo, Dem. Rep.
(formerly Zaire)

1994
Human and equine
morbillivirus
Australia

- The issue of health equity arises because, although public goods are defined as neither divisible nor excludable, public health policies nevertheless carry distributional issues of unequal access, biased priorities or benign neglect. The poor have different health priorities from the rich—and the rich have greater preventive and protective capabilities than the poor.

- The spread of the global private market, moreover, is accelerating the privatization of medical services and the commercialization of health knowledge. Private markets are inherently inequitable because without purchasing power the poor are excluded from commercial services and health technologies.

- Because globalization is being accompanied by a revolution in the life and communications sciences, unprecedented opportunities in health are likely to arise. A major challenge is whether these opportunities will be exploited to meet human health needs equitably. As argued by Rao (in this volume), the tension between global public goods and global equity with social justice poses vexing dilemmas.

Despite remarkable health advances, the 21st century will open with enormous inequities in world health. Average life expectancy in the most advanced countries (about 80 years) is twice that of the most health-backward countries (about 40 years). Equally sizable health gaps can be found within countries. Even in the United States life expectancy among the healthiest males in the best-off county is twice that of the unhealthiest males in the worst-off county (Murray and Lopez 1998).

Furthermore, the control of many global diseases of the poor can be considered a public good. For example, the successful eradication of smallpox, the near elimination of polio and the primary health care movement are global efforts for the public good.[8] But not all global efforts are necessarily equity-enhancing.

Take the surveillance for emerging infections. A recurring issue in building international cooperation for surveillance is the comparative importance of various threats to different population groups. The public in rich countries fears the importation of a devastating new virus, while ordinary people in poor countries suffer from common infections such as diarrhoea and respiratory diseases.[9] These different health concerns present divergent surveillance priorities, generated by the ready access of rich populations to effective vaccines and antibiotics that are financially or logistically inaccessible to many poor populations. Simply adopting a global goods perspective does not by itself resolve the dilemma of which disease should receive priority in global surveillance or how limited global resources should be prioritized.

Similar equity issues are associated with environmental and behavioural threats. The risk of skin cancer due to ozone depletion is higher among those unable, for reasons of education or work demands, to protect themselves from damaging sunlight. Toxic waste disposal is often situated near the residential sites of the poor, among and within countries. Such behavioural pathologies as violence and drug abuse disproportionately afflict the poor and excluded. Even some damaging health behaviour (such as tobacco consumption) is disproportionately concentrated among the poor or working class.

Equity issues are compounded by global imbalances in scientific and technical institutional capacity. Except perhaps modestly in Japan and Europe, no other country has the equivalent of the US Centers for Disease Control, Food and Drug Administration and Environmental Protection Agency. Such public capabilities are absent in most developing countries. Although their technical expertise and sophisticated laboratories are often used for global activities, the mandates and budgets of these industrial country institutions are entirely oriented to the protection of their citizens. Dependent on technical capabilities that are highly imbalanced, the global process of achieving equity in setting agendas and work priorities is skewed.

Perhaps the most powerful dimension of globalization is the integration of the world economy through private markets. Global markets have generated uneven growth, income maldistribution and economic instability, as reflected by the Asian financial crisis. Globalization has also facilitated the entry of private markets into health care systems. Often called "health sector reform", health policies are increasingly privatizing health care services to contain costs and promote efficiency. Private payments for health care naturally place fiscal barriers to universal coverage and service access by the poor. Some argue that a mixture of efficiency driven by the private sector and equity protected by the public sector provides an acceptable blend (World Bank 1993). Yet there is little empirical evidence for such optimality. Indeed, early experiments on the imposition of user fees in public systems to enhance efficiency and cost recovery have neither realized the presumed benefit nor enhanced equity of access (Dahlgren 1994).

With globalization partly driven by revolutionary scientific change, technological breakthroughs present exciting opportunities for global health. In the life sciences the decoding of the human genome holds enormous promise for the development of new and powerful drugs, vaccines and diagnostic tests. Some have even projected that gene typing will enable medical treatments to be tailored to the genomic characteristics of individual patients. Similarly, the communications revolution has the power to bring health information to all people, bypassing the mediation of governments, professional bodies and health care systems. Information technology can, moreover, enhance the performance of many health-related activities—such as primary education, health information, disease surveillance, management information systems and health research by scientists based in widely dispersed locations.

If knowledge is a public good, will these unprecedented opportunities be equitably exploited? Or will certain groups be excluded or marginalized? These questions are being played out in the race to produce newer and more effective health technologies. Although the public sector funds most basic research, applied drug and vaccine development is overwhelmingly conducted by the private sector. Protected by intellectual property rights, private industry naturally focuses its technology development on products to serve affluent consumers with effective purchasing power. Weak profit incentives discourage commercial research and development investments on diseases of the poor. Lacking market power, the diseases of the poor are "orphaned" by benign neglect.[10] Similar concerns over equitable access are expressed about health-related information. Information may be a global public good, but its meaning and utilization are likely to vary with literacy, education and communications infrastructure. Because information and communications systems are also commercially driven, neither information dissemination nor its content is likely to cater to the health needs of the disadvantaged.

Perhaps the most positive feature of globalization has been growing normative convergence on such basic issues as human rights, democracy and public demand for transparency and accountability in health decision-making. Health is positive-sum: one person's good health does not detract from another's. Indeed, better health usually has positive effects on entire populations—through, say, less disease transmission. The world-wide diffusion of information and normative convergence that preventable human suffering should not be tolerated may increasingly move the public to perceive good health universally shared as a basic human right. Good health is both an instrument as well as an expression of global solidarity, reflecting ultimately the indivisibility of health.

GLOBAL HEALTH GOVERNANCE

Stimulated in part by the 1998 election of a new director-general for the WHO, a rich literature has developed on reform of global health governance

(Chen, Bell and Bates 1996; Ministry of Foreign Affairs 1996). Three prestigious medical journals—*Lancet, British Medical Journal,* and *American Journal of Public Health*—featured series on reform proposals for international health organizations (Buse and Gwin 1998; Godlee 1997; Lucas 1998; Walt 1998; Yach and Bettcher 1998a, b). In a review of the literature, Lee (1997) concluded that organizations had failed to adapt to the rapidly changing global context, the shift in the pattern of disease, the improved understanding of the broader social determinants of health and the diversity of institutional actors. She recommended constitutional and management reforms of the WHO and other international bodies.

Among this literature, perhaps the most cogent is a framework proposed by Jamison, Frenk and Knaul (1998). They note that the WHO constitution (Article 2) lists 22 functions, far too many for organizational effectiveness. Instead they propose two types of international health functions—core and support (table 2). Core functions should be aimed at promoting global public goods, such as information, standards and regulations, health policy and research and development. All countries need these core functions. Support functions should be aimed at enhancing capacity and health sector performance—objectives of special importance for developing countries. The analogy is that while core functions correct for global market failures, support functions overcome national weaknesses. Whereas support functions can be considered to move countries from dependence to independence (national health sovereignty), core functions can be conceptualized as moving nations from independence to interdependence (global health solidarity). Where the constraining resource is knowledge, technical assistance should be provided, and where the bottleneck is financial, development financing is indicated. This framework naturally suggests complementary roles for the WHO and the World Bank, the main technical and financial institutions in world health.

However elegant, this framework pays insufficient attention to the pluralism of global health actors and to "power shifts" away from vertically organized formal institutions to horizontally linked coalitions in global health. Mathews (1997) argues that the most important political implication of globalization is the shift of power from government and intergovernmental agencies to private actors—to nongovernmental organizations (NGOs), private business and the press and media. The influence of industry is reflected by its political clout with powerful governments, and the power of NGOs is demonstrated by their impact at the recent global conferences in Rio, Vienna, Cairo and Beijing.

In health, as in other fields, the diversity of global actors has grown expo-
nentially in recent years, including agencies in the United Nations system.[11] With
a new director-general, the WHO has begun a bold reform process with as yet
uncertain outcomes. The World Bank, which began health lending in 1985, has
quickly become the largest source of concessional financing for health in the
developing world.[12] Growth in the private sector, however, has probably been
even greater. NGOs are increasingly active in health affairs. Academia remains an
important source of knowledge production and professional training. The pharmaceutical industry has gone global in production, distribution and marketing.
And health has become a significant feature in newspapers and the mass media.

TABLE 2

Essential objectives and functions of international health organizations

Basic objectives	Core functions	Rationale
Assure adequate levels of goods with benefits to all countries	Promotion of international public goods Research and development Databases to facilitate learning across countries Norms and standards for national use and to regulate international transactions Consensus building on health policy	Collective action is an economically rational approach to provision of public goods from which all can benefit, and international collective action responds to opportunities whose benefits cover many nations
Assure opportune response to global threats and control international transmission of health risks	Intervention to deal with international externalities Environmental risks Spread of pathogens Spread of antibiotic-resistant strains Transfer of unhealthy lifestyles Trade in legal and illegal harmful substances	If actions in individual countries have consequences for other countries (negative or positive), leaving decision-making to countries at the national level will fail to include all costs or benefits

TABLE 2 *continued*

Basic objectives	Core functions	Rationale
Supplementary objectives	Supportive functions	
Protect health of vulnerable groups	Agency for dispossessed The poor Particular countries Regions of countries Special groups Victims of human rights violations Female children in some countries Displaced people Victims of emergencies	Ethical imperative to protect people when their governments fail or when their human rights are violated; in self-interest of every nation state to prevent and resolve humanitarian crises
Support development in countries	Technical cooperation and development financing Capacity building Capacity strengthening Performance enhancement	Some countries require targeted investments in knowledge and financial resources to enhance conditions for sustainable development

Source: Jamison, Frenk and Knaul 1998.

The emergence of institutional pluralism is only one of the manifestations of the globalization of health. Global health increasingly demonstrates cross-border externalities. As a public good, health risks and responses are increasingly global. No individual or nation state can fully guarantee its own health. International cooperation within the health field and between the health sector and other development sectors will become mandatory. Future international health cooperation will be influenced by at least three factors—resource mobilization, systems of global governance and the creation of institutional space for organizational renovation and innovation.

"Donor fatigue" has affected the health field just as it has other sectors supported by foreign development assistance. Thus a formidable challenge is the mobilization of political support and the requisite resources to effectively produce global public health goods (Raymond 1997; IOM 1997). The case for

public expenditures to promote global health is strong on economic, moral
and practical grounds:

- Abundant evidence confirms that disease prevention saves money
  (WHO 1996). Huge economic losses are associated with infectious
  disease outbreaks—cholera in Latin America cost $1.7 billion, plague in
  India cost $770 million, and mad cow disease in the United Kingdom
  cost $3 billion (table 3). The total US investment in the global campaign
  to eradicate smallpox was $32 million, an amount that is returned to US
  taxpayers every 26 days in savings from eliminating vaccination and
  screening programs (IOM 1997).
- US public opinion surveys repeatedly confirm that Americans
  overwhelmingly support foreign assistance for poverty alleviation—
  including health— provided the aid genuinely reaches the needy and
  promotes self-reliance (Kull 1995).[13]

TABLE 3

Estimated annual financial costs to the United States of common infectious diseases

Disease	Estimated annual cost
HIV/AIDS	$3 billion in public health funds
Tuberculosis	$343 million in public health funds, $700 million in direct treatment costs
Nosocomial (hospital-acquired) Infections	$10 billion in direct treatment costs
Sexually transmitted diseases costs (excluding AIDS)	$5 billion in direct treatment
Intestinal infections	$23 billion in direct treatment and lost productivity costs
Drug-resistant infections	$4 billion (and rising) in direct treatment costs
Influenza	$5 billion in direct treatment costs $12 billion in lost productivity costs

Source: Adapted from CISET 1995.

- The morality of altruism is backed by the practicality of self-interest. Ordinary people recognize that we are ultimately an interdependent single species, and human security anywhere depends on unified global action everywhere.

Despite the permissiveness of public opinion, political leadership to maintain concessional resource flows to developing countries has been weak. One strategy for the health field is to build systematically on concrete incremental gains. An example would be an initial focus on visible health threats, such as infectious disease vulnerability, easily understood by the general public in the North. A global programme could be developed and targeted specifically at the control of infectious diseases among travellers and their contacts. Depending on its definition, the programme could include many of the infectious diseases that afflict the poor. Eschewing public taxes, the programme could be financed by imposing a health fee—say, $1 per international air ticket. The fee, resembling an airport facility charge, could generate $500 million a year, equivalent to the entire budget of the WHO.[14] If such a system were successful, the precedent could be built on incrementally to strengthen other parts of an overall system of global health governance.

An incremental step-wise approach is recommended because most previous efforts to reform global health governance have floundered on the design table. Proposals that envision a single unified global system, a "grand design", do not sufficiently recognize the growing pluralism of institutional actors, the shifts in power between formal institutions and informal alliances and the sheer complexities of developing international consensus over intractable political and bureaucratic bottlenecks. Unlike the first conference on international health in 1851—12 governments were represented—global decision-making today requires the participation of 185 member governments of the United Nations system.

Progress may come from the recognition that health as a global public good can be most effectively advanced not by a single top-down system but by the many actions of many actors. Conceptually and practically, many subsystems together could constitute a mosaic system of global health. Gaps and duplications will naturally emerge, but these flaws may not be fatal if the subsystems are adaptive, flexible and responsive to changing demands.

That future system should create space for institutional renovation and innovation. It seems likely, for example, that horizontally linked global health alliances or partnerships may increasingly challenge the traditional dominance of governments and multilateral institutions. Just as NGOs spearheaded the 1970s campaign against infant formula, global coalitions drawing together many actors are being formed on tobacco control, environmental health, essential drugs and infectious disease surveillance. In some countries "health watches" are being established to bring greater transparency and accountability to public institutions. Networking is assuming increasing importance in the conduct of global health affairs, as reflected in the exponential growth of health exchanges on the Internet.

Thus the future portends lively interactions between diverse actors—some conflictual and others harmonious. Controversy is likely to surface around such contentious issues as the international trade in tobacco. The authority of the World Trade Organization will be contested by NGO coalitions working in partnership with the WHO and the United Nations Children's Fund. Another area of potential conflict is equitable access to health products that could benefit poor populations in developing countries. Restrictive intellectual property rights owned by commercial companies could be contested by NGO-academic-United Nations alliances.

Other interactions, however, have the potential for synergism. Especially promising are partnerships between private industry and publicly spirited groups. One current example is industry's free donation of ivermectin and albendizole, drugs against onchocerciasis and filiariasis. Another is the mobilization of Rotary International to fund the global eradication of polio. And a third is the encouragement for industry to do research and development on an AIDS vaccine by the International AIDS Vaccine Initiative, a nonprofit organization.

These partnerships have the potential to draw on the comparative strengths, rather than expose the weaknesses, of different institutional actors. Networks or alliances among academic and international organizations, for example, could accelerate the political acceptance of scientific facts that Cooper (1989) described as so instrumental in moving self-interested nation states into formal international agreements of cooperation. When scientific evidence proves that the benefits of cooperation clearly outweigh the costs, individual actors move together in a positive-sum process. Public-private linkages could attempt to transform available knowledge into applied health products of use to the world's poor and excluded. Creative subsidies or multilateral research and development funds could be established to enhance research investments that advance global health.

The possible arrangements are diverse and interesting, offering opportunities for creativity. Indeed, it could be argued that any leading institution in global health should eschew in-house activities by its staff supported by its own budgets, and should instead function as a catalyst for shared work by other relevant institutional actors—academia, NGOs, industry and the press. And an international agency such as the WHO should, rather than operate as a "command and control" centre for world health, exert world leadership by becoming the central promoter and facilitator in the production of health as a global public good. Only time will tell whether such international health agencies have diagnosed the changing times and reshaped their institutional instruments to meet the new challenges of global health.

NOTES

1. The Athenian plague is reportedly the first recorded transnational epidemic recorded in the second book of Thucydides' histories (Zinsser 1963).

2. The term "quarantine" comes from the 40 days of isolation imposed on foreign sailors on ships arriving in Venetian ports.

3. Evidence for the devastating effects of measles and smallpox on previously unexposed populations is strong. In a related area, there is growing scientific consensus that syphilis was imported into Europe from the Americas (Berlinguer 1992).

4. As a new concept and phenomenon, there is no consensus on the precise definition of the term "globalization". Many interpret the term as the global integration of specific fields—for example, the global economy. We believe this to be excessively narrow and prefer to define globalization as integrative world-wide processes of economy, polity, culture and human life facilitated or driven by the revolution in information technology. As such, globalization is qualitatively different from other concepts, such as modernization and interdependence.

5. Indiscriminate use of antibiotics has accelerated the emergence of multidrug-resistant tuberculosis among the 8 million new cases a year and chloroquin-resistant malaria among some 500 million cases in 90 countries—90% in Sub-Saharan Africa—causing an estimated 2.7 million deaths a year (Nakajima 1997).

6. Health scientists have noted that the legality of international trade in addictive substances do not conform to health criteria. While illicit addictive drugs are considered illegal, world-wide trade in tobacco and alcohol, which cause far more health damage, is considered legal.

7. Upon her inauguration as the director-general of the WHO in July 1998, Dr. Gro Brundtland announced the global control of tobacco as one of the organization's top priorities.

8. One of the great success stories of global health in this century was the successful eradication of smallpox, which may soon be joined by the elimination of polio. Also technically feasible is the eradication of leprosy, guinea worm, river blindness, Chagas disease, tetanus and maybe measles.

9. Public fears about transmissible diseases can generate extreme xenophobia. A recent example is fear of HIV/AIDS among Haitians and Africans. Various ethnic groups have been blamed for historical epidemics—Jews for the Black Death, Irish for cholera in New York and Italians for polio in Brooklyn.

10. Some claim that several breakthroughs of significance to poor populations, like a new and effective cholera vaccine, are technically feasible but the fruits of this knowledge are not being applied, because private companies that own the patent rights lack the commercial incentives necessary to bring the products to market.

11. The premier United Nations agency for health is the WHO, which is charged with "directing and coordinating international health work." But many other United Nations bodies also pursue health work, including the United Nations Children's Fund (children's health), the United Nations Fund for Population Activities (women and reproductive health), the United Nations Development Programme (human development) and UNAIDS (multiagency AIDS programme).

12. World Bank lending in health approaches $2 billion a year. The Bank's health engagement accelerated after its seminal *World Development Report 1993: Investing in Health*, which is widely credited for bringing applied economic analysis to health policies.

13. In one of the few instances of an increase in foreign aid, the US Congress appropriated an extra $50 million in 1998 for the control of emerging infections.

14. There have been efforts in this direction. In 1995 the WHO and the International Civil Aviation Organization established an expert panel for updating the deterrence of insect-borne diseases, airplane disinfection and airport management.

References

Berlinguer, Giovanni. 1992. "Public Health Then and Now: The Interchange of Disease and Health between the Old and New Worlds." *American Journal of Public Health* 82: 1407–13.

Buse, Kent, and Catherine Gwin. 1998. "The World Bank and Global Cooperation in Health: The Case of Bangladesh." *Lancet* 351: 665–69.

Chen, Lincoln, David Bell and Lisa Bates. 1996. "World Health and Institutional Change." In *Enhancing the Performance of International Health Institutions.*

Rockefeller Foundation, Social Science Research Council and Harvard School of Public Health. Cambridge, MA: Harvard Center for Population and Development Studies.

CISET (Committee on International Science, Engineering and Technology). 1995. *Global Microbial Threats in the 1990s.* Working Group on Emerging and Re-emerging Infectious Diseases. Washington, DC: National Science and Technology Council.

Cooper, Richard N. 1989. "International Cooperation in Public Health As a Prologue to Macroeconomic Cooperation." In Richard N. Cooper and others, eds., *Can Nations Agree?* Washington, DC: Brookings Institution.

Dahlgren, Göran. 1994. "The Political Economy of Health Financing Strategies in Kenya." In Lincoln C. Chen, Arthur Kleinman and Norma C. Ware, eds., *Health and Social Change in International Perspective.* Harvard School of Public Health, Department of Population and International Health. Boston, MA: Harvard University Press.

Godlee, Fiona. 1997. "WHO Reform and Global Health." *British Medical Journal* 314: 1359–60.

IOM (Institute of Medicine). 1997. "America's Vital Interest in Global Health." Washington, DC: National Academy Press.

Jamison, Dean T., Julio Frenk and Felicia Knaul. 1998. "International Collective Action in Health: Objectives, Functions, and Rationale." *Lancet* 351(9101): 514–17.

Kull, Steven. 1995. *Americans and Foreign Aid: A Study of American Public Attitudes: A Poll Conducted by the Program on International Policy Attitudes.* A Joint Program of the Center for the Study of Policy Attitudes and the Center for International and Security Studies at the University of Maryland. Washington, DC: Program on International Policy Attitudes.

Lederberg, Joshua. 1997. "Infectious Disease As an Evolutionary Paradigm." *Emerging Infectious Disease* 3(4): 417–23.

Lee, Kelley. 1997. "The Reform of the World Health Organization: Where Can We Go from Here? A Review of Recent Studies and Initiatives." Stockholm: Swedish International Development Agency.

Lucas, Adetokunbo. 1998. "WHO at Country Level." *Lancet* 351: 743–47.

Mathews, Jessica T. 1997. "Power Shift." *Foreign Affairs* 76(1): 50–66.

McMichael, Anthony J., and Andrew Haines. 1997. "Global Climate Change: The Potential Effects on Health." *British Medical Journal* 315: 805–09.

McNeill, William. 1976. *Plagues and Peoples.* Garden City, NY: Anchor Books.

Ministry of Foreign Affairs. 1996. "Tomorrow's Global Health Organization: Ideas and Options." Division for Global Cooperation. Stockholm: Government of Sweden.

Murray, Christopher J.L,. and Alan Lopez. 1998. "The Global Burden of Disease Study." Harvard School of Public Health, Boston, MA.

Nakajima, Hiroshi. 1997. "Global Disease Threats and Foreign Policy." *Brown Journal of World Affairs* 4(1): 319–32.

Raymond, Susan U., ed. 1997. "Global Public Health Collaboration: Organizing for a Time of Renewal." New York: Academy of Sciences.

Walt, Gill. 1998. "Globalisation of International Health." *Lancet* 351: 434–37.

WHO (World Health Organization). 1996. *The World Health Report 1996: Fighting Disease, Fostering Development.* Geneva.

World Bank. 1993. *World Development Report 1993: Investing in Health.* New York: Oxford University Press.

Yach, Derek, and Douglas Bettcher. 1998a. "The Globalisation of Public Health: I. Threats and Opportunities." *American Journal of Public Health* 88(5): 735–38.

———. 1998b. "The Globalisation of Public Health: II. The Convergence of Self-Interest and Altruism." *American Journal of Public Health* 88(5): 738–41.

Zinsser, Hans. 1963. *Rats, Lice and History.* Boston, MA: Little Brown and Company.

KNOWLEDGE AND
INFORMATION

These chapters examine the global public good aspect of knowledge and information, and of the infrastructure needed to transmit information. Joseph E. Stiglitz concentrates on the former. Within the latter, Debora L. Spar concentrates on the Internet, while J. Habib Sy treats both the Internet and other forms of global telecommunications. All three authors argue that the global public good aspects of knowledge and information present challenges and opportunities that are only beginning to be recognized.

Stiglitz first describes why knowledge is not simply a public good, but a *global* public good. In grappling with the dilemma of collective action in the production and dissemination of knowledge, states must decide to what extent there should be public provision and to what extent private production should be encouraged through strengthened intellectual property rights. Designing the appropriate intellectual property rights regime entails balancing static and dynamic efficiency. Indeed, because research (knowledge) is one of the most important inputs into the production of further knowledge, raising the "price" of knowledge may actually reduce follow-on research and slow the pace of innovation. Thus it is essential to reward research and innovation by firms while ensuring widespread access to knowledge and protection against monopoly rents. Issues of equity and efficiency interplay here as well, as most innovations incorporate ideas that are part of the common pool of knowledge. Narrowing the knowledge gap between developing and developed countries requires the construction of strong domestic knowledge infrastructures, most notably in education. Because knowledge is a global public good, Stiglitz argues that successfully meeting the challenges posed by knowledge externalities depends critically on cooperative efforts at the international level.

Equity concerns permeate the chapter by Sy, which focuses on global telecommunications from the standpoint of dependency theory. Sy notes that publicness cannot be guaranteed unless users have low-cost access to the opportunities afforded by the new information technologies. Privatization of telecommunications carriers, he argues, will not guarantee low-cost access and may actually impede it. Sy notes that in absolute terms the prices of knowledge goods and services are higher in Africa than in high-income countries—which may confirm some of the fears expressed by Stiglitz. In addition, even though information and communications technologies have public good attributes, Sy argues, they are embedded in power relationships. In particular, they are crucial for access to developing country markets, for intelligence purposes and for the transmission of ideas and ideologies. Most of all, they have the potential to widen the gap between haves and have-nots. Accordingly, Sy calls for a renewed commitment to a public service agenda and, to that end, for increased cooperation between states on a regional basis.

In her treatment of the Internet as a global public good, Spar notes that there is a growing trend towards "privatization" of the Internet. In theory, the Internet is nonrival and nonexcludable, in that it provides a basic infrastructure that can be used by many future users. But congestion problems are appearing, and servers are beginning to charge for access. Spar also discusses the Internet's positive and negative externalities. On the positive side, there have been gains in health, education and commerce—and hence growth. On the negative side, it is easier to transmit objectionable material. Internet regulations intended to tackle negative externalities will fail unless they are undertaken in concert among all nations—and even then they will be difficult to implement. The most important item on the policy agenda, however, is to ensure that developing countries obtain adequate physical infrastructure to reap the benefits of the Internet, and that those who can benefit most are not deterred by high prices from using the services.

KNOWLEDGE AS A
GLOBAL PUBLIC GOOD

JOSEPH E. STIGLITZ

Thomas Jefferson, the third president of the United States, described knowledge in the following way: "he who receives an idea from me, receives instruction himself without lessening mine; as he who lights his taper at mine, receives light without darkening me". In doing so, Jefferson anticipated the modern concept of a public good. Today we recognize that knowledge is not only a public good but also a global or international public good. We have also come to recognize that knowledge is central to successful development. The international community, through institutions like the World Bank, has a collective responsibility for the creation and dissemination of one global public good—knowledge for development.

This chapter reviews the concept of global public goods, explains the sense in which knowledge is a public good and explores the implications for international public policy that derive from the fact that knowledge is a global public good. In particular, I emphasize the role of knowledge for development, articulated forcefully in the *World Development Report 1998/99* (World Bank 1998b), and the consequences thereof.

BASIC CONCEPTS

This chapter combines two concepts developed over the past quarter century: the concept of global public goods and the notion of knowledge as a global public good.[1]

A public good has two critical properties: nonrivalrous consumption—the consumption of one individual does not detract from that of another—and nonexcludability—it is difficult if not impossible to exclude an individual from enjoying the good. Knowledge of a mathematical theorem clearly satisfies both attributes: if I teach you the theorem, I continue to enjoy the knowledge of the theorem at the same time that you do. By the same token, once I publish the theorem, anyone can enjoy the theorem. No one can be excluded.

They can use the theorem as the basis of their own further research. The "ideas" contained in the theorem may even stimulate others to have an idea with large commercial value.

Nonrivalrousness

The fact that knowledge is nonrivalrous—that there is zero marginal cost from an additional individual enjoying the benefits of the knowledge—has a strong implication. Even if one could exclude someone from enjoying the benefits of knowledge, it would be undesirable to do so because there is no marginal cost to sharing its benefits. If information is to be efficiently utilized, it cannot be privately provided because efficiency implies charging a price of zero—the marginal cost of another individual enjoying the knowledge. However, at zero price only knowledge that can be produced at zero cost will be produced.

To be sure, to acquire and use knowledge, individuals may have to expend resources—just as they might have to expend resources to retrieve water from a public lake. That there may be significant costs associated with transmission of knowledge does not in any way affect the public good nature of knowledge itself: private providers can provide the "transmission" for a charge reflecting the marginal cost of transmission while at the same time the good itself remains free.

Nonexcludability

While its nonrivalrous property says that no one should be excluded from the enjoyment of a public good (since the marginal cost of benefiting from it is zero), nonexcludability implies that no one *can* be excluded. This too has important implications: it means that knowledge cannot be provided privately. Assume that someone produced a theorem. Assume that the theorem is valuable in providing insights into how to solve practical problems. But assume also that the theorem cannot be kept secret and must be immediately available. Then, since anyone can immediately enjoy the theorem, the individual could make no profit from it. Competition would drive its price to zero. At any positive price, it would pay someone to get the information (which by assumption he could do) and undercut the seller.

Some forms of knowledge are (or can be made) excludable. For example, in some industries, such as metallurgy, trade secrets are used. To be sure, firms relying on secrets run a risk: a competitor, observing a new alloy, could analyse its composition and infer the mix of metals (and with modern techniques, even the relative proportion of the atoms). The firm might have a hard time inferring precisely how the alloy is made, but there is no way that rivals can be excluded from knowledge of the chemical composition and the properties of the alloy. By the same reasoning, when a firm discovers that consumers love, say, yoghurt, others cannot be excluded from using that knowledge to put their own yoghurts on the market.

Patents provide the exclusive right to inventors to enjoy the fruits of their innovative activity over a limited period (17 years in the United States). In return, inventors must disclose the details of their invention. But the fact of the invention, let alone the details provided in the patent application, make an enormous amount of knowledge freely available. The development of rayon provided other researchers with important information: it demonstrated the feasibility of a synthetic fibre—knowledge that was of enormous commercial value and that enhanced incentives for others to look for other synthetic fibres. Indeed, research in chemicals often consists of looking for slight variations of the original chemical. It is precisely because of the high value of the knowledge disclosed through the patent process (and the limited duration of the patent) that some firms decide not to patent their inventions and to rely on trade secrecy—even though this may seem to offer less protection at first sight.

But because the returns to some forms of knowledge can to some extent be appropriated (there is some degree of nonexcludability), knowledge is often thought of as an *impure* public good.

Global public goods

Shortly after Samuelson (1954) articulated the general theory of pure public goods, it became recognized that the benefits of some public goods were limited geographically. These were called local public goods (see Tiebout 1956 and Stiglitz 1977, 1983). Of course, the public goods earlier theory had focused on—such as national defence—were also limited geographically to a particular country. At the same time, there are several public goods that are not so limited—the benefits of which accrue to everyone in the world. In Stiglitz (1995) I identify five such global public goods: international economic stability, international security (political stability), the international environment, international humanitarian assistance and knowledge.

Most knowledge is a global public good: a mathematical theorem is as true in Russia as it is in the United States, in Africa as it is in Australia. To be sure, some kinds of knowledge are of value only or mostly to those living in a certain country—for example, knowledge particular to a country's institutions, weather or even geography. But scientific truths—from mathematical theorems to the laws of physics and chemistry—are universal in nature. The problems that economics deals with, such as scarcity, are ubiquitous, and accordingly the laws of economics are universally applicable, even if idiosyncratic institutions exist within each country.

The role of the state

The central public policy implication of public goods is that the state must play some role in the provision of such goods; otherwise they will be undersupplied. If firms cannot appropriate the returns to producing knowledge, then they will have limited incentive to produce it: in deciding how much to invest, they will look only at the return that they acquire, not the benefits that accrue to others. The benefits that have accrued from the development of the transistor, the laser or the mathematical algorithms that underlay the modern computer have been enormous, extending well beyond the benefits accruing to those who made or financed these innovations and discoveries.

Governments have pursued two strategies in addressing these concerns. The first is to increase the degree of appropriability of the returns to knowledge, by issuing patents and copyright protection. In doing so, governments are engaged in a careful balancing act: after all, one of the basic properties of knowledge as a public good is that the marginal cost of usage is zero (nonrivalrous consumption). Inventors obtain a return on their innovative activity either by charging through the use of a patent (licensing) or by charging a monopoly price on the product. In either case there is an inefficiency. The gain in *dynamic* efficiency from the greater innovative activity is intended to balance out the losses from *static inefficiency* from the underutilization of the knowledge or from the underproduction of the good protected by the patent.

One part of the balancing act is to limit the duration of the patent. A very short patent life would imply a low level of appropriability—such that the limited returns to innovative activity would imply low levels of innovation. A very long patent life would mean large losses in static efficiency; most of the fruits of the innovation would accrue to the innovator, with little passed on to consumers (say, in the form of lower prices) because the inventor would never be subjected to competitive pressure. Patents typically last for 17 years, and in many cases by the time a patent has expired its value is limited because new products and innovations have superseded it. This is not the case, however, for many drugs (partly because there may be a long testing period before the drug is actually marketed.)

But other aspects of the patent system play an important role in how the dynamic efficiencies are balanced with the static inefficiencies: the breadth and scope of a patent claim (whether a patent for a new genetically altered tomato covers all genetically altered vegetables, all genetically altered tomatoes or only this particular genetically altered variety) can have profound implications.

Initial knowledge is a key input into the production of further knowledge, and thus the design of the patent system can dramatically affect the overall pace of innovation. An excessively broad patent system (for example, with long-lived patents of broad scope) can raise the price of one of the most vital inputs into the innovative process and thus reduce the pace of follow-on innovations, even as it may provide returns to those making the original innovation. As a result the overall pace of technical progress may be slowed.[2] Worries about the adverse effects of excessively strong intellectual property protection have been brought home by the US government's recent antitrust suit against Microsoft, which has allegedly attempted to leverage the power associated with its control of the dominant personal computer operating system (itself a consequence of important network externalities that result in huge advantages associated with the establishment of an industry standard; Katz and Shapiro 1985) to a broader dominance in application software. Many industry experts believe that in doing so, Microsoft may have retarded the pace of innovation in the computer industry.[3]

These concerns are of particular importance to developing countries. Innovations (research and development expenditures) are even more concentrated in advanced industrial countries than are incomes (figure 1), and many of the advances in less developed countries consist of adapting the technologies of more advanced countries to the circumstances of the developing world.

The second strategy for dealing with the appropriability problem entails direct government support. If government could costlessly raise revenues for financing the support and if government were effective in discriminating between good and bad research projects, clearly this strategy would dominate that of enhancing intellectual property rights, for the latter strategy entails static distortions (the monopoly prices associated with patent rights result in prices exceeding marginal costs) and the inefficient utilization of knowledge. The static distortions can be thought of as a tax used to finance the research and development; the tax, however, is not an optimal tax.[4] But the patent system provides an effective self-selection mechanism: those who are convinced that they have a good idea invest their own money and the money of those whom they can persuade of the attractiveness of their idea. Such selection mechanisms may not only be more effective than, say, government bureaucrats attempting to assess various applications, but the costs of mistakes are borne by those making the misjudgement, not by the public at large. Thus the system provides strong incentives for individuals to engage in due diligence when assessing the merits of alternative research proposals. It is because of

FIGURE 1

GDP and research and development expenditures by region, 1987

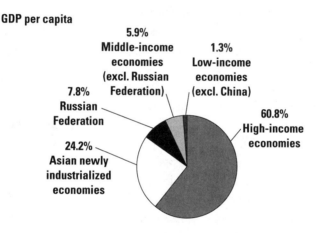

GDP per capita

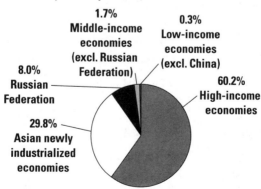

Research and development expenditures

Source: World Bank 1998b.

these strong incentive and selection properties that most economists believe that for a wide range of areas, the strategy of enhancing intellectual property rights is preferable to that of government subsidization.

But there are some important situations where the costs of the improved appropriability strategy are high. This is particularly the case for basic research because its benefits are widespread and diffuse, and because attempts to appropriate its returns may significantly slow the overall pace of innovation. Indeed, many advances in basic knowledge—such as mathematical theorems—are not patentable despite their importance and their potential practical applications.

This discussion should have made clear one central point: the concept of intellectual property—the breadth, scope and applicability of patent protection—is not just a technical matter. There are judgement calls and trade-offs, with different people and different countries all affected differently by alternative decisions. There are conflicts of interests between developed countries and less developed countries. But unfortunately, many of the key issues cannot even be summarized by a set of simply stated principles. In practice, decisions are made on a case-by-case approach.

For instance, two key issues in the granting of a patent are scope and novelty. Does the first person to develop a genetically engineered tomato get a patent for that specific tomato, for all genetically engineered tomatoes or for all genetically engineered vegetables? Is the idea of a genetically engineered plant sufficiently obvious that it is simply not patentable, with only specific and nonobvious genetic engineering processes being patentable? The consequences of answering these questions in different ways are enormous, as in the case of the automobile patent. In the early days of the automobile a lawyer-inventor named Selden received a patent for a horseless, self-propelled carriage. He attempted to use the patent not only to extract a royalty but also to enforce an industry cartel. Had Selden succeeded, he would have suppressed innovations such as those of Henry Ford, who subsequently attempted to provide a low-cost automobile. While most of the industry was willing to go along with Selden (because he offered the prospect of an industry cartel, which would raise their profits), Ford challenged the patent and won. Had he lost, there could have been a long delay before cars became a method of mass transportation.

The stance sometimes taken by producers of knowledge, that we need "strong" intellectual property rights, masks this underlying debate. Strong, in this context, becomes equivalent to "good", with the implication that the "stronger" the better. But I hope this discussion has brought out that the issues are far more complicated. Stronger, in the sense of "tighter" protection, could not only have large distributive consequences (between, say, developed countries and less developed countries), but also large efficiency consequences, with the pace of innovation actually impeded and living standards in less developed countries diminished.

Some industrial countries have effective competition policies that mitigate the risks that result from the abuse of monopoly power associated with a patent. But most countries do not have effective antitrust policies. For instance, drug companies can, and have an incentive to, act like discriminating monopolists, charging higher prices where the consumer surplus is higher or where they can extract more of the consumer surplus. Some European countries have policies that offset these monopolistic powers: given the large role of government in health care, they can effectively exercise their monopsonistic powers. Thus it is conceivable (and there are anecdotes supporting this possibility) that consumers in less developed countries could be charged higher prices for drugs than consumers in far richer countries. (In doing so, the consumers in less developed countries are in effect paying the fixed cost of research; consumers in more developed countries are partial free riders.)

Within the United States such price discrimination (not fully justified by differences in transactions costs) would probably be illegal. But there is no international competition policy that protects the poor country. Well-designed (but not excessively strong) intellectual property regimes can provide some protection. It is not clear the extent to which effective competition policies *within a country* might provide safeguards: presumably a country could pass a "most favoured nation" provision—no firm, enjoying the benefit of intellectual property protection, could charge the consumers of that country a higher price than the price charged for the same good elsewhere in the world.[5] (Today there is concern within the United States that Microsoft is using intellectual property protection in ways that thwart innovation, making it difficult for small, rival software firms to enter the market. The recent federal court case has presented allegations of a variety of anticompetitive practices—practices that stifle new entrants, sometimes with superior products.)

There are other issues in the design of an intellectual property regime. Every innovation makes use of previously accumulated knowledge—it draws on the global commons of pre-existing knowledge. How much of the returns to the innovation should be credited to this use of the global commons?

Current practice says zero—because it is a commons, there is no price. But this is not the way things need be. In many parts of the world there is a recognition that charges can and should be imposed for the use of commons (whether they are forests, grazing lands or fisheries). Such charges can be justified on both efficiency and equity grounds. The international community could similarly claim the right to charge for the use of the global knowledge commons. Because knowledge is a public good, the argument for charging a fee is largely based on an equity rationale. However, by recycling funds to support further research, an efficiency argument could also be developed. There are obvious practical problems in the implementation of such a scheme: what fraction of the returns to the innovation is due to the use of the global commons? But even a rough rule of thumb, in which a certain fraction of the returns to innovations is used to finance a "replenishment" of the global knowledge commons, might be an improvement.

This issue of the use of the global knowledge commons has been brought home forcefully in the context of biodiversity, where private firms have prospected for valuable drugs in natural settings. In many cases local people have long recognized the value of these local drugs, though they have not identified the particular chemicals in the plants that give the desired effects.

The contrast could not be more stark between the way this unpatented knowledge is treated and the way adaptations of innovations in developing countries of patented ideas from developed countries are treated. In the first case all of the return is credited to the "discoverer", with none to the pre-existing knowledge. In the second case the patent holder is allowed to act as a perfectly discriminating monopolist, regardless of the extent to which his or her innovation built on pre-existing knowledge.

The effective use of knowledge developed in industrial countries typically involves substantial elements of adaptation—combining global and local knowledge. Yet the intellectual property regime, as it has been evolving, assigns most of the bargaining power associated with how the fruits of these combinations are shared to the developed country, especially in larger developing countries, where there may be effective competition for the use of the patented idea.

An international intellectual property regime, designed to facilitate the production and use of the global public good—knowledge—in a way that sustains high rates of growth and is consistent with broad notions of equity, must balance a variety of subtle concerns, including dynamic and static efficiency and the use of the global knowledge commons.

Combining local and global knowledge

As I have just noted, a key part of successful development is combining global knowledge with local knowledge. The intellectual property regime affects how the gains are shared, and in doing so affects the pace of development within less developed countries. But many other aspects of the "knowledge infrastructure" within less developed countries can affect the pace of development and the extent to which developing countries can avail themselves of the fruits of the global public good of knowledge.

Perhaps the most important is education. The Republic of Korea and other newly industrialized countries that have closed the knowledge gap between themselves and more advanced industrial countries invested heavily in secondary and tertiary education, especially in science and technology. Poor developing countries have rightly stressed the importance of primary education, for primary education is the base of the entire education system. Even primary education can have a large impact on the pace at which innovations in agriculture or better fertility and health practices are spread. But a significant closing of the knowledge gap requires more than a strong primary education system.

In the past, some poor countries have been rightly criticized for investing too much in higher education, the benefits of which go to a small elite. But the criticism has been misinterpreted. The issue is not the importance of higher education. The criticism is of what is taught, the quality of the education and how it is financed. Science and technology are vital. They must be taught at international standards—otherwise the instruction does little good in closing the knowledge gap and it would be better to send students to study abroad. And the students should be made to bear as much of the costs as possible, if not now then later, by repaying student loans.[6]

Governments in newly industrialized countries often played other important roles in facilitating the transfer of knowledge. For example, they established standards laboratories to attain the kinds of international standards required for participation in global markets for high-technology commodities. Some countries not only showed an openness to foreign direct investment but also actively recruited those forms most likely to have knowledge spillovers and designed employment and other programmes to enhance the likelihood of such spillovers. Licensing policies also played a role in the transfer of knowledge.[7]

As essential as the adaptation and creation of new knowledge within a country is the dissemination of knowledge throughout a country. The movement of ideas within a country is affected by the effectiveness of its communications system. Recent advances in telecommunications have brought the costs of communication down tremendously and made possible the development of communications networks in parts of the world where it would have been decades, at best, before such systems would have been developed with older technologies. These new technologies mean that there is no longer a natural monopoly on communications, and by using competitive, market forces, access can be enhanced and prices lowered.[8]

This communications revolution, at the same time that it has made great strides in facilitating communication within countries, has also enhanced the ability of less developed countries to tap into the global knowledge pool. The Internet is proving to be a tool of immense power in sharing knowledge. Today developing countries face both great risks and great opportunities. Internet growth has been fastest in the United States and, not surprisingly, slowest in less developed countries. The enhanced ability to share and acquire knowledge in industrial countries may widen the knowledge gap because less developed countries may become even more disadvantaged.

At the same time, less developed countries can tap into a larger knowledge pool than they ever had access to before. Today a child anywhere in the world who has Internet access has access to more knowledge than a child in the best schools of industrial countries did a quarter century ago. He or she is no longer isolated. It is too soon to see how these contrasting forces will play out—whether the knowledge gap will be widened or narrowed. But it is clear that it is incumbent upon less developed countries to do everything they can to enhance their ability to tap into the reservoir of global knowledge.

Creating the knowledge infrastructure entails learning how to learn[9]— that is, creating the capacity to close the knowledge gap, an essential part of a successful development strategy.

KNOWLEDGE FOR DEVELOPMENT

Much of the knowledge that is required for successful development is not patentable; it is not the knowledge that underlies new products or new processes. Rather, it is equally fundamental knowledge: how to organize firms, how to organize societies, how to live healthier lives in ways that support the environment. It involves knowledge that affects fertility and knowledge about the design of economic policies that promote economic growth.

Those of us working in development institutions acquire much of this knowledge as a by-product of our general development activities. It is a form of learning by doing (see Arrow 1962). But knowledge for development goes beyond the collection of best practices and the accumulation of successful anecdotes and into analysis—why do certain policies and practices work in some circumstances and not others? Thus research is a central element of knowledge for development.

The ideas presented so far make clear that such knowledge is a global public good, and without active public support, there will be underprovision of this good. International institutions, including the World Bank and the United Nations Development Programme (UNDP) play a special role in the production and dissemination of this knowledge. We at the World Bank are increasingly thinking of ourselves as a Knowledge Bank,[10] and are organizing ourselves in ways that enhance our ability both to produce this knowledge and to disseminate it widely.

There is a natural complementarity between these new roles and the more traditional role of the World Bank in providing capital to less developed countries. Knowledge enhances the productivity of capital. Our research department's recent report on *Assessing Aid* shows that aid has a substantial impact on economic growth in countries that put into place good policies, while it has a negligible effect in countries that do not (World Bank 1998a). Knowing whether good policies are in place in developing countries and adapting World Bank lending programmes to reflect these realities is thus an important element of a successful lending programme.[11]

While we already know many elements of what makes for good policies, much needs to be learned. We need, for instance, to be able to better tailor policies to the different conditions and changing circumstances of individual countries. We have gradually come to recognize the adverse consequences of corruption, but we are only beginning to understand how to reduce corruption. While in the past we have focused, for instance, on the efficiency and equity aspects of tax structures; we are only beginning to pay attention to the susceptibility of different tax structures to corruption. Similarly, while there is widespread recognition of the advantages of privatization of certain public enterprises, we have only gradually come to recognize the problems that arise when privatization occurs prior to the establishment of effective regulatory or competition regimes. We have only slowly come to perceive the pervasiveness of corruption in the privatization process and the long-lasting adverse effects of that corruption. And we have all too late recognized that privatization prior to the establishment of effective market institutions may not necessarily lead to a vibrant market economy—because the incentives provided by privatization may be directed more towards stripping assets than creating wealth. It should be clear that this kind of knowledge is essential to all of the World Bank's lending programmes, in its project lending, in its sectoral lending and, perhaps most important, in its adjustment lending. More broadly, knowledge, aid and private capital work together in a successful development programme; they are complementary.[12]

But there is more. We have increasingly realized that isolated projects will have only limited effects in the transformation of societies that we call development. We have to go beyond projects, and we have to scale up projects. An essential aspect of this strategy is the design of projects from which we can learn, from which we can garner knowledge and that can constitute the basis of economy-wide transformations (see Wolfensohn 1998 and Stiglitz 1998).

CONCLUSION

The concept of global public goods is a powerful one. It helps us think through the special responsibilities of the international community. National public goods provide one of the central rationales for national collective action and for the role of government. Efficiency requires public provision and, to avoid the free-rider problem, the provision must be supported by compulsory taxation (see Stiglitz 1989). Similarly, global public goods provide a central rationale for international collective action. But today governance at the international level entails voluntary, cooperative actions. These include agreements to support an international property regime that facilitates the private production of certain kinds of knowledge. (We have raised questions of whether the current regime adequately reflects the broad interests of the international community, balancing equity and efficiency concerns among the affected parties.) But basic research and many other fundamentals forms of knowledge are not, and almost certainly should not be, protected by an intellectual property regime. In these areas efficiency requires public support. And this public support must be at the global level.

I have argued that knowledge is one of the keys to development and that knowledge is complementary to private and public capital. Knowledge is a global public good requiring public support at the global level. Current arrangements can be made to work effectively, but if they are to succeed we must be aware of the dangers and pitfalls. Some countries may try to free ride on others; they may try to capture more of the returns that are available from the use of the global knowledge commons; they may see their self-interest enhanced more by taking out of the global knowledge commons than contributing to it, in supporting research to design patentable applications rather in supporting basic research.

The efficient production and equitable use of global knowledge require collective action. The challenge facing the international community is whether we can make our current system of voluntary, cooperative governance work in the collective interests of all.[13]

Notes

The views presented here are solely those of the author and not those of any institution with which he is or has been affiliated.

1. See Stiglitz (1995) and US Council of Economic Advisers (1997). While the public good properties of knowledge had long been noted (Arrow 1962), early articulations of knowledge as a public good (in the sense defined by Samuelson 1954) include Stiglitz (1977) and Romer (1986). For an early textbook discussion, see Stiglitz (1986).

2. In theory, if the original innovator were a perfectly discriminating monopolist, such adverse effects might be limited because, it is alleged, he would never charge a fee for the usage of knowledge that would actually discourage a productive utilization (he would simply extract all of the users' producer surplus). But in practice there is not perfect discrimination, partly because the original innovator simply does not have the information required to be a perfectly discriminating monopolist. Moreover, competition in the product market is imperfect, and the innovator will discourage innovations that might result in the loss of some of his monopoly rents.

3. Aaron Edlin of the University of California at Berkeley (and a former staff economist at the US Council of Economic Advisors) has proposed an ingenious solution to spur innovation and limit the undue exercise of monopoly power: Microsoft would have to release its code, and the duration of its intellectual property protection would be limited to three years. If Microsoft continued to improve its product, the update versions of its software would be protected (for three years). Consumers would have a choice: they could avail themselves of the outdated (three-year-old) software or pay for the more advanced software. Microsoft would thus be forced to innovate at a fast pace to justify its dominant position in the market. Applications using the slightly outdated operating system would compete with those using the newer; and consumers would only be willing to pay for the new operating system if the improvements were worth the price.

4. According to the standards of optimal tax theory, which seeks to minimize deadweight losses. Moreover, the peculiar property of patents—imposing a high tax rate for a short period, followed by a zero tax rate—would (apart from the other considerations discussed in this section) appear to be far from optimal in terms of standard tax considerations. On the other hand, the tax is a "benefit" tax: those who enjoy the good pay the tax, and such taxes can be motivated by equity concerns.

5. This would, in a sense, be the opposite of antidumping laws, which stop firms from selling products at lower prices in international markets than they do domestically. While antidumping laws have the effect of hurting consumers at the same time that they protect producers, these "price gouging" laws would protect consumers.

6. One should note that to the extent that there are externalities associated with this education, there is an argument for public subsidies. The key question is, at the level of investment in education that maximizes a student's net present discounted value of income, is there a marginal externality—that is, is it desirable for government to encourage still further investment? Even without such marginal externalities, capital market imperfections provide a compelling argument for government intervention, but the interventions should be directed at reducing the impact of the imperfection.

7. This list is not meant to be exhaustive. For instance, some governments also created industrial and research parks, facilitating the exchange of ideas. Another important policy was the reduction of tariffs on intermediate goods, which allowed the import of essential inputs into more advanced technological processes.

8. Competition remains, however, far from perfect, so there is still an important role for an effective regulator. Chapter 2 of *World Development Report 1998/99* documents the success of countries that have used basic market competition with regulation (World Bank 1998b). Countries that have privatized without adopting a competitive framework have, at least in some cases, seen prices rise and access restricted: the private producer is more efficient in acting as a monopolist than the government was. In one instance the price of Internet access was raised to the point that a university could not afford to maintain connectivity. Thus the "reform" reduced the ability of those in the country to avail themselves of global knowledge.

9. I developed the concept of "learning to learn" and its implications for economic growth in Stiglitz (1987).

10. The concept of the Knowledge Bank was introduced in World Bank President James E. Wolfensohn's address to the 1996 Annual Meetings of the World Bank and International Monetary Fund (Wolfensohn 1996).

11. *Assessing Aid* points out that foreign aid is only significantly correlated with positive impacts in developing countries with sound economic policies and

institutions. In particular, in countries with sound economic management policies, 1% of GDP in aid leads to a sustained increase in growth of 0.5% and reduces poverty by 1%. In contrast, for those countries with poor economic environments, aid has no significant impact (the coefficient for growth as a result of aid inflow is actually negative, although not statistically different from zero).

12. Thus in countries that pursue good economic policies, aid "crowds in" private capital: $1 of aid helps bring in $2 of private capital. This helps explain aid's strong role in promoting economic growth. Similarly, the strong complementarity between knowledge and capital is one of the reasons that it is so difficult to parse out the extent to which growth is due to capital accumulation and the extent to which it is due to closing the knowledge gap. Improved knowledge stimulates higher investment, and the new investment embodies new technology. Without improvements in knowledge, East Asian countries presumably would have quickly experienced diminishing returns. As it was, they could maintain high rates of investment for an extended period without their incremental output-capital ratio falling. That is (only) one of the reasons that studies such as those of Young (1995), which purport to show that there was no East Asian miracle—that the region's growth can be explained entirely by investments, including investments in people—are so misleading. It was a miracle that these countries were able to maintain high returns with the levels of savings and investment—few if any other countries in the world succeeded in doing so. They did succeed in closing the knowledge gap, though to be sure, some of this knowledge was "purchased", like physical capital. For an alternative and more convincing interpretation (as well as a technical critique showing how sensitive Young's results are to the particular and unconvincing ways in which the variables entering the analysis are measured), see Klenow and Rodríguez-Clare (1997) and World Bank (1998b).

13. We can and should be more precise: since there are likely to be trade-offs, with some arrangements providing an advantage to some groups relative to others, the two key questions are standard efficiency and equity issues. Can international arrangements lead to a reasonably high level of efficiency (that is, not too large an undersupply of the global public good knowledge and not too high a level of "static inefficiency" from restrictive utilization of knowledge) in ways that comport with basic notions of equity?

REFERENCES

Arrow, Kenneth J. 1962. "The Implications of Learning by Doing." *Review of Economic Studies* 29: 155–73.

Katz, Michael L., and Carl Shapiro. 1985. "Network Externalities, Competition, and Compatibility." *American Economic Review* 75: 424–40.

Klenow, Peter J., and Andres Rodríguez-Clare. 1997. "Economic Growth: A Review Essay." *Journal of Monetary Economics* 40: 597–617.

Romer, Paul M. 1986. "Increasing Returns and Long-Run Growth." *Journal of Political Economy* 94(5):1002–37.

Samuelson, Paul. 1954. "The Pure Theory of Public Expenditure." *Review of Economics and Statistics* 36: 387–89.

Stiglitz. Joseph E. 1977. "Theory of Local Public Goods." In Martin S. Feldstein and Robert P. Inman eds., *The Economics of Public Services.* New York: Halsted Press.

———. 1983. "Public Goods in Open Economies with Heterogeneous Individuals." In Jean-François Thisse and Henry G. Zoller, eds., *Locational Analysis of Public Facilities.* Amsterdam and New York: North-Holland.

———. 1986. *Economics of the Public Sector.* New York: W.W. Norton.

———. 1987. "Learning to Learn, Localized Learning and Technological Progress." In Partha Dasgupta and Paul Stoneman, eds., *Economic Policy and Technological Performance.* New York and Sydney: Cambridge University Press.

———. 1989. "On the Economic Role of the State." In Arnold Heertje, ed., *Economic Role of the State.* Oxford: Basil Blackwell.

———. 1995. "The Theory of International Public Goods and the Architecture of International Organizations." *United Nations Background Paper 7.* New York: United Nations, Department for Economic and Social Information and Policy Analysis.

———. 1998. "Towards a New Paradigm for Development: Strategies, Policies, and Processes." Given as Raul Prebisch Lecture at the United Nations Conference on Trade and Development (UNCTAD), 18 October, Geneva.

Tiebout, Charles M. 1956. "A Pure Theory of Local Expenditures." *Journal of Political Economy* LXIV(October): 416–24.

US Council of Economic Advisers. 1997. *Economic Report of the President.* Washington, DC: US Government Printing Office.

Wolfensohn. James E. 1996. "1996 Annual Meetings Address." www.worldbank.org/html/extdr/extme/jdwams96.htm

———. 1998. "The Other Crisis: 1998 Annual Meetings Address." www.worldbank.org/html/extdr/am98/jdw-sp/am98-en.htm

World Bank. 1998a. *Assessing Aid: What Works, What Doesn't and Why.* A Policy Research Report. New York: Oxford University Press.

———. 1998b. *World Development Report 1998/99: Knowledge for Development.* New York: Oxford University Press.

Young, Alwyn. 1995. "The Tyranny of Numbers: Confronting the Statistical Realities of the East Asian Growth Experience." *Quarterly Journal of Economics* 110(3): 643–80.

GLOBAL COMMUNICATIONS FOR A MORE EQUITABLE WORLD

J. HABIB SY

Information and communications technologies are shaping the world views, understanding and behaviours of an increasing number of users and mass audiences. Overcoming the barriers of distance and time, ever faster, more complex and powerful systems are rapidly reshaping global politics, finance and strategy. In turn, globalization has significantly increased the need for, and reliance on, knowledge generation and processing. New technological frontiers have integrated digital computers, miniature microchips, cable, optical fibres and communication satellite systems for processing and disseminating information and have linked these to high-definition screens for display (Mosco and Wasko 1988, pp. 7–8).

Yet the world is more polarized than ever before between affluent and poor societies, disenfranchised and dominant social classes and information-rich and information-hungry nations. This chapter examines the world-wide trend towards increased privatization of both information and information and communications technologies, as well as the shrinking role of states and the effects on peoples' access to adequate information goods and services. Throughout, the focus is on Africa. The conclusion is that privatization is not a panacea, and that in developing countries, states appear to be preferred sources of funding for information services and information and communications technologies. A number of policy options can help level the playing field between nations that are rich in these technologies and nations that lack them .

INFORMATION AS A PUBLIC GOOD

Porat (1982, p. 79) describes the information economy as an aggregation of communication and information labour (information workers such as teachers, managers, clerks and agricultural extension agents) and information capital (telephones, business machines and so on). Porat further contends that the communication and information sector minimizes the private cost of coordination, increasing the division of labour and productive velocity. An increased division of labour boosts social and economic participation and influences an intricate collection of social variables such as mobilization, empathy, national integration, and modernization.

Whether information is the driving force for growth and increased wealth in the global economy (a false impression, as discussed below) or whether it is before all the expression of social relations and thus power relationships, information and communications technologies are generally considered a strategic investment in all respects. Wellenius and Stern (1994, pp. 2–3) stress the fact that "telecommunications constitute the core of, and provide the infrastructure for, the information economy as a whole. Telecommunications facilitate market entry, improve customer service, reduce costs, and increase productivity. They are an integral part of financial services, commodities markets, media transportation, and the travel industry, and provide vital links among manufacturers, wholesalers, and retailers. Countries and firms that lack access to modern telecommunications systems cannot effectively participate in the global economy".

There have been many attempts to understand information as a public or a private economic good (Bates 1988). Sinha (1991) raises the issue of the market as an inadequate tool for generating and equitably distributing a number of goods and services, especially public goods. He suggests that certain characteristics (network externalities and nonexcludability) make telecommunications eligible as a public good and that, when subjected to the imperfections of market forces, it is not equally accessible to end users—especially in peripheral economies where market efficiencies are wanting. Whether information is analyzed in terms of its flow (Pool 1984), aggregate value in "post-industrial" economies (Machlup 1962; Porat 1978), value and cost (Bates 1985; 1988) or competence (Gandy 1988), it has remained a problematic issue both as a commodity and as a social process.

Oscar H. Gandy has critiqued the neoclassical definition of information—as an "essence", a "natural" resource or a "product of labour"—from a political economy standpoint. He suggests the following characteristics for information goods and services:

As a public good, information presents considerable challenges to the idealized neoclassical marketplace. Consumption of information is nonrivalrous to the extent that consumption by one does not significantly reduce the possibility of consumption by another. These same attributes make it difficult to exclude non-payers from enjoying the direct benefits of consumption, especially as the ease of reproduction makes acceptable copies readily available. Indeed, because the cost of additional copies or exposures approaches zero at some scale, and because the demands of efficiency in a fully competitive market would move market price to cost, information markets without access constraints guaranteed by state action would be doomed to failure.

As with a great many goods and services, the production or consumption of information goods and services may generate costs or benefits for others not part of the market transaction. (Gandy 1992, p. 30)

Gandy further contends that neoclassical orthodoxy's assumption of stable tastes and preferences, which are determined by forces external to the market, cannot be sustained because of the presence of power within markets and in relationships that influence markets. Gandy also reviews several other critiques: that "markets are anything but perfect especially when one considers the highly concentrated communications industry worldwide"; that "public goods, especially information, generate critical distortions"; that "institutions, not individuals, are the dominant forces in the political economy"; that "there is substantial market power, the ability to influence price and supply"; that "a stable equilibrium is never achieved especially in an economy that is dynamic and variable over time"; and that "the state is not an objective, unbiased intervenor" (Gandy 1992, pp. 26–32).

Bates (1988, pp. 81–82) hypothesizes that the precondition for the production and consumption of information as an economic good and for conditions of optimality (that is, the satisfaction of various efficiency and social maximization criteria) may lie in the ability of markets to create significant levels of ancillary value, whether private or social.

Even if such optimal conditions were met, communications competence would still remain an unresolved issue, a blind spot in dominant information policies. Increased commoditization, privatization and social upheaval among powerless communities make them ineligible to use information resources to improve the quality of their lives (Gandy 1988, p. 109). Gandy rightly suggests that "this aspect of communications competence, the ability to understand the world so as to change it, is only one variable in the equation of inequality" (p. 109). Indeed, the growing trend to privatize or "liberalize" information services, markets and telecommunications carriers raises concerns about the widening gap between information-affluent and information-hungry social classes, nations and indeed entire regions of the world. In other words, access and equity are key issues for policy-makers to consider in this area.

INFORMATION ACCESS AND EQUITY

Four access and equity issues are particularly important for information and communications technologies: access to infrastructure and capabilities, international programmes to boost access, the direction of information flows and market shares in the communications industry.

Access to information infrastructure and capabilities
As a public good, information is undersupplied or unequally consumed—largely because of severe imbalances in the provision of global public communications services. At least 80% of the world's population lacks the most basic telecommunications. Countries with 55% of the world's people have less than 5% of the world's telephone lines, and more than half of the world's people have never used a telephone. Less than 6% of computers with Internet access are in Eastern Europe, Asia, Africa, the Middle East and Latin America and the Caribbean (Hamelink 1998, p. 71). Africa, in particular, will enter the 21st century with the poorest telecommunications infrastructure and services in the world. Africa accounts for 20% of the world's population but contains only 2% of the world's telephone lines (Cheneau-Loquay 1998, p. 2). Tokyo or Manhattan has more telephone lines than the entire continent.

Africa's involvement in and access to the Internet—which is used by more than 40 million people in 168 countries—is still marginal by international standards (except among the most privileged social segments in South Africa and northern Africa). But Internet technology is rapidly spreading across Africa. In 1997 Egypt, Kenya, South Africa and Tunisia were the only African countries with full international Internet links faster than 64 kilobytes per second. A year later 36 countries had full access, and by the end of the century almost all countries on the continent will have full access (Jensen 1998).

Yet cost remains a major constraint for end users. It costs three to four times more for an African to surf the Internet than for the average US or European user. A new $1,500 personal computer would take more than half the annual income of a university professor in Senegal and more than the annual income of a full professor in Nigeria. Africa's access to the Internet remains marginal and controlled mainly by external forces, both private and governmental. Access to the Internet may become even more elusive for farmers in distant locations or informal workers in the peripheries of poorly managed cities (see below). Africa's poor will not be connected to the Internet (or any other net for that matter). African women and children and millions of refugees abandoned on the battlefields of civil and economic confrontations will remain in the prehistory of communications, unable to enter the digital age.

Democracy and participation will not fully develop in Africa if access to the Internet, distance learning opportunities, computerized library packages and strategic databases remain out of reach for isolated and poor African nations unable to integrate their economies and intellects with a powerful and respected community of states. When such services are offered for free in Africa, it is usually just for a brief period, to create habits that will facilitate later price hikes. Is this the promise of the information age? Nothing will be free. Services will be available for all in theory—but they will be used only by those who can afford them.

International programmes to boost access

Over the years an enormous number of projects have been launched to salvage Africa from oblivion through virtual communications. An inventory of bilateral and multilateral programmes to enhance Africa's connectivity and cope with the situation just described is beyond the scope of this chapter. But a few examples can be reviewed.

The UNDP recently launched an $11.5 million programme called the Internet Initiative for Africa as part of the United Nations System-Wide Special Initiative on Africa. This programme focuses on policy, infrastructure and culture. It offers country-level support, but the recipient country must cover half the costs. Burkina Faso, Ethiopia, the Gambia, Mauritius, Nigeria and Swaziland are participants. The Sustainable Development Networking Programme at UNDP offers a wide range of consultancy and training services at the country level.

The World Bank recently launched the InfoDev Program with the aim of creating an enabling environment for markets in which the private sector has the primary responsibility in the areas of capital investment and provision of services. Universities are targeted in this scenario but only insofar as they are willing to commercialize online library services to already impoverished students and faculty members. (In Kenya and Nigeria, for instance, faculty members earn an average of $100 a month.) Francophone Africa, France and its

Western French-speaking allies have decided to launch a network offering access to the Internet, e-mail and databases on a moderate and promotional fee basis. In 1996 South African President Nelson Mandela, representatives of the G–7 group of industrial countries and partners from developing countries convened a meeting on the information society and development. The Leland Initiative, spearheaded by the US Agency for International Development, aims at privatizing and liberalizing telecommunications services and ensuring Internet expansion in Africa. In the meantime the European Union is about to launch an enormous electronic network in hopes of fostering international trade (Noumba-Um and others 1993).

A common denominator for most programmes intending to boost Africa's telecommunications is their central drive for the widespread use of new communications technologies. This goal may prove to be out of reach. Indeed, unless social revolutions with far-reaching consequences take place in Africa, the small number of end users will not grow significantly in the coming decades because of widespread and growing poverty, political unrest, poor telecommunications infrastructure and high illiteracy rates, coupled with small numbers of graduates and computer literate individuals. Thus Africa may be further marginalized between the 2000s and 2020s, which would represent a setback for the market expansion of concerned industries.

The direction of information flows
Africa's participation in the global Internet culture is marginal—quantitatively in the number of end users and qualitatively in feeding the Internet with data, information and news designed by Africans. Some of the knowledge, information and news resources available on the Internet may be relevant to African users. But the impressive quantity of information does not match the quality and content needed by Africans to harness information resources for development. Moreover, Africans must be able to feed into the Net their perspectives and strategic needs, news and research results. Otherwise, African Internet users will remain passengers on the information highway—not drivers. "Content creation" has, in fact, become a key preoccupation of donor agencies (such as UNDP) operating in this field.

The United States generates 65% of global communications and 80% of words and images circulated throughout the world. Until recently 90% of telephone traffic and 88% of telex traffic between African countries was routed through non-African countries. Two-thirds of this traffic is handled through former colonial powers as a result of inadequate communications links between neighbouring African countries (Adam and Hafkin 1992). Transborder data flows are also hampered by the lack of skilled personnel to install and configure data communications equipment and software, by insufficient mastery of computer-mediated communications software, by the unavailability of direct telephone lines for communications links, by management and administrative problems and by the unavailability of basic data communications supplies and equipment (Adam and Hafkin 1992). These deficiencies threaten to widen the gaps between the North and the South— and between Africa and the rest of the world.

Market shares in the communications industry

Information and communications technologies represent a highly concentrated transnational industry that generates close to $1.5 trillion a year (Hamelink 1998). The industry's leading conglomerates reside in countries that are members of the Organisation for Economic Co-operation and Development (OECD)—Canada, Germany, Japan, the United States and former colonial powers such as France, Italy, the Netherlands and the United Kingdom. Of a global telecommunications market estimated at $615 billion, Africa's share is only $9 billion, or 1.9% (Catroux 1998). South Africa alone represents $3.6 billion, or more than a third of the region's market.

African countries are one of the largest groups of nations in the International Telecommunications Satellite Organization (Intelsat) system and the most important users of Intelsat's Planned Domestic Service, which enables member and nonmember countries to purchase or lease transponders for nonpreemptible domestic communications on a long-term basis. Thus Africa is paying a tremendous price for not having its own regional satellite communications industry. Several developing countries—a pool of Arab countries, Brazil, China, Indonesia, Mexico—have launched indigenous satellite telecommunications networks to boost their national and international trade and handle their domestic needs for the transmission of data and television signals.

Although regional satellite systems have proliferated—as evidenced by Eutelsat, Arabsat and Asiasat—Africa has no satellite communications capacity. It plans to have a regional satellite system by 2020 through the Regional African Satellite Communication Organization (RASCOM). For the time being, RASCOM is pooling and commercializing African countries' unused telecommunications circuits, hoping to eventually secure investment funds from the international community and international financial institutions.

Giant telecommunications carriers—including France Telecom, AT&T, Alcatel, Motorola, NEC Corporation, Bell Canada, Ericsson, British Telecom and CTS (China)—have already positioned themselves. And a few have started to buy newly privatized national telecommunications carriers.

Africa also lacks a telecommunications industry. Telephones, computers, televisions and even radios are imported at prohibitive costs—as are optical fibres, microwave technology, switching equipment, earth stations technology, satellite dishes, connectors, transponder hardware and submarine cables. Moreover, Africa's involvement in global negotiations on global standards for technology such as Integrated Services Digital Network (ISDN), high-definition television (HDTV), Direct Broadcast Satellite (DBS) systems and the Internet is still marginal—this, despite the political, cultural, technological and economic implications and far-reaching consequences for present and future generations of Africans at home and abroad.

Africa's meaningful participation in the global information sector of the 21st century will depend on how communications manufacturing capabilities, know-how and specialized telecommunications and information labour are developed nationally, regionally and internationally. In a sense Africa's real challenge is to go beyond narrow consumerism and strive to find a respectable niche in global information and knowledge production sectors.

INTERNATIONAL BUSINESS AND INFORMATION TECHNOLOGIES

Global telecommunications underpin globalization. Companies need communications technology to do business internationally, and information technologies have helped markets become interconnected. Technology has also blurred the boundaries between "goods" and "services". For example, a software programme may be sold on diskette as a "good" and online as a "service" (Castells and Aoyama 1994, p. 8). Moreover, information and communications technologies have allowed companies to centralize finance, marketing, research and planning decisions in a headquarters office regularly updated through a global network of computers.

For example in the 1980s, Digital Equipment in the United States had keyboards made in Boston, Massachusetts, display monitors made in Taiwan (China), system boxes assembled in Westfield, Massachusetts, floppy disk drives made in Singapore and assembled and tested in Springfield, Massachusetts, disk drive heads made in Westboro, Massachusetts, and integrated circuits made in Hudson, Massachusetts that are sent to Taiwan (China) to be cut and packaged, then sent to Marlboro, Massachusetts to be made into hybrid circuits, then tested and sent to Westfield, Massachusetts to be incorporated into the computer memories made in Hong Kong (China) and Singapore (Mosco and Wasko 1988).

Globalization produces new types of relationships between labour, production, technology and capital, and above all a level of fluidity and interactivity among all factors of production. Under these circumstances small and medium-size enterprises and isolated public companies cannot compete on an equal footing with the giant conglomerates of the 21st century. Mergers and acquisitions, a dominant feature of the international business environment of the past 20 years, can be partly explained by this fact. And for a company, resisting this dominant trend may mean obsolescence, loss of competitiveness and therefore irrelevance.

Despite the competitive pressures, however, the Internet offers opportunities for small and medium-size businesses in Africa to have cheaper access to certain kinds of information than previously. Niche suppliers can also gain instantaneous access to a wider, global market. Here, pricing and availability will be crucial variables. While development assistance can help, current policies (such as the push for privatization) are sometimes counter-productive when it comes to universal access.

Information and communications technology and privatization
According to the World Bank, telecommunications reform usually consists of commercializing and separating operations from governments; increasing the participation of private enterprise and capital; containing monopolies, diversifying the supply of services and developing competition; and shifting government responsibility from ownership and management to policy and regulation (Wellenius and Stern 1994). In theory, the rationale for such reform is to generate substantial government revenues, reduce external debt, develop competition and enable countries to become stronger players in the global economy.

If that has happened, it has not benefited the poor. According to UNDP's *Human Development Report 1997*, "the greatest benefits of globalization have been garnered by a fortunate few. ... The least developed countries, with 10% of the world's people, have only 0.3% of world trade—half their share of two decades ago. ... The share of the poorest 20% of the world's people in global income now stands at a miserable 1.1%, down from 1.4% in 1991 and 2.3% in 1960. It continues to shrink. And the ratio of the income of the top 20% to that of the poorest 20% rose from 30 to 1 in 1960, to 61 to 1 in 1991—and to a startling new high of 78 to 1 in 1994" (UNDP 1997, p. 9).

Even though the World Bank has championed these policies, it admits that the tide of privatizations in the telecommunications sector may lead to "only five or six major operating companies dominating the world market in which state telecommunications enterprises are sold" (Wellenius and Stern 1994, p. 47) and that "privatization is not always a feasible option, nor does it by itself guarantee improved sector performance" (p. 45).

Sinha (1991) raises more fundamental questions in a cross-national evaluation of telecommunications policies in 65 developing countries divided into five groups ranging from low- to high-income countries. His results show that differences in telephone and line densities are closely related to national income. The critical difference between country groups relates to the extent of liberalization of their telecommunications policies, with group 2 countries having more liberalized policies than group 1 countries and group 5 countries having more liberalized policies than group 4 countries. A major finding of the survey is that while policy liberalization is not associated with significant differences in performance between different groups of countries, it is associated with adverse conditions of access and availability of services.

The study further suggests that "the liberalization of telecommunications policies in developing countries leads to a systematic worsening of conditions of access and availability of telephone service with little corresponding gains in improved sector performance" (pp. 209–210). The study concludes that if there are gains to be made from sector reform, they should be linked to high economic growth and pursued in highly industrialized countries. More important, Sinha argues convincingly that "government commitment (as reflected in increasing government investment) to stepping up the growth of the sector is the most important single factor in improving both performance and distribution at all levels of development and under all economic conditions" (pp. 209–10).

Sinha's study is a significant break from neoclassical views on telecommunications reforms in dominated countries. Indeed, he points out that the market mechanism is inadequate for generating and equitably distributing a number of goods and services—particularly a quintessential public good such as telecommunications. Sinha suggests that "subjecting the sector to imperfect markets could prevent any possibility of equitable access to telecommunications" in most dominated countries (p. 210). The creation and aggravation of such imbalances are among the root causes of bad development and the worsening quality of life in these countries.

Analyzing the consequences of Côte d'Ivoire's telecommunications privatization through its sale to France Telecom (a French multinational) without the introduction of competitive pressures, Sinha shows that the deal was a disaster for the country. It "resulted in the doubling of the price of basic residential service in the two years from 1988 to 1990 without any corresponding lowering of the price of business service or any additional tax revenues flowing to government coffers" (Sinha 1991, pp. 212–13).

In Senegal, France Telecom acquired SONATEL at a bargain price and then increased tariffs for certain categories of service (Niang 1998). Contrary to the claim that privatization brings higher salaries to telecommunications staff, the opposite happened in Senegal. SONATEL workers organized in a local trade union are considering renegotiating their agreements with France Telecom and even going on strike to force the company to keep its promises of better wages after privatization.

Thus privatization is not a panacea. It can lead to disaster where there is a lack of effective regulation and adequate specialized manpower with a progressive vision.

Geostrategic dimensions of information and communications technology

Packaging and repackaging information into a marketable commodity has become a central tool for consumerism, financial transactions and social control. As noted, information and communications technology are generally considered a strategic sector. Telecommunications make up the core of, and provide the infrastructure for, the entire information economy. Countries and firms that lack modern telecommunications cannot effectively participate in the global economy (Wellenius and Stern 1994, pp. 2–3). Thus telecommunications is a catalytic sector from the perspective of industrial policy.

Two additional dimensions of information make it a strategic good, and not just another commodity. The first is the power that information brings, especially in a negotiation. Asymmetric interdependence may be seen as the ability of more powerful states to have better access to and control of information in a negotiating situation. For instance, the expertise and personnel that can be marshalled by powerful countries engaged in global negotiations— for example, within the World Trade Organization, General Agreement on Tariffs and Trade (GATT) or World Administrative Radio Conference (WARC)—far exceed those available to dominated countries. The professional team backing the US negotiations at GATT numbered about 160—while that for the WARC was conservatively estimated at 930, including only government employees (O'Brien and Helleiner 1982, p. 124).

The second dimension covers all forms of intelligence, whether for security or commercial purposes. Technological espionage, satellite imagery, geographic information systems, remote sensing, transborder data flow, observatory satellite platforms—all have become prominent features of information gathering and processing. They are also essential tools for knowing what the neighbour or the enemy is doing in advanced technologies, microelectronics and sophisticated satellites legally acquired and then illegally duplicated. O'Brien and Helleiner (1982) pay attention to this issue and further suggest that "this type of information cannot be entirely separated from knowledge of underlying technical change, demand shifts, and the like" (pp. 102–03).

Africa deserves special attention in that respect. In the mid-1850s many African countries were militarily and administratively colonized. Companies started building huge communications empires from Cairo to Cape Town. Their goal was to integrate coastal trading ports into fully colonized territories, complete with cheap labour and raw materials. Telegraph and telephone networks became indispensable for monitoring colonial markets and their military and political situations (Sy 1996). Today there is the same need for efficient "wiring" of useful areas of raw materials and cheap labour.

In the process of privatization, developing countries have witnessed a major increase in foreign ownership of their telecommunications markets and industries. This development conflicts with objectives for independence and points to the strategic dimension of privatization, deregulation and trade liberalization, both for firms and for countries.

The partial privatization of Africa's telecommunications sector is perhaps a necessity, but the way it is taking place may represent a major threat to Africa's national and global security interests. Africa's telecommunications sector is increasingly under siege through pressures on African governments to sell their telecommunications industries to transnational corporations. These private interests have aggressively started positioning themselves— sometimes in a near-monopoly in local markets and in highly strategic sectors such as water, electricity, telecommunications and mineral extraction. Dominated countries have been forced to reorganize their markets into larger subregional or regional markets to prepare for integration with the global market. This process may significantly alter the sovereignty of African states: it may be an open invitation for foreign investors to capture strategic economic sectors even while they fail to alleviate problems such as low growth and investment.

PRIVATIZATION AND EQUITY

Pricing is never innocent for network goods such as transportation and communications. Because the marginal cost of using these services can be close to zero, user charges do not reflect the marginal cost, unlike for other types of goods. Instead, pricing is the result of a conscious, distributive decision on how to share the burden of the initial investment. With privatization, these distributive decisions are often taken out of the public domain and put into foreign hands.

The biggest challenge in the privatization of Africa's telecommunications will be to balance the needs of foreign private carriers for return and income and the needs of domestic users—including universities, research institutions, informal sector workers, nongovernmental organizations, individual and organized farmers and civil society organizations—in search of affordable telecommunications tariffs. Primary and secondary schools may also want to benefit from reduced tariffs. Who will subsidize such needs in countries where poverty has destabilized entire social groups—including civil servants, whose income has been slashed by reform, inflation, unemployment, devaluation and extremely costly imported goods?

Faced with budget constraints due in part to the marketization of information, schools, universities, libraries, international organizations and nonprofit servers and nodes around the world are bound to sell information and documentation to end users, whereas universal access to the world's scientific and cultural heritage should be guaranteed to all. In the face of tariff increases that sometimes come with privatization, equity questions become more pressing. Why should the limited purchasing power of African workers directly feed into the cash flows of the multinational corporations that are buying, at bargain prices, Africa's vital service providers in such areas as health, water, electricity and telephony? If privatization is needed to restore the balance of payments, why aren't the same structural adjustment and privatization programmes applied to industrial countries whose external debts have long since passed acceptable levels?

POLICY RECOMMENDATIONS

Over the past 20 years countless meetings, seminars, workshops, teleconferences and exhibits have been organized by bilateral, multilateral and private organizations in an effort to open Africa to the promises of the global telecom-

munications market. New utopias and crusades in the name of the information society, the global village and cyber communications have been presented
as magical formulas to remedy all of society's illnesses.

Many of these initiatives have been effective in extending the reach of
global telecommunications and promoting good domestic governance. Yet
many have failed to address the public good aspect of the issue. They have
not addressed, for example, the natural monopolies over key knowledge
and information industries held by a small number of transnational companies based in powerful countries. A more promising approach would be
to build capacity in various sectors so that developing countries can add
value to information and make it available to national and international
end users. The following offers a few principles for fair and effective policies in this field.

Regional and global policies

African participation in most of the negotiations dealing with international
regimes for information technologies has been less visible and efficient than
that of Asia and South America. But this does not mean that in the near future,
younger Africans will not play a more important role than they have been
allowed by generally conservative political systems. Directions for policy
renewal should concentrate on the following themes, some of which were
adopted at Africa Telecom 98, a meeting sponsored by the International
Telecommunication Union (Harrison 1998):

- Africa should own and operate a dedicated regional communications
  satellite through a flexible federation of human, financial and
  technological resources as well as adequate legal and political
  frameworks.

- Developing nations in general, and Africa in particular, should
  participate in global negotiations united around the same platform of
  action rather than on an individual basis.

- Privatization should be combined with transparent regulation and
  telecommunications policies. In addition, privatization under structural
  adjustment programmes must be carefully scrutinized to avoid a de facto
  recolonization of Africa's telecommunications sector by multinational
  corporations.

- Africa should be organized and strengthened as a regional
  telecommunications market for equipment and services and common
  procurement arrangements. Privatization should not be carried out at
  the expense of regional integration.

- Africa's industrial strategy should aim at learning how to manufacture both simple and more complex telecommunications parts and software through South-South cooperation and South-North ventures based on equitable agreements on a regional or subregional basis.

- High and arbitrary tariffs on imported products (such as computers) aggravate the problem of affordability and accessibility for scholars, citizens and small businesses in African countries (as in Senegal).

Revisiting public services

The notion of a public good or service should be revisited to reflect the true value of goods and services to people and to the improvement of their lives. In African and other developing countries, libraries, certain telecommunications services (distance learning, computerized health delivery systems) and education and health care should be subsidized by states from tax revenues based on fairness principles and assessed on a progressive scale. The rich and transnational corporations should pay higher taxes than the poor and informal workers. The same goes for tariffs and user fees. True, no African state can afford the telecommunications infrastructure it needs from tax revenue alone. Thus new forms of public-private partnerships will be necessary.

In fact, subsidization has played a role in some of the best success stories in the field of information technologies. In the United States, for example, the number of computers connected to the Internet has been stimulated by state subsidies for telecommunications infrastructure. Moreover, the Internet was heavily subsidized between 1968—when it was created as a Defense Department project—and 1995. In addition, the Internet has benefited from indirect financing through research development projects (mostly located in universities) and through subsidization of the purchase by universities of bandwidth for Internet use.

For whose benefit should such public services be recognized? Services that have intrinsic commercial value and few externalities should not be recognized as public services. Yet the notion that every service needed by humankind must be commercialized should be critically reassessed. The view that only defence, police, education and health are public services is wrong. Since the early 1980s international financial institutions have advocated the privatization of water and electricity, telephony and television, education and health. This process has led to the weakening of states already dominated on the political and economic fronts. Meanwhile, public spending on defence has not been discouraged—and indeed has sometimes been subsidized by donors.

This pattern of development has contributed to a situation in which Africa has the highest death toll from civil, ethnic and interstate wars and the highest number of refugees and displaced persons in the world.

Public services should have a universal reach and be made widely available for two reasons:

- *It is what people want.* Public services should be identified and promoted in a democratic manner and through participatory processes.

- *To level the playing field.* Given that firms and people interact and compete at the international level (thanks in large part to the development of telecommunications and information technologies), it makes sense to ensure that all are equally prepared and given the same opportunities for training and using basic services.

To finance public (or even privatized) telecommunications services, for instance, indigenous capital should be used to the extent possible. Internal capital (whether private or public) must be given priority over external borrowing and funding, especially in countries such as Angola, Egypt, Nigeria and South Africa, where internal savings and capital markets are significant. This approach would be consistent with dominant trends in OECD spending on knowledge and information industries.

In other countries international development assistance can help bridge the gap between savings and investment. This could be possible with a more democratic United Nations—one that paid more attention to distributional issues. Instead the telecommunications and information sectors show perpetuating global imbalances, unequal access to public resources and services, and increased poverty and turmoil, leading to wars within and between nations.

National governments will also have to do their part. Africa's public libraries are neglected, and no serious internal efforts are being made to build subregional or regional databases and strong research and development firms.

Thus policies to develop communications technologies in Africa and elsewhere can help—but they must be placed in the proper context. Communications technology alone cannot promote social fairness and place underdeveloped economies on a sound, sustainable and democratic track. In fact, inequitable development will impede the growth of telecommunications by shrinking the number of users. That could marginalize Africa further, even for countries or companies now best placed to take advantage of the emerging African market.

We can learn from past mistakes. The view that people matter more than market forces can regain ground, enabling telecommunications to offer vast potential for democratic development and for rebalancing a world that is becoming smaller every day.

NOTE

While writing this paper, I received comments or discussed some of the issues involved with Professor Oscar Gandy, Jr., Annenberg School of Communications, University of Pennsylvania; Professor Samir Amin, director, Third World Forum; and Ms. Yassine Fall, executive secretary, AAWORD. I wish to acknowledge their able assistance.

REFERENCES

Adam, James, and Nancy Hafkin. 1992. *Telematics for Development.* Addis Ababa: United Nations Economic Commission for Africa.

Bates, Benjamin J. 1985. "Information As an Economic Good: A Re-Evaluation of Theoretical Approaches." Paper presented at the 35th Annual Conference of the International Communication Association, 23–27 May, Honolulu, HI.

———. 1988. "Information As an Economic Good: Sources of Individual and Social Value." In Vincent Mosco and Janet Wasko, eds., *The Political Economy of Information.* Madison: University of Wisconsin Press.

Castells, Manuel, and Yuko Aoyama. 1994. "Paths towards the Informational Society: Employment Structure in G–7 Countries, 1920–90." *International Labour Review* 133(1): 5–33.

Catroux, Jean-Michel. 1998. "La renaissance." *Jeune Afrique Economie* 262 (13 April–3 May): 88.

Cheneau-Loquay, Annie. 1998. "Télécommunications : quel est l'état des lieux en Afrique et quelles sont les perspectives?" Centre National de la Recherche Scientifique. www.regards.cnrs.fr/Africanti/carto.html.

Gandy, Oscar H. Jr. 1988. "The Political Economy of Communications Competence." In Vincent Mosco and Janet Wasko, eds., *The Political Economy of Information.* Madison: University of Wisconsin Press.

———. 1992. "The Political Economy Approach: A Critical Challenge." *Journal of Media Economics* 5(2): 23–42.

Hamelink, Cees J. 1998. "The People's Communication Charter." *Development in Practice* 8(1): 68–74.

Harrison, Babatunde. 1998. "Combining Technologies Spur African Telecom Market." Africa Journal (May). *Electronic Newsletter on African Media Issues,* africa-journalist@idc.org.

Jensen, Mike. 1998. "African Internet Connectivity." http://www3.sn.apc.org/africa/afrmain.htm

Machlup, Fritz. 1962. *The Production and Distribution of Knowledge in the United States.* Princeton, NJ: Princeton University Press.

Mosco, Vincent, and Janet Wasko, eds. 1988. *The Political Economy of Information.* Madison: University of Wisconsin Press.

Niang, Bocar. 1998. "Les abonnés de Dakar supportent la 'baisse.'" *Sud Quotidien.* 23 August.

Noumba-Um, Paul, and others. 1993. "Etudes de cas: 14 pays d'Afrique." *Le Communicateur* 12(23–24): 357–96.

O'Brien, Rita Cruise, and G.K. Helleiner. 1982. "The Political Economy of Information in a Changing International Economic Order." In Meheroo Jussawalla and Donald M. Lamberton, eds., *Communication Economics and Development.* New York: Pergamon Press.

Pool, Ithiel de Sola. 1984. "Tracking the Flow of Information." *Science* 221: 609–13.

Porat, Marc Uri. 1978. "Global Implications of an Information Society." *Journal of Communication* 28(1).

————. 1982. "Information, Communication and Division of Labor." In Meheroo Jussawalla and Donald M. Lamberton, eds., *Communication Economics and Development.* New York: Pergamon Press.

Sinha, Nikhil. 1991. "Choices and Consequences: A Cross-National Evaluation of Telecommunications Policies in Developing Countries." Ph.D. dissertation. University of Pennsylvania, Annenberg School of Communications, Philadelphia.

Sy, Jacques Habib. 1996. *Telecommunications Dependency: The African Saga (1850–1980).* Nairobi: Alternative Communications.

UNDP (United Nations Development Programme). 1997. *Human Development Report 1997.* New York: Oxford University Press.

Wellenius, Bjorn, and Peter Stern. 1994. *Implementing Reforms in the Telecommunications Sector: Lessons from Experience.* Washington, DC: World Bank.

THE PUBLIC FACE
OF CYBERSPACE

DEBORA L. SPAR

Imagine a network that spans the world. A network that delivers—invisibly and inexpensively—the myriad bits of information that will be the key to prosperity in the 21st century. Imagine a network that links patients with doctors, students with teachers and markets with customers wherever they might exist. This network, of course, is the Internet. And according to many of its staunchest proponents, it already exists. Consider the words of Bill Gates (1995, p. 5), who predicts that "there will be a day, not far distant, when you will be able to conduct business, study, explore the world and its culture, call up any great entertainment, make friends, attend neighborhood markets, and show pictures to distant relatives—without leaving your desk or armchair". Or the vision of Nicholas Negroponte (1995, p. 6): "Early in the next millennium.... Mass media will be redefined by systems for transmitting and receiving personalized information and entertainment. Schools will change to become more like museums and playgrounds for children to assemble ideas and socialize with other children all over the world. The digital planet will look and feel like the head of a pin".

In these views, as in many similar scenarios, the Internet acts as a virtual and virtuous public good. It incorporates the activities of all who wish to use it. It allows these users to interact without any rivalry in their usage. And it serves the greater good of the community in which it exists, easing information flows and creating layers of positive externalities. But does this world really exist? Can it deliver the lofty ideals that its adherents predict? In 1998 it is not quite clear. Yes, the potential of the Internet is obvious. But its capacity to function as a public good is not. Particularly in the developing world, the promise of a networked society may be more hopeful than real.

This chapter examines the Internet as a public good. In a preliminary way I sketch out why the Internet may—or may not—be conceived of as a public good and how its public nature is likely to affect both its development and the development paths of the countries in which it operates. Like most writing on this subject, this chapter is mainly a thought piece. With cyberspace developing at breakneck speed, it is impossible to predict trends with any certainty. Thus my objective is modest: simply to consider the rapidly evolving realm of cyberspace as a possible public good and to chart the implications. If cyberspace, or some elements of cyberspace, are indeed public goods, how are they to be regulated? What policy-making forum is most appropriate for this vast new territory? And how will rules of any sort be imposed on the unruly reaches of the Net?

THE ORIGINS OF THE INTERNET

The Internet got its start in the late 1960s as a communications infrastructure called the ARPANET, run by the US Department of Defense and its Advanced Research Projects Agency (ARPA).[1] Consisting of a series of links joining discrete computer networks, the ARPANET was an experiment in "interworking" designed to give university research scientists an opportunity to create a solid "network of networks" that would facilitate the exchange of scientific and military information and save the costs of replicating computer capabilities at multiple sites. Taking advantage of recent developments in computer technology while also trying to make the system impervious to nuclear attacks or natural disasters, the developers of the ARPANET structured a highly decentralized system. Information flowed from one computer network to another through a variety of media (telephone wires, fibre optic links, satellites) and physical sites.

Over time this decentralized network of networks became known as the Internet. Following the model of the national telephone system, and even employing many of its connections, the Internet's pathways remained out of sight and mind to its users. No one needed to know how messages moved from one place to another—only that they got there securely. Unlike the telephone system, the logical structure of the Internet allowed any one user to broadcast a message simultaneously to any site on the network. This possibility reflected the Internet's scientific purpose: to enable a small, elite group of researchers to share critical information among themselves.

For roughly 20 years this community flourished quietly online. Expanding rapidly from just four host computers in 1969 to 2,000 in 1985, the Internet became a common mode of communication for university researchers, government scientists and outside computer engineers. Responsibility for its upkeep shifted in the 1980s to the National Science

Foundation (NSF), which underscored the Net's scientific focus and explicitly prohibited users from engaging in commercial or other nonresearch purposes.[2]

Its privatization

By the late 1980s, however, this scientific focus had effectively disappeared. Aware of the growing commercial interest in the Net, as well as its own budgetary limits, the NSF slowly began to privatize the Internet (see Lodge and Rayport 1995). At first private firms just provided infrastructure services to the Net's established user base. Then in 1989 commercial service providers emerged, offering Internet access to a wide new range of private and commercial customers. In 1990 the Internet was officially opened to commercial ventures.

Privatization transformed the Net. In the early 1980s the Internet community had consisted of about 25 linked scientific and academic networks. By 1995, when the last piece of the NSF backbone was retired in favour of higher-speed, privately owned backbones, the Net had grown to include more than 44,000 networks, including 26,000 registered commercial entities (*Time* 1995; Sullivan-Trainor 1995). Extending far beyond academia and the US Department of Defense, 40–50 million computers were connected to Internet hosts in 1995, and the number was growing at unprecedented rates.

Its globalization

At about this time the Internet sprang from its US origins to become a truly global phenomenon. To some extent, of course, the Net had always been global. Because it used the existing telecommunications network, the medium was inherently international in scope, following the pathways established decades earlier to link national communications infrastructures. Thus foreign scientists had long been connected to the US system, as eventually were academics and other researchers.

But the commercialization of the Net opened its pathways to substantially larger groups of users. The commercial outburst that began in the United States quickly spread to Europe, Asia and large swaths of the developing world. By 1992, 92 countries were fully connected to the Internet, and 45 more could exchange electronic mail (email). By 1993 non-US connections accounted for 40% of Internet connections and were growing at a much more rapid pace than US connections (Lodge and Rayport 1995). By 1996, 167 countries had their own Internet hosts, and even the poorer developing countries were experiencing significant growth in the number of new telephone lines and the number of Internet connections (ITU 1998). In China alone 620,000 users had connected to the Internet by late 1997, and an estimated 10,000 additional links were being added every month (Zhang 1997).

Its promises

By 1998 the Internet could truly be seen as a global medium—even, perhaps, as *the* global medium. Its connections crossed borders imperceptibly, linking markets and citizens in new and intriguing ways and destroying conventional notions of national borders. Continuing a trend made possible by phones, faxes and satellite dishes, the Internet promised to make information readily available to all corners of the globe. Cheaply, and without technological hassle, it promised to deliver to users whatever information they could find—and to link the purveyors of information to the potential consumers of that information with a speed and an ease that had never before been realized. In the process the Net also threatened to destroy many conventional aspects of business, society and the state.

Both the promise and the threat rested on the basic power of information. By moving information so widely and freely, the Internet could remove the information barriers that authoritarian states had long wielded over their citizens.[3] It could also put producers directly in touch with would-be customers, dismantling the cumbersome chains of wholesalers, distributors and retailers that have customarily separated producers from their sales and added significantly to final product costs (see *Chain Store Age* 1997, pp. 42–44 and *The Times of London* 1998, p. 10). In both the political and commercial spheres, therefore, the radical promise of the Internet was to dismantle existing chains of authority, giving citizens and consumers greater autonomy over their decisions and—more poetically—their fate.

Without the benefit of hindsight, it is difficult to evaluate the credibility of these promises, because their delivery rests on the passage of time and the interplay of countless unpredictable factors. Still, thinking about these predictions in the context of public goods is an interesting (if perhaps not entirely obvious) point of departure.

Public goods, after all, are essentially a way of conceiving economic activity that falls somewhere between the state and the market. Discussion of public goods implies a concern for the societal impact of commercial activity or for the provision of social goods outside normal commercial channels. In this volume public goods also offer a theoretical approach to questions of economic development. All these attributes and all these issues exist in cyberspace. Indeed, many of the more radical promises put forth by the Internet's most devoted proponents relate to the shifting boundary between private and public sectors, and to the provision of social goods by commercial forces. Viewing the Internet as a possible public good thus provides an intriguing lens into this evolving medium—and a means to examine how the development of a global Net is likely to affect the societies it connects.

THE CASE FOR THE INTERNET AS A PUBLIC GOOD

As the chapters in this volume make clear, defining a public good is no easy task. Nor is identifying one: areas treated as public goods in some contexts may elsewhere be treated as private; public goods may be converted back into privately delivered services; and even the clearest examples of public goods can also be conceived of as bundles containing both public and private attributes. Yet even within this ambiguity, the Internet undeniably has the makings of a public good.

Nonrivalry and nonexcludability

Consider the two most commonly cited attributes of public goods: they are nonexcludable and their consumption is nonrivalrous (see Baumol and Blinder 1982, p. 540 and Stiglitz 1993, pp. 180–82, and 1988, pp. 74–75). The Internet has both attributes. Theoretically, any number of users can simultaneously interact in cyberspace. Indeed, that is the beauty of both the underlying architecture of the system and the kind of communities that have emerged on it. Because the Internet spans so many modes of transmission and because it breaks any individual message into bits of information (known as "packets"), it is almost infinitely expandable. By ratcheting up the necessary physical infrastructure—adding servers, increasing telephone lines, building additional satellite capacity—new users can simply piggyback onto the existing system.

The parallel here to road-based highway systems is apt. Once the main structure has been constructed—the US interstate system or Germany's autobahn for the original highway; the NSF-supported backbone for this new information highway—new systems can be attached without tremendous difficulty. Local communities can build roads connecting to the interstate system; new users can access the Net through modems and phone lines. Unlike older highway systems, though, the Net is global. Users in, say, Tanzania, can connect directly to Yahoo! or the Microsoft Network. Moreover, their links to these US-based services do not come at the expense of existing connections within the United States. Instead the Tanzanian users are simply added to the system, expanding the network rather than constraining it.

It is this attribute of cyberspace that puts it, theoretically at least, into the category of public goods. So long as a user in Tanzania can gain access to a phone line, a computer and a modem, he or she cannot easily be denied access to the Internet's underlying architecture. The highway is there and it is open, and anyone with a direct connection can venture onto it. More formally, the use of the Internet's myriad pathways is thus nonexcludable. Likewise, its usage is also nonrivalrous, because the entry of the Tanzanians does not force other users offline.

To the contrary, one of the Internet's most touted features is its ability to bring together expanding communities of like-minded users. So the addition of Tanzanian users to, say, a chat room on development in Africa would presumably increase the value of the chat room to existing users. Seen in this way, online usage is clearly nonrivalrous, and thus classifies again as a public good. Architecturally, then, cyberspace would appear to fit the standard economic definition of a public good: its usage is nonexcludable and nonrivalrous.

Positive externalities

Cyberspace also bears another attribute of public goods, though this one is not necessarily contained within standard definitions. Specifically, cyberspace has the capacity—perhaps even the natural inclination—to foster all sorts of positive externalities. These externalities are the focus of much of the enthusiasm about the Internet's potential, and the source of its greatest societal links.

Consider the possibilities. For example, the Internet could be used—and already has been in a few small instances—as a vehicle for top-notch, long-distance medical treatment. Expert doctors could be brought to consult in remote areas, reviewing patients they will never meet, conducting training for local health providers, even assisting through video links with operations or emergency procedures (see Lawrence 1996, p. 3; Rhodes 1994; and Brandon 1995, p. 17). The result would be better health care, at lower cost, for the local community and all who come into contact with it.

Tele-education could likewise link students and teachers over what would otherwise be improbable distances. In areas where teachers are scarce, online instructors could reach huge numbers of needy students, once again bringing high-quality services at very low cost. Online learning materials could replace expensive books; and computers could (in some circumstances) replace classrooms. The economies of scale in this model would be dramatic, enabling poor or remote communities to access a level of education that they otherwise would be unlikely to obtain. And the results would presumably be dramatic as well, enhancing all the positive benefits that typically adhere to education, training and literacy.

Even at a purely commercial level, the Internet promises to create positive externalities, particularly in the realm of economic development. With access to the Net, small producers in remote locations can gain exposure in, and thus access to, wider markets. Rather than having to link themselves to intermediaries and retail distributors, producers can advertise their wares directly on the Net, attracting the kind of consumers most likely to purchase a particular product. Music companies, for example, can advertise particular recording artists to users who have indicated a fondness for particular types of music; similarly, hotels can tout their services to users who have used the Net to book airline tickets to a particular destination. If such online sales spur significant commerce—and online sales are predicted to grow to anywhere between $6 billion and $130 billion by 2000 (Data Analysis Group 1998, pp. 92–127; Forrester Research 1997; Willis 1998, p. 55)—they should spur economic growth and its accompanying benefits wherever they occur.

Formally, of course, none of these externalities conforms to the standard, or at least the narrowest, definition of a public good. Yet positive externalities are generally considered to be at least linked to public goods, even if they are not a defining characteristic. Stiglitz (1993, p. 180), for example, describes public goods as constituting an "extreme case of positive externalities" (see also Varian 1984, pp. 253–56). And many public policies treat positive externalities as if they were public goods, pulling their provision squarely into the public sector. Health care, for example, is often seen as the province of the state because higher levels of health are good for all citizens of the state (see Chen, Evans and Cash in this volume). Education is treated similarly in most countries, as are security and fire protection. None of these areas fits the strict definition of a public good: health care, for example, is excludable, and under some circumstances education is rivalrous. Not all citizens will necessarily receive health care just because some do; and the admission of one student to a top-notch university will mean that admission is denied to another. Yet because of the positive externalities associated with these services, public policy often treats them as the province of the state, assuring (through state control) that the service is widely available and often free of charge.[4]

Thus, in this respect as well, the Internet has many of the trappings of a public good. We might therefore expect it to be treated over time as a public good, with the state playing an active role in its provision or regulation. Yet several other factors seem to mitigate against that possibility. The first is that state activities in this realm are bound to be limited by the very nature of the Internet; the second is that in many respects cyberspace negates its identity as a public good. I will first address the second of these factors, reserving the first for the concluding section.

THE CASE AGAINST THE INTERNET AS A PUBLIC GOOD

As noted, cyberspace appears to have many of the attributes customarily associated with public goods. Yet, as with many apparently public goods, not all elements of cyberspace fit easily into the public goods camp. Most important, while the architecture of the Internet is inherently nonexcludable and nonrivalrous, the services performed on this architecture are not.

Excludability

Consider America Online (AOL), the world's largest commercial online service provider. AOL is a subscribers-only community. Members must pay a fee to join, and AOL reserves the right to exclude or expel users. Other communities—such as specialized chat rooms or networks of a particular company's suppliers and customers—are even more closed, with membership tightly restricted and usage controlled through passwords or encrypted key access. Increasingly, even basic news sites such as the Wall Street Journal Interactive Edition (WSJ.com) are providing information only to those who join their service, acquire a password and pay for the stories they read.

Commercially, such arrangements make great sense. They enable the provider to profit from the sale of its product and to gear its advertisements to a carefully selected mix of users. The impact on the consumer, though, is to convert what is often thought of as public good—information—into a more restricted commodity. Of course, this conversion has existed for a long time. Most newspapers, after all, sell their paper copies rather than distributing them for free. But the transition to a pay-per-view world in cyberspace means that nonexcludability no longer holds. Tanzanians cannot be excluded from the *Wall Street Journal's* site, but they may be excluded from reading its contents if they are unwilling or unable to pay. In this respect, the information highway becomes a toll road. It is still available and it is still linked into a broader community, but its use comes only for a fee.

Online exclusion can take other forms as well. Most chat rooms will expel members who violate the established norms of their community. Groups will prohibit foul speech, pornography or comments below a certain level of sophistication. Once again, such rules make great sense for those involved in their creation. They uphold the norms of a given community and preserve the values it has chosen. But they also make the Internet less of an all-encompassing, all-welcoming place. By creating means of exclusion, they too convert the Internet into a series of semiprivate enclaves rather than a publicly available good.

Congestion

As the Internet expands, assumptions about its nonrivalrous use have also come under attack. In theory the Net is almost infinitely expandable. But in practice congestion is an undeniable problem. The rapid multiplication of users, combined with their ever-expanding demand for data, has caused a noticeable strain along the Net's multiple pathways. Although the physical capacity of the Net continues to increase (OECD 1997, pp. 146–47), many users report growing delays in Internet transmission and a declining quality of service (Lewis 1996; *InfoWorld* 1996; Metcalfe 1995). Part of this strain is simply due to an expansion of the Net's user base; part is due to the increased transmission of images, audio and video files, all of which consume far more space than the basic email messages that dominated earlier use of the Net.[5]

Congestion will only worsen as these trends continue. Thus Internet engineers and service providers are working to find means for tagging and distinguishing particular packets: for transmitting some bits of information through the Net faster than others. The analogy here is to a restricted bus lane on a national highway or to an ambulance whose journey takes precedence over other drivers. Over time online congestion is likely to force a similarly tiered use of the Internet, with some users receiving preferential treatment and paying for the privilege to do so.

So what does this mean for the public good attributes of the Internet? As with many public goods, the picture is mixed. While some aspects of the Net, particularly its underlying architecture, function rather naturally as public goods, many of the developing uses of the Net break this public space into private spheres where usage can be excluded and consumption rivalrous. And the further commercialization proceeds on the Net, the wider those private spaces are likely to become—especially as more information providers begin to charge for services or monitor their user base. Meanwhile, of course, the positive externalities of cyberspace remain largely untouched: there is still tremendous potential for the Net to be used as a tool of learning, of medicine, of development. Reconciling these possibilities with the private aspects of cyberspace will be a complicated but critical task.

POLICY IMPLICATIONS

Any policy directed towards cyberspace must begin with the realization that the Internet is largely ungovernable. It transcends national borders. It thrives on a deep-seated culture of anarchy. And its development is outpacing nearly all government efforts to track it, much less regulate it. Despite its beginnings as a state-run enterprise, the commercial Internet has embraced a fiercely individualistic culture, a culture that often verges on the libertarian and displays a pronounced disdain for government involvement of any sort (Frezza 1997, p. 103).

The restricted scope for policy

To date, governments have been largely, perhaps surprisingly, eager to comply with demands for nonintervention. In 1997 the Clinton administration issued an influential Framework for Global Electronic Commerce that set out the US government's policy towards the commercial Internet and electronic commerce. Notable in this document was its nearly unrelenting focus on market forces. It argues, for example, that "governments must adopt a non-regulatory, market-oriented approach to electronic commerce" and that "governments should refrain from imposing new and unnecessary regulation, bureaucratic procedures, or taxes and tariffs on commercial activities that take place via the Internet" (White House 1997). Within a week similar sentiments were vigorously echoed by policy-makers in the European Union: at a ministerial conference members of the Union jointly declared that "the expansion of Global Information Networks must essentially be market-led and left to private initiative ... private enterprise should drive the expansion of electronic commerce in Europe"(Ministerial Declaration at Global Information Networks 1997). Cyberspace, both statements seemed to suggest, would indeed be as free as many "Netizens" demanded.

In practice, moreover, even tentative movements towards regulation have been met with vehement opposition from Internet groups, forcing governments to back away from policy initiatives. In 1996, for instance, the US Congress passed the Communications Decency Act, a law intended to prohibit the transmission of indecent material across the Net. The act was immediately attacked by a broad array of Internet users and interest groups, who argued that the law constituted a bar to the development of the Net and an unconstitutional attack on free speech (Lapin 1996, p. 84). In June 1997 the Supreme Court essentially agreed and struck down the law.

A similar fight—and fate—surrounded the Clinton administration's controversial "Clipper chip" proposal. First suggested in 1993, Clipper was the brainchild of the US National Security Agency, which saw it as a relatively unobtrusive way for the government to retain access to those Internet communications that might constitute a national security threat to the United States. The notion behind Clipper was that every computer used in the United States would contain a Clipper chip—essentially an encryption algorithm. Because the government would keep a decryption key under its control, it could eavesdrop as appropriate on all electronic transmissions. Although the White House pledged that the Clipper key would be used only with a warrant, making it just a high-tech version of standard wire tapping, the Internet community resoundingly denounced the proposal, labelling it an unconstitutional invasion of privacy and ban on free speech (Levy 1994, pp. 42–51, 60–70). Under a barrage of criticism, the White House eventually retreated.

In Europe too, industry and user groups have generally kept regulatory impulses to a minimum. The European Commission has taken a remarkably hands-off approach to electronic commerce and has imposed no restraints on the content of online communications—except Germany, which has developed prohibitions against the posting or transmission of offensive material.[6] Where European regulation has been more forthcoming, though, is for privacy. In October 1998, a controversial data protection directive went into effect in the European Union. Designed to protect individuals from undue scrutiny of their personal information, the directive laid forth stringent rules on the collection and use of personal data on the Internet and other computer systems. Most dramatically, the directive also threatened to block the transfer of personal information to countries that lack what the Europeans consider adequate protection of privacy.

As expected, US firms and the US government responded vigorously to this objective and quickly launched discussions to prevent what was quickly dubbed a "cyber trade war" (Kehoe 1998, p. 15). As of mid-1998 the two sides were still working to resolve their differences, though the Americans remained largely wed to industry-led controls on privacy rather than government regulation (Dunne 1998, p. 4, Jonquieres 1998, p. 6; Singleton 1998, p. A18).

Even in Asia, where governments have been considerably more eager to constrain and channel Internet use, the ideology and architecture of the Net have made regulation difficult to enforce. In 1996, for example, Singaporean authorities required local Internet providers to filter out offensive material before it reached users; they also demanded that any organization posting political or religious information on the Web first register with the country's broadcasting authority (*The Economist* 1996, pp. 43–43; McDermott 1996, p. B6; Rodan 1998, pp. 63–89). China imposed similar regulations in 1996, requiring computer networks to register with the central government and forbidding online pornography or political criticism (Brauchli 1996, p. A10; Fluendy 1996, pp. 71–72). Almost at once, however, these regulations encountered opposition and obstacles. In China authorities quietly lifted most (though not all) curbs on Internet use just months after proclaiming them; and in Singapore a 1998 Electronic Transactions Bill explicitly relieved Internet access providers of any liability for the content they transmit (*Asiaweek* 1998; Fletcher and Hsieh 1997, p. 25). Thus both governments quietly backed down, implicitly acknowledging the difficulties of controlling cyberspace while still allowing it to flourish.

Such official balancing acts reflect a broader tension of any Internet policy. Though no one quite knows how commerce will ultimately develop online, it seems clear that a great deal of commerce will eventually migrate to cyberspace, letting loose a flurry of economic activity and presumably growth. Governments, eager to spur and capture this growth, are understandably reluctant to adopt measures that would hamper the development of online commerce or dampen the enthusiasm of its pioneers. Thus the US government has been unwilling to tax commercial activity in cyberspace; Europeans have moved slowly with efforts to protect privacy; and Chinese and Singaporeans have let information flow more freely than they might have desired. All have adopted a basic policy of not constraining private activity in this realm. This appears to be an inevitable policy choice—and a wise one during this phase of the Internet's evolution.

Approaches to intervention

Despite such constraints, however, the public nature of cyberspace implies that at some point governments will have to play some role. Typically, government policy for public goods is either to provide them or to regulate their private sale. For the Internet the first option is clearly unworkable, because private firms have already moved successfully and definitively into cyberspace. And the second option is unwieldy, for the reasons described above: cyberspace vehemently does not want to be regulated, and governments have limited means for enforcing rules or regulation on this unruly space. If firms do not like the regulation emanating from their home state, they can easily move elsewhere or simply route their activities through a more accommodating state.

Facing these constraints, governments are likely to move towards a third, hybrid, model of intervention. As they do in other realms, they will be pushed to provide services that the market will not provide by itself—those with a high public benefit but unsustainable private costs. Telemedicine and tele-education both fit into this camp, especially in poor areas or developing countries, where the benefits are perhaps the greatest but the profit potential limited.

In these areas governments that want to reap the tremendous potential of cyberspace will have to expend considerable resources to do so—or else find some means of harnessing the private sector to service the public good. Where the provision of these services demands the installation of new infrastructure (telephone lines, computers, servers) governments will likely have to assume the role of provider as well. For developing countries with little existing infrastructure, this will almost certainly be expensive and time-consuming. In Tanzania, for example, there were only 3 Internet hosts and 500 Internet users in 1996, and only 0.9 residential phone lines per 100 households (ITU 1998, pp. A-20, A-76). Similar statistics are common throughout the developing world. Thus governments will almost certainly have to play some role in creating the basic infrastructure that their countries will need to venture along the information highway. Yet even here the solutions are likely to involve private sector involvement, either on a contractual basis or perhaps in regulated partnerships akin to those that helped develop other public utility sectors.

Another inevitable role for government will be to prevent the negative externalities—the public bads—that are also inherent in cyberspace. As the Internet develops, the negative aspects that have already been unearthed will almost certainly become more evident, and the public outcry against them larger. Citizens will worry about the easy availability of information they deem unsavoury or illegitimate for public transfer. They will worry about the sanctity of their personal information, about easy access to information on criminal activity or about their children's access to pornography or particular political or religious views. All these worries will undoubtedly manifest themselves in public debate, and eventually in public policy. Governments will need to find some means of squashing the transfer of bad information without restricting the flow of good information. This will likely involve new kinds of legislation and innovative means of interpretation and enforcement. It will also undoubtedly require international cooperation, because the mobility of Internet activity will once again make it difficult for any single state to prevent disruptive activity.

The need for multilateral policy and the dilemma of developing countries

The strategic tension between good and bad flows of information highlights two of the most important aspects of any Internet policy. First, at some basic level the public good that adheres to the Internet is information: the facts, knowledge and know-how that are relayed so rapidly and inexpensively along the Internet's intricate paths. Ultimately, the value of the Net does not lie in its hardware but in its software, in the information that it conveys. For the most part this information is the source of positive externalities: it imparts the learning and the skills that create societal value. In its consumption this information also bears the attributes of a true public good: knowledge is largely nonrivalrous and largely (though not entirely) nonexcludable. Yet these same attributes adhere to bad information—to the personal data or offensive material that many Internet users do not want to see carried through cyberspace. This tension makes any government policy inherently fragile, because it must walk a narrow and ill-defined line between the positive and negative attributes of information transfer.

A second aspect of Internet policy relates to the fundamentally international nature of cyberspace. As noted, the Internet ignores territorial borders and disdains unilateral policies. To be truly effective, any Internet policy will need to be multilateral, spanning all countries in which the relevant activity occurs. This need has several implications. First, it means that any nation that wishes to push its Internet policy in a particular direction will need to move quickly to the international sphere, trying to influence a still-unformed agenda. Second, it means that global coalitions will need to be created and global consensus arrived at—even though the Internet is still in its infancy and countries vary widely in their use and familiarity with it. Third, it means that developing countries risk exclusion from a policy that will likely be global in scope.

This last implication is particularly unfortunate because it is in the developing world where the positive externalities from the Internet promise to be most powerful. It is in the developing world where telemedicine and tele-education have the potential to create the largest benefits and where local producers stand to gain the most from the expanded access to markets that the Internet can provide. Thus it is developing countries that in many ways have the greatest stake in the orderly and open development of the Internet. They cannot afford to have information in cyberspace restricted to private enclaves or to have this flow of information slowed by a priority system that works against poor users. Developing countries also desperately need to create the physical infrastructure that will bring the Internet to the doorsteps and desktops of their citizens. Yet having unilateral policies towards these ends undoubtedly will not suffice, and waiting for an international consensus means leaving the initiative in the hands of rich states with different policy agendas.

It is not clear how developing countries can avoid these outcomes or achieve the policy objectives just outlined. Events in cyberspace remain chaotic, and governments will need to respond to policy demands as they arise. In general, though, it seems that developing countries could benefit by keeping a few general principles or guidelines in mind:

- The Internet will be a dominant feature of the 21st century and a powerful tool for commerce and communication. All nations, regardless of their stage of development, need to watch the evolution of the Internet with care and concern.

- As much as possible, developing countries need to position themselves strategically in any intergovernmental negotiations or discussions regarding the Net. They need to get a seat at the table before the table is set by other countries with different policy agendas.

- Developing countries should also concentrate on building the "nuts and bolts" of the communications infrastructure that will convey their citizens onto the Net. Basic telecommunications, at a reasonable cost, are a necessary precursor to Internet activity. Thus policies to ensure the construction of this infrastructure are essential, whether they be undergirded by public procurement, private liberalization or aid policies underwritten by wealthier states.

- Finally, as the information age proceeds, developing countries need to recognize the importance of building negotiating links not just with other countries but also with the private groups that are increasingly shaping the rules of cyberspace. Corporations are obviously key in this regard, but so are the private interest groups and nongovernmental organizations that have been so important in prodding the direction of policy in the developed world.

In all of the principles it seems that conceiving of the Internet as a public good helps to at least point policy-makers in an appropriate direction. The Net is undeniably a boon for private business and a revolution in communications. But it is also a powerful medium capable of delivering—or restricting—significant societal benefits. Thinking of it in this way, and probing policy options along these lines, are the first steps towards harnessing this tremendous power.

NOTES

1. This section comes from Spar (1996).

2. The NSF's acceptable-use policy statement read in part: "NSFNET Backbone Services are provided to support open research and education in and among US research and instructional institutions, plus research arms of for-profit firms when engaged in open scholarly communication and research. *Use for other purposes is not acceptable*" (cited in Sullivan-Trainor 1995, p. 175; emphasis added).

3. In Indonesia, for instance, the Net was a major source of communication for the student groups that ultimately pushed Suharto from power in 1998. See Thoenes (1998 p. 1) and Marcus (1998 p. 26A). For more on these general trends, see Spar (1998 pp. 7–13).

4. State services are not really free of charge, of course, because tax revenues are gathered to pay for state expenditures. But they are free of charge at the point of delivery, and provision of the service is not dependent on the level of taxation paid. Rich and poor people, for example, receive similar levels of protection from the local fire station.

5. For a description of these trends, see OECD (1997 pp. 144-45). Supporting statistics are available at http://nic.merit.edu/nsfnet/statistics/.

6. A 1997 law holds content providers liable for the posting of offensive material, including pornography, hate speech and information deemed excessively violent. The law also allows for access providers to be held responsible for the transmission of this material if they are "aware of the content" and fail to use "reasonable and technically possible" means to block it (Bonfante 1997, p. 30).

REFERENCES

Asiaweek. 1998. "Taming the Wild Internet." 21 July.

Baumol, William J., and Alan S. Blinder. 1982. *Economics.* 2nd ed. New York: Harcourt Brace Jovanovich.

Bonfante, Jordan. 1997. "The Internet Trials." *Time,* 14 July.

Brandon, Karen. 1995. "In Experiment, Urban Doctors Make Rural Calls by TV." *Chicago Tribune,* 26 February.

Brauchli, Marcus W. 1996. "China Requires Computer Networks to Get Registered." *Wall Street Journal,* 5 February.

Chain Store Age. 1997. "Nonstore Retailing Leads the Way on the Internet." August.

Data Analysis Group. 1998. *Computer Industry Forecasts.* Third quarter. Cloverdale, CA.

Dunne, Nancy. 1998. "US-EU in 'Productive' Talks on Internet Privacy." *Financial Times,* 3 July.

The Economist. 1996. "Not too Modern Please." 16 March.

Fletcher, Matthew, and David Hsieh. 1997. "Easing the Net Curbs." *Asiaweek,* 31 January.

Fluendy, Simon. 1996. "Pandora's Box." *Far East Economic Review,* 26 September.

Forrester Research. 1997. "Retails Revs Up." *Forrester Report* 4(6). Cambridge, MA.

Frezza, Bill. 1997. "Can the Government's Black Helicopters Fly in Cyberspace?" *Communications Week,* 5 May.

Gates, Bill. 1995. *The Road Ahead.* New York: Viking.

InfoWorld. 1996. "The World Wide Wait." August 26.

ITU (International Telecommunication Union). 1998. *World Telecommunication Report 1998: Universal Access.* Geneva.

Jonquieres, Guy de. 1998. "Bid to Avert Threat of 'Cyber Trade War.'" *Financial Times,* 10 September.

Kehoe, Louise. 1998. "US, EU at Odds over Cyber Privacy." *The Financial Post,* 29 August.

Lapin, Todd. 1996. "Internet v. United States Department of Justice, Janet Reno, et al." *Wired* (May).

Lawrence, Mark. 1996. "Different Facets of Telemedicine." *The Age,* 7 May.

Levy, Steven. 1994. "Battle of the Clipper Chip." *New York Times Magazine,* 12 June.

Lewis, Peter H. 1996. "Traffic Jam on the Internet." *International Herald Tribune*, 25 June.

Lodge, George C., and Jeffrey Rayport. 1995. *The National Information Infrastructure: Information Technology and Industry Evolution.* Harvard Business School Case 9–396–111. Cambridge, MA: Harvard Business School.

Marcus, David L. 1998. "Internet Notches First Successful Coup." *Ft. Lauderdale Sun-Sentinel,* 24 May.

McDermott, Darren. 1996. "Singapore Unveils Sweeping Measures to Control Words, Images on Internet." *Wall Street Journal,* 6 March.

Metcalfe, Bob. 1995. "Predicting the Internet's Collapse." *InfoWorld,* 4 December.

Ministerial Declaration at Global Information Networks. 1997. Ministerial Conference, Bonn, 6–8 July. Available at www2.echo.lu/bonn/final.html.

Negroponte, Nicholas. 1995. *Being Digital.* New York: Vintage Books.

OECD (Organisation for Economic Co-operation and Development). 1997. *Information Technology Outlook 1997.* Paris.

Rhodes, Tom. 1994. "From a Theatre of War to the Operating Room." *The Times of London,* 16 August.

Rodan, Garry. 1998. "The Internet and Political Control in Singapore." *Political Science Quarterly* 113(1): 63–89.

Singleton, Solveig. 1998. "The Future of the Net: Don't Sacrifice Freedom for 'Privacy.'" *Wall Street Journal,* 24 June.

Spar, Debora L. 1996. *Cyberrules: Problems and Prospects for On-Line Commerce. Program on Information Resources Policy.* Cambridge, MA: Harvard University, Center for Information Policy Research.

———. 1998. "The Spotlight and the Bottom Line." *Foreign Affairs* 77(2): 2–7.

Stiglitz, Joseph E. 1988. *Economics of the Public Sector.* 2nd ed. New York: W. W. Norton.

———. 1993. *Economics.* New York: W.W. Norton.

Sullivan-Trainor, Michael. 1995. *Detour: The Truth about the Information Superhighway.* Foster City, CA: San Mateo Books.

Thoenes, Sander. 1998. "High-Tech Battle Lines in Indonesia." *Christian Science Monitor,* 5 May.

Time. 1995. "Welcome to Cyberspace." Special issue.

The Times of London. 1998. "Quote: Nicholas Negroponte." Special section: "Controlling the Future." 28 April.

Varian, Hal R. 1984. *Microeconomic Analysis.* 2nd ed. New York: W.W. Norton.

White House. 1997. "A Framework for Global Electronic Commerce." Available at www.ecommerce.gov/framewrk.htm#2.

Willis, Clint. 1998. "Future Shop: Does Amazon.com Really Matter?" *Forbes*, 6 April.

Zhang, Mo. 1997. "China Issues New Rules Strengthening Regulatory Structure over Internet." *East Asian Executive Reports*, 15 November.

PEACE AND
SECURITY

At the national level, security is a traditional public good, even in the work of Adam Smith. This is also true at the global level, argue David A. Hamburg, Jane E. Holl and Ruben P. Mendez. Mendez maintains that, unlike defence, peace fulfils substantive, and not just formal, public good criteria. Indeed, defence may have negative as well as positive externalities, nationally and globally. Taking the substantive argument a step further, Hamburg and Holl talk about "just peace" as the true public good. Granted, certain conflicts may have only local effects in the short term. But preventing deadly conflict has truly universal externalities because it acts on any potential source of violence, and therefore potentially protects anyone from violence and death.

What kinds of mechanisms are needed to maintain peace? According to Kenneth Waltz in *Man, the State and War* (1959), the roots of conflict are found at three levels: the psychological level, the level of a society or political system and the level of the international system. Mendez focuses on the third, while Hamburg and Holl focus on the first two. Hamburg and Holl depict peace as the result of comprehensive and ongoing efforts to build social systems where differences can be settled peacefully. Human rights, the rule of law, basic needs, justice and environmental sustainability are all part of the equation, and the actors may involve public and private institutions or individuals. Hamburg and Holl present a bottom-up, multiactor and multidisciplinary approach to world peace.

Mendez focuses at greater length on the more strictly political and institutional aspects of peace, and the structures required at the level of the international system. Reviewing the historical record as well as the situation since the end of the Cold War, Mendez contrasts three models of international order: collective security, balance of power and hegemony. He argues that only collective security fully takes into account the public good nature of international peace, and that such a system is the most effective in the long run. International organizations such as the United Nations and regional bodies have key roles to play in such a system.

REFERENCE

Waltz, Kenneth. 1959. *The Man, the State and War: A Theoretical Analysis.* New York: Columbia University Press.

PREVENTING DEADLY CONFLICT

From Global Housekeeping to Neighbourhood Watch

DAVID A. HAMBURG AND JANE E. HOLL

Most people do not think of conflict prevention as a collective, or public, good. Yet efforts to prevent, contain or stop a war, if successful, surely result in conditions that convey broad benefits—not only for the parties to the conflict but also for wider circles of people and states. Even more important, putting in place conditions that prevent the outbreak of conflicts has broader benefits than containing a specific war. This chapter considers how preventing deadly conflict is—like clear air or clean water—a global public good that the international community can secure and maintain.

The indivisible and nonexcludable characteristics of public goods mean that any individual can enjoy a commodity (or condition) without diminishing others' ability to enjoy it to the same extent and that no one can be excluded from that enjoyment. These characteristics raise some questions. Who should provide and maintain public goods? Are they provided as a grant of nature or created by some agent? Does responsibility for maintaining them fall to that agent or another? Or is this handled through some regime to regulate use, so that the good is neither depleted nor corrupted through overuse? We might also ask ourselves whether it is useful to apply these concepts to preventing deadly conflict.

Few systemic restraints exist to prevent grievances from turning into disputes that develop into full-fledged violence. Moreover, the availability of cheap, highly destructive weapons means that more disputes can now lead quickly to widespread destruction. This reality leads us to conclude that responsible leaders and societies must (and can) strengthen all levels of social interaction to resolve disputes before they become violent and threaten wider consequences. Conflicts do not exist in isolation; they have what economists would call externalities, or costs to the broader community, which must find ways to bear and share those costs.

We argue here for an approach to preventing deadly conflict that takes into account three interdependent conditions: security, well-being and justice, each of which might be thought of as a public good. But our emphasis is on their combination and interaction in ways that not only make people better off but also inhibit the need to resort to violence. The result of this represents an international public good. And it is not difficult to imagine the beneficial and widespread effects of mutually reinforcing institutions, regimes and habits of interaction among states that would be set up to achieve this outcome.

If certain principles are observed—among them, that the processes established to ensure basic security, well-being and justice are based on the rule of law—preventing deadly conflict creates conditions that are indivisible and nonexcludable. Everyone would enjoy equal access to the environment of "just peace" that is created. And no one would be excluded from its general advantages. For example, preventing deadly conflict in Kosovo—by establishing sound mechanisms for representative governance, widespread access to economic opportunity and observance of the rule of law—offers advantages to all inhabitants of the region, not simply Kosovar Albanians. In this sense preventing deadly conflict can be thought of as a public good.

We do not equate preventing deadly conflict with simplistic notions of "peace". Humanity has witnessed many examples of societies at so-called peace under repressive regimes that deny all or parts of their people basic security, well-being or justice. The practices of such regimes do not prevent deadly conflict as much as they suppress it—at great cost and only for as long as coercive power is applied. Rather than ameliorate conditions that give rise to grievances, such repressive regimes foster them. So, like prevention, peace should not be thought of as a public good unless important conditions that characterize a just peace are also present.

One important result of thinking of the prevention of deadly conflict as a public good is precisely to establish a culture of prevention—much like the norms of public health. A widespread orientation of people and leaders towards possibilities for preventive action and responsibilities for taking such action can help create a climate of expectations that mass violence does not have to emerge, even in serious disputes. Towards this end, we can begin to make progress by looking to our governments, our leaders, our international institutions and our organizations of civil society to build on the foundation for preventive action that is already in place.

PREVENTION OF DEADLY CONFLICT AS A PUBLIC GOOD

Carnegie Commission on Preventing Deadly Conflict (1997) presents two broad strategies for prevention. The first is operational prevention, or measures to respond to an immediate crisis. The second is structural prevention, or measures to keep crises from arising in the first place or to keep them from recurring.

Operational prevention relies on early engagement and combines political, economic and (if necessary) military measures to help stop the spiral of potential violence. Its successful application involves clear leadership. It involves a coherent political-military approach that will stop the violence and address humanitarian needs. It involves the timely deployment of adequate resources to meet acute needs. And it involves a means for integrating responsible local leadership in each phase of the process.

Structural prevention combines top-down and bottom-up approaches that not only make people better off but also inhibit the need to resort to violence. It emphasizes the need to promote effective, mutually reinforcing, international regimes—for rule-making, economic cooperation, arms control and disarmament, dispute resolution and cooperative problem solving. It also emphasizes the need to promote stable and viable countries—that is, thriving states with representative government, the rule of law, robust civil societies and open economies with social safety nets.

Governments

Major preventive action remains the responsibility of states, especially their leaders. States must decide whether they do nothing, act alone, act in cooperation with other governments, work through international organizations or work with the private sector. It should be an accepted principle that those with the greatest capacity to act have the greatest responsibility to do so.

To be sure, the leaders, governments and people closest to potentially violent situations bear primary responsibility for taking preventive action. They stand to lose the most if their efforts fail. The best approach to prevention is the bottom-up approach, one that emphasizes local solutions to local problems where possible and new divisions of labour—involving governments and the private sector—based on comparative advantage and augmented as necessary by help from outside.

Civil society

Many elements of civil society can work to reduce hatred and violence and to encourage attitudes of concern, social responsibility, and mutual aid within and between groups. In difficult economic and political transitions, the organizations of civil society can do much to alleviate the dangers of mass violence. Many private actors around the world, dedicated to helping prevent deadly conflict, have declared a public commitment to the well-being of humanity in their activities. They have raised considerable sums of money on the basis of this commitment, bringing them great opportunities but also great responsibilities.

As pillars of any thriving civil society, the best nongovernmental organizations (NGOs) provide an array of human services unmatched by government or the market. They are the self-designated advocates for action on virtually all matters of public concern. The rapid spread of information technology, market-driven economic interdependence and easier and less expensive ways of communicating within and among states have allowed many NGOs—through their world-wide operations—to become key global conduits for ideas, financial resources and technical assistance.

Three broad categories of NGOs offer especially important potential contributions to the prevention of deadly conflict: human rights and other advocacy groups, humanitarian and development organizations and the small but growing number of unofficial, so-called track-two groups, which help open the way to more formal peace processes through mediation, negotiation and confidence-building measures.

Human rights, track-two and grassroots development organizations provide early warnings of rising local tension and help open or protect the political space between groups and the government that can allow local leaders to settle differences peacefully. Humanitarian NGOs also have great flexibility and access in responding to the needs of victims (especially the internally displaced) during emergencies. Development and pro-democracy groups have become vital to peaceful transitions from authoritarian rule to more open societies and, for violent conflicts, in helping to make peace processes irreversible. The work of international NGOs and their connection to each other and to indigenous organizations throughout the world reinforce a sense of common interest and common purpose and demonstrate the political will to support collective measures for preventive action.

International regimes

A top-down approach to prevention begins with governments and their relations with each other in the international system. Various regimes help manage relations between states through treaties, historical convention and common practice. They undergird international behaviour in economic interaction, management of the global commons, arms control and protection of human rights. In this context the theory of democratic peace—that democracies tend not to fight each other—is important (see Brown, Lynn-Jones and Miller 1996; Bremer 1992, pp. 309–41, and 1993, pp. 231–49; Bueno de Mesquita and Lalman 1992; Doyle 1983, pp. 205–35; Ray 1995; Rummel 1983, pp. 27–72, 1985, pp. 419–55, and 1975-81; and Russet 1993). We would go further. The world's democracies have also taken the initiative on the basis of their shared values to collaborate in nearly all the global regulating regimes in the areas noted above.[1]

This collaboration created the UN Charter, which prohibits aggression between states and entered into force in 1945. With this prohibition, and many subsequent reaffirmations by regional organizations world-wide, the rudiments of a global system of preventing violent conflict are apparent. In addition, the end of the Cold War marked a turning point—a largely peaceful end to the nuclear rivalry that could have destroyed human society. Current agreement among the nuclear powers on many issues has improved prospects for a more unified international response to crises.

But a regime to prevent violent conflict does not exist. True, the incidence of violence between states has decreased markedly as we approach the end of the 20th century. Yet violence within states continues with alarming frequency.

Even so, the post–Cold War climate and the growing (though still inadequate) consensus about the importance of human rights and democratic governance provide the opportunity for a new international effort to curb violent conflict. Through their economic, political and social policies, responsible leaders world-wide must develop an awareness in governments of preventive opportunities. They must grasp what strategies work best under various conditions and work together to draw on all available resources—governmental and nongovernmental—to prevent deadly conflict.

The intuitive attraction of preventive efforts should dominate thinking and policy-making in international peace and security. After all, it makes more sense to take less costly, less intrusive measures early enough to avoid the need for more drastic and expensive interventions later. But perhaps wishful thinking dominates, or problems are too complex to suggest easy or obvious solutions. All too often, circumstances must become grave before effective action is taken. A study comparing the cost of preventive action with the cost of conflict found that in Rwanda prevention would have cost about $1.3 billion while humanitarian actions following the genocide cost $4.5 billion (Brown and Rosecrance 1999). Although studies of this type are controversial, the authors quantify the dramatic cost-effectiveness of preventive action.

CONFLICT PREVENTION: THREE INGREDIENTS FOR BUILDING PEACE

Since the Berlin Wall fell in 1989 more than 4 million people have been killed in violent conflicts. In January 1997 there were more than 35 million refugees and internally displaced persons around the world. Some violence has been chronic, as in Bosnia and Chechnya. Some has been a tremendous spasm of destruction, as with the massive genocide in Rwanda, an extraordinary and tragic example of the failure of the world community to take effective preventive action. With nearly 1 million people killed in three months, this is one of the most horrifying chapters in human history.

Whatever model of self-government societies ultimately choose, it must meet the three core needs of security, well-being and justice and give people a stake in nonviolent efforts to improve their lives. Meeting these needs enables people to live better lives and reduces the potential for deadly conflict.

Security
Many violent conflicts have been waged by people trying to establish and maintain a safe living space. Today the main sources of insecurity are the threat posed by nuclear and other weapons of mass destruction, the possibility of conventional confrontation between states and such internal violence as terrorism, insurgency, organized crime and repressive regimes.

The nuclear detonations by India and Pakistan in the first half of 1998 show that the retention of nuclear weapons by any state stimulates others to acquire them. Thus the only durably safe course is to work towards the elimination of such weapons. For this, stringent conditions have to be set with security for all, including rigorous safeguards against any nuclear weapons falling into the hands of dictatorial and fanatical leaders. Needed promptly are credible mechanisms and practices to:
- Account for nuclear weapons and materials.
- Monitor their whereabouts and operational condition.
- Ensure the safe management and reduction of nuclear arsenals.

Chemical and biological weapons also pose grave security threats. With the entry into force of the Chemical Weapons Convention in 1997, a significant international legal regime was established banning the production, possession and use of chemical weapons. The convention treads a fine line between abolishing deadly poisons as weapons without unnecessarily fettering legitimate commerce in chemicals, one of the world's largest industries. Importantly, the Chemical Weapons Convention established a rigorous verification process of routine and challenge (that is, surprise) inspections that reinforces the integrity of the convention as an important component in the nonproliferation regime. A rigorous inspection component is precisely what the 1972 Biological Weapons Convention lacks. State parties to the Biological Weapons Convention are currently negotiating a protocol designed to add a more vigorous verification component. Progress towards a more effective bulwark against biological weapons remains slow, however.

While these international legal norms are essential for maintaining an effective nonproliferation regime, arms control measures alone are not enough to guarantee the elimination of the threat posed by these types of weapons. The international community of nations must also actively reinforce measures to eliminate chemical and biological weapons. Moreover, international efforts must be complemented by national efforts in the form of defensive measures, export controls, consequence management preparations, conventional deterrent capabilities and aggressive national intelligence means to identify potential proliferant nations or subnational groups.

It is impossible to completely control biological weapons or to deny access to materials and information. But it may be possible to control the most dangerous pathogens through mechanisms to monitor their possession and the construction of facilities for their manufacture. A registry could be established in which governments and other users would record strains under their control and publish details of their experiments. This registry would create a legal and professional expectation that those working with these strains would be obligated to reveal themselves. In addition, the professional community of researchers and scientists must engage in expanded and extensive collaboration in this field and establish a close connection to the public health community.

For conventional weapons, governments must keep arms control near the top of their national and multilateral security agendas. The North Atlantic Treaty Organization and other regional arrangements that offer the opportunity for sustained dialogue among professional military establishments can promote transparency and civilian control of the military. Part of the challenge is to rein in the global arms trade, dominated by the five permanent members of the United Nations Security Council and Germany. Together these states account for 80–90% of the world-wide flow of conventional arms. There have been few efforts to control the flow of conventional weapons, and trade in small arms and ammunition—which account for most deaths in today's conflicts—remains largely unregulated. One effort in the right direction is the international movement for a world-wide ban on the production, stockpiling, distribution and use of land mines.

Human security may also depend on natural resources, which often lie at the heart of conflicts that hold the potential for mass violence. In some cases antagonists deliberately manipulate resource shortages for hostile purposes (using food or water as a weapon). Other conflicts arise over competing claims of sovereignty over resource endowments (such as rivers or oil and other fossil fuel deposits). And increasingly there is environmental degradation and resource depletion in areas characterized by political instability, rapid population growth, chronic economic deprivation and societal stress.

Global population and economic growth, along with high consumption in industrial countries, have led to the depletion, destruction and pollution of the natural environment. Nearly every region has a major resource endowment whose responsible management will require cooperation among states. Science and technology can help reduce environmental threats, but more effort is required to develop sustainable strategies for social and economic progress. This sustainability is likely to become a key principle of development—and a major incentive for global partnerships.

Well-being

Decent living standards are a universal human right. Development efforts to meet these standards are a prime responsibility of governments, and the international community has a responsibility to help through development assistance. Assistance programs are vital to many developing states, crucial to sustaining millions of people in crises and necessary to help build otherwise unaffordable infrastructure. But long-term solutions must also be found through a state's own development policies, attentive to the needs of the economic and social sectors.

The general well-being of a society requires government action to help ensure widespread economic opportunity. Whether and how to undertake such interventions in the economy are controversial issues and should be decided and implemented democratically by societies on their own. But economic growth without widespread sharing in the benefits of growth will not reduce prospects for violent conflict—and it could exacerbate tensions. The resentment and unrest likely to be induced by drastically unbalanced or inequitable economic opportunity may outweigh whatever prosperity is generated by that opportunity.

The distribution of economic benefits in a society is a political concern resolved through decisions on the kind of economic organization a society will construct, including the nature and level of governmental engagement in private sector activity. Poverty is often a structural outgrowth of these decisions, and when poverty runs in parallel with ethnic or cultural divisions, it often creates a flash point. A durable, just peace is most commonly found where economic growth and the opportunities to share in that growth are broadly distributed.

There is great preventive value in initiatives that focus on children and women—not only because they are the main victims of conflict but also because in many vulnerable societies women are an important source of community stability and vitality. A focus on children entails providing access to education and basic health services and prohibiting the recruitment of child soldiers and the industrial exploitation of child labour. A focus on women entails national programs that encourage education for girls, women-operated businesses and other community-based economic activities. And in rebuilding violence-torn societies, women, who are usually the majority of the surviving population, must be involved in all decision-making and implementation.

What is the role of development assistance in promoting well-being and preventing deadly conflict? Good governance has become the keynote of development assistance in the 1990s, along with building skills for participating in the modern global economy. The new approach requires the state to equip itself with a professional, accountable bureaucracy to handle macroeconomic management, poverty reduction, education and training, and environmental protection. Development assistance can also reduce the risk of regional conflicts by tying border groups in one or more states to their shared interests in land and water development, environmental protection and other concerns.

The emphasis on good governance has also encouraged a more robust and responsible private sector in many countries. The emergence of world-wide markets through rising economic activity in the private sector is a strong signal that people are taking advantage of the opportunities in the global economy.

Sustained growth requires investment in people, and programs must prevent deep, intergenerational poverty from becoming institutionalized. Development assistance can include transitional budgetary support, especially for maintenance and for the buffering of the human cost of conversion to market economies. Extensive technical assistance, specialized training and broad economic education are all badly needed. So too is the building of indigenous institutions to sustain the vital knowledge and skills for development.

Improving well-being thus requires a multifaceted approach to mobilize and develop human capacities, broaden and diversify the economic base, remove barriers to equal opportunity and open countries to participation in the global economy and other political and social processes in the international community.

Justice

The rule of law forms the basis for the just management of relations between and among people. It also helps ensure the protection of fundamental human rights, political access through participatory governance, social accommodation of diverse groups and equitable economic opportunity. States' efforts to promote justice should include the development of international law with an emphasis on three areas: human rights, humanitarian law and nonviolent alternatives for resolving disputes, including more flexible intrastate mechanisms for mediation, arbitration, grievance recognition and social reconciliation.

Beyond these measures to help improve the security environment between states, mechanisms to help prevent and manage violence within states are also necessary. Four essential elements provide a framework for maintaining a just regime for internal stability:

- A body of law that is legitimately derived and widely promulgated and understood.
- A consistent, visible, fair and active network of police authority to enforce laws, especially at the local level.
- An independent, equitable and accessible system to redress grievances, especially an impartial judicial system.
- A penal system that is fair and prudent in meting out punishment.

Although vital, these basic elements of internal security are hard to achieve, and they require constant attention through democratic processes.

No political right is more fundamental than the ability to have a say in how one is governed. Democracy achieves this by accommodating competing interests through regular, widely accessible and transparent processes at many levels of government. Sustainable democratic systems also need a military under civilian control and civil services that are competent, honest and accountable.

While the right to a say in how one is governed is a fundamental human right and the foundation of a political framework within which disputes among or within groups can be brokered in nonviolent ways, merely giving people a say does not ensure political accommodation. People must believe that their government will minimize corruption, maintain law and order, provide for their basic needs and safeguard their interests without compromising their core values.

Engineering transitions to participatory governance, or restoring legitimate governance following conditions of anarchy, may require temporary power sharing. Many forms of power sharing are possible, but all provide for widespread participation in the reconstruction effort and for the constructive involvement of outsiders. But in the process of these transitions, and in the aftermath of authoritarian regimes or civil wars characterized by atrocities, the legitimacy of the reconciliation mechanisms is paramount. At least three ways exist to bring perpetrators to justice and help move societies forward: using the existing judicial system aggressively and visibly, establishing a special commission for truth and reconciliation and relying on international tribunals.

TOWARDS A CULTURE OF PREVENTION

During the next century human survival may well depend on our ability to learn a new form of adaptation, one in which intergroup competition is largely replaced by mutual understanding and human cooperation. Curiously, a vital part of human experience—learning to live together—has been badly neglected.

During the past few decades valuable insights have emerged from field studies and experimental research on intergroup behaviour. Among the most striking is the finding that the propensity to distinguish between in-groups and out-groups and to make harsh, invidious distinctions between *us* and *them* is a pervasive human attribute. These easily learned responses may have had adaptive functions beneficial to human survival in the ancient past, but they have also been a major source of conflict and human suffering. And they are no longer adaptive. Indeed, the immense human capacity for adaptation should make it possible for us to learn to minimize harsh and hateful distinctions.

A greater comprehension of other, often unfamiliar cultures is essential for reducing negative preconceptions. Those who have a deep sense of belonging to groups that cut across ethnic, national or sectarian lines may serve as bridges between groups and help move them towards a wider, more inclusive social identity. Building such bridges will require many people interacting with mutual respect across traditional barriers. Developing a personal identification with people beyond one's primary group has never been easy. Yet broader identities are possible, and in the next century it will be necessary to encourage them on a larger scale than ever before.

At a time when many countries are struggling with the new and uncertain challenges of democratization, the international community must champion the norm of responsible leadership and support opportunities for leaders to engage in negotiated, equitable solutions to intergroup disputes. Leaders who demonstrate good will and who engage in these practices should be recognized and rewarded. By the same token, conditions should be fostered that allow electorates to hold their leaders accountable when they depart from democratic norms of peaceful conflict resolution. The international community must expand efforts to educate the public everywhere that preventing deadly conflict is both necessary and possible. To miss the opportunity for preventive action is a failure of leadership.

Any effort to promote tolerance, mutual assistance, responsible leadership and social equity is valuable in its own right. The prevention of deadly conflict has a practical as well as a moral value: where peace and cooperation prevail, so do security and prosperity. Witness the steps after the Second World War to lay the groundwork for today's flourishing European Union. Leaders such as Jean Monnet and George Marshall looked beyond both the wartime devastation and the enmities that had caused it—and envisioned a Europe in which regional cooperation would transcend adversarial boundaries and traditional rivalries. Correctly, they foresaw that large-scale economic cooperation would facilitate not only the postwar recovery but also the long-term prosperity that has helped Europe achieve a degree of peace and security once thought unattainable. Postwar reconstruction is an excellent example of building structural prevention by creating conditions that favour social and economic development and peaceful interaction.

Realizing this vision was not easy. It required constant and creative efforts to educate the public, mobilize key constituencies and persuade reluctant partners. Maintaining this support has required the prudent use of scarce political and social capital. To take just one example, the Marshall Plan initially enjoyed very little support among the US public. If it had not been for the determination and skill of US President Harry S. Truman, the program that made the most important contribution to Europe's postwar reconstruction and development probably would not have been implemented. The Marshall Plan is a model of what sustained international cooperation can accomplish. It also shows the importance of visionary and courageous leadership.

In short, the effort to avert deadly conflict is a matter of humanitarian obligation and of enlightened self-interest. Establishing a culture of prevention is a key public good: it is nonrivalrous and nonexclusionary. Indeed, the more people that practice it, the better off everyone becomes.

The role of the United Nations

The United Nations can have a central, even indispensable role in preventing deadly conflict by helping governments cope with incipient violence and organizing the help of others. Its legitimizing function, its ability to focus world attention on key problems, its considerable operational capacity in many of its specialized agencies—all these make it an important asset in any prevention regime.

The long-term role of the United Nations in helping to prevent deadly conflict resides in its central purposes: promoting peace and security, fostering sustainable development, inspiring widespread respect for human rights and developing the rule of international law. Three major reports combine to form a working program for the United Nations to fulfil these roles: *An Agenda for Peace* (Boutros-Ghali 1992); *An Agenda for Development* (Boutros-Ghali 1995); and *An Agenda for Democratisation* (Boutros-Ghali 1996). Each report focuses on major tasks essential for reducing the global epidemic of violence, preserving global peace and stability, preventing the spread of weapons of mass destruction, promoting sustainable economic and social development, championing human rights and fundamental freedoms and alleviating massive human suffering. Each is an important statement of the broad objectives of peace, development and democracy—as well as a valuable road map to achieving those objectives. In combination, they suggest how states might use the United Nations more effectively to reduce the incidence and intensity of global violence.

More recently, Secretary-General Kofi Annan sounded a clarion call for the United Nations to return to its "cardinal" mission—ensuring human security. He has repeatedly emphasized the importance of prevention and the possibilities for action, not only for the United Nations and its operating agencies but also for regional organizations and for the private sector (see Annan 1997, 1998a, b, c). He has emphasized the applicability and benefit of preventing conflict for every region and highlighted Africa for special attention in this regard.

While most observers agree that the United Nations must be strengthened, few can find common ground on how to do so. For preventing deadly conflict, a number of steps can be taken to enhance prospects that preventive engagement by the United Nations will be successful:

- Establish a rapid reaction capability.
- Use Article 99 of the UN Charter more frequently to bring potentially violent situations to the attention of the Security Council.
- Have member states contribute to the newly created Fund for Prevention to strengthen the hand of the Secretary-General for preventive diplomacy.
- Make greater use of good offices, envoys and special representatives to help defuse developing crises.
- Use the considerable convening power of the office of the Secretary-General more assertively to assemble groups of "friends" that can help coordinate the international response to worsening situations.
- Reform the Security Council to reflect the world's capacities and its needs.

Other measures are desirable and possible. A renewed commitment must be made to the preventive purposes of the United Nations, precisely because of the all-pervasive, public good nature of conflict prevention (see United Nations 1997). Widespread opportunity for prosperity in an environment of just peace maintained at every level of human society would permit all to partake of prosperity. Achieving this is surely a worthy goal.

NOTES

This chapter draws heavily from the Carnegie Commission on Preventing Deadly Conflict (1997).

1. See, for example, arrangements regulating economic interaction such as the International Bank for Reconstruction and Development, which together with its affiliate the International Development Association is known as the World Bank. The Bank was established in 1945 along with the International

Monetary Fund (Stremlau and Sagasti 1998, p. 91). Other arrangements include regional agreements creating security arrangements like the North Atlantic Treaty Organization, Organization of American States, Organization of African Unity and Organization for Security and Cooperation in Europe; economic organizations such as the European Union and North American Free Trade Agreement (Carnegie Commission on Preventing Deadly Conflict 1997, pp. 169–73); arrangements on international dispute resolution such as the International Court of Justice (created in 1945) and World Trade Organization (created in 1994); arrangements on arms control such as the Nuclear Non-Proliferation Treaty, 1992 Biological Weapons Convention and 1993 Chemical Weapons Convention (Carnegie Commission on Preventing Deadly Conflict 1997, pp. 73–75); and arrangements on the protection of human rights such as the Universal Declaration of Human Rights (issued in 1948), Convention on the Elimination of All Forms of Discrimination against Women (issued in 1979), and Convention on the Rights of the Child (issued in 1989).

References

Annan, Kofi. 1997. "The United Nations: New Directions, New Priorities." The Sorensen Distinguished Lecture on the United Nations. Council on Foreign Relations, 22 April, New York.

———. 1998a. "Challenges of Prevention." Address to the James A. Baker III Institute of Public Policy. Rice University, 24 April, Texas.

———. 1998b. "Intervention." The 35th Annual Ditchley Foundation Lecture, 29 June, Ditchley Park, United Kingdom.

———. 1998c. "The United Nations As a Conflict Prevention Device." Address to the Conference on Preventing Deadly Conflict among Nations in the Twenty-first Century, University of California at Los Angeles, 23 April.

Boutros-Ghali, Boutros. 1992. *An Agenda for Peace.* New York: United Nations.

———. 1995. *An Agenda for Development.* New York: United Nations.

———. 1996. *An Agenda for Democratisation.* New York: United Nations.

Bremer, Stuart. 1992. "Dangerous Dyads: Conditions Affecting the Likelihood of Interstate War 1816–1965." *Journal of Conflict Resolution* 36(2): 309–41.

———. 1993. "Democracy and Militarized Interstate Conflict, 1816–1965." *International Interactions* 18(3): 231–49.

Brown, Michael E., and Richard N. Rosecrance. 1999. *The Costs of Conflict: Prevention and Cure in the Global Arena.* Lanham, MD: Rowman & Littlefield.

Brown, Michael E., Sean M. Lynn-Jones and Steven E. Miller, eds. 1996. *Debating the Democratic Peace.* Cambridge, MA: MIT Press.

Bueno de Mesquita, Bruce, and David Lalman. 1992. *War and Reason: Domestic and International Imperatives.* New Haven, CT: Yale University Press.

Carnegie Commission on Preventing Deadly Conflict. 1997. *Preventing Deadly Conflict: Final Report.* Washington, DC.

Doyle, Michael. 1983. "Kant, Liberal Legacies, and Foreign Affairs." *Philosophy and Public Affairs* 12(3): 205–35.

Ray, James Lee. 1995. *Democracy and International Conflict: An Evaluation of the Democratic Peace Proposition.* Columbia: University of South Carolina Press.

Rummel, Rudolph J. 1975–81. *Understanding Conflict and War.* 5 vols. Los Angeles, CA: Sage.

———.1983. "Libertarianism and International Violence." *Journal of Conflict Resolution* 27(1): 27–72.

———. 1985. "Libertarian Propositions on Violence within and between Nations: A Test against Published Results." *Journal of Conflict Resolution* 29(3): 419–55.

Russett, Bruce. 1993. *Grasping the Democratic Peace: Principles for a Post-Cold War World.* Princeton, NJ: Princeton University Press.

Stremlau, John, and Francisco Sagasti. 1998. *Preventing Deadly Conflict: Does the World Bank Have a Role?* Washington, DC: Carnegie Commission on Preventing Deadly Conflict.

United Nations. 1945. *Charter of the United Nations and Statute of the International Court of Justice.* New York.

———. 1997. *Renewing the United Nations: A Programme for Reform.* Report of the Secretary-General. Fifty-first session, United Nations Reform: Measures and Proposals, Agenda Item 168; 14 July.

Peace As a
Global Public Good

Ruben P. Mendez

World history is largely a history of wars. All have been fought in a world without governance—where national "defence", regional military alliances, balance of power and hegemonic imperialism have been the prevailing regimes. There is a manifest need for a system under universal auspices for maintaining global peace and security. The notion of a global public good is a logical starting point for considering how such a system would operate. In the literature of public economics, defence has traditionally been held up as a pure public good in the domestic sphere. But there are problems, as this chapter will show, with this formalistic approach—and even more so at the international level. In contrast, peace meets the substantive (that is, welfare) as well as formal criteria of a public good.

This chapter first analyses the maintenance of peace and security as a public good in terms of these criteria. It shows how the conventional treatment of a public good neglects the substance of its putative benefits—which are what ultimately concern humankind. Theories of public goods and related subjects of public finance theory, such as free riding, externalities and other market failures, have focused on the level of states and smaller political entities. The chapter transposes these basic elements to the international level. It then contrasts two generic models of the maintenance of international peace and security: traditional *realpolitik* approaches, through balance of power or hegemony, and collective security. It argues that collective security is more effective and sustainable, and that the United Nations has a central role in such a system. Finally, the chapter describes practical, incremental steps to bring the current regime closer to a true and effective system of collective security.

DEFINING THE PUBLIC GOOD: PEACE AND DEFENCE

The essence of what is meant by "public goods" was encapsulated by Paul Samuelson in his landmark 1954 article, "The Pure Theory of Public

Expenditure". He defined public goods as "*collective consumption goods . . . which all enjoy in common in the sense that each individual's consumption of such a good leads to no subtraction from any other individual's consumption of that good*" (Samuelson 1954, pp. 387-89). Public goods are thus described in the literature as nonrival (in their consumption)—which actually means nonrivalrous.[1] For instance, the sailors and passengers on ships in the vicinity of a lighthouse can simultaneously consume (use) the lighthouse beacon for guidance without detracting from each other's use.[2] In the jargon of economics, there is no marginal (additional) cost in the extra use of a public good.

Public goods are also nonexcludable or, more accurately, nonexclusionary.[3] A good is nonexclusionary if no one—not even nonpayers—can be excluded from using it, and it thus attracts free riders. In these circumstances the private sector is not apt to provide the good because it cannot obtain revenues by charging for its use. It is for this reason that the public sector (governments in states and smaller political entities) normally finances the provision of public goods, obtaining the funding from taxes or user charges.

The general literature of public economics contains extensive formal methodological analysis of public goods but little on the nature of their benefits. Anthony Atkinson and Joseph Stiglitz defend this focus on the grounds that "there is a substantial gain in terms of clarity of argument and the avoidance of ambiguity" (Atkinson and Stiglitz 1980, pp. 562–63). Formal, especially mathematical, analysis is one way of achieving and demonstrating precision and clarity. At times, however, such analysis is overdone—at the expense of learning the content of the actual benefits (or adverse effects) generated by the putative public good.[4]

Yet substantive criteria are important, especially if the analysis is to be useful in formulating policy. Even though defence is conventionally studied as a public good, it does not meet substantive criteria as well as does peace.

Defence as a public good

Textbooks on economics and public finance generally cite national defence as the example par excellence of a pure public good, demonstrating that it is:

- Nonrivalrous—that is, the consumption, or enjoyment, of the protection afforded by national defence to a resident of a country does not detract from another resident's consumption of that protection. The protection is indivisible, and its enjoyment by an additional person involves no marginal, or additional, cost.

- Nonexclusionary—no one in the country can be excluded from benefiting from the protection of national defence, regardless of whether he or she contributes directly to the defence budget.

The analyses go on to point out that because the private sector cannot profitably provide defence—because it cannot charge the beneficiaries and exclude those who do not pay—the government provides it directly, financing its costs through taxation. More detailed discussions delve into programme budgeting, project cost-effectiveness, monitoring of expenditures and production, ways of reducing costs and the like (see Hyman 1990, pp. 323–31; Mankiw 1997, p. 222; Mansfield 1989, p. 14; Rosen 1988, pp. 79–82; Samuelson and Nordhaus 1989, pp. 770–71; and Stiglitz 1988, ch. 12).

The "utility" conferred by defence expenditures, conventionally assumed to be mainly protection, is taken for granted.[5] The term "defence" has positive connotations. But the analyses do not deal with the substance and consequences of its assumed goodness.[6] The term is a euphemism for more concrete and accurate words like war, weapon, military and arms (Keller 1995). Former war ministries are now invariably called defence ministries. In its latent state defence involves weapons systems, the arms industry, military technology, nuclear testing, the arms trade and the arms race. In its active form it is called war.

A number of core questions may be asked in this respect. First, is there really such a thing as a nuclear umbrella? Do alliances whose main defence is the threat of nuclear strikes protect their members? Or put them at risk of becoming victims of massive retaliation?[7] One characteristic of a public good is that although people or nations may value it differently, they receive it equally. Does the deterrence effect—if, in fact, it exists—outweigh the danger of war by accident or of catastrophe if there is retaliation? How much retaliatory capacity is necessary to serve as a deterrent?

Second, what private benefits and positive externalities does military spending bring? Employment and income for the military and support personnel? Increased economic activity and income from construction, rental payments, food purchases, tourism, spending for entertainment, and various multiplier effects? Increased production and revenues for suppliers? Scientific and technological progress? National pride? What are the costs to taxpayers and to military and support personnel, voluntary or conscripted? Is military spending the most efficient way of increasing economic activity and welfare, even where there is less than full employment? What are the alternatives and the opportunity costs? Isn't spending on productive economic activities, long-term civilian-oriented research or space exploration more efficient and wel-fare-enhancing? Wouldn't direct grants be a less costly way of compensating the unemployed?

It would help in understanding how the military establishment influences public spending priorities to use some insights of public choice theory, which applies market principles (self-interest, rational expectations) to nonmarket situations. The way self-interest operates in the behaviour of civilian bureau-crats, legislators and voters has been extensively scrutinized and criticized. But public choice specialists have neglected the military, failing to consider how self-interest influences legislators, military bureaucrats, think tanks on mili-tary matters (like the US RAND Corporation), and lobbyists and corporate leaders connected with the military-industrial complex (in terms of, say, mil-itary empire building or deliberate overestimation of the enemy and of required military expenditures). A stark example of a military-industrial establishment that helped initiate war, studied by historians but not by pub-lic choice economists, is that of Japan before the Second World War.

There have been increasing references in the literature to economic inef-ficiency resulting from the self-interest of the bureaucrats and business exec-utives of the military-industrial establishment.[8] There have also been revelations recently about how US generals, for instance, deliberately overes-timated the Soviet Union's military strength during the Cold War. This mis-statement was an important factor in increasing US military outlays (Schwartz 1998). But in addition to issues of national economic waste and inefficiency, there is a global welfare consideration that should not be over-looked: that self-serving behaviour in the military establishment has pro-duced colossal disasters and remains extremely dangerous.

Sandler and Hartley (1995, p. 341) note that public sector economics has made the greatest contribution to the economics of defence in recent years. But this contribution has been at the level of the state and of microeconom-ics. It covers questions of increasing the efficiency and cost-effectiveness of military expenditures within nations or, at most, alliances. It does not deal with the international market failures of a world of states and exclusive alliances acting in their own self-interest, nor with what action should be taken to correct these failures and increase global welfare. Table 1 gives exam-ples of market failures and policy responses and how they are transposable from the national to the international level.

A third set of questions to ask when evaluating defence as a public good is, what are the negative externalities? Damage to the environment and social

TABLE 1

Market failures and policy responses: national and international

Form of market failure	National (mainly the United States)	
	Example	Policy response
Public goods	Lighthouses and highways	Government provision, financed by taxes and user charges
	Maintaining law and order	National Guard, conscription
Negative externalities	Urban air pollution	Clean Air Act
	River pollution by paper mill	Regulation
Positive externalities	Education	Government provision, financed by subsidies and tax breaks
	Polio vaccination	Government provision
	Home ownership	Tax deductibility of interest costs
Competitive breakdowns	Standard Oil Co. (US)	Sherman Antitrust Act
	Railroad monopsony	Promotion of competition
	Natural monopolies	Regulated public utility
Information failures	Effects of tobacco	Surgeon General's warning
	Interest rates on loans	Truth-in-lending laws
	Investment information	Full disclosure at New York Stock Exchange and Securities and Exchange Comission
Incomplete markets	Credit for small business	Small Business Investment Corporation
	Insurance for the elderly	Medicare
Merit goods	Music and the arts	Subsidies and tax breaks

International and global	
Example	Policy response
Protecting the ozone layer	Montreal Protocol
The Internet	None
Peacekeeping	UN peacekeeping, NATO
CFC Emissions	Montreal Protocol
Marine oil pollution	None
Education ("reverse brain drain")	None
Smallpox vaccination	WHO programme
Maintaining rain forests	Debt-for-nature swaps
OPEC	Petrodollar recycling, International Energy Agency
US and EU auto markets	None
Agricultural subsidies	GATT/WTO negotiations
Nuclear testing	Test ban treaty
Two-tier foreign currency market	None
Capital and credit for least-developed countries	World Bank/IDA
Balance of payments insurance	IMF (in theory)
Preservation of historic treasures	UNESCO's Abu Simbel programme

fabric of the areas adjacent to domestic and foreign military bases? Spread of prostitution and venereal diseases? Feelings of danger, insecurity, frustration and anger by nonmembers or "enemies" of the defence alliance? Did the North Atlantic Treaty Organization (NATO) provoke the creation of the Warsaw Pact through such negative externalities? Did both "defence" alliances escalate the arms race by generating negative externalities against each other? What are the economic costs of the arms race? To taxpayers? In terms of alternative, forgone opportunities for expenditure? Even when technically there was peace among the world's leading military powers, did the people feel there was security?

Finally, doesn't the matching of expenditures by each side decrease the marginal benefit of each additional expenditure? Wouldn't a lower equilibrium be less costly and less threatening?

Peace as a public good

Although not as popular a subject as defence, peace is also a public good cited by teachers of public finance and other economists (Kindleberger 1986). Unlike defence, it unarguably meets the public goods criteria from a substantive (welfare) as well as a formal perspective. It is a state of relations among peoples and nations that everyone aspires to or wishes to maintain. Excepting pathological would-be conquerors and profiteers, as well as sadists and masochists, who would prefer war, peace can be said to be a universal public good. It is the best state of society for human survival and a necessary condition for the satisfaction and welfare of society's members. Without peace, one cannot enjoy the conveniences of daily life. It is a prerequisite for the pursuit of happiness and social and human development.

How does peace meet the formal as well as substantive criteria of being a public good? In terms of being nonexclusionary, if a country is at peace, it is a benefit that no resident can be excluded from enjoying. At the international level global peace benefits all, much like the public good of law and order at the national level. Where peace and security prevail, everyone can enjoy the fact that there is no war or threat of it, international travel and trade are unimpeded, people can go about their work without fear and the like. Under this state of affairs everyone everywhere can enjoy the benefits of peace, the enjoyment of one not detracting from that of another. Welfare economists, in fact, may deem peace even more fundamental than a public good. They may consider it an enabling institution of the market mechanism and an essential element of the first fundamental theorem of welfare economics (Mendez 1992, p. 58).

Global and regional peace

How do we appraise regional or local peace—for instance, peace in Cyprus? In a sense such peace is a universal public good in that it has existence value: the fact that there is peace in Cyprus is perceived as good, and this perception is available to everyone. In itself, however, the good feeling associated with the knowledge of a localized peace may not rank high in the scale of benefits. It would intrinsically be a form of "enjoyment from afar", akin to but even less intense than, say, the enjoyment felt by a reader of *National Geographic* in learning that there are still rain forests in the Amazon and gorillas in the mountains of Rwanda (Mendez 1995b, p. 46).

Peace in Cyprus, however, is also a public good in that it is an element—a building block—of world order. It enhances peace in Greece, Turkey and the Mediterranean, and it contributes to peace in the world and to the peace process. While the private benefits (to Cypriots, Greeks and Turks) are the strongest, a local Cypriot peace thus has positive externalities that give it public goods attributes. A regional public good in the international arena, furthermore—provided it does not infringe on another region or country—is analogous to regional peace within a nation. The maritime law and order provided by the US Coast Guard, for instance, may be enjoyed by sailors in Boston but not directly by farmers in Iowa. But it is still something that the US government provides, using tax revenues, because it is needed and can be financed by the public but not the private sector. Although some members of society have a larger stake than others, all benefit from the externalities and efficiency of national provision.

Peacekeeping services in specific countries and regions have public goods characteristics but nonetheless are akin to what public sector economists call private goods publicly provided. Expanding peacekeeping forces to cover additional countries (such as Burundi and Rwanda) would incur increased costs and detract from funds available for other countries (such as Bosnia). As illustrated by the Cyprus example, however, peacekeeping has extensive positive externalities, and in national systems of public finance these are grounds for subsidies. In addition, there are benefits in providing such services under international public auspices—with the neutrality and universality of the United Nations—rather than by individual nations. This is why within states, governments rather than militias, gangs or private armies are the preferred enforcers of peace.

PRODUCING PEACE: POWER POLITICS AND COLLECTIVE SECURITY

Collective security brings the international sphere closer to the kind of security management provided domestically, in that breaches of security are deemed a matter of concern to all and mechanisms exist to deter violent behaviour. According to some authors (notably in the Realist tradition), however, the traditional balance of power also offered order and security. This section briefly reviews the historical record, as well as the analytical background, of this ongoing debate.

Balance of power, hegemony and the Cold War

THE HISTORICAL RECORD. Balance of power theory took root and bloomed in Europe (Sheehan 1996; Gulick 1955). Stability was supposedly ensured by checking the military buildup of one political entity or alliance with an equally strong alliance of others. Yet Europe has experienced many cases where this putative balance of power failed to prevent war, as in the Wars of the League of Augsburg (1688–97) and of the Spanish Succession (1701–14), despite the supposed balance of power between the Bourbon and Hapsburg dynasties; the Seven Years' War (1756–63), pitting Austria, France, Russia, Saxony and Sweden against Britain, Portugal and Prussia; and World War I (1914–18), following the division of Europe into the Triple Alliance (Britain, France and Russia) and the Triple Entente (Germany, Austria-Hungary and, until 1915, Italy).

Whether a balance of power existed during the Cold War is questionable given recent revelations that the Soviet bloc was much weaker than Western strategists claimed. But the perception of a balance of power may have been what mattered—or perhaps it was a balance of terror, because every country with nuclear arms and delivery capabilities *ipso facto* had a nuclear deterrent.

In fact, what bipolarity produced was at best an uneasy peace, punctuated by rampant armed conflicts in North-East and South-East Asia, the Middle East and Africa. The main accomplishment—some call it fortuitous—was the containment of these conflicts and the happy avoidance of a global nuclear holocaust. But the period did include real, medium-size and dangerous wars in Korea and in the former Indochina.

A FLAWED SYSTEM. Although it may temporarily deter states from going to war, a "balance of power" suffers from shortcomings and inefficiencies. One reason is to be found in Robert Jervis's (1976) security dilemma: to feel truly secure, a state needs to be more than just equal, in military capability, to its neighbours. It needs to be more powerful. If this logic is applied to all, then all states cannot be secure at the same time, and general equilibrium is impossible. The result is usually an arms race. The impossibility of achieving a perfect balance leads to a compulsion to have a credit balance. Feeding the spiral are imperfect information about the actual strength of each counterpart and a tendency to escalate military buildups.

In an arms race the putative marginal benefits of additional military expenditures fall even as the level of danger rises with the growth of expenditures. Competing parties often practice escalation to attain or maintain a balance of power. A cascading balance through disarmament, on the other hand, has never been realized. Real disarmament did not take place until the end of the Cold War. This casts doubts on the efficiency—and desirability—of a balance of power in other than a truly anarchic environment.

In addition, there are doubts about the effectiveness of a balance of power in an age of weapons of mass destruction, given their far-ranging negative externalities. During the Cold War an exchange of hydrogen bombing raids by the United States and the Soviet Union or even one bombing would have caused such widespread destruction that it is doubtful that even the victor, if any, could have enjoyed survival. Even a more limited nuclear war, say, between India and Pakistan, would wreak destruction and negative externalities of disastrous proportions—for the victor as well as the vanquished.

PEACE THROUGH HEGEMONY. The Cold War has ended, and for the present, at least, there is no global balance of power. Former Cold War antagonists are trying to reduce their nuclear arsenals and convert from military to civilian economies while manufacturing military hardware and selling it to developing countries. There is now only one super economic and military power—the United States. Does this mean that the United States will now keep the peace? Although it takes a more active role than any other country—as in the case of disputes between Israelis and Palestinians and in the former Yugoslavia—the United States does not want to become the world's police officer. It would, furthermore, be criticized if it intervened in other situations, such as disputes elsewhere in the Middle East, in most of Latin America and much of Africa and in many other parts of the world.

These are some of the flaws in the theory of benevolent hegemony, another Western concept.[9] There are claims in history of eras of hegemonic peace: the *pax romana*, the *pax britannica* and—although unlike the others it is a target of vilification by Western historians—the *pax mongolica* of the era of Central Asia's famous silk route. A closer examination of these periods reveals that a *pax hegemonica* (to use a Graeco-Roman hybrid) consisted, in fact, of suppressive imperialistic regimes. The peace was geographically limited and highly selective. The main beneficiaries were the elites and perhaps other citizens of the hegemonic power, but there was much oppression and suffering elsewhere.

There have also been recent references to a *pax americana* and *pax sovietica*. It is questionable that these existed or that the former Cold Warriors will try to establish or reinvent them.[10] It is also improbable that Western Europe will try to embark on a new military imperialism. The former imperialist powers are so war averse, so unwilling to risk lives and have lost so much power that they are reluctant to intervene (or even to authorize UN interventions) in what they consider strategically marginal areas such as Burundi, Liberia, Somalia and Rwanda. This is less true in the former Yugoslavia—which Europe sees as in its own backyard—where these powers have assigned NATO, a part of their regional public sector, to intervene.

Collective security

History shows that neither hegemony nor a balance of power can ensure sustainable peace. Hegemony, like dictatorship, leads to unrest and upheavals. A balance of power also fails, partly because groups of governments and groups of people face prisoner's dilemmas—the temptation of their members to cheat or defect[11]—and other problems of voluntary collective action. The arms race is, in fact, a type of prisoner's dilemma.

The collective security model, by contrast, recognizes the public nature of international peace. It views global peace as an indivisible whole—a truly collective good—and therefore makes even local conflicts a binding matter of concern for the international community (along the principle of "one for all and all for one"). The collective security model aims, while not for Immanuel Kant's "Perpetual Peace", at least for an enduring and universal system for resolving conflict with as little violence as possible.

The three pillars of the system of collective security as it is developed in the UN Charter (1945) are:

- A mutual undertaking of pacific behaviour: "All members shall settle their international disputes by peaceful means" and "shall refrain in their international relations from the threat or use of force against the territorial integrity or political independence of any state" (Article 2, see also Chapter XIV).

- A menu of graduated responses or mechanisms for settling disputes (negotiation, enquiry, mediation, conciliation, arbitration, judicial settlement and other peaceful means; Chapter VI) and dealing with threats to or breaches of the peace and with aggression (all the way to sanctions, blockades, embargoes and full-scale military action as mandated by the Security Council; Chapter VII).

- An extensive preventive programme comprising international economic and social cooperation, decolonization and development, social progress, better standards of living and human rights (Chapters IX, XI and XII).

The global analogue of law and order in states is peace and security. This is a responsibility of the international public sector. Emma Rothschild gives an apt sociological description:[12]

> *Common security . . . is seen as a sort of social contract between states. The "individuals" who seek security are themselves nation-states. International order—like war, in Rousseau's description—is a "relation between states, not a relation between men." Nations-states choose to organize their security in common; they sacrifice certain individual freedoms, such as the freedom to try to overthrow other nation-states by force, for the common good of avoiding nuclear war.*
>
> (Rothschild 1995, p. 97)

The United Nations provides the framework for this contract and is itself the contract. Russett, Oneal and Davis (1998) recently carried out a comprehensive and mathematically rigorous study of militarized disputes and memberships in international organizations during 1950–85. The study provides statistically significant evidence that shared memberships in many international organizations substantially reduce the chances of armed conflict between two states—an effect strengthened when the states are also democratic and interdependent. This is an indication of the value of international organizations not only as providers of public goods but also as global public goods.

INTERNATIONAL PEACE AFTER THE COLD WAR

What is the new post-Cold War system, and what are the chances that a true and universal system of collective security will emerge?

The new security equation

The Cold War has been replaced by an easier, less tense global peace. While the current peace no longer appears to be under the shadow of nuclear warfare between big powers, it is still punctuated by small wars—most of which are considered mere brush fires by Western powers—all over the world: Recent conflicts have occurred in Afghanistan, Angola, Burundi, Congo, Eritrea-Ethiopia, Haiti, Iraq-Kuwait, Liberia, Rwanda, Somalia, western Sahara and the former Yugoslavia—not to mention those that have arisen in successor states of the former Soviet Union since the demise of the *pax sovietica,* or the problems still simmering in Cambodia, Cyprus, El Salvador, Mozambique, the Middle East and elsewhere. The victims are mainly people in low-income countries.

While there is now more focus on "mini-wars", the number of major armed conflicts has actually decreased since the end of bipolarity (figure 1). The number of wars catapulted in the late 1940s and early 1950s and continued to increase until peaking in 1989, the eve of the end of the Cold War. Since then they have declined.[13] The number of deaths has also declined, after peaking during the conflicts in Korea and the former Indochina, which were clear manifestations of the conflict between what were then called East and West.

The nature of strife has also changed. In the past eight years there have been more than 100 cases of armed conflict, almost all within states (the most notable exceptions being Iraq-Kuwait and, most recently, Eritrea-Ethiopia) and involving more than 175 subnational groups and organizations. This new breed of international problem involves not so much regular armies as militias, armed civilians, guerrillas and ethnic groups. Small arms are the predominant weapons. While the world's big powers manufacture and export small arms extensively, their military edge is more in high-tech weapons of the type used in the Gulf wars.

Because the strategists of the big powers see these post-Cold War conflicts as of marginal importance, international action has been limited. Witness the lack of action to stem the mass killings in Rwanda. This is in contrast to the attitudes of the big powers during the Cold War, when they showed great interest in the parties to conflict and tried to secure their support or use them as bases or spheres of influence. This included supplying them with arms and training and equipping their armed forces, in what have been called "proxy wars".

A related development is "collapsed"—and collapsing—states, characterized by a breakdown of public institutions and of governance, law and order. A classic example is Cambodia, where a UN Transitional Authority supervised national elections and helped carry out many other functions of government during the transition period from 1992 to 1993.

Although most of today's wars are within states, they reflect tensions between ethnic groups and historical nations that were previously controlled or sublimated by supraethnic and supranational governments. These tensions have been given full rein in the more permissive ethos of the new, post-Cold War environment. Armed conflicts often lead to crop failures, famines, epidemics, genocide and mass movements of refugees—invariably causing spillovers across national borders into not only neighbouring, but also more distant countries.

Intrastate conflicts thus generate massive negative externalities. At the end of 1997 there were more than 22 million refugees and displaced persons.[14] This figure does not include movements of emigrants seeking to escape poor and deteriorating economic conditions. The budget of the UN High

FIGURE 1

Wars and war-related deaths in the 20th century

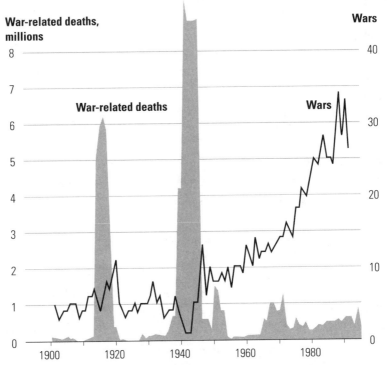

Source: Reproduced, with permission, from *World Military and Social Expenditures 1996* by Ruth Leger Sivard. Copyright 1996 by World Priorities, PO Box 25140, Washington, DC 20007.

Commissioner for Refugees has been the fastest growing of the voluntarily financed UN programmes—tragic testimony to the soaring numbers of refugees, of whom Haitians, Hutus, Tutsis and south Slavs are recent examples. Displaced populations not only move to territories adjacent to the areas of conflict but also to other countries, developed as well as developing.

With the advance of globalization and the intensification of international interconnections and interactions, wars can no longer be considered private, national affairs. They are matters of concern to the entire world community.

The regional approach

One of the consequences of these changed realities is a growing recognition of the importance of multilateral action. Such action can be carried out by regional as well as global multilateral institutions. The UN Charter, in fact, "encourage[s] the development of pacific settlement of local disputes through such regional arrangements or by such regional agencies either on the initiative of the states concerned or by reference from the Security Council," provided that "no enforcement action shall be taken ... without the authorisation of the Security Council" (Article 52, para. 3, and Article 53, para. 1).[15]

Regional public organizations deal with regional disputes in various parts of the world, and this may be considered part of a decentralized approach to achieving peace—as contrasted, for instance, with the centralized, hegemonic approach. In the context of international public goods theory, it may also find justification as a form of action within a region by the "public sector" of the region. For example, the Commonwealth of Independent States is providing buffer and peacekeeping forces in Georgia, Moldova and the Tajikistan-Afghan and Georgian-Abkhazian borders; and the Economic Community of West African States carries out "monitoring" in Liberia and Sierra Leone (International Institute for Strategic Studies 1997).

These missions have operated in agreement or cooperation with the United Nations and are often patterned on UN peacekeeping models. Action or approval by the international public sector is needed to give legitimacy to interventions in matters of peace and security. These interventions have met with varying degrees of success. A number of factors influence the volume and scope of activity of these peacekeeping missions. One is financing. Most time and money have been spent on the territories of the former Yugoslavia, a commitment made possible by Europe's economic wealth. In Africa, on the other hand, although the Organization of African Unity has shown perhaps the most concern about regional political unity and cooperation of any regional institution, a lack of resources has prevented it from carrying out as much peacekeeping as it would like. With its mistrust of Western countries, Africa has relied more on the United Nations than have other regions.[16]

Regional groupings, except those in Africa, often use nationals of other regions in staffing their missions—another reflection of globalization. The membership of regional institutions, moreover, often does not coincide with the countries and regions involved. This is the case, for instance, in disputes or potential disputes involving Afghanistan and Tajikistan, and the countries of Western and Eastern Europe, Central Asia and the Baltic Sea. Outside Africa, many parties to regional conflicts prefer to have the good offices of nationals of neutral countries. An example was the Neutral Nations Supervisory Commission, comprising Swedish and Swiss observers, for the Korean armistice in 1953. A more recent example is the US involvement that led to the Dayton Agreement on the former Yugoslavia. The US efforts seemed more realistic than the moral high ground taken by the European Community in its initial intervention, which endorsed and sealed the start of Yugoslavia's dismemberment—and the ineluctable strife that followed.

Still, it would be rare to have an international public institution of one region intervene in another region. It could become the norm were there global hegemony in the form of a regional organization, such as NATO. But this approach would not be accepted outside the Western world.

THE ROLE OF THE UNITED NATIONS IN PEACE AND SECURITY

While certain conflicts can best be settled by regional public institutions, there is a danger where global interests are involved that these institutions will give priority to the region they represent rather than the interest of peace in general. As can be inferred from the composition of the national, regional and global public sectors (table 2), regional public institutions can be, like states, among the free riders of the larger global arena. There is a clear advantage in such an arena to having neutral, impartial and universal auspices for resolving armed conflicts and potential conflicts.

Hence the need for a universal peacekeeper—the equivalent on a global scale of a municipal police force, or of a national guard or constabulary—to keep law and order. This peacekeeper's services might be compared to the national public good of defence, except there is no external enemy and its goals are inner-directed rather than expansionist. The maintenance of peace and security, in fact, is the primary function of the United Nations.

TABLE 2

Composition of the private and public sectors

Level	Private sector	Public sector
National	Individuals and households Private firms Nongovernmental organizations (NGOs)	Government Government corporations

Regional	Individuals, firms and NGOs
	  with regional activities
	Regional states
		Public regional
		  organizations (such as the
		  EU, or NATO)

Global	States
	Regional organizations
	Individuals, firms and NGOs
	  with global relations
		Public international
		  organizations

During its first 45 years bipolarity and the veto power of its permanent members rendered the Security Council largely ineffective. With the end of the Cold War the Council unanimously authorized action against Iraq following its invasion of Kuwait, in what many hoped would presage a new era of world cooperation in the maintenance of peace and security. The euphoria about a new role for the United Nations was followed by action in Somalia, but when the US-directed operation suffered widely publicized casualties, there was an about-face and a resistance to engage in peacekeeping operations, with the United Nations taking the blame.

Since then the Security Council has been extremely tight and selective in deciding when to authorize UN action, and poor and small states are increasingly concerned over the dismissal of their cases. This imbalance is largely a consequence of the skewed composition of the Security Council and points to a need for more representation for non-Western countries to redress this imbalance. Unless this is done, the Security Council's credibility and legitimacy will suffer.

United Nations peacekeeping

The United Nations organizes peacekeeping activities at the request of the Security Council. Although the term "peacekeeping" is not in the UN charter, it started being used during the operations of the first UN Emergency Force, which kept the peace for more than 10 years after British, French and Israeli forces withdrew from Egyptian territory during the 1956 Suez war (Urquhart 1987). The term has since been applied to any noncombatant UN military presence. It does not cover "enforcement", which has been carried out only by individual states or groups of states with UN authorization, as in the Korean and Gulf wars.

UN peacekeeping missions have taken a number of forms, including:

- Logistical support and protection for the supply of food, clothing and medicine, as in Bosnia and Herzegovina and Rwanda.

- Observer missions, such as those to monitor peace and conflict in Georgia, Liberia and Tajikistan; this includes truce supervision, as with the Arab-Israeli armistice.

- De facto buffers, as with the peacekeeping force separating the Greek- and Turkish-speaking populations in Cyprus and with the interim force in Lebanon.

- Transitional administrations such as the mission in eastern Slavonia, Baranja and western Sirmium (in Croatia) and the comprehensive operation that conducted elections and provided government services in Cambodia until the formation of a new government, from 1992 to 1993. The UN role may also be solely for conducting or monitoring democratic elections (or both), as in Haiti, Central America and western Sahara (see annex).

The mandates of UN peacekeeping missions, however, have often been so tightly circumscribed or left so vague and without support that they were doomed to ineffectiveness or failure from the beginning. Even in combat-prone situations UN forces are not supposed to fight and are often unarmed. While in theory the forces can act in self-defence, in practice they have to rely on the good will of the authorities and populations in the host country. This approach has resulted in extensive fatalities—including 1,551 noncombatants by mid-1998—and kidnapping or hostage taking. Although the Security Council designated safe havens in the former Yugoslavia, UN missions were not given the mandates or wherewithal to protect the areas. Thus UN peacekeeping operations have no teeth and exist in limbo. While the original premise of peacekeeping is that there is a peace to be maintained and that the parties to the conflict have arrived at terms of agreement, today this is often not the case, so the term is a misnomer.

The UN *Agenda for Peace* articulates the idea of special "peace enforcement" contingents, equipped with appropriate armaments and the authority to use them to achieve their goals, as distinguished from regular peacekeeping (Boutros-Ghali 1995). But this approach received a setback in Bosnia and Somalia, where the transformation of peacekeeping into provisional peace enforcement was not accompanied by the necessary authority or wherewithal for the task. It would be useful if the nature of future UN peace-related operations were clearly defined and they were given the appropriate mandates and resources, so that their implications would be clear to all.[17]

The United Nations has severe shortcomings in its capacity to maintain peace and security on a global scale. These handicaps and the possibilities for reform and strengthening can be better understood if their historical causes are considered. While the Allied Powers established the United Nations at the end of the Second World War to maintain global peace and security, the emergence of bipolarity transformed their treatment of the United Nations as they focused on NATO, the Warsaw Pact and other regional alliances in the Middle East and East Asia and the Pacific.

The major powers' handling of the United Nations was at best one of neglect, but more often one of cynicism. These attitudes were reflected in the selection and treatment of the Secretary-General, in the high-level staffing of the Secretariat, in the diversion of authority and resources to other public international organizations (such as the Bretton Woods institutions, over which they had direct control) and in the withholding of obligatory financial contributions to UN budgets.

Support for the United Nations and its specialized agencies must include realistic mandates so that they are not placed in "lose-lose" situations. Peacekeeping, properly construed, should be accompanied by the continuum of actions necessary for sustained peace: relief and rehabilitation, assistance in transitional arrangements where public authority has broken down, governance and economic development. These complementary actions could be undertaken by the United Nations, other agencies of the UN system and other appropriate parties.

Financing United Nations peace and security activities

The method of financing UN peacekeeping operations is a far cry from the method of financing analogous public goods and goods with positive externalities in nation-states. At the national level such goods are normally provided by the public sector and financed from tax revenues. This approach is used because of the extensive scope of their benefits, the difficulty of excluding nonpayers from enjoying those benefits and the lack of incentives for the private sector to provide the goods.

The United Nations has three sources of financing: its regular budget, peacekeeping special accounts and extrabudgetary programmes for development, the environment, refugees and other assistance, which are financed from voluntary contributions. The regular budget covers mainly the administrative expenses of the organization. It is financed from assessed contributions by all member states, ranging from 25% of the budget for the United States to 0.01% for small and poor countries such as Fiji and Somalia. The assessment formula is thus based on the principle of progressive taxation, such as is found in states.

The costs of peacekeeping operations were initially charged to the regular budget. The cost of the first UN Emergency Force in 1956, however, was such a strain on the regular budget that a separate special account was established. This arrangement has been adopted for all subsequent peacekeeping operations except the Peacekeeping Force in Cyprus, which is financed in part from voluntary contributions. The scale of assessments for peacekeeping accounts is more progressive than for the regular budget, meaning that richer states (especially the permanent members of the Security Council) pay more and poorer states pay less. Under the present system the United Nations reimburses governments for the costs of the forces and materials they provide and pays for the direct costs of maintaining these forces and its own operations.

The amounts involved in financing the UN's regular budget and peacekeeping accounts are relatively small relative to government budgets in developed countries. They catapulted immediately after the end of the Cold War until a brake was applied in 1995 amid controversies over arrears, the decision to assign NATO direct responsibility for peacekeeping in Bosnia and expressions of concern that UN peacekeeping operations were too costly. Even at their peak, however, UN peacekeeping expenditures amount to a small fraction of world military expenditures (table 3).

Overall, the financial situation of the United Nations is one of chronic crisis. Besides being generally underfunded, it has perpetual cash-flow dilemmas and is constantly off balance. Troubles in Burundi, Liberia, Rwanda and other countries were not properly addressed by the Security Council because of lethargy and ostensibly financial considerations—with disastrous and tragic results. In addition to the cavalier treatment of UN finances by the world's richest members—which is the organization's most serious immediate predicament—the following are some of the concrete financial problems of the UN financing system:

- There are no penalties for late payments except the loss of the right to vote in the General Assembly if a government's arrears equal or exceed the amount it should have paid during the previous two years (Article 19 of the UN Charter).

- The United Nations reimburses governments that contribute troops and materials to peacekeeping operations or pays its missions directly, but payments are often late. Because cash-flow problems are typical and financial crises recurrent with the regular budget and the peacekeeping

TABLE 3

United Nations, United States and world military spending, 1986–99

(millions of nominal US dollars)

Year	UN regular budget[a]	UN peacekeeping budget[b]
1986	855.9	234.7
1987	855.9	233.0
1988	886.2	253.8
1989	886.2	618.1
1990	1,084.0	410.0
1991	1,084.0	480.2
1992	1,205.7	1,734.7
1993	1,205.7	3,008.0
1994	1,316.2	3,264.6
1995	1,316.2	3,260.0
1996	1,271.0	740.0
1997	1,271.0	1,295.2
1998	1,266.2	992.1
1999	1,266.2	826.0

a. Annualized figures of final biennial budgetary appropriations by the General Assembly.

b. 1996 figures are for the first six months. Figures from 1997 on are for a new 1 July–30 June financial reporting period for peacekeeping accounts.

c. Outlays are for 1 October–30 September US fiscal years.

d. Estimates are for calendar years.

Source: US Council of Economic Advisers 1998; US Arms Control and Disarmament Agency 1996; International Institute of Strategic Studies 1997; UN data.

reserve fund is usually depleted early in the year, the United Nations has to dip into the peacekeeping special accounts to avert bankruptcy.

- Having a special account for each peacekeeping operation is cumbersome and time-consuming.[18]
- The increasing costs of peacekeeping are the subject of complaints by both rich and poor countries and have been a factor in the Security Council's decisions to curtail operations in countries such as Angola, Liberia and Rwanda.

US national defence spending[c]	World military spending[d]	UN peacekeeping budget as % of	
		US spending	World spending
273,400	997,400	0.086	0.024
282,000	1,029,600	0.083	0.023
290,400	1,058,600	0.087	0.024
303,600	1,068,900	0.204	0.058
299,300	1,081,200	0.137	0.038
273,300	1,027,300	0.176	0.047
298,400	931,500	0.581	0.186
291,100	867,100	1.033	0.347
281,600	840,300	1.159	0.389
272,100	827,700	1.198	0.394
265,700	796,600	—	—
270,500		0.479	—
264,100		0.376	—
265,500		0.311	—

- The present system obviously cannot support the establishment and maintenance of a standing military force for emergencies and prolonged operations.

Certain conventional proposals for reform have been presented and could possibly cover the short term. These include charging interest or imposing fines for late payments, having a unified peacekeeping budget, authorizing the Secretary-General to obligate up to, say, one-third of the estimated cost of an operation once it is approved by the Security Council,[19] increasing the level of the Peacekeeping Reserve Fund (and having it funded), exhorting deadbeat countries to pay their arrears, depriving delinquent countries of their right to participate in the Security Council and General Assembly[20] and proposing that governments fund their contributions to the peacekeeping budget from their national defence budgets.

There is a pressing need for radical surgery to place the UN's peacekeeping and other operations on a sound financial footing.[21] The problems stem from the club-like nature of the UN's financing system. While this system may work for exclusive clubs, it cannot be effective for financing the provision of universal public goods.

CONCLUSION

World history, as noted at the beginning of this chapter, is strewn with myriad wars and their tragic and devastating results. Donald Kagan notes one estimate, made in 1968, that of the previous 3,421 years only 268 years were free of war (Kagan 1995, p. 4). While one may question the accuracy and methodology of such an estimate, there is no doubt that world history is largely a history of wars. Ruth Sivard has counted 250 wars between 1900 and 1995 (Sivard 1996, pp. 7–8 and 18–19; see also Sollenberg and Wallensteen 1998, p. 17). Their adverse effects include widespread destruction, devastation and dislocation of populations, simmering and escalating tensions, famines, devastation of economies, disabling injuries and loss of human life, which she estimates at 110 million for the period.

As this chapter has shown, the maintenance of global peace and security is the quintessential global public good, in both substance and form. As with most public goods and goods with positive externalities, it is a function best carried out on a global scale by the international public sector, and in appropriate regional situations by regional public sectors. Governments acting individually in their national self-interest are not apt to carry out this mandate, just as firms and individuals in national states act as free riders when it comes to sharing group responsibility. Thus international public institutions are the logical providers of global public goods—and the United Nations, in particular, is the logical guardian of peace and security.

Yet while traditional peacekeeping by national states acting on their own or as groups of allies acting beyond the groups' borders has been subject to market failures, the United Nations has been subject to government failures. This is a major obstacle to an effective institutional structure for the maintenance of peace and security, and there is an urgent need for international institutional reform. Such reform requires not simply action by the UN Secretariat but the active and genuine support of member governments, especially the world's big powers.

In other writings I have suggested an approach similar to that used by the General Motors Corporation's "Saturn" project as one that might provide a solution to the UN's capacity problems (see Mendez 1995a, 1997a). To compete with high-quality Japanese-made automobiles, General Motors decided to bypass its bureaucracy and establish a new and independent unit from scratch, unfettered by the stubborn problems of producing a high-quality car. Thus the Saturn project had its own management, employment and procurement methods, manufacturing processes, quality control and the like. The result was an automobile superior in quality to other General Motors products and competitive with high-quality imports. Such an approach could be adopted to strengthen the UN Secretariat's capacity to provide the public goods of peace and security.

The Saturn project demonstrates the possibilities of improving performance even in seemingly intractable situations. Effective peacekeeping and peace enforcement require highly specialized skills, equipment, personnel, communications, transport, technical operations and a variety of other elements. The UN's capacity for the physical provision of peace and security could be increased by establishing a new, specialized agency. The new institution would be involved only in the operational aspects of peacekeeping and peace enforcement and could also be empowered to subcontract certain activities. It would act as an executing agency for the Security Council and General Assembly, which would retain their responsibilities for policy-making, decision-making and financing. The agency could adopt fresh new practices and procedures to help ensure the vitality and efficiency of its operations. While starting from scratch, it could benefit from a wealth of accumulated knowledge and experience, of existing hardware and technology, and of trained military personnel who could apply their skills to the cause of world peace.

Support for the United Nations and its new specialized agency must include realistic mandates so that they are not placed in "lose-lose" situations. As noted, in its proper form peacekeeping should be accompanied by the conditions or continuum of actions necessary for sustained peace: relief and rehabilitation, assistance in transitional arrangements where public authority has broken down, governance and economic development. These complementary actions could be undertaken by other agencies of the UN system and other appropriate parties.

All exhortations and efforts to "reform" the United Nations will come to naught unless it is put on a sound financial footing—unless countries in arrears pay their debts and unless there is true financial reform. Reform will require concerted action on basic issues. While it is difficult to get self-interested states to agree on such action, it is not an unrealistic goal and has been done before. One need only review the international institutions and regimes established since the United Nations was created, including its specialized agencies, UNDP and the United Nations Children's Fund, the World Health Organization's smallpox eradication programme, the Law of the Sea, the Montreal Protocol, the General Agreement on Tariffs and Trade and World Trade Organization and others. Reforming the United Nations—including the behaviour of its members towards the organization—would be a decisive step in harnessing international free riding and establishing effective global governance.

The world would get closer to these goals if those involved in research, policy-making and advocacy were to work actively to promote the role and capacity of international public institutions to provide those essential goods and services not provided, or severely underprovided, under the present economic and political structure of the international community. Such action, I hope, will result from this collection of essays on the provision of global public goods as a new rationale for international cooperation.

ANNEX

UN PEACEKEEPING OPERATIONS, PAST AND PRESENT

1. **UNTSO:** United Nations Truce Supervision Organization (Middle East), June 1948–present.
Current mission strength: 168.
Budget in 1998: $26.4 million.

2. **UNMOGIP:** United Nations Military Observer Group in India and Pakistan, January 1949–present.
Current mission strength: 43.
Budget in 1998 : $7.8 million.

3. UNEF I: First United Nations Emergency Force (Middle East), November 1956–June 1967.

4. UNOGIL: United Nations Observation Group in Lebanon, June 1958–December 1958.

5. ONUC: United Nations Operation in the Congo, July 1960–June 1964.

6. UNSF: United Nations Security Force in West New Guinea (West Irian), October 1962–April 1963.

7. UNYOM: United Nations Yemen Observation Mission, July 1963–September 1964.

8. **UNFICYP:** United Nations Peacekeeping Force in Cyprus, March 1964–present.
Current mission strength: 1,267.
Cost: $43 million (UN assessment $22.7 million; voluntary contributions: Cyprus $13.8 million, Greece $6.5 million).

9. DOMREP: Mission of the Representative of the Secretary-General in the Dominican Republic, May 1965–October 1966.

10. UNIPOM: United Nations India-Pakistan Observation Mission, September 1965–March 1966.

11. UNEF II: Second United Nations Emergency Force (Middle East), October 1973–July 1979.

12. **UNDOF:** United Nations Disengagement Observer Force (Golan Heights), June 1974–present
Current mission strength: 1,046.
Cost: $35.1 million.

13. **UNIFIL:** United Nations Interim Force in Lebanon, June 1974–present
Current mission strength: 4,480.
Cost: $136.7 million.

14. UNGOMAP: United Nations Good Offices Mission in Afghanistan and Pakistan, May 1988–March 1990.

15. UNIIMOG: United Nations Iran-Iraq Military Observer Group, August 1988–February 1991.

16. UNAVEM I: United Nations Angola Verification Mission I, January 1989–June 1991.

17. UNTAG: United Nations Transition Assistance Group (Namibia), April 1989–June 1990.

18. ONUCA: United Nations Observer Group in Central America, November 1989–January 1992.

19. **UNIKOM:** United Nations Iraq-Kuwait Observation Mission, April 1991–present.
Current mission strength: 1,120. Cost: $50.6 million (two-thirds of it paid by Kuwait).

20. **MINURSO:** United Nations Mission for the Referendum in Western Sahara, April 1991–present. Current mission strength: 316. Cost: $65.1 million.

21. UNAVEM II: United Nations Angola Verification Mission II, June 1991–February 1995.

22. ONUSAL: United Nations Observer Mission in El Salvador, July 1991–April 1995.

23. UNAMIC: United Nations Advance Mission in Cambodia, October 1991–March 1992.

24. UNPROFOR: United Nations Protection Force (former Yugoslavia), March 1992–December 1995.

25. UNTAC: United Nations Transitional Authority in Cambodia, March 1992–September 1993.

26. UNOSOM I: United Nations Operation in Somalia I, April 1992–March 1993.

27. ONUMOZ: United Nations Operation in Mozambique, December 1992–December 1994.

28. UNOSOM II: United Nations Operation in Somalia II, March 1993–March 1995.

29. UNOMUR: United Nations Observer Mission Uganda-Rwanda, June 1993–September 1994.

30. UNOMIG: United Nations Observer Mission in Georgia (Central Asia), August 1993–present.
Current mission strength: 81. Cost: $20.7 million.

31. UNOMIL: United Nations Observer Force in Liberia, September 1993–September 1997.

32. UNMIH: United Nations Mission in Haiti, September 1993–June 1996.

33. UNAMIR: United Nations Assistance Mission in Rwanda, October 1993–March 1996. .

34. UNASOG: United Nations Aouzou Strip Observer Group (Chad-Libya), May 1994–June 1994.

35. **UNMOT:** United Nations Mission of Observers in Tajikistan, December 1994–present.
Current mission strength: 83.
Cost: $22.3 million.

36. UNAVEM III: United Nations Angola Verification Mission III, February 1995–June 1997.

37. UNCRO: United Nations Confidence Restoration Operation in Croatia, March 1995–January 1996.

38. **UNPREDEP:** United Nations Preventive Deployment Force (former Yugoslav Republic of Macedonia), March 1995–present.
Current mission strength: 809.
Cost: $22.3 million.

39. **UNMIBH:** United Nations Mission in Bosnia and Herzegovina, December 1995–present.
Current mission strength: 1,962.
Cost: $190.9 million.

40. UNTAES: United Nations Transitional Administration for Eastern Slavonia, Baranja and Western Sirmium (Croatia), January 1996–January 1998.

41. **UNMOP:** United Nations Mission of Observers in Prevlaka (Croatia), January 1996–present.
Current mission strength: 28.
Costs are included under UNMIBH.

42. UNSMIH: United Nations Support Mission in Haiti, July 1996–July 1997.

43. MINUGUA: United Nations Verification Mission in Guatemala, January–May 1997.

44. **MONUA:** United Nations Observer Mission in Angola, July 1997–present.
Current mission strength: 1,213.
Cost: $140.8 million.

45. UNTMIH: United Nations Transition Mission in Haiti, August–November 1997.

46. **MIPONUH:** United Nations Civilian Police Mission in Haiti, December 1997–present Current mission strength: 284. Cost: $18.5 million.

48. **MINURCA:** United Nations Mission in the Central African Republic, April 1998–present Current mission strength: 1, 379. Cost: $28.8 million.

47. **UNITED NATIONS CIVILIAN POLICE SUPPORT GROUP** (Danube region of Croatia), January 1998–present. Current mission strength: 210. Cost: $7.1 million.

49. **UNOMSIL:** United Nations Observer Mission in Sierra Leone, July 1998–present. Mission not yet complete. Estimated cost: $18.3 million.

Note: Current peacekeeping operations (shown above in bold) are as of 31 July 1998. Costs are estimates for 1 July 1998 to 30 June 1999, the new reporting period for peacekeeping budgets, except for UNTSO and UNMOGIP, which are funded from the regular budget.

Summary of peacekeeping operations, personnel and financing

Personnel (as of 30 June 1998)

Military and civilian police personnel serving 14,570

   (10,658 troops, 2,984 civilian police and 928 military observers)

Countries contributing military and civilian police personnel 76

Fatalities 1,551

Financial Aspects

Estimated total cost of operations
from 1948 to 30 June 1998 ....$18.3 billion

Estimated cost of operations
from 1 July 1998 to 30 June 1999 ....$826 million

Outstanding contributions to peacekeeping operations
on 30 April 1998 ....$1.55 billion

Source: United Nations Departments of Peace-keeping Operations and Public Information (1996).

NOTES

1. Properly speaking, a public good is not nonrival with any other good but rather does not involve any rivalry among its consumers and is therefore nonrivalrous. It is consumers who may be rival or nonrival with each other in the use of the good. I have also noted this in previous writings (Mendez 1997b, pp. 332–33).

2. John Stuart Mill (1921 [1848], pp. 387–89) was the first to make this observation. Coase (1974) notes periods in the past when lighthouses were provided privately, and Sandler (1977) notes how defence can be rivalrous when one region of a country is being defended rather than another. If one looks hard enough, many public goods situations can be shown to lack some formal characteristics. While the ideal type is rare, it does serve as a useful concept.

3. As with "rival", the term "excludable" is misleading because it describes the consumer, not the good. Thus the good may be "exclusionary," indicating that certain consumers may be excluded from using it, or "nonexclusionary" if no one is excluded.

4. Martha Nussbaum laments that "it is unfortunately difficult for economists to undertake a searching philosophical critique of foundations over which so much technically sophisticated work has by now been built" (Nussbaum 1998, p. 17).

5. As noted below, other putative benefits include national pride, the multiplier effects of defence expenditures, other stimuli to the economy, and scientific and technological progress through research and development.

6. Russett, Oneal and Davis (1998) and Sandler (1977) point out that defence may involve choosing which countries, frontiers, bridges, cities, and the like to defend while leaving others less protected and as such fails the pure public goods test. "Deterrence," on the other hand, is arguably closer to a public good in that once forces are in place they provide protection for everyone formally under the protective umbrella. Although the term also begs the question of its goodness, deterrence—if it in fact served its defined purpose—would be a public good not only for citizens of the country or alliance that produces it but also for other countries and even the world at large as beneficiaries of the resulting peace. Thus deterrence could be a global and not only a national public good.

7. The capacity for massive retaliation, a concept espoused by US Secretary of State John Foster Dulles, is not necessarily a US monopoly, because other countries with nuclear and delivery capabilities can also cause extensive damage.

8. This interest is recent. For instance, Mueller's (1979) survey of the literature on public choice makes no reference to the military-industrial establishment. Neither does the recent Cullis and Jones (1998) textbook. Compare Sandler and Hartley (1995).

9. Like balance of power theory, hegemonic theory is chameleonic, with varying interpretations in economics (such as Kindleberger), political science (Gramsci, Hobbes, Keohane), history (P. Kennedy, Thucydides) and other fields (Kipling). The theory seems to have found credibility only among Western theorists. Grunberg (1990) presents an interesting interpretation of the mythology of benevolent hegemony.

10. Russett (1985) gives an authoritative and devastating critique of some of the better-known hegemonic theories.

11. There are variations of this model, which may be generalized as follows: if a gang of arrested criminals is to be interrogated, it would serve their collective good if no member confessed or informed on the others. Each prisoner, however, would have the incentive to do so when interrogated separately if he or she were promised leniency or freedom—even if the others were punished more severely. But if each prisoner behaved in this self-interested way, all of them would be worse off.

12. She notes that "the economic security of individuals, and the political security of groups, are ends of a rather different sort" (Rothschild 1995, p. 98).

13. These estimates are based on the Stockholm Institute for Peace Research's (SIPRI) definition of major armed conflict: "prolonged combat between the military forces of two or more governments, or of one government and at least one organized armed group, and incurring the battle-related deaths of at least 1000 people for the duration of the conflict". The latest SIPRI statistics indicate 25 major armed conflicts in 24 locations around the world in 1997, with all but one—between India and Pakistan—being internal. The number of conflicts dropped from 27 in 1996 and 32 in 1989, when the conflict statistics were started (Sollenberg and Wallensteen 1998, p. 17). Thus intrastate conflicts have declined in recent years, especially if one factors in the increased number of states in the system.

14. This figure is based on estimates provided by the Statistical Unit of the UN High Commissioner for Refugees.

15. The one exception provided for was "measures against any enemy state"—that is, any enemy of the Second World War UN alliance.

16. An example is the offer by the United States to finance half the cost of an African crisis response force, which African governments rejected, asserting their preference for UN auspices.

17. This is one of the recommendations of the report of the Independent Working Group on the Future of the United Nations (1995). For an analysis and clarification of the conceptual distinctions and consequences of the different kinds of UN activities in this area, see pages 19–25 of the report.

18. As noted, the General Assembly has asked the Secretary-General to provide estimates of total peacekeeping costs for each year. Small countries under-

standably prefer having a separate account for each peacekeeping operation, which maintains their prerogative of reviewing each operation ordered by an otherwise completely uncheckable Security Council.

19. Under the Charter only the General Assembly can approve budgets. According to standing arrangements the Secretary-General has to formulate budget proposals for each peacekeeping operation and present them to two intergovernmental committees before they are submitted for General Assembly approval. There is room for streamlining, provided it addresses the objections of poor countries, which want to preserve this prerogative of the General Assembly as a potentially useful balance to the otherwise absolute power of the Security Council.

20. It is not certain whether this move would require amending the Charter or could be mandated under their rules of procedure or through other means. In any case, it would be difficult to obtain the agreement of member governments.

21. A detailed discussion of a new system of financing is beyond the scope of this chapter. I have made proposals in other writings, some of which are listed in the references.

References

Atkinson, Anthony B., and Joseph E. Stiglitz. 1980. *Lectures on Public Economics.* London: McGraw Hill.

Boutros-Ghali, Boutros. 1995. *An Agenda for Peace.* 2nd ed. New York: United Nations.

Coase, Ronald H. 1974. "The Lighthouse in Economics." *Journal of Law and Economics* 17(October): 357–76.

Cullis, John, and Philip Jones. 1998. *Public Finance and Public Choice.* 2nd ed. New York: Oxford University Press.

Grunberg, Isabelle. 1990. "Exploring the 'Myth' of Hegemonic Stability." *International Organization* 44(4): 431–77.

Gulick, Edward Vose. 1955. *Europe's Classical Balance of Power.* Ithaca, NY: Cornell University Press.

Hyman, David. 1990. *Public Finance: A Contemporary Application of Theory to Policy.* 3rd ed. Chicago, IL: Dryden.

Independent Working Group on the Future of the United Nations. 1995. *The United Nations in Its Second Half-Century.* A project supported by the Ford Foundation and the Yale University Secretariat. New York: Ford Foundation.

International Institute for Strategic Studies. 1997. *The Military Balance 1997/98.* London: Oxford University Press.

Jervis, Robert. 1976. *Perception and Misperception in International Politics.* Princeton, NJ: Princeton University Press.

Kagan, Donald. 1995. *On the Origins of War and the Preservation of Peace.* New York: Doubleday.

Keller, William W. 1995. *Arm in Arm: The Political Economy of the Global Arms Trade.* New York: Basic Books.

Kindleberger, Charles P. 1986. "International Public Goods without World Government." *American Economic Review* 5(1): 1–13.

Mankiw, N. Gregory. 1997. *Principles of Economics.* New York: Dryden Press.

Mansfield, Edwin. 1989. *Principles of Microeconomics.* 6th ed. New York: Norton.

Mendez, Ruben P. 1992. *International Public Finance: A New Perspective on Global Relations.* New York: Oxford University Press.

————. 1995a. "Harnessing the Global Foreign Currency Market: Proposal for a Foreign Currency Exchange (FXE)." In Commission on Global Governance, *Issues in Global Governance.* Amsterdam: Kluwer Law International.

————. 1995b. "The Provision and Financing of Universal Public Goods." In Desai, Meghnad and Paul Redfern, eds., *Global Governance: Ethics and Economics of the World Order.* London: Pinter.

————. 1997a. "Financing the United Nations and the International Public Sector: Problems and Reform." *Global Governance* 3: 283–310.

————. 1997b. "War and Peace from a Perspective of International Public Economics." In Jürgen Brauer and William Gissy, eds., *Economics of Peace and Conflict.* Aldershot, UK: Avebury.

Mill, John Stuart. 1921 [1848]. In W.J. Ashley, ed., *Principles of Political Economy.* London: Longmans.

Mueller, Dennis C. 1979. *Public Choice.* Cambridge: Cambridge University Press.

Nussbaum, Martha. 1998. "Family Models [letter to the editor]." *Times Literary Supplement.* 5 June.

Rosen, Harvey. 1988. *Public Finance.* 2nd ed. New York: Irwin.

Rothschild, Emma. 1995. "The Changing Nature of Security." In Commission on Global Governance, *Issues in Global Governance.* Amsterdam: Kluwer Law International.

Russett, Bruce. 1985. "The Mysterious Case of Vanishing Hegemony; Or, Is Mark Twain Really Dead?" *International Organization* 39(2): 207–31.

Russett, Bruce, John R. Oneal and David R. Davis. 1998. "The Third Leg of the Kantian Tripod for Peace: International Organizations and Militarized Disputes, 1950–85." *International Organization* 52(3): 441–67.

Samuelson, Paul A. 1954. "The Pure Theory of Public Expenditure." *Review of Economics and Statistics* 36 (November): 387–89.

Samuelson, Paul A., and William D. Nordhaus. 1989. *Economics.* 13th ed. New York: McGraw Hill.

Sandler, Todd. 1977. "Impurity of Defense: An Application to the Economics of Alliances." *Kyklos* 30(3): 443–60.

Sandler, Todd, and Keith Hartley. 1995. *The Economics of Defense.* Cambridge: Cambridge University Press.

Schwartz, Stephen I. 1998. *Atomic Audit: The Costs and Consequences of U.S. Nuclear Weapons, 1940–1995.* Washington, DC: Brookings Institution.

Sheehan, Michael. 1996. *The Balance of Power: History and Theory.* London: Routledge.

SIPRI (Stockholm International Peace Research Institute). 1997 and 1998. *SIPRI Yearbooks.* New York: Oxford University Press.

Sivard, Ruth Leger. 1996. *World Military and Social Expenditures 1996.* 16th ed. Washington, DC: World Priorities.

Sollenberg, Margareta, and Peter Wallensteen. 1998. "Major Armed Conflicts." In Stockholm International Peace Research Institute, S*IPRI Yearbook* 1998. New York: Oxford University Press.

Stiglitz, Joseph E. 1988. *Economics of the Public Sector.* 2nd ed. New York: W.W. Norton.

United Nations. 1945. *Charter of the United Nations and Statute of the International Court of Justice* (including amendments to Articles 23, 27, 61 (twice) and 109). New York.

———. 1996. *Proposed Budgetary Requirements of Each Peace-keeping Operation for the Period from 1 July 1996 to 30 June 1997; Note by the Secretary-General.* Document A/C.5/50/63. Presented to the Fifth Committee under agenda item 138(a), "Administrative and Budgetary Aspects of the Financing of the United Nations Peace-Keeping Operations." New York.

———. 1998. *Proposed Budgetary Requirements of Each Peacekeeping Operation for the Period from 1 July 1998 to 30 June 1999; Note by the Secretary-General.* Document A/C.5/52/52. Presented to the Fifth Committee under agenda item 142 (a), "Administrative and Budgetary Aspects of the Financing of the United Nations peacekeeping operations." New York.

———. Various years. *Programme Budget, Supplement(s) No. 6* of the *Official Records of the General Assembly* for the 42nd through 52nd sessions (document symbols A/[# of session]/6). New York.

———. Various years. General Assembly resolutions. New York.

United Nations Department of Public Information. 1996. *United Nations Peace-Keeping Operations, Background Note.* DPI/1634/Rev.2. Plus unrestricted data provided by the Department of Peace-Keeping Operations and the United Nations High Commissioner for Refugees.

US Arms Control and Disarmament Agency. 1996. *World Military Expenditures and Arms Transfers,* 1995. Washington, DC.

US Council of Economic Advisers. 1998. *The Economic Report of the President* 1998. Washington, DC: Government Printing Office.

Urquhart, Brian. 1987. *A Life in Peace and War.* New York: Harper and Row.

POLICY
IMPLICATIONS

INTERNATIONAL PUBLIC GOODS AND THE CASE FOR FOREIGN AID

RAJSHRI JAYARAMAN AND RAVI KANBUR

Public discourse and debate on foreign aid, defined as official flows of resources to developing countries, have undergone an interesting transformation since the fall of the Berlin wall and the end of the Cold War. Twenty years ago the rationale for foreign aid was security or solidarity. Official flows—military assistance and flows for development purposes—helped keep countries in one of the two main global blocs. But there was also a strong sentiment in industrial countries that resource transfers from rich to poor countries were a moral obligation. These two influences led to high and increasing aid flows.

Today the Cold War rationale has disappeared. And "aid fatigue" has gripped the other major rationale—the result of budget pressures in donor countries and considerable scepticism about the efficacy of foreign aid in actually helping poor countries, particularly the poor. This scepticism is unusual in that it is found on both the political right and the political left. On the right there has been a revival of an old argument that foreign aid, because it consists of flows to governments from governments, simply swells bloated and inefficient public sectors—an argument that has gained strength as private capital flows have vastly outstripped public flows in the aggregate (Bauer and Yamey 1981). On the left there have been similar concerns about flows going to corrupt elites in recipient countries and about the use of flows to leverage market-oriented development strategies, as well as a preference for channelling flows through the newly resurgent civil society in developing countries (Oxfam 1995).

The analytical literature on the efficacy of aid in achieving its stated objectives has provided further grist to this mill. It seems clear that the "middle ground" has shifted in the past decade, from the relatively positive assessments of Cassen (1987) and Riddell (1987) to the scepticism of Boone (1996) and

Burnside and Dollar (1997). Burnside and Dollar, for example, conclude that there is generally no correlation between aid flows and development as measured by growth in per capita GNP (similar results hold in the literature for other indicators, such as infant mortality rates). Detailed econometric analysis reveals this to be the result of a combination of forces. While aid does increase growth rates when it flows into good policy environments, it typically does not flow into such environments—or induce such environments to emerge.

Although there are variations among aid donors, this is a devastating critique given that, at least since the 1980s, the international community has tried to apply conditionality on aid flows (recent theoretical analyses of conditionality include Coate and Morris 1996 and Svensson 1997b). This outcome also calls into question the left-leaning critique that aid has failed because it has been directed toward the wrong model of development (so if only the model was right, conditional aid would help development). But what these recent results suggest most strongly is that aid cannot leverage domestic policy change. This has in turn led to the discussion and literature on "ownership" and on how this is to be identified and monitored (Gwin and Nelson 1997).

It is perhaps not surprising that, at the end of this exhausting analytical and policy debate on the efficacy of conventional aid, some in the policy and analytical realm have turned to the newly emerging area of international public goods—almost in relief, one feels! There is no question that the rapidly globalizing world has created major problems of cross-border and global externalities, and highlighted others. Population, environment, migration and refugees, drugs and crime and disease control are all topics likely to emerge at any conference that deals with the foreign policy agenda of the future, and are all areas where developing countries can affect industrial countries (Cassen 1997). This view characterizes the emergence of a newly articulated rationale for foreign aid, closer to the security than to the solidarity agenda. It rests much more on the direct spillovers of the lack of development in poor countries on to the well-being of rich countries.

But there is also a strand in this literature recognizing that attempts to deal with cross-border externalities may well involve implicit transfers. As Schelling (1997, p. 8) notes, "any action [in rich countries] to combat global warming will be, intended or not, a foreign aid program". He goes on to make the intriguing suggestion that it might be more efficient for the United States to reduce global warming gases and allow Bangladesh, say, a higher emission level, rather than make financial transfers in the old-fashioned mode. Similarly, Jamison, Frenk and Knaul (1998, p. 515) argue that "continuing global integration reduces the control that governments have over a growing number of health status determinants that derive from the international transfer of risks. In addition, many of the means to solve health problems—such as knowledge and technology—have become international public commodities that no individual government or corporation is likely to produce in adequate measure on its own".

Through an interesting dynamic, therefore, we find ourselves at the intersection of two literatures—that on conventional foreign aid and that on global externalities and public goods.

- Could international public goods and cross-border spillovers provide a revived rationale for old-fashioned transfers intended to spur development in poor countries?
- When faced with the choice of making transfers or contributing to an international public good, what should a donor country do—even if its objectives are governed by self-interest rather than solidarity?
- What happens to the many issues (like conditionality and ownership) in old-fashioned solidarity-driven aid, so exhaustively and exhaustingly debated over the past 20 years or more, in this new world of international public goods?

The objective of this chapter is to begin the discussion of these questions, which seem to have been neglected in the rush to embrace international public goods as a new rationale for maintaining international development cooperation and even traditional aid flows. We set out a simple model of interaction between two countries that share a common public good and pose the problem of the richer "donor" country deciding between making a transfer or contributing to a public good, while being concerned only about the impact of outcomes on its own well-being. We next analyse the problem with different specifications of the public good. We conclude by discussing the implications of this analysis and the areas for further research.

THE BASIC MODEL AND THE NEUTRALITY RESULT

To think systematically about the interaction between international public goods and conventional aid transfers—in light of the literature on donor-recipient interactions (such as Svensson 1997a and 1997b) and that on contributions to public goods (such as Cornes and Sandler 1996)—the simplest model needs the following components:

- Two agents with differing endowments.
- The possibility of direct transfers from one (the richer, say the donor) to the other (the poorer, say the recipient).
- A public good formed out of contributions of the two parties but which both parties enjoy.
- A setup where the donor is the "Stackleberg leader" and the decision on transfers versus contributing to the international public good is made to maximize the donor's objective function, taking into account the recipient's reaction function.

The literature on private contributions to public goods provides a model that comes very close to the above specification, except that instead of a Stackleberg leader-follower setup, a Nash equilibrium between the two players is used as the main tool of analysis. We start with a brief statement of the Nash equilibrium framework—to allow us to introduce notation and serve as a benchmark for the more appropriate Stackleberg formulation.

In the basic Nash model two goods enter each agent's utility function. One is a private good, the other is an international public good. Given their incomes, countries play a noncooperative game in contributing towards a single international public good—in other words, a good whose consumption is nonexcludable and nonrival. This is a seemingly natural way to model the interaction between the donor and the recipient. It allows for an analysis of the effect of an income transfer from one agent to another, and it captures the essence of the international public goods problem. Each agent optimizes his or her objective function, taking other agents' strategies as given. Contributions to the public good are made simultaneously by each country. The Nash equilibrium is then characterized by the intersection of the best response functions of each player. For the sake of clarity, analysis will be restricted to the case where there is one donor and one recipient. Without loss of generality, suppose hereafter that agent 1 is the donor and agent 2 is the recipient. The two-player game can be described as follows:

Game 1: Simultaneous contributions to an international public good

Definition. A game $P1$ in voluntary, simultaneous contributions to a public good consists of a set of players (I), strategies $g_i \in R_+$ and payoffs $\left(u_i, \forall i \in I\right)$ such that

$$i \in I = [1, 2]$$
$$g_i \in R_+$$

$u_i = \max u_i(x_i, G)$

subject to $x_i + G = w_i + g_{-i}$

$x_i \geq 0$

where i is 1 or 2, g_i is government i's contribution to the international public good, x_i is government i's consumption of a private good, w_i is government i's wealth, u_i is government i's value function, G is $(g_1 + g_2)$, which is the public good enjoyed by both parties, and g_{-i} is $(G - g_i)$.

Assumption 1. Utility is continuous, increasing in both arguments and strictly concave.

Denote agent i's demand function for the public good by $f_i(m)$, where $(m = g_{-i} + w_i)$ is i's full income.

Assumption 2.[1] $0 < f_i'(m) < 1$.

Definition. A Nash equilibrium of P1 is a vector (g_1, g_2) such that for $i = 1, 2$ (g_i^*, x_i^*) solves

Max $u_i(x_i, g_i + g_{-i}^*)$
x_i, g_i

subject to $x_i + g_i = w_i$

$x_i, g_i \geq 0$

A key assumption in the specification is that the public good is simply the sum of the two contributions. As will be seen, this additive formulation drives many of the basic results, and departures from additivity change the results considerably.

For the purpose of P1, we restrict our attention to the case where both governments contribute a positive amount to the public good in equilibrium—the Nash equilibrium is an interior one.[2] Within this framework, foreign aid might be conceptualized, as has been done by Sandler (1997) and others, as a transfer of Δw from government 1 (the donor) to government 2. Consider the following comparative statistics exercise. Suppose we are originally at an interior Nash equilibrium. Now suppose a "world government" mandates the donor to make a transfer $\Delta w < g_1^*$ to the recipient. After the redistribution it can be shown that there is a new Nash equilibrium in which both the recipient and the donor change their contributions to the public good by precisely the same amount by which their wealth has changed. Consumption of both the public and private goods, and hence indirect utilities, are therefore unaltered in the new Nash equilibrium.

This is the so-called "neutrality theorem" (see Warr 1983 and Bergstrom, Blume and Varian 1986). What it means for our purposes is that aid in the form of a wealth transfer from donor to recipient has no effect on international public goods provision or on donor and recipient well-being. Furthermore, the recipient views any increase in the donor's contribution towards the public good—say, Δg_1—as identical to a wealth transfer of $\Delta w = \Delta g_1$. There is a second sort of neutrality result here in that agents are indifferent between aid in the form of public good contributions and aid in the form of transfers.

The Nash framework is a useful means of conceptualizing how the presence of an international public good alters the case for conventional resource transfers. But the Nash approach, standard in the literature on public goods, is problematic here for at least two reasons. First, in the foreign aid arena, it is natural to think of the "donor" as a "leader". The notion of a world government that "orders" a transfer from donor to recipient, rationalizing the Nash comparative statistic exercise, does not sit well with the aid literature. Indeed, almost all the theoretical literature on conditionality is in the Stackleberg leader-follower framework.

Second and related, it was argued earlier that conventional resource transfers and public good contributions could be regarded as dual instruments. They should thus ostensibly be considered simultaneously as part of a coherent strategy if we are to be capable of addressing the question of balance between contributions and direct transfers. These features can be better captured in a Stackleberg leadership game in which the recipient plays the best response to the donor's transfer and contribution level, and the donor chooses transfer and contribution levels that maximize his own welfare, taking into account the recipient's reaction function (see Pedersen 1996, who models foreign aid as a Stackleberg game). The Stackleberg game in contributions may be modelled as follows.

Game 2: Stackleberg—donor is the leader and recipient is the follower

$$P2 = \left[I, \left(g_i, u_i \right)_{i=1,2} \right] \text{ where:}$$

The recipient (follower) solves:

Max $u_2(x_2, g_1 + g_2)$

x_2, g_2

   subject to $x_2 + g_2 = w_2$

   $x_2, g_2 \geq 0$

Denote the recipient's reaction function by

$$g_2(g_1) = \text{argmax } u_2(x_2, g_1 + g_2)$$

Then, the donor (leader) solves

Max $u_1[x_1, g_1 + g_2(g_1)]$

x_1, g_1

   subject to $x_1 + g_1 = w_1$

   $x_1, g_1 \geq 0$

Definition. A Stackleberg equilibrium of $P2$ is a contribution g_1 and a reaction function $g_2(\cdot)$ such that (g_1^*, x_1^*) solves the donor's problem and $(g_2(g_1^*), x_2^*)$ solves the recipient's problem.

We have argued that $P2$ is a more appropriate formulation for foreign aid than $P1$. But formulating the problem in this way does not get rid of the neutrality outcome. If the same conditions mentioned in the Nash equilibrium neutrality theorem are satisfied, the Stackleberg equilibrium is also characterized by neutrality following an aid transfer (for a proof, see Bruce 1990 or Sandler 1992). In particular, starting from an interior Stackleberg equilibrium to $P2$ (and provided the conditions from the Nash neutrality result are also satisfied): a comparative static redistribution of income from 1 to 2 will leave public goods provision as well as welfare unaltered, and agents will be indifferent between aid in the form of increased public goods contributions and direct income transfers. The donor will not care, in its own interests, whether it gives "conventional" aid or contributes to international efforts to mitigate cross-border externalities.

The neutrality result is a sobering one for those who would advocate a transition from conventional aid to international public goods contributions—or those who would strengthen the case for conventional aid in the name of cross-border spillovers. It says that the two are perfect substitutes. Clearly, therefore, we must explore deviations from this benchmark if we are to obtain interesting insights on the relationships between conventional aid and contributions to international public goods. The next section takes up this story.

TYPES OF INTERNATIONAL PUBLIC GOODS AND THE CASE FOR FOREIGN AID

As noted, the neutrality result renders moot the choice between conventional aid and contributions to international public goods. But as is well known from the public goods literature (see Cornes and Sandler 1996), neutrality can be overturned when the technology for the public good is not simply additive.[3] Following the literature, we consider three special cases.

- The first case considers outcomes when there are differing efficiencies in the production of the public good. An example would be pollution abatement—it may be cheaper for country 1 to produce clean air than it is for country 2. This can be captured in the simplest possible manner by supposing that the total public goods provision is still $G = g_1 + g_2$, but that each country's budget constraint is of the form $(x_i + \pi_i g_i = w_i)$, where $\pi_i \neq \pi_j$. In particular, $\pi_i < \pi_j$ means that country i produces the public good more efficiently than country j.

- The second case is a "min" technology, where $G = \min[g_1, g_2]$. This relates directly to Hirshleifer's (1983) notion of a "weakest link" technology in public goods provision, with a good example in the international public goods arena being infectious disease control.

- The third case is a "max"(or "best-shot") technology, where $G = \max[g_1, g_2]$. This type of view would be pertinent to high-tech research and development (R&D)—with the obvious caveat that the R&D in question is in fact a public good.[4]

Non-neutrality results in the Nash game for alternative public goods production technologies have been documented elsewhere, most notably in Cornes and Sandler (1996) and Sandler (1997). Here we summarize simplified versions for the three cases mentioned above.

- When two countries produce a public good with an additive technology (clean air) with differing efficiencies, non-neutrality results. Furthermore, a transfer from 1 to 2 increases (decreases) public goods provision and indirect utility of the donor and recipient if and only if the recipient produces clean air more (less) efficiently than the donor.

- Suppose agents are identical, differing only in wealth levels, where $w_1 > w_2$. Then, in the case of a weakest-link technology, a transfer from donor to recipient that does not fully equalize incomes increases public

425

goods provision and makes the recipient unambiguously better off. It also makes the donor better off if the increased utility from increased public goods provision more than offsets the reduction in utility following the donor's diminished private goods consumption.

- Suppose agents are identical, differing only in wealth levels, where $w_1 > w_2$. Then, in the case of a best-shot technology, a transfer from donor to recipient that does not fully equalize incomes reduces public goods provision and makes the donor worse off. But the recipient will be better off if the increased utility from increased private goods consumption more than offsets the reduction in utility following the diminished public goods provision. (For proofs of these propositions, see Jayaraman and Kanbur 1998.)

The fact that in the Nash case we can talk about whether the donor is better off or not following a transfer highlights the problem with the Nash approach: why should a donor make a transfer if it makes the donor worse off? So we really do have to move to a Stackleberg framework. The Nash excursion turns out to have been useful, however, because the results in the Stackleberg case basically follow the Nash intuitions.

Analogous to the Nash case, non-neutrality arises in the Stackleberg case when the public good technology is nonadditive or efficiencies vary. As before, we consider three cases—differing efficiencies, weakest-link and best shot technologies—but this time in a Stackleberg framework. The game is a little more complex than that described in $P2$ above because the donor's strategy consists of an income transfer t to agent 2 (the recipient) as well as its contribution to the international public good. But in some cases, rather than have the donor maximize directly over t, we deduce the optimal transfer from the best response function of the recipient and the indirect utility function of the donor.

In the presence of corner solutions in the transfer contributions strategy of the donor, this approach simplifies the analysis considerably. The recipient is the follower, and the strategy simply is a contribution to the public good given the donor's transfer and contribution level. Here we summarize the results in three propositions and briefly outline the intuition behind the results. Proofs of these propositions are in the appendix.

Differing efficiencies $(\pi_1 \neq \pi_2)$, $\pi_i \in (0, 1)$, $G = g_1 + g_2$
Proposition 1. In a Stackleberg game with differing efficiencies any transfer $(t < g_1^*)$ from agent 1 to agent 2 will be characterized by non-neutrality. Furthermore, faced with a choice between income transfers and con-

tributions towards the public good, the donor will set $t = 0$ when $\pi_2 > \pi_1$, and $g_1 = 0$ when $\pi_2 < \pi_1$.

So when the donor and the recipient produce the public good with differing efficiencies, a corner solution in "transfers" will result. More specifically, the basic intuition is that if the donor is more efficient, it should set direct transfers equal to 0 and concentrate solely on public goods provision as a means of enhancing welfare. Inasmuch as the recipient directly benefits from the public good, such contributions on the part of the donor may be regarded as a more efficient form of foreign aid, echoing the sentiment of Schelling (1997).

Weakest link $G = min[g_1, g_2]$

Proposition 2. In a Stackleberg framework with identical preferences, characterized by a weakest-link technology, there are conditions under which a new equilibrium exists with positive transfers and increased public goods provision that Pareto dominates the pre-transfer equilibrium.

Thus when the technology is of the weakest-link variety, the donor will want to use a combination of direct resource transfers and contributions to the public good. The reasons for this should be quite intuitive. If the public good is a normal good, contributions to the good increase with income. The "min" technology means that to ensure a given level of contributions, both countries must contribute towards public goods provision. So, if the donor wishes to attain a given level of provision, it must encourage the recipient to contribute to it through income transfers, and must itself make contributions—complementarity of contributions is what drives this result.

Best-shot $G = max[g_1, g_2]$

Proposition 3. In a Stackleberg framework with a best-shot technology and identical agents, the Stackleberg equilibrium will be characterized by zero direct income transfers.

The outcome here is no different than that in the Nash equilibrium. It is clear that with a "max" technology, the donor is better off making no direct income transfer to the recipient, but rather, devoting its resources to public goods investments. Given the technology, this result should be relatively intuitive. Even with identical preferences, the degree of difference in income levels between donor and recipient typically implies that public goods provision is likely to be determined by donor rather than recipient contributions—even when some income transfer is made. The donor therefore has no reason to believe that the recipient will devote any direct income transfers towards public goods contributions and therefore has no self-interest in making such transfers.

DISCUSSION AND CONCLUSION

To those who might have thought that cross-border externalities and international public goods would lead to a significant strengthening of the argument for conventional aid—not by relying on solidarity but by appealing to the self-interest of the donor—the results of this chapter are only half comforting. It turns out that for international public goods to come to the rescue of conventional aid through this channel, one of two situations must hold:

- The public good must be an additive combination of the two contributions, and the recipient country must be more efficient at producing the public good than the donor country.
- The total public good must be largely determined by the lower of the two contributions.

If, on the other hand, the public good is additive in individual contributions but the donor country is more efficient in producing it, or the total public good is determined by the larger of the two contributions, it is in the donor's interest to minimize the conventional transfer. These cases highlight the fact that the international public goods argument for conventional aid is more complex than meets the eye. Depending on the nature of the public good, a variety of outcomes are possible.

It is worth stressing the importance of setting out exactly the nature of the public good. Start with fundamental genomic research. This has the characteristics of a max technology, and there is an argument for richer countries to undertake this research and make the findings freely available to poorer countries. But three issues arise. Will the research be specific to the needs of poorer countries? Will the findings indeed be made freely available to poorer countries? Even if they are, will the poorer countries have the capacity to use them?

These questions take us deeper into the nature of the good at hand. The fact that different types of research (on tropical or temperate agriculture, for example) affect rich and poor countries differently cautions us against lumping things together in a single "public goods" category. The second question reminds us that the publicness or otherwise of a good is technologically as well as socially and politically determined—privately conducted research into tropical crops, with private patents for seeds and so on, is not what we mean by the "max" technology specification. The third question reminds us also to think about the whole process before specifying the public good.

Take infectious diseases as another example. The development of vaccines, and fundamental research into the nature and evolution of such diseases, is probably a "max" technology and, according to our analysis, the donor would be well advised to conduct such research and make the results freely available to the recipient. But implementation of an immunization programme is probably a "min" technology—no matter how well developed the programme is in the donor country, ultimately the level of immunization in the recipient country will determine the global level of infection. The focus should thus be on improving the recipient's capacity and willingness to implement an immunization programme.

Now consider a class of public goods that seems to satisfy the additive technology characterization—clean air, or its converse the public bad, greenhouse gases. Here, whoever reduces their emission, the whole world benefits. Is it better for the United States to undertake the reduction, at some cost to its income level, or to give Bangladesh foreign aid and rely on it to cut its emissions as it gets wealthier? The answer depends on which of the two countries can reduce emission at least cost per unit reduction.

This is an empirical question. But if it turns out that the United States is more efficient, it would be rational for the United States to achieve emission reductions not through making Bangladesh richer and then relying indirectly on Bangladesh's choice to use some of this increased wealth to get cleaner air—but by directly reducing its (the Unites States') own emissions. But if the issue is biodiversity, and the focus is on the biodiversity present in, say, the Amazon basin, then almost by definition the United States is less efficient in preserving this than is Brazil. The United States, in its own interests, will have to rely on giving Brazil the resources to preserve biodiversity in the Amazon.

Thus the presence of international public goods does not necessarily strengthen the case for conventional aid across the board. But it should also be clear that the presence of international public goods by no means eliminates the need to worry about the "conventional" problems of "conventional" aid—since it is really only in areas where implementation is not needed in the recipient country that the donor country can go it alone. In the min technology, certainly, even optimally the donor will wish to make transfers as well as contribute to the public good. The efficiency of these transfers then becomes a concern of the donor, and we are back to the literature on conditionality. For example, the way that transfers have been modelled here assumes full fungibility of resources. Clearly, the donor could get a bigger bang for its buck by trying to tie transfers to expenditures on infectious disease control. But to do this there needs to be an effective contracting system with sanctions for non-compliance.

The literature on conditionality has pointed, for example, to the "Samaritan's dilemma" of a donor who cares about the well-being of the recipient (see Buchanan 1975 and Coate 1995), hence the inability to implement contracted sanctions and the inefficiency of the time inconsistency that results. These issues are not avoided— indeed, they are perhaps sharpened—even when the donor only cares about consequences for itself. At the same time, when current efficiency differences in public goods production dictate that the donor specializes in contributing to the public good rather than making transfers, there is still the question, not modelled in this chapter, of whether it is better to try to improve the efficiency of public good production in the recipient country—but this takes us right back to implementation issues in the recipient country.

The basic objective of this chapter is to insert a note of caution into the current excitement about international public goods as a new rationale for aid. International public goods certainly provide a rationale for international cooperation based on self-interest. But only in certain circumstances do they provide a rationale for donors to continue conventional transfers based on self-interest. At the same time, in the actual implementation of many public goods interventions, conditionality, fungibility, monitoring. sanctions and the like are ever present.

To investigate these issues, further research will have to develop richer models that incorporate a combination of altruistic and self-interested motives in making transfers, choices between contributing to different types of public goods, and contractual agreements on the transfers and on the public goods contributions, and enforcement mechanisms. This will allow us, among other things, to address the question of whether, even when altruism is involved, it is better for the donor country to express it through contributions to the types of public goods that do not lead it into the tangle of conditionality—essentially, by supplying public goods that it can produce and then make freely available.

APPENDIX

PROOF OF PROPOSITION 1: DIFFERING EFFICIENCIES

Assume that
$$(\pi_1 \neq \pi_2), [\pi_i \in (0, 1)], G = g_1 + g_2$$

Denote agent 2's reaction function in the Stackleberg game by $G = f[(w_2 + t)/\pi_2 + g_1]$. Then agent 1's (the leader's) problem is

Max $\quad\quad\quad u_1\{x_1, f[(w_2 + t)/\pi_2 + g_1]\}$
x_1, g_1

$$\text{subject to } x_1/\pi_1 + g_1 = (w_1 - t)/\pi_1$$
$$x_1, g_1 \geq 0$$

Let "stars" denote pre-transfer Stackleberg equilibrium levels and "primes" denote post-transfer Stackleberg equilibrium levels.

Neutrality requires that $G' = G^*$—that is, that aggregate public goods provision remain unaltered following the transfer and that consumption of the private goods remain unaltered (that is, that individuals' indirect utilities are unaltered). The first of these conditions implies that

$$G' = f\left[\left(w_2 + t\right)\Big/\pi_2 + g_1'\right] = f\left[\left(w_2\right)\Big/\pi_2 + g_1^*\right] = G^*$$

By the strict convexity of preferences, this can only hold if

$$g_1' = g_1^* - t/\pi_2$$

Note however, that differing efficiencies implies that $t/\pi_2 \neq t/\pi_1$. Therefore, when the above equality holds, the donor is strictly better off when $\pi_2 < \pi_1$ and strictly worse off when $\pi_2 > \pi_1$. This contradiction completes the proof of nonneutrality.

For the second half of the proposition, consider the utility of the donor, keeping G fixed at G^*. Before the transfer the donor's indirect utility is

$$u_1\left[w_1 - \pi_1 g_1^*, \ f\left(w_2 / \pi_2 + g_1^*\right)\right]$$

After the transfer the donor's indirect utility is

$$u_1\left[w_1 - \pi_1 g_1^* + \left(\pi_1 t\right) / \pi_2 - t, \ f\left(w_2 / \pi_2 + g_1^*\right)\right]$$

Suppose $\pi_2 > \pi_1$. Then it should be clear from the expression above that a utility-maximizing donor will wish to set $t = 0$. Suppose, alternatively, that $\pi_2 < \pi_1$. Then, analogously, the donor should set $g_1 = 0$.

PROOF OF PROPOSITION 2: WEAKEST LINK $G = \min[g_1, g_2]$

Suppose agents 1 and 2 have identical preferences and differ only in wealth levels, where $w_1 > w_2$. Then, clearly:

$$G^* = \min(g_1^*, g_2^*) = \text{argmax } u_2(w_2 - g_2, g_2)$$

Now suppose there was a transfer from 1 to 2 that was not perfectly equalizing (that is, $w_1 - w_2 > t$). Then, clearly:

$$G' = \min(g_1', g_2') = \text{argmax } u_2(w_2 + t - g_2, g_2)$$

Clearly, agent 2 is better off following a transfer and by assumption 2, $G' > G^*$.

As before, denote agent 2's demand for the public good by $f(w_2 + t)$. Then agent 1's problem is

$$\text{Max } u_1\left[w_1 - t - f\left(w_2 + t\right), \ f\left(w_2 + t\right)\right]$$
$$t \geq 0$$

To see when it would be expedient for the donor to make a transfer to the recipient, consider the first-order condition to the donor's maximization problem, assuming that the second-order condition is strictly negative.

$$- \left\{ \delta u_1 \left[w_1 - t - f(w_2 + t),\ f(w_2 + t) \right] / \delta x_1 \right\} \left[1 + f'(w_2 + t) \right] +$$
$$\left\{ \delta u_1 \left[w_1 - t - f(w_2 + t),\ f(w_2 + t) \right] / \delta G \right\} \left[f'(w_2 + t) \right] \le 0$$

$$\lim_{t \to 0} - \left\{ \delta u_1 \left[w_1 - t - f(w_2 + t),\ f(w_2 + t) \right] / \delta x_1 \right\} \left[1 + f'(w_2 + t) \right] +$$
$$\left\{ \delta u_1 \left[w_1 - t - f(w_2 + t),\ f(w_2 + t) \right] / \delta G \right\} \left[f'(w_2 + t) \right]$$

$$= - \left\{ \delta u_1 \left[w_1 - f(w_2),\ f(w_2) \right] / \delta x_1 \right\} \left[1 + f'(w_2) \right] +$$
$$\left\{ \delta u_1 \left[w_1 - f(w_2),\ f(w_2) \right] / \delta G \right\} \left[f'(w_2) \right]$$

Agent 1 will therefore find it worthwhile making a positive transfer if and only if:

$$\left\{ \delta u_1 \left[w_1 - f(w_2),\ f(w_2) \right] / \delta x_1 \right\} / \left\{ \delta u_1 \left[w_1 - f(w_2),\ f(w_2) \right] / \delta G \right\} <$$
$$\left[f'(w_2) \right] / \left[1 + f'(w_2) \right]$$

Therefore, when this condition is satisfied, both agents are made better off by the transfer.

PROOF OF PROPOSITION 3: BEST-SHOT $G = \max[g_1, g_2]$

When agents are identical, differing only in terms of income, we know that in equilibrium $g_2 = 0$. Then agent 1's problem becomes:

Max $u(w_1 - t - g_1, g_1)$
g_1, t

$$\text{subject to} \qquad g_1 \ge 0$$
$$t \ge 0$$

It is clear that the second constraint will be binding. So, g_1 will solve the first-order condition:

$$\delta u_1(x_1,\ g_1) / \delta x_1 = \delta u_1(x_1,\ g_1) / \delta g_1$$

NOTES

The authors are grateful to Todd Sandler and to seminar participants at Cornell University, the United Nations Development Programme (UNDP) and Overseas Development Council (ODC) for helpful comments. The work on this paper is part of a larger project at the ODC on the future of multilateral assistance.

1. This assumption simply requires that both the private and the public goods be normal goods and follows Andreoni (1988) and Bergstrom, Blume and Varian (1986).

2. The literature also considers corner solutions (see for instance, Cornes and Sandler 1996 and Bergstrom, Blume and Varian 1986). These will be mentioned later but not be considered in detail in the Nash framework.

3. Even a technology of the form $f(\Sigma g_i)$ generates the neutrality result.

4. Note that in the "max" and "min" technology cases, assumption 2 must be modified slightly to $0 < f_i'(w_i) < 1$.

REFERENCES

Andreoni, James. 1988. "Privately Provided Public Goods in a Large Economy: The Limits of Altruism." *Journal of Public Economics* 31(1): 57–73.

Bauer, Peter, and Basil Yamey. 1981. "The Political Economy of Foreign Aid." *Lloyds Bank Review* 142: 1–14.

Bergstrom, Theodore C., Lawrence Blume and Hal Varian. 1986. "On the Private Provision of Public Goods." *Journal of Public Economics* 29(1): 25–49.

Boone, Peter. 1996. "Politics and the Effectiveness of Foreign Aid." *European Economic Review* 40: 289–329.

Bruce, Neil. 1990. "Defence Expenditures by Countries in Allied and Adversarial Relationships." *Defence Economics* 1(3): 179–95.

Buchanan, James M. 1975. "The Samaritan's Dilemma." In Edmund S. Phelps, ed. *Altruism, Morality and Economic Theory.* New York: Russell Sage.

Burnside, Craig, and David Dollar. 1997. "Aid Spurs Growth—In a Sound Policy Environment." *Finance and Development* (December): 4–7.

Cassen, Robert. 1987. *Does Aid Work?* Oxford: Oxford University Press.

———. 1997. " The Case for Concessional Aid." *OECF Newsletter* (September). Overseas Economic Cooperation Fund, Tokyo.

Coate, Stephen. 1995. "Altruism, the Samaritan's Dilemma, and Government Transfer Policy." *American Economic Review* 85(1): 46–57.

Coate, Stephen, and Stephen Morris. 1996. "Policy Conditionality." World Bank, Washington, DC.

Cornes, Richard, and Todd Sandler. 1996. *The Theory of Externalities, Public Goods and Club Goods.* 2nd ed. Cambridge: Cambridge University Press.

Gwin, Catherine, and Joan Nelson, eds. 1997. *Perspectives on Aid and Development.* Washington, DC: Overseas Development Council.

Hirshleifer, Jack. 1983. "From Weakest-Link to Best-Shot: The Voluntary Provision of Public Goods." *Public Choice* 41: 371–86.

Jamison, Dean T., Julio Frenk and Felicia Knaul. 1998. "International Collective Action in Health: Objectives, Functions and Rationale." *Lancet* 35(9101): 514–17.

Jayaraman, Rajshri, and Ravi Kanbur. 1998. "International Public Goods and the Case for Foreign Aid." Cornell University, Ithaca, NY.

Oxfam. 1995. *The Oxfam Poverty Report.* Oxford.

Pedersen, Karl R. 1996. "Aid, Investment and Incentives." *Scandinavian Journal of Economics* 98(3): 423–38.

Riddell, Roger C. 1987. *Foreign Aid Reconsidered.* Baltimore, MD: Johns Hopkins University Press.

Sandler, Todd. 1992. *Collective Action: Theory and Applications.* Ann Arbor: University of Michigan.

————. 1997. *Global Challenges: An Approach to Environmental, Political, and Economic Problems.* Cambridge: Cambridge University Press.

Schelling, Thomas. 1997. "The Cost of Combating Global Warming: Facing the Tradeoffs." *Foreign Affairs* 76(6): 8–14.

Svensson, Jakob. 1997a. "Foreign Aid and Rent-Seeking." Policy Research Working Paper 1880. World Bank, Washington, DC.

————. 1997b. "When Is Foreign Aid Policy Credible? Aid Dependence and Conditionality." Policy Research Working Paper 1740. World Bank, Washington, DC.

Warr, Peter G. 1983. "The Private Provision of a Public Good Is Independent of the Distribution of Income." *Economics Letters* 13: 207–11.

REGIONAL PUBLIC GOODS IN INTERNATIONAL ASSISTANCE

Lisa D. Cook and Jeffrey Sachs

One of the basic lessons of modern economic development is that the public sector should focus its scarce energies, talents and resources on those activities that will not be provided adequately by private markets. Such activities include those involving a clear natural monopoly (law enforcement), problems of collective action because of the nonrival or nonexcludable nature of goods (basic research, national defence, macroeconomic policy, definition of property rights) or serious externalities not easily overcome by the assignment of property rights because of high transactions costs (infectious disease control, watershed management, fisheries management). It is also increasingly appreciated that international development assistance should have a similar focus, supporting desirable activities that will not be provided adequately either by private markets or by the local and national governments that are the recipients of such aid. While some aid is simply redistributional in purpose (such as humanitarian assistance in the wake of a natural disaster), a considerable amount of aid aims to correct market failures through the provision of public goods.

During the 1980s and 1990s aid programmes increasingly became a kind of surrogate national government, with outside agencies (usually led by the Bretton Woods institutions) attempting to foster the provision of public goods at the local and national levels. The basic motivation, sometimes explicit but more often implicit, was that national governments could not be trusted to provide public goods within their own territories as a result of some kind of "political failure". In this vision the International Monetary Fund (IMF) and the World Bank would lead reform on behalf of the national polity because the government receiving the aid was too weak, too corrupt, too prone to backsliding or too incompetent to mobilize the needed actions on its own. Thus during the 1980s and especially in the first half of the 1990s aid was closely tied to policy conditions to ensure that the aid was linked to appropriate policies and the appropri-

436

ate provision of public goods by the national government. In principle, if the aid was not used in the way agreed with the outside agencies, it would be cut off.

We know from a large number of studies and frustrating case histories that this model is deeply flawed. First, money is fungible. Even if foreign agencies succeed in ensuring that particular funds are directed towards particular purposes, they cannot be sure that the aid funds are truly incremental in support of those purposes. Thus an outside agency may desire to boost spending on education, only to find that the international aid dollars directed towards education are offset by a reduction in the government's own budgetary outlays on education. In this way foreign aid becomes a mere income transfer, not a promoter of public goods. Second, donor agencies have their own policy agendas that may have little overall coherence. Each donor is driven by its own local politics. The sum of the aid does not add up to coherent development assistance. Third, conditionality is extremely weak. Aid agencies often do not know enough about local conditions to make strong demands on the recipients about the use of the funds. And even when they do, the agencies generally lack the incentive to carry through on threats to cut off aid when the monies are misspent, because the recipient countries may be politically important to key donor countries. Fourth, it seems that many World Bank and IMF loans are simply defensive loans, in the sense that they are made so that countries will pay back previous loans from these institutions.

A new approach to aid is needed. In our view donors should get back to basics, to ensure that aid really delivers public goods that otherwise will not be provided either by markets or recipient governments in the absence of the aid. Without a doubt, there is one hugely neglected area of public goods: goods that can only be provided effectively at the level of the region (defined here to mean a grouping of neighbouring governments)[1] or on a global scale. The first category may be called "regional public goods" and the second category "international public goods". This chapter focuses on regional public goods, partly because international public goods are covered in other chapters and partly because very little work has been undertaken on the actual and desirable levels of public goods provision at the regional level.

THE CASE FOR REGIONAL PUBLIC GOODS

It is easy to offer pertinent examples of regional public goods—that is, public goods that must be delivered on the supranational level by a number of national governments acting in concert. A nonexhaustive list includes:

- *Environment.* Many issues of environmental management inherently cut across national boundaries. Watershed management inevitably requires the cooperation of all countries along the watershed to define issues of property rights, monitoring, analysis and enforcement. Many kinds of pollution (acid rain, effluent runoffs) cross national borders and so involve one country imposing external costs on another. Management of natural reserves often cuts across national boundaries (Serengeti-Masai Mara, Peru-Ecuador Amazonia, Nicaraguan-Honduran Atlantic Coast rainforest). Scientific research on issues of ecozone management (biodiversity, desertification, impacts of climate change) are inherently regional or global public goods because the benefits of research accrue to all who share the ecozone, which typically involves a number of neighbouring countries.

- *Public health.* Management of infectious disease inherently involves cross-border issues because migrant workers typically are pathways for the spread of disease. This is emphatically and disastrously true for the greatest epidemic now striking Africa—the human immunodeficiency virus (HIV) and acquired immune deficiency syndrome (AIDS). It is also true for more traditional and devastating diseases such as malaria. Large migratory populations in many parts of the developing world (East Africa, West Africa, Southern Africa, South-East Asia, the Middle East) also mean that national health systems are overwhelmed by demands from non-nationals. Cross-country financial or administrative arrangements rarely meet the health needs of migratory populations. Basic research on diseases endemic to a particular region (for example, onchocerciasis in West Africa) raises issues of regional cooperation, again because of the lack of ability and incentive for any one country to bear the costs of effective research and development on its own. Intellectual property rights raise cross-border issues as well, because the incentive for private pharmaceutical companies to develop effective responses to endemic diseases depends on the intellectual property rights regime governing an entire affected region, not just an individual country.

- *Financial market regulation and stabilization.* Cross-border links between financial markets are inevitable because financial markets are characterized by various increasing returns to scale in their operations (as vehicles for managing risk as well as for reducing unit costs of financial services). These links raise important questions about the regulatory environment because the quality of oversight of financial markets in one country will sharply affect financial markets in neighbouring countries. Similarly, a financial panic that starts in one country can quickly spread to neighbouring countries, as occurred in the "tequila crisis" following Mexico's 1994 devaluation and in the East Asian crisis of 1997–98. For these reasons, regional groupings of governments are increasingly looking for ways to harmonize their financial regulations and to ensure that all countries in a region are appropriately monitoring their financial policies, lest the mistakes in one redound to the detriment of the others.

- *Transport.* The coordination of cross-border transport networks is crucial to economic development, yet extremely difficult to manage in practice. The historical record suggests, for example, that inland countries are deeply disadvantaged relative to coastal countries, in part because of inadequate cooperation between them. Roads that lead from the inland to ports are in poor shape because the coastal country often lacks the incentive to build, maintain and police roads on behalf of the inland country. In general, the location and maintenance of roads is largely driven by local politics rather than by the optimization of the transport network. Similarly, a single national port facility may serve a number of countries, raising claims for regional governance over basic utilization of the port (private concessioning, operations of customs agents, policing and so on).

- *Telecommunications and data transmission.* As with asphalt highways, information highways pose tremendously important cross-border issues. Satellite systems and fibre-optic cables service regions rather than nations. The regional scale of competition among providers of telecommunications services will determine, to a significant extent, the pricing and quality of service within any individual nation.

- *Power grids.* Power systems at the national level almost always require regional cooperation, management and financing. This is plainly true in the case of hydroelectric power, where rivers are not only the source of power but also often the border of neighbouring countries. Similarly, countries that tap hydroelectric power upstream may have huge negative effects on downstream countries that require cooperative solutions. Electricity is increasingly transmitted across national borders by regionally linked grids, enhancing competition in energy provision and lowering unit costs. Pipelines typically must cross national borders to take oil from inland sites (as in Central Asia) to world markets, provoking difficult regional issues of economics and security.

- *Agricultural research and extension.* Agriculture research has deep public goods aspects, and these often inhere to the regional rather than national scale. The development of new seed varieties, for example, generally requires strong public sector support because hybrid seeds are nonrival and generally nonexcludable goods, and therefore the benefits of hybrid seed development cannot easily be appropriated by the original research team. Similar regional issues inhere to a wide range of agricultural problems: weather monitoring stations, weather modelling and forecasting, crop insurance, conservation research and management, and biotechnology research.

- *Law enforcement.* Many types of criminal activities (drug trafficking, car theft, financial fraud, tax evasion, money laundering) operate at a regional scale, often with one country serving as a transit point or safe haven for criminal operations in another country. In many activities law enforcement is only as good as its weakest point. A road from an interior state to a coastal port will be nearly useless to the interior if the road is underpoliced in the coastal state.

In each of these areas public goods arise at all levels of governance: international, regional, national and even local. Public health measures may involve vaccine research appropriately financed and undertaken at the international level, testing and inoculation programmes at the regional level (given specificity of disease types within regions, high levels of cross-border mobility and so on), public health system maintenance at the national level and operational control of health clinics at the local level. Similarly, in the area of agricultural productivity, basic biotechnology research on tropical foodstuffs may take place in an international research institute, specific seed development for a regional ecozone (such as the African Sahel) at the regional level, agricultural extension planning at the national level and implementation at the local level. As a third example, in the area of financial market regulation, public goods provision involves international norms (Article VIII standards on currency convertibility under the IMF charter, proposed standards on cross-border capital flows), regional undertakings (regional stock markets, supervisory agencies and accounting standards), national macroeconomic management and local government fiscal control within the national arrangements.

One extremely pertinent general category of regional public goods is scientific research on regionally focused problems of health, agriculture and environmental management. For well-known reasons, basic research is almost always a public good, at least in part. This is mainly because the gains from basic scientific research cannot easily be appropriated by the researchers (and even when they can be—say, through patent rights that give a temporary monopoly on the supply of a new discovery—there are often huge efficiency losses resulting from the underutilization and monopoly pricing of the new discovery).

Recent research on development problems carried out at the Harvard Institute for International Development stresses that most developing countries, and particularly those in the tropics, face profound problems in public health, agriculture and environment that will require new scientific and technological approaches that cannot simply be "borrowed" or taken from advanced economies (Gallup and Sachs 1999; Bloom and Sachs 1999). Advanced country scientific research pays relatively scant attention to tropical problems such as malaria, schistosomiasis, helminths or tropical agriculture. Moreover, health and agricultural technologies developed in advanced economies are not directly applicable in the tropics. And scientific funding for problems of tropical health, agriculture and environment is a pittance of the funds mobilized for temperate zone problems in these areas. To name just one striking example, the 1989 expenditures of the US state of Georgia on agricultural research stations exceeded the budgets of each of the five largest global research centres on tropical agriculture, such as the International Rice Research Institute (IRRI).[2]

As poor as the delivery of public goods may be at the national and local levels, it is even more exiguous at the regional and international levels. In many cases regional needs are particularly neglected because while international programmes, research institutes and the like have been created, they lack the needed counterpart institutions and funding at the regional level. This hypothesis is not easy to prove because there is little careful cataloguing of the needs and actual provision of public goods at the international, regional, national and local levels. Indeed, part of the hope of this chapter is to spur a much more careful empirical analysis of this claim. In any event, we have good reason to believe that regional public goods are generally under-provided—and often completely neglected. Transactions costs in managing public goods provision at the national level are already very high. At the regional level, they are often insurmountable. Why?

- Neighbouring states are often in direct military conflict, and thus are busy uprooting regional infrastructure (cross-border bridges, roads, power systems) rather than creating it.
- Neighbouring states are often in diplomatic competition ("cold war") when they are not in outright military competition. Thus Chile and Bolivia have lacked diplomatic relations since the War of the Pacific (1879) despite the fact that Chile provides Bolivia's natural outlet to the Pacific Ocean. The main road from Bolivia to the Pacific Port of Arica was unpaved for a century, until 1995. Similarly, the notorious feuding in East Africa has left interior states cut off from natural outlets to world markets.
- Regional bodies are often politically weak and dramatically underfunded by participating national governments. As a US Congressional leader once famously observed, "all politics is local". In the nationalistic political environment that has gripped and still grips many countries, cross-border cooperation is looked on with extreme suspicion—consider US

public opinion towards the North American Free Trade Agreement (NAFTA)—and is typically extremely underfunded. Even the European Union, after 40 years of successful European integration, commands resources on the scale of around 1% of GDP of member governments, or about one-fiftieth of the resources mobilized at the national level.

• International assistance programmes are mostly directed to national governments rather than supranational entities. As documented below, this pattern is partly the result of the charters of aid-granting institutions, both at the international level (for example, the IMF and World Bank) and at the national level (for example, donor agencies in high-income countries). It is also the result of the fact that the political weakness of regional bodies becomes self-fulfilling. Donor agencies do not give to "weak" regional bodies, and as a result those bodies do not gain strength, capacity and financial viability.

The result is that around the world, regional bodies that aim to provide regional public goods are underfunded and often nothing short of incapacitated. In Africa, for example, regional groupings such as the Southern African Development Community (SADC), East African Community and similar bodies in West and Central Africa are extremely promising in concept. But in practice they generally fall far short of their aims because of limited authority (which is jealously guarded by national politicians) and, even more damaging, weak national capacity as a result of meagre budgets and uncertain future planning periods. One finds little difference in most other parts of the world, as with institutions for Central American integration, the Andean Pact and the Association for South-East Asian Nations (ASEAN). In most cases the stated regional goals are admirable, and the funding of regional activities, minuscule.

MODEST EVIDENCE ON THE PROVISION OF REGIONAL PUBLIC GOODS

Despite the magnitude of international assistance, surprisingly little can be gleaned about its composition from publicly available data. We do not really know, for example, how much foreign aid is directed at public goods provision rather than at activities that could be directly financed by the private sector. Most observers recognize, for example, that many World Bank activities in infrastructure financing essentially substitute for project financing that could be raised in private markets. Indeed, in many cases a project is the object of direct competition between the World Bank and private firms. These private firms often complain bitterly that the Bank has edged them out of activities for which they are well-suited. Even when money is spent on health or education, it is not really clear whether the funds are substitutes for private activity. And as noted, even when international assistance is directed at public goods provision, it is analytically difficult to discern whether the project financing is truly incremental. Recent evidence regarding African aid, for example, suggests that a considerable amount of aid funds are fungible, and thus more in the character of generalized income transfers than incremental provision of public goods.

The insufficiency of the empirical record is largely the result of two shortcomings:

*   *Lack of systematic classification of aid programmes.* While the Organisation for Economic Co-operation and Development (OECD) has made major strides in the classification of international assistance, such classifications remain incomplete, especially for the purposes of systematic analysis. The OECD does not allocate multilateral aid programmes on the same basis as bilateral aid programmes, and OECD data certainly do not distinguish between the provision of public goods and private goods.

*   *Lack of distinction between local, national and regional projects.* There is no attempt to classify aid projects according to whether such aid is directed at national or local projects versus regional projects. For example, some assistance programmes involve coordinated transfers to neighbouring countries so that the two countries can coordinate the provision of public goods. Thus international aid might finance a hydroelectric plant on the river boundary of two countries, designed to provide electricity to both. Such aid would typically be classified as two national projects rather than one integrated regional project.

Despite these severe limitations, it is possible to look at the provision of international assistance for regional public goods. We have sought evidence, albeit indirect and incomplete, on the amount of funding that international assistance programmes direct towards regional as opposed to national efforts. There seems, in short, to be precious little such funding, though there are certainly some notable cases, and success stories, of regional assistance.

Bilateral assistance

The most comprehensive source on bilateral assistance is the OECD Development Assistance Committee (DAC) reporting system (OECD 1998). We use this source to classify aid programmes on a national or regional basis. We define a national programme as aid from a donor government or multilateral institution to a single recipient country. We classify a programme as a regional assistance programme if it is allocated to a region but unallocated by country. This accounting is imperfect, but it is the best that we can do with the published data. It will misclassify aid programmes in three ways. First, bilateral aid to individual countries can be closely coordinated, so that in effect the aid is providing a regional public good. Second, a regional aid programme (unallocated by country) could be providing national public goods to countries in the region, without a true regional component. Third, some aid that is unallocated by country and region (and is designated simply as "LDCs [least developed countries] unspecified" in DAC reports) may include regional assistance.

Net official development assistance (from countries and multilateral institutions) in 1996 is shown in table 1. We see immediately that regional aid programmes unallocated by country represent a very small portion of total assistance: just 7.4% in Africa, for example.

TABLE 1

Net official development assistance by region, 1996

Recipient region	Country	Unallocated	Total	Unallocated as % of total
Europe	2,371	122	2,493	4.9
Africa				
North	3,308	54	3,362	1.6
Sub-Saharan	15,831	915	16,746	5.5
Total	19,140	1,538[a]	20,678	7.4
Americas				
North and Central	3,198	71	3,269	2.2
South	3,110	114	3,224	3.5
Total	6,308	1,877	8,185	2.3
Asia				
Middle East	4,696	94	4,790	2.0
South and Central	6,643	20	6,663	0.3
Far East	6,848	88	6,936	1.3
Total	18,186	710	18,896	3.8
Oceania	1,667	116	1,783	6.5

a. The total unallocated for Africa is not the sum of unallocated for North Africa and Sub-Saharan Africa because there is also $569 million of unspecified aid for Africa as a whole, not separated into North and Sub-Saharan Africa. Similar discrepancies occur in the other regions.
Source: OECD 1998.

World Bank

Under its charter the World Bank is to lend to member countries. Some Bank projects take on a regional public goods character, however, through the coordination of country-level programmes. Indeed, several projects in recent years have been "conceived as border-insensitive, jointly and severally implemented, with identical financing arrangements, and bundled and approved by the Board as a single venture" (Bhattasali 1998). Examples of such projects include agricultural research and dissemination within the purview of the Consultative Group on International Agricultural Research (CGIAR); water projects such as the Aral Sea Basin Program for Water and Environmental Management, which coordinates activities among Kazakhstan, the Kyrgyz Republic, Tajikistan, Turkmenistan and Uzbekistan; disease control efforts such as the Onchocerciasis Control Programme, which coordinated efforts among Benin, Burkina Faso, Côte d'Ivoire, Ghana, Mali, Niger and Togo; and infrastructure projects such as the rehabilitation of the Abidjan-Ouagadougou-Kaya railway. Given the published data, however, it is not possible to estimate overall World Bank lending for regional programmes. Based on discussions with Bank officials, and in view of the difficulties under the Bank's charter of lending to regional bodies, we believe that region-based lending is very small, though with notable successes (such as the Onchocerciasis Control Programme).

United Nations

The United Nations was established in large part to solve problems of international coordination and to enhance regional and international cooperation. The 81 UN organizations, including the World Health Organization, United Nations High Commissioner for Refugees (UNHCR), United Nations Educational, Scientific and Cultural Organization (UNESCO), and UNDP, are core providers of regional and international public goods. This is clearly the case in programmes of disease control (World Health Organization), refugee resettlement (UNHCR), dispute resolution and peacekeeping, and so forth. Yet even with the United Nations it is not possible on the basis of published data to ascertain the actual flow of funds directed towards national-level programmes and those that are truly regional or international in character.

Regional development banks

Regional development banks, such as the Inter-American Development Bank (IDB) and African Development Bank (AfDB), would seem to be ideally suited to help finance the provision of regional public goods. Regrettably, this generally seems not to be the case, as these banks have increasingly modelled their lending activities to match the country-level projects of the World Bank. As one AfDB staff member reportedly said, "we trade on our African identity, as an institution close to Africa's problems, but all we do is repeat what the World Bank has done with fewer resources and less efficiency" (*The Economist* 1998). The AfDB reported the allocation of African Development Fund loans and grants during 1974–97 using a breakdown among three categories of countries (lowest-income, higher-income, and highest-income borrowing members) as well as "multinational" projects. On this basis it appears that 98.1% of the allocations went to country programmes, and just 1.9% went to multinational projects (AfDB 1998, p. 7). This is especially ironic for a region rife with regional problems involving transport (given that Africa has the highest proportion of landlocked countries of any region), infectious disease, cross-border conflict and so on.

The IDB seems to have a growing portfolio of regional projects, though it is still modest relative to overall lending. As of 1997 the IDB had made 58 regional loans totalling $2.77 billion, with cumulative disbursements of $1.71 billion. Total IDB disbursements were $61.4 billion, so regional projects amounted to 4.5% of the total. In 1997 the IDB made 18 regional loans totalling $833 million in commitments, compared with $6.02 billion in overall loans. Thus regional loans accounted for 13.8% of the total, suggesting an increase in region-based lending (IADB 1998). Regional projects in 1997 included:

- Regional infrastructure (Bolivia-Brazil gas pipeline, Central American electric interconnection system).
- Regional financial markets (credit programme for the Central American Bank for Economic Integration).
- Research and development (technology programme for agriculture and natural resource management, digital mapping and geographic information systems).
- Regional policy reform (support for the Free Trade Area of the Americas Initiative).
- Regional training initiatives (fellowships and other support for advanced training of public officials).

RECOMMENDATIONS FOR ENHANCING THE PROVISION OF REGIONAL PUBLIC GOODS

The shortfall of international assistance in the area of regional public goods is stark, even though it cannot be precisely determined with published data.

Nonetheless, it is clear that international donors, both bilateral and multilateral, focus the vast bulk of their attention and financial resources on country-level programmes. Country-level programmes are sometimes coordinated across borders, but this is the exception rather than the rule. And there is very little direct financing of regional institutions, such as the secretariats of regional bodies like SADC, or projects initiated and overseen by such regional institutions.

This chapter is a very preliminary look at the issue, meant to spur further analysis and action. We therefore recommend the following five operational steps in the near term:

- Coordination between UNDP, the World Bank, the OECD and regional development banks to develop a more accurate accounting of the allocation of activities between national projects and regional projects.

- Development of analytical methods within UNDP, the World Bank and the OECD to examine the allocation of aid flows between public goods, private goods and income transfers.

- Review of the governing principles of the World Bank, IMF, UN agencies, regional development banks and principal bilateral donor agencies to examine biases or legal limitations on the provision of aid to regional projects and regional bodies.

- Canvassing by UNDP of regional bodies (SADC, Economic Community of West African States, Mercosur, ASEAN, Andean Pact and so on), to determine operating budgets, regional projects under their supervision and support received from national and international agencies.

- A series of UNDP workshops around the world to explore policy options for increased regional public goods provision in key areas such as infrastructure, public health and research and development.

Sceptics of regional public goods provision repeatedly point to the current weakness of regional bodies such as SADC in fulfilling the mandate of public goods provision. This is a mistaken, static view of the issue. Regional bodies will inherently be weak until they are given both the mandate and—especially—the financing to do more. Who would have thought, at the conclusion of the Second World War, that France and Germany, after three bitter wars in 75 years, would form the nucleus of an unprecedentedly effective regional grouping in Western Europe? And yet the European Union found its origins in decisions by the United States to channel postwar reconstruction aid through a regional body (the Organization for European Economic Cooperation, or OEEC, later OECD) in the context of the Marshall Plan. The Marshall Plan, together with a group of European visionaries, effectively created European regional cooperation and public goods provision by pressing the war-torn continent to work together as a condition of receiving US assistance.

In this context, the possibility of creating a new set of OEECs (or OECDs) for the major developing regions has been raised. The idea is a powerful one that draws strength from the success of the Marshall Plan. On a practical level, assuming that the decision were rightly made to vastly enhance the provision of regional public goods, it would often be desirable to build on existing (admittedly weak and underfinanced) regional bodies rather than reinvent them from the start.

Our common longer-term goal should surely be to work towards a reassessment and redesign of the international aid strategy in general, to make sure that international assistance serves the most important needs of the developing world—mainly by focusing on activities that cannot otherwise be addressed by national and local governments or private actors. Public action, urgently and amply supported, will be crucial in generating the ideas and technologies needed to overcome the crises in health, demography, environment and food productivity facing so much of the developing world in coming years.

Notes

1. Even the term "regional" is fraught with ambiguity. In some usages "regional" refers to a grouping of neighbouring countries like the Central American Common Market (CACM) or Southern African Development Community (SADC). In other cases "regional" is reserved for continent-wide activities (such as within Africa) while "subregional" is applied to groups like the CACM and SADC. We use the first sense of the term.

2. Eicher (1994 p. 89). IRRI's budget for core and special projects was $36.2 million, compared with Georgia's budget of $40 million. The combined US state spending on agricultural research stations by the 10 largest programmes— California, Florida, New York, Texas, Georgia, North Carolina, Minnesota, Nebraska, Louisiana, Ohio—exceeded by a wide margin the combined spending by the 10 largest international research centres on tropical agriculture—IRRI, International Crops Research Institute for the Semi-Arid Tropics (ICRISAT), International Maize and Wheat Improvement Center (CIMMYT), International Center for Tropical Agriculture (CIAT), International Institute of Tropical Agriculture (IITA), International Center for Agricultural Research in the Dry Areas (ICARDA), International Potato Center (CIP), International Livestock Centre for Africa (ILCA), International Livestock Research in Animal Diseases (ILRAD) and International Food Policy Research Institute (IFPRI).

REFERENCES

AfDB (African Development Bank)/African Development Fund. 1998. *Annual Report 1997*. Abidjan.

Bhattasali, Deepak. 1998. Personal communication. World Bank, Africa Region, Washington, DC. 24 June.

Bloom, David, and Jeffrey Sachs. 1999. "Geography, Demography, and Economic Growth in Africa." *Brookings Papers on Economic Activity 2*. Washington, DC: Brookings Institution.

The Economist. 1998. "The Bank That Likes to Say No." 6 June.

Eicher, Carl K. 1994. "Building Productive and International Agricultural Research Systems." In Vernon W. Ruttan, ed., *Agriculture, Environment, and Health: Sustainable Development in the 21st Century*. Minneapolis: University of Minnesota Press.

Gallup, John Luke, and Jeffrey D. Sachs, with Andrew D. Mellinger. 1999. "Geography and Economic Development." In Boris Pleskovic and Joseph E. Stiglitz, eds., *Annual World Bank Conference on Development Economics 1998*. Washington, DC: World Bank.

IADB (Inter-American Development Bank). 1998. *Annual Report 1997*, "Regional", http://www.iadb.org/exr/doc98/pro/paisrg.htm

OECD (Organisation for Economic Co-operation and Development). 1998. *Development Co-operation: Efforts and Policies of the Members of the Development* Assistance Committee, 1997 Report. Paris.

GLOBAL PUBLIC GOODS

Concepts, Policies and Strategies

INGE KAUL, ISABELLE GRUNBERG AND MARC A. STERN

Many crises dominating the international policy agenda today reflect an underprovision of global public goods. That was the idea advanced in the introduction. To test it, we explored two main questions. Are global public goods a useful concept for describing and analysing current global challenges? And what policy options exist to enhance the provision of these goods?

We have found that, indeed, today's challenges are global public goods—and that they represent in large measure a new emerging class of such goods. Up to now, global public goods consisted primarily of "traffic rules" between countries and such at-the-border issues as tariffs. But increasingly, the initiatives for international cooperation reach behind national borders. Global concerns are penetrating national agendas, and national concerns are becoming the subject of international debate and of policy coordination and harmonization. Today, concrete outcomes and targets—such as disease control, pollution reduction, crisis prevention, and harmonized norms and standards—matter. The reasons for these new exigencies: enhanced openness, growing systemic risks, and the policy demands of the growing number of transnational actors in both business and civil society.

A major reason for the underprovision of this new class of global public goods—we call them global policy outcomes—is that public policy-making has not yet adjusted to present-day realities. There are three major gaps:

- A jurisdictional gap—the discrepancy between the global boundaries of today's major policy concerns and the essentially national boundaries of policy-making.

- A participation gap—which results from the fact that we live in a multiactor world but international cooperation is still primarily intergovernmental.

- An incentive gap—because moral suasion is not enough for countries to correct their international spillovers or to cooperate for the global public good.

Because of these gaps, nation states will witness continuing erosion of their capacities to implement national policy objectives unless they take further steps to cooperate in addressing international spillovers and systemic risks. But that cooperation must be of a new type. Not just cooperation that keeps global public bads at bay (until they reach crisis proportions) but cooperation that centres on creating global public goods and internalizing externalities. And not just cooperation that mistakenly assumes that the sphere of "public" ends at national borders, but cooperation that recognizes that an efficient system of global public policy is a necessary ingredient of an efficient global economy.

To make cooperation work along these lines, its current structure must be re-engineered to create:

- A clear jurisdictional loop, reaching from the national to the international (regional and global) level and back to the national.
- A participation loop, bringing into the process all actors—governments, civil society and business; all population groups, including all generations; and all groups of countries.
- An incentive loop to ensure that cooperation yields fair and clear results for all.

These are the main messages from the previous chapters. Here we elaborate on each of them in more detail to show how they could be realized, turned from postulates for change into concrete reform measures. The suggested proposals for action include, among others: preparing national externality profiles; reconfiguring responsibility for "foreign affairs" at the national level; reversing the logic of globalization to place greater emphasis on national capacity-building and regionalism; establishing new mechanisms for externality exchanges (or "trade" in global public goods); and creating a new international institutional architecture. This new architecture, we emphasize, should rely primarily on existing organizations, adding new ones only as needed. Examples of suggested new institutions include a United Nations Global Trusteeship Council, a knowledge bank, and a participation fund, self-administered by developing countries, to allow them to enter international negotiations on a more equal footing.

As the discussion will make clear, the concept of global public goods does not aim to replace the present rationale for aid in any way. Development assistance to poor countries remains a compelling challenge since the numbers of poor countries and poor people are high and rising. The absolute number of poor people has reached more than 1.5 billion, a regrettable record. Thus, the ethical and moral justifications for aid remain as strong as ever. But global public goods present an added rationale for international cooperation as well as for aid. Since the provision of these goods in many instances starts from the national level, it is in the self-interest of the international community to assist developing countries not only because they are poor but also to enable them to make their contribution to the provision of essential global public goods.

These and the other suggested actions require someone to take a first step—to jump-start change. We see essentially two main possibilities for this. One is for G–8 leaders to recognize the need for a more cooperative, participatory approach to managing the international economy and society. If they expand into a G–16—as we have suggested here and as other observers have recommended (Sachs 1998)—we are confident that a new political dynamic would be unleashed to set in motion important forces of political reform. The other option—not alternative, but complementary—could be a drive for change emanating from the public, from global civil society.

We believe that we have entered a new era of public policy—one in which international cooperation and the internalization of cross-border spillovers of national actions have to be at the core of public policy. We find the concept of global public goods to be a powerful tool for understanding this new era. And we feel that it should be shared beyond specialized, rarefied circles of microeconomists and introduced into the vocabulary of those who grapple daily with real-world challenges. Facilitating this process is one of the main purposes of this book. But there is first yet another challenge—to fully understand the concept of global public goods in all its manifold dimensions and complexities.

GLOBAL PUBLIC GOODS—A USEFUL CONCEPT, A NEW TYPOLOGY

In the first chapter we defined global public goods as having nonexcludable, nonrival benefits that cut across borders, generations and populations. At a minimum, the benefits of a global public good would extend to more than just one group of countries and not discriminate against any population group or any set of generations, present or future. Here we note simply what we did not know when we began looking at public goods. That global public goods is an apt term for many of today's international policy challenges, and that the concept offers us new insights into the many issues under consideration.

Some issues, we thought, were likely candidates for being global public goods, such as environmental sustainability and peace. But some, such as equity and market efficiency, looked less likely to fit the definition. Interestingly, however, all selected concerns passed the global public good test—though as table 1 shows, some meet the qualifying criteria of nonexcludability and nonrivalry more than others.

Based on the case studies, we now propose a typology of global public goods to distinguish more clearly among three main classes—according to the policy challenges they pose (see table 1). In class 1 are *natural global commons,* such as the ozone layer or climate stability, where the policy challenge is sustainability and the collective action problem is one of overuse. *Human-made global commons,* class 2, encompass a range of diverse issues: scientific and practical knowledge, principles and norms, the world's common cultural heritage and transnational infrastructure such as the Internet. For these global public goods, the main challenge is underuse.

The main collective action problem of the human-made commons, underuse, can take different forms, depending on the issue. For example, the global stock of knowledge, including essentially freely available nonpatented knowledge, is often so dispersed that actors find it difficult to identify what is known, how valid the knowledge is and under what conditions it applies. This makes gaining access to knowledge difficult—hence, its underuse. For the Internet, underuse can result from a variety of factors—illiteracy, language barriers or lack of money to buy computers.

If we take basic human rights as an example of a universally accepted norm, we see yet another type of underuse: repression. Some countries limit people's options to act and contribute to society—their freedom to travel or speak, or the inopportunity to obtain basic education and health care. But doing this results in developmental costs and inefficiencies. A consensus on what constitutes a universal norm, though difficult to achieve, seems to be emerging. On its fringes, the accumulating stock of universal norms and principles will always be somewhat fluid, as new norms and values are coming close to being universal but are not yet firmly accepted as such. Judging from present political debates, issues such as basic labour rights are possible new entries into the global stock of norms.

Class 3, *global policy outcomes,* includes peace, health and financial stability. The collective action problem associated with these less tangible global public goods is the typical challenge of undersupply. What sets the goods in class 3 apart from those in class 2 is that they are flow variables: a continuous

TABLE 1

Global concerns as global public goods: a selective typology

Class and type of global good	Benefits		Nature of the supply or use problem
	Nonexcludable	Nonrival	
1. Natural global commons			
Ozone layer	Yes	No	Overuse
Atmosphere (climate)	Yes	No	Overuse
2. Human-made global commons			
Universal norms and principles (such as universal human rights)	Partly	Yes	Underuse (repression)
Knowledge	Partly	Yes	Underuse (lack of access)
Internet (infrastructure)	Partly	Yes	Underuse (entry barriers)
3. Global conditions			
Peace	Yes	Yes	Undersupply
Health	Yes	Yes	Undersupply
Financial stability	Partly	Yes	Undersupply
Free trade	Partly	Yes	Undersupply
Freedom from poverty[c]	No	No	Undersupply
Environmental sustainability[c]	Yes	Yes	Undersupply
Equity and justice[c]	Partly	Yes	Undersupply

Note: This typology includes primarily issues that are the subject of the case studies in this volume. In addition, it refers only to final global public goods and bads, not to intermediate ones such as global regimes and institutions.

a. Here nonexcludable means that it is difficult for anyone to avoid bearing the costs of the bad.

b. Here nonrival means that one person's being affected by a bad—such as a disease—does not reduce the extent to which others are affected.

c. The demand for these goods emerges to the extent that the overuse of natural global commons or the underuse of human-made global commons assumes alarming proportions.

Corresponding global bad	Costs	
	Nonexcludable[a]	Nonrival[b]
Depletion and increased radiation	Yes	Yes
Risk of global warming	Yes	Yes
Human abuse and injustice	Partly	Yes
Inequality	Partly	Yes
Exclusion and disparities (between information rich and information poor)	Partly	Yes
War and conflict	Partly	Yes
Disease	Yes	Yes
Financial crisis	Yes	Yes
Fragmented markets	Yes	Yes
Civil strife, crime and violence	Yes	Yes
Unbalanced ecosystems	Yes	Yes
Social tensions and conflict	Yes	Yes

effort is required to ensure that they are supplied. The goods in class 2, by contrast, are stock variables: they have already been produced. Human activity can neglect and ignore them, as often happens with existing knowledge, or it can limit and repress them, as with human rights. The goods in class 1, the natural commons, are also stock variables: they precede human activity. We need to worry about their preservation and rehabilitation.

So while the goods in class 1 are natural, those in classes 2 and 3 are human. Particular cases of human-made global public goods are those that are network-based, such as the Internet or technical standards. For such goods, we have an extreme form of nonrivalry in consumption—in the sense that the addition of a new customer, far from taking away from existing consumers (or members of the network), benefits them. The larger the network, the larger the benefits to its members. As Debora Spar shows, this relationship holds for the Internet, below the point of congestion. And as Mohan Rao points out, the principle also applies to equity: the more enshrined that equity becomes as a universally acceptable principle, the more that people will come to expect justice and fairness.

Global public bads

Many of the global public goods examined here are still more of a hope or policy vision than a reality. While these goods sit on the policy agenda as objectives, the corresponding global public bads actually surround us in our daily lives. Interestingly, several authors found it easier to describe the bad than the good. For example, Charles Wyplosz relies, for his analysis of global financial stability, on a systematic examination of global financial instability. Why? Because the bad is often present, while the good has yet to be realized. Indeed, the good is often intangible, and one tends to take it for granted until it is lacking. Bads are more concrete. For example, good health is a general condition, disease a concrete fact. Human rights are hardly noticeable until they are violated and free speech or free movements are no longer possible. Or consider clean air—we take it for granted until smoke darkens the sky and blackens our lungs.

Global bads seem to be more public than global goods, as indicated by comparing the "benefits" column of table 1 with the "costs" column. This may also explain why policy agendas nationally and internationally are often focused just on reducing bads rather than producing goods. As several authors emphasize, such bads as disease, increased ultraviolet radiation, acts of terrorism or other types of violence often affect people at random. The means to protect oneself against these effects are limited, if they exist at all. Wyplosz noted that normal volatility can be priced, but excessive volatility and the effects of financial crises cannot. Hence, the concern about avoiding too severe an underprovision of global public goods and the attempt, once things are back to a certain level of normalcy, to give preference to private goods rather than public goods.

The rich have the wealth, knowledge and other powers to arrange some protection on their own. This may be access to the latest, and often highly priced, pharmaceuticals—or, for countries, the ability to build seawalls to stem the tides of rising water levels resulting from global warming. The poor, however, typically cannot afford such private protection. So, a lack of public goods affects equity adversely because the poor cannot avoid the problems as easily as the rich—they are exposed to scorching sun and ultraviolet radiation, they have no savings when civil unrest or war destroys their home, and they have no insurance when disease takes away their ability to work.

Note, however, that private protection against public bads often provides only short-lived and highly inefficient solutions. It is an avoidance strategy, not a solution to the problem. And often problems are allowed to accumulate, causing higher costs to all when a crisis ultimately erupts. Thus the underprovision of such global public goods as environmental sustainability or peace gives rise to the need for "anti-bads"—such facilities, arrangements or devices as scrubbers to avoid pollution, diplomats to avoid war or regional bodies to avoid financial instability. These facilities are what we called intermediate global public goods in chapter one. They contribute to the adequate supply of the ultimate outcomes of peace, sustainability or financial stability.

While global public goods are undersupplied and current realities are troubled by the corresponding global public bads, it is important not to limit one's sights just to keeping bads under wraps. This could lead the world into a lowest common denominator of international cooperation limited to avoiding disaster. While this approach may allow us to survive, it would fail to exploit opportunities for more dynamic growth with greater equity and sustainability. So, the focus here is on controlling bads as well as providing goods.

In addition, there are dynamic interlinkages between the various global public goods. Ensuring an adequate supply of a particular global public good (or adequate access) will have spillovers in other issue areas. The typical example is the link between peace and development, but other linkages have been suggested (such as the health-growth linkage that Ethan Kapstein emphasizes).

The global commons of classes 1 and 2 become policy issues only when their scarcity or absence creates a global public bad. For the natural global commons, this often takes the form of overexploitation of natural resources—and thus, nonsustainability of present policies and strategies. For human-made global commons, the problem is more often one of unequal access—and hence growing disparities, such as those between rich and poor. When such overuse or underuse assumes critical proportions—approaching limits of nonsustainability in the first case or explosive inequity in the second—these concerns move into class 3, global policy outcomes. The reason is that as long as everything is normal, commons command little policy and management attention. This explains why the international community began to focus in earnest on the importance and value of the natural global commons (such as nonrenewable energy sources) only in the early 1970s. When mismanagement of the commons produces too many negative externalities, international cooperation is seen as necessary, at least at the level of intent, and agreements on desirable conditions are formulated—specifying such aspects as pollution levels, poverty targets or standards of good governance. This shift in priority and approach gives the commons a new character and moves them into class 3 of global public goods.

Externalities and systemic effects

When a public good or bad has nonexcludable or only partly excludable effects, it brings costs or benefits to innocent bystanders. So, nonexcludability is an extreme form of externality. As discussed in the first chapter, the standard definition of an externality is the effect of an activity or good that arises when an individual, firm or any other actor takes an action but does not bear the full costs (negative externality) or receive the full benefits (positive externality). Examples of negative externalities are transborder pollution, such as carbon dioxide emissions, or human rights curtailments, which can produce poverty and ethnic strife and result in conflict, war and even genocide, as in Bosnia, Haiti and Rwanda. Positive externalities are generated by, for example, the preservation of rainforest or the creation of national communicable disease response teams that are available when needed for worldwide deployment.

Global public goods and bads can have two sources. They can be the product of positive or negative cross-border spillovers of country-level action, or they can be generated by global systemic effects. And the externalities can be direct or indirect—travelling directly from country to country or person to person, as with contagious diseases, or affecting other countries and actors indirectly, notably through the global commons. Health risks, such as skin cancer from ozone depletion, are indirect externalities.

Systemic effects emerge from both natural and human-made systems. Take the public benefits of such ecosystems as the oceans or the atmosphere, which are largest when these systems are undisturbed by human activity. They have pre-existing utility. Human-made commons also generate public benefits, though their utility emerges only once they have been constructed.

As the chapters reveal, human-made commons often operate with inherent flaws. For example, Wyplosz draws attention to the fact that financial crises can result not just from capacity shortfalls or policy weaknesses within countries but also from inherent market risks. Widespread information asymmetries can lead to multiple equilibria, which he argues were the cause of self-fulfilling exchange rate crises in Europe in 1992–93, Mexico in 1995 and Asia in 1997–98. Externalities are one type of market failure. Multiple equilibria, adverse selection, moral hazard and the other phenomena analysed by Wyplosz are other types, which individually and together can create systemic risk.

Systemic risk exists in other areas, too, and often translates into a problem of governability. (We return to this point below when discussing the jurisdictional gap.) For example, Spar refers to the Internet as the quintessential global infrastructure element. As she argues, the Net is truly transnational, so governments will find it difficult to regulate Internet-related activities. Or as Kapstein and Rao show, international inequity has reached such proportions that it has taken on a life of its own. It creates serious global social strains and might well put to the test the durability of the global social fabric. International travel, for example, is now more dangerous because of the rise in crime and poverty that followed the financial crises of the 1990s, and political frustration and despair express themselves in acts of terrorism and other violence (*Financial Times* 1999).

Public goods as multiactor products

Several authors underscore the fact that public goods are not necessarily state-produced, and global public goods are not necessarily the products just of intergovernmental action. Even private goods and private action can generate externalities, positive and negative. Nonstate groups can also provide global public goods. Amartya Sen makes the point that such goods as global equity can result from a plurality of identities and affiliations that people have.

Many of these identities or affiliations might not, as he puts it, be parasitic on the person's nationality or citizenship. He reminds us that the Hippocratic oath, by which members of the medical profession abide, was not mediated by any national or international contract. Similarly, a feminist would probably be concerned about the deprivation of women in general rather than just the situation of women in a particular country. Whether individuals or civil society organizations support universal human rights or other concerns of justice and fairness, they make a direct contribution to the production of global equity.

Sen therefore stresses that it is important to distinguish between within-country equity, international equity and global equity. The first two relate to the existence of states, while the third often materializes despite national borders and other human-made divides. As Rao remarks, solidarity and social cohesion know no boundaries or frontiers other than those erected by history.

Nancy Birdsall and Robert Lawrence present similar arguments for the business community. They point out that the demand for policy harmonization is often promoted by commercial actors. In fact, business has often been the driving force behind international regime-building, notably in transport, communication and the environment. As the authors extensively discuss, the question is to what extent these business interests relate to particular private or global public goods. Geoffrey Heal uses the term "privately produced global bads" to refer to phenomena, such as greenhouse gas emissions, to which most people are in one way or another contributing. Thus from many points of view it holds that public goods, including global public goods, are multiactor products rather than just state-provided.

Even so, the more public a good is, the more it will be undersupplied by the normal operation of the market or the international system—and if it is a public bad, the more likely it will be oversupplied.

Variability of publicness

Another point that emerges clearly from the discussions, notably in the chapters by Heal, Spar, Joseph Stiglitz and Habib Sy, is that publicness and privateness are not fixed attributes. Indeed, if the requisite technologies are available, the publicness of a good can be influenced by policy. Making a good more private will increase the chance that it will be provided, even in a decentralized setting. Two methods may be used: assigning property rights or internalizing externalities. Both are elaborated at further length in the section on providing global public goods below. Conversely, enhancing access to a global public good such as knowledge, say through education, reveals the latent publicness of that good—which could not be taken advantage of before. Thus it seems that the term global public good adequately represents the variety of global policy challenges outstanding, whether the depletion of the earth's carrying capacity, the underuse of technology or human rights norms, or the outcomes (such as peace) that remain neglected without global leadership. The reach of global spillovers is variable, and we have a continuum along the public-private dimension and along the global-regional-national dimension.

NEW CHALLENGES FOR INTERNATIONAL COOPERATION

If the concept of global public goods offers a useful lens for understanding current problems, does it also help point the way to new policy solutions and actions to manage them? Yes. Looking at the international policy agenda through this lens draws attention to three important facts: the emergence of a new type of global public good, the changed realities that bring this new class to the fore, and the gaps in the present system of public policy-making, which explain the persistence of so many global public bads.

An emerging class of global public goods
Global public goods are not new. Concern with them goes back to early 17th century negotiations on freedom on the high seas, and the Grotian principle of *mare liberum* (Kingsbury 1996). At that time, international cooperation was primarily concerned with between-country issues. The international transport and communications regimes that emerged in the late 19th century and early 20th century are essentially of this type (Zacher and Sutton 1996). These have been called, in the cooperation literature, "international traffic rules"(Bryant 1980), or regimes concerning nations' shared use of global commons and the regulation of movements between countries. Early on, international cooperation also began—of course, with various ups and downs—to address at-the-border issues, such as lowering trade barriers or removing capital controls.

Throughout the history of international cooperation, there have also been cases of behind-the-border policy coordination or harmonization. An example is the gold-standard policy practised in the late 19th century and until the First World War—and again, though less successfully, in the 1920s (Eichengreen 1992). Another case, more attempted than realized, was the adoption of the Universal Declaration of Human Rights in 1948 (United

Nations 1948). The Cold War soon stalled this effort, with the East-West conflict cutting the initially integrated set of civil, political, economic and social rights into a dichotomy that lasted until the 1990s. Now, however, the international policy agenda appears to be more focused on behind-the-border issues—not in lieu of, but in addition to, other concerns.

Behind-the-border issues consist of two closely intertwined concerns. They include public goods that have so far been primarily a domestic concern—such as poverty, health, competition policy and banking standards. They also include issues pertaining to previously global issues, such as the ozone shield, linking them to national-level actions, such as the reduction of chlorofluorocarbons. Today's concerns about global public goods are different because they reach behind national borders and because they are a blend of "national" and "international". Many of them now fall in class 3 (see table 1). They blur the lines between "domestic" and "foreign", and "national" and "international".

New realities

Why are we witnessing the emergence of a new class of global public goods? Judging from the chapters here and from other studies on global trends (Hirst and Thompson 1996; Keohane and Nye 1989; Reinicke 1998; and Rodrik 1997), it is clear that a wide range of factors have contributed to their emergence. Three stand out: openness, systemic risk and the power shift away from the state.

With the lowering of at-the-border controls, but also with enhanced political pluralism and democracy, countries have become more open. Combined with technological advances, this has encouraged more international economic activity—more foreign trade, more foreign investment and more international travel and communications. As Wyplosz points out, international economic activities act as ever more powerful *transmission belts* of externalities. It is this fact that makes Kapstein conclude that the time has come when many hitherto domestic issues, such as labour rights and taxation, can no longer adequately be dealt with at the national level, but ought to be taken to the international level. Lincoln Chen, Tim Evans and Richard Cash remark that with the integration of markets—and the internationalization of marketing—even noncommunicable diseases today are a global health issue. The authors refer, among other things, to the spread of unhealthy consumption patterns, such as smoking, which worldwide advertisements inflict on new consumer groups that may lack the information to make an informed choice about whether to consume the product. Clearly, openness has increased the meaning of interdependence, which used to be de facto connectedness among legally sovereign nations.

The growing number and higher level of systemic risks is linked to openness. While we would not like to join the ranks of analysts predicting chaos and conflict for the future (Huntington 1996 or Kaplan 1994), there is little doubt that some problems require urgent attention. Among them are the challenges of global warming, the growing international inequality, the crisis-prone financial markets, the emergence of new drug-resistant disease strains, the rapid loss of biodiversity and genetic engineering. While these challenges are quite different, they all have the potential to affect deeply the way in which societies and economies work.

It is encouraging to see that many of these concerns are already prominent on the international agenda. As Scott Barrett points out, there is merit in not being too overanxious on some of the issues, including global warming, because all the facts are not yet known. But as Cooper (1994) stresses, even if problems are not fully measured or understood, we can undertake preventive measures that even from our current points of view would be desirable investments—such as advancing the present generations' frontiers of knowledge and technological capacities to meet future challenges.

The third factor is the far-reaching power shift away from the state in the past few decades but particularly during the 1990s (Boyer and Drache 1996; Mathews 1997; Ndegwa 1996; Strange 1996). Here we want to highlight a related, additional dimension of this issue: that nonstate actors in international policy-making often pursue a transnational perspective. For example, governments must now meet market expectations or subject their policy actions to monitoring by intergovernmental organizations, such as the International Monetary Fund, and even to assessments by such private bodies as credit rating agencies. In addition, their actions are coming under closer scrutiny by nongovernmental organizations (NGOs), such as Amnesty International, the Human Rights Watch, the World Watch Institute, Transparency International or the Social Watch. This holds for both developing and industrial countries.[1]

In many respects, governments today are accountable to both domestic and international constituencies. Governments are transmission belts between internal and external demands, intermediaries rather than myopic agents of "purely" national self-interest. No doubt, politicians are elected by domestic constituencies, their primary point of reference. But to serve domestic interests well, policy-makers have to take the outside into account, certainly not to build protectionist barriers or just to defend the country against outside influences, but in a much more demanding task, to combine national interests with international exigencies in a way that maximizes the country's welfare. Put differently, the challenge is to tackle the interlinked, internal-external issues that the new class of global public goods presents.

Today's policy deficits

Given the new policy challenges and a new policy environment, can the present system of policy-making deal adequately with the exigencies at hand? At first sight, it seems that all is well. International cooperation is an active field. As Young (1989, p. 11) notes, "we live in a world of international regimes". He is right: the body of joint international policy statements, resolutions and treaties is expanding fast.[2] And in some areas, international cooperation is working quite well, with exchange and consultation on shared concerns and often even accords on next steps. But to turn intentions into policy actions, cooperation seems to move only hesitantly, if at all. Yet this step is critical to providing the new class of global public goods—the global conditions and outcomes that often depend on coordinated action by a multitude of decentralized actors.

The obstacles to this more operational type of follow-up to international agreements are several. Many have already been identified in the literature on international relations.[3] Here we highlight just two. The first factor that often impedes cooperation (and typically for good reason) is uncertainty about the exact nature of the problem or the feasibility of possible policy responses. It is precisely for this reason that Lisa Martin and others in this book place such strong emphasis on the importance of information and on the role of international organizations in helping governments reduce uncertainties about the problem under negotiation. This can be done by providing empirical facts and figures as well as through forward-looking policy research. Hence, epistemic communities have a major role to play in facilitating international cooperation (Haas 1992). Their input is particularly important during times of change and transition—as at present.

The second set of collective action problems that frequently block cooperation involve free riding on the efforts of others. The case studies here provide evidence of free riding in a number of policy areas, including aid, health and peace.

But at the same time, the analyses in the book suggest that the cause for the present underprovision of global public goods lies deeper than these two problems, as is typical of collective action dilemmas. The more fundamental issue is the organization of policy-making today, both nationally and internationally. While the studies clearly show that each issue requires specific solutions, the analyses point to three cross-cutting policy deficits that we label the jurisdictional, participation and incentive gaps. It is not that the international relations and public policy literatures have overlooked these gaps. Instead, the gaps have taken on greater significance because of the emergence of the new class of global public goods—global policy outcomes—and the growing relevance of nonstate actors on the international stage. Filling these gaps is thus a new policy exigency, so in what follows we focus on suggestions to that effect.

We have seen that the concept of global public goods is not only fitting but also informative. It draws attention to the important policy difference between global public goods and bads, as well as that between externalities and systemic effects. Moreover, the global publicness that is a common property of all the policy issues examined here alerts us to the fact that their current underprovision, also, has a common, structural root—the issue to which we now turn.

PROVIDING GLOBAL PUBLIC GOODS BY CLOSING THE THREE GAPS

To be clear, we are not suggesting that cooperation as such is inherently good or desirable. Nor do we think that where market failures occur, governments always have to be brought in to salvage the situation. Nor are we arguing that supranational institutions are required to address all failures of international cooperation. The world is much more complicated than this—especially today, with more international cooperation in both the private sector and civil society. The policy recommendations suggested by the contributors to this book reflect the ample evidence of failures of markets, of government and of international cooperation. They span a wide range of possible options—from correcting global public bads through market-based mechanisms, as Heal suggests, to banking strongly on civil society, as David Hamburg and Jane Holl and Sen do, to strengthening the role of the United Nations, as Ruben Mendez suggests. Intriguingly, there is strong agreement that the provision of global public goods has to start from the national level.

Agreement also exists on the point that there is no one-size-fits-all policy approach. Strategies have to be tailored to the issue and the context. For example, where the overall political climate is more supportive of private initiative, property rights and markets can play a more important role in economic life, including the provision of public goods. And where human rights and democracy are curtailed, civil society's input will be constrained.

In searching for future policy solutions to enhance the provision of global public goods, we must be aware of the institutional context—how it influences our perceptions and the feasibility of various policy measures.[4]

CLOSING THE JURISDICTIONAL GAP

The "jurisdictional gap" refers to the discrepancy between the boundaries of global public goods—which are by definition essentially global—and those of today's main locus of policy-making, the nation-state—whose boundaries are by definition national. Theoretically, one could address the problem of boundaries by strengthening supranational governance or by attempting to trim issues back to the size of nation-states, which could involve rebuilding protectionist barriers. We prefer to follow a third path: creating a jurisdictional loop that runs from the national to the international and back to the national—by way of several intermediate levels, regional and subregional.

The nation-state is the key actor in this loop. As Barrett stresses, other actors may play a role, but governments are unique in possessing legislative and coercive powers. Building a jurisdictional loop can recreate effective sovereignty—what some analysts, starting with Bull (1977), have termed "operational" or "internal" sovereignty, as opposed to "de jure" or "external" sovereignty.

Reinicke (1998, p. 57) defines internal sovereignty as "the ability of government to formulate, implement, and manage public policy", adding that "a threat to a country's operational internal sovereignty implies a threat to its ability to conduct policy".[5] Since this threat exists in today's world of growing interdependencies and globalization, governments will be more effective in serving their country and constituencies if they can take their operational sovereignty to the source of the problem. If the problem is international in scope, decision making to address it will have to be done at that level. The fact that governments are responsible for, and accountable to, the citizens of a particular territory does not mean they cannot seek domestic results in the international sphere. The growing number of international resolutions, treaties, organizations and other cooperation mechanisms shows that in some respects this is a well-recognized fact. Yet what the analyses in this book seem to suggest is that domestic policy-making and international cooperation are still too separate and disjointed. They need to be more systematically integrated—for everybody's national interest as well as the interest of the global common good.[6]

How can this be done, practically? A good start would be the following six steps:

- Establishing national externality profiles.
- Internalizing cross-border spillovers.
- Re-engineering national approaches to international issues.
- Linking national and global policy agendas.
- Strengthening regional cooperation.
- Bringing cooperation gains back to the national level.

Establishing national externality profiles

As Barrett and Martin emphasized, an important precondition for international cooperation is certainty—certainty about the existence of a problem, the possible solutions and the net benefits from addressing a problem rather than letting it drag on. Today most countries—from politicians and government officials to business, civil society and the general public—have little awareness of the cross-border externalities, positive or negative, that they produce. Not only that, there is often considerable uncertainty and unawareness of the many ways in which the country depends on, and is affected by, outside events. So, one of the most important ingredients of international cooperation is lacking: a clear idea of why, from a national perspective, cooperation makes sense. National externality profiles could encourage a debate on this topic—and could thus be an important first step towards closing the current jurisdictional gap and bringing global concerns into national policy and vice versa.

Such profiles could help establish what nations receive and generate in positive and negative cross-border spillovers—and what they require in global public goods to attain their national objectives. These profiles would reveal interdependence by indicating where individual countries might benefit from cooperation with others—or where others might expect cooperation from them. If these profiles were to show that all countries have a negative overall balance on their outgoing and incoming externality accounts, it would be clear that the world is caught in a serious prisoner's dilemma with potentially large implications—be it faltering world economic growth, global warming or the spread of disease and ill health. Or if the profiles were to point to missed development opportunities (as with underuse of the world's knowledge stock, an inefficiency highlighted by Stiglitz), opportunities could emerge for more optimal development outcomes at relatively modest cost.

Table 2 presents a preliminary depiction of a national externality profile, with two main elements:

- Cross-border effects (or spill-ins), both positive and negative, from other countries, other regions, the global commons or global infrastructure, either directly or indirectly.
- Externalities (or spillovers), both positive and negative, generated by the country and affecting other countries, other regions, the global commons or global infrastructure, either directly or indirectly.

We are talking, of course, of externalities that arise from within a given territory by any kind of actor—public, corporate, individual. The effects (or spillovers) are also felt inside another territory by a wide range of actors. In most instances, however, it is up to governments to agree on corrective policy measures. In a way, the suggestions to formulate national externality profiles is analogous to calculating national income figures or national levels of greenhouse gas emissions—governments are recording the effects of other nongovernmental actors as well as their own.

In table 2 the spill-ins are grouped by their origin and by the issue area or national policy concern they affect. For the spillovers the table could, accordingly, indicate the national source. Based on such a profile, a country can clearly identify its stake and vested interests in international cooperation, as well as its own responsibilities in reducing undesirable, negative cross-border spillovers from its territory. The profile also signals which outside actors or systems are likely to make cooperation requests on the country. Comparing the list of countries on the "outgoing" and "incoming" side of the externality profile could point to rich possibilities for bargaining and arranging quid pro quos, bilaterally or multilaterally.

To create a meaningful profile, countries need a frame of reference to determine which externalities are negative and which positive, and what level of a positive (negative) externality is desirable (tolerable). National efforts to establish such reference points will likely be revealing in identifying and ranking issues.[7] Another possible instrument is a global issue profile, such as reports on major final and intermediate global public goods, analysing their current provision and the steps needed to boost supply. In fact, global issue profiles are already emerging.

Take the report by the Development Assistance Committee of the Organisation for Economic Co-operation and Development on *Shaping the*

21st Century (OECD/DAC 1996). It presents a sort of joint global public good and externality analysis for OECD countries as a whole. The focus is on linkages between OECD countries and developing countries and, here again, primarily on externalities flowing from the South to the North. Some analysts characterize the OECD report as recasting international development assistance to serve the aims of a "globalized internal policy" (Raffer 1998).

Other global reports relevant in this context are those covering topics such as human development (UNDP, various years), drug control (UNDCP 1997), HIV/AIDS (UNAIDS 1998), refugees (UNHCR, various years), environment (World Resources Institute, various years), monetary and financial issues (BIS, various years; IMF, various years), trade and development (UNCTAD, various years), economic development (World Bank, various years) and population (UNFPA, various years). With some modifications in their concepts and statistical tables, these reports could provide starting points for the type of global issue reports suggested here. Certainly, developing the analytical tools and measurements needed for systematic externality assessments will take time and require extensive research and policy debate, but their importance for the future management of global policy challenges would seem to justify the effort.

As these remarks indicate, externality profiles would provide a rich basis for cross-country and cross-issue analyses, debates and bargaining—and for cooperative policy-making in the mutual interest of all.

Internalizing cross-border spillovers

The paradox of global public goods, as many contributors point out, is that their provision has to start nationally—except for the most extraterritorial of them. As Wyplosz underscores, international financial stability needs a strong national foundation. International efforts can complement, coordinate and monitor national endeavours but cannot substitute for them. The measures he suggests for building national financial strength include national-level policy changes, such as adequate macroeconomic and structural policies and legal frameworks, as well as capacity development efforts in such areas as accounting and banking supervision.

The chapters by Chen, Evans and Cash and by Mark Zacher reach similar conclusions. They make it clear that ensuring global health will remain a Sisyphian endeavour unless health services are strengthened nationally. And Hamburg and Holl add that without conflict prevention, including such measures as local community development, peace will remain fragile, and

TABLE 2

National externality profile: a schematic illustration

| | Spill-ins (by origin) | | | | | |
| | Positive | | | Negative | | |
Affected domestic policy concern	Countries ⇩	Regions ⇩	Global ⇩	Countries ⇩	Regions ⇩	Global ⇩
1 ⇐						
2 ⇐						
3 ⇐						
4 ⇐						
5 ⇐						
6 ⇐						
7 ⇐						

Policy implication — National requests for cooperation with other countries

Note: A fully developed profile would have separate tables for each major country, region, global common and system. For the global dimension, it would also be important to distinguish between indirect externalities (that is, cross-border spillovers that affect domestic policy concerns by way of their direct impact on global commons) and systemic effects.

	Spillovers (by recipient)					
	Positive			Negative		
	Countries	Regions	Global	Countries	Regions	Global
Domestic source of externality	⇧	⇧	⇧	⇧	⇧	⇧
1 ⇨						
2 ⇨						
3 ⇨						
4 ⇨						
5 ⇨						
6 ⇨						
7 ⇨						

Policy implication   Requests for cooperation likely to be received from outside stability may be attainable only through such undesirable means as political repression. Zacher further notes that little will come of the increasing calls for international monitoring and surveillance of global development trends unless countries' capacities to generate, analyse and report necessary data are strengthened—along with their ability to respond swiftly and decisively when problems are spotted. Similarly, sound national energy policies can go a long way in alleviating global environmental problems. All these arguments point in the same direction, and that is that the first step towards addressing externality issues must be undertaken nationally.

But why would countries be willing to accept this principle of internalizing externalities if, as noted before, they are self-interested, country-focused actors? Here we return to the notion of effective sovereignty.

The attainment of national objectives in many countries today depends on what is happening abroad, and that means primarily what is happening with other countries' externalities. One solution, widely practised, consists of making detailed, bilateral externality trade-offs (for example, we discourage the activities of terrorist groups in our territory and in exchange you provide additional development assistance or security cooperation). Countries could either seek to reduce the generation of negative externalities through national-level change, offer compensation to affected countries or, where it can be arranged, seek to swap implementation credits with other countries. Similarly, they could request rewards for any positive externalities they generate. Below we explore how to determine which strategy might be the most appropriate in which context.

But there is also a broader multilateral formula that may prevail because of its simplicity: it requires that each country accept the principle of national responsibility, so that others are prepared to do the same. If countries agree to avoid negative cross-border spillovers as much as possible, there is less need for international negotiations and special cooperative efforts that might prove more costly to countries than implementing necessary adjustments voluntarily. Thus the principle of national responsibility for internalizing externalities is not only the most politically feasible—it also makes economic sense.

There are signs that this broader bargain is already taking place. Indeed, the international community has accepted "national responsibility" as an important guidepost for managing international relations. This principle clearly underpinned the debates at the 1972 United Nations Conference on the Human Environment (United Nations 1972), as well as those at the subsequent 1992 United Nations Conference on Environment and Development

(United Nations 1992). The 1997 Kyoto Conference of the Parties to the United Nations Framework Convention on Climate Change also saw a debate on this issue (United Nations 1998b). At this conference the European Union stressed that such international mechanisms as emissions trading or joint implementation should not be allowed to distract from the need for policy change at home. The possibility that a country could avoid responsibility at home through the use of joint implementation or emissions trading was an important reason for some developing countries at Kyoto to express reservations about these mechanisms (Cutajar 1998).

The principle of national responsibility resembles the principle of "extended reciprocity" in gift giving: one usually gives gifts without expecting, in return, another gift of equal value, and sometimes even without expecting anything in return. The principle usually applies in smaller cohesive groups. But there are signs that as a result of economic globalization and interdependence a global society is emerging, allowing us to reap the advantages of this system internationally.

Re-engineering national approaches to international issues

For enhanced awareness to translate into more cooperative action, there needs to be clearly identified "national counterparts", or government entities whose mandate is to deal with the rest of the world and who are responsible for the common provision of global public goods. In most countries international affairs have traditionally been concentrated in a separate government entity: a ministry of foreign affairs specialized in representing national interests abroad. But these interests have primarily concerned such issues as border security, international relations or the promotion of national exports. The objectives were "defence", "outreach" or "competition". Other government entities—such as ministries of health, labour or even the economy—were largely oriented towards internal affairs. While this division of responsibilities has changed in many countries, a global public goods approach to international cooperation will require a further re-engineering of national approaches to international issues.

An important objective of such reorganization would be to ensure that thematic and sectoral government entities have the capability to address and manage global interdependence in their respective areas of work. This can be achieved by introducing foreign affairs responsibilities into relevant ministries or by incorporating domestic concerns more systematically into foreign affairs. Whatever the pattern, the objective is to overcome the traditional divide between "internal" and "external" that economic liberalization and globalization have de facto eroded. This is not to say that borders have become meaningless—instead, they are porous.[8]

If governments lack the capacity to take the outside into account, they will end up being "policy-takers" and feeling that globalization is eroding their policy-making sovereignty. But, if they adopt a proactive stance and determine what they need from external players in order to meet national objectives, they can still be "policy-makers". As the UN experience shows (Krause and Knight 1995), even small countries can, within a multilateral forum, sometimes yield significant political influence and turn global public goods from alien policy concerns into home-grown policy outcomes.

Linking national and global policy agendas

National policy alone, though often an important starting point (due to the goods in question), will rarely suffice to ensure an adequate provision of global public goods. So, what advice do the case studies offer for putting into practice the full "policy loop" that many of the goods will require? One set of measures pertains to externalities that can be managed through cooperative but decentralized actions; the other set concerns joint management of global systemic issues.

Turn first to the case of country-to-country (or direct) externalities. What international mechanisms are needed to facilitate the management of this type of cross-border externality? A basic requirement would be to share information. And indeed, most chapters in this book stress the growing importance of monitoring and surveillance, and see the provision of critical information as the key role of international organizations.

Yet as the recognition of externalities grows, governments and other actors are likely to expect international organizations to play a second role—becoming more strongly involved in addressing existing problems and facilitating externality exchanges among countries. This goes beyond the traditional types of international agreements specifying what countries will do, individually, and it goes beyond mere monitoring and surveillance or traditional development assistance. Externality exchanges involve a new type of operational activity for international organizations: the supervision and management of international quid pro quos. Wyplosz's proposal for ex ante conditionality falls into this category. According to his proposal, countries would have to qualify for full participation in the international financial market, analogous to applying for membership in the Organisation for

Economic Co-operation and Development (OECD) or the World Trade Organization (WTO).

The clean development mechanism or the joint implementation scheme, foreseen in the Kyoto Protocol, are also examples, as are the "aid for policy change" stipulations in OECD/DAC (1996). To be sure, these activities will continue to involve information-gathering—on, say, how well a country is complying with good and prudent banking or financial practices, or how far it has curbed its emissions of heat-trapping gases. But international organizations could also work as mediators to salvage the agreements in cases of noncompliance.

As Lisa Cook and Jeffrey Sachs stress, a major shortcoming of the present system of international organizations, including the IMF and the World Bank, is that they are country focused: they deal primarily with internal matters rather than externalities. Externalities are addressed only when a crisis has arisen, rather than preventively or proactively. Assuming the role of a broker to facilitate externality exchanges between governments will also add a new dimension to the information function of international organizations.

Turning now to cooperation on global systemic issues, recall the types of issues that fall into this category. Global systemic issues are so transnational, so nonterritorial, that they cannot easily be analysed in terms of one country's externality towards another or towards the rest of the world. As Wyplosz shows, financial boom and bust cycles are a clear example (although these can be prevented, to some extent, with national-level action). Underuse of the global knowledge stock, raised by Stiglitz, is another. As he points out, few countries on their own and out of national interest would gather or develop knowledge that has no commercial value. Yet such knowledge is critical to the progress of developing countries on which balanced and stable future world economic growth will depend. Being transnational, the Internet may also qualify, as does inequity. Inequity creates cross-border externalities in the form of social instability, ethnic tensions and environmental damage. But in a truly global sense (as articulated by Sen) it is also an inherently transnational issue and an issue of global, systemic risk. The reason is that inequality has assumed such proportions that policies "merely" aimed at creating a level playing field no longer suffice (UNDP, *Human Development Report 1998*). Equal opportunities for *unequal* players produce more inequity.

There is thus a need for an international policy dialogue on the social fundamentals underpinning our emerging global society. One possible way of redressing the current trend towards growing global inequity is to review carefully the justice of present international regimes and institutions (an issue discussed in detail below in the section on closing the participation gap). Another is to revalue certain goods and services, notably those that constitute critical inputs into the provision of public goods such as the service of pollution reduction. If this were done, the actual wealth—not just the income wealth—of countries would become apparent, possibly resulting in a fairer distribution of development opportunities (an issue taken up in more detail below in the section on closing the incentive gap).

We will not attempt here to open a debate on the grossly neglected issue of equity. Our comments are meant to illustrate that even with the best of efforts, global systemic risks cannot be fully resolved nationally through individual country efforts. They call for global mechanisms and joint provision of the good in question. Although in some areas a dominant nation or group of nations may act directly to reduce systemic risks, in most policy areas cooperative efforts that include most—if not all—nations are required.

Strengthening regional cooperation

In devising national-global policy loops, the regional level cannot be overlooked. Cook and Sachs point out that many issues are regional. While these issues no doubt also contribute to global public goods, it is more efficient to deal with them at the regional level rather than the global. As Wyplosz shows, even global agreements can sometimes be better implemented regionally— rather than globally or nationally.

Regional forums often have advantages over global ones in the sense that they present fewer information problems. Countries in a region know each other better. As Birdsall and Lawrence point out, they may be able to identify more appropriate solutions. At the same time, Cook and Sachs identify a large number of obstacles that can impede regional cooperation, such as a common history of conflict and war, or shared poverty. To help overcome these obstacles, countries within a region could invite outside parties, including international organizations, to act as facilitators. Although no standard policy advice can apply in all cases, international cooperation can gain from regional specialization—in both negotiating priorities and implementing agreements.

The debate on regional and global forums has been reinvigorated recently with discussions of the need for a new financial architecture (Eichengreen 1999; Wade and Veneroso 1998). The analyses here suggest that this debate might usefully be extended to other pressing global topics.

Bringing cooperation's gains back to the nation

Bringing the gains from cooperation back to the national level is the responsibility of national actors. But as Barrett and Martin explain, a host of cooperation techniques help ensure that countries comply with international commitments. To close the jurisdictional loop, we would like to stress accountability. For national policy-makers to be able to accept responsibility for global affairs, it is important for them to return from international negotiations with clear net gains to show to their electorates. Not only that, they should be able to demonstrate that the results constitute a fair outcome. If international cooperation is to enjoy broadly based public support, it has to prove its worth at the local level, with local constituencies. Ideally, the identification of cooperation needs should start there, and the fruits from cooperation should also flow back there. Only if this condition is met will international cooperation and the provision of global public goods avoid being perceived as external affairs—as a diversion of efforts and resources rather than an investment in local well-being. And only then will global issue boundaries and jurisdictional boundaries truly coincide.

If one were to follow the six steps suggested here, a jurisdictional loop would close, and nation-states could regain the policy-making sovereignty that they so often fear they have lost to globalizing markets and other transnational pressures. Yet the design of the loop, as suggested here, would best follow a strict principle of subsidiarity. Recall that, under subsidiarity, decisions should be made at the lowest possible level, as close to the locus of action as possible—at the national level rather than the regional, at the regional level rather than the global.

As Bryant (1995, p. 31) defines it, subsidiarity is the presumption that "lower-level, local jurisdictions should make decisions unless convincing reasons exist for assigning them to higher-level, more central authorities, with the burden of proof always resting on the proponents of centralization". The intention is to reduce information problems, promote peer reviews, facilitate more diversified policy advice and ultimately create better-fitting solutions. But subsidiarity is also an answer to the challenge of representativeness in global policy-making—to the question of who makes decisions, on behalf of whom. Subsidiarity can be seen as an antidote to the potential pitfalls of "behind-the-border policy convergence".[9]

Indeed, the growing convergence of standards and domestic policies begs the question of who decides what the common standards are. Birdsall and Lawrence discuss this question in their chapter. In addition, one could also ask who decides who complies with the common policy standards, and who does not? There is a danger that declaring "noncompliance" would amount to an insidious form of sanction, and become a foreign policy tool with private benefits. Examples have been seen in the realm of economic policy or good governance. But there is potential for abuse in apparently more technical spheres, such as the safety of airports. Noncompliant states may easily drift into rogue status. Consequently, the harmonization of standards could force individual countries to conform across a much broader range of issues and activities, regardless of the democratic choices in the internal policy-making process.

Policy-making under conditions of globalization and for global public goods poses tremendous challenges of balance—because it entails the need to complement decentralization with centralization, and commonality with diversity. Thus domestic affairs and external affairs have to blend so that international cooperation becomes an integral part of national public policy-making.

CLOSING THE PARTICIPATION GAP

As Birdsall and Lawrence argue, the harmonization of domestic rules and standards is beneficial for trade and efficiency if it is arrived at through a democratic process. Rao stresses that the absence of fully representative forums is probably the most important handicap of international cooperation today. Cook and Sachs revisit how deeply flawed past development assistance often was because it was delivered, quasi ready-made, by outside agencies. Chen, Evans and Cash as well as Zacher see a new era of development management dawning, one marked by horizontal networking rather than by vertical organizational structures. Wyplosz calls for more diversity and pluralism in policy advice, including the creation of regional IMFs. And Kapstein suggests placing representatives of social issues into organizations such as the IMF in order to ensure enhanced public scrutiny and more consistency between financial and social concerns.

The assumptions behind all these suggestions are that process matters and that enhanced representativeness of international organizations will lead to greater equity in outcomes. As Rao puts it, equity is an important lubricant of international cooperation and hence an important ingredient in the provision of global public goods. Where it is absent, distrust and noncooperation will result.

There is thus broad agreement among the authors that a focus on global public goods and bads goes beyond value-free discussions of global interdependence. Instead, it is also important to address squarely the political issue of final outcomes and priorities—the question of what cooperation is good for. As noted, the test of whether a good is public is only partly technical— whether, and to what extent, the good exhibits properties of nonexcludability and nonrivalry in consumption. This is the theoretical side of its publicness. But there is also a practical-political side of publicness. This involves questions concerning whether a good is not merely nonexcludable but also accessible to all—and whether the public, including all interested groups, actually has a say in the decision-making process on how much of the good to produce and how to organize the production process. In short, the message is that participation is a critical dimension at all stages of the provision process. Accordingly, the key elements of the suggested institutional reforms are voice, access and the power to contribute.[10]

Voice

Many of today's international institutions were founded in the second half of the 1940s, when the political process, nationally and internationally, was strongly state-centred. Many countries had not yet won their political independence, and our understanding of development was quite different from what it is now. To reflect the ongoing process of change, organizational adjustments are needed. Among the authors' recommendations on this point, four stand out.

First, there is a need for more equitable North-South representation. Take the United Nations and its original membership of just 51 countries. Today more than 180 countries belong. Not only that, familiar categories of countries have, over the past five decades, lost much of their relevance. Today's distinctions include such new categories as middle-income countries, newly industrialized economies and transition economies. The industrial countries are really post-industrial—with the service sector often the most important part of the economy. Yet the unmet social agenda in these richer countries— poverty, ill health, social disintegration and reversals of human development (UNDP, *Human Development Report 1998*)—sometimes rivals that in developing countries.

At the same time, some poor countries such as China are now joining the league of major economic powers. Others, such as India and Pakistan, have entered the group of nuclear powers. Environmental goods, once considered free, are now recognized as valuable and are beginning to be priced, so some income-poor countries may soon see their natural resources revalued dramatically upwards. Other countries are population-rich. In previous decades this was seen more as a liability than an opportunity. But this perception is also changing with the emerging role of knowledge and human capital in development—and the growing purchasing power of some of the developing countries.

In the light of these changes, there is an urgent need to reconsider the composition of international forums. Rao in particular stresses the importance of more equitable North-South representation, and Spar emphasizes that it is important for developing countries to be fully present even in areas where they may not yet be active players, such as the Internet, a point strongly echoed by Sy. Efforts to enhance representativeness should not spare any organization. As Mendez points out, there is also a need for a more democratic United Nations Security Council (on this, see also Russett 1997). Yet the real question is where the momentum for these reforms could come from: who could jump start this process? Expanding the G–8 into a G–16, as suggested earlier, could be a start.

Second, there is a need for a new form of tripartism, a tradition in the International Labour Organization and its legislative body with representatives of governments, employers and labour. But various authors have in mind a new (and broader) tripartism when emphasizing the need to encourage more systematic consultation and cooperation among government, civil society and business.

Underpinning this proposal is the realization that the roles and the political balances among the different groups of actors have changed significantly. Take civil society. NGOs have increased in number in virtually all countries as well as at the global level. Barrett refers to the role of NGOs at the 1992 United Nations Conference on Environment and Development. And Chen, Evans and Cash as well as Zacher refer to increasingly active processes of worldwide informal networking among professional organizations as well as individual experts in the health field. Sen's major point is that global equity and justice do not depend on just governmental or intergovernmental initiatives. In fact, the issue is not only bringing NGOs into intergovernmental decision-making. The negotiations on the international treaty to ban land mines have shown that, at times, governments are also brought into NGO movements.[11] Human rights also presents numerous examples of NGOs being the prime provider of a global public good and of governments joining in the effort only hesitantly.

Birdsall and Lawrence remind us that many corporations have become multinational and some even transnational, and that this group of actors is the main lobby for behind-the-border policy convergence. Business also took a keen interest in the 1992 United Nations Conference on Environment and Development (see, for example, Schmidheiny and the Business Council for Sustainable Development 1992) and other environmental negotiations. Barrett highlights the important role of business (notably DuPont) in shaping international cooperation on ozone depletion—and of major energy companies in ongoing negotiations on climate change. Involvement of business in international cooperation is not a new phenomenon. Many international agreements, especially those on communications, transportation, trade and finance, have always had significant private sector inputs (see the historical accounts in Zacher and Sutton 1996). A growing number of corporations have become transnational and "footloose", and therefore more alienated from the communities where they operate (see Reinicke 1998 and Helliwell 1998). They are thus less accountable—both in a strict, legal sense and in a wider, political sense—to national governments.

Against this backdrop, Chen, Evans and Cash conclude that we will likely see more horizontally linked alliances, including all actors and levels, drawing on the comparative strengths rather than on the weaknesses of the different partners. In this scenario, intergovernmental organizations will be forums—platforms for consultations, negotiations, as well as information providers and information screening mechanisms—rather than the main providers of global public goods.

Intergovernmental organizations have undoubtedly begun to open their doors and conference rooms to civil society—and, increasingly, to business—but change has been haphazard. Strategies for how to organize the emerging tripartism, in policy-making and implementation, remain a major challenge. As Korten (1990, p. 201) points out, one obvious difficulty is to determine "which NGOs are better representatives of the people's view than official government representatives". This question is even more complex when applied to corporations.[12]

Another crucial issue in this respect is how to balance the direct influence of nonstate actors at the international level with the indirect influence they have through their channels to national governments.[13] Sen's chapter might offer an answer by drawing attention to civil society actors who think and act transnationally. Similarly, an argument could be made that transnational business is not necessarily fully represented by any one nation state—and that to have a voice, space must be provided for them in international policy-making. No doubt, this proposition requires further debate.

Another question is to what extent governments as governments (as institutions in the business of governing, rather than as country representatives) can avoid prisoner's dilemmas. Can they avoid destructive competition and meet the challenges posed by the growing mobility of capital? Kapstein refers to tax competition among states. But many other cases of policy arbitrage by nonstate actors could be mentioned. Interestingly, consultation and coordination among governments to address this challenge already seems to be happening, although more at the technical than at the political level (Slaughter 1997). It might thus become necessary to differentiate between traditional intergovernmental cooperation where states negotiate with one another on behalf of domestic constituencies, and international cooperation that allows states to work together towards shared public policy objectives.

Third, as Todd Sandler's analysis shows, even with the best of intentions, present generations typically overlook important concerns of future generations (on this, see also Schelling 1997). But tomorrow's generations are not the only ones excluded from policy-making. Older people and youth are often by-passed as well. From these observations, Sandler proposes new mechanisms to ensure wider participation of at least all present generations—young, middle-aged and old—and to encourage present generations to weigh the impact of their actions on future generations.

One possibility for ensuring that the interests of all generations, present and future, receive full consideration could be to create a new United Nations Global Trusteeship Council to act as a custodian of sustainable, or "steady-course", development.[14] The council's primary mandate would be to advise the Secretary-General when a prisoner's dilemma threatens to undermine collective action in the long-term interest of all. The council would provide guidance when short-term interests make it attractive for countries not to cooperate—even though that could result in a common tragedy, such as worldwide recession, social upheaval or irreversible environmental damage. Comprised of eminent individuals, the council could help the Secretary-General to "blow the whistle"—alerting the international community to the emerging collective action problem, supporting him as a disinterested intermediary, assisting negotiating parties with creating stronger incentives to cooperate.

Finally, representative decision-making, especially when it concerns global public goods, must reflect all interest groups to ensure that the many facets of reality are taken into account. As recent development literature, notably UNDP's *Human Development Report* (various years) have repeatedly reminded us, economic growth and income expansion are not the sum-total of human experience. Balanced development needs to be just that—balanced among economic, social, cultural, environmental and political concerns. Most of these issues have professional or other civil society organizations as their advocates. So it would be possible, as Hamburg and Holl suggest, for local populations to participate in designing peace strategies—to ensure that these strategies include not only military and strategic considerations but also concerns about national reconciliation, nation building and just and equitable development.

Power to contribute

As discussed throughout this volume, the provision of global public goods often has to start from the national level, with national—and often even local—change in policies and in development outcomes. But many countries, especially the least developed, do not have the national capacity, let alone the financial resources, to honour certain international commitments.

Zacher points out that in some instances this may even constitute a serious obstacle to forging international agreements. The case he had in mind concerned monitoring health conditions. A country without requisite capacity to respond to a problem will worry (understandably) about the consequences of reporting a disease outbreak. Disclosure of such a fact could have many adverse consequences, from loss of tourism to trade sanctions. Obviously, it is not in the interest of the developing country or the international community to abandon disease surveillance for such reasons. A more appropriate response is for the richer countries to help poorer countries develop their national capacities. Wyplosz makes a similar point about creating conditions for enhanced financial stability.

Without capacity convergence, today's globalizing world will continue to be prone to crises, and international cooperation will continue to be preoccupied with emergency rescue operations. Not only that, international cooperation will be increasingly top-heavy, trying to do at the global level what could be done much more efficiently and effectively at the regional or national. The risk that crisis management will divert scarce resources away from long-term investments is real and seems to be growing (see, for example, Chote 1998). National capacity development—globalization from below—is the more promising and sustainable route.

Access

As Sy demonstrates, the growing divide between the world's income rich and income poor is beginning to replay itself in the information area: the gap between the information rich and information poor. Sy attributes this trend mainly to privatization and liberalization, which have swept through the communications sector. Telecommunications infrastructure is a critical conduit for information and knowledge. When this infrastructure is privatized without adequate government controls, the wall between the world's growing knowledge stock and the world's information poor becomes even more difficult to bring down.

This illustrates the importance of Stiglitz's proposal to build a knowledge bank: to assemble, sort and store knowledge of special relevance to developing countries (and possibly to other poor people). Such an arrangement could significantly reduce today's tremendous underuse of knowledge. In line with the emphasis various authors place on the value of decentralized and participatory policy-making, Stiglitz's proposal could be expanded to envision the knowledge bank as an institution built from the ground up and consisting of a network of local, national and regional centres. In this way the world could benefit from a more diverse range of knowledge—that of indigenous people and of international scientists.

Similar access problems exist in other areas. As Chen, Evans and Cash as well as Cook and Sachs point out, medical advances often fail to benefit the most disease-stricken people because pharmaceutical companies tend to research and develop "profitable" diseases, those that primarily afflict rich populations. The far more crippling and lethal health hazards of the poor receive much less attention.

Of course, it should be stressed that the privatization of public goods, such as knowledge, is often a well-intended policy choice. As Stiglitz elaborates, patents and copyrights encourage private producers to provide a product. But as he also stresses, this involves judgement calls and trade-offs. While the overall intent is a gain in dynamic efficiency flowing from greater innovative activity, a loss of static efficiency is likely, from thwarted competition and underuse of the protected knowledge. Obviously, different people and countries will be affected differently by alternative decisions on this point.

A fairer process holds the promise of fairer outcomes. But recall Mendez's point about the need to distinguish between form and substance. Fairer representation in form but not in substance might fail to yield the desired result. Much depends on the weight assigned to different interests. Should the wealthy enjoy a double advantage—in resources and in agenda setting—as in many institutions at present? Or to achieve fair outcomes, would it be necessary to give special consideration to less fortunate population groups in order to end their repeated, renewed marginalization? To answer this question, we can take guidance from Rawls's two principles of justice, discussed in both Sen's and Rao's chapters. According to Rawls (1971), institutions and the outcomes they produce are just if they effectively guarantee equal opportunity for all to pursue their interests (the first principle) and if the outcomes bring the greatest benefit to the least advantaged (the second principle).

Perhaps the new United Nations Global Trusteeship Council proposed here could also be custodian of Rawls' second principle. And NGOs, in addition to their role in monitoring human rights, social and environmental concerns, might also launch a new "watch" to help monitor organizational justice, and how well international organizations meet Rawls' two principles of fairness.

CLOSING THE INCENTIVE GAP

Any progress towards closing the jurisdictional loop and making international cooperation more participatory will help narrow the incentive gap identified earlier in this chapter. But there are still opportunities for joint gains through cooperation—gains ignored today because the balance of short-term costs and benefits seems unfavourable to at least one of the parties. Cooperation is not an end in itself—it is a means to an end. International partners often have common goals but fail to reach them jointly. Unless international cooperation is incentive compatible, this could also lead to more empty resolutions, widening the implementation gap rather than narrowing it.

Incentive compatibility means that international cooperation is seen by all concerned parties to be a worthwhile outcome, leading to clear national net benefits. It is important to emphasize "net" because rational actors will consider both the gross benefits from cooperation as well as the costs, including the linkage costs or transactions costs. More than financial, the costs can include a loss of independence.

Whether participants care mostly about absolute or relative gains, cooperation is unlikely to happen or be sustainable without net positive benefits. Barrett leaves no doubt on this point. Finding the right incentive structure is the key to ensuring that internationally agreed policy priorities translate into cooperative action. The first issue we explore here concerns the techniques available to improve the incentive structures for international cooperation for the provision of global public goods.

What is an incentive? Some people are motivated more by immaterial rewards, and others more by financial gains. Within the context of international cooperation, one could imagine that some countries would feel adequately rewarded if they received added recognition as a world leader, a principled member of the international community or a nation that places altruism and concern about global equity at the core of its identity. These moral and ethical motives are also often the motivating force of NGO involvement in international affairs. Similarly, business ethics and reputation are often a critical consideration for engaging private corporations in social and environmental matters—a form of bundling private and public benefits, to which we return later.

Offering convincing incentives is not costless. They must be backed by financial resources. In particular, it takes some extra inducements to persuade actors to forgo immediate profits for the sake of future generations, as Sandler's chapter shows. We will turn later to the issue of financing, examine the current infrastucture for development financing and the modifications that could make it fit better in a global public good context.

Identifying the right supply technology

As Jayaraman and Kanbur point out, the starting point for designing cooperation strategies, including related incentive structures, is to be absolutely clear on the nature of the good to be produced. The nature of the good, in turn, largely determines the best method for supplying the good.

At the beginning of this chapter we noted that global public goods can be broken down into different classes according to the nature of the supply problem involved: overuse, underuse or undersupply (see table 1). There is a growing literature on methods (or technologies) for coping with the undersupply problem, particularly in the field of game theory (see, for example, Hirshleifer 1983; Cornes and Sandler 1996; and Sandler 1997, 1998). As a backdrop to our discussion here on incentive techniques, we briefly review the distinctions offered by Jayaraman and Kanbur. They differentiate among three supply strategies according to whether all actors have an equal role in the supply of the public good or whether some actors are more pivotal than others.

SUMMATION. Some goods are supplied by adding up many contributions of equal importance. They include global policy outcomes, such as reduced carbon dioxide emissions or reduced use of CFCs. In these cases all contributions equally affect the desired outcome because all contributions are functionally identical. In other words, a ton of greenhouse gases not emitted in Bangladesh is no different from a ton of emission reductions in France. The contribution of one actor can theoretically substitute for that of another, so it does not really matter who contributes.

Where public goods are supplied by summation, collective action problems are likely to abound. For example, a prisoner's dilemma can arise when each actor relies on the other ones to supply the good. In other cases some actors may attempt to play "chicken", threatening not to contribute in hopes that others will lose their nerve and make a contribution on which they can eventually free ride. Not surprisingly, contribution problems are common in the domain of aid, where one donor could foot the total bill and each donor's financial contribution is functionally equivalent to that of others. To overcome the incentive problem in these situations, countries can provide sanctions or inducements to contribute, or they can bundle the public good with private benefits, as described below.

WEAKEST LINK. In these cases the provision of the public good is limited by the effort of the weakest member. Prophylactic measures by countries to prevent the spread of diseases or avoid international terrorism fit this strategy. Many global regimes, from the prevention of marine pollution to prudential financial supervision, are only as strong as their weakest link. Thus provision strategies must be aimed at bringing all on board and strengthening the capacity of weak partners. Wyplosz emphasizes that efforts at enhancing financial stability must start in each country; and Zacher stresses for the same reason that a well-functioning international disease surveillance system depends on the capacity of all members to undertake national monitoring.

Yet at times, weakest-link situations also give rise to "assurance" games: the cooperating parties limit their contributions to that of the weakest member, because anything above that may well prove to be wasted. Take the arms trade dilemma, where no country has an incentive to curb exports unilaterally unless major exporters move first. Providing assurances and verification—a major role of international organizations—is one way to overcome the incentive problem in that case.

BEST SHOT. This method is called for when addressing a global concern requires the best possible and most immediate contribution, such as the most advanced medicine, the latest insights into agricultural technology or the fastest response to an emergency. The contribution of the best player defines the overall contribution of the public good. Jayaraman and Kanbur label this "max technology". Providing an example for best-shot technology in the health field, Zacher refers to the US Centers for Disease Control, often called on when a serious international risk emerges.

One danger of relying on the best-shot approach for an expanded range of goods is that it can easily be turned into a hegemonic model of public good provision. Although it is often important to have centres of excellence to rely on, overreliance on best-shot approaches can have its problems, as Cook and Sachs remind us. Excessively centralized provision of global services can stifle national ownership and produce inappropriate solutions, a point echoed by Birdsall and Lawrence as well as Wyplosz.

Another issue is burden-sharing and cost recovery: Does the best actor have enough incentive to provide the good on behalf of others? Moreover, once a good exists, there is often plenty of scope for free riding, making cost recovery difficult for the provider. Private benefits might be tacked on to the public good to induce the main actor to provide the public good. But then, the provider in a best-shot scenario may not maximize the interests of the larger community that relies on its actions. As Stiglitz notes, this tends to happen in the knowledge field where innovations can be patented. So, best-shot solutions can entail efficiency losses.

For goods that fit the best-shot or the weakest-link strategies, it is also important to assess which countries are pivotal, because cooperation is easier to arrange when the number of parties is small than when it is large (Kahler 1992; Chase, Hill and Kennedy 1999). Only a few countries are key to preserving forests that serve as global carbon sinks. Similarly, world economic trends can be strongly influenced by the macroeconomic choices of a few major economic powers.

All three methods for providing global public goods imply that additional measures are needed to induce actors to contribute—whether all actors or only pivotal actors. How can these incentives be shaped, and what form could they take?

Enhancing the incentive structure

The use of incentives is a familiar instrument of national public policy. Fiscal incentives, taxes and subsidies are perhaps the most popular tools. But there is no international taxation authority that could, by levying taxes, influence the choices of governments and private actors. In addition, most international agreements are nonbinding, and even binding ones have to be translated into national law before they take effect. Thus international incentive mechanisms must be less direct and more persuasive than coercive. From the chapter analyses we glean advice on five possible incentive measures.

COMBINING PUBLIC GAINS WITH PRIVATE GAINS. This can be done if, say, a desired public benefit can be realized through the enhanced provision of joint products, such as those with a mix of private and public benefits. Sandler refers in this connection to tropical forests. Their protection can be an important global service, but they also provide large local and national benefits that in the long run may be higher than the costs of protection. Sandler also suggests that investments in economic growth can alleviate poverty by creating jobs—and so can find more political support than "growth only" or "poverty reduction only" strategies. In the same vein, the Kyoto Protocol proposes that industrial countries supporting emission-reduction initiatives in developing countries under the Clean Development Mechanism can claim credit towards their own emission targets in return. Girls' education is another joint product. It entails private benefits for the girls, their families and the national economy, while also producing global public benefits such as lower fertility rates, thus slowing globally unsustainable population growth.

PROMOTING ADOPTION SPILLOVERS. As Heal points out, many public goods have large fixed costs, often those of research and development or infrastructure development. These costs have to be paid only once. Whoever makes these investments first confers benefits on others. For example, stricter emissions laws in some major industrial countries have compelled car manufacturers and fuel producers to improve their products globally—to the benefit of the environment and consumers everywhere. When other states adopted similar laws later, the costs were far lower because of the earlier steps by the larger economies—manufacturers already knew how to make cleaner cars. For adoption spillovers, major economies have a de facto standard-setting role—they are pivotal actors, so to speak. When research and development efforts are financed from national public resources, adoption spillovers can mean indirect development assistance. Thinking back to the national externality profile, a country could list such contributions as a positive externality.

However attractive this strategy may be, it requires the leader or best-shot provider to take the first step. Consumers, citizens and private actors in these major markets should be aware of the global spillovers of their decisions, and this awareness can create an added incentive for setting the right standards. For the private sector, new business opportunities have been a powerful incentive for, say, auto manufacturers to comply with the standards set in the major markets.

But adoption spillovers can also provide deterrents. The labelling of products as "no child labour" or "dolphin-safe" compels other producers—if consumers respond to the label—to move to a new standard. In this case standard-setting can be accomplished by NGOs and the private sector, or in public-private collaboration.

FORMING CLUBS. According to Cornes and Sandler (1996, pp. 33–34), "a club is a voluntary group deriving mutual benefit from sharing one or more of the following: production costs, members' characteristics . . . or a good characterized by excludable benefits". Several authors suggest that forming an issue-based club can help avoid free riding where a global public good is at least partly excludable and offers highly desirable benefits. The incentive problem then becomes easier, because those who fail to contribute their share of the public good are not admitted into the club.

Accordingly, Wyplosz suggests a club approach to capital account liberalization that relies on pre-qualification. Instead of thrusting capital account liberalization on ill-prepared countries, one could define preconditions for a country's full international financial liberalization. The country could meet the conditions at its own pace and in its own way and then apply for membership. On qualification, it would be authorized to have full entry into international financial markets. This could bring several benefits, such as lower costs for borrowing capital and the benefit of bailout insurance should the country suffer a financial crisis. Even without qualification, countries could enter international financial markets, but without the expectation of international public support in a crisis.

Birdsall and Lawrence suggest the possibility of regional clubs for common trade-related policy approaches. Cook and Sachs suggest taking the territorial—often regional or subregional—boundaries of development challenges as a basis for "aid clubs". One could also envision that some of the other organizational proposals by the authors could, at least initially, take the form of a club. Kapstein—based on Tanzi (1996)—calls for an international taxation organization. Such an organization could facilitate intergovernmental consultations on fiscal issues and reduce the problems of policy arbitrage.

As noted, the benefits of some clubs increase with more members. This applies to networks and network benefits. Clearly, the knowledge bank could be seen as a network, as could norms and standards clubs of the kind recommended by Wyplosz. Since some clubs have an interest in expanding membership, it is often efficient for them to support new members in qualifying for membership. Accordingly, several authors emphasize the importance of technical assistance for potential members. (Such support would be a joint product—providing private benefits to applicants and club benefits to members.)

Much technical cooperation today, especially for governance, aims to ensure that statistics, say, are up to par and internationally comparable, or that procurement rules conform to a given model. That is, international cooperation already focuses on helping countries enter technical clubs, benefiting both the existing and new members of the club. But to be a relevant policy instrument for the provision of global public goods, clubs would have to function openly and transparently to establish their legitimacy (on this point, see also Lawrence, Bressand and Ito 1996).

REPOSITIONING THE GOOD ON THE PUBLIC-PRIVATE SCALE. Early in this chapter we noted that the publicness or privateness of a good is not an invariable quality. It often depends on the policy choice—and, of course, on the technologies available. The authors discuss various ways of enhancing the provision of global public goods by making these goods—or critical inputs into their production—more private. This may sound like a contradiction. Yet enhanced privateness—say, through the definition of new property rights— can avoid free riding and prisoner's dilemmas and return to the optimal incentive structure of the private markets.

Take the famous tragedy of the commons and the problem of the over-grazing of communal land. To avoid a free-for-all depletion of the commons, one solution is to define property rights and give owners responsibility for sustaining and managing their land plots. Property holders are expected to use their assets more efficiently. Of course, this approach is simple enough with land, which can be enclosed and is thus physically (but not always legally) excludable.

Property rights can also manage scarcities, as with pollution permits, described by Heal. But the problems of defining the property rights—pollution entitlements in this case—should not be underestimated (Cooper 1994). As Heal underscores, a judicious allocation of pollution entitlements (or any other quotas), is important to allow markets to function efficiently. He suggests that the allocation of quotas may have to favour developing countries proportionately more than industrial countries to meet the efficiency requirement.

The Coase theorem (Coase 1960) has contributed to our understanding of how to tackle public good issues with private mechanisms. According to the theorem: if there are no transactions costs and if liability laws and property rights are clear, there is no need for a central authority to tackle externalities— the market failures will correct themselves. In such an environment the victim of a negative externality can threaten to sue for redress and then negotiate a mutually agreeable compensation. But as Cooper (1994) and Streeten (1994) note, these mechanisms are not well suited to the international environment, where there are many jurisdictions, high levels of uncertainty, and typically large transactions costs.

The opposite—making private goods more public—is also a familiar strategy, especially for human-made commons that suffer from underuse and insufficient access, but also for such private goods as finance. An example: the recourse to public development finance for countries that are excluded from private financial flows. Development assistance consists of subsidized loans, such as those provided by the World Bank, notably through the International Development Association (World Bank 1998). It also consists of grant money, such as the funds channelled through UNDP (see UNDP 1998a). These organizations facilitate developing countries' access to financial resources that they would otherwise not be able to claim. Technical assistance—delivered bilaterally or multilaterally through the agencies of the UN system, such as the Food and Agriculture Organization, World Health Organization, United Nations Children's Fund and United Nations Population Fund—performs a similar role. It promotes access to such essential private goods as food and shelter. In so doing, it also enhances the global public good of economic and social stability and progress.

PAYING THE RIGHT PRICE. Getting prices right can be critical in making international cooperation work—through cost sharing, refunds and the like (see Sandler 1998). As Barrett shows, the Montreal Protocol offers side-payments to developing countries (through the Multilateral Fund) and transition economies (through the Global Environment Facility) for the additional or incremental costs they incur from participating in the global effort. The United Nations Framework Convention on Climate Change and the United Nations Convention on Biodiversity make similar provisions. For example, with the Clean Development Mechanism of the Kyoto Protocol, rich countries can fulfil part of their commitments to reduce emissions by providing assistance and incentives to poor countries—rather than by adjusting themselves (UNDP 1998b). But side-payments may be too vague and too undifferentiated a concept to ensure an effective functioning of externality exchanges in the future.

Contributions to global public goods can be exchanged, but in such an exchange the goods have be priced. More research and policy debate is needed on how to calculate costs—and judge offers—on both sides of the bargain. Should one consider only direct costs or include opportunity costs in the equation? Should the scarcity of the good be taken into account? How should potential windfall profits be provided? Such profits could accrue if one country asks another that can provide a good more efficiently to do so, allowing the requesting country to enjoy considerable savings. As experience with permit trading shows, the trading of fish quotas under the European Common Fisheries Policy (*The Economist*, 21 November, 1998) has brought out the true value of the good and made trading attractive. Clearly, if the price or the compensation is at the right level, externality trading can work, and such schemes as the Clean Development Mechanism could yield significant results.

A key question to resolve in this context is whether to manage trade bureaucratically or to let markets work. If side-payments simply reimburse actors for the direct costs of their cooperation, a long-term commitment to reciprocal cooperation will be necessary—so that cooperation costs and benefits can be expected over time to even out fairly for all parties concerned (Axelrod 1984). Without such a strong, long-term commitment to cooperation, each "game" will have to yield attractive net benefits. In that case, direct cost reimbursement may be too modest an incentive.

Clearly, designing an international public incentive system is an intricate matter. But it is doable. And it provides hope. By developing the techniques for making cooperation incentive-compatible, we have a way out of the grim logic of the prisoner's dilemma and the collective irrationality of free riding. In a globalizing world of mounting externalities and systemic risks, the idea of going it alone, playing chicken and opting for other noncooperative strategies will bring only short-lived gains. A more appropriate and sustainable strategy is to aim for inclusion—by bringing everyone on board and avoiding defection.

RESTRUCTURING DEVELOPMENT FINANCE

Efforts to strengthen international public incentives do not necessarily entail financial implications, but the question of finance is important precisely because of the need to provide extra incentives or to strengthen weak links in the global system. How well does today's system of development financing meet the requirements of providing for global public goods? Is it equipped to facilitate the necessary financial transactions?

To simplify matters, we focus on official development finance, by which we mean all official, government-supported financial transactions— side-payments, incremental cost payments, and payments of costs priced through market mechanisms, such as a pollution permit trading. We will not totally leave aside private payments, especially where they complement official transactions. But we will not address in this synthesis how to make financial markets work more efficiently and more in support of development. Private payments are critical in the total picture of financing development (and as discussed in the chapter by Wyplosz), but our concern here is limited to financing international development cooperation. In particular, we discuss the key features of the present financing mechanisms for development cooperation—and some possible adjustments of that system to the new exigencies.

Present financing arrangements

The term "international development cooperation" today means primarily aid. It refers to the official development assistance (ODA) provided by richer donor countries to poorer recipient countries. About two-thirds of ODA is provided through bilateral channels; the rest through multilateral aid agencies and, increasingly, NGOs.[15] As Cook and Sachs point out, ODA flows and the programmes they support are primarily directed at nations and at national governments. Country allocations, rather than issue allocations, are the norm. Within countries, funds often flow through a specialized agency such as the United Nations Educational, Scientific and Cultural Organization or World Health Organization, reflecting a sectoral approach to development. In some cases sectors are also important from a global public good perspective, because they are linked to an important global challenge. This applies to health and population. But many of today's challenges are more cross-sectoral than sectoral: the environment, equity, market efficiency, knowledge and food security. So too would be macroeconomic coordination, if one day it were to move to the centre of international cooperation.

New financing arrangements

This situation has several implications for cooperation aimed at the provision of global public goods. Here are some of the changes that could be envisioned:

EXPANDING THE CATEGORIES OF ACTORS. Today's system offers only two roles: donor or recipient of ODA. The criterion for being a recipient is primarily a country's income with other factors that may cause special vulnerability, such as being land-locked or drought-prone. But as the discussion on incentives has shown, a public goods strategy needs more differentiated roles. For example, there is a need to distinguish between producers and recipients of externalities. Recipients fall into two groups: the beneficiaries of positive externalities, and the victims of negative externalities. Correspondingly, the generators of externalities can be a source of benefits (possibly "donors") or a source of negative spillovers (possibly "polluters"). Who has what role in relation to whom will obviously vary from issue to issue. There is also the role of pivotal actors, whether they are weak links in a regime of underprovided goods or preferred providers (such as countries with large reserves of biodiversity or cultural goods).

The picture becomes even more complex with financing. Take the case, described by Jayaraman and Kanbur, of a traditional aid donor who concludes that investing in pollution abatement in a developing country is more efficient than undertaking investments for this purpose at home. So the "donor" offers an investment incentive to a developing country. Is this aid? Is the "donor" a donor? Or is this the "procurement of a service"? Who is the actual donor in this relationship? The same question was posed earlier when we discussed assistance to allow developing countries to enter technical and policy clubs: are we still talking about aid here? Unlike the transfers and incentives necessary to procure global public goods, traditional aid has to be refocused on humanitarian imperatives.

A reliable answer to these questions requires greater clarity and certainty about precisely how the deal is structured and what financial and other resource transfers are involved. We will not settle such questions here. The discussion is meant to illustrate that the current system of development cooperation needs an expanded typology of actors if it is to accommodate global public good strategies. We still need the traditional roles of "donor" and "recipient". But development cooperation will be even more important—and more complicated—in a global public good context.

ALLOCATING RESOURCES BY COUNTRY AND ISSUE. Future financing for international development cooperation will require more than a country focus. It will also require an issue focus: for allocations of global public good resources. This change could be facilitated by differentiating in the future between two types of ODA: country allocations of ODA, (ODA-C) and global ODA allocations, (ODA-G). Global ODA could also include regional allocations (ODA-R), in line with the proposal by Cook and Sachs.

CREATING FOCUSED GLOBAL PUBLIC GOOD FUNDS. Several authors suggest that adequate financing of global public goods requires special financing facilities for the good in question. Hamburg and Holl propose a facility for conflict prevention. Ismail Serageldin makes a case for a global culture facility, modeled along the lines of the Global Environment Facility (GEF 1994). And Wyplosz mentions a global financial insurance fund, which also needs financing. If the knowledge bank proposed by Stiglitz were set up like a foundation, it too would need an endowment. This list is not exhaustive, but it shows the general need for re-examining the present system of development financing from the viewpoint of whether each major concern has an adequate arrangement for its funding.

CREATING A GLOBAL PARTICIPATION FUND. One global public good is obviously missing from both the list of organizations and funding arrangements: equity, which may be so cross-sectoral that it can hardly be separated from the issue areas where it applies. It is also a broad concept that needs to be made operational. As suggested earlier, an important starting point for equity is participation—having the option to be fully and effectively involved in decisions that affect one's life. Equity in participation, should be embedded in the structures of international governance, as Kapstein and Rao argue.

One way to do this is to create a global participation fund. This fund would provide developing countries with a resource pool that they could administer independently to strengthen their capacity to participate in international negotiations on global public goods. For example, countries could use fund resources to coordinate their policy stance or strengthen their negotiating skills in different areas—or to participate in international debates where they would not otherwise be heard. The fund's resources could consist of an additional 0.1% of the traditional aid donor countries' GNP, on a time-bound basis of, say, five years.

PROMOTING REGIONAL, SELF-ADMINISTERED FUNDS. Several authors have presented strong arguments for a more regional approach to identifying policy priorities and implementing cooperation initiatives. A natural complement of these proposals, as argued by Cook and Sachs, is to allocate funding on a more regional basis in the key issue areas. The precedent for this suggestion: the Marshall Plan, under which the United States provided assistance to the war-torn societies of Europe after the Second World War. The plan's implementation was self-administered by the recipient countries, which reviewed each other's assistance requests, and through peer review and monitoring, ensured the proper use of funds.[16] Analysts agree that the Marshall Plan process was critical in laying a foundation for the subsequent integration of Europe. The OECD also had its origin in this process.[17] Now, more than 50 years later, perhaps the time has come to replicate the Marshall Plan model and create more regional OECDs, possibly integrated into such regional bodies as the Andean Pact, the Association for South-East Asian Nations, the Economic Community of West African States, Mercosur and the Southern African Development Community.[18]

ADJUSTING NATIONAL PUBLIC FINANCE. One aspect of national sovereignty that governments guard most jealously is their taxation authority. That is why the bulk of development finance has to come from national budgets. So, it is important to ensure that the external dimensions of national concerns—as well as the country's obligations to internalize its negative cross-border spillovers—are adequately reflected in national budgets. To establish clear national responsibility for global public goods, sectoral ministries could maintain two main budget lines, one for domestic expenditures and one for meeting the financial implications of international cooperation. Alternatively, ministries of foreign affairs or development cooperation authorities could add special global public goods accounts to their traditional aid allocation. Some countries are already moving in this direction. Denmark recently increased its aid allocation by 0.5% of its GNP in order to support global environmental concerns and international human disaster relief.

To the extent that a clearer focus on global public goods means more expenditures, resources could be freed by reducing perverse fiscal incentives, or incentives that encourage public bads (UNDP, *Human Development Report 1998*). If governments were to aim at discouraging bads more decisively, there would also be huge scope for mobilizing additional resources. According to Cooper (1998), OECD models suggest that a worldwide tax on carbon emissions would in 2020 yield some $750 billion in revenue, or 1.3% of that year's gross world product.

Another option is the one suggested by Chen, Evans and Cash, to revisit the idea of a surcharge on international air travel—in effect, a fee for enjoying the benefit of good global health conditions worldwide. The revenue from such a fee could be channeled back into financing international health initiatives. Stiglitz mentions a fee for inventors seeking patents to pay for the global knowledge stock that they undoubtedly made use of, and from which they will profit. Interestingly, the World Intellectual Property Organisation (WIPO) recently cut its fees by 15% because record numbers of patent applications have allowed it to accumulate large surpluses (Williams 1997). Perhaps a link could be forged between patent fees and the financing of a global knowledge bank. For example, a part of WIPO's earnings could be used to support neglected research—for example on tropical diseases and agriculture—and basic education for all. It could also be used to support access of poor countries to critical but still patented knowledge. Constructing a closer link between the United Nations Educational, Scientific and Cultural Organization (UNESCO) and WIPO could thus be a step towards creating a knowledge bank, or at least towards creating a global hub for such an institution.

Clearly, traditional aid mechanisms are far too confining to accommodate the new and varied financing requirements of a global public good strategy. Traditional aid is one of its elements, but the strategy will not succeed without a wider framework of international development cooperation offering additional financing sources and methods.

*   *   *

The concept of global public goods can help us understand and respond to the new global policy challenges likely to face nations in the 21st century. Tackling this growing agenda of common concerns will require fresh thinking, intense research efforts, new political instruments and innovative policy responses. But it is clear that more research and debate are needed to refine and apply the ideas presented here to individual policy problems. We hope that this book is a start.

NOTES

The views presented here are those of authors and not necessarily those of the institution with which they are affiliated.

1. For examples of these NGOs, see Social Watch (1998); Human Rights Watch (1998); Amnesty International (1998); Brown, Renner and Flavin (1998); Brown and Flavin (1999); and Transparency International (1998).

2. More treaties were signed in the four decades after the Second World War than in the previous four centuries (Grenville and Wasserstein 1987, p.1). In 1972, at the United Nations Conference on Human Environment, there were only three dozen multilateral agreements concerned with the environment. When countries met 20 years later at the Earth Summit in Rio de Janeiro, there were more than 900 agreements and significant nonbinding legal instruments concerned with the environment (Weiss and Jacobson 1996, p.1). In addition, from the Congress of Vienna in 1815 until the 1990s, the number of international organizations has increased steadily. For example, from about 30 in 1910, the number of interna-

tional organizations grew to almost 70 in 1940 and then to more than 1,000 in 1980, with 1,147 recorded in 1992. (Shanks, Jacobson and Kaplan 1996, pp. 593 and 598).

3. A review of the literature on international cooperation reveals that some practices are critical to successful negotiations and effective follow-up. Besides certainty, they include clearly defined and "doable" objectives, a fair and credible treaty design that provides gains for all and is self-enforcing through built-in incentives, an incremental approach building from framework agreements to precise commitments, a realistic expectation that cooperation is an ongoing exercise, a culture of altruism and concern for others and global issues, and, of course, political leadership. See, in particular, Axelrod (1984), Barrett (in this volume), Cooper (1989), and Kindleberger (1986).

4. As North (1995, p. 22) puts it, "successful development policy entails an understanding of the dynamics of economic change if the policies pursued are to have the desired consequences. And a dynamic model of economic change entails as an integral part of that model analysis of the polity, since it is the polity that specifies and enforces the formal rules".

5. According to Reinicke (1998, p. 57), "external sovereignty implies the absence of a supreme authority and therefore the interdependence of states in the international system". However, both sides of sovereignty are closely interrelated: "given the nature of the origin of external sovereignty, any threat to it would ultimately also affect its internal counterpart. Similarly, a sustained challenge to a country's internal sovereignty will eventually affect its external sovereignty" (p. 58).

6. In this connection it is useful to take a closer look at the term "cooperation". According to Bryant (1995), it is best defined as an umbrella term for the entire spectrum of interactions among national governments. But it would also apply to interactions among other actors or actor groups. Bryant distinguishes four types, or levels, of cooperation: consultation, mutual recognition, coordination and explicit harmonization (p. 6). He adds that "consultation alone involves only a small degree of cooperative management. Mutual recognition and coordination are more ambitious, and explicit harmonization still more so. At the opposite extreme of the spectrum, which entails no cooperation and may be labeled 'national autonomy', the decisions of governments are completely decentralized" (pp. 6-7). In part, today's problems of cooperation may stem from the fact that we are, in more and more issue areas, attempting a step forward: from consultation to mutual recognition, or from mutual recognition to coordination and, increasingly, harmonization.

7. A particularly complex issue, which could arise when identifying and ranking externalities, relates to effects transmitted through markets—such as foreign trade and investments—from country to country. Wyplosz, for example, distinguishes between pecuniary and nonpecuniary externalities. Pecuniary externalities are calculable and subject to pricing. For example, the price of

borrowing capital is typically risk-adjusted. In that case, financial risk really ceases to be an externality because it is being taken into account in economic decision-making. Nonpecuniary externalities, such as financial contagion effects, on the other hand, are less predictable, and therefore less amenable to pricing.

A related issue is the "export" of low environmental or social standards, sometimes—but not always rightly—referred to as "ecodumping" or "social dumping". In this case, environmental or social conditions, which have no border-transgressing externalities, nevertheless affect other countries because they are embodied in traded goods or services. The main challenge here is not to confuse externalities with comparative advantage (or competitiveness). Additionally, if cultural sensitivities are touched (that is, psychological externalities exist), then it may be necessary to seek an appropriate corrective means—for example, social or economic labelling (which would provide consumers with better information and allow them to make a well-informed choice between buying or boycotting a good) or appropriate compensation and aid (which, for example, could be targeted at reducing a problem such as child labour). For a more detailed discussion on such market-transmitted effects, see Bhagwati (1997) and Cooper (1994).

8. Helliwell's (1998) comparative analysis of economic linkages within and across countries shows that, among other things, internal economic linkages are still much tighter than those between nations. The author thus concludes that "the shrinking size and pervasiveness of border effects reveal that the global economy of the 1990s is really a patchwork of national economies, stitched together by threads of trade and investment that are much weaker than the economic fabric of nations" (p. 118).

9. The principle of subsidiarity is extensively debated within the context of the European Union. An interesting analysis of its pros and cons in various issue areas, which could provide policy guidance for the application of the principle at the international level, is presented in CEPR (1993). The authors conclude that "coordinating policies yield benefits when scale economies or spillovers between member states are important.... [But centralization] also has costs. By diminishing accountability it offers scope for policies to diverge from the best interest of constituent states, regions or localities.... By laying the burden of proof on those wishing to centralize, subsidiarity recognizes the initial sovereignty of member states and emphasizes that problems of accountability of 'government failure' at the centre may be substantial.... Even within issues, the case for centralization is much weaker for some policies than for others.... Regulation of drinking water quality, for instance, is inconsistent with subsidiarity, but there is a better case for an EC role in management of problems such as the pollution of the Rhine" (pp. xv–xvii).

10. Some analysts (Gilpin 1987; Kindleberger 1986) have pointed to the possibility of a "benevolent hegemon" assuming major responsibility for providing global public goods, such as military security or financial rescue packages. However, past experience in that respect (for example, the role of the United

States in international peacekeeping) demonstrates the limits of such a hegemonic approach. A hegemonic provision process may be unfair, and can stifle the initiative of other actors and thus prove inefficient.

11. The Convention on the Prohibition of the Use, Stockpiling, Production and Transfer of Anti Personnel Mines and on Their Destruction was signed by 121 states on 3–4 December 1997 in Ottawa, Canada. The convention represents a milestone in international cooperation: it was initiated by a group of like-minded states and NGOs, notably the International Campaign to Ban Landmines (ICBL), outside the auspices of the concerned intergovernmental forums and without the backing of some of the major powers (see http://www.armscontrol.org/FACTS/aplfact.htm). The ICBL was awarded the 1997 Nobel Peace Prize for its role in this campaign. Another example of the growing influence of NGOs on international policy-making is the lobbying effort they staged to postpone discussions at the OECD on a Multilateral Agreement on Investment. See de Jonquieres (1998).

12. For background information on private sector partnerships with multilateral organizations, see United Nations 1998a, 1999 and www.un.org/partners (particularly "New Dimensions on Cooperation: Case Studies from the UN System") and www.worldbank.org/html/extdr/business/bpcpartners.htm.

13. This point was brought to our attention by Ralph C. Bryant.

14. A similar proposal was put forward by the Commission on Global Governance (1995) and is also included in the report of the Secretary-General of the United Nations on reform of the organization (United Nations 1997). Unlike these earlier proposals, we do not recommend revising the mandate of the existing Trusteeship Council, whose role it was to supervise the administration of former Trust Territories. Instead, we suggest a new United Nations Global Trusteeship Council be established based on a fresh General Assembly mandate.

15. For a definition of the different types of flows and relevant statistics, see OECD/DAC (1998).

16. For descriptions of the plan, see Kunz (1997) and Reynolds (1997).

17. To facilitate a joint and self-administered process to implement the Marshall Plan, the recipient countries formed the Organisation for European Economic Co-operation (OEEC), the forerunner of today's OECD (Raffer and Singer 1996). Looking back at the Marshall Plan experience and ahead to the 21st century, Rostow (1997, pp. 211–12) concludes that "one cannot overestimate the importance of the Marshall Plan's multilateral character. It provided an essential element of dignity and partnership to even the smallest powers. In the 21st century, the diffusion of power makes it even more essential that plans of action be arrived at on a multilateral basis.... The Marshall Plan did not merely put the economies of Western Europe back on their feet. It was part of an effort to create a world unlike that of the failed interwar years...it was the matrix within which the Europeans drew together and learned from a parochial past". As DeLong and

Eichengreen (1993, p. 191) argue, "the Marshall Plan should thus be thought of as a large and highly successful structural adjustment program".

18. The call for a new Marshall Plan for developing countries has resurfaced at various times since the Second World War. Among others, Austria's former Federal Chancellor Bruno Kreisky was a strong advocate of this proposal (Raffer and Singer 1996, p. 62). Other advocates include Streeten (1994), Raffer and Singer (1996) and Schelling (1997).

REFERENCES

Amnesty International. 1998. *Amnesty International Report 1998.* London.

Axelrod, Robert. 1984. *The Evolution of Cooperation.* New York: Basic Books.

Bhagwati, Jagdish. 1997. "The Global Age: From a Sceptical South to a Fearful North." *World Economy* 20(3): 259–83.

BIS (Bank for International Settlements). Various years. *Annual Report.* Basle.

Boyer, Robert, and Daniel Drache, eds. 1996. *States against Markets: The Limits of Globalization.* London and New York: Routledge.

Brown, Lester R., and Christopher Flavin. 1999. *State of the World 1999: A Worldwatch Institute Report on Progress toward a Sustainable Society.* New York: W.W. Norton.

Brown, Lester R., Michael Renner and Christopher Flavin. 1998. *Vital Signs 1998.* New York: W.W. Norton.

Bryant, Ralph C. 1980. *Money and Monetary Policy in Independent Nations.* Washington, DC: Brookings Institution.

———. 1995. *International Coordination of National Stabilization Policies.* Washington, DC: Brookings Institution.

Bull, Hedley. 1977. *The Anarchical Society.* New York: Columbia University Press.

CEPR (Centre for Economic Policy Research). 1993. *Annual Report 1992–93.* London.

Chase, Robert, Emily Hill and Paul Kennedy, eds. 1999. *The Pivotal States: A New Framework for U.S. Policy in the Developing World.* New York: W.W. Norton.

Chote, Robert. 1998. "World Bank Sounds Alarm over Risky Emergency Loans." *Financial Times.* 25 September.

Coase, Ronald H. 1960. "The Problem of Social Cost." *Journal of Law and Economics* 3(1): 1–44.

Commission on Global Governance. 1995. *Our Global Neighborhood: The Report of the Commission on Global Governance.* New York: Oxford University Press.

Cooper, Richard N. 1989. "International Cooperation in Public Health As a Prologue to Macroeconomic Cooperation." In Richard N. Cooper and others, eds., *Can Nations Agree? Issues in International Economic Cooperation.* Washington, DC: Brookings Institution.

————. 1994. *Environment and Resource Policies for the World Economy.* Washington, DC: Brookings Institution.

————. 1998. "Toward a Real Global Warming Treaty." *Foreign Affairs* 77(2): 66–79.

Cornes, Richard, and Todd Sandler. 1996. *The Theory of Externalities, Public Goods and Club Goods.* 2nd ed. Cambridge: Cambridge University Press.

Cutajar, Michael Zammit. 1998. "The Complex Process towards Consensus: The State of the Climate Talks before the Buenos Aires Meeting." *Development and Cooperation* 6: 8–11.

de Jonquieres, Guy. 1998. "Network Guerillas." *Financial Times.* 30 April.

DeLong, J. Bradford, and Barry Eichengreen. 1993. "The Marshall Plan: History's Most Successful Structural Adjustment Programme." In Rüdiger Dornbusch,Wilhelm Nölling and Rilard Lagard, eds., *Postwar Economic Reconstruction and Lessons for the East Today.* Cambridge, MA: MIT Press.

The Economist. 1998. "Financial Trawling." 21 November.

Eichengreen, Barry. 1992. *Golden Fetters: The Gold Standard and the Great Depression 1919–1939.* New York: Oxford University Press.

————. 1999. *The New Financial Architecture.* Washington, DC: Institute of International Economics.

Financial Times. 1999. "Security Advice Goes Online." 8 February.

GEF (Global Environment Facility). 1994. *Instrument for the Establishment of the Restructured Global Environment Facility.* Washington, DC.

Gilpin, Robert G. 1987. *The Political Economy of International Relations.* Princeton, NJ: Princeton University Press.

Grenville, J.A.S., and Bernard Wasserstein. 1987. *The Major International Treaties since 1945: A History and Guide with Texts.* New York: Methuen.

Haas, Peter, ed. 1992. "Epistemic Communities and International Policy Coordination." *International Organization* 46 (1).

Helliwell, John F. 1998. *How Much Do National Borders Matter?* Washington, DC: Brookings Institution.

Hirshleifer, Jack. 1983. "From Weakest-Link to Best-Shot: The Voluntary Provision of Public Goods." *Economica* 61(1): 79–92.

Hirst, Paul, and Grahame Thompson. 1996. *Globalization in Question: The International Economy and Possibilities of Governance.* Cambridge: Polity Press.

Human Rights Watch. 1998. *World Report 1999.* New York: Human Rights Watch.

Huntington, Samuel P. 1996. "The West: Unique, Not Universal." *Foreign Affairs* 75(6): 28–46.

IMF (International Monetary Fund). Various years. *World Economic Outlook.* Washington, DC.

Kahler, Miles. 1992. "Multilateralism with Small and Large Numbers." *International Organization* 46 (3): 681–708.

Kaplan, Robert D. 1994. "The Coming Anarchy." *Atlantic Monthly* (February): 44–76.

Keohane, Robert O., and Joseph S. Nye. 1989. *Power and Interdependence.* 2nd ed. New York: HarperCollins.

Kindleberger, Charles P. 1986. "International Public Goods without International Government." *American Political Review* 76(1): 1–13.

Kingsbury, Benedict. 1996. "Grotius, Law and Moral Scepticism: Theory and Practice in the Thought of Hedley Bull." In Ian Clark and Iver B. Neumann, eds., *Classical Theories of International Relations.* New York: St. Martin's Press.

Korten, David C. 1990. *Getting to the 21st Century: Voluntary Action and the Global Agenda.* Hartford, CT: Kumarian Press.

Krause, Keith, and W. Andy Knight, eds. 1995. *State, Society, and the UN System: Changing Perspectives on Multilateralism.* Tokyo: United Nations University Press.

Kunz, Diane B. 1997. "The Marshall Plan Reconsidered." *Foreign Affairs* 76(3): 162–70.

Lawrence, Robert Z., Albert Bressand and Takatoshi Ito. 1996. *A Vision for the World Economy: Openness, Diversity, and Cohesion.* Washington: The Brookings Institution.

Mathews, Jessica. 1997. "Power Shift." *Foreign Affairs* 76(1): 50–66.

Ndegwa, Stephen N. 1996. *The Two Faces of Civil Society: NGOs and Politics in Africa.* Hartford, CT: Kumarian Press.

North, Douglass. 1995. "The New Institutional Economics and Third World Development." In John Harris, Janet Hunter and Colin M. Lewis, eds., *The New Institutional Economics and Third World Development.* London and New York: Routledge.

OECD/DAC (Organisation for Economic Co-operation and Development/ Development Assistance Committee). 1996. *Shaping the 21st Century: The Contribution of Development Co-operation.* Paris.

————. 1998. *Development Cooperation: Efforts and Policies of the Members of the Development Assistance Committee 1997 Report.* Paris.

Raffer, Kunibert. 1998. "ODA and Global Housekeeping: A Trend Analysis of Past and Present Spending Patterns." ODS Working Paper. United Nations Development Programme, Office of Development Studies, New York.

Raffer, Kunibert, and Hans Singer. 1996. *The Foreign Aid Business: Economic Assistance and Development Cooperation.* Cheltenham, UK: Edward Elgar.

Rawls, John. 1971. *A Theory of Justice.* Cambridge, MA: Harvard University Press.

Reinicke, Wolfgang H. 1998. *Global Public Policy: Governing Without Government?* Washington, DC: Brookings Institution.

Reynolds, David. 1997. "The European Response: Primacy of Politics." *Foreign Affairs* 76(3): 171–84.

Rodrik, Dani. 1997. *Has Globalization Gone Too Far?* Washington, DC: Institute for International Economics.

Rostow, Walt W. 1997. "Lessons of the Plan: Looking Forward to the Next Century." *Foreign Affairs* 76(3): 205–12.

Russett, Bruce. 1997. *The Once and Future Security Council.* New York: Saint Martin's Press.

Sachs, Jeffrey. 1998. "Making it Work." *The Economist.* 12 September.

Sandler, Todd. 1997. *Global Challenges: An Approach to Environmental, Political, and Economic Problems.* Cambridge: Cambridge University Press.

————. 1998. "Global and Regional Public Goods: A Prognosis for Collective Action." *Fiscal Studies* 19(1): 221–47.

Schelling, Thomas C. 1997. "The Cost of Combatting Global Warming: Facing the Tradeoffs." *Foreign Affairs* 76(6): 8–14.

Schmidheiny, Stephan and the Business Council for Sustainable Development. 1992. *A Global Business Perspective on Development and the Environment.* Cambridge, MA: MIT Press.

Shanks, Cheryl, Harold K. Jacobson and Jeffrey H. Kaplan. 1996. "Inertia and Change in the Constellation of International Governmental Organizations, 1981–1992." *International Organization* 50 (4): 593–627.

Slaughter, Anne-Marie. 1997. "The Real New World Order." *Foreign Affairs* 76(5): 183–97.

Social Watch. 1998. *Social Watch.* Uruguay: Instituto del Tercer Mundo.

Strange, Susan. 1996. *The Retreat of the State.* Cambridge: Cambridge University Press.

Streeten, Paul. 1994. "A New Framework for Development Cooperation." In Terenzio Cozzi, Pier Carlo Nicola, Luigi Pasinetti and Alberto Quadrio

Curzio. *Benessere Equilibrio e Sviluppo: Stidu in Onore di Siro Lombardini.* Milan: Vita e Pensiero.

Tanzi, Vito. 1996. "Is There a Need for a World Tax Organization?" Paper presented at the International Institute of Public Finance, 26–29 August, Tel Aviv, Israel.

Transparency International. 1998. *1998 Annual Report—Combating Corruption: Are Lasting Solutions Emerging?* Berlin, Germany.

United Nations. 1948. *Universal Declaration on Human Rights.* General Assembly Resolution 217 III. New York.

———. 1972. "Report of the United Nations Conference on the Human Environment." A/CONF.48/141Rev.1. Stockholm. Also reprinted in *International Legal Materials* 31(1992): 849–73.

———. 1992. "Agenda 21." Adopted by the United Nations Conference on Environment and Development. A/CONF.151/26/Rev.1 (vol.1) (93.I.8). Rio de Janeiro, Brazil.

———. 1997. "Renewing the UN: A Programme for Reform." Report of the Secretary-General. A/51/950. New York.

———. 1998a. "Joint Statement on Common Interests by UN Secretary-General and International Chamber of Commerce." United Nations Department of Information Press Release SG/2043.9.New York.

———. 1998b. "Report of the Conference of the Parties on its Third Session." FCCC/CP/1997/7. Kyoto, Japan.

———. 1999. Secretary-General's Address to World Economic Forum in Davos. SG/SM.6881/Rev/1. New York.

UNAIDS (United Nations Joint Programme on HIV/AIDS). 1998. *UNAIDS Progress Report 1996/97.* Geneva.

UNCTAD (United Nations Conference on Trade and Development). Various years. *Trade and Development Report.* Geneva and New York.

UNDCP (United Nations International Drug Control Programme). 1997. *World Drug Report.* New York: Oxford University Press.

UNDP (United Nations Development Programme). 1998a. *Annual Report of the Administrator 1997.* DP/1998/17. New York.

———. 1998b. *The Clean Development Mechanism—Issues and Options.* New York.

———. Various years. *Human Development Report.* New York: Oxford University Press.

UNFPA (United Nations Population Fund). Various years. *The State of the World Population.* New York.

UNHCR (United Nations High Commissioner for Refugees). Various years. *The State of the World's Refugees.* New York: Oxford University Press.

Wade, Robert, and Frank Veneroso. 1998. "Two Views on Asia: The Resources Lie Within." *The Economist.* 7 November.

Weiss, Edith Brown, and Harold K. Jacobson. 1996. "Why Do States Comply with International Agreements? A Tale of Five Agreements and Nine Countries." *Human Dimensions Quarterly* 1(4): 1–5.

Williams, Frances. 1997. "UN Agency Cuts Patent Fees by 15%." *Financial Times.* 3 October.

World Bank. 1998. *The World Bank Annual Report 1998.* Washington, DC.

———. Various years. *World Development Report.* Washington, DC.

World Resources Institute. Various years. *World Resources: A Guide to the Global Environment.* New York: Oxford University Press.

Young, Oran R. 1989. *International Cooperation: Building Regimes for Natural Resources and the Environment.* Ithaca, NY, and London: Cornell University Press.

Zacher, Mark W., and Brent A. Sutton. 1996. *Governing Global Networks: International Regimes for Transportation and Communication.* New York: Cambridge University Press.

GLOSSARY

club good: an intermediate case between a pure public good and a pure private good. With a club good exclusion is feasible but the optimal size of the club is generally larger than one individual. An example would be a film screening. Here it is possible for the good to be priced (exclusion can be practised) and for a number of people to share the same good without diminishing each other's consumption of it. The size of the optimal sharing group is that which maximizes their joint utility.

Coase's theorem: the assertion that if property rights and liability are properly defined and there are no transactions costs, then people can be held responsible for any negative externalities they impose on others, and market transactions will produce efficient outcomes.

externality: a phenomenon that arises when an individual or firm takes an action but does not bear all the costs (negative externalities) or receive all the benefits (positive externalities).

free rider: someone who enjoys the benefits of a (public) good without paying for it. Because it is difficult to preclude anyone from using a pure public good, those who benefit from the good have an incentive to avoid paying for it—that is, to be free riders.

global public good: a public good with benefits that are strongly universal in terms of countries (covering more than one group of countries), people

---

Definitions are drawn from Joseph E. Stiglitz's second edition of *Economics* (New York: W. W. Norton, 1997), from the fourth edition of *The MIT Dictionary of Modern Economics* (Cambridge, MA: MIT Press, 1992) or from Richard Cornes and Todd Sandler's second edition of *The Theory of Externalities, Public Goods and Club Goods* (New York: Cambridge University Press, 1996). The definition of global public goods is taken from the first chapter of this volume.

(accruing to several, preferably all, population groups) and generations (extending to both current and future generations, or at least meeting the needs of current generations without foreclosing development options for future generations).

market failure: the situation in which a market fails to attain economic efficiency.

mixed good: a mixed good lies between the polar extremes of a private good and a public good, containing elements of both. For example, inoculation against disease is a mixed good since it benefits the community at large (by reducing risks of illness) as well as the individual. In such a case, private consumption confers a beneficial externality on the rest of the community.

moral hazard: the tendency for those who purchase insurance to be less cautious, as they have a reduced incentive to avoid what they are insured against.

nonexcludability: benefits that are available to all once a good is provided are termed nonexcludable. Goods whose benefits can be withheld costlessly by the owner or provider generate excludable benefits. Fireworks displays, pollution control devices and street lighting yield nonexcludable benefits because once they are provided, it is difficult if not impossible to exclude individuals from their benefits.

nonrivalry: a good is nonrival or indivisible when a unit of the good can be consumed by one individual without detracting from the consumption opportunities available to others from that same unit. Sunsets are nonrival or indivisible when views are unobstructed.

Pareto efficient: a resource allocation is said to be Pareto efficient if there is no rearrangement that can make anyone better off without making someone else worse off.

Prisoner's dilemma: a situation in which the independent pursuit of self-interest by two parties makes them both worse off.

public good: public goods have the properties of nonrivalry in consumption and nonexcludability. For example, peace costs little or nothing for an extra individual to enjoy. In addition, the costs of preventing any individual from the enjoyment of this good are high.

transactions costs: the extra costs (beyond the price of the purchase) of conducting a transaction, whether those costs are in money, time or convenience.

FURTHER READING

COMPILED BY PRIYA GAJRAJ

Axelrod, Robert. 1984. *The Evolution of Cooperation.* New York: Basic Books.

Barrett, Scott. 1990. "The Problem of Global Environmental Protection." *Oxford Review of Economic Policy* 6: 68–79.

Bergstrom, Theodore C., Lawrence Blume and Hal Varian. 1986. "On the Private Provision of Public Goods." *Journal of Public Economics* 29(1): 25–49.

Brookings Institution. 1994–98. Project on Integrating National Economies. Washington, DC.

Bryant, Ralph C. 1995. *International Coordination of National Stabilization Policies.* Washington, DC: Brookings Institution.

Chase, Robert, Emily Hill and Paul Kennedy, eds. 1999. *The Pivotal States: A New Framework for U.S. Policy in the Developing World.* New York: W.W. Norton.

Coase, Ronald H. 1974. "The Lighthouse in Economics." *Journal of Law and Economics* 17 (October): 357–76.

Conybeare, John A.C. 1984. "Public Goods, Prisoners' Dilemmas and the International Political Economy." *International Studies Quarterly* 28: 5–22.

Cooper, Richard N. 1989. "International Cooperation in Public Health As a Prologue to Macroeconomic Cooperation." In Richard N. Cooper and others, eds., *Can Nations Agree? Issues in International Economic Cooperation.* Washington, DC: Brookings Institution.

———. 1994. *Environment and Resource Policies for the World Economy.* Washington, DC: Brookings Institution.

———. 1995. "The Coase Theorem and International Economic Relations." *Japan and the World Economy* 7: 29–44.

Cooper, Richard N., and others, eds. 1989. *Can Nations Agree? Issues in International Economic Cooperation.* Washington, DC: Brookings Institution.

Cornes, Richard, and Todd Sandler. 1996. *The Theory of Externalities, Public Goods and Club Goods.* 2nd ed. Cambridge: Cambridge University Press.

Cowen, Tyler. 1992. "Law As a Public Good." *Economics and Philosophy* 8: 249–67.

Dasgupta, Partha. 1995. *An Inquiry into Well-Being and Destitution.* Oxford: Clarendon Press.

Dasgupta, Partha S., and Geoffrey M. Heal. 1979. *Economic Theory and Exhaustible Resources.* Cambridge: Cambridge University Press.

Dasgupta, Partha, Karl-Göran Mäler and Alessandro Vercelli, eds. 1997. *The Economics of Transnational Commons.* Oxford: Clarendon Press.

DeLong, J. Bradford, and Barry Eichengreen. 1993. "The Marshall Plan: History's Most Successful Structural Adjustment Programme." In Rüdiger Dornbusch,Wilhelm Nölling and Rilard Lagard, eds., *Postwar Economic Reconstruction and Lessons for the East Today.* Cambridge, MA: MIT Press.

Eden, Lorraine and Fen Osler Hampson. 1997. "Clubs Are Trump: The Formation of International Regimes in the Absence of a Hegemon." In J. Rogers Hollingsworth and Robert Boyer, eds., *Contemporary Capitalism.* Cambridge: Cambridge University Press.

European Commission. 1998. *Towards a More Coherent Global Economic Order.* Forward Studies Series. New York: St. Martin's Press.

Ffrench-Davis, Ricardo, and Stephany Griffith-Jones, eds. 1995. *Surges in Capital Flows to Latin America.* Boulder, CO: Lynne Reiner.

Gordon, David, Catherine Gwin and Steven W. Sinding. 1996. "What Future for Aid?" *Occasional Paper 2.* Overseas Development Council, Washington, DC.

Graham, Carol. 1998. *Private Markets for Public Goods: Raising the Stakes in Economic Reform.* Washington, DC: Brookings Institution.

Griffin, Keith, and Terry McKinley. 1996. *New Approaches to Development Cooperation.* ODS Discussion Paper 7. New York: United Nations Development Programme, Office of Development Studies.

Haggard, Stephen. 1995. *Developing Nations and the Politics of Global Integration.* Washington, DC: Brookings Institution.

Hardin, Garrett. 1968. " The Tragedy of the Commons." *Science* 162 (December): 1243–48.

Hardin, Russell. 1982. *Collective Action.* Baltimore, MD: Johns Hopkins University Press.

Helm, Dieter, ed. 1991. *Economic Policy Towards the Environment.* Oxford: Blackwell.

Hirshleifer, Jack. 1983. "From Weakest-Link to Best-Shot: The Voluntary Provision of Public Goods." *Economica* 61(1): 79–92.

Hook, Steven W. 1996. *Foreign Aid Toward the Millenium.* Boulder, CO: Lynne Rienner.

Jamison, Dean T., Julio Frenk and Felicia Knaul. 1998. "International Collective Action in Health: Objectives, Functions, and Rationale." *Lancet* 351(9101): 514–15.

Kahler, Miles. 1995. *International Institutions and the Political Economy of Integration.* Washington, DC: Brookings Institution.

Kennedy, Paul. 1993. *Preparing for the Twenty-First Century.* London: Harper Collins.

Keohane, Robert O. 1984. *After Hegemony: Cooperation and Discord in the World Political Economy.* Princeton, NJ: Princeton University Press.

Killick, Tony. 1997. "What Future for Aid?" In United Nations Department for Policy Coordination and Sustainable Development, *Finance for Sustainable Development: The Road Ahead.* New York: United Nations.

Kindleberger, Charles P. 1986a. "International Public Goods without International Government." *The American Political Review* 76(1): 1–13.

———. 1986b. *The World in Depression 1929–1939.* Berkeley: University of California Press.

———. 1989. *The International Economic Order: Essays on Financial Crisis and International Public Goods.* Cambridge, MA: MIT Press.

Krasner, Stephen D. 1986. *International Regimes.* Ithaca, NY and London: Cornell University Press.

Lawrence, Robert Z. 1996. *Regionalism, Multilateralism, and Deeper Integration.* Washington, DC: Brookings Institution.

Malinvaud, Edmond, Jean-Claude Milleron, Mustapha Nabli, Amartya K. Sen, Arjun Sengupta, Nicholas Stern, Joseph E. Stiglitz and Kotaro Suzumura. 1998. *Development Strategy and Management of the Economy.* Oxford: Clarendon Press.

Martin, Lisa. 1993. "The Rational Choice of Multilateralism." In John G. Ruggie, ed., *Multilateralism Matters: The Theory and Praxis of an Institutional Form.* New York: Columbia University Press.

Mendez, Ruben P. 1992. *International Public Finance: A New Perspective on Global Relations.* New York: Oxford University Press.

———. 1995. "The Provision and Financing of Universal Public Goods." In Meghnad Desai and Paul Redfern, eds. *Global Governance: Ethics and Economics of the World Order.* London: Pinter Publishers.

Murdoch, James C., and Todd Sandler. 1997. "The Voluntary Provision of a Pure Public Good: The Case of Reduced CFC Emissions and the Montreal Protocol." *Journal of Public Economics* 63(2): 331–49.

North, Douglass C. 1990. *Institutions, Institutional Change and Economic Performance: Political Economy of Institutions and Decisions.* Cambridge: Cambridge University Press.

O'Hanlon, Michael, and Carol Graham. 1997. *A Half Penny on the Federal Dollar: The Future of Development Aid.* Washington, DC: Brookings Institution.

Olson, Mancur. 1971. *The Logic of Collective Action.* Cambridge, MA: Harvard University Press.

Ostrom, Elinor, Roy Gardner and James Walker. 1994. *Rules, Games, and Common Pool Resources.* Ann Arbor: University of Michigan Press.

Oye, Kenneth A., ed. 1986. *Cooperation under Anarchy.* Princeton, NJ: Princeton University Press.

Raffer, Kunibert, and Hans Wolfgang Singer. 1996. *The Foreign Aid Business: Economic Assistance and Development Co-operation.* Brookfield, VT: Edward Elgar.

Randel, Judith, and Tony German, eds. 1998. *The Reality of Aid 1998–1999.* London: Earthscan.

Reinicke, Wolfgang H. 1998. *Global Public Policy: Governing Without* Riddell, Roger. 1996. *Aid in the 21st Century.* ODS Discussion Paper 6. New York: United Nations Development Programme, Office of Development Studies.

Riddell, Roger. 1996. *Aid in the 21st Century.* ODS Discussion Paper 6. New York: United Nations Development Programme, Office of Development Studies.

Rittberger, Volker, and Peter Mayer. 1993. *Regime Theory and International Relations.* New York: Oxford University Press.

Rosecrance, Richard. 1992. *Cooperation in a World Without Enemies: Solving the Public Goods Problem in International Relations.* Working Paper 2. Department of Political Science. University of California, Los Angeles.

Rosenau, James N. 1997. *Along the Domestic-Foreign Frontier: Exploring Governance in a Turbulent World.* Cambridge: Cambridge University Press.

Rosenau, James N., and Ernst-Otto Czempiel. 1992. *Governance without Government: Order and Change in World Politics.* Cambridge: Cambridge University Press.

Rosenthal, Joel H., ed. 1995. *Ethics and International Affairs: A Reader.* 1st ed. Washington, DC: Georgetown University Press.

Ruggie, John G. 1972. "Collective Goods and Future International Collaboration." *The American Political Science Review* 66: 874–93.

Ruggie, John G., ed. 1993. *Multilateralism Matters: The Theory and Praxis of an Institutional Form.* New York: Columbia University Press.

Russett, Bruce M., and John D. Sullivan. 1971. "Collective Goods and International Organization." *International Organization* 25(4): 845–65.

Samuelson, Paul A. 1954. "The Pure Theory of Public Expenditure." *Review of Economics and Statistics* 36 (November): 387–89.

Sandler, Todd. 1992. *Collective Action: Theory and Application.* Ann Arbor: University of Michigan Press.

———. 1997. *Global Challenges: An Approach to Environmental, Political, and Economic Problems.* Cambridge: Cambridge University Press.

————. 1998. "Global and Regional Public Goods: A Prognosis for Collective Action." *Fiscal Studies* 19(1): 221–47.

Schelling, Thomas C. 1960. *Strategy of Conflict.* Cambridge, MA: Harvard University Press.

Sen, Amartya K. 1987. *On Ethics and Economics.* Oxford and New York: Basil Blackwell.

Stiglitz, Joseph. 1995. "The Theory of International Public Goods and the Architecture of International Organizations." Background Paper 7. United Nations, Department for Economic and Social Information and Policy Analysis, New York.

————. 1998. "An Agenda for Development in the Twenty-First Century." In Boris Pleskovic and Joseph E. Stiglitz, eds., *Annual World Bank Conference on Development Economics 1997.* Washington, DC: World Bank.

Stokke, Olav, ed. 1996. *Foreign Aid Toward the Year 2000: Experiences and Challenges.* London: Frank Cass.

Streeten, Paul. 1989. "Global Institutions for an Interdependent World." *World Development* 17(9): 1349–59.

————. 1995. *Thinking about Development.* New York: Cambridge University Press.

Takahashi, Kazuo, ed. 1998. *Agenda for International Development 1998.* Tokyo: Foundation for Advanced Studies on International Development.

UNDP (United Nations Development Programme). Various years. *Human Development Report.* New York: Oxford University Press.

World Bank. 1997. *Private Capital Flows to Developing Countries: The Road to Financial Integration.* A Policy Research Report. New York: Oxford University Press.

————. 1998. *Assessing Aid: What Works, What Doesn't, and Why.* A Policy Research Report. New York: Oxford University Press.

————. Various years. *World Development Report.* Washington, DC.

Young, Oran R. 1989. *International Cooperation: Building Regimes for Natural Resources and the Environment.* Ithaca, NY and London: Cornell University Press.

————. 1997. *Global Governance: Drawing Insights from the Environmental Experience.* Cambridge, MA: MIT Press.

ABOUT THE
CONTRIBUTORS

SCOTT BARRETT

Scott Barrett is associate professor of economics at the London Business School. He is a graduate of the University of Massachusetts at Amherst, University of British Columbia and London School of Economics. He has written a number of papers on international cooperation, particularly relating to environmental protection, and received the Erik Kempe Prize for this work. He has also advised a number of international organizations on treaty negotiations, and was a lead author of the second assessment report by the Intergovernmental Panel on Climate Change.

NANCY BIRDSALL

Nancy Birdsall is senior associate at the Carnegie Endowment for International Peace, where she directs the economics programme. She was executive vice president of the Inter-American Development Bank from 1993 until 1998, and is the author of numerous publications on economic development. Her most recent work is on the relationship between income distribution and growth. Birdsall holds an M.A. in international relations from the Johns Hopkins School of Advanced International Studies and a doctorate in economics from Yale University.

RICHARD A. CASH

Richard A. Cash, M.D., M.P.H., is a fellow at the Harvard Institute for International Development and senior lecturer in the Department of Population and International Health at the Harvard School of Public Health. He was one of the developers of oral rehydration therapy in Bangladesh and helped conduct the first clinical trials of this therapy. He has continued to pursue his interest in infectious diseases in developing countries, directing an applied research programme that has focused on capacity strengthening, the role of research in policy development and most recently on childhood diseases and on ethical issues in international health research.

Lincoln C. Chen

Lincoln C. Chen, M.D., is vice president of the Rockefeller Foundation and oversees its international programmes in health, population, education, agriculture and the environment. Before joining the foundation in 1997, Chen was Taro Takemi Professor of International Health at the Harvard School of Public Health, where he served as chair of the Department of Population and International Health. At Harvard University he was director of the Harvard Center for Population and Development Studies. He has written extensively on health and development policies.

Lisa D. Cook

Lisa D. Cook is research associate at the Harvard Institute for International Development and Center for International Development at Harvard University. Her current research interests include emerging markets, financial institutions and markets (in Africa, Russia and Central and Eastern Europe) and macroeconomic policy in transition and developing economies. She recently served as an economic adviser to the government of Rwanda. She is the author of a number of publications and working papers. She received her Ph.D. in economics from the University of California at Berkeley and joined Harvard in 1997.

Tim G. Evans

Tim G. Evans is team director of the Health Sciences Division at the Rockefeller Foundation. He is on leave of absence from the Harvard School of Public Health, where he is assistant professor of population and international health.

He holds degrees in agricultural economics (D.Phil, Oxford University) and clinical medicine (M.D., McMaster University) and has completed residency training in internal medicine (Brigham and Women's Hospital).

PRIYA GAJRAJ

Priya Gajra is a research associate in the Office of Development Studies at the United Nations Development Programme. She holds an M. A. in international relations from Cambridge University and a B. A. in history from Yale University. Before joining UNDP, she worked at the European Commission Humanitarian Office.

ISABELLE GRUNBERG

Isabelle Grunberg is senior policy adviser in the Office of Development Studies at the United Nations Development Programme. Previously, she was associate director of United Nations studies at Yale University and a MacArthur fellow and lecturer at Yale. She was also a lecturer at the London School of Economics and the Institut d'Etudes Politiques in Paris. She received a French doctoral equivalent (agrégation) from the Sorbonne University and the Ecole Normale Supérieure. Her areas of publication include international political economy and theories of the international system.

DAVID A. HAMBURG

David A. Hamburg is president emeritus at Carnegie Corporation of New York, having been president from 1983 to 1997. From 1975 to 1980 he was president of the Institute of Medicine at the National Academy of Sciences, and from 1980 to 1983 he was director of the Division of Health Policy Research and Education and John D. MacArthur Professor of Health Policy at Harvard University. He also served as president and chairman of the board of the American Association for the Advancement of Science. He is a member of the Defense Policy Board and the President's Committee of Advisers on Science and Technology, and co-chair (with Cyrus Vance) of the Carnegie Commission on Preventing Deadly Conflict.

GEOFFREY HEAL

Geoffrey Heal is Paul Garrett Professor of Public Policy and Corporate Responsibility and professor of economics and finance, Program on Information and Resources, in the Graduate School of Business at Columbia University. He has held teaching positions at many leading universities in Europe and the United States. His books and articles cover a wide range of topics in the area of environmental economics, including environmental markets, exhaustible resources and economic interpretations of sustainability. He obtained his Ph.D. in economics from Cambridge University.

JANE E. HOLL

Jane E. Holl is executive director of the Carnegie Commission on Preventing Deadly Conflict, a programme of the Carnegie Corporation of New York. Before joining Carnegie she served as director for European affairs at the National Security Council under President Bush and President Clinton. She was a career officer in the US Army and retired in 1994. She holds a Ph.D. in political science from Stanford University.

RAJSHRI JAYARAMAN

Rajshri Jayaraman is a third-year Ph.D. student in the Department of Economics at Cornell University. She has an M.A. in international and development economics from Yale University and a B.A. in economics and finance from McGill University. Before joining Cornell she worked at the World Bank's resident mission in India and its Europe and Central Asia department in Washington DC, and in the Human Development Report Office at the United Nations Development Programme in New York.

RAVI KANBUR

Ravi Kanbur is T.H. Lee Professor of World Affairs and professor of economics at Cornell University. His main areas of interest are public economics, development economics and agricultural economics. His work spans conceptual, empirical and policy analysis. He is particularly interested in bridging the worlds of rigorous analysis and practical policy-making. He is widely published on a range of topics, including risk taking, inequality, poverty, structural adjustment, debt, agriculture and political economy. Kanbur is director of the World Bank's *World Development Report 2000*.

ETHAN B. KAPSTEIN

Ethan B. Kapstein is Stassen Professor of International Peace at the Humphrey Institute of Public Affairs and Department of Political Science at the University of Minnesota. Previously, he was vice president and director of studies at the Council on Foreign Relations, and principal administrator at the Organisation for Economic Co-operation and Development in Paris. He has written several books and many professional articles on international economic relations.

INGE KAUL

Inge Kaul is director of the Office of Development Studies at the United Nations Development Programme. From 1990 to 1995 she served as director of the Human Development Report Office at UNDP, where she coordinated a team of authors producing the annual *Human Development Report*. Before that she held senior policy positions at UNDP. She has extensive research experience in developing countries and is the author of a number of publications and reports on development financing and aid.

ROBERT Z. LAWRENCE

Robert Z. Lawrence is chief economist at the Council of Economic Advisers, Albert L. Williams Professor of Trade and Investment at the John F. Kennedy School of Government at Harvard University, and new century senior fellow at the Brookings Institution. He is also a research associate at the National Bureau of Economic Research, edits the Brookings Trade Policy Forum and chairs the Project on Middle East Trade at the John F. Kennedy School of Government. His current research focuses on global integration, trade in the Middle East and the impact of trade on labour markets. His publications focus on domestic and international economic problems and he has co-authored *Globaphobia: Confronting Fears About Open Trade* (Brookings Institution Press, 1998).

LISA L. MARTIN

Lisa L. Martin received her Ph.D. in government from Harvard University in 1990. She then moved to the University of California at San Diego, teaching in the Political Science Department. She spent the academic year 1991–92 as a national fellow in the Hoover Institution at Stanford University. In 1992 she moved to Harvard University as associate professor in the Government Department, and in 1996 she was promoted to full professor. Her publications include *Coercive Cooperation: Explaining Multilateral Economic Sanctions* (Princeton University Press, 1992) and a forthcoming book titled *Democratic Commitments: Legislatures and International Cooperation.*

RUBEN P. MENDEZ

Ruben P. Mendez is a former senior career official at the United Nations Development Programme. He currently teaches at New York University and Yale University, where he is affiliated with the Yale Center for International and Area Studies, and is writing an independent history of UNDP. He served as special adviser to the chairman of the Philippines's National Economic Council and as economist in the Planning Department at Merrill Lynch, Pierce, Fenner and Smith. He pioneered the discipline of international public finance with his book *International Public Finance: A New Perspective on Global Relations* (Oxford University Press, 1992) and other writings.

J. MOHAN RAO

J. Mohan Rao is professor of economics at the University of Massachusetts at Amherst. His main research interests are economic development, income distribution and institutional change in developing countries. He has made a number of contributions to the microeconomics of agrarian institutions and the macroeconomics of development. He has also written extensively on the constraints and options in agricultural development policy. He recently published major studies on environment-economy linkages, economic liberalization and industrial productivity growth in India. His current research focuses on the logic of state action and on the long-run connection between development and globalization.

JEFFREY SACHS

Jeffrey Sachs is Galen L. Stone Professor of International Trade at Harvard University, director of the Harvard Institute for International Development and director of the Center for International Development at Harvard University. Between 1986 and 1990 he advised the governments of Argentina, Bolivia, Brazil, Ecuador, Estonia, Mongolia, Russia, Slovenia and Venezuela, as well as Poland's Solidarity movement, on various aspects of economic and financial reform. His current research interests include the transition to market economies in Eastern Europe and the former Soviet Union, international financial markets, international macroeconomic policy coordination and macroeconomic policies in developing and developed countries.

TODD SANDLER

Todd Sandler is distinguished professor of economics and political science at Iowa State University. In addition to writing articles on a wide range of topics, he co-authored *The Theory of Externalities, Public Goods and Club Goods* (2nd ed., Cambridge University Press, 1996). His recent book, *Global Challenges,* applies simple economic methods to study a range of problems, including terrorism, acid rain, global warming, revolutions and treaty formation. He and Keith Hartley have just finished a forthcoming book, *The Political Economy of NATO: Past, Present, and into the 21st Century* (Cambridge University Press, 1997).

AMARTYA SEN

Amartya Sen is master of Trinity College at Cambridge University and Lamont University Professor Emeritus at Harvard University. Previously, he was Drummond Professor of Political Economy at Oxford University and fellow of All Souls College, and he has taught at the London School of Economics, Delhi University and Cambridge University. He is a past president of the American Economic Association, Indian Economic Association, Development Studies Association and Social Choice and Welfare Society. In 1998 he received the Nobel Prize in economics.

ISMAIL SERAGELDIN

Ismail Serageldin is vice president for Special Programs at the World Bank and chairman of the World Commission on Water for the 21st Century. He also serves as chairman of the Consultative Group on International Agricultural Research, Consultative Group to Assist the Poorest and Global Water Partnership, and co-chairs the World Bank-NGO Committee. The World Bank's Special Programs seek to, among other goals, integrate culture with the development paradigm and support efforts by the Bank's member countries to preserve history, culture and identity. Serageldin has published widely on development, economics, the environment and culture.

DEBORA L. SPAR

Debora L. Spar is associate professor at Harvard Business School. She has co-authored several books on business-government relations, international economic cooperation and foreign direct investment. Her current work focuses on foreign trade and investment, how firms compete in foreign markets and how government policies shape the climate for international business. She is particularly interested in exploring how the growth of trade in information is reshaping the global economy and redefining the strategies of firms in information-intensive industries such as media and entertainment. She is also involved in projects examining the links between foreign direct investment and human rights.

MARC A. STERN

Marc A. Stern is senior policy analyst in the Office of Development Studies at the United Nations Development Programme and a doctoral candidate in international affairs at the University of California at San Diego. His thesis focuses on the effects of economic integration on environmental policy in developing countries. He has published several articles on Mexican environmental policy and is co-editor of *Latin American Environmental Policy in International Perspective* (Westview, 1996). Before joining UNDP, he served as editor-in-chief of the *Journal of Environment and Development*.

Joseph E. Stiglitz

Joseph E. Stiglitz is senior vice president for Development Economics, and chief economist at the World Bank. Previously, he served as chairman of the US Council of Economic Advisers and was a member of the council and an active member of President Clinton's economic team since 1993. He is on leave from Stanford University, where he is professor of economics. As an academic he helped create a branch of economics—the economics of information—that has received widespread application throughout economics. He is also a leading scholar on the economics of the public sector.

J. Habib Sy

J. Habib Sy is director of a Senegal-based nongovernmental organization, Partners for African Development. He has held various academic posts and positions in the print and television fields. In addition, he was senior programme specialist at the International Development Research Centre. He is the author of several books and articles on African telecommunications systems and policies and African history and sociopolitical systems. His areas of interest include mass communications theory, the impact of new communications technologies, education communications, transcultural communications, African telecommunications systems, information superhighways and African history.

Charles Wyplosz

Charles Wyplosz is professor of international economics in the Graduate Institute in International Studies at the University of Geneva, and research fellow at the Centre for Economic Policy Research. He is also managing editor of *Economic Policy* and serves on the scientific boards of several professional journals. Since 1992 he has advised the government of Russia, and he is a consultant to various international organizations. He holds a Ph.D. in economics from Harvard University and has published extensively on exchange rates, macroeconomic policy and labour markets. His recent research focuses on currency crises, European Monetary Union and exchange rates in transition economies.

MARK W. ZACHER

Mark W. Zacher is professor of political science and research director of the Institute of International Relations at the University of British Columbia. From 1971 to 1991 he was director of the Institute of International Relations. He is a specialist on international regimes and organizations. Zacher is the author of *Dag Hammarksjold's United Nations* (Columbia University Press, 1970) and *International Conflicts and Collective Security, 1946–1977* (Praeger, 1979). He is the co-author of *Pollution, Politics and International Law: Tankers at Sea* (University of California Press, 1979), *Managing International Markets: Developing Countries and the Commodity Trade Regime* (Columbia University Press, 1988) and *Governing Global Networks: International Regimes for Transportation and Communications* (Columbia University Press, 1996).

INDEX

Vercelli, Alessandro, 5
Vernon, Raymond, 82
Vienna Convention for the
    Protection of the Ozone Layer
    (1985), 195
Vienna Declaration (1993), 78

Wade, Robert, 476
Wallensteen, Peter, 404
Walt, Gill, 295
Warner, Andrew, 179
Warr, Peter G., 423
Wasko, Janet, 326, 334
Watts, Sheldon, 271
Weindling, Paul, 271
Weingast, Barry, 56
Welfare state: Keynesian theory as
    core of postwar, 91; as provider
    of social justice, 93–97; social
    justice in postwar, 93–97
Well-being: as factor in conflict pre-
    vention, 367, 373–75
Wellenius, Bjorn, 327, 334, 335, 336
Wheeler, David, 141
Wijkman, Per Magnus, 5
Williams, Frances, 497
Williams, Green, 270, 497
Williams, Jr., 243
Willis, Clint, 350
Willis, Ken, 248
Wilson, Theodore, 89
Winpenny, James T., 247
Wolfensohn, James, 320
Wollstonecraft, Mary, 83
Woodall, Jack, 276
Worksett, Roy, 242
World Bank, 275, 281; financial sec-
    tor reform task of, 165; financing
    for health, 296; financing of large
    loans by, 174; InfoDev program,
    330; International Development

Association, 492; lending for
    regional public goods, 445; rec-
    ommendation for conditional
    lending of, 109–10; role in pro-
    duction and dissemination of
    knowledge, 319
World Commission on Environment
    and Development (Brundtland
    Commission), 11
World Federation of Trade Unions
    (WFTU), 92–93
World Health Organization (WHO):
    assistance during ebola
    outbreak in Zaire, 274;
    Collaborating Centers, 275, 278,
    280; Division for Emerging
    Communicable Diseases, 277,
    279; establishment (1948), 266;
    International Health
    Regulations of, 272, 279–80,
    284; reform process, 296; role
    of, 271–72; Rumor Outbreak
    Page, 269, 277
World Intellectual Property
    Organization (WIPO),
    xxviii–xxix, 497
World Trade Organization (WTO),
    129, 141, 144, 148
World Watch Institute, 463
Wyplosz, Charles, 108, 161, 162, 167,
    168, 456–57, 459, 525

Yach, Derek, 295
Yamey, Basil, 418
Yermakov, Waldermar, 270, 271
Young, Oran R., 464

Zacher, Mark, 60, 461, 481
Zhang, Mo, 347
Zinsser, Hans, 284
Zurn, Michael, xxiii